Lecture Notes in Computer Science

Vol. 142: Problems and Methodologies in Mathematical Software Production. Proceedings, 1980. Edited by P.C. Messina and A. Murli. VII, 271 pages. 1982.

Vol. 143: Operating Systems Engineering. Proceedings, 1980. Edited by M. Maekawa and L.A. Belady. VII, 465 pages. 1982.

Vol. 144: Computer Algebra. Proceedings, 1982. Edited by J. Calmet. XIV, 301 pages. 1982.

Vol. 145: Theoretical Computer Science. Proceedings, 1983. Edited by A.B. Cremers and H.P. Kriegel. X, 367 pages. 1982.

Vol. 146: Research and Development in Information Retrieval. Proceedings, 1982. Edited by G. Salton and H.-J. Schneider. IX, 311 pages. 1983.

Vol. 147: RIMS Symposia on Software Science and Engineering. Proceedings, 1982. Edited by E. Goto, I. Nakata, K. Furukawa, R. Nakajima, and A. Yonezawa. V. 232 pages. 1983.

Vol. 148: Logics of Programs and Their Applications. Proceedings, 1980. Edited by A. Salwicki. VI, 324 pages. 1983.

Vol. 149: Cryptography. Proceedings, 1982. Edited by T. Beth. VIII, 402 pages. 1983.

Vol. 150: Enduser Systems and Their Human Factors. Proceedings, 1983. Edited by A. Blaser and M. Zoeppritz. III, 138 pages. 1983.

Vol. 151: R. Piloty, M. Barbacci, D. Borrione, D. Dietmeyer, F. Hill, and P. Skelly, CONLAN Report. XII, 174 pages. 1983.

Vol. 152: Specification and Design of Software Systems. Proceedings, 1982. Edited by E. Knuth and E. J. Neuhold. V, 152 pages. 1983.

Vol. 153: Graph-Grammars and Their Application to Computer Science. Proceedings, 1982. Edited by H. Ehrig, M. Nagl, and G. Rozenberg. VII, 452 pages. 1983.

Vol. 154: Automata, Languages and Programming. Proceedings, 1983. Edited by J. Díaz. VIII, 734 pages. 1983.

Vol. 155: The Programming Language Ada. Reference Manual. Approved 17 February 1983. American National Standards Institute, Inc. ANSI/MIL-STD-1815A-1983. IX, 331 pages. 1983.

Vol. 156: M.H. Overmars, The Design of Dynamic Data Structures. VII, 181 pages. 1983.

Vol. 157: O. Østerby, Z. Zlatev, Direct Methods for Sparse Matrices. VIII, 127 pages. 1983.

Vol. 158: Foundations of Computation Theory. Proceedings, 1983. Edited by M. Karpinski, XI, 517 pages. 1983.

Vol. 159: CAAP'83. Proceedings, 1983. Edited by G. Ausiello and M. Protasi. VI, 416 pages. 1983.

Vol. 160: The IOTA Programming System. Edited by R. Nakajima and T. Yuasa. VII, 217 pages. 1983.

Vol. 161: DIANA, An Intermediate Language for Ada. Edited by G. Goos, W.A. Wulf, A. Evans, Jr. and K.J. Butler. VII, 201 pages. 1983.

Vol. 162: Computer Algebra. Proceedings, 1983. Edited by J.A. van Hulzen. XIII, 305 pages. 1983.

Vol. 163: VLSI Engineering. Proceedings. Edited by T.L. Kunii. VIII, 308 pages. 1984.

Vol. 164: Logics of Programs. Proceedings, 1983. Edited by E. Clarke and D. Kozen. VI, 528 pages. 1984.

Vol. 165: T.F. Coleman, Large Sparse Numerical Optimization. V, 105 pages. 1984.

Vol. 166: STACS 84. Symposium of Theoretical Aspects of Computer Science. Proceedings, 1984. Edited by M. Fontet and K. Mehlhorn. VI, 338 pages. 1984.

Vol. 167: International Symposium on Programming. Proceedings, 1984. Edited by C. Girault and M. Paul. VI, 262 pages. 1984.

Vol. 168: Methods and Tools for Computer Integrated Manufacturing. Edited by R. Dillmann and U. Rembold. XVI, 528 pages. 1984.

Vol. 169: Ch. Ronse, Feedback Shift Registers. II, 1-2, 145 pages. 1984.

Vol. 170: Seventh International Conference on Automated Deduction. Edited by R.E. Shostak. IV, 508 pages. 1984.

Vol. 171: Logic and Machines: Decision Problems and Complexity. Proceedings, 1983. Edited by E. Börger, G. Hasenjaeger and D. Rödding. VI, 456 pages. 1984.

Vol. 172: Automata, Languages and Programming. Proceedings, 1984. Edited by J. Paredaens. VIII, 527 pages. 1984.

Vol. 173: Semantics of Data Types. Proceedings, 1984. Edited by G. Kahn, D.B. MacQueen and G. Plotkin. VI, 391 pages. 1984.

Vol. 174: EUROSAM 84. Proceedings, 1984. Edited by J. Fitch. XI, 396 pages. 1984.

Vol. 175: A. Thayse, P-Functions and Boolean Matrix Factorization, VII, 248 pages. 1984.

Vol. 176: Mathematical Foundations of Computer Science 1984. Proceedings, 1984. Edited by M.P. Chytil and V. Koubek. XI, 581 pages. 1984.

Vol. 177: Programming Languages and Their Definition. Edited by C.B. Jones. XXXII, 254 pages. 1984.

Vol. 178: Readings on Cognitive Ergonomics – Mind and Computers. Proceedings, 1984. Edited by G.C. van der Veer, M.J. Tauber, T.R.G. Green and P. Gorny. VI, 269 pages. 1984.

Vol. 179: V. Pan, How to Multiply Matrices Faster. XI, 212 pages. 1984.

Vol. 180: Ada Software Tools Interfaces. Proceedings, 1983. Edited by P.J.L. Wallis. III, 164 pages. 1984.

Vol. 181: Foundations of Software Technology and Theoretical Computer Science. Proceedings, 1984. Edited by M. Joseph and R. Shyamasundar. VIII, 468 pages. 1984.

Vol. 182: STACS 85. 2nd Annual Symposium on Theoretical Aspects of Computer Science. Proceedings, 1985. Edited by K. Mehlhorn. VII, 374 pages. 1985.

Vol. 183: The Munich Project CIP. Volume I: The Wide Spectrum Language CIP-L. By the CIP Language Group. XI, 275 pages. 1985.

Vol. 184: Local Area Networks: An Advanced Course. Proceedings, 1983. Edited by D. Hutchison, J. Mariani and D. Shepherd. VIII, 497 pages. 1985.

Vol. 185: Mathematical Foundations of Software Development. Proceedings, 1985. Volume 1: Colloquium on Trees in Algebra and Programming (CAAP' 85). Edited by H. Ehrig, C. Floyd, M. Nivat and J. Thatcher. XIV, 418 pages. 1985.

Vol. 186: Formal Methods and Software Development. Proceedings, 1985. Volume 2: Colloquium on Software Engineering (CSE). Edited by H. Ehrig, C. Floyd, M. Nivat and J. Thatcher. XIV, 455 pages. 1985.

Vol. 187: F.S. Chaghaghi, Time Series Package (TSPACK). III, 305 pages. 1985.

Vol. 188: Advances in Petri Nets 1984. Edited by G. Rozenberg with the cooperation of H. Genrich and G. Roucairol. VII, 467 pages. 1985.

Vol. 189: M.S. Sherman, Paragon. XI, 376 pages. 1985.

Vol. 190: M.W. Alford, J.P. Ansart, G. Hommel, L. Lamport, B. Liskov, G.P. Mullery and F.B. Schneider, Distributed Systems. Edited by M. Paul and H.J. Siegert. VI, 573 pages. 1985.

Vol. 191: H. Barringer, A Survey of Verification Techniques for Parallel Programs. VI, 115 pages. 1985.

Lecture Notes in Computer Science

Edited by G. Goos and J. Hartmanis

243

ICDT '86

International Conference on Database Theory
Rome, Italy, September 8–10, 1986
Proceedings

Edited by Giorgio Ausiello and Paolo Atzeni

Springer-Verlag
Berlin Heidelberg New York London Paris Tokyo

Editors

Giorgio Ausiello
Dipartimento di Informatica e Sistemistica
Università di Roma, "La Sapienza"
Via Eudossiana 18, Rome, Italy

Paolo Atzeni
IASI-CNR
Viale Manzoni 30, Rome, Italy

CR Subject Classification (1985): H.2, H.1, E.1, F.2, F.4

ISBN 3-540-17187-8 Springer-Verlag Berlin Heidelberg New York
ISBN 0-387-17187-8 Springer-Verlag New York Berlin Heidelberg

Printed in Germany

Printing and binding: Druckhaus Beltz, Hemsbach/Bergstr.
2145/3140-543210

FOREWORD

The International Conference on Database Theory (ICDT'86) was held on September 8-10, 1986, at the headquarters of Consiglio Nazionale delle Ricerche, the Italian Research Council, in Rome. It was conceived to provide a European forum for the international research community working on theoretical issues related to database systems.

The topics of the Conference covered all major themes of research in database theory: relational theory, logic and databases, conceptual models, deductive databases, database semantics, concurrency control, analysis and design of data structures. The interaction between database theory and logic programming was extensively considered, both in the submitted papers and in the invited lectures.

ICDT'86 was organized by CRAI, Universitá di Roma "La Sapienza" (Dipartimento di Informatica e Sistemistica), and IASI-CNR, and it was sponsored by EATCS and the Middle and South Italian Section of IEEE. The Organizing Committee consisted of P. Atzeni, A. D'Atri, M. Moscarini, D. Saccá.

The Program Committee consisted of S. Abiteboul, G. Ausiello (chairman), F. Bancilhon, A. D'Atri, M. Moscarini, J. Mylopoulos, J.-M. Nicolas, J. Nievergelt, C.H. Papadimitriou, J. Paredaens, D. Saccá, N. Spyratos, J.D. Ullman, M.Y. Vardi.

There were 83 papers submitted, from 20 different nations, and 24 of them were selected during a meeting held in Rome on May 23, 1986, attended by S. Abiteboul, G. Ausiello, A. D'Atri, M. Moscarini, J. Paredaens, D. Saccá. The members of the Program Committee were assisted by the following referees: M. Adiba, P. Atzeni N. Bidoit, J. Biskup, P. Borlu, P. Bosc, P. De Bra, C. Delobel, R. Demolombe, P. Di Felice, A. Doucet, P. Faudemay, H. Gallaire, G. Gambosi, G. Gardarin, G. Grahne, M. Gyssens, K. Hinrichs, R. Hull, N. Le Thanh, C. Lecluse, N. Lerat, S. Miranda, A. Motro, E.J. Neuhold, D. Plateau, M. Regnier, F. Remmen, S. Salza, M. Scholl, M. Terranova, D. Van Gucht, L. Verbeeck, D. Vermeir, V. Vianu, L. Vieille, K.M. van Hee, J. van Leeuwen.

The scientific program also included three invited lectures, given by A.K. Chandra, P. Kanellakis, C. Zaniolo, two of which are included in this volume.

We gratefully acknowledge the economic support provided by Banca Nazionale del Lavoro, Consiglio Nazionale delle Ricerche, Enidata S.p.A., IBM Italia, Selenia S.p.A., Universitá di Roma "La Sapienza".

Giorgio Ausiello
Program Committee

Paolo Atzeni
Organizing Committee

CONTENTS

Logic Programming and Parallel Complexity

Paris C. Kanellakis[1]

Dept. of Computer Science, Brown Univ., Providence, RI, USA

July 1986

Abstract: This paper is a survey of the many applications of the theory of parallel algorithms and complexity to logic programming problems. The mathematical tools relevant to the analysis of parallel logic programs include: the concept of alternation, the complexity class NC, and parallel algorithms using randomization and/or achieving optimal speed-ups. The logic programming problems addressed are related to query optimization for deductive databases and to fast parallel execution of primitive operations in logic programming languages, such as, fixpoint operators, term unification, and term matching. The formal language we use to illustrate the addition of recursion to database queries is the language of *logical query programs* (or programs), whose evaluation has been the object of much recent research. Our presentation highlights the fact that all of these results can be stated using the *stage function* $s_H(n)$ of a program H, where n is the size of the database queried. In this context we also present two new observations. (1) Given a linear single rule program H, it is NP-hard to decide whether $s_H(n)=O(1)$; this extends the bounded recursion analysis of [57, 42]. (2) There is a program that can be evaluated in $s(n)=O(\log n)$ stages, but whose derivation trees (of width 1) are of size exponential in n. An extension of derivation trees from width 1 to constant width properly strengthens the fast evaluation method of [76].

1. Introduction

Programming in logic has been a fundamental theme in Computer Science theory and practice, ever since their early days, and is in large part motivated by the elegant and precise qualities of mathematical logic. The 1965 seminal paper "A Machine Oriented Logic Based on the Resolution Principle" of J.A. Robinson was a breakthrough in theorem proving and in the use of first-order predicate calculus as a programming language [63]. This theme was further developed in the 70s [50, 4, 81, 46], largely through the programming language PROLOG [64, 15]. Another (seemingly unrelated) important development was the identification by E.F. Codd in 1970 of first-order relational calculus, with finite interpretations, as the natural formalism for database description and manipulation [16]. The 70s was also a decade of relational database systems

[1] Supported partly by an IBM Faculty Development Award and partly by ONR-DARPA grant N00014-83-K-0146, ARPA Order No. 4786.

and database theory, e.g. [74].

Today, the challenge of deductive databases and of knowledgebase systems is to combine the technology of logic programming (exemplified by PROLOG, LISP or other artificial intelligence tools) with the efficiency of database technology. This would be a concrete step towards a new generation of computing; some already refer to it as the fifth generation. The technological advance driving this ambitious effort is, as so often happens in Computer Science, new hardware. Parallel computers, a reality of the 80s, offer the new element which has made major advances in logic programming and databases feasible. A thornier issue, as is also usual in Computer Science, is the development of efficient software for these multiprocessor machines.

Logic programming languages for parallel machines have been the object of much recent study, (e.g., [13, 72]). AND-parallelism and OR-parallelism have been the most celebrated qualitative measures of parallelism in logic programs. In this paper we would like to "complete the picture" through the use of the theory of parallel algorithms and complexity. We believe that this connection sheds much light on the algorithmic aspects of parallel logic programming. For example, one of the most fundamental contributions to complexity theory has been the concept of alternation [12]. Alternating Turing Machines (ATMs) with simultaneous resource bounds capture the complexity of derivation trees, rule-goal trees, and AND-OR trees, all familiar concepts in logic programming [46, 15].

The logic programming problems addressed in this paper are related to deductive database retrieval [30], as well as, to algorithms for primitive operations of logic programming languages, (i.e., fixpoint operators, term unification and term matching). *Logical query programs* are the "toy" formal language we use to illustrate the addition of recursion or fixpoint operators to database queries, (see [9]).

This survey can be viewed as complementing the exposition in [7]. The major theme is parallel computation, whereas [7] reviews advances in sequential algorithms for logical query program evaluation. Another important issue in the same area, which is outside the scope of our paper, is the use and expressive power of negation, [14, 4, 9].

In Section 2 we present the mathematical tools relevant to the analysis of parallel logic programs. These include: alternation, the complexity class NC (problems solvable in polylogarithmic time with a polynomial number of processing elements), and parallel algorithms using randomization and/or achieving optimal speed-ups. We use the ATM model of parallel computation.

The complexity theory developed around the class NC, first defined in [59], accurately describes the problems which can be considerably sped-up through the use of polynomial-bounded hardware. Problems in NC are exactly those with a great deal of potential parallelism. In contrast significant speed-ups cannot be achieved for logspace-complete problems in PTIME, unless PTIME=NC, [18] (one more unlikely fact of complexity theory, such as, NP=P, NP=co-NP etc.). Logspace-complete problems in PTIME are, in a worst case sense, inherently sequential and represent the type of lower bounds that can be shown given the state-of-the-art in Computer Science theory.

As with sequential computation and the class PTIME, polynomial (e.g. n^{100}) does not necessarily mean practical time or number of processors or processing elements. Moreover, even low degree polynomials, which are satisfactory time bounds for sequential algorithms, are sometimes unsatisfactory processor bounds. It is however widely accepted that PRAM algorithms (for the Parallel Random Access Machine model of computation) with "small" processor bounds are quite close to algorithms for "real" multiprocessor machines. Well how small is "small"? For primitive combinatorial operations, such as, sorting or unification, PRAM algorithms using O(n) processors are potentially useful. For database applications, where n is the database size, processor bounds beyond O(log n) are positively unrealistic. The formal tools of optimal parallel algorithms and randomization have been developed to address precisely these concerns.

In Section 3 we review recent developments in the study of logic programs on unstructured data. Our presentation highlights the fact that all of these results deal with the *stage function* $s_H(n)$ of a logical query program H, (n is the database size). Section 3.1 has definitions, Section 3.2 lower bounds, and Sections 3.3, 3.4 programs with inherent parallelism. In this context we also present two new results. (1) We show that deciding whether $s_H(n)=O(1)$, for a linear single rule program H is NP-hard; this extends the analysis of [57, 42], (Section 3.4). (2) We show that extending the polynomial fringe property of [76] to constant width derivation trees leads to a stronger sufficient condition for evaluating programs in $s(n)=O(\log n)$ stages, (Section 3.3).

The topic of Section 4 is unification of terms, the primitive operation of logic programming on structured data defined by Robinson in [63]. Robinson's unification algorithm required time exponential in the size of terms. The following years saw a sequence of unification algorithms culminating with the linear-time algorithm of [60]. Unification can also be generalized to higher-order logics and equational theories [38]. These generalizations although quite interesting usually lead to hard computational questions outside PTIME. We concentrate on parallel first-order uninterpreted unification, (Section 4.1). In Sections 4.2, 4.3 we review the lower and upper bounds appearing in [22, 86, 23, 84, 83].

In order to complete the picture of the state-of-art we include two sections with open questions (Sections 3.5 and 4.4). Finally, in our conclusions (Section 5) we comment on the potential impact of these theoretical results to practice.

2. Parallel Algorithms and Complexity

For sequential computation we use the standard models of *Deterministic Turing Machines* (DTMs), *Nondeterministic Turing Machines* (NTMs), their *time* and *space* resource definitions, as well as, *log-space reducibility* [37]. A decision problem is in the class LOGSPACE = DTM-space(log n) if it can be decided by a DTM, which uses O(log n) auxiliary space on inputs of size n. Similarly we define NLOGSPACE = NTM-space(log n) and PTIME = DTM-time($n^{O(1)}$), that is, PTIME consists of those decision problems, which can be decided by some DTM using O(n^k) time (for some constant k) on inputs of size n. We use the terms *polynomial* for $n^{O(1)}$, *polylogarithmic* for $\log^{O(1)} n$, and *superpolynomial* for $2^{\log^{O(1)} n}$.

Alternating Turing Machines (ATMs) are generalizations of NTMs, defined in [12]. We assume that their input (of size n) is on an end-marked, read-only input tape. They can informally, but fairly intuitively, be described as follows.
The ATM states are partitioned into *existential* and *universal* states. As with a NTM, the transitions of an ATM on an input string determine a relation among *configurations* (IDs), where (ID_i, ID_j) is in this relation if and only if the machine can move in one step from ID_i to ID_j. A *computation tree* of an ATM on an input string consists of a tree. The nodes of this tree are configurations of the ATM on the input string and constrained so that: the children in a computation tree of any non-leaf configuration ID_i with a universal (resp. existential) state include all (resp. one) of the configurations that are possible one step next moves from ID_i of the ATM. A computation tree is accepting if the root is labeled with the initial configuration and all leaves with accepting configurations. The input string is accepted if and only if there is an accepting computation tree. A NTM is an ATM all of whose states are existential.
An ATM uses (a) time T(n), (b) space S(n), (c) tree-size Z(n), if for all accepted inputs of size n there is an accepting computation tree (a) whose longest path has at most T(n) nodes, (b) each of whose nodes is labeled by a configuration using auxiliary space at most S(n), (c) whose number of nodes is at most Z(n). ATM-time(T(n)) is the class of decision problems each of which can be decided be an ATM using time O(T(n)). Similarly we define ATM-space(S(n)), ATM-treesize(Z(n)). The importance of the *tree-size* resource was demonstrated in [65]. The following fundamental identity is shown in [12]:
PTIME = ATM-space(log n) (or ALOGSPACE)

Problems decided by ATMs using *simultaneously* space O(S(n)) and time O(T(n)), or simultaneously space O(S(n)) and tree-size O(Z(n)) form the complexity classes ATM-space-time(S(n), T(n)) and ATM-space-treesize(S(n), Z(n)). Complexity classes with simultaneous resource bounds can be used to make precise the notions of "problems with inherent parallelism" or "problems which can be solved very fast in parallel using a bounded amount of processing elements". The complexity class NC, defined in [59], is such a class. As we shall see it is largely independent of the choice of parallel computation model.

For expository reasons we start with the characterization of NC based on ATMs [65]:

$$NC = \text{ATM-space-time}(\log n, \log^{O(1)} n) = \text{ATM-space-treesize}(\log n, 2^{\log^{O(1)} n}).$$

NC is a subset of PTIME=ALOGSPACE, because of the additional simultaneous polylogarithmic time or superpolynomial tree-size restrictions. For PTIME we have in fact:

$$PTIME = \text{ATM-space}(\log n) = \text{ATM-space-time}(\log n, n^{O(1)}) = \text{ATM-space-treesize}(\log n, 2^{n^{O(1)}}).$$

Refining the space-time bounds we have NC^k, $k=2,3,...$

$$NC^k = \text{ATM-space-time}(\log n, \log^k n), \text{ for } k=2,3,...$$

Refining the space-treesize bounds we have the class LOGCFL, important for the study of context free languages as well as logic programs [65]:

$$LOGCFL = \text{ATM-space-treesize}(\log n, n^{O(1)}).$$

Many parallel algorithms are expressed using the model of *Parallel Random Access Machines* (PRAMs) of [27]. NC is also equal to the class of problems solvable on a PRAM using simultaneously polylogarithmic PRAM-time and a polynomial number of PRAM-processors.

Another perhaps more fundamental model of parallel computation is *Uniform Circuits of bounded fan-in*, (UCs); see [18, 66] for the technical uniformity conditions. Once again NC captures "parallel solutions in very fast time and bounded hardware", because it is equal to the class of problems solvable by UCs using simultaneously polylogarithmic circuit-depth and polynomial circuit-size. The classes NC^k $k=2,3,...$ can be defined using UCs. In addition NC^1 is also defined in this model
$NC^k = \text{UC-size-depth}(n^{O(1)}, \log^k n)$, for $k=1,2,3,...$

We can close our review of these complexity classes, all subsets of PTIME, with the following containements which are believed (but not yet proven) to be proper:

$$NC^1 \subseteq LOGSPACE \subseteq NLOGSPACE \subseteq LOGCFL \subseteq NC^2 \subseteq NC^3 \subseteq NC \subseteq ALOGSPACE.$$

Since the containement $NC \subseteq PTIME = ALOGSPACE$ is strongly conjectured to be strict, a proof that a problem is *logspace-complete* in PTIME is evidence of its inherently sequential nature. On the other hand, membership in NC denotes the presence of a high degree of potential parallelism [18]. Many natural problems are known to be logspace-complete in PTIME. Such problems that are also relevant to our exposition are: *path system accessibility* the first such problem discovered [17]; *monotone circuit value* [31]; *propositional Horn clause implication* [44] the propositional formulation of deductive databases [30]; *unification of terms* [22, 86, 23] the fundamental operation of logic programming [63]. These problems are complete in PTIME under more strict notions of reducibility than logspace-reducibility. They are complete under *NC^1-reducibility* [18] and even *first-order-reducibility* [41]. This last reducibility is useful for proving less general but unconditional lower bounds [39].

An optimal parallel algorithm is a PRAM algorithm which using m processors runs in time O(Seq(n)/m), where Seq(n) is the best known sequential time bound for the problem. Optimal parallel algorithms achieve the greatest speed-up possible given m processors. In addition most common PRAM algorithms using m processors and using T(n) time can be modified to use k processors, for $1 \leq k \leq m$, and run in time O(T(n)m/k), (by having k machines simulate m machines). Whereas membership in NC is a certificate of parallelizability, an optimal parallel algorithm for m processors is a potentialy useful algorithm for the entire range of 1 up to m processors. For a discussion of these issues see [19].

Example 2.1: Given a graph G and two distinguished nodes u and v in G the graph accessibility problem GAP is: does there exist a path in G from u to v? If G is undirected we have u-GAP and if G is directed acyclic of bounded degree we have dag-GAP.
GAP is in NLOGSPACE, in fact dag-GAP is logspace-complete in this class. For u-GAP there are optimal parallel algorithms (see [19] for the history and recent developments on this problem). For dag-GAP it is easy to see that Seq(n)=O(n). However the known NC algorithms for dag-GAP use M(n)/log n processors to achieve $O(\log^2 n)$ time. $M(n)=n^{2.49...}$ is the best sequential-time bound for n by n matrix multiplication [20, 10]. Thus for m processors the best known time bound is order *min*(n, M(n)log n/m) $1 \leq m \leq M(n)/\log n$. For $m=O(n^{1.49..})$ the best known solution effectively uses only one processor! The existence of an optimal parallel algorithm for dag-GAP is one of the more important open questions in parallel computation.

Randomization can also play an important role, combined either with NC or with optimal parallel algorithms. Randomized algorithms are like PRAM algorithms, where each processor can at any step flip an unbiased coin (the coin flips of different processors are independent). Without any assumptions on the distribution of their inputs randomized algorithms compute the correct answer with overwhelming probability, e.g., [61, 71, 49]. For example, the algorithm in [49] is a randomized polylogarithmic time algorithm, which uses a polynomial number of processors for finding a maximum matching in a graph, (this matching is not to be confused with the term matching of Section 4). Without randomization, an algorithm with this running time and number of processors is not known. Processor requirements for certain problems can be substantially reduced using randomization [62, 82, 23].

3. Parallelism and Unstructured Data

3.1. Databases, Data Complexity, and Logical Query Programs

Let our *universe* be a fixed, countably infinite set of constants. A *database* is a vector $B=(D,r_1,...,r_p)$, where D is a finite subset of the universe called the *database domain*, and for each i, $1 \leq i \leq p$, $r_i \subseteq D^{k_i}$ (for some integer $k_i \geq 0$) is a *relation* of *arity* k_i. An element of a relation is called a *tuple*. Database B is said to have *sort* $(k_1,...,k_p)$. A *query* of sort $(k_1,...,k_p) \rightarrow k$ for some integer $k \geq 0$, is a function Q from databases of sort $(k_1,...,k_p)$ to databases of sort k, such that, if $B=(D,r_1,...,r_p)$, then $Q(B) \subseteq D^k$. Note that when $k=0$ we have a *boolean* query, which returns either ø (false) or D^0 the set containing the empty tuple (true). The tuples in relations represent unstructured data.

The *data complexity* of query Q, [8, 77], is the computational complexity of testing membership in the set $\{(w,B) \mid \text{tuple } w \in Q(B)\}$. With a slight abuse of notation, we say that query Q is in the class LOGSPACE, NC, PTIME, ... iff the set $\{(w,B) \mid \text{tuple } w \in Q(B)\}$ can be decided in LOGSPACE, NC, PTIME ... . Similarly query Q is logspace-complete in PTIME (or PTIME-complete) if the corresponding decision problem is logspace-complete in PTIME. For the purposes of measuring data complexity, the *size* of database B, $|B|=n$, is the length of the representation of B in some standard encoding. Note that the database size and not the size of a program for Q is the asymptotically growing parameter.

First-order queries are the queries expressible in first-order relational calculus (with finite interpretations). First-order logic has been recognized as a powerful declarative language for expressing queries [16]. The ability to translate first-order queries into relational algebra, a procedural language, and their low data complexity are the theoretical foundations of database theory [16, 1, 74]. First-order queries are in LOGSPACE and thus contain a great deal of potential parallelism. Not all queries in LOGSPACE are first-order queries. This limitation of first-order logic is true even if we augment it with an order predicate $\leq$, or other interpreted predicates, or even weak monadic second order quantification. The finiteness of the interpretations makes this an interesting issue [25, 1, 39, 41, 8, 21, 29, 34].

Fixpoint queries are obtained by augmenting first-order logic with the *fixpoint operator* μ. Detailed expositions of these queries and their expressive power can be found in [56, 5, 8, 35]. Fixpoint queries are in PTIME. However, in order to be able to express every PTIME query as a fixpoint query we need to add to the language an order predicate $\leq$, see [26, 40, 77, 33, 70, 21, 58] for this robust expressibility result.
The expressive power of negation in fixpoint queries has been examined in [8, 25, 21]. An important observation [40, 32] is that negation interacts differently with fixpoint operator μ in the finite case (the database case) than it does for infinite interpretations [56, 5]. For the finite case application of μ once on a first-order query suffices to express all fixpoint queries; for the infinite case negation and μ might have to alternate.

An interesting subset of the fixpoint queries, without negation, can be expressed using function-free Horn clauses as a programming language [9, 30]. This approach lies at the heart of the programming language PROLOG, whenever it is used to handle unstructured data. These *logical queries* are queries expressible in the language of *logical query programs* [76], (also known as Horn clause query programs [9], deductive database query programs [30], recursive rule query programs [11], or popularly as DATALOG programs). We now define the syntax and semantics of these programs.

SYNTAX

We assume we have a countably infinite set of variables $\{x,y,z,...\}$ and of predicate symbols of all arities $\{R,R_0,R_1,...\}$. A *rule* is an expression of the form:

$A \leftarrow A_1,...,A_e.$ for $e \geq 0$,

where $A,A_1,...,A_e$ are *atomic formulas* of the form $R_i(x_1,...,x_{k_i})$ and each x_j, $1 \leq j \leq k_i$, is a variable and $k_i \geq 0$ is the arity of R_i, (for $k_i=0$ there are no variables in the atomic formula). We call A the *consequence* and $A_1,...,A_e$ the *antecedents* of this rule, (for $e=0$ there are no antecedents in the rule).

Note that a rule does not contain any instantiated variables or any interpreted predicates (e.g. order or inequality), and that equality is expressed using equal variables.

A *logical query program* (program) H is a finite set of rules. A predicate symbol in program H is said to be an *intentional database predicate* (IDB) iff it appears in the consequence of some rule; otherwise it is an *extentional database predicate* (EDB).

SEMANTICS

Let $B=(D,r_1,...,r_q)$ be a database, and let program H have EDBs $R_1,...,R_q$ and IDBs $R_{q+1},...,R_p$.

A *valuation* ρ is a function from variables to finite set D. If A is the atomic formula $R(x_1,...,x_k)$ then $A\rho$ is the tuple $(\rho(x_1),...,\rho(x_k))$. In addition, if predicate symbol R is interpreted as relation r in database $B=(D,...,r,...)$ then the notation $A\rho \in B$ means that tuple $(\rho(x_1),...,\rho(x_k)) \in r$. We define a sequence of databases $I^s_H(B)$ $(s=0,1,...)$:

$I^s_H(B)=(D, r^s_1,..., r^s_q, r^s_{q+1},..., r^s_p)$, where we have, $r^0_i=r_i$, $1 \leq i \leq q$, $r^0_j=\emptyset$, $q+1 \leq j \leq p$, and

$r^{s+1}_i=r^s_i \cup \{ A\rho \mid \rho$ is a valuation and there is a rule $A \leftarrow A_1,...,A_e.$ in H such that, the predicate symbol of A is R_i and each $A_j\rho$ is in $I^s_H(B)$, $1 \leq j \leq e\}$, $1 \leq i \leq p$.

Note that $r^s_i \subseteq r^{s+1}_i \subseteq D^{k_i}$, for all i, s. The EDB relations are not modified, $r^s_i=r_i$ for all i, s, $1 \leq i \leq q$.

$I^\omega_H(B) = (D, r^\omega_1,..., r^\omega_q, r^\omega_{q+1},..., r^\omega_p)$, where we have, $r^\omega_i = \bigcup_{s \geq 0} r^s_i$, $1 \leq i \leq p$.

The *minimum model* of program H on database B is $I^\omega_H(B)$. This operational definition is equivalent with the fixpoint definition in [4, 50, 81]. We have adopted it because of our emphasis on the concept of the *stage function.*

The database $I_H^{s+1}(B)$ can be computed from the database $I_H^s(B)$ using only logarithmic auxiliary space, so this computation can be done with an NC algorithm. We call this computation the s<u>th</u> *naive iteration.* The *naive evaluation* of the minimum model $I_H^\omega(B)$ is to perform successive naive iterations until for some s we have $I_H^s(B)=I_H^{s+1}(B)$. Since D is finite such an s_0 exists and therefore for $s \geq s_0$ $I_H^\omega(B)=I_H^s(B)$.

Definition 3.1.1: For program H, the *stage function* of n, $s_H(n)$ is the least s such that $I_H^\omega(B)=I_H^s(B)$, for all databases B of size at most n.

As is shown in [8], for each fixed H we have $s_H(n)=O(n^k)$, for some constant $k \geq 0$, which depends on the arities of predicates in H. Whenever $s_H(n)=O(\log^k n)$, for some constant $k \geq 0$, $I_H^\omega(B)$ can be computed in NC by performing $s_H(n)$ naive iterations. Is $s_H=O(1)$ we will say that H is *bounded*, else it is *unbounded.*

A program H can be used to define a query by designating the EDBs as inputs and a single IDB as output. When the output choice is clear from the context we will refer to the query defined by H as Q_H.

EXPRESSIVE POWER

Logical query programs can define a strict subset of the fixpoint queries. This is because of the absence of negation, even of inequality. They are therefore in PTIME, although not necessarily in NC. Precise expressibility results are investigated in [9]. Logical query programs do define a natural class of queries. Important combinatorial problems can be defined, such as, transitive closure and path system accessibility. Logical query programs combine recursion (a single application of fixpoint operator μ) with *a union of untyped, tagged, tableaux*, the most common first-order queries [74].

Definition 3.1.2: A query Q is in class STAGE(f(n)) if there exists a program H such that $Q=Q_H$ and $s_H(n)=O(f(n))$.

A query in STAGE(f(n)) can be evaluated in O(f(n)) naive iterations, where each iteration is a first-order query. In fact each iteration is a union of untyped tagged tableaux queries. Also each bounded query, i.e., in STAGE(O(1)), is easily seen to be a union of untyped tagged tableaux. These STAGE classes are similar to the iterated query classes of [40], without negation. Clearly, for each program H and any output choice the query Q_H is in STAGE[$s_H(n)$].

The following inclusions indicate the natural STAGE analogs of the classes NC^2,NC and PTIME.
STAGE(log n) $\subseteq NC^2$,

$STAGE(\log^{O[1]} n) \subseteq NC$,
$STAGE(\log^{O(1)} n) \subseteq STAGE(n)$,
$STAGE(n^{O(1)}) \subseteq PTIME$.

Because of the absence of interpreted predicates (e.g., order) in logical query programs, it is possible to demonstrate that these inclusions are *proper* [39].

Example 3.1.3: In addition to their other rules let the following programs always contain rule $R(x,y) \leftarrow R_0(x,y)$.

a. Transitive closure of R_0 is defined using rule, $R(x,y) \leftarrow R(x,z),R(z,y)$.
Here we have $s(n) = \Theta(\log n)$.

b. This transitive closure is also defined using rule, $R(x,y) \leftarrow R(x,z),R_0(z,y)$.
Here however we have $s(n) = \Theta(n)$.

c. Undirected transitive closure is defined using rules, $R(x,y) \leftarrow R(x,z),R(z,y)$. and $R(x,y) \leftarrow R_0(y,x)$.
With $s(n) = \Theta(\log n)$.

d. Bipartite transitive closure is defined using rule, $R(x,y) \leftarrow R(x,y_1),R(x_1,y),R(x_1,y_1)$.
With $s(n) = \Theta(\log n)$.

e. If 0-ary IDB predicate R_c is true, directed graph R_0 has a cycle, $R_c \leftarrow R(x,x)$. and $R(x,y) \leftarrow R(x,z),R(z,y)$.
With $s(n) = \Theta(\log n)$.

f. Context free language $\{a^n c b^n \mid n \geq 0\}$ can be simulated by rule, $R(x,y) \leftarrow R_1(x,z),R(z,z_1),R_2(z_1,y)$.
Here $s(n) = \Theta(n)$, but as we shall see this query is in $STAGE(\log n)$.

g. All tableaux queries can be trivially written in this language and are bounded. It is possible to write less trivial programs, which are also bounded. $R(x,y) \leftarrow R(z,z_1),R_1(x,y),R_1(z,z_1)$.
This query is bounded with $s(n) = 1$.

SUBLANGUAGES

There are various syntactically restricted subsets of logical query programs, which are of independent interest.

I. We say that program H is *linear* if the antecedents of each rule contain at most one IDB symbol. The programs in Example 3.1.3 (b,f,g) are linear.

Linear programs can be generalized as follows. Let G_H be the following directed labeled multigraph:

a. The set of nodes is $\{i \mid R_i$ is a predicate symbol in $H\}$.

b. The multiset of labeled arcs is constructed as follows:

for the j-th rule in H $R_i(...) \leftarrow R_{i_1}(...),R_{i_2}(...),...,R_{i_e}(...)$ *add* the arcs $(i_1, i), (i_2, i),...,(i_e, i)$ labeled j.

The nodes of G_H can be partitioned uniquely into *strongly connected components.* Each labeled arc of G_H is either contained in a component or is between nodes in different components. We call H *piecewise linear* iff no strong component of contains two arcs with the same label.

Each linear rule is clearly also piecewise linear. If G_H is acyclic we say that H is *nonrecursive*, else it is *recursive*. Clearly any union of untyped tagged tableaux can be written as a nonrecursive program, and is bounded.

Piecewise linear programs form a large, natural syntactic class of programs. All first-order queries expressible using logical query programs can be written using piecewise linear programs. All piecewise linear queries are in STAGE(log n).

II. There are certain syntactic restrictions on programs, which facilitate their analysis.

One such class of programs are those consisting of *elementary chain rules*. A rule with consequence R(x,y) is an elementary chain rule if the variables in its antecedents form a chain from x to y (see [76] for a precise definition). Example 3.1.3 (a,b,f) clearly illustrate such rules. The theory of context free grammars is useful in the analysis of elementary chain programs.

A logical query program with IDB predicates R, R',... is *uniform* if it contains *initialization* rules $R(x,y,...) \leftarrow R_0(x,y,...)$. and $R(x,y,...) \leftarrow R_0'(x,y,...)$. ... and in addition EDBs $R_0, R_0', ...$ appear in no other rules. The programs in Example 3.1.3 (a,d,f,g) are uniform. This restriction is equivalent to arbitrarily initializing every IDB. Homomorphism techniques from database dependency theory are useful in the analysis of uniform programs.

III. The simplest recursive logical query programs are the *single rule programs* (sirups). A sirup H is a uniform, recursive program with one IDB predicate R. In addition to the initialization rule $R(x,y....) \leftarrow R_0(x,y,...)$ program H has one *defining* rule.

Note that, because H is uniform and recursive, the defining rule has consequence R, does not contain R_0, and contains R in its antecedents. A sirup can have one possible output R.

The sirup is *pure* if R is the only predicate in the defining rule. The sirup is *typed* if it is pure and there is a partition of the variables into k blocks such that if $R(x_1,...,x_k)$ appears in H then x_i is in the ith block.

Typed sirups and full template dependencies [74] are identical. Examples 3.1.3 (a,d,f,g) are sirups, (a) is pure, (d) is typed, (f,g) are linear, (a,f) are elementary chains. When we refer to a sirup we need only describe its defining rule.

3.2. Inherently Sequential Programs

Logical query programs express queries in PTIME. Despite the lack of features, such as, negation, order, etc... in the language there are simple programs defining queries, whose data complexity is as high as that of any PTIME query. These are typically nonlinear sirups. The most celebrated one is path system accessibility [17]

$R(x) \leftarrow R(y), R(z), R_3(x,y,z).$

We call this sirup *monadic* since R is 1-ary. Path system accessibility is logspace-complete in PTIME. In addition, [39] has shown using a combinatorial game argument that its is in STAGE(n)\STAGE($\log^{O(1)} n$). This strict lower bound (the proof depends on the lack of an order predicate) applies to all other PTIME-complete queries in this section.

Syntactically tight PTIME-complete elementary chain sirups are examined in [76, 2], typed and pure sirups in [11], and monadic sirups in [48]. The following sirup is in a syntactic sense the simplest hard sirup. The theorem is from the unpublished notes [48].

Theorem 3.2.1: The query defined by sirup,
$R(x) \leftarrow R(y), R(z), R_1(y,x), R_1(x,z)$. is logspace-complete in PTIME and in STAGE(n)\STAGE($\log^{O(1)} n$).

Proof Sketch: Logspace-hardness follows from a reduction from monotone circuit value. W.l.o.g. the circuit consists of alternating layers of AND and OR gates; AND gates have indegree 2 and outdegree 1; OR gates have indegree 2 and outdegree $k \geq 2$. Every wire w in the circuit is associated with a constant w in the EDB relations, such that, wire w has value 1 iff R(w) is true in the minimum model.

The 0,1 inputs to the circuit are encoded using the initialization rule $R(x) \leftarrow R_0(x)$ and EDB relation r_0. The AND and OR gates are simulated by patterns of tuples in EDB relations r_0 and r_1. These patterns are presented graphically in Figure 1. Pairs in r_1 are arcs labeled r_1 and elements of r_0 are nodes labeled r_0.

This reduction technique works for most monadic sirups although care has to be taken each time in showing that wire w has value 1 iff R(w) is true. The strict lower bound follows from the results in [39] and the nature of these reductions, they are first-order translations [41].
Q.E.D.

3.3. Parallelizable Programs

Let H be a program to be evaluated on database B. If D is the (finite) domain of B then the (finite) *Herbrand Base* of H on B are all possible ground atomic formulas, *atoms*, which are instantiations of IDBs of H with elements of D. Note that, since for EDBs the only relevant atoms are the tuples of B, we define the Herbrand Base with IDB atoms. A natural notion associated with the evaluation of H on B is the derivation tree.

Definition 3.3.1: Let w be an element of the Herbrand Base of H on B. A *derivation tree of width* k for w is a tree, each of whose nodes is labeled with a subset V of the Herbrand Base of size at most k, and such that:
a. If v is the root node then w is an element of V,
b. If v is a leaf node then V is empty,

c. If v is an internal node, whose children are labeled by sets $V_1,...,V_i$, then all elements of V can be derived in *one naive iteration* of H on relations $B \cup V_1 \cup ... V_i$.

Clearly w is in the minimum model of H on B iff there is a derivation tree for w (of some width). A derivation tree, which is a path of polynomial in n length, but unfortunately polynomial in n width is provided by naive evaluation (n is the size of B).

Example 3.3.2: Consider the following monadic sirup,
$R(x) \leftarrow R(y), R(z), R_1(y,x), R_1(x,z), R_1(z,y)$.
Database $B=(D,r_0,r_1)$ is represented pictorially in Figure 2a, using the obvious notation. R(7) is in the minimum model. A derivation tree for R(7) of width 2 is shown in Figure 2b and one of width 1 in Figure 2c. It is easy to see that the database in this example can be extended downwards, so that, the top node has a width 2 derivation tree that is a long path, but its best derivation tree of width 1 is of exponential size.

With every program H and constant k we can associate an Alternating Turing Machine $ATM_{H,k}$, which uses O(log n) space on inputs of size n. The inputs to this machine are pairs (w,B), where B is a database and w an element of the Herbrand Base of H on B. $ATM_{H,k}$ accepts (w,B) iff w is in the minimum model of H and B. The accepting computation trees of $ATM_{H,k}$ on input (w,B) are the derivation trees of width k of w. In an existential state the configuration of $ATM_{H,k}$ has in logarithmic auxiliary storage a subset V of the Herbrand Base. The machine guesses sets $V_1,...,V_i$ and verifies that condition (c) of the derivation tree definition holds. This brings it to a universal state, with i children existential states whose configurations are $V_1,...,V_i$. From our review of Section 2 it is clear that, if for some constant k $ATM_{H,k}$ uses polynomial (superpolynomial) tree-size the queries defined by H are in LOGCFL (NC).

Definition 3.3.3: A program H has the polynomial (superpolynomial) tree-size property if there exists a constant k, such that, for every database B and atom w in the minimum model of H on B, atom w has a derivation tree of width k and size polynomial (superpolynomial) in the size of B.

The *polynomial fringe property* of [76] is based on this insight (for width 1 derivation trees). It can be used to characterize parallelizable programs. In fact [76] show something far more interesting and (not) surprisingly related to the stage function. Given a parallelizable program H [76] provide a simple syntactic transformation of H into an equivalent program H'. The transformation is such that, the naive evaluation of H' takes at most polylogarithmic naive iterations of H'. The method used has many other interesting applications in parallel computation [85, 3, 54]. The following is essentially Theorem 6.2 of [76], extended to width k derivation trees, which are strictly more powerful.

Theorem 3.3.4:
(a) A program H with the polynomial (superpolynomial) tree-size property is in STAGE(log n) (STAGE($\log^{O(1)}$ n)).
(b) There is a program with the polynomial tree-size property, which does not satisfy the polynomial fringe property of [76].

Proof Sketch: (a) As in the proof of [76] each naive iteration is augmented by one step of a logarithmic transitive closure algorithm on an implication graph. The old naive iteration takes care of "bushy but short" derivation trees, the transitive closure of "skinny but long" derivation trees. This new *fast iteration* is the naive iteration of a new program H´and handles all derivation trees of reasonable size fast. The stage function of H´ is logarithmic (polylogarithmic) if H has the polynomial (superpolynomial) tree-size property.
The only modification of the implication graph for the width k case, is that its nodes are all subsets of size k of the Herbrand base. An arc in the implication graph from V to V´denotes the sylogism that from a proof of V and the minimum model discovered up to this point one naive iteration of H would produce V.´
As in [76] each naive iteration of H´can be performed with polynomial in n (the size of B) number of PRAM-processors in O(log n) PRAM-time. The exponent however depends on the maximum arity c in H and on k, $O(n^{3ck})$. Since the implication graph might involve large parts of the Herbrand Base (in each iteration) this is the unrealistic part of the transformation.

Part (b) is based on Example 3.3.2. The query in this example is logspace-complete in PTIME [48], i.e., there are more complex databases to evaluate it on than that of Figure 1a. It is possible to modify the example to produce a query expressed by a logical query program H and in STAGE(log n) with the following property:
"it does not always have derivation trees of width 1 of polynomial size, although it does have width 2 polynomial size derivation trees". The basic intutition is to notice the "triangle" symmetry in the sirup and to create databases where recursion takes place only if two "triangles" share a side; for triangle adjacency we use transitive closure. Here is this logical query program H:
$R_2(x,x_1,y_1,z_1) \leftarrow R_0(x), R_1(x_1,y_1),R_1(y_1,z_1),R_1(z_1,x_1).$
$R_3(x,y,z,x,y,z_1) \leftarrow R_1(x,y),R_1(y,z),R_1(z,x),R_1(y,z_1),R_1(z_1,x).$
$R_3(x,y,z,x_1,y_1,z_1) \leftarrow R_3(x,y,z,x_2,y_2,z_2), R_3(x_2,y_2,z_2,x_1,y_1,z_1).$
$R_2(x,x_1,y_1,z_1) \leftarrow R_2(y,x_1,y_1,z_1), R_2(z,x_1,y_1,z_1), R_3(x,y,z,x_1,y_1,z_1).$
Q.E.D.

The proof of this theorem may be viewed as an abstract interpreter. This interpreter will, without testing for parallelizability, work in polylogarithmic iterations in the presence of the superpolynomial tree-size property and otherwise degenerate into naive evaluation (perhaps even worse). In order to utilize other, more realistic interpreters or compilers, one would like syntactic characterizations of parallelizability. Syntactic characterizations will be sufficient conditions, because of the undecidability [76, 2] of testing for parallelizability.

All known syntactic sufficient conditions follow from Theorem 3.3.4. and involve the class STAGE(log n). For example, piecewise linear programs are in STAGE(log n) [76, 11, 79]. Some elementary chain programs in STAGE(log n) are described in [76] and some typed sirups in this class are in [11]. Bounded programs are in STAGE(log n), but they deserve their own section.
Some of the most elegant combinatorial results involve sirups and new insights into context free languages: (1) all elementary chain sirups are syntactically classified as in STAGE(log n) or PTIME-complete in [2], (2) There exists an inherently nonlinear parallelizable sirup [76].

3.4. Unbounded vs Bounded Programs

A program H may be used to define a set of queries, one for each choice of output predicate. If these are all first-order queries we say that H is first-order. Under what conditions is H first-order? Consider the graph G_H, used to define piecewise linear programs. It captures the dependencies among the various predicates. If it is acyclic we called H nonrecursive and clearly H is then first-order and bounded. As illustrated in Example 3.1.3. (g) this condition is not necessary. Once again the stage function is a central notion.

Recall that H is bounded if its stage function is bounded by a constant. As shown in [57], boundedness characterizes first-order programs. Furthermore the queries defined by bounded programs are finite unions of untypped tagged tableaux. For unbounded programs they are infinite unions of untypped tagged tableaux. There is an interesting fact also about unbounded programs. Because of their restricted syntax there is a *gap* [37] theorem for these programs. Namely, as shown in [11], if the program is unbounded the stage function is $\Omega(\log n)$. The proofs of these theorems are based on homomorphism techniques from database theory. They are summarized as follows, where part (a) is from [57] and part (b) from [11]:

Theorem 3.4.1: Program H is,
(a) first-order iff $s_H = O(1)$.
(b) not first-order iff $s_H = \Omega(\log n)$.

The problem of boundedness has received a fair amount of attention. The first sufficient condition for boundedness was formulated in [55]. Boundedness is decidable for elementary chain programs, since it corresponds to context free language finiteness. It is also decidable for typed sirups (and sets of typed rules) [67], although it is NP-hard in the size of the sirup [87]. The decision procedure of [67] for typed rules may be extended to certain (but not all) pure rules using [11]'s proof technique.

For linear programs sufficient conditions for boundedness appear in [42, 57]. These lead to efficient decision procedures for certain subsets of the linear sirups. An example of such a subset from [57] is "linear sirups with no repetitions of EDB symbols in the defining rule of the sirup". Unfortunately boundedness of linear programs is undecidable even for linear programs [28], and uniform linear programs [51]. It is sufficient for undecidability that the program consist of the union of one recursive linear rule and a constant number of nonrecursive rules; its predicates can be binary (monadic recursion is used if inequality is allowed), [80].

The decidability of boundedness of sirups is still open, even for pure or linear sirups. We complete this review of the state-of-the-art of boundedness with a new observation about linear sirups. This theorem generalizes certain example sirups in [57] not covered by known efficient criteria.

Theorem 3.4.2: Boundedness of linear sirups is NP-hard, in the size of the sirups. This is true even for a linear sirup with IDB of arity 4 and one EDB of arity 2 in the defining rule.

Proof Sketch: The reduction is from three colorability of an undirected graph G [37]. Given graph G construct the following sirup H(G),

$R(x,y,z,v) \leftarrow R(x,y,z,w), R_1(x,v),R_1(y,v),R_1(z,v),R_2(w,x),R_2(w,y),R_2(w,z),$
$R_3(x,y),R_3(y,x),R_3(z,x),R_3(x,z),R_3(z,y),R_3(y,z),$
$\ldots,R_1(x_i,v),R_1(w,x_i),\ldots$ (where x_i is a node in G)
$\ldots,R_3(x_i,x_j),R_3(x_j,x_i),\ldots$ (where x_ix_j is an edge in G).

One can show that H(G) is bounded with bound 1 iff G is three-colorable. Moreover, the three EDB symbols R_1,R_2,R_3 can be encoded by a single EDB symbol.
Q.E.D.

3.5. Open Questions

We are now going to outline a number of interesting open questions about these logical query programs.

ANALYSIS

1. First a concrete technical question. Is boundedness of sirups decidable, even for linear or pure sirups?

2. The most fundamental question in this area is to develop techniques to estimate the stage function of a given program. Boundedness is a special case. For example, find sufficient conditions on typed sirups that guarantee $s(n)=O(\log n)$.

3. Naive evaluation is a simple algorithm. Is it possible to use tools from the mathematical analysis of

algorithms to compute expected time bounds for the stage function, for random input databases?

4. Is there a way of quantifying the complexity of operational definitions of negation, such as, negation as failure [14]? Because of the finiteness assumption, negation and fixpoints may interact in unexpected ways [40, 32, 56]. The use of negation by an interpreter might speed-up the evaluation of a logical query program.

EQUIVALENCE

1. A technical question here from [11] is: let H be a type sirup and Q a tableau query, is $Q_H \subseteq Q$ decidable? The containement $Q \subseteq Q_H$ is decidable.

2. Theorem 3.3.4. is based on an equivalence preserving transformation. Unfortunately equivalence of programs is undecidable [58]. One interesting features of uniform programs and sirups in particular is that their equivalence is decidable [69], by database dependency techniques. The fundamental question here is to develop equivalence preserving transformations for use in the query optimizer. An interesting such example is the *magic sets* of [6].

3. An algebraic theory of logical query programs would be very useful. Context free grammars for elementary chain programs have provided many technical tools; graph grammars capture only some aspects of the full theory.

CLASSIFICATION

1. A technical question here is to classify typed sirups and monadic sirups with respect to their parallel complexity, as was done for elementary chain sirups [2].

2. Study the gap and hierarchy properties [39, 37] of the STAGE complexity classes.

3. The author knows of no NC problem, which is expressible as a logical query and which is not in STAGE(log n). Is it possible to express, as logical queries, problems known to be in random NC but not known to be in NC [49]? Is Theorem 3.3.4.(a) a necessary condition for parallelizability?

4. The classification questions are related to finding the *dimension of inductive definitions* [56, 5, 21, 8], intuitively the minimum arity of the fixpoint definitions. Even for small dimensions there are hard open expressibility questions in this area [8].

PARALLEL EVALUATION

1. Restricted fixpoint operators, such as, transitive closure, undirected transitive closure, etc... have interesting expressibility properties [41]. Study parallel algorithms for these operations on databases. A

difference, from conventional parallel algorithms for such problems as u-GAP [19, 62], is the emphasis on external storage costs [43, 78].

2. The fundamental question here is: what are good top-down and bottom-up evaluation methods using m processors, where $m = O(\log n)$. In the presence of "goals with bound arguments" top-down evaluation might be a better method than bottom-up evaluation. Much recent work in the area [7, 36, 6, 68, 75] could be combined with parallel evaluation algorithms.

3. Is there an optimal parallel algorithm for the dag-GAP problem? This theoretical question is well motivated by the unreasonable PRAM processor bounds of Theorem 3.3.4.

4. Parallelism and Structured Data

4.1. Terms, Unification and Matching

PROLOG and other logic programming languages, in addition to their recursive control structure, provide primitive operations for the definition and manipulation of structured data. The most important such primitive for symbolic computation is the operation of unification of terms [63, 60, 53]. A special case of unification is term matching, with many applications in term rewriting, equational reasoning [38, 45] and even in PROLOG compilation [52].

We start with a countably infinite set of *variables* {x,y,z,...} and a disjoint countably infinite set of *function* symbols {f,g,...} of all *arities*. A *constant* is a funcion symbol of arity 0. The set of *terms* is the smallest set of finite strings, such that:
Every variable and constant is a term.
If f is a k-ary function symbol, $k \geq 1$, and $t_1,...,t_k$ are terms then $ft_1...t_k$ is a term.

A term t_v is usually represented by a labeled directed, acyclic, graph rooted at node v (dag v, for short), as follows:
Every node is labeled by either a variable or a k-ary function symbol.
A node labeled by variable x has outdegree 0 and represents the term x.
A node labeled by constant g has outdegree 0 and represents the term g.
A node labeled by k-ary function symbol f with $k \geq 1$ has k outgoing arcs labeled 1 to k. The term represented by the dag rooted at this node is $ft_1...t_k$, where t_i is represented by its subdag rooted at the head of the outgoing arc labeled i.
Since dag v is rooted at v all of its nodes are reachable from v. A dag v could be a *tree* (with root v). A dag v is *compact* if for all pairs of different nodes w and w' of this dag t_w and $t_{w'}$ are different terms, that is, a compact dag contains no repeated subdags. Note that although each node of a dag v determines a single

term the converse is only true for compact dags. It is easy to see that the dag representation can be very concise; a dag v of size n may represent a term of (string) length 2^n. Since term representations are not unique the first problem is one of equivalence of representations. We use = for syntactic equality of strings.

INPUT: Throughout our presentation we assume that the input consists of two *disjoint* dags respectively rooted at u and v. They represent terms t_u and t_v. Their size is n, and we explicitly state if one or both of them are trees or compact dags.

EQUAL: The *term equivalence* problem is given dags u,v is $t_u = t_v$?

A *substitution* is a mapping σ from variables to terms, for example, the valuations of Section 3.1 are substitutions where the terms are constants in D. The action of substitution σ on a term t, written $\sigma(t)$, is the result of replacing each variable x in t by $\sigma(x)$, where these replacements take place simultaneously. A substitution σ is *more general* that a substitution τ if there exists a substitution ρ, such that, $\tau(t) = \rho(\sigma(t))$, for all terms t. Term matching and unification are defined in terms of substitutions.

MATCH: The *term matching* problem is given dags u,v is there a substitution σ, such that, $\sigma(t_u) = t_v$?

UNIFY: The *term unification* problem is given dags u,v is there a substitution σ, such that, $\sigma(t_u) = \sigma(t_v)$?

A basic fact about unification is that whenever two terms are unifiable there is a unifier which is more general than any other unifier, the mgu. The mgu is unique up to renaming of variables. For example, terms fxy and fgygz are unifiable with mgu $\sigma(x) = ggz$ $\sigma(y) = gz$ and $\sigma(z) = z$; after the substitution both terms become fggzgz. Two canonical examples of ununifiable terms are x and gx, as well as, fxy and gz. Term matching of t_u and t_v is a subcase of unification where w.l.o.g. t_v contains no variables. Algorithms for UNIFY and MATCH also produce the mgu.

Naive Unification: Let us describe term unification using a naive algorithm for UNIFY. First given the input dags u,v, for each variable x identify all nodes with label x into a single node with label x. Let us call the resulting dag G. Let r be the smallest binary relation on the nodes of G such that:
r(u,v) is true.
r is an equivalence relation.
If node $a_i(b_i)$ is the ith child of node a(b) and r(a,b) then $r(a_i,b_i)$, (i.e., propagation to children)
Given an instance of UNIFY, t_u and t_v are unifiable iff relation r is *homogeneous* and *acyclic.*
Relation r is homogeneous if whenever r(a,b) then nodes a and b are not labeled by different function symbols, that is the nodes in each r-equivalence class are either labeled by variables or by a unique function

symbol. Relation r is acyclic if the r-equivalence classes are partially ordered by the arcs of the input dags. If r is homogeneous and acyclic then shrinking the r-equivalence classes to single nodes results in a rooted dag representing $\sigma(t_u)=\sigma(t_v)$ and σ is the mgu. A detailed example follows.

Example 4.1.1: Let 0 be a constant and f a binary function symbol, (e.g., "nil" and "cons"). The input terms $t_u=ff...f0x_k...x_2x_1$, $t_v=fx_1fx_2...fx_k0$ are represented by the (disjoint) dags u,v in Figure 3a. Note that t_u and t_v share variables. If we identify nodes labeled by the same variable we get Figure 3b. In this same figure the undirected edges represent r-equivalence classes of relation r of naive unification. If we shrink each r-equivalence class to a node we get the mgu σ. Note that $\sigma(t_u)=\sigma(t_v)$ is an exponentially long string in k represented by the compact dag of Figure 3c.

Let the structure of these terms be described in three EDB relations. r_0 contains the pair to be unified (u,v), r_i contains pairs of nodes (p,c) where c is the ith child of p, i=1,2. r is the minimum model of the following program H on these relations.

$R(x,y) \leftarrow R_0(x,y).$

$R(x,x) \leftarrow .$

$R(x,y) \leftarrow R(y,x).$

$R(x,y) \leftarrow R(x,z),R(z,y).$

$R(x,y) \leftarrow R(x_1,y_1),R_1(x_1,x),R_1(y_1,y).$

$R(x,y) \leftarrow R(x_2,y_2),R_2(x_2,x),R_2(y_2,y).$

For the above logical query program the stage function is linear, each naive iteration alternating between maintaining equivalence and propagating to children. This type of alternating behavior is the intuitive cause of the logspace-completeness of unification.

4.2. Inherently Sequential Operations

The operation of unification of terms is logspace-complete in PTIME. [22, 86]. Furthermore, as shown in [22] this lower bound does not depend on the conciseness of the dag representation. They hold for tree inputs. A different operation, which has some similarities with unification is *congruence closure* [24, 47]; congruence closure is also PTIME-complete [47].

If a variable appears in both input terms we say that they *share variables.* Variable sharing is a major cause of difficulty of unification as indicated by Example 4.1.1. and quantified in [23]. In a PROLOG interpreter, where each rule is really a local procedure, unification may be performed without any variable sharing. We say that a term t is *linear* if no variable appears in (string) t twice. Nonlinearity of both input terms is the major difficulty of unification in PROLOG [22]. We summarize the basic bounds of [22, 23] in the following theorem.

Theorem 4.2.1:

(a) For trees, UNIFY is logspace-complete in PTIME even if, either, both input terms are linear, or, do not share variables.

(b) For dags, UNIFY is in NC^3 provided the input terms do not share variables and one of them is linear. For dags MATCH is in NC^2.

The parallel algorithms for UNIFY of case (b) involve a modification of the parallel algorithms for MATCH. This is in order to account for unifying a set of trees representing linear terms that do not share variables. In the next section we will therefore concentrate on algorithms for MATCH. It is interesting to note that the acyclicity test of naive unification (i.e., the notorious "occur" check in PROLOG) may be omitted in case (b). The only possible ways for this case to fail invole inhomogeneity.

Apart from case (b), which we believe characterizes many unifications in the PROLOG interpreter, there has been work (in [84]) on how limited parallelism can be used to give limited speed-ups for the general unification problem.

4.3. Parallelizable Operations

Recall that in MATCH w.l.o.g. we are given a dag u and a disjoint dag v with no variables. We want, either to find a substitution of terms for the variables of u to make it syntactically equal to v, or determine that no such substitution exists. Different results can be obtained depending on the form of dag v (e.g., tree or compact dag). We can assume that each variable in dag u labels exactly one node, multiple copies of variable x can be merged in one copy.

It is instructive to present the four main steps M1-M4 of the algorithm from [23]. For the parallel implementation, which is the more technical part we refer to [23].

M1: A spanning tree T of dag u is formed by having each node of dag u arbitrarily choose one of the arcs which are directed into it. T is produced because the dag is rooted at u.

M2: T is embedded in dag v. Formally an embedding of T in dag v is a mapping ρ from the nodes of T to those of dag v (not necessarily a one-to-one mapping), such that:

ρ maps u (the root of T) to v.

For all nodes w of T, w and $\rho(w)$ are labeled by the same function symbol or w is labeled by a variable.

For all nodes w and w′ of T, if there is an arc in T labeled i from w to w′ then there is an arc in dag v labeled i from $\rho(w)$ to $\rho(w')$.

If there is no embedding then clearly t_u and t_v are not unifiable.

M3: The embedding ρ gives a substitution for all the variables of t_u. Specifically, if variable x is the label of (the unique) node w in dag u then the subdag rooted at $\rho(w)$ represents the term substituted for x. The substitution is performed by replacing all arcs in T of the form (w',w) by (w',ρ(w)). If terms t_u,t_v are unifiable then clearly this substitution is the only one possible. However, this substitution is not necessarily a unifying substitution since spanning tree T may not contain all the edges of the dag u. There is one more thing to check.

M4: Let dag c be the dag without variables obtained from dag u by making the substitution defined in M3. Check whether dags c,v are equivalent, i.e., $t_c = t_v$. This is like the EQUAL problem, only the input dags are not necessarily disjoint. The answer to MATCH is yes iff $t_c = t_v$.

Steps M1-M3 can be implemented using $O(n^2)$ processors in NC^2. Step M4 can also be implemented using $O(n^2)$ processors in NC^2 provided dag v is compact or a tree, (for the tree case the time bounds are logarithmic). The proofs use techniques from [73]. Step M4 is the only step that for general dag v seems to require M(n) processors. Recall from Section 2 that M(n) is the best sequential time for multiplying n by n matrices and for practical applications $O(n^3)$. In general, step M4 is the dominating step. In [23] it is implemented in NC^2 using $M(n^2)$ processors, and in random NC^2 using M(n) processors. The proofs for the randomized algorithm use techniques from [71, 61].

There is some "circumstantial" evidence that no deterministic NC^2 algorithm can improve on the M(n) processor bound of this randomized algorithm for MATCH. The dag-GAP problem (Example 2.1) reduces to EQUAL [23]. As defined in Section 4.1 the inputs to EQUAL in this reduction are disjoint dags rooted at u,v. The reduction is in constant time (first-order reducibility of [41]) and using $O(n^2)$ processors. Thus an NC^2 algorithm with better than M(n) processor bounds for EQUAL would imply one for dag-GAP. We summarize these results from [23] in the following theorem.

Theorem 4.3.1:
(a) For input dags MATCH is in NC^2 using $M(n^2)$ processors and in random NC^2 using M(n) processors.
(b) The problem dag-GAP first-order reduces to EQUAL using $O(n^2)$ processors.

Use of M(n) processors would also allow us to dispense with our disjoint and rooted character of input dags u,v. With M(n) processors the input could be one labeled directed acyclic graph with two special nodes u,v. If dag v is a tree or a compact dag the algorithm outlined is almost optimal. Another such case is investigated in [83]. For input trees [83] has an NC^2 algorithm using O(n) processors. As noted in [22] this special case of MATCH is in LOGSPACE, and MATCH is in the complement-of-NLOGSPACE$\subseteq NC^2$.

4.4. Open Questions

Improving the processor bounds for the dag-GAP problem or showing lower bounds (also the last problem of Section 3.5) is the most elegant and probably hardest open question. Also,

1. Is it possible to improve Theorem 4.3.1. to NC^2 using M(n) processors, but no randomness?

2. A practical problem is how to incorporate the various algorithmic techniques for the special cases in the design of specialized hardware for unification.

3. What is the exact role of the acyclicity test? Surprisingly the fastest known algorithm to compute relation r of naive unification uses UNION-FIND and is slightly faster than linear-time. Acyclicity is an integral part of the linear-time algorithm of [60]. There are similar open questions about congruence closure [24]. In congruence closure propagation to parents replaces propagation to children. Is computing the congruence closure of *pair (u, v* on a cyclic graph) in NC?

4. Which is the best expected time algorithm for unification, [53, 60]?

5. Rewrite rule systems [38, 45] are a good example of the use of term matching as a primitive. More analysis is needed of the overall parallel complexity of these systems.

5. Conclusions

AND-parallelism and OR-parallelism have been the most celebrated qualitative measures of parallelism in logic programming languages. We believe that the complexity class NC is the quantitative criterion for identifying those computational problems in logic programming, with large amounts of potential parallelism.

Although evaluation of logical query programs and unification of terms in their full generality are inherently sequential tasks, many important parallelizable cases have been identified. Lower bounds based on PTIME-completeness indicate some basic limitations (e.g., differences from arithmetic operations) but make no statements about average performance or constant factor speed-ups. They are worst-case asymptotic lower bounds. From a practical point of view much remains to be done both in software for parallel evaluation of database queries and special hardware for primitive operations. The theory of parallel computation contributes to a better understanding of these "real world" problems.

Some of the theoretical results that we reviewed here could be directly applicable to practice. Let us close our exposition with two such examples. (1) Piecewise linear programs are rich in expressive power, easy to use, and parallelizable programs. They are the natural candidates for efficient database system extensions.

(2) There are almost optimal parallel algorithms for unification of arbitrary and linear PROLOG terms, (given the appropriate representations). These could be incorporated in special hardware for unification.

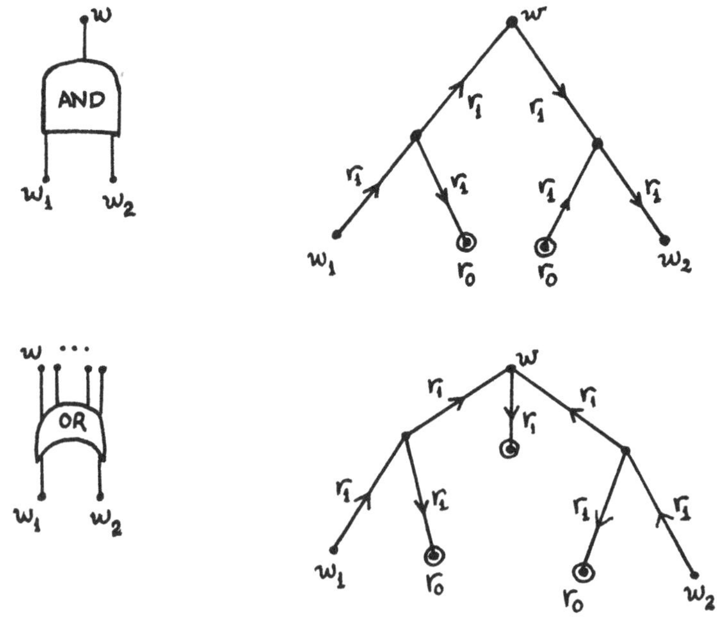

Figure 1

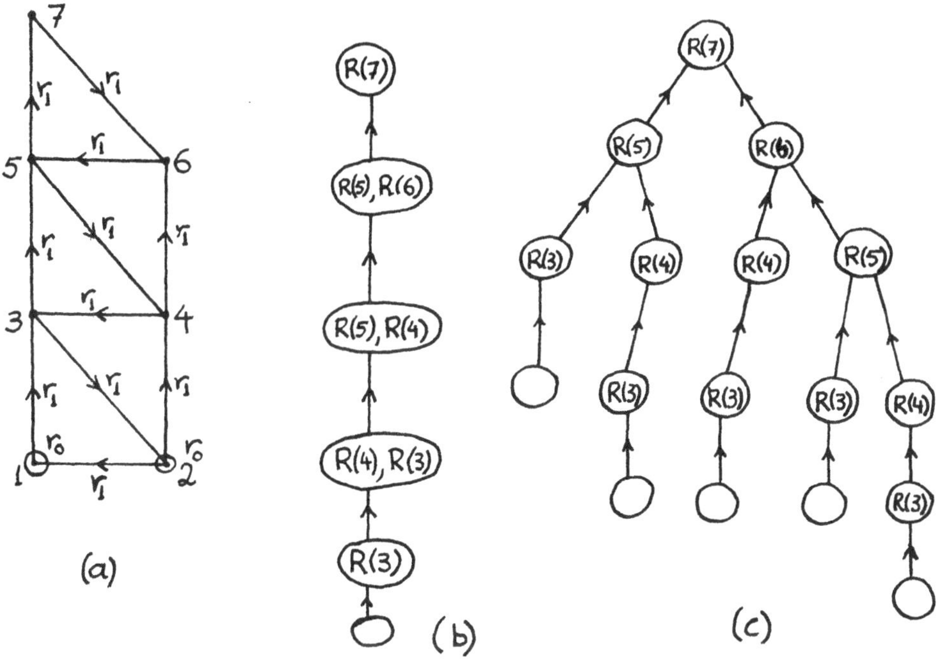

Figure 2

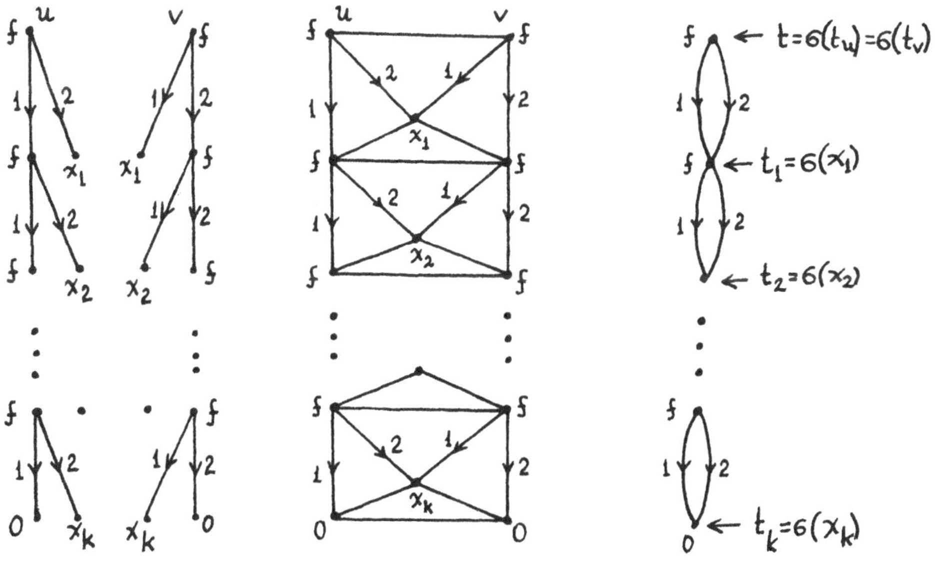

Figure 3

References

1. Aho, A.V. and Ullman, J.D. Universality of Data Retrieval Languages. Proceedings of the 6th POPL, ACM, 1979.

2. Afrati, F. Papadimitriou, C.H. The Polynomial Stack Theorem and its Applications. Tech. Rep., National Technical Univ. of Athens, May 1986.

3. Atallah, M.J., Hambrusch, S.E. Solving Tree Problems on a Mesh-connected Processor Array. Proceedings of the 26th FOCS, IEEE, 1985.

4. Apt, K.R., van Emden, M.H. "Contributions to the Theory of Logic Programming". *JACM 29*, 4 (1982), 841-862.

5. Barwise, J. Moschovakis, Y.N. "Global Inductive Definability". *Journal of Symbolic Logic 43*, 3 (1978), 521-534.

6. Bancilhon, F., Maier, D., Sagiv, Y., Ullman, J.D. Magic Sets and Other Strange Ways to Implement Logic Programs. Proceedings of the 5th PODS, ACM, 1986.

7. Bancilhon, F., Ramakrishnan, R. An Amateur's Introduction to Recursive Query Processing Strategies. Proceedings of the 86 SIGMOD, ACM, 1986.

8. Chandra, A.K., Harel, D. "Structure and Complexity of Relational Queries". *JCSS 25*, 1 (1982), 99-128.

9. Chandra, A.K., Harel, D. "Horn Clause Programs and Generalizations". *J. Logic Programming 2* (1985), 1-15.

10. Chandra, A.K. Maximal Parallelism in Matrix Multiplication. RC 6193, IBM, 1976.

11. Cosmadakis, S.S., Kanellakis, P.C. Parallel Evaluation of Recursive Rule Queries. Proceedings of the 5th PODS, ACM, 1986.

12. Chandra, A.K., Kozen, D.C., Stockmeyer, L.J. "Alternation". *JACM 28*, 1 (1981), 114-133.

13. Clark, K.L., Gregory, S. A Relational Language for Parallel Programming. Proceedings of the ACM Conference on Functional Programming Languages and Computer Architecture, ACM, 1981.

14. Clark, K.L. Negation as Failure. In *Logic and Databases*, Gallaire, H. and Minker, J., Eds., Plenum Press, 1978, pp. 293-324.

15. Clocksin, W.F., Mellish, C.S.. *Programming in Prolog*. Springer Verlag, 1981.

16. Codd, E.F. "A Relational Model for Large Shared Data Banks". *CACM 13*, 6 (June 1970), 377-387.

17. Cook, S.A. "An Observation on a Time-Storage Trade-off". *JCSS 9*, 3 (1974), 308-316.

18. Cook, S.A. "A Taxonomy of Problems with Fast Parallel Algorithms". *Information and Control 64* (1985), 2-22.

19. Cole, R., Vishkin, U. Deterministic Coin Tossing and Accelerating Cascades: Micro and Macro Techniques for Designing Parallel Algorithms. Proceedings of the 17th STOC, ACM, 1986.

20. Coppersmith, D., Winograd, S. "On the Asymptotic Complexity of Matrix Multiplication". *SIAM J. of Computing 11*, (1982), 472-492.

21. deRougemont, M. Uniform Definability of Finite Structures with Successor. Proceedings of the 16th STOC, ACM, 1984.

22. Dwork, C., Kanellakis, P.C., and Mitchell, J.C. "On the Sequential Nature of Unification". *J. Logic Programming 1*, 1 (1984), 35-50.

23. Dwork, C., Kanellakis, P.C., Stockmeyer, L.J. Parallel Algorithms for Term Matching. Proceedings of the 8th International Conference on Automated Deduction, Springer Verlag LNCS, 1986.

24. Downey, P.J., Sethi, R. and Tarjan, R.E. "Variations on the Common Subexpression Problem". *JACM 27*, 4 (1980), 758-771.

25. Fagin, R. "Monadic Generalized Spectra". *Zeitschr. f. math. logik 21*, (1975), 89-96.

26. Fagin, R. "Generalized First-Order Spectra and Polynomial-Time Recognizable Sets". *SIAM-AMS Proc. 7*, 1 (1974), 43-73.

27. Fortune, S., Wyllie, J. Parallelism in Random access Machines. Proceedings of the 10th STOC, ACM, 1978.

28. Gaifman, H. January 1986. NAIL Seminar.

29. Gaifman, H., Vardi, M.Y. "A Simple Proof that Connectivity of Finite Graphs is Not First-Order Definable". *Bulletin of the EATCS 26*, June (1985), 44-45.

30. Gallaire, H., Minker, C., Nicolas,J.M. "Logic and Databases: A Deductive Approach". *Computing Surveys 16*, (1984), 153-185.

31. Goldschlager, L.M. "The Monotone and Planar Circuit Value Problems are Logspace-complete forP". *SIGACT News 9*, 2 (1977), 25-29.

32. Gurevich, Y., Shelah S. Fixed-Point Extensions of First-Order Logic. Proceedings of the 26th FOCS, IEEE, 1985.

33. Gurevich, Y. Algebra of Feasible Functions. Proceedings of the 24th FOCS, IEEE, 1983.

34. Gurevich, Y., Lewis, H.R. "A Logic for Constant Depth Circuits". *Information and Control 61*, (1984), 65-74.

35. Harel, D., Kozen, D.C. "A Programming Language for the Inductive Sets, and Applications". *Information and Control 63*, (1984), 118-139.

36. Henschen, L.J., Naqvi, S.A. "On Compiling Queries in Recursive First-Order Databases". *JACM 31*, 1 (1984), 47-85.

37. Hopcroft, J.E. and Ullman, J.D.. *Introduction to Automata Theory, Languages, and Computation.* Addison-Wesley, 1979.

38. Huet, G. and Oppen, D. Equations and Rewrite Rules: a Survey. In *Formal Languages: Perspectives and Open Problems*, Book, R., Ed., Academic Press, 1980, pp. 349-403.

39. Immerman, N. "Number of Quantifiers is Better than Number of Tape Cells". *JCSS 22*, 3 (1981), 65-72.

40. Immerman, N. Relational Queries Computable in Polynomial Time. Proceedings of the 14th STOC, ACM, 1982.

41. Immerman, N. Languages which Capture complexity Classes. Proceedings of the 15th STOC, ACM, 1983.

42. Ioannidis, Y.E. A Time Bound on the Materialization of Some Recursively Defined Views. Proceedings of the 85 VLDB, Stockholm, 1985.

43. Ioannidis, Y.E. On the Computation of the Transitive Closure of Relational Operators. Proceedings of the 86 VLDB, Tokyo, 1986.

44. Jones, N.D., Laaser, W.T. "Complete Problems for Deterministic Polynomial Time". *TCS 3*, 2 (1977), 105-117.

45. Knuth, D.E. and Bendix, P.B. Simple Word Problems in Universal Algebras. In *Computational Problems in Abstract Algebra*, Leech, J., Ed., Pergamon, Oxford, 1970, pp. 263-297.

46. Kowalski, R.A.. *Logic for Problem-Solving.* North Holland, 1979.

47. Kozen, D. Complexity of Finitely Presented Algebras. Proceedings of the 9th STOC, ACM, , 1977.

48. Kanellakis, P.C., Papadimitriou, C.H. February 1986. Notes on Monadic Sirups-unpublished.

49. Karp, R.M., Upfal, E., Wigderson, A. Constructing a Perfect Matching is in Random NC. Proceedings of the 17th STOC, ACM, 1985.

50. Kowalski, R. Predicate Logic as a Programming Language. Proceedings IFIP 74, Amsterdam, 1974, pp. 569-574.

51. Mairson, H., Sagiv, Y. February 1986. Personal Communication.

52. Maluszynski, J., Komorowski, H.J. Unification-free Execution of Horn-clause Programs. Proceedings of the 2nd Logic Programming Symposium, IEEE, 1985.

53. Martelli, A., Montanari, U. "An efficient Unification Algorithm". *ACM Trans. on Programming Languages and Systems 4*, 2 (1982), .

54. Miller, G.L., Reif, J.H. Parallel Tree Contraction and its Applications. Proceedings of the 26th FOCS, IEEE, 1985.

55. Minker, J., Nicolas, J.M. "On Recursive Axioms in Relational Databases". *Information Systems 8* (1982), 1-13.

56. Moschovakis, Y.N.. *Elementary Induction on Abstract Structures.* North Holland, 1974.

57. Naughton, J. Data Independent Recursion in Deductive Databases. Proceedings of the 5th PODS, ACM, 1986.

58. Papadimitriou, C.H. "A Note on the Expressive Power of PROLOG". *Bulletin of the EATCS 26*, June (1985), 21-23.

59. Pippenger, N. On Simultaneous Resource Bounds. Proceedings of the 20th FOCS, IEEE, 1979.

60. Paterson, M.S., Wegman, M.N. "Linear Unification". *JCSS 16*, (1978), 158-167.

61. Rabin, M.O. "Probabilistic Algorithm for Testing Primality". *J. Number Theory 12*, (1980), 128-138.

62. Reif, J. Optimal Parallel Algorithms for Integer Sorting and Graph Connectivity. Proceedings of the 26th FOCS, IEEE, 1985.

63. Robinson, J.A. "A Machine Oriented Logic Based on the Resolution Principle". *JACM 12*, (January 1965), 23-41.

64. Roussel, P. PROLOG: Manuel de Reference et d' Utilisation, Groupe de !A, UER Luminy. Univ. d' Aix-Marseille, France, 1975.

65. Ruzzo, W.L. "Tree-size Bounded Alternation". *JCSS 21*, 2 (1980), 218-235.

66. Ruzzo, W.L. "On Uniform Circuit Complexity". *JCSS 22*, 3 (1981), 365-383.

67. Sagiv, Y. On Computing Restricted Projections of Representative Instances. Proceedings of the 4th PODS, ACM, 1985.

68. Sacca, D., Zaniolo, C. On the Implementation of a Simple Class of Logic Queries for Databases. Proceedings of the 5th PODS, ACM, 1986.

69. Sagiv, Y. February 1986. Notes on Uniform Equivalence-unpublished.

70. Sazonov. A Logical Approach to the Problem P=NP. Proceedings of the MFCS, Springer LNCS 88, 1980.

71. Schwartz, J.T. "Fast Probabilistic Algorithms for the Verification of Polynomial Identities". *JACM 27*, 4 (1980), 701-717.

72. Shapiro, E.Y. A Subset of Concurrent PROLOG and its Interpreter. No. 3, ICOT, Tokyo, 1983.

73. Tarjan R.E., Vishkin, U. Finding Biconnected Components and Computing Tree Functions in Logarithmic Parallel Time. Proceedings of the 25th FOCS, IEEE, 1984.

74. Ullman, J.D.. *Principles of Database Systems.* Computer Science Press, 1983.

75. Ullman, J.D. "Implementation of Logical query Languages for Databases". *ACM Trans. on Database Systems 10* (1985), 289-321.

76. Ullman, J.D., Van Gelder, A. Parallel Complexity of Logical Query Programs. Proceedings of the 27th FOCS, 1986, to appear.

77. Vardi, M.Y. Complexity of Relational Query Languages. Proceedings of the 14th STOC, ACM, 1982.

78. Valduriez, P., Boral, H. Evaluation of Recursive Queries Using Join Indices. Proceedings of the 1rst International Conference on Expert Database Systems, Charleston, South Carolina, 1986.

79. Vardi, M.Y. May 1985. Personal Communication.

80. Vardi, M.Y. February 1986. Personal Communication.

81. van Emden, M.H., Kowalski, R.A. "The Semantics of Predicate Logic as a Programming Language". *JACM 23*, 4 (1976), 733-742.

82. Vishkin, U. Randomized Speed-ups in Parallel Computation. Proceedings of the 16th STOC, ACM, 1984.

83. Verma, R.M., Krishnaprasad, T., Ramakrishnan, I.V. An Efficient Parallel algorithm for Term Matching. Tech. Rep., SUNY Stony Brook, June 1986.

84. Vitter, J.S., Simons, R. "New Classes for Parallel Complexity: a Study of Unification and Other Complete Problems for P". *IEEE Trans. on Computers* (1986), .

85. Valiant, L.G., Skyum, S., Berkowitz, S., Rackoff, C. "Fast Parallel Computation on Polynomials Using Few Processors". *SIAM J. of Computing 12*, 4 (November 1983), 641-644.

86. Yasuura, H. On the Parallel Computational Complexity of Unification. ER 83-01, Yajima Lab., October 1983.

87. Yannakakis, M. March 1986. Personal Communication.

Table of Contents

The Generalized Counting Method for Recursive Logic Queries

Domenico Saccà †

CRAI, Rende, Italy

Carlo Zaniolo

MCC, Austin, Texas, USA

ABSTRACT

This paper treats the problem of implementing efficiently recursive Horn Clauses queries, including those with function symbols. In particular, the situation is studied where the initial bindings of the arguments in the recursive query goal can be used in the top-down (as in backward chaining) execution phase to improve the efficiency and, often, to guarantee the termination, of the forward chaining execution phase that implements the fixpoint computation for the recursive query. A general method is given for solving these queries; the method performs an analysis of the binding passing behavior of the query, and then reschedules the overall execution as two fixpoint computations derived as results of this analysis. The first such computation emulates the propagation of bindings in the top-down phase; the second generates the desired answer by proving the goals left unsolved during the previous step. Finally, sufficient conditions for safety are derived, to ensure that the fixpoint computations are completed in a finite number of steps.

1. Introduction

This work is motivated by the belief that an integration of technologies of Logic Programming and Databases is highly desirable, and will supply a corner stone of future Knowledge Based Systems [P, U2]. Prolog represents a powerful query language for database systems, and can also be used as a general-purpose language for application development, particularly in the symbolic manipulation and expert system areas [Z1]. However, Prolog's sequential execution model and the spurious non-logical constructs thus grafted on the language constitute serious drawbacks for database applications, since

---

† Part of this work was done while this author was visiting at MCC.

i) they imply a one-tuple-at-the-time, nested-loop join strategy which is not well-suited for parallel processing, and tends to be inefficient when the fact base is stored on disk, and

ii) the programmer must guarantee the performance and the termination of the program by carefully ordering rules and goals— a policy that limits the ease-of-use of the language and the data independence of applications written in it.

Thus, we should move beyond Prolog, to a pure Logic-based language amenable to secondary storage and parallel implementation, where the system assumes responsibility for efficient execution of correct programs — an evolution similar to that of databases from early navigational systems to relational ones. Towards this ambitions objective, we take the approach of compiling the intentional information expressed as Horn clauses and queries into set-oriented processing primitives, such as relational algebra, to be executed on the extensional database (fact base). This is a simple process for Horn Clauses containing only non-recursive predicates with simple variables, inasmuch as these rules basically correspond to the derived join-select-project views of relational databases [U1]. Horn clauses, however, contain two powerful constructs not found in the Relational calculus: one is recursion, that, e.g., entails the computation of closures, the other is general unification that, via the use of function symbols, can be used to support complex and flexible structures (not just flat tuples as is relational databases). The efficient implementation of these two powerful constructs poses some interesting problems [HN, MS, CH, U2, L, BMSU1, SZ1, Z2, GD, Vg, Vi]. For instance, the technique of using the query constants to search the database efficiently (pushing selection) is frequently inapplicable to recursive predicates [AhUl]. Moreover, the issue of safety, which in relational databases is solved by simple syntactic conditions on the query language, here requires a complex analysis on the bindings passed upon unification [UV,Z3].

This paper studies the problem of implementing safely and efficiently recursive Horn clauses in the presence of query constants and thus it introduces a powerful technique, called *the generalized counting method,* that is more effective in dealing with recursive predicates with function symbols than those previously known [HN, U2, BMSU1, BMSU2, SZ1].

2. Fixpoint Evaluation of Recursive Queries

Take the recursive rule of Figure 1,

r_0: $SG(x,y)$:- $P(x,x_1)$, $SG(x_1,y_1)$, $P(y,y_1)$
r_1: $SG(x,x)$:- $H(x)$.

Fig. 1. *The same-generation example.*

where $P(x,x_1)$ is a database predicate describing that x_1 is the parent of x, and $H(x)$ is a database predicate describing all humans[1]. Then, a query such as:

G1: $SG(x,y)$?

defines all persons that are of the same generation. The answer to this query can be computed as the least fixpoint of the following function over relations:

$$f(\mathbf{SG}) = \pi_{1,1}H \bigcup \pi_{1,5}((\mathbf{P} \bowtie_{2=1} \mathbf{SG}) \bowtie_{4=2} \mathbf{P}))$$

Our function f is defined by a relational algebra expression having as operands the constants H and P and the variable $\mathbf{SG}$ (H and P denote the database relations with respective function symbols H and P and respective arities one and two — whereas $\mathbf{SG}$ is an unknown relation with arity two). Therefore, the computation of the least fixpoint can proceed by setting the initial value of $\mathbf{SG}$ to the empty set and computing $f(\mathbf{SG})$. Then $f(\mathbf{SG})$ becomes the new value for $\mathbf{SG}$ and this iterative step is repeated until no more tuples can be added to $\mathbf{SG}$, which then becomes the answer to the query. Since all goals in a Horn clause are positive, the corresponding relational expression is monotonic, w.r.t. the ordering on relations defined by set containment. Thus, there exists a unique least fixpoint [T1]. The fixpoint computation approach, refined with the differential techniques, such as those described in [B, BGK], supplies an efficient algorithm for implementing queries with no bound argument. This approach, however, becomes inefficient for common queries, such as $G2$ below, where arguments are either constant or otherwise bound to a small set of elements:

G2: $SG(john,y)$?

This query retrieves all humans of the same generation as "john". A naive application of the fixpoint approach here implies generating all possible pairs of humans in the same generation, to discard then all but those having "john" as their first component. Much more efficient strategies are possible; Prolog's backward chaining, for instance, propagates all the bindings downwards, during the top-down phase (from the goal to database), then, during the bottom-up phase, performs a fixpoint computation using only those database facts that were found

[1] A predicate that only unifies with facts will be called a database predicate. By database relation we mean a set of facts with the same predicate symbol and number of arguments.

relevant in the previous phase. (For the example at hand, the only relevant facts are those describing ancestors of "john".) In traditional databases this top-down binding propagation strategy corresponds to the well-known optimization technique of pushing selection inside the relational algebra expressions. We need here to extend and generalize this technique to the case of recursive predicates. The importance of the problem considered is underscored by the safety issue for "computational" predicates, such as the merge example of Figure 2, which are normally defined using both recursion and function symbols.

r_0: $MG(x \bullet y, x_1 \bullet y_1, x \bullet w)$:- $MG(y, x_1 \bullet y_1, w)$, $x \geq x_1$
r_1: $MG(x \bullet y, x_1 \bullet y_1, x_1 \bullet w)$:- $MG(x \bullet y, y_1, w)$, $x < x_1$
r_2: $MG(nil, x, x)$
r_3: $MG(x, nil, x)$

Fig. 2. *Merging two sorted lists.*

The problem of supporting *non-recursive* Horn clauses with function symbols was studied in [Z2]. Since predicates have structured arguments (for instance the first argument in the the head of r_1 in Figure 2 has x and y as subarguments), an Extended Relational Algebra (ERA) was proposed in [Z2] to deal with them. A first operator, called *extended select-project,* entails the selection of subcomponents in complex arguments (in this particular case where the dot is our (infix) function symbol, this operator performs "car" and "cdr" operations on dotted lists). The second operator, called a *combine,* allows one to build complex arguments from simpler ones (on a dotted list, this corresponds to the "cons" operator). Non-recursive Horn clauses can be implemented as ERA expressions [Z2, Z3]. Moreover, since functions defined using ERA expressions are still monotonic, the basic fixpoint computation approach (bottom-up execution) remains applicable to predicates with function symbols.

However, there are safety issues which limit the applicability of the fixpoint approach, since Herbrand's universe is infinite when function symbols are involved. For instance, the relations representing all possible sets of values for x and x_1 in our rules of Figure 2, are infinite; furthermore even if we restrict these variables to a finite set, rules r_1 and r_2 would generate longer and longer lists at each step of the fixpoint computation, which therefore becomes a non-terminating one.

In reality, the potential safety problem previously described are avoided because a procedure, such as that of Figure 2, is only invoked as a goal with certain arguments bound, to derive the the unbound ones. Typically for instance, the first two arguments are given to derive the third one (or perhaps, the third argument is given to generate all the pairs of lists that merge into this one, or some combination of these two situations). This observation also extends to predicates without function symbols; for instance, the same-generation example might be written without the $H(x)$ goal in the second rule of Figure 1, because of an implicit assumption that SG will only be called with some arguments bound — an assumption that better be verified before an relational algebra equivalent can be generated for the SG rules.

In conclusion, an effective usage of the binding information available during the top-down phase is vital for performance reasons and to avoid the non-termination pitfall. The purpose of this paper is to propose a general framework and efficient algorithms to deal with this problem. The basic approach consists of the following steps:

i) a symbolic analysis of the binding propagation behavior during the top-down phase, and using the results of this analysis,

ii) the computation of special sets (i.e., the counting sets and the supplementary counting sets) that actually implement the top-down propagation of bound values,

iii) a modified bottom-up computation that generates the values satisfied by the queries.

The method presented here, is more powerful than methods previously proposed in the literature with respect to the treatment of recursive predicates with function symbols. For instance, the queries on the MG example of Figure 2, can not be handled with the methods proposed in [U2] that doe not allow for function symbols on the right side of rules.

3. Binding Passing Property.

In a logic program LP, a predicate P is said to *imply* a predicate Q, written $P \rightarrow Q$, if there is a rule in LP with predicate Q as the head and predicate P in the body, or the exists a P' where $P \rightarrow P'$ and $P' \rightarrow Q$ (transitivity). Then any predicate P, such that $P \rightarrow P$ will be called *recursive*. Two predicates P, and Q are called *mutually recursive* if $P \rightarrow Q$ and $Q \rightarrow P$. Then the sets of all predicates in LP can be divided into recursive predicates and non-recursive ones (such as database predicates). The implication relationship can then be used to partition the recursive predicates into disjoint subclasses of mutually recursive predicates, which we will call *recursive cliques,* with their graph representation in mind. All predicates in the same recursive clique must be solved together — cannot be solved one at a time.

For the LP of Figure 1, SG is the recursive predicate (a singleton recursive clique), and H and P are database predicates. However, in the discussion which follows, H and P could be any predicate that can be solved independently of SG; thus they could be derived predicates — even recursive ones— as long that they are not mutually recursive with SG. Finally, it should be clear that "john" is here used as a placeholder for any constant; thus the method here proposed can be used to support any goal with the same binding pattern.

Formally, therefore, we will study the problem of implementing a query Q that can be modeled as triplet $<G, LP, D>$, where:

LP is a set of Horn clauses, with head predicates all belonging to one recursive clique, say, C.

G is the goal, consisting of a predicate in C with some bound arguments.

D denotes the remaining predicates, in the bodies of the LP-rules, which are either non-recursive or belong to recursive cliques other than C.

The predicates in C will be called the *constructed predicates* (c-predicates for short) and those in D the *datum predicates.* For instance, if our goal is $G2{:}SG(john, x)?$ on the LP of Figure 1, then SG is our c-predicate (a singleton recursive clique) and P and H are our datum predicates.

In general, datum predicates are those that can be solved independently of the c-predicates; therefore, besides database predicates they could also include predicates derived from these, including recursive predicates not in the same recursive clique as the head predicates. Take for instance the LP of Figure 2, with goal

$$MG(L_1, L_2, y)?$$

where L_1 and L_2 denote arbitrary given lists. Here MG is our c-predicate and the comparison predicates $\geq$ and $<$ are our datums. The $<$ predicate could, for instance, stand for a database predicate (e.g., if there is a finite set of characters and their lexicographical order is explicitly stored: $a < b$, $b < c$, $\cdots$) or it could stand for a built-in predicate that evaluates to false or true when invoked as a goal with both arguments bound, or, with integers defined using Peano's axioms, it could be the recursive predicate of Figure 3,

r_0: $x < s(x)$.
r_1: $x < s(y)$:– $x < y$.

Fig. 3. *The "less-than" relationship for integers represented using the successor notation.*

Exit rules and recursive rules:

A rule with a recursive predicate R as its head will be called *recursive* if its body contains some predicate from the same recursive clique as R; it will be called an *exit rule,* otherwise.

For notational convenience, we will always index the recursive rules starting from zero, $r_0, \cdots, r_{m-1}$; thus, the total number of recursive rules under consideration is always m. For instance, in Figure 2, r_0 and r_1 are the recursive rules, while

r_2 and r_3 are the exit rules.

3.1. Binding Propagation

Datum predicates propagate bindings from the bound arguments in the heads of the rules to arguments of the c-predicate occurrences in their bodies. Let us, *for now,* say that our only datums are database and comparison predicates; then the binding propagation in a rule r_i can be defined as follows. Say that B is a set of (bound) variables of r_i. Then *the set of variables bound in* r_i *by* B will be denoted B^{+r_i} (or B^+ when r_i is understood) and is recursively defined as follows:

i) (basis)

Every variable appearing in B is also in B^+

ii) (induction)

database predicates: If some variable in database predicate is bound then all the other variables are bound.

comparison predicates: If we have an equality, such as $x = expression$ or $expression = x$, and all the variables in *expressions* are bound, then x is bound as well.

Let P be a predicate in the body of r_i. Then, an *argument* of P will be said to be *bound* when all its variables are bound.

Say that S denotes the bound arguments in the head predicate of r_i and B the (bound) variables in these arguments, moreover, say that T denotes the set of arguments bound by B in a c-predicate occurrence P; then we will say that r_i *maps the set of bound arguments* S *of its head, into the set of bound arguments* T *of* P.

Solved Predicates:

A datum predicate of r_i will be said to be *solved* when all its variables are bound.

Say for instance that the first argument of SG is bound in Figure 1. Then x is bound and so is x_1 (via the database predicate P). Thus in r_0 of Figure 1, the bindings propagate from SG^1 to SG^1. Thus $P(x, x_1)$ is a solved predicate in r_0, whereas $P(y, y_1)$ is not. $H(x)$ is solved in r_1.

3.2. Binding Graph of a Query

The *binding graph* of a query is a directed graph having nodes of the form P^S where P is a c-predicate symbol and S denotes its bound arguments, and whose arcs are labeled by the pair $[r_i, v]$, where r_i is the index to a recursive rule, and v is a zero-base index to c-predicate occurrences in the body of this rule, i.e, 0 is the index to the first c-predicate occurrence, 1 to the second one, etc. (the zero base is chosen to simplify the counting operations). The binding graph M_Q for a query $Q =< G, LP, D >$ is constructed as follows:

i) If S is the non-empty set of bound arguments in G, then G^S is the *source node* of M_Q,

ii) If there exists a node R^S in M_Q and there is a rule r_i in LP that maps the bound arguments of R into the bound arguments T of the v-th c-predicate occurrence and this has symbol P, then P^T is also node of M_Q, and there is an arc labeled $[r_i, v]$ from R^S to P^T.

Figure 4 shows a binding graph for a query $SG^{1,2}$ on the rules of Figure 1, and Figure 5 shows the graph for a query $MG^{1,2}$ on the rules of Figure 2.

Let r_i be a rule and S be the set of the bound arguments in the head of r_i. Then we say that r_i is *solved by* S if all its variables are bound by the variables in $B_S \bigcup B_c$, where:

B_S are the bound variables in the head (i.e., those contained in the S-arguments), and

B_c are the variables of c-predicates in the body of r_i.

We can now enunciate our key property.

Binding passing property:

A query Q will be said to have the *binding passing property* when the following properties hold for each node R^S of its binding graph:

(a) S is not empty, and

(b) each rule r_i such that the predicate symbol of its head is R, is *solved* by S.

Thus our examples in Figures 1 and 2, with binding graphs of Figure 4 and 5, have the binding passing property. This property guarantees that (a) bindings can be passed down to any level of recursion, and that (b) all predicates in the recursive rules can be solved either in the top-down or in the bottom-up execution phase. Our binding graph is similar to the rule/goal graph described in [U2] and is an extension of the query binding graph presented in [SZ1].

We point out that we assume that the binding is propagated through an argument of a c-predicate only if the whole argument is bound. A more detailed analysis could consider that the binding can be also passed through partially bound arguments of c-predicates. The binding passing property needs to be checked only once for any given binding pattern in the query (e.g., at compile time), moreover the following proposition guarantees that binding graphs can be constructed efficiently [SZ3].

PROPOSITION 1. *Let* $Q = <G, LP, D>$ *be a query such that there is a bound on the arity of the predicates in* LP*, then*

a) *The binding graph of* Q *can be constructed in time polynomial in the size of* LP*.*

b) *The binding passing property of* Q *can be tested in time polynomial in the size of* LP*.*

4. The Generalized Counting Method.

We now present a method to implement logic queries which have the binding passing property defined in the previous section. This method, called the *generalized counting method*, is an extension of the counting method described in [SZ1] for solving a particular class of logic queries without function symbols and without comparison predicates. An informal description of the counting method was first given in [BMSU1].

The generalized counting method recasts a query that is inefficient or unsafe to compute in a single fixpoint computation, into a pair of safe and efficient fixpoint computations. While this pair could be expressed directly in terms of relational algebra [SZ1], reasons of simplicity, expressivity and independence from the target implementation language suggest to represent it by recursive rules. Thus the generalized counting method can be viewed as a rule rewriting system that maps a query $Q = <G, LP, D>$ into an equivalent query $\overline{Q} = <\overline{G}, \overline{LP}, D>$ that can be computed safely and efficiently using the fixpoint approach described in Section 2. In $\overline{LP}$ we find two new sets of rules, called *counting rules* and *supplementary counting rules*, that perform the top-down propagation of bound values; in addition, we find every rule of LP transformed into one or more rules (*modified rules*) that perform the bottom-up computation of the final anwer.

4.1. Counting and Supplementary Counting Rules

The overall translation process consists of (i) the generation of counting and supplementary counting sets to perform the top-down propagation of bound values, and (ii) the modification of the original goal and rules to take advantage of the counting sets.

To generate counting sets, a number of new predicate symbols are introduced, one for each node of the binding graph M_Q of Q. Thus, for each node R^S we introduce a new predicate $cnt.R^S$ with $|S|+3$ arguments. Thus, there is an argument for each bound argument in the head of the original rule, plus three additional integer arguments respectively recording (i) the level of the recursive call, (ii) the recursive rule used and (iii) the c-predicate occurrence used in the

G : SG(a, b)?

LP: r_0: SG(x, y):- P(x, x_1),P(y, y_1),SG(x_1, y_1)

r_1: SG(x, x):- H(x).

Binding Graph

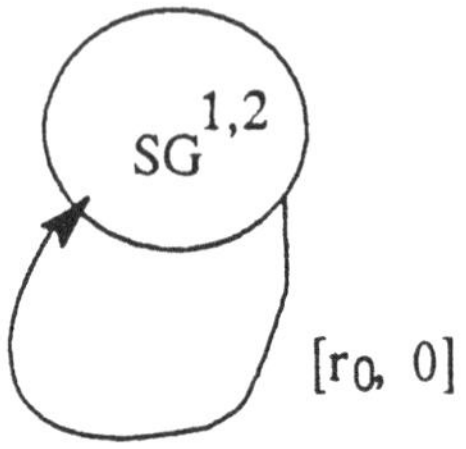

Counting Rules:

cnt.$SG^{1,2}$ (0, 0, 0, a, b).

cnt.$SG^{1,2}$ (j+1, 1*k+0, 1*h+0, x_1, y_1):- cnt.$SG^{1,2}$ (j, k, h, x, y), P(x, x_1), P(y, y_1).

Supplementary Rules: None

Modified Rules and Goal:

$SG^{1,2}$ (j−1, (k−0)/1, h/1) :−$SG^{1,2}$ (j, k, h).

$SG^{1,2}$ (j, k, h) :- cnt.$SG^{1,2}$ (j, k, h, x, x), H(x).

$\overline{G}$: $SG^{1,2}$ (0, 0, 0)?

Figure 4. The Same Generation Example for G: SG(a,b)?

body of the rule.

Exit Counting Rules:

The first counting rule is generated by the source node in M_Q, say P^S which corresponds to the query goal. Say that the query goal has $n = |S| \geq 1$ bound arguments with respective values $a_1, \cdots, a_n$. Then we add the following clause for the counting set:

$$cnt.P^S(0,0,0,a_1, \cdots, a_n).$$

Recursive Counting Rules:

There is a recursive counting rule for each arc in M_Q as follows: for an arc labeled $[r_i, v]$ from node R^S to node P^T, we add the rule

$$cnt.P^T(j+1, m \times k+i, p \times h+v, y_1, \cdots, y_l) :-$$
$$cnt.R^S(j, k, h, x_1, \cdots, x_n),\ Q_1, \cdots, Q_q$$

where:

i) $x_1, \ldots, x_n$ are the bound arguments in the head of r_i (i.e., those in S),

ii) $y_1, \cdots, y_l$ are the bound arguments in the v-th c-predicate of r_i (i.e., those in T),

iii) $Q_1, \cdots, Q_q$ are the predicates of r_i, solved for bound arguments S.

iv) j, k and h are the running indices, while m and p are constants characterized as follows:
m is the total number of recursive rules,
p denotes the total number of c-predicates in the body of r_i.

It should be clear, that in the rule above we have taken liberties with the notation by representing operations on indexes directly by their arithmetic expression rather than introducing new goals, such as "j' is $j+1$", "k' is $m \times k+i$" and "h' is $p \times h+s$", and then writing the head as $cnt.P^T(j', k', h', y_1, \cdots, y_l)$, as required, say, in Prolog. But we have used this more concise notation since it is suggestive of the counting operations to be performed during the fixpoint computation.

Informally described, the counting rules are constructed by eliminating all unbound arguments and unsolved datum predicates, exchanging the a c-predicate in the body with that in head, and adding the two indexes. Note that, while there are as many counting rules as arcs in the graph, there are only as many counting predicates as there are nodes — see Figure 5 for an example.

In the top-down generation of the counting sets we often generate values that are needed in the successive bottom-up computation. For instance, in the merge example of Figure 2, we generate the values of x in rule r_0 and those of x_1 in r_1;

since these will not be part of the c-predicates in the modified rules, they must be saved for later use in the bottom-up phase. The supplementary rules provide the means to this end.

Supplementary Counting Variables:

Consider a node R^S in M_Q. In M_Q, there is arc labeled $[r_i, v]$ out of R_S for each occurrence of a c-predicate in the body of r_i. Say that

a) B^+ denotes the set of the variables bound in r_i by the (bound) variables in the S-arguments of the head of r_i,

b) V_U denotes the set of all variables either appearing in unsolved predicates of r_i, or in unbound arguments of the head of r_i (i.e., those not in S)

c) V_C the set of variables appearing in some unbound arguments of a c-predicate in the body of r_i,

then we need to save the values of every variable in $V_U \cap B^+$, but those in V_C whose values are recomputed in the bottom-up computation anyway (see modified rules). Thus we need to keep the values of all variables in $V_{sp} = (B^+ \cap V_U) - V_C$, which will be called the set of *supplementary counting variables*. For rules where V_{sp} is empty there is no need for a supplementary counting set. Such is the case for the *SG* example of Figure 4.

Consider however the example of Figure 5. For rule r_0 we have $B^+ = \{x, y, x_1, y_1\}$, while $V_U = \{x\}$. Since $V_C = \{w\}$, the set of supplementary counting variables is $V_{sp} = \{x\}$. Likewise for r_1, the only supplementary counting variable is x_1.

Supplementary Counting Rules:

Then we can add the supplementary counting rules, one for each bundle of arcs labeled with the same rule out of a node for which the set of supplementary counting variables is not empty. If r_i is the rule labeling a bundle leaving, say, node R^S, then, using the counting rule for R^S, we write:

$$spcnt.r_i.R^S(j, k, h, z_1, \cdots, z_t) \text{ :- } cnt.R^S(j, k, h, x_1, \cdots, x_n),\ Q_1, \cdots, Q_q$$

where,

i) $x_1, \ldots, x_n$ denote the bound arguments in the head of r_i (i.e., these in S),

ii) $z_1, \cdots, z_t$ are the supplementary counting variables.

iii) $Q_1, \cdots, Q_q$ are the predicates of r_i, solved for bound arguments S.

For an example see Figure 5.

G : MG(L_1, L_2, W)?

LP:

r0: $MG(x \bullet y,\ x_1 \bullet y_1,\ x \bullet w)$:- $MG(y,\ x_1 \bullet y_1,\ w),\ x \geq x_1$.

r1: $MG(x \bullet y,\ x_1 \bullet y_1,\ x_1 \bullet w)$:- $MG(x \bullet y,\ y_1,\ w),\ x < x_1$.

r2: MG(**nil**, x, x).

r3: MG(x, **nil**, x).

Binding Graph

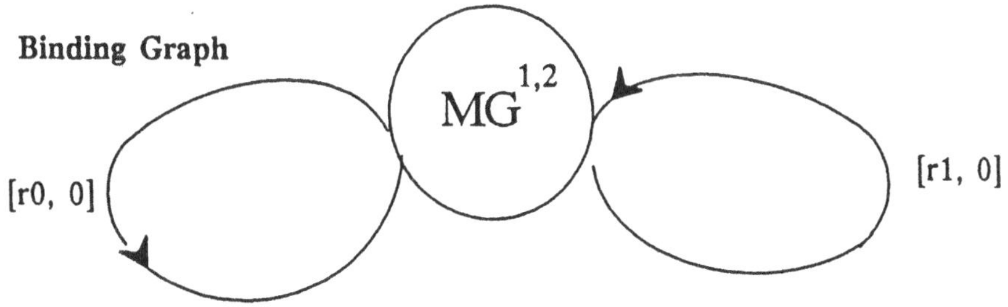

Counting Rules:

$cnt.MG^{1,2}$ (0, 0, 0, L_1, L_2).

$cnt.MG^{1,2}$ $(j+1,\ 2^*k+0,\ 1^*h+0,\ y,\ x_1 \bullet y_1)$:- $cnt.MG^{1,2}$ $(j,\ k,\ h,\ x \bullet y,\ x_1 \bullet y_1),\ x \geq x_1$.

$cnt.MG^{1,2}$ $(j+1,\ 2^*k+1,\ 1^*h+0,\ x \bullet y,\ y_1)$:- $cnt.MG^{1,2}$ $(j,\ k,\ h,\ x \bullet y,\ x_1 \bullet y1),\ x < x_1$.

Supplementary Counting Rule:

$spcnt.MG^{1,2}.r0$ $(j,\ k,\ h,\ x)$:- $cnt.MG^{1,2}$ $(j,\ k,\ h,\ x \bullet y,\ x_1 \bullet y_1),\ x \geq x_1$.

$spcnt.MG^{1,2}.r1$ $(j,\ k,\ h,\ x_1)$:- $cnt.MG^{1,2}$ $(j,\ k,\ h,\ x \bullet y,\ x_1 \bullet y_1),\ x < x_1$.

Modified Rules and Goal:

$MG^{1,2}$ $(j-1,\ (k-0)/2,\ h/1,\ x \bullet w)$:- $spcnt.MG^{1,2}.ro(j-1,\ k/2,\ h,\ x)$, $MG^{1,2}(j,\ k,\ h,\ w)$.

$MG^{1,2}$ $(j-1,\ (k-1)/2,\ h/1,\ x_1 \bullet w)$:- $spcnt.MG^{1,2}.r1(j-1,\ (k-1)/2,\ h,\ x_1)$, $MG^{1,2}(j,\ k,\ h,\ w)$.

$MG^{1,2}$ (j, k, h, x) :- $cnt.MG^{1,2}$ (j, k, h, **nil**, x).

$MG^{1,2}$ (j, k, h, x) :- $cnt.MG^{1,2}$ (j, k, h, x, **nil**).

$\overline{G}$: $MG^{1,2}$ (0, 0, 0, w)?

Figure 5. The List Merge Example

4.2. Modified Rules

Modified Recursive Rules:

A number of new predicate symbols are introduced, one for each node in M_Q, to replace the c-predicate symbols in LP. For each node in M_Q, there are as many modified rules as there are bundles of arcs from the node labeled with the same rule. Thus, let R^S be a node in M_Q and r_i be the label of a bundle of arcs leaving R^S; then, we introduce the following rule (again we take liberties with the notation by denoting with $k-i/m$ an integer division that succeds only if the remainder is zero):

$$R^S(j-1, (k-i)/m, h/p, u_1, \cdots, u_n) :-$$

$$spcnt.R^S.r_i(j-1,(k-i)/m, h/p, z_1, \cdots, z_t),\ \hat{P}_0, \cdots, \hat{P}_{p-1},\ W_1, \cdots, W_q.$$

where:

i) $u_1, \ldots, u_n$ are the unbound arguments in the head of r_i (i.e., those that do NOT belong to S),

ii) $spcnt.R^S.r_i(j-1,(k-i)/m, h/p, z_1, \cdots, z_t)$ is the supplementary counting predicate, if any, with $z_1, \cdots, z_t$, $t>0$ supplementary counting variables.

iii) $W_1, \cdots, W_q$ are the predicates of r_i, NOT solved for bound arguments S.

iv) $\hat{P}_0, \cdots, \hat{P}_{p-1}$ are the modified c-predicate occurrences in the body of r_i, constructed as follows. Say that there is an arc labeled $[r_i, v]$ from R^S to P^T, and $x_1, \cdots, x_l$ are the unbound arguments in the v-th predicate of r_i (i.e., those NOT in T), then

$$\hat{P}_v = P^T(j, k, h+v, x_1, \cdots, x_l).$$

v) j, k and h are the running indices, while m, i and p are constants respectively denoting the total number of recursive rules, the index of the rule labeling the arc, and the total number of c-predicates in the body of this rule. These indexing operations reverse those performed when building the counting sets.

In other words, one has to take the original rule r_i, eliminate all solved variables and bound predicates, add the three indexes (after suitable indexing operations) in each c-predicate, and, finally, add the the supplementary counting predicates, if any. In addition to the modified recursive rules so generated we need some modified exit rules.

Modified Exit Rules:

Say that R^S is a node of M_Q and there is each exit rule r_i with head predicate R. Then we add the following modified exit rule:

$$R^S(j, k, h, u_1, \cdots, u_n) :-\ cnt.R^S(j, k, h, x_1, \cdots, x_l),\ W_1, \cdots, W_q.$$

where:

i) $u_1, \ldots, u_n$ are the unbound arguments in the head of r_i (i.e, those which do NOT belong to S),

ii) $cnt.R^S(j,k,h,x_1, \cdots, x_l)$ is the counting predicate, with $x_1, \cdots, x_l$ the bound arguments in r_i's head.

iii) $W_1, \cdots, W_q$ are the predicates in the body of r_i.

Thus the exit rules are generated by replacing the bound predicates in the head by the indexes and then adding the counting set to the body of the rule.

Modified Goal:

If $\hat{P}$ is the original query goal with bound arguments S and predicate symbol P, then let $x_1, \cdots, x_n$ denote the unbound arguments (i.e., those not in S). Then, the modified query goal is

$$P(0,0,0, x_1, \cdots, x_n)?$$

It thus follow that the fixpoint computation of the modified rules should be stopped after zero values are generated for the indices.

Figure 6 illustrates the application of the method to the a situation involving mutually recursive predicates and more than one c-predicate in the body of a recursive rule (non-linear rule).

4.3. Properties of the Generalized Counting Method.

From a formal viewpoint the Generalized Counting Method can be viewed as a rule rewriting system. In this framework, both the original set of Horn Clauses and the modified one have a pure fixpoint-based semantics that defines the sets of answers satisfying the query [VK] (arithmetic predicates can be treated in this framework as being defined by infinite comparison relations over complex arithmetic terms [Z3]). Then we can prove the following basic result [SZ3]:

THEOREM 1. *Let $Q = <G, LP, D>$ be a query that has the binding passing property. If $\overline{Q} = <\overline{G}, \overline{LP}, D>$ denotes the modified query produced by the generalized counting method, then Q and $\overline{Q}$ compute the same answer.*

(Note however, that in the theorem above, the answer to both queries could be infinite, a problem treated in Section 5.)

From a computational viewpoint, the generalized counting rules prescribe an abstract computation plan having some desirable performance characteristics. First of all, counting and modified rules can be generated efficiently:

PROPOSITION 2. *Let $Q = <G, LP, D>$ be a query such that Q has the binding passing property and there is a bound on the arity of the predicates in LP. Then the generalized counting method constructs the modified query*

G : P(a, y)?

LP : r_0: P(x, y) :- B1(x, x_1), Q(x_1, y), B2(x, x_2), Q(x_2, y), B3(y, z).

r_1: Q(x, y) :- B4(x, z), P(z, y).

r_2: P(x, y) :- B5(x, y).

A recursive clique of two mutually recursive predicates: P and Q.

Binding Graph:

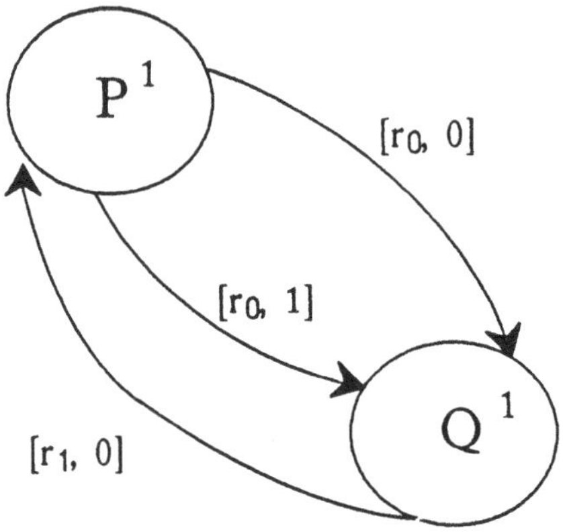

Counting Rules:

cnt.P1 (0, 0, 0, a).

cnt.Q1 (j+1, 2*k+0, 2*h+0, x_1):- cnt.P1 (j, k, h, x_1), B1(x, x_1), B2(x, x_2).(from [r_0,

cnt.Q1 (j+1, 2*k+0, 2*h+1, x_2):- cnt.P1 (j, k, h, x), B1(x, x_1), B2(x, x_2). (from [r_0,

cnt.P1 (j+1, 2*k+1, 1*h+0, z):- cnt.Q1 (j, k, h, x), B4(x, z). (from [r_1,

Supplementary Rules: None

Modified Rules and Goal:

P1 (j−1, (k−0)/2, h/2, y):- Q1 (j, k, h, y), Q1 (j, k, h+1, y), B3(y,z).

Q1 (j−1, (k−1)/2, h/1, y):- P1 (j, k, h, y).

P1 (j, k, h, y):- cnt.P1 (j, k, h, x), B5(x, y).

$\overline{G}$: P1 (0, 0, 0, y)?

Figure 6. François' Example

$\overline{Q} = <\overline{G}, \overline{LP}, D>$ *in time polynomial in the size of LP*.

As today, we still lack a general framework that allows us to characterize the performance of the various methods proposed for the compilation of recursive predicates. However, a clear understanding of the behavior of these methods has emerged from the study of typical examples [BR]. These examples strongly suggest that the counting method is superior to the others (in terms of database accesses and computational steps required), particularly in situations that do not require the elimination of duplicates. Thus, the method is ideally suited for situations involving function symbols, where a new term is generated at each step in the fixpoint computations (either by adding some level of nesting in the structure or by removing some). Recursive predicates such as appending two lists, extracting all the elements of a list, searching and manipulating tree structures, etc., are ideal candidates for the generalized counting method.

Our confidence in the ability of the generalized counting method to deal with recursive predicates with function symbols is reinforced by the authors' experience with Prolog and the observation that the generalized counting can be implemented to emulate Prolog very closely. To illustrate this point let us consider the two fixpoint computation prescribed by the generalized counting method. A possible implementation strategy consists of computing all counting set and supplementary counting sets values, before going into the fixpoint computation of the modified rules (a strategy similar to that used in implementing magic sets [BMSU1, BMSU2, SZ2]). However, a modified exit rule with a certain index value, can be fired as soon as the counting set value for that particular index value is obtained. Assuming that no duplicate elimination is needed, the overall strategy then becomes quite similar to that of Prolog (and also to that of [HN]). However, the generalized counting method also allows for massive joins since it does not imply a one-tuple-at-the-time join strategy, and the top-down binding propagation is independent from the ordering of rules and goals.

4.4. Simplifications and Extensions.

A number of simplifications of the overall generalized counting method can be introduced to deal with various subcases.

Single Recursive Rule:

When there is a single recursive rule, the second index remains constant and can be eliminated (see for instance Figure 4).

Single c-predicate in the rule bodies:

When there is a single c-predicate in the body of every rule, the third index remains constant and can be eliminated (see Figure 4).

Shared Solved Predicates

Counting rules and supplementary counting rules might share the same solved predicates. For instance, in Figure 5, the comparison predicates are evaluated in both the counting rules and in the supplementary counting ones; this duplicate work could be eliminated. A general solution to this problem consists in introducing an *allcnt* predicate that computes both the bound arguments and the supplementary counting variables [SZ3]. Then, the counting and special counting predicates can simply be derived from the *allcnt* by projecting out variables not needed in the specific case.

Arbitrary Datum Predicates.

As previously mentioned, datum predicates need not be restricted to database and comparison predicates; all is required is that these predicates can be solved independently of the recursive clique under consideration. For instance, the technique presented in [Z3] can be used to deal effectively with *non-recursive rules,* possibly containing function symbols. Said technique provide a a generalization of the binding propagation rules described in Section 3.1.

Let us now turn to the problem of determining whether recursive predicates (not in the same recursive clique as our c-predicates), can be used as solved datum predicates. This tantamounts to determining whether the corresponding goal in the rule can be solved for the given set of bindings. To this end, we can apply the known techniques for solving recursive predicates, in particular the generalized counting method described here. Take for instance a query $G: MG(L_1, L_2, X)$, defined against a LP consisting of the rules of Figure 2 and 3 combined. Then, in order to solve this query, we will also have to solve the goal $G2$: $C_1 < C_2$, where C_1 and C_2 stand for arbitrary constants. Thus we get the modified set of rules of Figure 7 (since we only have one recursive rule we only use one index).

Finally, we need to link the rules of Figure 7 with the last counting rule of Figure 5. This can, for instance, be accomplished by redefining the goal $x < x_1$ of Figure 5 as follows:

$$x < s_1 \text{:- } assert(cnt. <^{1,2}(x, x_1)),\ <^{1,2}(0).$$

(This is a rather coarse solution, presented here only as a quick illustration on how things could function; more refined solutions will be given in future reports.)

Trivial Modified Rules

It is easy to see that the only function of the modified recursive rule in Figure 7, is to decrement the index to zero one step at the time. We can thus dispense with this rule and write a new modified goal:

$$\overline{G}: cnt. <^{1,2}(\_, x, s(x))?$$

We have thus eliminated the second fixpoint computation (tail recursion); moreover, we can also drop the index from the counting set computation.

G: $C1<C2?$

LP:

r_0: $x < s(y)$:- $x < y$.

r_1: $x < s(x)$.

Binding Graph

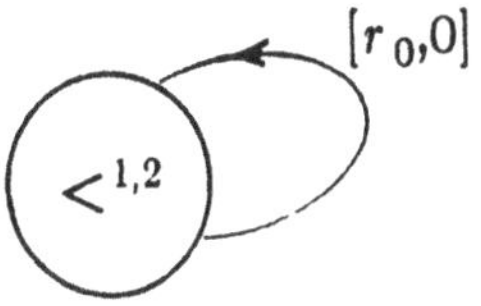

Counting rules:

cnt. $<^{1,2}(0, C1, C2)$

cnt. $<^{1,2}(j+1, x, y)$:- *cnt.* $<^{1,2}(j, x, s(y))$

Supplementary Counting rules: None.

Modified Rules and Goal:

$<^{1,2}(j)$:- *cnt.* $<^{1,2}(j, x, s(x))$.

$<^{1,2}(j-1)$:- $<^{1,2}(j)$.

$\overline{G}$: $<^{1,2}(0)?$

Fig. 7. *Implementation of the "less-than" rules of Figure 3.*

Symmetrically, it easy to identify many situations where the counting set computation becomes trivial and can be eliminated. Therefore, the counting method also supplies a good framework for identifying simple cases where recursive queries with constants can be implemented safely and efficiently by a single fixpoint [AhUl].

5. Safety of Queries

A safe query is one that generates only a finite number of answers. Safety for recursive queries with function symbols is undecidable; thus the best a person can do is to provide sufficient conditions that cover the cases of practical interests. Our domain of interest consists of recursive queries having the binding passing properties for which we want to ensure that the our methods terminate. Note that the generalized counting method recasts the original query Q into two fixpoint computations: whenever both these computations terminate in a finite number of steps, we will say that *the generalized counting method is safe w.r.t. to the query Q*.

The following property follows immediately from the definitions:

PROPOSITION 3. *The generalized counting method is safe w.r.t. a query having the binding passing property if and only if the counting set fixpoint computation converges in a finite number of steps.*

We will now assume that our c-predicates are either database predicates or comparison predicates (including equality).

We now give a sufficient condition for the generalized counting method to be safe, which appears to cover most of the situations of practical interest.

Term Length

The length of a term t denoted $|t|$ is defined as follows:

(a) if t is a constant, then $|t|=1$,

(b) if $t=f(t_1, \cdots, t_k)$, then $|t|=|t_1|+\cdots+|t_k|+1$.

This definition allows to determine the length of constant terms. When the terms contain variables, then we can express the length of the term in function of those of the variables. For instance $|x \bullet x|=|x|+|x|+1=2|x|+1$ In general, there is no information on the actual length of x, except that $|x| \geq 1$. Thus $|x \bullet x| \geq 3$.

The length of a set of terms S is the sum of the length of all terms in S. For instance the length of the bound arguments (i.e., $x \bullet y, x_1 \bullet y_1$) in rule r_0 of the *MG* example in Figure 5 is $|x|+|y|+|x_1|+|y_1|+2$.

Arc Length Balance.

Let (R^S, P^T) be an arc in the binding graph with label $[ri, v]$. The length balance associated with this arc is defined as difference between the length of the bound arguments in the head of r_i (i.e., those denoted by S) and the length of the bound arguments of the v-th c-predicate in the body (i.e., the arguments denoted by T). For instance the length balance for the arc labeled $[r_0, 0]$ in the binding graph of Figure 5 is:

$$(|x|+|y|+|x_1|+|y_1|+2)-(|y|+|x_1|+|y_1|+1)=|x|+1.$$

A lower-bound of the arc length balance can be obtained by replacing the length of the variables by the lower bound of their length if the coefficient is positive, or by the upper bound if the coefficient is negative. For instance, in the previous example, a lower bound of the arc length balance is 2, since the variable x has length one or greater.

Cycle Length Balance.

Given a cycle of the binding graph, the length balance associated to it is defined as the sum of the length balances of its arcs. A lower bound of the cycle length balance can be obtained as the sum of the lower bounds of the arc length balances.

THEOREM 2. *If the the length balance associated with every cycle in the binding graph of a query is positive, then the fixpoint computation of the counting sets converges in a finite number of steps.*

Thus, the examples in Figures 5 and 7 are safe. While Theorem 2 is very useful for determining the safety of recursive predicates with function symbols, including typical situations, such as appending two lists and searching and manipulating trees and lists, there are many situations where more elaborated or completely different techniques must be used.

For instance, if the arc length balance computed over all bound arguments is not positive, one may try to find a subset of the bound arguments for which it is (also a sufficient condition for safety). Often, the cycle length balance depends upon the lengths of variables, which is in turn determined by other predicates (including recursive ones). An interesting technique to deal with some of the more complex situations is given in [UlVg]. For variables that belong to some database predicate, it is often reasonable to assume that their length is one. This additional assumption enables one to infer the safety of the counting method applied to the following example, where Q is a database relation with no function symbols in the second column:

$$P(b \bullet b \bullet x)?$$

$$P(b \bullet b \bullet x) :- Q(x, y), P(x \bullet y).$$

$$P(b).$$

Finally, there are situations such as those of examples of Figure 4 and 6, where all the solved predicates are database predicates, and the arc balance is null. Therefore, there is no a priori assurance that duplicates cannot occur in the computation of the counting sets. Even for these situations, if the underlying database is known to be acyclic, the generalized counting method remains safe and efficient [SZ1]. When the acyclicity of the underlying database cannot be guaranteed, two solutions are possible. The first is to use methods such as the magic set [BMSU1] and minimagic method [SZ2], that have a built-in check for and elimination of duplicates. The second approach consists of starting with the computation of generalized counting sets while checking for duplicates. If duplicates show up then one will fall back on the standard counting method. This hybrid approach, known as *magic counting* is described in [SZ1].

6. Conclusion

We have presented a new method, named generalized counting, that is very efficient [BR] and appears particularly useful in dealing with recursive rules containing function symbols. The method implements recursive queries by two fixpoint computations. The first propagates the initial bindings into the recursive loop, while the second solves the remaining goals and constructs the desired answer. The method is applicable to arbitrary recursive predicates, including those featuring mutual recursion and non-linear recursion.

The paper also discussed the application of the method to solve nested recursive predicates. A sufficient condition for the finiteness of the fixpoint computations was finally given; although quite simple, this condition seems adequate for many common cases involving recursive predicates with function symbols. It thus appears that the generalized counting method provides a very valuable tool towards compiling pure logic programs with good performance and an a-priori guarantee of termination.

Acknowledgments:
The authors are grateful to François Bancilhon, Ravi Krishnamurthy and Raghu Ramakrishan for many inspiring discussions.

References

[AhUl] Aho A. V. and J. Ullman, " Universality of Data Retrieval Languages," *Proc. POPL Conference,* San Antonio Tx, 1979.

[AC] Aiello, L. and Cecchi, "Adding a Closure Operator to the Extended Relational Algebra ...", Rome Univ. Technical Report, 1985.

[B] Bancilhon, F., "Naive Evaluation of Recursively defined Relations", Unpublished Manuscript, 1985.

[BGK] Bayer, R., U. Guntzer and W. Kiessling, "On the Evaluation of Recursion in Deductive DB Systems by Efficient Differential Fixpoint Iteration," Technical Report, Technische Univ. Munich, 1985.

[BMSU1] Bancilhon, F., D. Maier, Y. Sagiv, J. Ullman, "Magic sets and other strange ways to implement logic programs", *Proc. 5th ACM SIGMOD-SIGACT Symp. on Principles of Database Systems,* 1986.

[BMSU2] Bancilhon, F., D. Maier, Y. Sagiv, J. Ullman, "Magic sets: algorithms and examples", unpublished manuscript, 1985.

[BR] Bancilhon, F., Ramakrishan, R., "An amateur's introduction to recursive query processing strategies", *Proc. ACM SIGMOD Int. Conference on Management of Data,* Washington, D.C., May 1986.

[CH] Chandra, A.K., Harel, D., "Horn clauses and the fixpoint hierarchy", *Proc. ACM SIGMOD-SIGACT Symp. on Principles of Database Systems*, 1982, pp. 158-163.

[GD] Gardarin, G., DeMaindreville, C., " Evaluation of Database Recursive Logic Programs as Recursive Function Series," *Proc. ACM SIGMOD Int. Conference on Management of Data,* Washington, D.C., May 1986.

[HN] Henschen, L.J., Naqvi, S. A., "On compiling queries in recursive first-order databases", *JACM 31,* 1, 1984, pp. 47-85.

[L] Lozinskii, E.L., "Inference by generating and structuring of deductive databases", Report 84-11, Dept. of Computer Science, Hebrew

University, Israel.

[MS] McKay, D., Shapiro, S., "Using active connection graphs for reasoning with recursive rules", *Proc. 7th IJCAI, 1981*, pp. 368-374.

[P] Parker, S. et al., "Logic Programming and Databases," in *Expert Database Systems,* L. Kerschberg (ed.), Benjamin/Cummings, 1986.

[R] Reiter, R., "On closed world databases", in *Logic and Databases* (Gallaire, H., Minker, J., eds), Plenum, New York, 1978, pp. 55-76.

[SZ1] Saccà, D., Zaniolo, C., "On the implementation of a simple class of logic queries for databases", *Proc. 5th ACM SIGMOD-SIGACT Symp. on Principles of Database Systems,* 1986.

[SZ2] Saccà, D., Zaniolo, C., "Implementation of recursive queries for a data language based on pure Horn clauses", unpublished manuscript, 1986.

[SZ3] Saccà, D., Zaniolo, C., "Techniques for Solving Recursive queries in a Logic Based Language," in preparation.

[U1] Ullman, J.D., *Principles of Database Systems*, Computer Science Press, Rockville, Md., 1982.

[T1] Tarski, A. "A Lattice Theoretical Fixpoint Theorem and its Application," *Pacific Journal of Mathematics No. 5,* pp. 285-309, 1955.

[UV] Ullman, J.D. and A. Van Gelder, "Testing Applicability of Top-Down Capture Rules," Stanford University, Report STAN-CS-85-1046, 1985.

[U2] Ullman, J.D., "Implementation of logical query languages for databases", *TODS 10,* 3, 1985, pp. 289-321.

[VK] van Emden, M.H., Kowalski, R., "The semantics of predicate logic as a programming language", *JACM 23,* 4, 1976, pp. 733-742.

[Vg] Van Gelder, A., "A Message Passing Framework for Logical Query Evaluation," *Proc. ACM SIGOD Int. Conference on Management of Data,* Washington, D.C., May 1986.

[Vi] Vieille, L. "Recursive Axioms in Deductive Databases: the Query-Subquery Approach," *Proc. First Int. Conference on Expert Database Systems,* Charleston, S.C., 1986.

[Z1] Zaniolo, C. "Prolog: a database query language for all seasons," in *Expert Database Systems,* L. Kerschberg (ed.), Benjamin/Cummings, 1986.

[Z2] Zaniolo, C. "The Representation and Deductive Retrieval of Complex Objects," *Proc. 11-th VLDB,* pp. 459-469, 1985.

[Z3] Zaniolo, C. "Safety and Compilation of Non-Recursive Horn Clauses," *Proc. First Int. Conference on Expert Database Systems,* Charleston, S.C., 1986.

Restructuring of Complex Objects and Office Forms
(Extended Abstract)

Serge Abiteboul
I.N.R.I.A.
Domaine de Rocquencourt
78153 Le Chesnay
FRANCE

Richard Hull[1]
Computer Science Department
University of Southern California
Los Angeles, CA 90089-0782
USA

Abstract: A model of structures arising in Semantic Database Models (complex objects) and Office Information Systems (forms) is studied. An algebra based on rewrite operations is introduced. The problem of restructuring is investigated. Some basic result are presented.

1. INTRODUCTION

A recent trend in the database field is to consider hierarchical data structures. Hierarchical data structures are central in the non-first-normal-form relational model [ABi,FT,RKS,SP], and have been studied under the name formats [HY], and complex objects [ABe,BK]. These structures also arise naturally in semantic database models offering aggregation, grouping, and generalization [AH1,HK,HM,SS]. In fact, forms in Office Information Systems are similar kinds of structures [PFK,SLTC,T]. The purpose of this paper is to develop tools to manipulate typed hierarchical objects.

The focus of the paper is on typed hierarchical objects obtained using:

- tuple constructor (aggregation),
- set constructor (grouping), and
- union constructor (generalization).

[1] Work by this author supported in part by the National Science Foundation grant IST-83-06517, and IST-85-11541. Part of this work was performed while he was visiting I.N.R.I.A.

These objects are similar to the objects found in [HY,K,AH1]. Most other investigations have considered data structures involving the first two constructors only. The use of the third constructor allows us to handle sets of objects of possibly different types. (In [BK], sets of objects of possibly different structures are considered without emphasizing the use of strict typing.) Another novel feature of our model is the utilization of particular constants which can serve as nonapplicable nulls, and are also used to model boolean and other finite domains.

One of the major research problems facing the field of databases is to understand how to manipulate hierarchical structures. Languages were already presented for typed objects built using the first two of these constructors [ABe,ABi,FT,J,KV,SP]. The first theme of the paper is to present an algebraic language capable of handling objects obtained using all three constructors. The central operator of the algebra is a rewrite operator. Rewrite operators are directly inspired by the rewrite rules of [BK], although our approach is different in fundamental ways. To perform complex manipulations deep in a structure, nesting of rewrite similar to nesting of selections in [ABi,SP], or nesting of extend/replace in [ABe] is used.

The second theme of the paper is to study the problem of data restructuring. In virtually all database models, it is possible to represent essentially the same data in different ways. This notion of "data relativism" arises in a variety of contexts like database integration, view construction, form modification. It is thus crucial to understand data relativism at a fundamental level [H1,HY,HM], so that systems can effectively translate between alternative data representations.

Our study of restructuring is based on transformations of types. Some of these transformations are information preserving, and lead to a characterization of "structural equivalence" which generalizes results of [HY]. Other transformations provide ways to augment the information capacity of a type. The effect of all these transformations can be achieved using only "simple" rewrite operations. This class of simple rewrite operations is closed under composition. As a consequence, if a user specifies the restructuring of the database using a sequence of transformations as defined here, the system can compute the new database state using a single rewrite operation.

The paper is organized as follows. Types are presented in Section 2 together with their corresponding objects. Section 3 introduces the algebra. Results concerning structural equivalence are exhibited in Section 4. Finally, augmentation is studied in Section 5.

2. TYPES AND OBJECTS

The purpose of this section is to motivate and formally define types and objects.

We first present an example concerning two versions of information that might be stored in a personnel database. Consider the two form templates shown in Figure 2.1. The structure of these forms is described by the types shown in Figure 2.2. Speaking roughly, a "type" is a tree with certain kinds of nodes. All leaf nodes of a type correspond to "basic types". This includes such types as "alpha", "9-dig", etc., and also some special type $\perp$ which has a one element domain. There are three kinds of internal nodes. Intuitively, $\times$-nodes correspond to the tuple constructor; *-nodes correspond to the set constructor; finally, +-nodes correspond to the union constructor.

Types as described here generalize the notion of "format" [HY] to include particular types with one element domain. As we shall see, these types can be used to represent nonapplicable

Last Name:	
First Name:	
SS:	
Sex:	(M/F)
If male,	military position:
If female,	names of children:
	Married:(Y/N)
	If married, maiden name:
Form 1	

Last Name:
First Name:
SS:
If applicable, military position:
Married:(Y/N)
Names of children:
If applicable, maiden name:
Sex: (M/F)
Form2

Figure 2.1: Two form templates for a personnel database

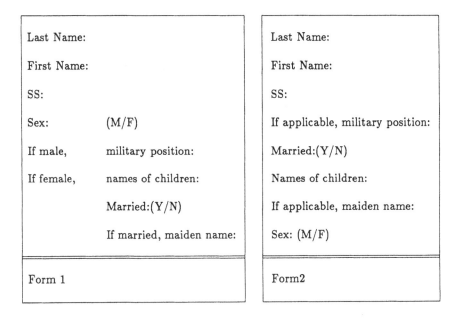

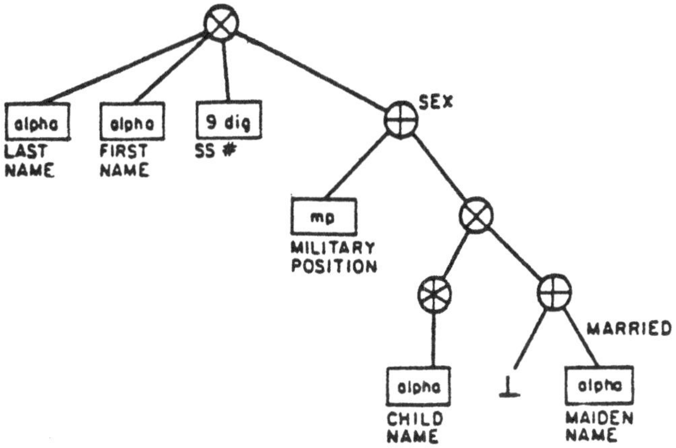

Type of Form 1

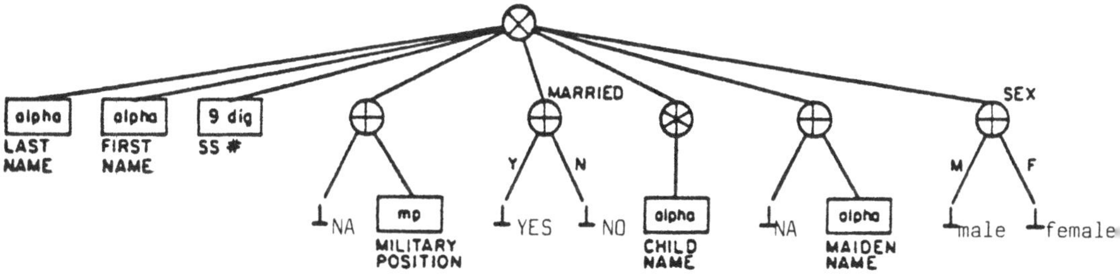

Type of Form 2

Figure 2.2: Types for Form1 and Form2

nulls, and finite domains. Furthermore, they play an important role in our study of restructuring.

As mentioned in the introduction, types can serve as a formal model for representing data structures used in various disciplines. First, types subsume the family of form structures considered in Office Automation Systems [PFK,SLTC,T]. Furthermore, as indicated in the example, this model provides the possibility of faithfully representing forms in which different parts are to be filled out under different circumstances. (On the other hand, as described here the model does not directly incorporate the occurrence of dependent fields, such as one field which is to be the sum of two other fields). Also, types can be used to model classes of objects arising in Semantic Database Models [AH1,SS,HK,HM] which incorporate aggregation, grouping, and generalization. Finally, it should be noted that the structures of non-first-normal-form relations correspond to types in which tuple and set constructors alternate.

We now present the formal notions of type and object.

We assume the existence of *domains* $D_1,\ldots,D_n,\ldots$ of *atomic values*. These domains are all countable and pairwise disjoint. We also assume the existence of a particular atomic value, denoted $\perp$, which is not in D_i for any i. The set $\{\perp\}$ will serve as the unique one-element domain.

We assume the existence of an infinite set of symbols called *attributes*. A function dom assigns a domain to each attribute. We suppose that there is an infinite supply of attributes for each domain. To distinguish between attributes with infinite domain, and attributes with one-element domain,

- attributes with infinite domain are denoted with letters from the beginning of the alphabet; and
- attributes with one element domain are denoted $\perp$ with subscripts (e.g., $\perp_{male}$, $\perp_2$).

Finally, we assume the existence of an infinite set of symbols called *tokens* which contains the set of attributes.

Intuitively, a type is a tree. Leaves of the tree denote atomic types, and are labelled by attributes. Internal nodes correspond to applications of the constructors, and are labelled by non-attribute tokens. Formally, we have:

Definition: A *type* is a rooted tree (V,E) where $V = V_+ \cup V_* \cup V_\times \cup V_b$ is the disjoint union of +-nodes, *-nodes, $\times$-nodes, and basic nodes such that

(i) a node is a basic node iff it is a leaf, and

(ii) each *-node has exactly one child.

The nodes of a type are labelled by tokens with the following restrictions:

(iii) a node is assigned an attribute iff it is a leaf, and

(iv) distinct siblings (i.e., distinct children of the same node) are assigned distinct tokens.

We use a natural syntactic representation for types where: square brackets correspond to tuple constructors, braces correspond to set constructors, and angle brackets correspond to union constructors. The following are examples of types:

P: <B; R:[B,B']>
P:[Q_1: { R: [B,B',B"] }, Q_2: { S: [C,C'] }]
P:{ Q:[R:{C}, R':<C';S':{B}>] }

Note that the second example is the description of a relational schema.

With each type, we associate a set of objects in the following way:

Definition: For each type T, the *domain* of T, denoted dom(T), is defined recursively by:

(1) For each attribute A, dom(A) has already been defined,

(2) if T ≡ P:[T_1,...,T_n], and Q_i is the root token of T_i for each i, then dom(T)= {[Q_1:O_1,...,Q_n:O_n] | $O_i \in$ dom(T_i) for each i},

(3) if T ≡ P:{T'}, then dom(T)= {{O_1,...,O_n} | $O_i \in$ dom(T') for each i}, and

(4) if T ≡ P:<T_1;...;T_n>, and Q_i is the root token of T_i for each i, then dom(T)= {<Q_j:O_j> | $O_j \in$ dom(T_j) for some j in [1..n]}.

Each element in dom(T) is called an *object* of type T.

To illustrate the previous two definitions, we now give examples of objects, and their corresponding types:

(1) <B:b> and <R:[B:b_1,B':b_2]> are objects of type P: <B; R:[B,B']>.

(2) [Q_1:{[B:b,B':b',B":b"], [B:b',B':b,B":b] }, Q_2: {}] is an object of type
P:[Q_1: { R: [B,B',B"] }, Q_2: { S: [C,C'] }]

(where it is assumed that dom(B)= dom(B')= dom(B")).

When the type is understood, and an implicit ordering of siblings assumed, we can simplify the syntactic description of objects. For instance, the object of (2) can be written as

[{[b,b',b"], [b',b,b]}, {}]

3. AN ALGEBRA FOR TYPED OBJECTS

In this section, we introduce an algebra for typed objects. In particular, we concentrate on one operation that is going to be essential for restructuring objects, namely rewrite.

As mentioned in the introduction, one of the major problems in the database field is to understand how to manipulate hierarchical structures. Several proposals have been made recently in this direction. A calculus-based language has been proposed in [J], and also used in [ABe,KV,RKS]. Algebraic languages for non-1NF models have also been developed [ABi,KV,SP,FT,H2]. Although these languages sometimes use quite different operators, they generaly have comparable expressive power. Indeed, in [ABe,KV], it is shown that a calculus based on [J] is equivalent to particular algebras.

These various investigations do not allow the use of the union constructor. In this section, we introduce a powerful language to manipulate objects in the presence of the union constructor. The central operator of our language is a "rewrite". This operator allows easy manipulation of hierarchical data. As in [BK], a rule is used to describe how an object should be "rewritten". The nesting of rewrites as used here is related to nesting of extend/replace functions in [ABe], and also to nesting of selections in [ABi] or [SP]. Another approach for defining an algebra for objects permitting the union constructor is developed in [K].

The rewrite operation is defined using some "rewrite rules". To specify the form of the rules, we need the concept of "variables". Like objects, variables in our context are strictly typed.

Definition: For each type R, there is an infinite set Var_R of symbols ($R \neq R' \Rightarrow Var_R \cap Var_{R'} = \phi$). Let $Var = \cup_R Var_R$. *(Complex) variables* are recursively defined by:

(i) each object of type T is a variable of type T,

(ii) each element of Var_T is a variable of type T,

(iii) if $T \equiv P:[T_1,...,T_n]$ is a type, Q_i is the root token of T_i for each i, and X_i a variable of T_i for each i, then $[Q_1:X_1,...,Q_n:X_n]$ is a variable of T,

(iv) if $T \equiv P:<T_1;...;T_n>$ is a type, Q_i is the root token of T_i for each i, and X_j a variable of T_j for some j in [1..n], then $<Q_j:X_j>$ is a variable of T,

(v) if $T \equiv P:\{T'\}$ is a type, and X_i a variable of T' for each i, then $\{X_1,...,X_n\}$ is a variable of T,

Note that this definition permits the specification of variables with components of arbitrary granularity. For instance, X, $[Q_1:Y,Q_2:Z]$, and $P:[\ Q_1: \{U_1,U_2\}, Q_2: Z\ ]$ are objects of type

$$P{:}[\ Q_1{:}\ \{\ R{:}\ [B,B',B'']\ \},\ Q_2{:}\ \{\ S{:}\ [C,C']\ \}\ ].$$

We are now ready to define the rewrite expressions. Due to the recursive nature of their definition, we present both rewrite rules, and rewrite expressions, at the same time. Motivating examples are given afterwards.

Definition: Let X be a variable of type S. *(Rewrite) rules* and *rewrite expressions* are defined recursively in the following way:

(i) if Y is a variable of type T appearing in X
 (i-a) $X \rightarrow Y$ is a rule from S to T,
 (i-b) if ρ is a rewrite expression from T to T', $X \rightarrow \rho(Y)$ is a rule from S to T',

(ii) (ii-a) if $X \rightarrow Y_1, \ldots, X \rightarrow Y_n$ are rules from S to $T_1, \ldots, T_n$, respectively, where Q_i is the root token of T_i for each i, then $X \rightarrow [Q_1{:}Y_1, \ldots, Q_n{:}Y_n]$ is a rule from S to $P{:}[T_1, \ldots, T_n]$,
 (ii-b) if $X \rightarrow Y$ is a rule from S to T_i for some i in [1..n], and Q_i is the root token of T_i, then $X \rightarrow <Q_i{:}Y>$ is a rule from S to $P{:}<T_1;\ldots;T_n>$,
 (ii-c) if $X \rightarrow Y_1, \ldots, X \rightarrow Y_n$ are rules from S to T', then $X \rightarrow \{Y_1, \ldots, Y_n\}$ is a rule from S to $P{:}\{T'\}$,
 (ii-d) if $X \rightarrow Y_1, \ldots, X \rightarrow Y_n$ are rules from S to T, and T is a set type, then $X \rightarrow Y_1 \cup \ldots \cup Y_n$ is a rule from S to T.

A rewrite expression from $S{=}A{:}\{S'\}$ to $T{=}B{:}\{T'\}$ is an expression of the form rew(Δ) where Δ is a set of rules from S' to T'.

The semantics of rewrite rules and expressions is given by the following definition:

Definition: An *assignment* is a partial mapping α which maps elements in Var into objects of the appropriate type. This assignment is extended to expressions in the following way:

(1) $\alpha(O)=O$ for each object O,

(2) $\alpha([Q_1{:}X_1, \ldots, Q_n{:}X_n]) = [Q_1{:}\alpha(X_1), \ldots, Q_n{:}\alpha(X_n)]$,

(3) $\alpha(<Q{:}X>) = <Q{:}\alpha(X)>$,

(4) $\alpha(\{X_1, \ldots, X_n\}) = \{\alpha(X_1), \ldots, \alpha(X_n)\}$,

(5) $\alpha(X_1 \cup \ldots \cup X_n) = \alpha(X_1) \cup \ldots \cup \alpha(X_n)$,

(6) $\alpha(\text{rew}(\Delta)(X)) = \{\beta(V) \mid U \rightarrow V \in \Delta, \text{ and } \beta(U) \in \alpha(X)\}$,

Now we have:

Definition: Let ρ=rew(Δ) from S, and O be an object of S. Then the *effect* of ρ on O is defined by

ρ(O)= {α(Y) | X→Y in Δ, and α(X) in O}.

We now present three examples of rewrite expressions. The first example shows how rewrite expressions specify selection and projection. (As with objects, tokens are omitted from variables if understood from the context.)

Example 3.1: Again using Form 1, the set of names of females with first name 'Mary' having exactly one child is given by

rew([X,'Mary',Z,<Female:[{U},V]>] → X)

The second example illustrates the use of several rules to obtain different treatment of alternative structures resulting from the union constructor.

Example 3.2: Consider Forms 1 and 2 of Section 2. It is easily seen that a mapping transforming a set of forms 1 into a set of forms 2 is obtained using the rewrite operation rew($\{r_1,r_2,r_3\}$) where

$$r_1 = [X,Y,Z,<MP{:}W>] \rightarrow [X,Y,Z,<MP{:}W>,<\bot_{no}>, \{\},<\bot_{NA}>,<\bot_{male}>]$$

$$r_2 = [X,Y,Z,<Female{:}[V,<\bot_0>]>] \rightarrow [X,Y,Z,<\bot_{NA}>,<\bot_{no}>, V,<\bot_{NA}>,<\bot_{female}>]$$

$$r_3 = [X,Y,Z,<Female{:}[V,<Maiden\text{-}name{:}U>]>] \rightarrow [X,Y,Z,<\bot_{NA}>,<\bot_{yes}>, V,<U>,<\bot_{female}>]$$

The last example presents the use of rewrite rules in a nested way, and also the utilization of union of rewrites.

Example 3.3: Consider the following two types:

P:{ P':[Dept, Pers:{R:[Emp, M:{Name}, F:{Name}]} }

Q:{ Q':[Dept, Pers:{R:[Emp, S:{ S':[Name, Sex:$<\bot_{male};\bot_{female}>$]}]}

which might be used to store, for each department, each employee along with his/her children, differentiated by sex. We now give a rewrite expression which maps objects of the first type into objects of the second in the natural manner. (The corresponding mapping is information preserving.)

ρ_{male}= rew(W → [Name:W, Sex:<$\bot_{male}$>])
ρ_{female}= rew(W → [Name:W, Sex:<$\bot_{female}$>])
ρ= rew([Emp:X, M:Y, F:Z] → [Emp:X, S:ρ_{male}(Y) ∪ ρ_{female}(Z)])
rew([Dept:U, Pers:V] → [Dept:U, Pers:ρ(V)])

Following [ABe], the other operations that are in the algebra are basic set operations.

- Four binary operations. Three of these operations deal with two sets of objects over the same type: *union, intersection, and difference.* One deals with two arbitrary sets of objects: *cross product* (and produces a set of pairs).
- Two unary operations: The *power set* operation which takes a set O of objects and returns the set of all subsets of O, and *set collapse* which takes a set O' of sets, and returns the set of all objects belonging to some element of O'.

The use of variables in our context is closely related to the use of variables in the extend operation of [ABe]. Indeed, it is possible to generalize the rules by allowing dynamic constants as in [ABe]. We conjecture that the algebra generalized in this manner is equivalent to the algebra of [ABe] for types not using the union construct. Thus, results of [ABe] would imply that the algebra is "complete" in the sense of the calculus of [J]. A more precise proof of completeness would involve extending a calculus in the style of [J] to handle complex objects *with* the union construct, and proving that the algebra presented here is equivalent to the resulting calculus. In the remainder of the paper, we do not consider dynamic constants.

4. EQUIVALENCE PRESERVING TRANSFORMATIONS

In the last two sections of this paper, the problem of restructuring is considered. In particular, natural local transformations on types preserving information capacity (Section 4), and augmenting it (Section 5) are introduced. A fundamental result (Theorem 4.3) states that the equivalence preserving transformations are "complete" in a formal sense. In both sections, the semantics of transformations are expressed using "simple" rewrite operations. A fundamental result of Section 5 states that each sequence of these transformations can be expressed using a single rewrite operation.

We first present an example which illustrates the structural manipulations on types which forms the basis for the definitions of "structural" equivalence and dominance given below. The example involves the two related types shown in Figure 4.1, which might be used to represent family units in some culture. Assume for a moment that in this culture, a family unit consists of either an adult female, or a married couple. (Unmarried adult males in this culture have no "legal" status). The type shown in part (a) can represent family units under this assumption: objects of this type consists in either a female or an ordered pair, with first coordinate a female and second coordinate a male. Suppose now that a new law has been enacted within this culture, which allows women to take more than one husband. Then the type in part (b) can be used to represent family unit. It is clear in this case that existing data stored in the structure of (a) can be translated into the structure of (b). However, as illustrated by other examples presented in the full paper [AH2], it may be difficult to know whether this is possible in the general case.

As mentioned in the introduction, previous work on data relativism [ABi,AABM,HM,H,HY,MB] suggests that an intuitively appealing formalism for comparing the information capacity of two structures can be based on local structural manipulations. This is substantiated in particular by results in [HY], which show that a family of 6 transformations and their inverses are "complete" for proving equivalence of information capacity. Two of these transformations are illustrated in Figure 4.2 (a) and (b). A capacity increasing transformation is shown in Figure 4.2 (c).

Returning to the example, Figure 4.3 shows a sequence of information capacity preserving and increasing transformations which indicates that the type of Figure 4.1(a) is naturally dominated by the type of Figure 4.1(b). Note that the first four transformations are information

Figure 4.1: The Polyandry Example

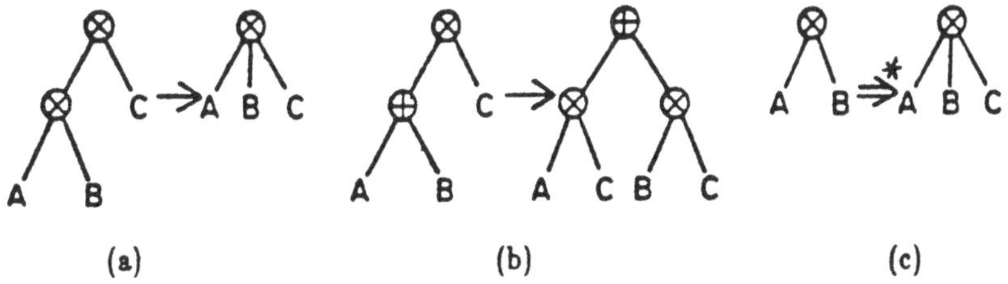

Figure 4.2: Two equivalence preserving transformations and one capacity increasing transformation

capacity preserving, and the last one strictly increases information capacity.

We now define the nine local structural transformations on types. As we shall see, these transformations preserve the information capacity of types. The transformations are presented in five groups; the first three of these are essentially trivial, while the latter two are more provocative. The transformations are first defined as they occur at the root of a type, and then generalized to permit their occurrence at an arbitrary node of a type. Three simple examples of e-transformations are shown in Figure 4.4 below.

Definition: The *equivalence preserving transformations (e-transformations)* are as follows:
Renaming e-transformations:

(i) B:T' is obtained from A:T' by a renaming transformation.

Simple × e-transformations:

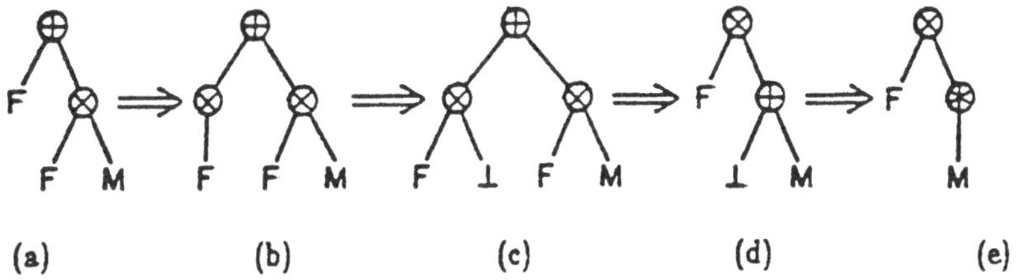

Figure 4.3: Structural transformation of a type which utilizes ⊥ types

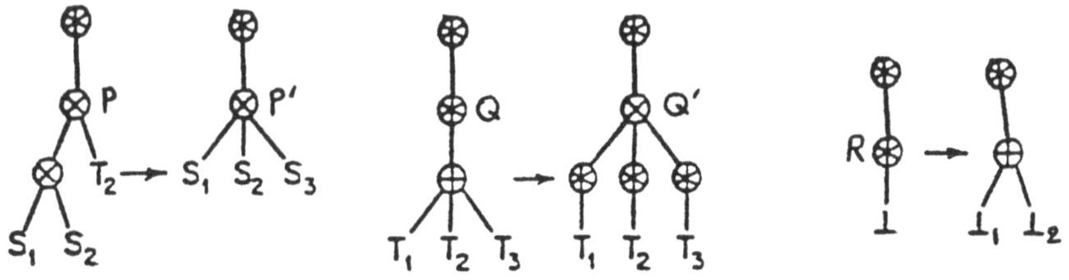

collapse ⊗ (a) | ⊕ through ⊛ (b) | ⊥ through ⊛ (c)

Figure 4.4: Examples of e-transformations

(ii) replace $[T_1,...,T_{i-1},Q:[S_1,...,S_m],T_{i+1},...,T_n]$ by $[T_1,...,T_{i+1},S_1,...,S_m,T_{i+1},...,T_n]$;

(iii) replace $Q:[T]$ by T;

Simple + e-transformations:

(iv) replace $<T_1;...;T_{i+1};Q:<S_1;...;S_m>;T_{i+1};...;T_n>$ by $<T_1;...;T_{i-1};S_1;...;S_m;T_{k+1};...;T_n>$;

(v) replace $Q:<T>$ by T;

Rising + e-transformations:

(vi) replace $[T_1,...,T_{i+1},Q:<S_1,...,S_m>,T_{i+1},...,T_n]$ by $<[T_1,...,T_{i-1},S_1,T_{i+1},...,T_n];...;[T_1,...,T_{i-1},S_m,T_{i+1},...,T_n]>$;

(vii) replace $\{<T_1;...;T_n>\}$ by $[Q_1:\{T_1\},...,Q_n:\{T_n\}]$;

e-transformations with $\perp$:

(viii) replace $[T_1,...,T_{i-1},\perp,T_{i+1},...,T_n]$ by $[T_1,...,T_{i-1},T_{i+1},...,T_n]$;

(ix) replace $\{\perp\}$ by $<\perp_1;\perp_2>$;

Suppose now that S is a type with a root node P and the type R below it, that R' is constructed from R using an e-transformation, and that S' is constructed from S by replacing R by R' at P. Then S' is the *result* of applying an e-transformation to S, written S $\rightarrow$ S'. The reflexive, transitive closure of $\rightarrow$ is denoted by $\rightarrow^*$.

With each of these transformations, one can associate a function from objects to objects.

The corresponding functions are called *restructuring functions*. The semantics of most restructuring functions should be obvious. For instance, for transformation (ix), we have:

Let T≡P:{⊥} be a type. Then transformation (ix) maps the object {} of type T to $\bot_1$, and the object {⊥} to $\bot_2$.

We now present a result that states that these functions are in fact bijective rewrite functions.

Theorem 4.1: Let R and S be two set types such that R → S (resp., S → R), then there is a rewrite operation ρ which is a bijection from dom(R) to dom(S). Furthermore ρ defines the same mapping as R → S (resp., the inverse of S → R).

Note that the restriction that R and S be of set-type is necessary since rewrite functions operate exclusively on set types. We now illustrate the previous result. Consider the e-transformations of Figure 4.4. Then they correspond to the following rewrite operations.

(a) rew([[X,Y], Z] → [X,Y,Z]);

(b) rew(X → [ρ_1(Z), ρ_2(Z), ρ_3(Z)]) where
Q_i is the root token of T_i for each i,
ρ_1= rew(<Q_1:V>→V),
ρ_2= rew(<Q_2:V>→V), and
ρ_3= rew(<Q_3:V>→V); and

(c) rew({}→$\bot_1$,{⊥}→$\bot_2$)

The next two results of this section imply that the application of e-transformations is essentially Church-Rosser, transforming each type into a "normal-form" type which is unique up to renaming of some internal nodes. For this, we need two definitions: the first defines the normal form for types; and the second allows us to "ignore" the internal names in types.

Definition: A type S is in *normal form* if:

a. there is at most one +-node in S, in which case the root is the +-node and it has more than one child;

b. ⊥ is not a child of any *-node or ×-node;

c. no child of ×-node is a ×-node; and

d. each ×-node has more then one child.

Definition: Two normal form types S and T are *isomorphic* (up to renaming),denoted S ≡ T, if S can be transformed to T using only renamings.

Generalizing arguments of [HY], we now state that the application of the e-transformations is essentially Church-Rosser:

Theorem 4.2: Let S be a type. Then there is a type T in normal form such that $S \rightarrow^* T$. Also, if R is a type such that $S \rightarrow^* R$, then $R \rightarrow^* T$. In particular, if T1 and T2 are normal form types such that $S \rightarrow^* T1$ and $S \rightarrow^* T2$, then T1 ≡ T2.

We now present two notions for comparing information capacity of database structures that were introduced by [HY], namely absolute equivalence, and dominance. We then use these concepts to prove the "completeness" of our transformations thereby generalizing results of [HY] for formats.

Intuitively, absolute dominance roughly captures the intuition that natural database transformations should not "invent" data values. (See [H] for more motivation.) To formally define this notion, we first define the "active domain" of objects. Speaking informally, if O is an object, the active domain of O, denoted by act(O), is the set of all atomic elements occuring in O. Using this, we define particular subsets of the domain of a type. Specifically, for a type T and a set X, $\mathrm{dom}_X(T) = \{O \in \mathrm{dom}(T) \mid \mathrm{act}(O) \subseteq X\}$. We now have:

Definition: Let S and T be types. Then S is *dominated by* T *absolutely,* denoted $S \leq T$ (abs), if there is some k such that for each finite set satisfying[2] $|X \cap \mathrm{dom}(A)| \geq k$ for each A appearing in S or T, $|\mathrm{dom}_X(S)| \leq |\mathrm{dom}_X(T)|$. S is *absolutely equivalent* to T, denoted $S \sim T$ (abs), if $S \leq T$ (abs) and $T \leq S$ (abs).

We now present a characterization of absolute equivalence between types which demonstrates that (i) the collection of nine natural local transformations is "complete" for absolute equivalence (Theorem 4.3), and (as a result) (ii) virtually any natural notion of equivalent information capacity is identical to it (Corollary 4.4).

---

[2] This condition is included to prevent certain combinatorial technicalities from having an impact.

Theorem 4.3: Let S1 and S2 be two types. Then S1 $\sim$ S2 (abs) iff there is some normal form type T such that S1 $\to^*$ T and S2 $\to^*$ T.

Note that by Theorem 4.3, the e-transformations and their inverses are "complete" for proving absolute equivalence. Thus, by Theorems 4.1, rewrite operations are also "complete" for absolute equivalence. Also, it is decidable whether two types are absolutely equivalent (although it appears that testing this is co-NP and requires exponential time). Perhaps the most important implication of Theorem 4.3 is the following, which implies that essentially all notions of information capacity equivalence for types are identical to absolute equivalence.

Corollary 4.4: Let xxx-dominance be any reflexive, transitive binary relation on types such that

a. if S $\to$ T or T $\to$ S, then S $\leq$ T (xxx), and

b. if S $\leq$ T (xxx) then S $\leq$ T (abs);

and let xxx-equivalence be defined from xxx-dominance in the natural manner. Then S $\sim$ T (xxx) ifff S $\sim$ T (abs).

5. STRUCTURAL DOMINANCE

In this section, we define "structural dominance" (and "structural equivalence"), an intuitively appealing notion of information capacity dominance between types. This notion is based primarily on the transformations introduced in the previous section, together with three new transformations. We prove that the new transformations also correspond to some rewrite operations. Indeed, we show that these transformations, and the transformations introduced in the previous section correspond to "simple" rewrite operations. A major result of this section is that simple rewrite operations are closed under composition. This shows that any finite sequence of transformations correspond to a single rewrite.

To begin the formal development, we define the three information increasing transformations, here called "augmentations", and use them to define the general notion of structural dominance.

Definition: The three *augmentations* on types are defined as follows:

(x) replace $<T_1;...;T_n>$ by $<T_1;...;T_n;Q:\perp>$.

(xi) replace $<Q_1:\perp_1;...;Q_n:\perp_n>$ by A.

(xii) replace $<T,Q_2:\perp>$ by {T}.

For formats S and T, write S => T if one of the following holds:

(α) S $\rightarrow$ T, or T $\rightarrow$ S, or

(β) T is the tree obtained from S by replacing a subtree S' of S by one augmentation of S'.

The relation =>* is the reflexive, transitive closure of =>. Finally, S is *structurally dominated by* T, denoted S $\leq$ T (struct), if S =>* T; and S is *structurally equivalent to* T, denoted S ~ T (struct), if S $\leq$ T (struct), and T $\leq$ S (struct).

A straightforward application of Theorem 4.4 shows that for each S and T, S ~ T (abs) iff S ~ T (struct).

With each of these transformations, one can associate an *(augmenting) restructuring function.* The semantics of these functions is now briefly presented:

(x) is the identity ;

(xi) maps $<\perp_i>$ to a_i for each i in [1..n], and some values $a_1,...,a_n$ in dom(A); and

(xii) maps $<Q_1:O>$ to {O}, and $<Q_2:\perp>$ to {} (where Q_1 is the root of T).

In the full paper, we introduce the notion of *simple rewrite operation.* Intuitively, a rewrite operation is simple if it uses rewrite rules with only $\perp$ constants in the premise, and if each variable appears at most once in the premise.

We now present a result that states that the restructuring functions are in fact simple one-to-one rewrite functions.

Theorem 5.1: Let R and S be two set types such that R => S, then there is a simple one-to-one rewrite operation ρ from dom(R) to dom(S). Furthermore ρ defines the same mapping as R => S.

It follows from Theorem 5.1 that:

Corollary 5.2: Let R and S be two set types. If R $\leq$ S (struct) then there exists simple rewrite operations $\rho_1,...,\rho_n$ such that $\rho_1 o...o\rho_n$ is a one-to-one mapping from dom(R) to dom(S).

The previous result exhibits one reason why composition of simple rewrite operations is important. The next result shows that such compositions can be realized by a single rewrite. (The proof of this result is intricate. It remains open whether the result holds for larger classes of rewrite operations.)

Proposition 5.3: Let ρ_i for i in [1..n] be simple rewrite operations from R_i to R_{i+1} for each i in [2..n]. Then there exists a simple rewrite operation ρ such that $\rho_1 o ... o \rho_n = \rho$.

It should be clear from the definition of rewrite operations that each rewrite operation can be computed efficiently using parallelism. A consequence of the above proposition is that sequences of simple rewrite operations can also take full advantage of parallelism.

Using Proposition 5.3, we have:

Theorem 5.4: Let R and S be two set types such that R =>* S. Then there exists a one-to-one simple rewrite ρ from R to S.

It remains open whether the converse of this result holds.

REFERENCES

[ABe] Abiteboul, S., and C. Beeri, On the power of languages for complex objects, in preparation.

[ABi] Abiteboul, S. and N. Bidoit, Non first normal form relations: an algebra allowing data restructuring, Inria Internal Report, to appear in JCSS.

[AH1]
Abiteboul, S. and R. Hull, IFO : a formal semantic database model, USC Technical Report 1984, to appear in TODS.

[AH2]
Abiteboul, S. and R. Hull, Restructuring of complex objects and office forms, in preparation.

[AABM]
Atzeni, P. G. Ausiello, C. Batini and M. Moscarini, "Inclusion and equivalence between relational database schemata", Theor. Computer Science 19 (1982), 267-285.

[BK] Bancilhon, F., S. Khoshafian, A calculus for complex objects, PODS, Boston (1986).

[FT] Fisher, P., S. Thomas, Operators for non-first-normal-form relations, Proc. of the 7th International Comp. Soft. Applications Conf., Chicago (1983).

[HM] Hammer, M., D. McLeod, Data description with SDM: a semantic database model, TODS 6,3 (1981), 357-386.

[H1] Hull, R., Relative information capacity of simple relational database schemata, USC Technical Report (1984), to appear in SIAM J. Computing.

[H2] Hull, R., A survey of theoretical research in typed complex database objects, USC Technical Report (1986).

[HK] Hull, R., R. King, Semantic database modelling: survey, applications, and research issues, USC Technical Report (1986).

[HY] Hull, R., C.K. Yap, The format model: a theory of database organization, JACM 31,3 (1984), 518-537.

[K] Kuper, G.M., The logical data model: a new approach to database logic, Ph.D. thesis, Stanford University (1985).

[MB] Motro, A., P. Buneman, Constructing superviews, SIGMOD 1981.

[PFK]
Purvy, R., J. Farrell, and P. Klose, The design of Star's records processing: data processing for the noncomputer professional, ACM Trans. on Office Automation Systems 1, 1 (1983), 3-24.

[RKS]
Roth M.A., H.F. Korth, A. Silberschatz, Theory of non-first-normal-form relational databases.

[SP] Scheck, H-J., P. Pistor, Data structures for an integrated data base management and information retrieval system, VLDB, Mexico (1982).

[SS] Smith, J., D. Smith, Database abstractions: aggregations and generalzation, ACM TODS (1977).

[SLTC]
Shu, N.C., V.Y. Lum, F.C. Tung, and C.L. Chang, Specification of forms processing and business procedures for office automation, IEEE Trans. on Software Engineering SE-8,5 (1982), 499-512.

[T] Tsichritzis, D., Form management, Comm. ACM 25, 7 (1982), 453-478.

SET CONTAINMENT INFERENCE

Paolo Atzeni[1] - D. Stott Parker Jr.[2]

(1) IASI-CNR - Viale Manzoni 30 - I-00185 Roma

(2) UCLA Computer Science Dept. & Sylogic, Inc., Los Angeles, CA, USA

ABSTRACT

Type hierarchies and type inclusion inference are now standard in many knowledge representation schemes. In this paper, we show how to determine consistency and inference for collections of statements of the form

mammal isa **vertebrate.**

These containment statements relate the contents of two sets (or types). The work here is new in permitting statements with negative information: disjointness of sets, or non-inclusion of sets. For example, we permit the following statements also:

mammal isa non(**reptile**)

non(**vertebrate**) isa non(**mammal**)

not(**reptile** isa **amphibian**)

Among the various types of containment, we consider "binary containment inference", the problem of determining the consequences of positive constraints P and negative constraints **not(P)** on sets, where positive constraints have the form **P**: $X \subseteq Y$, where **X**, **Y**, are types or their complements. A negative constraint is equivalent to a statement of the form $X \cap non(Y) \neq \emptyset$. Positive constraints assert containment relations among sets, while negative constraints assert that two sets have a non-empty intersection. We show binary containment inference is solved by rules essentially equivalent to Aristotle's Syllogisms. The containment inference problem can also be formulated and solved in predicate logic. When only positive constraints P are specified, binary containment inference is equivalent to Propositional 2-CNF Unsatisfiability (unsatisfiability of conjunctive propositional formulas limited to at most two literals per conjunct). In either situation, necessary and sufficient conditions for consistency, as well as sound and complete sets of inference rules are presented. Polynomial-time inference algorithms are consequences, showing that adding negation does not result in intractability for this problem.

1 INTRODUCTION

In this paper we are interested in exploring inference properties of collections of statements like **X** isa **Y**, where **X** and **Y** are types. For example, we can assert

mammal isa **vertebrate**

reptile isa **vertebrate**

Statements of this kind form an interesting class of constraints for real knowledge representation problems, which permits declaration of containment relationships among types. 'Taxonomic' knowledge of this kind is (apparently) basic to human intelligence.

This paper departs from previous work by permitting negation in two ways:

- First, we let the types **X** and **Y** represent complements of types. For example, we permit statements of the form

  mammal isa non(**reptile**)

  where non(**reptile**) represents the complement of the type **reptile**. This statement asserts that **mammals** are disjoint from **reptiles**.
- Second, we allow negative statements to be made. For example, we permit statements like

  not (**reptile** isa **amphibian**)

  which asserts that a **reptile** is **not** a type of **amphibian**, or equivalently, that **reptile** must intersect with non(**amphibian**). In other words, some non-amphibian reptiles exist.

We are interested in developing inference systems for type containment statements. The examples above are assertions that we would like to be able to store in a knowledge base and derive inferences from. For example, we would like to be able to ask: "Is **mammal** a **reptile**"? and have a system correctly infer that the answer is **NO**. In general we wish to be able to make queries of the forms: "**X** isa **Y**?", "not(**X** isa **Y**)?"

We call this problem the Binary Containment Inference Problem, a special case of a general containment inference problem permitting inclusion statements (and their negations) involving more than two types. It is a limited fragment of set theory of practical use.

An initial purpose of this paper was to investigate how negation affects inference in specific knowledge domains, thus extendeing previous work done in [1], where we discussed a restricted version of the binary containment inference problem. Generally, of course, permitting negation causes inference to become computationally intractable; combinatorial explosions arise as soon as a negation operator is introduced. This is puzzling, since humans deal with at least certain kinds of negation without either becoming befuddled or taking long periods of time to arrive at correct conclusions. As a matter of fact, we discovered that, for the binary containment problem, negation does not result in computational intractability. Thus binary containment assertions are at the same time expressive, yet not general enough a fragment of set theory to cause complexity problems.

Indeed, the binary containment problem can be solved somewhat elegantly. When all the statements are inclusions, we show here that the inference problem is equivalent to Propositional 2-CNF Unsatisfiability (the complement of the 2-SAT problem) [4]. More generally, the binary containment problem can be expressed and solved efficiently with predicate logic. We show that the problem is also solvable using a small set of inference rules. $O(n^3)$ time, where n is the number of types, is sufficient in all cases.

Interestingly, <u>syllogisms</u> turn out to be precisely the rules for binary containment inference. There are 24 valid syllogisms. These rules have been used for millenia, and were actually held as synonymous with the word <u>logic</u> until the mid-nineteenth century after the work of George Boole. While syllogisms were discarded eventually as being 'less general' than boolean logic, they clearly fit here naturally.

It seems likely that all the results in this paper have been discovered by other researchers at one time or another, in one form or another. After all, binary containment inference has been studied for millenia. However we are not aware of a reference covering the results here. Indeed, we were motivated by a study of existing knowledge representation systems, which uniformly lacked general containment inference processing.

It is possible to focus exclusively on logic when studying containment inference, by expressing the problem in predicate logic and then applying resolution proof techniques. The approach of this paper is broader, developing several formal systems to handle containment inference problems. This approach has certain benefits. First, it clarifies the model theory of the binary set containment problem, the problem's relationship to syllogisms, and identifies degenerate cases of constraints precisely. Second, it sets the foundation for fast algorithms not based directly on logic. Finally, it permits generalization to formal systems handling more complex types of 'syllogisms'.

2 TERMINOLOGY

2.1 Syllogisms

Aristotle apparently defined a syllogism to be any valid inference [3], but concentrated on inferences that can be made from four kinds of propositions:

Every **S** is **P**
No **S** is **P** (i.e., Every **S** is not **P**)
Some **S** is **P**
Some **S** is not **P**

A syllogism is composed of three propositions involving three <u>types</u> **S**, **M**, and **P**, representing respectively its 'Subject', 'Middle', and 'Predicate'. For example, the following is a syllogism:

```
Major premise:  every P is M
Minor premise:  some  S is not M
               -------------------
Conclusion:     some  S is not P
```

Since the conclusion always involves the subject and predicate, while the premises use the middle type **M** in 4 nontrivial ways (called 'figures' by Aristotle, although he developed only the first three figures shown below), there are a total of $4 \times 4 \times 4 \times 4 = 256$ possible syllogisms, of which 24 are valid. These 24 are listed below, divided into the four figures:

S11:	every	*S*	is	*P*	if	every	*M*	is	*P*	and	every	*S*	is	*M*.	
S12:	some	*S*	is	*P*	if	every	*M*	is	*P*	and	every	*S*	is	*M*.	*
S13:	some	*S*	is	*P*	if	every	*M*	is	*P*	and	some	*S*	is	*M*.	
S14:	every	*S*	is not	*P*	if	every	*M*	is not	*P*	and	every	*S*	is	*M*.	
S15:	some	*S*	is not	*P*	if	every	*M*	is not	*P*	and	every	*S*	is	*M*.	*
S16:	some	*S*	is not	*P*	if	every	*M*	is not	*P*	and	some	*S*	is	*M*.	
S21:	every	*S*	is not	*P*	if	every	*P*	is not	*M*	and	every	*S*	is	*M*.	
S22:	some	*S*	is not	*P*	if	every	*P*	is not	*M*	and	every	*S*	is	*M*.	*
S23:	some	*S*	is not	*P*	if	every	*P*	is not	*M*	and	some	*S*	is	*M*.	
S24:	every	*S*	is not	*P*	if	every	*P*	is	*M*	and	every	*S*	is not	*M*.	
S25:	some	*S*	is not	*P*	if	every	*P*	is	*M*	and	every	*S*	is not	*M*.	*
S26:	some	*S*	is not	*P*	if	every	*P*	is	*M*	and	some	*S*	is not	*M*.	
S31:	some	*S*	is	*P*	if	every	*M*	is	*P*	and	every	*M*	is	*S*.	*
S32:	some	*S*	is	*P*	if	every	*M*	is	*P*	and	some	*M*	is	*S*.	
S33:	some	*S*	is	*P*	if	some	*M*	is	*P*	and	every	*M*	is	*S*.	
S34:	some	*S*	is not	*P*	if	every	*M*	is not	*P*	and	every	*M*	is	*S*.	*
S35:	some	*S*	is not	*P*	if	every	*M*	is not	*P*	and	some	*M*	is	*S*.	
S36:	some	*S*	is not	*P*	if	some	*M*	is not	*P*	and	every	*M*	is	*S*.	
S41:	every	*S*	is not	*P*	if	every	*P*	is	*M*	and	every	*M*	is not	*S*.	
S42:	some	*S*	is not	*P*	if	every	*P*	is	*M*	and	every	*M*	is not	*S*.	*
S43:	some	*S*	is not	*P*	if	every	*P*	is not	*M*	and	every	*M*	is	*S*.	*
S44:	some	*S*	is not	*P*	if	every	*P*	is not	*M*	and	some	*M*	is	*S*.	
S45:	some	*S*	is	*P*	if	every	*P*	is	*M*	and	every	*M*	is	*S*.	*
S46:	some	*S*	is	*P*	if	some	*P*	is	*M*	and	every	*M*	is	*S*.	

These 24 syllogisms are all valid under the assumption that the sets denoted by the types **S**, **M**, and **P** are nonempty. If this assumption does not hold, the 9 entries above marked with stars (*) are invalid. In other words, although we would normally assume that whenever "every **X** is **Y**" then also "some **X** is **Y**", this inference is invalid when the set denoted by the type **X** is empty.

The structure of the syllogisms has fascinated philosophers and mathematicians for millenia. At this point the reader may be asking questions such as:

- Is the set of 24 rules (or 15, eliminating starred ones) complete?
- Is there a more compact presentation of these rules?
- Can the rules be used in an efficient inference system?

We address these questions later in the paper.

2.2 Syntax Of Containment Propositions

Some readers will have noticed that syllogisms involve containment propositions. Specifically, if **X** and **Y** represent sets, and non(Y) represents the set complement of Y:

every X is Y $\equiv$ $X \subseteq Y$
some X is Y $\equiv$ $X \cap Y \neq \emptyset$
not every X is Y $\equiv$ $X \cap \text{non}(Y) \neq \emptyset$
not some X is Y $\equiv$ $X \subseteq \text{non}(Y)$

This collection of syllogistic propositions is thus equivalent to the binary propositions one can make up with the standard set predicates $\subseteq$ and $\cap \neq \emptyset$. In an effort to follow [1], as well as simplify notation ($\cap \neq \emptyset$ is tedious to write), we define the following two predicates on type descriptors X, Y:

Definition. X isa Y if the set denoted by X is a subset of the set denoted by Y.

Definition. X int Y if the set denoted by X intersects the set denoted by Y. The intersection must be nonempty.

Remark. X int Y $\equiv$ not (X isa non(Y)).

2.3 The Set Containment Problem

Our goal in this section is to set up a framework for expressing containment problems. We differentiate between the scheme of a containment problem, and its interpretations or models. The scheme specifies the structure of the problem, while interpretations of the scheme give instances of objects in the types in the scheme.

Definition. A type scheme T/U is a collection of type symbols $\{U, T_1, \ldots, T_n\}$. The type symbol U is a special symbol and is called the universe of the type scheme.

Each type symbol T_i will denote a subset of U. The universe symbol U is needed in order to define what we mean by complements $\text{non}(T_i)$ of types:

Definition. A type descriptor X of a type scheme T/U is either

1. a type symbol T_i or U.
2. non(Y), where Y is a type descriptor of T/U.

Definition. An interpretation I of a type scheme T/U is a map associating to each type descriptor of T a possibly empty subset of a finite domain D. In other words, for each I, $I(T_i)$ is a subset of D. We require finite interpretations here for simplicity.

Each interpretation I must satisfy the following conditions:

- The universe contains all types and their complements.

  For each type symbol T_i in the scheme T/U,

  1. $I(T_i) \subseteq I(U)$,
  2. $I(\mathrm{non}(T_i)) \subseteq I(U)$.

- The universe defines complementation.

  If '-' represents set difference, then:

  1. $I(T_i) = I(U) - I(\mathrm{non}(T_i))$
  2. $I(\mathrm{non}(T_i)) = I(U) - I(T_i)$

For any type descriptor X, in other words, non(X) denotes the complement under U of the set denoted by X.

Remark. In any interpretation, non(non(X)) denotes the same set as X, and non(U) denotes the the empty set ∅.

Definition. A type descriptor X is trivial in interpretation I if $I(X) = \emptyset$. The trivial interpretation I assigns $I(X) = 0$ for every type descriptor X.

Definition. A positive constraint P has the form

$$P:\ X_1 \cap \ldots \cap X_p \ \underline{\text{isa}}\ \ Y_1 \cup \ldots \cup Y_q$$

where each X_j, $1 \le j \le p$, and each Y_k, $1 \le k \le q$, is a type descriptor.

The constraint is satisfied by the interpretation I if

$$I(X_1) \cap \ldots \cap I(X_p) \subseteq I(Y_1) \cup \ldots \cup I(Y_q).$$

Definition. A negative constraint has the form not(P), where P is a positive constraint. It is satisfied if P is not.

Note that positive constraints can be rewritten as

$$P:\ \mathrm{non}(X_1) \cup \ldots \cup \mathrm{non}(X_p) \cup Y_1 \cup \ldots \cup Y_q = U$$

or, equivalently,

$$P:\ X_1 \cap \ldots \cap X_p \cap \mathrm{non}(Y_1) \cap \ldots \cap \mathrm{non}(Y_q) = \emptyset;$$

so the negative constraint not(P) is equivalent to

$$\mathbf{not(P)}:\ X_1 \cap \ldots \cap X_p \cap \mathrm{non}(Y_1) \cap \ldots \cap \mathrm{non}(Y_q) \neq \emptyset$$

In other words, positive constraints make assertions about inclusions among types, while negative constraints make assertions about intersections among types.

Definition. A containment scheme is a pair S=(T/U,C) where U is a universe symbol, T/U is a type scheme {U, $T_1, \ldots, T_n$}, and C is a set of containment constraints on type symbols in T.

Definition. A model of a containment scheme (T/U,C) is an interpretation I of T/U that satisfies all constraints in C.

Containment constraints can be 'degenerate'. Consider the following constraints: 1) **X** isa **non(X)**; 2) **non(X)** isa **X**; 3) **not(X** isa **X)**. The first constraint is satisfied only when **X** denotes ∅. Similarly, the second is satisfied only when **non(X)** denotes ∅, so **X** denotes the same set as **U**. The first two constraints together can be satisfied only when both **X** and **U** denote ∅. In other words, the first two constraints imply that there can be only one model: the trivial one. The third constraint is the negation of (**X** isa **X**), which is true of every interpretation for **X**. Thus, any scheme with the third constraint can satisfy no interpretation, and will have no model.

Definition. A containment scheme is unsatisfiable if it has no model; otherwise it is satisfiable.

Now consider the following general problem:

Set Containment Problem

Input: a containment scheme (T/U,C)

Question: Is the containment scheme satisfiable? (That is, is there an interpretation for T/U that satisfies each constraint C_j in C?)

Not surprisingly, the set containment problem is NP-complete in general. The proof of this claim, omitted here for the sake of brevity, is based on the reduction of the SAT problem [4] directly to our problem. However, in the special case in which all constraints are positive, the set containment problem is always satisfiable, because the trivial interpretation (in which I(U)=∅) is always a model satisfying C.

In this paper we are interested only in the special case **p=q=1**, where all constraints are binary. This restricted version is called the Binary Set Containment Problem. In the remainder of the paper we first consider the special case where all binary constraints are positive, then study the general binary containment problem.

Example Consider the containment scheme

S = ({**pacifist**, **quaker**, **republican**}/U, C)

where the constraint set C is:

republican isa non(**pacifist**)
republican int **quaker**
quaker isa **pacifist**.

The binary set containment problem for this scheme is to determine whether it is satisfiable or not. It turns out this scheme is unsatisfiable; we will see why shortly.

2.4 Containment Inference

We first recall some terminology concerning inference rules. The reader unfamiliar with this material may wish to consult texts in database theory, such as [6,7]. We remind the reader that classes of constraints studied in database theory do not involve negation, for the most part. That is, collections of data dependencies (functional dependencies, join dependencies, etc.) do not imply that a specific data dependency does not hold, but only that one does hold. These systems are always satisfiable. Unsatisfiability can occur with containment, as we have already seen. Therefore, the inference problem here is somewhat different than in these texts.

Implication and inference are important concepts in dealing with constraints of the general kind proposed here. If we are given a set of constraints, we are frequently interested in deducing whether other constraints must also hold. A constraint c is implied by a set of constraints C (C |== c) on a scheme S if it holds in all models of S. Given C and c, the inference problem is to tell whether C implies c. Algorithms for the solution of the inference problem (called inference algorithms) have correctness proofs that are usually based on sound and complete sets of inference rules. If C is unsatisfiable, then C has no models, and so we can say that C |== c for every constraint c.

Set Containment Inference Problem

Input: a containment scheme (T/U,C), and a constraint c.

Question Is it true that C |== c?

This problem can be reduced to the Set Containment Problem mentioned earlier simply by determining satisfiability of the scheme with constraints $C \cup$ {not(c)}. Alternatively, we can approach the inference problem with inference rules.

Definition. An inference rule C |-- c is a rule asserting that the constraint c holds whenever the set of constraints C holds. For example, the rule

X isa Y, Y isa Z |-- X isa Z

asserts that the inclusion predicate isa is transitive. X, Y, and Z represent arbitrary type descriptors.

Definition. Relative to a specific set of inference rules, C |-- c if c can be derived from C using applications of the rules.

The basic requirement for each inference rule is to be sound, i.e., that it derive from C only constraints c such that C |== c. Moreover, it is important to have sets of inference rules that are complete, i.e., that allow the derivation of all the constraints c such that C |== c. Thus, a set of rules is sound and complete when |-- is equivalent to |==.

Definition. A scheme (T/U,C) is inconsistent if there is a constraint c such that C |-- c and C |-- not(c). Otherwise the scheme is consistent.

Clearly, an inconsistent scheme is also unsatisfiable. We will see later that the converse also holds.

3 DEGENERATE PROPERTIES OF CONTAINMENT SCHEMES

This section characterizes when a containment scheme has certain degenerate properties, namely, triviality of types, triviality of schemes, unsatisfiability.

Most of the proofs in this work make use of an algorithm, called 'Model Extension Algorithm', which we present here informally, because the proofs are not presented in full. The algorithm takes as input a containment scheme (T/U,C), an assignment I to the type descriptors and a constant t (which I may or may not include in its image), and produces an assignment I′ which definitely uses t (unless the scheme is trivial). It is called a 'model extension' algorithm since it always produces a model when given one. The algorithm somehow resembles the 'closure' or 'chase' algorithms common in relational database theory, but differs from them because has to take into account negation, especially with respect to the complement of types. Essentially, the algorithm has to make sure that, for every type descriptor **T**, the constant **t** is either in I(T) or in I(**non**(T)).

Theorem 1. A type descriptor **X** is trivial in every model of C iff C |== **X** isa **non**(**X**).

A corollary of Theorem 1 is that a pair of constraints X isa **non**(**X**), **non**(**X**) isa X, must be implied by any scheme with only the trivial model. (U, and consequently both **X** and **non**(**X**), must denote ∅.)

We showed earlier that containment constraints can actually be unsatisfiable, giving as an example **not**(**X** isa X). In fact, this constraint is not only sufficient for unsatisfiability, it is also necessary:

Theorem 2. A containment scheme (T/U,C) is unsatisfiable iff for some **X**, C |== **X** int **non**(**X**).

Sketch of the Proof. The if part is easy. With respect to the only if part, the proof shows how, if no constraint of the form **X** int **non**(**X**) is implied by C, a model for the scheme can be built. This is done by first considering an assignment that satisfies all the intersection constraints, and accumulatively applying the model extension algorithm to it in order to satisfy the containment constraints.

4 POSITIVE BINARY CONTAINMENT

Let us now devote our attention to the containment problem. Consider first the important special case of the set containment inference problem where all constraints are of the form X isa Y with **X** and **Y** type descriptors denoting subsets of U.

In [1] a similar problem was studied and solved. A complete set of inference rules is presented for two containment predicates, isa and dis.

The proposition (X isa Y) states that the type X denotes a subset of the type Y, while the proposition (X dis Y) states that X and Y denote disjoint sets. In [1] it is shown that, for arbitrary types X, Y, Z, the following rules for isa and dis are sound and complete:

I1: |-- X isa X.
I2: X isa Y, Y isa Z |-- X isa Z.
M1: X dis Y, Z isa X |-- Z dis Y.
M2: X dis X |-- X isa Y.
D1: X dis X |-- X dis Y.

We can use set complementation to simplify these rules. Since, for example,

$$\text{X dis Y} \equiv \text{X isa non(Y)},$$

then we can informally replace the five rules above with

I1: |-- X isa X
I2: X isa Y, Y isa Z |-- X isa Z
D1: X isa non(X) |-- X isa Y,

provided we let X, Y, Z, be arbitrary type descriptors, and treat non(non(X)) as being equivalent to X.

In the statements X isa Y, X dis Y of [1], X is required to be a type symbol (not a type descriptor). Without this requirement the 5 rules above are incomplete. For example, the rule

X isa Y |-- non(Y) isa non(X)

is not inferrable from the 5 rules, but is sound.

Consider, then, the following set of rules:

ISA0: |-- X isa U.
ISA1: |-- X isa X.
ISA2: X isa Y, Y isa Z |-- X isa Z.
ISA3: X isa Y |-- non(Y) isa non(X).
TRIV0: U isa non(U) |-- X isa non(U).
TRIV1: X isa non(X) |-- X isa non(U).
TRIV2: X isa non(U) |-- X isa Y.
EQ0: e(non(non(X))) |-- e(X) [e any expression].
EQ1: e(X) |-- e(non(non(X))) [e any expression].

Theorem 3. The set of rules ISA0-3, TRIV0-2, EQ0-1 is sound and complete

For positive binary containment inference. That is, if **C** contains only positive constraints and |-- represents derivability using these rules, then

C |-- (**X** _isa_ **Y**) _iff_ C |== (**X** _isa_ **Y**).

5 GENERAL BINARY CONTAINMENT

We show in this section that the 24 syllogisms listed earlier are essentially the rules we need for general set containment inference. However, although these 24 rules are elegant, they are also somewhat verbose. We show first that we can reduce the syllogism rules to a set of 5 simple rules (involving really only two basic syllogisms, S11 and S13), and then that an extension of these 5 rules dealing with degenerate conditions is a sound and complete set for containment inference.

5.1 Compressed Syllogisms

Let **X**, **Y**, **Z** be type descriptors. Consider the following rules:

R1: every **X** is **Z** _if_ every **Y** is **Z** **and** every **X** is **Y**.
R2: some **X** is **Z** _if_ every **Y** is **Z** **and** some **X** is **Y**.
R3: some **X** is **Y** _if_ every **X** is **Y**.
R4: some **X** is **Y** _if_ some **Y** is **X**.
R5: every **X** is **non(Y)** _if_ every **Y** is **non(X)**.

Here R1 and R2 are syllogisms mentioned earlier. Rule R3 requires the assumption that types are nonempty; this is actually necessary only where the existential quantifier ''some'' implies actual existence of some object, as it often does in natural language. R4 and R5 state that both intersection and disjointness of types are symmetric relations.

Theorem 4. All valid syllogisms follow from the rules R1-R5.

The proof of the theorem is based on a simple case analysis, showing how the various syllogisms can be reduced to the five rules.

5.2 Formal Containment Rules

Consider the following rules:

INT0: X <u>int</u> Y |-- X <u>int</u> U.
INT1: X <u>int</u> Y |-- X <u>int</u> X.
INT2: X <u>int</u> Y |-- Y <u>int</u> X.
INT3: X <u>int</u> Y, Y <u>isa</u> Z |-- X <u>int</u> Z.
INT4: X <u>int</u> U, X <u>isa</u> Y |-- X <u>int</u> Y.
INC0: X <u>int</u> non(X) |-- Y <u>isa</u> Z.
INC1: X <u>int</u> non(X) |-- Y <u>int</u> Z.
ISA0: |-- X <u>isa</u> U.
ISA1: |-- X <u>isa</u> X.
ISA2: X <u>isa</u> Y, Y <u>isa</u> Z |-- X <u>isa</u> Z.
ISA3: X <u>isa</u> Y |-- non(Y) <u>isa</u> non(X).
TRIV0: U <u>isa</u> non(U) |-- X <u>isa</u> non(U).
TRIV1: X <u>isa</u> non(X) |-- X <u>isa</u> non(U).
TRIV2: X <u>isa</u> non(U) |-- X <u>isa</u> Y.
EQ0: e(non(non(X))) |-- e(X) [e any expression].
EQ1: e(X) |-- e(non(non(X))) [e any expression].

These rules extend the compressed syllogism rules R1-R5 to deal with trivial types and unsatisfiable constraint sets, but otherwise express the same information.

<u>Theorem</u> 5. The rules INT0-4, INC0-1, ISA0-3, TRIV0-2, EQ0-1 are sound and complete for general binary containment inference.
<u>Sketch of the Proof</u>. For any constraint c nonderivable from C by means of the rules, the proof shows a model that satisfies C and does not satisfy c. This is done by using a variant of the model extension algorithm.

<u>Corollary</u>. A containment scheme (T/U,C) is unsatisfiable if and only if it is inconsistent.

The rules listed above involve an amount of 'overhead' in dealing with trivial types and unsatisfiable constraint sets. This overhead complicates ordinary use in making inferences. In most real situations we would assume that: 1) the constraints are satisfiable; 2) no type is trivial except non(U). If these assumptions are known to be true the rules simplify considerably. Since the type descriptor non(U) is always trivial, it must be distinguished from the others. We write $X \not\equiv T$ to specify that X is none of the type descriptors {T,non(non(T)),...}. Now, if we verify that our containment scheme is satisfiable, and formally make the non-triviality assumptions,

INT0: X ≢ non(U) |-- X int U.
INT1: X ≢ non(U) |-- X int X.
ISA0: |-- X isa U.
ISA1: |-- X isa X.

then the rules analyzed earlier can be replaced with the following set:

INT2: X int Y |-- Y int X.
INT3: X int Y, Y isa Z |-- X int Z.
INT4: X ≢ non(U), X isa Y |-- X int Y.
ISA2: X isa Y, Y isa Z |-- X isa Z.
ISA3: X isa Y |-- non(Y) isa non(X).
EQ0: e(non(non(X))) |-- e(X) [e any expression].
EQ1: e(X) |-- e(non(non(X))) [e any expression].

These rules are intuitive, and match the compressed syllogism rules R1-R5 closely.

6 CONTAINMENT AND LOGIC

It is possible to map all containment constraints into first-order predicate logic. The table below shows how this can be done, giving not only a logical equivalent, but also its "skolemized" clausal form.

Constraint	*Predicate Logic Equivalent*	*Clause Equivalent*
X isa Y	$\forall x \; U(x) \supset (X(x) \supset Y(x))$	**not** $U(x) \vee$ **not** $X(x) \vee Y(x)$
X int Y	$\exists x \; U(x) \wedge X(x) \wedge Y(x)$	$U(\gamma) \wedge X(\gamma) \wedge Y(\gamma)$

Here γ is a (unique) skolem constant representing an object that is simultaneously a member of the types X, Y, and U. Resolution can be used directly on the clauses to derive inferences. For example, the resolvent of the clauses (not X(x) or Y(x)) and (not Y(x) or Z(x)) is (not X(x) or Z(x)), mirroring the inference rule ISA2. A thorough introduction to resolution proof techniques may be found in [5].

The use of U in the clauses is necessary to handle degeneracy properly. The key problem is that the predicate logic sentence $\forall \mathbf{x}\ P(\mathbf{x})$ is not well-defined when the quantification is over an empty domain. Including U in each clause makes the domain of quantification explicit. Specifically, with a set of positive constraints C implying both (**X** isa **non**(**X**)) and (**non**(**X**) isa **X**), we now know from Theorem 1 that U must be trivial, and only the trivial interpretation is a model for C. However, if we were to omit the use of U(**x**) in the clauses corresponding to C, resolution would be able to derive from C the clauses (**not X**(**x**) or **not X**(**x**)) and (**X**(**x**)or**X**(**x**)), i.e., (**not X**(**x**)) and (**X**(**x**)). The resolvent of these two clauses is **false**, indicating incorrectly that C is unsatisfiable. By including U we obtain the clauses (**not**(U(**x**)) **or not**(**X**(**x**))) and (**not**(U(**x**)) **or X**(**x**)), with resolvent (**not** U(**x**)). This resolvent asserts there is no **x** for which U(**x**) is true. In other words, U denotes ∅, as desired.

There are other connections between containment constraints and logic. Boole [2] points out that containment constraints correspond to propositional logic equations. He gives essentially the following table:

Containment constraint	*Propositional equation*
T_1 *isa* T_2	$T_2 = V \wedge T_1$
T_1 *isa* non(T_2)	not $T_2 = V \wedge T_1$
T_1 *int* T_2	$V \wedge T_2 = V \wedge T_1$
T_1 *int* non(T_2)	$V \wedge$ not $T_2 = V \wedge T_1$
non(T_1) *isa* T_2	$T_2 = V \wedge$ not T_1
non(T_1) *isa* non(T_2)	not $T_2 = V \wedge$ not T_1
non(T_1) *int* T_2	$V \wedge T_2 = V \wedge$ not T_1
non(T_1) *int* non(T_2)	$V \wedge$ not $T_2 = V \wedge$ not T_1

A new propositional variable V is generated for each containment constraint. We can infer then that (T_1 isa T_2) if we can show that T_1= **W and** T_2, and infer (T_1 int T_2) if we can show that W_1 **and** T_1= W_2 **and** T_2, where W, W_1 , W_2 are conjunctions of zero or more (possibly negated) variables.

In fact, when only positive constraints are considered, there is a direct connection between containment inference and logic:

Theorem 6. Positive Binary Set Containment Inference and Propositional

2-CNF Unsatisfiability are equivalent. That is, for every scheme (T/U,C) there is a propositional formula **f(C)** in conjunctive normal form with at most two literals per clause, such that

1. C implies (X <u>isa</u> Y) <u>iff</u>

   f(C) and (X) and (**not**(Y)) is unsatisfiable.

2. C has only the trivial model <u>iff</u> **f(C)** is unsatisfiable.

This theorem shows there is an inference procedure using resolution on the propositional equivalent **f(C)** of a set of positive clauses. We check only for a proof of **false** from the propositional logic equivalent of the containment constraints conjoined with the negation of the constraint whose inferrability we wish to test.

7 CONCLUDING REMARKS

This paper generalizes the results in [1] to consider negation in various ways. The results are encouraging, in that only a few rules are needed for complete binary containment inference. As long as we are interested only in binary properties of containment among sets, this gives us a complete inference system for set theory.

Perhaps the first work to be done is in developing algorithms using the inference systems presented here. Algorithms are beyond the scope of what we wished to present here, but the inference systems developed in this paper all run in polynomial time. A simple upper bound is $O(n^3)$ where n is the number of types. Improved bounds will follow where more is known about the type structure. For instance, few real type hierarchies seem to be very deep. Even the standard biological taxonomy of living creatures is only about 10 levels deep.

When we begin to consider more complex forms of knowledge about types, such as sentences involving unions and intersections, the containment problem becomes NP-complete, and the inference problem co-NP-complete. Still, it would be interesting to extend the binary rules in this paper for the more general inference problem.

Other directions for further research lie in exploring graphical interpretations of the constraints, as in [1], and in providing efficient algorithms for containment problems. Also, there are a variety of ways to generalize the problems discussed here that the reader has no doubt already considered. These include investigating alternative types of 'syllogisms', restricting values of U in interpretations (for example, specifying I(U) in advance), and so forth. The general area of containment inference is a large new area in which many problems wait to be studied.

Acknowledgement

Richard Huntsinger, Karen Lever, and Tom Verma gave the paper a careful reading and suggested important improvements in the presentation.

REFERENCES

1. Atzeni, P. and D. Stott Parker, Formal Properties of Net-based Knowledge Representation Schemes, Proc. 2nd International Conference on Data Engineering (Los Angeles, CA, February 5-7, 1986), IEEE Computer Society, Washington, D.C., 1986.
2. Boole, G., An Investigation of The Laws of Thought, Dover, 1958.
3. Gardner, M., Logic Machines and Diagrams, University of Chicago Press, 1982.
4. Garey, M.R. and D.S. Johnson, Computers and Intractability: A Guide to the Theory of NP-Completeness, W.H. Freeman and Co., San Francisco, 1979.
5. Loveland, D., Automated Theorem Proving, North-Holland, 1976.
6. Maier, D., The Theory of Relational Data Bases, Computer Science Press, Rockville, MD, 1983.
7. Ullman, J.D., Principles of Data Base Systems, 2nd Ed., Computer Science Press, Rockville, MD, 1982.

A Domain Theoretic Approach to Higher-Order Relations

Peter Buneman
Atsushi Ohori†

University of Pennsylvania
Philadelphia, PA 19104

Many database programming languages [Atki85] share with relational database theory the constraint that relations (or whatever bulk data structures are used) should be *flat*. This means that the values stored in a relation may only belong to the base types of the language, integer, boolean, string etc. and may not be compound types such as arrays and records. In relational database theory one usually makes the *first normal form* assumption [Ullm82], which similarly demands that values stored in a a relation be atomic, i.e. they cannot be decomposed by operators of the relational calculus or algebra.

The flatness constraint in database programming languages is rather annoying because, unlike array types and record types, relation types cannot be freely parameterized by other types. This is extremely limiting in the case that relations are the only persistent type allowed for one then has no method of storing arrays, for example, in the database. The flatness constraint also limits the development of database adjuncts for programming languages like Ada [Ichb79] and ML[Gord79] with generic or polymorphic type systems because relations cannot be made "first class" types. In particular one cannot write generic code for data types with this limitation. The first normal form assumption for relational database theory is also restrictive in that it does not allow the relational data model to be cleanly combined with other data models such as the functional data model [Ship81, Bune82]. Moreover it has recently been argued [Banc85, Zani84b] that the first normal form assumption is incompatible with representation of databases in logic programming and with the requirements of various kinds of application.

In this paper we will attempt to show that by exploiting a form of inheritance on objects rather than types, one can naturally provide a unifying framework for records, relations and other data types that are common in databases and at the same time relax the constraint that they are flat. Moreover, several of the basic ideas of relational database theory have a remarkably simple characterization within this framework. The concept of inheritance has been around for some time in programming languages [Gold80], databases

---

† Much of this work was carried out while Peter Buneman was a visiting SERC research fellow at the University of Glasgow, Scotland and while Atsushi Ohori was on leave from OKI Electric Co., Japan. It was also supported by an NSF CER grant MCS82-19196.

[Smit77] and AI [Brac85]. Only recently has it received a formal treatment in the context of type systems in functional programming [Card84, Card85] and in relationship to logic programming AïtK84]. The ideas presented here are based on this work and are also closely related to those described in [Banc85].

The structure of what follows is first to introduce the notion of inheritance informally, the following section then provides a formal description of this in simple domain-theoretic terms and provides a generalized definition of relations. The final two sections show how some of the basic ideas of database theory, such as functional dependencies fit with this description.

Preliminaries

Our starting point is to describe partial functions that behave properly with respect to inheritance. To give some motivation for this, let us introduce a provisional notation for partial functions. The expression {*'Susan'* ⇒ 3490; *'Peter'* ⇒ 7731; *'Karen'* ⇒ 8535} describes a small telephone directory, a partial function from character strings to integers. We could use the same notation to describe records such as {*Name* ⇒ *'J. Doe'*; *Department* ⇒ *'Sales'*; *ShoeSize* ⇒ 10}. Here the inputs are a set of labels (perhaps a subset of some larger set) and the outputs are a set of heterogeneous values. Later in this exposition, we shall want to describe partial functions whose output set consists of one understood value. Let us use the notation {2; 3; 5; 7} to describe the partial function {2 ⇒ {};3 ⇒{};5 ⇒{};7 ⇒{}}, where {} is the single output value. There is an obvious, though somewhat misleading as it turns out, correspondence between such single-valued partial functions and sets.

There is a sense in which we can say one partial function is better defined than another. For example {*'Susan'* ⇒ 3490; *'Peter'* ⇒ 7731; *'Karen'* ⇒ 8535} is better defined than {*'Susan'* ⇒ 3490; *'Karen'* ⇒ 8535} because it is defined for more input values; moreover, wherever the second partial function is defined, it agrees with the first. Another way in which one partial function may be better defined than another is by being defined on the same values and having better defined outputs. For example

{*Name* ⇒ *'John Doe'*; *Address* ⇒{*City* ⇒ *'Philadelphia'*; *Zip* ⇒ 19101}}

is better defined than

{*Name* ⇒ *'John Doe'*;*Address* ⇒{*City* ⇒ *'Philadelphia'*}}

because one of the outputs is better defined in the first expression than in the second. The last two examples are "higher order" partial functions: the values are themselves partial functions.

A problem arises when we use higher order partial functions. We have to ask whether any partial function we write down in this notation makes sense. Compare the following three examples

$$\begin{array}{lll}\{\{Emp\# \Rightarrow 1234 & \} \Rightarrow \{Name \Rightarrow \text{'J. Brown'};\;\; Office \Rightarrow \text{'Paris'}\}; & \\ \;\{Emp\# \Rightarrow 1234;\; ShoeSize \Rightarrow 10 & \} \Rightarrow \{Name \Rightarrow \text{'K. Smith'} \qquad \}\} & (a)\end{array}$$

$$\begin{array}{llll}\{\{Stud\# \Rightarrow 3456 & & \} \Rightarrow \{Name \Rightarrow \text{'D. Dare'}\}; & \\ \;\{ & Course\# \Rightarrow \text{'CIS123'} & \} \Rightarrow \{CName \Rightarrow \text{'Algebra'}\}; & \\ \;\{Stud\# \Rightarrow 3456; & Course\# \Rightarrow \text{'CIS123'} & \} \Rightarrow \{Name \Rightarrow \text{'D. Dare'}; & (b) \\ & & \qquad CName \Rightarrow \text{'Algebra'}; & \\ & & \qquad Grade \Rightarrow \text{'A'} \qquad \}\} & \end{array}$$

$$\begin{array}{lll}\{\{Emp\# \Rightarrow 1234 & \} \Rightarrow \{Name \Rightarrow \text{'J. Brown'};\;\; Office \Rightarrow \text{'London'}\}; & \\ \;\{Emp\# \Rightarrow 1234;\; ShoeSize \Rightarrow 10 & \} \Rightarrow \{Name \Rightarrow \text{'J. Brown'};\;\; Office \Rightarrow \text{'London'}\}; & (c) \\ \;\{Emp\# \Rightarrow 1234 & \} \Rightarrow \{Name \Rightarrow \text{'J. Brown'} \qquad \}\} & \end{array}$$

Example (a) is badly behaved. In return for a better input it has produced a less informative - and contradictory - output. Example (b) is the sort of behavior one might expect from a database system. There is extra information to be gained by providing a better specified input. Example (c) is redundant in that we can infer the second and third input-output pairs from the first, but we can nevertheless consider these pairs as part of the partial function. In order to exclude partial functions like (a) we need to impose the condition that if a given input x produces an output y, then any input that is better defined than x will produce an output that is at least as well-defined as y. Looking at example (c) we see something that is not even a partial function; a given input $\{Emp\# \Rightarrow 1234\}$ has produced two outputs. Given that there is an ordering on the input and output spaces, we need to define formally what we mean by a partial function.

Maps, Records and Relations

The examples in the previous section were mostly composed of records, i.e. partial functions from labels to values. In order to describe what it means for a partial function to be well behaved, we shall assume the input and output spaces are partially ordered. Specifically, we shall assume that they are complete partial orders (c.p.o.s). If V and W are the input and output c.p.o.s, we can represent a partial function by a subset F of $V \times W$ that is subject to the following restrictions.

$$(1) \qquad \text{if} \quad (x, y) \in F, x' \sqsupseteq x \quad \text{and} \quad y \sqsupseteq y' \quad \text{then} \quad (x', y') \in F$$

(2) if $(x, y_1) \in F$ and $(x, y_2) \in F$ then $(x, y_1 \sqcup y_2) \in F$

(3) $(\bot_1, \bot_2) \in F$

The first of these says that if a given input-output pair belongs to F then any better defined input and worse defined output will belong to F. The second says that F is *functional*, i.e. there is a unique best output associated with a given input. (3) indicates that every input in V has at last one associated output (namely $\bot_2$). Since a given input can have more than one output, it is inappropriate to call F a function (partial or total). Instead, we shall refer to any subset of $V \times W$ that satisfies these conditions as a *map* from V to W and denote the set of such maps by $V \mapsto W$. It is interesting to note that the conditions for a map are almost the same as those used by Scott [Scot82] for an *approximable function* in his "Information Systems" approach to the semantics of programming languages, and a recent paper by Ohori [Ohor86] describes this connection in detail and promises to provide a denotational semantics for relational databases.

Now it is readily seen that maps are ordered by (set) inclusion and that if F_1 and F_2 are in $V \mapsto W$ then $F_1 \cap F_2$ is also in F. We can therefore define

$$F_1 \sqcap F_2 = F_1 \cap F_2$$

$$F_1 \sqcup F_2 = \cap\{F | F \in V \mapsto W,\ F \supseteq F_1,\ F \supseteq F_2\}$$

The join ($\sqcup$) is defined only if there is at least one map F such that $F \supseteq F_1$ and $F \supseteq F_2$. Thus maps themselves form a c.p.o. Moreover, if $F \in V_1 \mapsto V_2$ and $G \in V_2 \mapsto V_3$ their composition, defined by $F_1 \circ F_2 = \{(x,z) | \exists y.(x,y) \in F_1,\ (y,z) \in F_2\}$, is a map. For maps in $V \mapsto V$ the ordering that defines V (note that it is a map) is the identity for composition.

A particularly simple map is that specified by a single pair of points (x, y), i.e. $\{x', y' | x' \in V, y' \in W, x' \sqsupseteq x, y \sqsupseteq y'\}$. Call such a map *elementary* and call a map *finite* if it is of the form $E_1 \sqcup E_2 \sqcup \ldots \sqcup E_n$ where $E_1, E_2, \ldots, E_n$ are elementary. If F_1 and F_2 are finite maps in $V \mapsto W$, then so are $F_1 \sqcap F_2$ and $F_1 \sqcup F_2$ (if it exists). If at least one of F_1 and F_2 is finite, then so is $F_1 \circ F2$.

We are now in a position to be more precise about the notation of the previous section. The notation $\{x_1 \Rightarrow y_1; x_2 \Rightarrow y_2; \ldots; x_n \Rightarrow y_n\}$ defines the finite map which is the join ($\sqcup$) of the n elementary maps generated by the pairs $(x_1, y_1), (x_2, y_2), \ldots, (x_n, y_n)$. Note that this join is not always defined, which is demonstrated by example (a) of the previous section.

All we have done so far is to re-hash some of the basic definitions of domain theory [Stoy77] in a somewhat unusual manner. Let us try to see how this is connected to databases by taking some examples.

1. Suppose V is a flat domain and $TRIV$ is the trivial domain which contains one non-bottom element $\{\}$. Now the elements of $V \mapsto TRIV$ correspond to the subsets of elements of V (other than $\bot$). The $\sqcup$ and $\sqcap$ operations correspond to union and intersection, and the ordering on $V \mapsto TRIV$ corresponds to set inclusion.
2. Now suppose $\mathcal{L}$ is a flat domain of *labels* and V is any domain. We can identify $\mathcal{L} \mapsto V$ with the *records* over V. The ordering on $\mathcal{L} \mapsto V$ is the ordering we used informally in the previous section. Call this domain $\mathcal{R}(V)$. $\sqcup$ and $\sqcap$ respectively define "unifiers" and "generalizers" of two records. Note that for records r_1 and r_2, $r_1 \sqcup r_2$ is not necessarily defined. This ordering on records is a generalization of that described by Zaniolo in his treatment [Zani84a] of null values, and is closely related to Lipski's [Lips79] semantics for null values.
3. We can now consider the maps in $\mathcal{R}(V) \mapsto TRIV$. These are the *relations* over V, with $\sqcap$ defining the *natural join*. Note that there is a difference between relations and sets as defined in (1) above. The input domain $\mathcal{R}(V)$ is not, in general, flat.

This result that natural join is a "meet" operation ($\sqcap$) is not so surprising if one considers two relations with the same columns. Here the natural join gives us the intersection of the tuples in the two relations. What is more interesting is that this definition extends to "non-first-normal-form" relations, where the components may themselves be structures such as records or other relations. For example, the natural join of

$$\begin{array}{llll}
\{\{Name \Rightarrow \text{'J. Doe'}; & Dept \Rightarrow \text{'Sales'}; & Addr \Rightarrow \{City \Rightarrow \text{'Moose'} & \}\}; \\
\{Name \Rightarrow \text{'M. Dee'}; & Dept \Rightarrow \text{'Manuf'} & & \}; \\
\{Name \Rightarrow \text{'N. Bug'}; & & Addr \Rightarrow \{ & State \Rightarrow MT\}\}\}
\end{array}$$

and

$$\begin{array}{lll}
\{\{Dept \Rightarrow \text{'Sales'}; & Addr \Rightarrow \{ & State \Rightarrow WY\}\}; \\
\{Dept \Rightarrow \text{'Admin'}; & Addr \Rightarrow \{City \Rightarrow \text{'Billings'} & \}\}; \\
\{Dept \Rightarrow \text{'Manuf'}; & Addr \Rightarrow \{ & State \Rightarrow MT\}\}\}
\end{array}$$

is

$$\begin{array}{llll}
\{\{Name \Rightarrow \text{'J. Doe'}; & Dept \Rightarrow \text{'Sales'}; & Addr \Rightarrow \{City \Rightarrow \text{'Moose'}; & State \Rightarrow WY\}\}; \\
\{Name \Rightarrow \text{'M. Dee'}; & Dept \Rightarrow \text{'Manuf'}; & Addr \Rightarrow \{ & State \Rightarrow MT\}\}; \\
\{Name \Rightarrow \text{'N. Bug'}; & Dept \Rightarrow \text{'Manuf'}; & Addr \Rightarrow \{ & State \Rightarrow MT\}\}; \\
\{Name \Rightarrow \text{'N. Bug'}; & Dept \Rightarrow \text{'Admin'}; & Addr \Rightarrow \{City \Rightarrow \text{'Billings'}; & State \Rightarrow MT\}\}\}
\end{array}$$

We identified relations with maps from $\mathcal{R}(V)$ to a trivial domain because it corresponds to our intuition that a relation is something like a set of records, and we would need to keep this characterization if we wanted to assign data types to relations. However, in the following discussion of functional dependencies, we do not need to be so restrictive. We can identify relations with maps in $V \mapsto TRIV$ for any domain V. In fact, the maps in $V \mapsto TRIV$ correspond to the upward-closed subsets of V, and this is the basis of the semantics presented in [Ohor86], where V is a space of finite approximations to a set of "real world" objects. An upward-closed subset of V then describes the finite approximations to a set of objects. Upward-closed subsets are specified by their minimal elements and we can think of these sets of minimal elements as relations, i.e. sets of finite approximations to real-world objects. The space $\mathcal{R}(V)$ provides an obvious example of a space of finite descriptions of (possibly infinite) record structures that constitute the "real world". In what follows, we shall use the ordering on records to provide concrete examples.

Functional Dependencies

Having found a simple characterization of the natural join, can we do the same for other relational operations such as projection; and how do we characterize functional dependencies and other concepts in relational database theory using this domain-theoretic approach? We have characterized relations as elements of $V \mapsto TRIV$ and noted that this is equivalent to saying that relations are upward-closed subsets of V. (A subset S of V is *upward-closed* if $x \in S$, $x' \in V$ and $x' \sqsupseteq x$ imply $x' \in S$). The natural join is the intersection of such sets, which itself is upward closed. Moreover, if we are dealing with finite maps we can characterize such sets by their minimal elements. Suppose R and S are two such sets of minimal elements and $\overline{R}$ and $\overline{S}$ are their respective upward closures. The ordering on $V \mapsto TRIV$ is the containment ordering on upward closed subsets, and

$$\overline{R} \supseteq \overline{S} \qquad \text{iff} \qquad \forall s \in S. \exists r. r \in R, s \sqsupseteq r.$$

The natural join of two relations is given by the intersection, and

$$\overline{T} = \overline{R} \cup \overline{S} \qquad \text{iff} \qquad T = minset\{r \sqcap s | r \in R, s \in S\}.$$

Where $minset(S)$ is the set of minimal elements of a set S. When we are talking about the joins of relations defined by their minimal representatives, we shall use the notation $R \bowtie S$ i.e. $R \bowtie S = minset(\overline{R} \cap \overline{S})$. These minimal elements are pairwise incomparable (i.e. they form cochains). This definition of the $\bowtie$ operation is used by Aït-Kaci to provide to provide semantics for the interpreter for his knowledge-base language.

Now in order to talk about functional dependencies and projections we need to place a slightly stronger constraint on what constitutes these sets of minimal elements. We shall require, for reasons that will shortly become apparent, that they be pairwise inconsistent. David S. Warren also requires this condition for the data base component of his logic programming system. We shall call a set of pairwise inconsistent elements *independent*; and if V is a c.p.o. we shall use $\mathcal{I}(V)$ to denote the set of independent sets in V.

Prop 1. *If V is a c.p.o. then $\mathcal{I}(V)$ is a c.p.o. under the ordering $\leq$ defined by $R \leq S$ iff $\overline{S} \subseteq \overline{R}$with $\bowtie$ being the lub operation.*

The proof that any two members I_1 and I_2 have a *lub* is immediate. That they have a *glb* follows by considering, for each $v \in I_1 \cup I_2$, the *lub*s of the set

$$\{w | w \sqsubseteq v \text{ and } \exists I \in \mathcal{I}(V). I \leq I_1, I \leq I_2 \text{ and } w \in I\}.$$

It is an immediate consequence of this result that $I_1 \bowtie I_2$ is an independent set whenever I_1 and I_2 are independent. It is also something of a relief that "natural joins" are once again "joins" under the ordering $\leq$ (they were "meets" under the ordering we defined on $V \mapsto TRIV$.)

The usual way to think of a *functional dependency* is as a constraint on a relation. We shall adopt a slightly different approach and think of a functional dependency as a map induced by a relation. Of course, some such maps will be "accidental" and must later be ruled out since they are not part of the intended structure of the relation. However, this approach will allow us to characterize relationships among functional dependencies in a particularly simple way. Suppose R is a member of $\mathcal{I}(V)$. Just as we defined $\overline{R}$ to be the set of points in V *above* points in R, we can define $\underline{R} = \{x | \exists r. r \in R, r \sqsupseteq x\}$, the set of points *below* points in R. Roughly speaking, we can say that there is a functional dependency from A to B if R induces a map from $\overline{A}$ to $\underline{B}$, where A and B are in $\mathcal{I}(V)$. But we usually think of functional dependencies as being defined on sets of column names. What do these have to do with independent sets? Think of the set of all records whose *Name* and *Age* fields are defined to the point that they are character strings and integers respectively. Take the set of minimal members of this set. It is clearly a set of pairwise inconsistent records, hence independent; and we may think of it as characterizing the data type {*Age*: *string*; *Name*: *int*}. In fact we can define

$$\{Name\text{: } string;\ Age\text{: } int\} = \{\{Name \Rightarrow s; Age \Rightarrow i\} | s \in string, i \in int\}.$$

We shall occasionally refer to such sets as *types* although there is no formal distinction between types and relations; they are both independent sets. No immediate connection is intended with the definition of *type* given by programming language semanticists in, for example, [MacQ82]. However in [Bune85] a simple type system for relations is described based upon this domain theoretic approach, which appears to combine cleanly with Cardelli's work on multiple inheritance [Card84]. Although our example of {*Name*: *string*; *Age*: *int*} is an example of a flat " record" type, there are more interesting independent sets such as those defined by the set of records that have an *Address* whose *City* is defined or the set of records whose *Age* and *ShoeSize* are defined and equal. Note that the set of records for which *either* the *Name or* the *Age* is defined does not give rise to an independent set. We must not therefore expect to be able to define functional dependencies for such disjunctive types.

To be precise about how relations generate functional dependencies, suppose A, B, R are sets in $\mathcal{I}(V)$ with $A \leq R$. Consider the set of pairs

$$\{(a,b)|a \in \overline{A}, b \in \underline{B}, \exists r \in \overline{R}.r \sqsupseteq a \sqcup b\} \cup \{(x,\bot)|x \in V\}. \tag{A}$$

If this is a map, we shall say that $(A, B) \in R^+$ or, in database parlance, R satisfies a functional dependency from A to B. What this means is that if the pairs of points in $\overline{A}$ and $\underline{B}$ that are bounded above by some point in $\overline{R}$ form a map, then R "generates" a function from $\overline{A}$ to $\underline{B}$, i.e. R satisfies the functional dependency (A, B). The term $\{(x,\bot)|x \in V\}$ is added to take care of the constraint that any map must contain $(\bot,\bot)$. To give an example to justify the claim that this is a functional dependency, let A be the set of points with a defined *Name* (e.g. $\{$*Name*: *string*$\}$, and B the set of points with a defined *Age* (e.g. $\{$*Age*: *int*$\}$). The relation

$\{\{$*Name* ⇒'*J.Doe*'; *Dept* ⇒'*Sales*'; *Age* ⇒*21*$\}$;
$\{$*Name* ⇒'*M.Mack*'; *Dept* ⇒'*Manuf*' $\}$;
$\{$*Name* ⇒'*N.Bug*'; *Age* ⇒*21*$\}\}$

will induce a map (according to the above definition) from $\overline{\{Name\text{: }string\}}$ to $\underline{\{Age\text{: }int\}}$, namely $\{\{$*Name* ⇒ '*J. Doe*'$\}$ ⇒ $\{$*Age* ⇒*21*$\}$; $\{$*Name* ⇒ '*N. Bug*'$\}$ ⇒ $\{$*Age* ⇒*21*$\}\}$, but the relation

$\{\{$*Name* ⇒'*J.Doe*'; *Dept* ⇒'*Sales*'; *Age* ⇒*21*$\}$;
$\{$*Name* ⇒'*M.Mack*'; *Dept* ⇒'*Manuf*' $\}$;
$\{$*Name* ⇒'*J.Doe*'; *Age* ⇒*22*$\}\}$

will not.

Another way of thinking about functional dependencies is that R satisfies a dependency from A to B if B gives us no more information about R than A, i.e. that members of R that are not discriminated by A will not be discriminated by B. Stated mathematically,

Prop 2. *$(A, B) \in R^+$ iff for any $r_1, r_2 \in R$, $a \in A$, $b \in B$, if $r_1 \sqsubseteq a, r_2 \sqsubseteq a$ and $r_1 \sqsubseteq b$ then $r_2 \sqsubseteq b$.*

In the case that $A \leq R$ and $B \leq R$, this means that for $(A, B) \in R^+$ the partition of R induced by B must be *coarser* than the partition of R induced by A. There is obviously a relationship here with the partition semantics for relations described in [Cosm85]; this characterization of functional dependencies is also used in [Ohor86] where the denotation of a functional dependency (A,B) is the set of all relations that satisfy it, $\{R|(A, B) \in R^+\}$.

We can therefore view a functional dependency either as a function generated by a relation or as a constraint on a relation. There are various ways of characterizing the structure of R^+. First, R^+ is a subset of $\mathcal{I}(V) \times \mathcal{I}(V)$ and is a map with some additional properties, which are given in the following result.

Prop 3. *If $R \in \mathcal{I}(V)$ then R^+ is a map (i.e. $R^+ \in \mathcal{I}(V) \mapsto \mathcal{I}(V)$). Moreover, for all $A, B, C \in \mathcal{I}(V)$,*

if $A \geq B$ then $(A, B) \in R^+$, and

if $(A, B) \in R^+$ and $(B, C) \in R^+$ then $(A, C) \in R^+$.

In fact, the condition $R \in \mathcal{I}(V)$ is not needed in this result it is sufficient that R should be a cochain in V.

Not surprisingly, these conditions are direct generalizations of Armstrong's axioms for functional dependencies, where we generalize the subset ordering on column names to the ordering $\leq$ in independent sets. The following result, which applies to any c.p.o. V, states this formally.

Prop 4. *For any $F \in V \times V$ and $A, B, C, W \in V$ the following two sets of conditions are equivalent:*

a_1	*F is a map*
b_1	*if $A \sqsupseteq B$ then $(A, B) \in F$*
c_1	*if $(A, B) \in F$ and $(B, C) \in F$ then $(A, C) \in F$*

a_2	*if $A \sqsupseteq B$ then $(A, B) \in F$*
b_2	*if $(A, B) \in F$ and $(B, C) \in F$ then $(A, C) \in F$*
c_2	*if $W \in V$ and $(A, B) \in F$ then $(A \sqcup W, B \sqcup W) \in F$*

It is an immediate consequence of this result that R^+ satisfies Armstrong's axioms as defined in (a_2), (b_2) and (c_2) above.

It was noted earlier that our definitions concerning maps were simply re-statements of some standard results in lattice theory. To be specific, for any F in $V \mapsto W$ we can associate a *monotone function* from V to W by defining, for any $x \in V$, the function $F(x) = \sqcup\{y \in W | (x, y) \in F\}$. We shall briefly use this overloaded notation to describe both the map F and the function F.

Prop 5. *F satisfies Armstrong's axioms iff the associated function from V to V is a closure. That is, for all x in V*

$$F(x) \sqsupseteq x, \text{ and}$$

$$F(F(x)) = F(x).$$

Now a closure is uniquely characterized its set of fixed points, i.e. those values $x \in V$ for which $F(x) = x$. Moreover, the set of such points must be a meet-closed subset of V, i.e. if x_1 and x_2 are fixed-points of F then so is $x_1 \sqcap x_2$. Let us redirect our attention to $\mathcal{I}(V)$. We have seen that any relation (independent set) in V generates a map R^+ in $\mathcal{I}(V) \mapsto \mathcal{I}(V)$ which satisfies a generalized form of Armstrong's axioms. However, Armstrong's axioms are intended to describe *constraints* on a relation, not the relation itself. What this means is that given a map Q in $\mathcal{I}(V) \mapsto \mathcal{I}(V)$ which satisfies Armstrong's axioms or, equivalently, given a closure on $\mathcal{I}(V)$, a relation R *satisfies* Q iff $R^+ \sqsupseteq Q$, where we take the ordering on maps to be that defined earlier.

There are some consequences of this connection with database theory that are quite straightforward. For example, if R satisfies Q then so does any relation that is above R in the ordering on $\mathcal{I}(V)$. In particular, if R satisfies Q then so does $R \bowtie S$. Also, restricting our attention to first-normal-form relations, if we are given a set Q of pairs of subsets of column names that satisfy Armstrong's axioms, we can characterize Q by the fixed points of the associated closure. These are the sets of column names that are not expanded by any pair in Q, i.e. a set C of column names is a fixed-point of Q iff for no $C' \geq C$ is (C, C') in Q. To take a standard example [Ullm82] of the relation scheme C(ity), S(treet), Z(ip), with functional dependencies generated by $Z \rightarrow C$ and $\{C, S\} \rightarrow Z$, the fixed points are $\{C, S, Z\}$, $\{C\}$, $\{S\}$.

The observation that maps satisfying Armstrong's Axioms correspond to closures has been made by [Simo85]. The results above show how they generalize to non first-normal-form relations. The completeness and consistency of Armstrong's axioms in this more general case is immediate.

Projections

Unlike the natural join, which gives rise to "higher" relations in the lattice $\mathcal{I}(V)$ of independent sets, we would expect the projection operator to loose information and to produce results that are "lower" in $\mathcal{I}(V)$. Suppose A is what we have been informally calling a type, e.g. $\{$*Name*: *string*; *Age*: *int*$\}$ and R is a relation such that $R \sqsupseteq A$. We could very simply define the projection A' of R onto A as the set of points in A below some point in R, i.e. $A' = \{a \in A | \exists r \in R. a \sqsubseteq r\}$. By this definition $A' \in \mathcal{I}(V)$ and $A' \leq R$.

However, this definition is not very satisfactory because of the constraint that R must be above A. If, for example, R were to have some null values for *Age* this would not be the case.

To produce a more satisfactory definition of projection, one approach is to go back to our definition of R^+ (equation A of the previous section) and note that for any $A \in \mathcal{I}(V)$, the pair (R, A) is always in R^+. Stated informally, no independent set A can give us more information about R than R itself. We may therefore ask for the image of R under the map induced from $\overline{R}$ to $\underline{A}$, and call this the projection of R onto A. one way of characterizing this set is to introduce a new ordering, $\preceq$ defined by

$$R \preceq S \quad \text{iff} \quad \forall r \in R. \exists s \in S. r \sqsubseteq S.$$

There is an obvious symmetry between $\preceq$ and $\leq$, and $R \preceq S$ iff $\underline{R} \subseteq \underline{S}$. The projection of A on R is characterized by the following result:

Prop 6. *A' is the image of R under the map induced by (A, R) iff $A' = maxset(\underline{A} \cap \underline{R})$.*

maxset is defined analogously to *minset* in the previous section. In fact, the projection of R on A is nothing more than the *glb* of R and A under the ordering $\preceq$, and projection is a *symmetrical* operation on R and A. Unfortunately, this still does not give us exactly what we want, because this *glb* may not be an independent set. This is readily seen by trying to project

$$\begin{array}{lll}\{\{Name \Rightarrow \text{'J. Doe'}; & Dept \Rightarrow \text{'Sales'}; & Age \Rightarrow 21\}; \\ \{Name \Rightarrow \text{'M. Mack'}; & Dept \Rightarrow \text{'Manuf'} & \}; \\ \{Name \Rightarrow \text{'N. Bug'}; & & Age \Rightarrow 22\}\}\end{array}$$

onto $\{Dept\text{: } string;\ Age\text{:}int\}$.

At this point we have two options. We could either decide that projection is not always defined, or we could relax the condition that relations should be independent sets. Under the first option, the projection above is not defined; under the second it is

$$\{\{Dept \Rightarrow \text{'Sales'}\}\{\ Age \Rightarrow 21\}\}$$

In order to provide some mathematical conclusion, we take the first option and define $A \between B$ as the greatest lower bound, under $\preceq$, of A and B, when this is defined.

Under this definition of projection $\between$ is a commutative, associative operator that also associates with $\bowtie$, i.e. $(A \between B) \bowtie C = A \between (B \bowtie C)$. We might also ask under what conditions $\between$ "distributes" over $\bowtie$. The following result gives us a sufficient condition.

Prop 7. *For any* $A, B, R \in \mathcal{I}(V)$, *if there exists* $W \in \mathcal{I}(V)$ *such that* $W \leq A$, $W \leq B$ *and* $(W, A) \in R^{+}$ *then* $(R \mathbin{\overline{\underline{\times}}} A) \bowtie (R \mathbin{\overline{\underline{\times}}} B) = R \mathbin{\overline{\underline{\times}}} (A \bowtie B)$ *provided all projections are defined.*

This is a generalization of the lossless join condition for relational instances [Ullm82]. In order to obtain the lossless join condition for relational schemata one needs to be assured that there are some points above A and B, i.e. that the "types" A and B have some instances. The representation of relational schemata is a problem that is left for further investigation. However, it should be noted here that the condition of independence is not quite adequate for some other desirable properties of projection that occur, for example, in describing universal relations. The orderings that have been used to define join and projection are essentially those that occur in the study of power domains [Smyt78]

Conclusions

We have tried to show that the notion of inheritance leads to a natural representation of the operators of the relational algebra and that some of the basic properties of relational database theory, such as Armstrong's axioms, can be derived from some very simple domain theoretic relationships. If these ideas have any value one would expect to be able to represent other notions in database theory, such as multi-valued dependencies and the universal relation assumption within the same framework. However, given the apparent connection with Scott's "Information Systems", a more pressing need is to work out a proper denotational semantics for relational databases.

In the longer term we hope that it will be possible to use an approach such as this to produce better type systems for database programming languages.

Acknowledgements

The ideas presented here were largely stimulated by Aït-Kaci's notation and semantics for type subsumption and Cardelli's work on multiple inheritance. Malcolm Atkinson's proposals for a relational data type for PS-Algol were also useful in thinking about the connection between relations and maps. We are also grateful to David MacQueen and Gopalan Nadathur for several discussions concerning lattice theory and some of the ideas in this paper.

References

[AïtK84] Aït-Kaci, H. "A Lattice Theoretic Approach to Computation based on a Calculus of Partially Ordered Type Structures", PhD. Dissertation, Department of Computer and Information Science, Moore School/D2, University of Pennsylvania, Philadelphia, PA 19104. (1984)

[Atki85] Atkinson, M.P. and Buneman, O.P. "Types and Persistence in Database Programming Languages", ACM *Computing Surveys.* To appear.

[Banc85] Bancilhon, F. and Khoshafian, S., "A Calculus for Complex Objects", Technical Report, MCC, Austin Texas, October 1985.

[Brac85] Brachman, R.J. and Schmolze, J.G., " An Overview of the KL-One Knowledge Representation System", Cognitive Science, 9,2, April 1985.

[Bune82] Buneman, P., Frankel, R.E. and Nikhil, R., An Implementation Technique for Database Query Languages, ACM Transactions on Database Management, 7, 2, June 1982

[Bune85] Buneman, O.P., "Data Types for Data Base Programming", Proceedings of the Appin Conference on Data Types and Persistence, Technical Report, Department of Computing, Glasgow University, September, 1985.

[Card84] Cardelli, L., "A semantics of Multiple Inheritance", *Semantics of Data Types* Kahn, G., MacQueen, D.B. and Plotkin, G. (eds), Springer-Verlag, Berlin, June 1984

[Card85] Cardelli, L. and Wegner, P., "On Understanding Types, Data Abstraction, and Polymorphism", ACM *Computing Surveys* January, 1986.

[Cosm85] Cosmadakis, S.S., Kanellakis, P.C., Spyratos, N. "Partition Semantics for Relations", Technical Report, Brown University, December 1985.

[Gold80] Goldstein, I. P. and Bobrow, D. G., "Extending object oriented programming in Smalltalk", Proceedings of the 1980 Lisp Conference, August, 1980.

[Gord79] Gordon, M.J., Milner, A.J.R.G., and Wadsworth, C.P., *Edinburgh LCF*, Springer-Verlag, Lecture Notes in Computer Science, 1979.

[Lips79] Lipski, W. "On Semantic Issues Connected with Incomplete Information Databases, ACM *Transactions on Database Systems* 4,3 (1979).

[Smit77] Smith, J.M. and Smith, D.C.P., "Database Abstractions - Aggregation and Generalization" ACM Transactions on Database Systems, 2, 2, June 1977.

[Ichb79] Ichbiah *et al.*, Rationale of the Design of the Programming Language Ada,

ACM Sigplan Notices, 14, 6, 1979

[MacQ82] MacQueen, D.B. and Sethi, R., "A semantic model of types for applicative languages", Technical Report, Bell Laboratories, 1982.

[Ohor86] Ohori, A. *Personal Communication*, 1986.

[Scot82] Scott, D. "Domains for Denotational Semantics" ICALP '82, Aarhus, Denmark, 1982.

[Smyt78] Smyth, M.B. "Power Domains" *Journal of Computer and System Science* 16, 23-26 (1978)

[Ship81] Shipman, D.W., The Functional Data Model and the Data Language DAPLEX, ACM Transactions on Database Systems, 140-173, 6, 1, March 1981

[Simo85] Jurgensen, H and Simovici, D.A., "Towards an Abstract Theory of Dependency Constraints in Relational Databases", Technical Report 1/85, Department of Mathematics and Computer Science, University of Massachussetts, 1985.

[Stoy77] Stoy, J. *Denotational Semantics: The Scott-Strachey approach to Programming Language Theory.* MIT Press, 1977

[Ullm82] Ullman, J.D., *Principles of Database Systems* (2nd ed.), Computer Science Press, Rockville Md. (1982)

[Zani84a] Zaniolo, C., "Database Relations with Null Values," JCSS, 28 1, pp. 142-166, February 1984.

[Zani84b] Zaniolo, C. "Prolog: A Database Query Language for All Seasons", Proc. IEEE-ACM International Expert Database Systems Workshop, Kiawah Island, October 1984.

On the Desirability of γ-acyclic BCNF Database Schemes

Edward P.F. Chan
Héctor J. Hernández

Department of Computing Science
The University of Alberta
Edmonton, Alberta, Canada T6G 2H1

ABSTRACT

In this paper, we show that γ-acyclic Boyce-Codd Normal Form database schemes are highly desirable with respect to query processing and updates. We first prove that this class of schemes is bounded with respect to the set of functional dependencies embodied in the database scheme. This result enlarges the class of known bounded database schemes. We then show that this class of schemes is simple in semantics by proving that there is a simple and efficient way to compute the X-total projection of the representative instance. As a consequence, answers to many queries for this class of schemes can be computed easily and efficiently. We also show that if a γ-acyclic Boyce-Codd Normal Form database scheme is lossless, then it is connection-trap-free. Finally, we derive a simple and efficient algorithm that determines if an updated state is consistent. This allows the system to enforce the satisfaction of functional dependencies embodied in the database scheme incrementally and efficiently.

1. Introduction

A central problem in relational database theory is the schema design problem. The problem of schema design may be loosely stated as follows: given a description of an application, construct a database scheme that is "good" or "desirable" for the application. The "desirability" or "goodness" of a scheme depends on the criteria we use to evaluate it.

Codd [Co] was the first to observe that with the presence of functional dependencies, certain anomalies may exist when a relation is updated. He proposed normal forms as a way to avoid the anomaly problems. Since then, several normal forms have been proposed. A survey of these normal forms can be found in standard texts like [Da][Ma][U]. Among these normal forms, Boyce-Codd Normal Form (BCNF) is one of the most important normal forms. Although there are problems with the construction of BCNF database schemes in general [BB][BG][LO][O], under certain reasonable assumptions, it has been shown that BCNF database schemes are free of the anomaly problems [LeP]. In fact, LeDoux and Parker [LeP] suggested that BCNF is a useful design criterion and showed that the problems with BCNF database schemes do not exist in most real-life applications. With functional dependencies as the constraints imposed on the database schemes, we believe BCNF is a good design goal toward which a database designer should strive, since this class of schemes seems to capture the principle of separation stated in [BBG].

Freedom from the anomaly problems is an important design criterion a database designer should consider. Simplicity in semantics, ease in information retrieval, and efficient enforcement of constraints are also important in most applications.

Query answering is an important function in any database system. Hence it is desirable to have a database scheme that would allow information to be retrieved easily and efficiently. Some work has been done on this problem and recently a class of database schemes known as the connection-trap-free schemes [CA] was proposed to fulfill such a requirement. Connection-trap-free schemes have the properties that they are simple in semantics and the user is able to retrieve correct answers efficiently and easily from the database. Because of these properties, connection-trap-free schemes are desirable for query processing.

In this paper, we first prove that the class of γ-acyclic BCNF schemes is bounded [GM][MUV]. We then show that this class of schemes is simple in semantics by proving that there is a simple and efficient way to compute the X-total projection of the representative instance. Since the set of total tuples represents the information content of a database [GMV][M][MUV][NG][S1][S2], the user is able to understand the semantics of the application easily. Answers to many queries for this class of schemes can also be generated efficiently. We then show that if a γ-acyclic BCNF database scheme is lossless, then it is connection-trap-free. This demonstrates that the class of γ-acyclic BCNF database schemes is highly desirable with respect to query processing.

Efficient enforcement of constraints is a difficult problem in general. Some work has been done on this problem, see for example [BBC][St]. Enforcement of constraints is concerned with updates in a database. Even with only functional dependencies, it is not clear if they can be enforced efficiently in real-life applications. One way to resolve this problem is to find a class of database schemes that would allow a cost-effective way to determine if an updated state satisfies the constraints. In the context of the weak instance model, we regard an algorithm for incrementally testing functional dependencies as cost-effective if it does not require the generation of the representative instance and the verification process is done on some specific relations efficiently. Some work has been done on this problem and a class of database schemes called independent schemes has been identified [GY][IIK][S1][S2]. For an independent scheme, ensuring that the constraints imposed on each relation are satisfied is sufficient to guarantee that the state satisfies the constraints. Therefore the problem of ensuring a database is satisfying is reduced to the problem of verifying that each relation satisfies the constraints locally. Since checking that each relation satisfies the local constraints is much less expensive than checking satisfaction globally, this class of schemes allows enforcement of constraints to be carried out cost-effectively. In this paper, we show that the class of γ-acyclic BCNF database schemes also allows enforcement of constraints to be performed cost-effectively. This demonstrates the desirability of this class of schemes with respect to updates.

The only other known class of database schemes with all these desirable properties is the class of independent and connection-trap-free database schemes [CA]. So our result is another effort in identifying classes of desirable database schemes with respect to query processing and updates.

We give most of the definitions of relational theory required for this paper in Section 2. In Section 3, we present an algorithm to chase a consistent state of a γ-acyclic BCNF database scheme. In Section 4, we prove that γ-acyclic BCNF database schemes are bounded. In Section 5, we show that there is a simple and efficient method for computing the X-total projection of the representative instance for a γ-acyclic BCNF database scheme. In Section 6, we prove that lossless γ-acyclic BCNF database schemes are connection-trap-free. In Section 7, we present an efficient algorithm to test incrementally the satisfaction of functional dependencies for a γ-acyclic BCNF database scheme. After that, we give our conclusions in Section 8.

2. Relational Background

We shall follow traditional relational database theory notation [Ma][U]. We consider only database schemes ($\mathbf{R}$, F), where $\mathbf{R}$ is a nonempty set of relation schemes and F is a set of functional dependencies (fds) defined on $\mathbf{U} = \bigcup \mathbf{R}$.

The universal relation model we are working with in this paper is the *weak instance model* [GMV][H2][M][S1][V][Y]. Given a consistent state $\mathbf{r}$ of ($\mathbf{R}$, F) and its tableau T_r, we shall denote the final nonempty tableau in a chase of T_r with respect to (w.r.t.) F as $CHASE_F(T_r)$ [ABU][BV][MMS]. The *X-total projection* of the representative instance for $\mathbf{r}$ shall be denoted as $[X]$.

A database scheme ($\mathbf{R}$, F) is *bounded* w.r.t. F if for every tuple t in the representative instance of any consistent state $\mathbf{r}$ of ($\mathbf{R}$, F), t's total part can be obtained in at most k fd-rule applications starting from T_r, for some constant $k \geq 0$ [GM][MUV].

The largest class of database schemes known to be bounded w.r.t. fds is the class of independent database schemes [AtC][C1][IIK][MRW][S3].

A *hypergraph* is a pair $H = \langle V, E \rangle$, where V is a set of nodes and E is a collection of nonempty subsets of V [B]. Given a database scheme $(\mathbf{R}, F)$, its hypergraph, denoted by $H_{\mathbf{R}}$, has $\mathbf{U}$ as its set of nodes, and $\mathbf{R}$ as its set of edges. If $(\mathbf{R}, F)$ is a BCNF database scheme, we are also interested in the hypergraph of R_i^+, $R_i \in \mathbf{R}$, denoted by $H_{R_i^+}$. $H_{R_i^+}$ has R_i^+ as its set of nodes, and its set of edges is formed by the R_j's included in R_i^+. It is clear that $H_{R_i^+}$ is a subgraph of $H_{\mathbf{R}}$.

Let $H = \langle V, E \rangle$ be a hypergraph. A *path* from x_1 (E_1) to x_m (E_m) is a sequence $\langle E_1, E_2, \ldots, E_m \rangle$ such that: (a) $x_1 \in E_1$ and $x_m \in E_m$; (b) $E_1, E_2, \ldots, E_m$ are edges in E, $m \geq 1$; (c) $E_k \cap E_{k+1} \neq \emptyset$, for $k = 1, 2, \ldots, m-1$; (d) no proper subsequence of it satisfies the above properties. Two nodes (edges) are *connected* if there exists a path from one to the other. H is *connected* if every pair of nodes (edges) in H are connected. A γ-*cycle* of length m is a sequence $\langle E_1, x_1, E_2, x_2, \ldots, E_m, x_m, E_{m+1} \rangle$ such that: (a) $x_1, x_2, \ldots, x_m$ are all distinct nodes of H; (b) $E_1, E_2, \ldots, E_m$ are all distinct edges in E, and $E_1 = E_{m+1}$; (c) $m \geq 3$; (d) x_k is in E_k and E_{k+1}, for $k = 1, 2, \ldots, m$; (e) if $1 \leq i < m$, then x_i is in no E_j except E_i and E_{i+1} [DM][F]. H is γ-*acyclic* if H does not have a γ-cycle; otherwise it is γ-cyclic. Similarly, a database scheme $(\mathbf{R}, F)$ is γ-*acyclic* if $H_{\mathbf{R}}$ does not have a γ-cycle; otherwise it is γ-cyclic.

Given a family of sets $E = \{E_1, \ldots, E_m\}$, $Bachman(E)$ is defined as follows: (a) if $E_i \in E$, then $E_i \in Bachman(E)$; (b) if X and Y are in $Bachman(E)$, then $X \cap Y$ is in $Bachman(E)$. E is *connected* if the hypergraph $H = \langle \bigcup_{i=1}^{m} E_i, \bigcup_{i=1}^{m} \{E_i\} \rangle$ is connected. A connected set $V = \{V_1, \ldots, V_m\} \subseteq$ Bachman($\mathbf{R}$) is the *unique minimal connection (u.m.c.) (among)* $X \subseteq \mathbf{U}$, if (a) $\bigcup_{i=1}^{m} V_i \supseteq X$, and (b) for all connected subsets $\{W_1, \ldots, W_k\}$ of Bachman($\mathbf{R}$) such that $\bigcup_{i=1}^{k} W_i \supseteq X$, there exists $\{W_{i_1}, \ldots, W_{i_m}\} \subseteq \{W_1, \ldots, W_k\}$ such that $W_{i_j} \supseteq V_j$, for $1 \leq j \leq m$.

In the rest of this paper when we refer to (a)cyclicity we shall be referring to γ-(a)cyclicity.

3. Algorithms for Proving Boundedness of Acyclic BCNF Database Schemes

In this section, we present the algorithms used in this paper to prove that acyclic BCNF database schemes are bounded. We present first Algorithm 1, below, the algorithm we use to compute $H_{R_i^+}$ for each $R_i \in \mathbf{R}$, and for any BCNF database scheme $(\mathbf{R}, F)$.

Algorithm 1

Input: A BCNF Database scheme $(\mathbf{R}, F)$.

Output: Hypergraph of R_i^+, for each $R_i \in \mathbf{R}$.

Notation: K_j stands for a key of R_j.

for each R_i in $\mathbf{R}$ **do begin**
    Let $H_{R_i^+} = \langle V = R_i, E = \{R_i\} \rangle$
    $Rest = \mathbf{R} - \{R_i\}$
    while there is an R_j in $Rest$ such that $V \supseteq K_j$ **do begin**
        $E = E \cup \{R_j\}$; $V = V \cup R_j$;
        $Rest = Rest - \{R_j\}$;
    end
end

Algorithm 2, shown below, is an algorithm to chase a consistent state of an acyclic BCNF database scheme. We are going to prove that this algorithm obtains the total part of any tuple in $CHASE_F(T_r)$ in a fixed number of applications of fd-rules. We shall do this by proving that Step 2 of Algorithm 2 equates only nondistinguished variables (ndv's). Unlike previous approaches [AtC][C1][IIK][MRW][S3], which assume independence, proving that Step 2 equates only ndv's is a difficult task in our case since we are no longer guaranteed that each attribute in a closure is "added" by a unique fd embedded in a unique relation scheme. In fact, this property makes our proof of boundedness much more difficult than in the independent case. To illustrate how tuples in T_r are extended using Algorithm 2, let us consider the following example.

Example 1: Let $(\{R_1(AB), R_2(BC), R_3(BCD)\}, \{B \rightarrow CD\})$ be an acyclic BCNF database scheme. The edges in $H_{R_1^+}$ are R_1, R_2, and R_3. Then in Algorithm 2 tuples originating from r_1 can be extended with tuples from r_3 or with those from r_2. Therefore if we want to compute the AC-total projection, then we will show in Section 5 that the expression to compute it is $\pi_{AC}(R_1 \bowtie R_2) \cup \pi_{AC}(R_1 \bowtie R_3)$. □

Algorithm 2

Input: T_r for a consistent state **r** of an acyclic BCNF database scheme (**R**, F).
For each $R_i \in \mathbf{R}$, $H_{R_i^+} = \langle V_i, E_i \rangle$ as computed by Algorithm 1.

Output: $CHASE_F(T_r)$.

Notation: K_j stands for a key of R_j.

Step 1:
for each $R_i \in \mathbf{R}$ **do begin**
  for each t in T_r originating from r_i **do begin**
    $Rest = E_i - \{R_i\}$
    while there is R_j in $Rest$ such that there exists
      t' in T_r from r_j and $t'[K_j] = t[K_j]$ **then do begin**
      $t[R_j] = t'[R_j]$
      $Rest = Rest - \{R_j\}$
    end
  end
end

Step 2:
Let T_r' be the outcome from Step 1.
Obtain $CHASE_F(T_r)$ from T_r'.

In the rest of this paper, we refer to a computation of $H_{R_i^+}$ (by Algorithm 1) simply as a computation of R_i^+ (by Algorithm 1).

4. γ-acyclic BCNF Database Schemes are Bounded

In this section, we prove that acyclic BCNF database schemes are bounded. We do this by proving that if we chase the tableau T_r for a consistent state of an acyclic BCNF database scheme using Algorithm 2, then Step 2 of Algorithm 2 equates only ndv's. This implies that the total part of every tuple in $CHASE_F(T_r)$ is obtained in Step 1 of Algorithm 2 in a fixed number of applications of fd-rules.

We give now most of the definitions needed in this section. Let (**R**, F) be a BCNF database scheme and let $R_i \in \mathbf{R}$. Let us consider a computation of R_i^+ by Algorithm 1. Let $H_{R_i^+} = \langle V, E \rangle$ be the partial hypergraph for R_i^+ before an execution of the while-loop in Algorithm 1. Let $R_j \in \mathbf{R}$ be such that it can be chosen at line (4) in Algorithm 1. We say that R_j *can be added* to $H_{R_i^+}$ (R_i^+). Assume R_j is chosen at line (4) in Algorithm 1. We say that R_j is a relation scheme that *is added* to

$H_{R_i^+}(R_i^+)$. $R_j \bigcap V$ is called *a connection point* of R_j (*in* R_i^+) and it is denoted by CP_j. Now, let $K_{j_1}, \ldots, K_{j_q}$ be the keys of R_j in CP_j. Then, for $1 \leq l \leq q$, if $A \in R_j - K_{j_l}$, we say that K_{j_l} (CP_j, or R_j) *adds* A to R_i^+; if $A \notin V$, we say that K_{j_l} (CP_j, or R_j) *A-extends* R_i^+; we say that R_j *uses* K_{j_l} (CP_j) in R_i^+.

Let $K_{i_1}, \ldots, K_{i_m}$ be the keys of R_i. We regard K_{i_l}, for $1 \leq l \leq m$, as adding A to R_i^+, for any $A \in R_i$. Also, we make the conventions that $CP_i = \bigcup K_{i_l}$, and that R_i (K_{i_l}, or CP_i) A-extends R_i^+, for any $A \in R_i$. We say that R_j in R_i^+ *can A-extend* R_i^+ if there is a computation of R_i^+ in which R_j A-extends R_i^+. Notice that if $A \in R_i$, then R_i is the only relation scheme that A-extends R_i^+. Let $A, B \in R_i^+$. We say that AB is (or A and B are) *not split* in R_i^+ if for all computations of R_i^+ (by Algorithm 1), R_j A-extends R_i^+ if and only if R_j B-extends R_i^+. The following example illustrates some of these definitions.

Example 2: Let $(\mathbf{R}, F) = (\{R_1(ED), R_2(DB), R_3(DBC), R_4(DBCAF)\}, \{D \rightarrow B, D \rightarrow BC, D \rightarrow BCAF, F \rightarrow ABCD\})$ be a BCNF database scheme. $(\mathbf{R}, F)$ is an acyclic BCNF database scheme. Let us consider $<R_1, R_4, R_3, R_2>$, a computation of R_1^+ by Algorithm 1. In this computation of R_1^+, $CP_4 = \{D\}$. Since $\{D\}$ is the only key of R_4 in CP_4 and since $ABCF \subseteq ABCDF - \{D\}$ (i.e., $R_4 - K_4$), R_4 adds A, B, C, and F to R_1^+. In fact, R_4 A-, B-, C-, and F-extends R_1^+ since A, B, C, and F are not in V when R_4 is added to R_1^+. R_2 adds B to R_1^+, since $B \in DB - \{D\}$ (i.e., $B \in R_2 - K_2$). Another connection point of R_4 in R_1^+, which can C-extend R_1^+ is DB; this occurs in the following computation of R_1^+: $<R_1, R_2, R_4, R_3>$. Other computations of R_1^+ in which $CP_4 = DBC$ can A-extend R_1^+ are: $<R_1, R_3, R_4, R_2>$ and $<R_1, R_2, R_3, R_4>$. AF is not split in R_1^+, but B and C are split in R_1^+. It is worth noting that the connection points of R_4 in different computations of R_1^+ are totally ordered by set inclusion. □

This section is organized as follows. In Section 4.1, we prove first that for every A in R_i^+ there is a unique maximal set of attributes (CP_{iA}) which A-extends R_i^+. This result is used in Section 4.2, in Lemma 4.1, to prove that when computing $CHASE_F(T_r)$ the A-component of a tuple t in T_r originating from r_i can be equated only by keys in CP_{iA} and that if the A-component of t in T_r is not an ndv, then t consists of constants on CP_{iA}. The facts in Section 4.2 are required in Section 4.3 for proving that acyclic BCNF database schemes are indeed bounded.

4.1. Some Properties of CP_j in R_i^+

We study first the connection points that can A-extend R_i^+ and prove that there exists a unique maximal connection point that can A-extend R_i^+. Example 2 above shows that the connection points of R_4 in R_1^+ are ordered by set inclusion. The following proposition proves that in general this is the case, provided that the BCNF database scheme is acyclic.

Proposition 4.1: Let $(\mathbf{R}, F)$ be an acyclic BCNF database scheme and let $R_i \in \mathbf{R}$. Let R_j in R_i^+ and let $CP_{j_1}, CP_{j_2}, \ldots, CP_{j_q}$ be a sequence of connection points of R_j corresponding to q different computations of R_i^+. Then $CP_{j_1}, CP_{j_2}, \ldots, CP_{j_q}$ are totally ordered by set inclusion.

Sketch of Proof: By contradiction. Assume that $CP_{j_1}, CP_{j_2}, \ldots, CP_{j_n}$, $1 < n \leq q$, is a sequence of connection points as defined above such that CP_{j_n} is the first connection point that violates the set inclusion total ordering. Observe this implies $R_j \neq R_i$; else there is only one connection point. Then, there exists CP_{j_l}, for some $1 \leq l < n$, such that CP_{j_l} and CP_{j_n} are not comparable. (Two sets are ***not comparable*** if neither one contains the other one.) But we can prove that this leads to a contradiction.

Hence $CP_{j_1}, CP_{j_2}, \ldots, CP_{j_n}$ must be totally ordered by set inclusion. □

Let R_j in R_i^+ be such that it can A-extend R_i^+. We shall denote the ***maximal connection point*** of R_j that can A-extend R_i^+ as CP_{jA_i}.

Let us now consider the connection points of two relation schemes in R_i^+ that can A-extend R_i^+. The following proposition states that if there is more than one R_j in R_i^+ which can A-extend R_i^+, then their maximal connection points that can A-extend R_i^+ are identical, provided that $(\mathbf{R}, F)$ is an acyclic BCNF database scheme.

Proposition 4.2 [CH]: Let $(\mathbf{R}, F)$ be an acyclic BCNF database scheme and let $R_i \in \mathbf{R}$. Let $R_{j_1}, R_{j_2}, \ldots, R_{j_q}$ in R_i^+ be such that for all $1 \leq l \leq q$, R_{j_l} can A-extend R_i^+. Then $CP_{j_1 A_i} = CP_{j_2 A_i} = \ldots = CP_{j_q A_i}$.

We shall refer to the ***(unique) maximal connection point*** that can A-extend R_i^+ by CP_{iA}.

4.2. Some Properties of $CHASE_F(T_r)$

In this subsection, we prove the facts about any computation of $CHASE_F(T_r)$ which are required in the next section to prove that acyclic BCNF database schemes are bounded.

Before deriving the proofs in this subsection, we need the following definitions. Let t_1 be a tuple in T_r which originates from r_i, $R_i \in \mathbf{R}$, and assume $A \in R_i^+$. We say that K_j (CP_{jA_i}, or CP_{iA}) *A-extends* t_1, if K_j (CP_{jA_i}, or CP_{iA}, respectively) A-extends R_i^+. We shall denote some time the maximal connection point that A-extends t_1 by CP_{t_1A}. We also say that AB *is not split* (or A and B *are not split*) in t_1, if AB is not split (A and B are not split) in R_i^+.

We want to point out that the fds considered are the ones embodied in the relation schemes in the database scheme. Therefore any fd-rule is of the form $K_p \to R_p - K_p$, where K_p is a nontrivial key of R_p. In the following we denote a sequence of fd-rules by $\tau_1 \ldots \tau_k$, and $\tau_1 \ldots \tau_k(T)$ denotes $\tau_k(\ldots(\tau_1(T))\ldots)$, where $\tau_i(T)$ is the tableau obtained from applying the fd-rule τ_i to the tableau T.

Lemma 4.1 [CH]: Let $(\mathbf{R}, F)$ be an acyclic BCNF database scheme. Let $\mathbf{r}$ be a state of $(\mathbf{R}, F)$, and let T_r be the tableau of $\mathbf{r}$. Suppose $T_r' = \tau_1 \ldots \tau_k(T_r)$ is nonempty, t_1, t_2 are in T_r', and $A \in \mathbf{U}$.

A: If $t_1[A] = t_2[A]$ and is an ndv, then

(1) $CP_{t_1A} = CP_{t_2A}$;

(2) $t_1[CP_{t_1A}] = t_2[CP_{t_1A}]$;

(3) if AB is not split in t_1, then $t_1[B] = t_2[B]$.

B: If $t_1[A]$ is a constant, then

(1) $t_1[CP_{t_1A}]$ are constants;

(2) if AB is not split in t_1, then $t_1[B]$ is a constant.

Corollary 4.1 [CH]: Let $(\mathbf{R}, F)$ be an acyclic BCNF database scheme. Let $\mathbf{r}$ be a state of $(\mathbf{R}, F)$ and let T_r be the tableau of $\mathbf{r}$. Let $\tau_1 \ldots \tau_k$ be a sequence of fd-rules applied to T_r. Suppose $T_r'' = \tau_1 \ldots \tau_{k-1}(T_r)$ is nonempty and t_1, t_2 are in T_r''. Assume we can apply τ_k: $K_p \to R_p - K_p$ to equate t_1 and t_2 such that the ndv $t_2[A]$ is equated to the constant $t_1[A]$, for some $A \in R_p - K_p$. Suppose $T_r' = \tau_k(T_r'')$ is nonempty. Then

A: $K_p \subseteq CP_{t_2A}$.

B: $t_1[CP_{tA}]$ are constants in T_r'' and for any t in T_r'' such that $t[A] = t_2[A]$ in T_r'', $t_1[CP_{tA}] = t[CP_{tA}]$ in T_r'.

Lemma 4.2: Let $(\mathbf{R}, F)$ be an acyclic BCNF database scheme. Let $\mathbf{r}$ be a state of $(\mathbf{R}, F)$ and let T_r be the tableau of $\mathbf{r}$. Let $\tau_1 \ldots \tau_k$ be a sequence of fd-rules applied to T_r. Suppose $T_r'' = \tau_1 \ldots \tau_{k-1}(T_r)$ is nonempty and t_1, t_2 are in T_r''. Assume we can apply τ_k: $K_p \rightarrow R_p - K_p$ to equate t_1 and t_2 such that the ndv $t_2[A]$ is equated to the constant $t_1[A]$, for some $A \in R_p - K_p$. Suppose $T_r' = \tau_k(T_r'')$ is nonempty. Then for all $B \in R_p - K_p$, if $t_1[B]$ is an ndv in T_r'', then $t_2[B]$ is an ndv in T_r''.

Sketch of Proof: By contradiction. Assume there is $B \in R_p - K_p$ such that $t_1[B]$ is an ndv in T_r'' and $t_2[B]$ is a constant in T_r''; it is clear that $A \neq B$. Assume t_1 and t_2 originate from r_1 and r_2 respectively, for some R_1 and R_2 in $\mathbf{R}$.

By assumption, τ_k equates the ndv $t_2[A]$ to the constant $t_1[A]$ and equates the ndv $t_1[B]$ to the constant $t_2[B]$. Since K_p is the key used by τ_k to equate t_1 and t_2, from Corollary 4.1.A, K_p is in CP_{1B} and K_p is in CP_{2A}. Since $B \notin R_1$ and $A \notin R_2$, it is not difficult to see that R_p can both B-extend R_1^+ and A-extend R_2^+, and that then R_p contains both CP_{1B} and CP_{2A} as well as A and B.

By Corollary 4.1.B, $t_1[CP_{2A}]$ are constants in T_r''. Hence since $t_1[B]$ is an ndv in T_r'', $B \notin CP_{2A}$. Similarly, by Corollary 4.1.B, $t_2[CP_{1B}]$ are constants in T_r''. Hence since $t_2[A]$ is an ndv in T_r'', $A \notin CP_{1B}$. Since $A \notin R_2$ and $B \notin R_1$, we can prove that $A \notin CP_{2A}$ and $B \notin CP_{1B}$. Therefore neither A nor B are in $CP_{1B}CP_{2A}$.

Since R_p can B-extend R_1^+ and $B \notin R_1$, $A \notin R_1$; else it is not difficult to see that $CP_{1B} \supseteq \{A\}$. Similarly, $B \notin R_2$. Observe $CP_{1B} \cap CP_{2A} \neq \emptyset$, since they share K_p. Since $R_p \supseteq CP_{1B}CP_{2A}AB$, and AB is in $R_p - CP_{1B}CP_{2A}$, and neither A nor B is in R_1R_2, we can prove that $CP_{1B} = CP_{2A}$ and that this leads to a contradiction. □

A class of schemes called embedded-complete database schemes was recently proposed to capture the intuition that every piece of information on some relation scheme is explicitly represented in a database. We define that class of schemes now. Let $W \subseteq \mathbf{U}$. We define $\downarrow W \downarrow = \bigcup \{\pi_W(r_j) | \ r_j$ is a relation on $R_j \in \mathbf{R}$ and $R_j \supseteq W\}$. A database scheme $(\mathbf{R}, F)$ is *embedded-complete* w.r.t. F if for any consistent state $\mathbf{r}$ of $(\mathbf{R}, F)$, $[X] = \downarrow X \downarrow$, for any $X \subseteq R_i$, for some $R_i \in \mathbf{R}$ [CM]. Before we can show that an acyclic BCNF database scheme $(\mathbf{R}, F)$ is bounded w.r.t. F, we need to show that it is embedded complete w.r.t. F.

Lemma 4.3 [CH]: Let ($\mathbf{R}$, F) be an acyclic BCNF database scheme. Then ($\mathbf{R}$, F) is embedded-complete w.r.t. F.

4.3. Acyclic BCNF Database Schemes are Bounded

The only thing left to do in order to show that acyclicity is a sufficient condition for BCNF database schemes to be bounded is to prove that Step 2 of Algorithm 2 does indeed equate only ndv's.

Lemma 4.4: Let ($\mathbf{R}$, F) be an acyclic BCNF database scheme. Let $\mathbf{r}$ be a consistent state of ($\mathbf{R}$, F). Let T_r be the tableau for $\mathbf{r}$. Then Step 2 of Algorithm 2 equates only ndv's.

Proof: Assume otherwise. Then, there is a sequence of fd-rule transformations $\tau_1 \ldots \tau_l$ used in Step 2 of Algorithm 2 such that τ_l: $K_l \rightarrow R_l - K_l$, $R_l \in \mathbf{R}$, is the first fd-rule to equate an ndv with a constant. Assume τ_l equates the ndv in $t_2[A]$ with a constant from $t_1[A]$, $A \in R_l - K_l$. Also assume t_2 originates from r_2 and t_1 originates from r_1, for some R_1 and $R_2 \in \mathbf{R}$. R_l must be in both R_2^+ and R_1^+ [BDB].

There are two cases to be considered depending on whether $t_2[K_l]$ consists of constants.

Case 1: $t_2[K_l]$ are constants. Hence $t_1[K_lA]$ are constants. Since $K_lA \subseteq R_l$, by Lemma 4.3, $t_1[K_lA] \in \downarrow K_lA \downarrow$. Thus there exists t' from r_p in T_r such that $t'[K_lA] = t_1[K_lA]$, for some $R_p \in \mathbf{R}$ such that $R_p \supseteq K_lA$. Observe K_l is a key of R_p. By Corollary 4.1.A, $K_l \subseteq CP_{2A}$. Since $A \in R_2^+ - R_2$ and $R_p \supseteq K_lA$, it is not difficult to see that R_p is in R_2^+. Also $t_2[K_l] = t_1[K_l]$, hence $t'[K_l] = t_2[K_l]$. Therefore $t_2[A]$ should have been equated to a constant in Step 1 of Algorithm 2, since t' and R_p satisfy the conditions in while-loop in Algorithm 2.

Case 2: $t_2[K_l]$ has some ndv's. Then $t_1[K_l]$ has some ndv's. Since, by Corollary 4.1.A, $K_l \subseteq CP_{2A}$, $t_1[CP_{2A}]$ has some ndv's before applying τ_l. But this is impossible since, by Corollary 4.1.B, $t_1[CP_{2A}]$ are constants before applying τ_l.

Since both cases lead to contradiction, the lemma is proven. □

Theorem 4.1: Let ($\mathbf{R}$, F) be an acyclic BCNF database scheme. ($\mathbf{R}$, F) is bounded w.r.t. F.

Proof: It follows from Lemma 4.4. □

5. Efficient Computation of X-total Projection

In this section we show that there is a simple and efficient way of computing $[X]$ for an acyclic BCNF database scheme, for any $X \subseteq \mathbf{U}$. Hence answers to many queries can be generated efficiently. Clearly if for all $R_i \in \mathbf{R}$, R_i^+ does not contain X, then $[X]$ is an empty set. We will show that if there exists $R_i \in \mathbf{R}$ such that $R_i^+ \supseteq X$, then $[X]$ can be computed by a simple and efficient method. This also demonstrates that the semantics of relationships among attributes is simple.

We first give some definitions required for the rest of this paper. Let $S = \{S_1, \ldots, S_k\}$ and $\bigcup_i S_i \subseteq \mathbf{U}$. Let I be a universal relation. I is said to satisfy the *embedded join dependency* $\bowtie S$ if $I[\bigcup_i S_i]$ satisfies the join dependency $\bowtie S$. S is *lossless w.r.t.* F if for all I satisfying F, I satisfies $\bowtie S$. Let $S' = <S_0, \ldots, S_n>$ be a sequence of distinct relation schemes from $\mathbf{R}$. Then $\pi_X(S_0 \bowtie \ldots \bowtie S_n)$ is an *extension join* of S_0 *covering* X [C1][IIK][H1] if $[S_i \cap (\bigcup_{j=0}^{i-1} S_j)] \to [S_i - (S_i \cap (\bigcup_{j=0}^{i-1} S_j))] \in F^+$, where $S_i - (S_i \cap (\bigcup_{j=0}^{i-1} S_j)) \neq \emptyset$, for all $0 < i \leq n$, and $\bigcup_i S_i \supseteq X$.

Lemma 5.1: Let $(\mathbf{R}, F)$ be an acyclic BCNF database scheme, $X \subseteq \mathbf{U}$ and $V = \{V_1, \ldots, V_k\}$ the u.m.c. among X. If there exists $R_i \in \mathbf{R}$ such that $R_i^+ \supseteq X$, then V is lossless w.r.t. F.

Proof: Let $H_{R_i^+}$ be the set of relation schemes of $\mathbf{R}$ in R_i^+. Let $H = H_{R_i^+} \cup V$. Since $(\bigcup_{i=1}^{k} V_i) \subseteq R_i^+$, H is a database scheme defined on R_i^+. It is easy to see that H is a lossless decomposition of R_i^+ w.r.t. the embodied fds in $H_{R_i^+}$ since $H_{R_i^+}$ is lossless [U]. Since H is acyclic and lossless, by a result in [Y], V is a connected subset of H implies V is lossless w.r.t. the embodied fds in $H_{R_i^+}$ and hence is lossless w.r.t. F. □

Lemma 5.2 [CA]: Let $(\mathbf{R}, F)$ be an acyclic database scheme. Suppose $\{V_1, \ldots, V_k\}$ is the u.m.c. among X and $\{S_1, \ldots, S_k\} \subseteq \mathbf{R}$ such that $S_i \supseteq V_i$, for all $1 \leq i \leq k$. Then $\pi_X(\bowtie_{i=1}^{k} S_i) = \pi_X(\bowtie_{i=1}^{k} \pi_{V_i}(S_i))$.

In Section 4, we proved that Algorithm 2 correctly computes the total tuples in the representative instance. It is not difficult to see that every X-total tuple is computed by an extension join of a R_p covering X, for some $R_p^+ \supseteq X$ [AtC][C1][IIK][H1]. Let us denote $[X]_{R_p^+}$ as the union of all the extension joins of R_p covering X. Let $E_X = \bigcup_{R_p^+ \supseteq X} [X]_{R_p^+}$.

Theorem 5.1: Let (**R**, F) be an acyclic BCNF scheme. Suppose $X \subsetneq \mathbf{U}$ and $V = \{V_1, \ldots, V_k\}$ is the u.m.c. among X. If there exists $R_i \in \mathbf{R}$ such that $R_i^+ \supsetneq X$, then $[X] = E_X = \pi_X(\bowtie_{j=1}^{k} \downarrow V_j \downarrow)$.

Proof: $\pi_X(\bowtie_{j=1}^{k} \downarrow V_j \downarrow) \subsetneq [X]$. By Lemma 5.1, V is lossless w.r.t. F. Hence $\pi_X(\bowtie_{j=1}^{k} \downarrow V_j \downarrow) \subsetneq [X]$ follows [CA][MUV].

$[X] \subsetneq E_X$. Since every X-total tuple is generated by some extension join of some R_p such that $R_p^+ \supsetneq X$, $[X] \subsetneq E_X$.

$E_X \subsetneq \pi_X(\bowtie_{j=1}^{k} \downarrow V_j \downarrow)$. Since every extension join in $[X]_{R_p^+}$ is a connected subset of **R** that contains X, by the definition of u.m.c. among X and Lemma 5.2, $[X]_{R_p^+} \subsetneq \pi_X(\bowtie_{j=1}^{k} \downarrow V_j \downarrow)$. Hence $E_X \subsetneq \pi_X(\bowtie_{j=1}^{k} \downarrow V_j \downarrow)$. □

By Theorem 5.1 for any $X \subsetneq \mathbf{U}$, the relationship among X in an acyclic BCNF database scheme is simple. That is, either there is no relationship among X or the relationship is represented by the u.m.c. among X. Furthermore, this relationship (i.e., the X-total projection) can be computed easily and efficiently. In fact, the expression $\pi_X(\bowtie_{j=1}^{k} \downarrow V_j \downarrow)$ that computes the X-total projection is in some sense optimal, since $\{V_1, \ldots, V_k\}$ is the u.m.c. among X; in other words, it requires, in some sense, the minimal number of joins to compute the X-total projection.

6. Lossless γ-acyclic BCNF Database Schemes are Connection-trap-free

A class of database schemes known as the connection-trap-free schemes has recently been proposed to allow users to easily retrieve correct information from a database [CA]. These schemes have the properties that they are simple in semantics and hence users are able to understand the application easily. Moreover, the information retrieval process is simple and answers to many queries can be generated easily and efficiently. We now define the class of connection-trap-free schemes.

Let $X \subsetneq \mathbf{U}$ and let (**R**, F) be a database scheme. A state **r** of (**R**, F) is said to have a *complete unique minimal connection among* X if $[X] = \pi_X(\downarrow V_1 \downarrow \bowtie \ldots \bowtie \downarrow V_k \downarrow)$, where $\{V_1, \ldots, V_k\}$ is the unique minimal connection among X. Then we say that (**R**, F) is *connection-trap-free (ctf)* w.r.t. F if for any consistent state **r** of (**R**, F), **r** has a complete unique minimal connection among X, for any $X \subsetneq \mathbf{U}$.

In this section we prove that lossless acyclic BCNF database schemes are ctf w.r.t. the fds embodied in the relations in the database scheme.

Theorem 6.1: Let (**R**, F) be a lossless acyclic BCNF database scheme. Then (**R**, F) is ctf w.r.t. F.

Proof: Since **R** is lossless w.r.t. F, there is $R_i \in$ **R** such that R_i^+ = **U** [ABU]. By Theorem 5.1, the theorem follows. □

7. Incremental Testing of Satisfaction

Constraints are logical restrictions imposed on data so that the information in a database correctly represents the part of real world that an application is interested in. Hence ensuring that the data satisfies the constraints is important in data management. In the context of the weak instance model, testing satisfaction of fds might be as expensive as generating the representative instance from the tableau of the state [H2]; it requires polynomial time and space in the size of the database state. Since database size is large in general and existing systems do not provide facilities for chasing, testing satisfaction of fds by generating the representative instance might not be practical. We regard an algorithm for incrementally testing fds as cost-effective if it does not require the generation of the representative instance and the verification process is done on some specific relations and can be carried out in polynomial time.

Under the weak instance model, several authors proposed the class of independent schemes to solve this problem [GY][IIK][S1][S2]. For the class of independent schemes, ensuring each relation satisfies the constraints locally guarantees the state is consistent. Hence this restricts the scope of verification to single relation and the representative instance is not generated in the verification process. Therefore, independence allows a cost-effective way to test satisfaction of constraints incrementally.

In this section, we show that if (**R**, F) is an acyclic BCNF database scheme, then there is also a cost-effective way to test satisfaction of F incrementally. Let **r** be a consistent state of an acyclic BCNF database scheme (**R**, F). Let r_p be a relation being updated, where $r_p \in$ **r**. Let t be the tuple being inserted in r_p. Let $\{K_{p_1}, \ldots, K_{p_m}\}$ be the set of nontrivial keys of R_p. Consider Algorithm 3, shown below. We claim that if no contradiction is found, that is, if Algorithm 3 prints *yes*, the updated state is consistent w.r.t. F. Theorem 7.1, below, proves this claim.

We need the following definitions for proving Theorem 7.1. Let **K** = $\{K_i \to A \mid K_i \to A$ is a nontrivial fd embodied in some R in **R**$\}$. Let us index the elements of **K** as

---

Algorithm 3

Input: A consistent state **r** of an acyclic BCNF database scheme (**R**, F).
A tuple t to be inserted in $r_p \in \mathbf{r}$, $R_p \in \mathbf{R}$.

Output: *no*, if $\mathbf{r} \cup \{t\}$ is not consistent w.r.t. F; *yes* otherwise.

Notation: $\{K_{p_1}, \ldots, K_{p_m}\}$ is the set of nontrivial keys of R_p.

for each K_{p_i} **do begin**
  for each $A \in R_p - K_{p_i}$ **do begin**
    for all $R_q \in \mathbf{R}$ such that $R_q \supseteq K_{p_i}A$ **do begin**
      if $\pi_{K_{p_i}A}(r_q) \cup \pi_{K_{p_i}A}(\{t\})$ does not satisfy $K_{p_i} \to A$ **then do begin**
        print *no*; **halt end**
    end
  end
end
print *yes*

$\{f_1{:}K_1 \to A_1, \ldots, f_q{:}K_q \to A_q\}$. We define $\downarrow f_i \downarrow = \downarrow K_i A_i \downarrow$, which, by definition in Section 4.2, is $\bigcup_{R_p \supseteq K_i A_i} \pi_{K_i A_i}(r_p)$.

Theorem 7.1 [CH]: Let **r** be a state of an acyclic BCNF database scheme (**R**, F). Let T_r be the tableau for **r**. If for all $1 \leq i \leq q$, $\downarrow f_i \downarrow$ satisfies the fd f_i, then **r** is a consistent state w.r.t. F.

We have proven our claim that Algorithm 3 is an algorithm to test incrementally the satisfaction of fds for an acyclic BCNF database scheme.

Therefore for acyclic BCNF schemes, the satisfaction of fds is basically enforced by creating indices. Since relational systems allow indices to be created for keys in a relation scheme, the enforcement of fds can be done in polynomial time and without generating the representative instance, that is, cost-effectively.

8. Conclusions

We showed that the class of γ-acyclic BCNF database schemes is highly desirable with respect to query answering and updates. We proved this by showing that it is bounded, the set of total tuples can be computed efficiently and it allows enforcement of constraints to be performed incrementally and cost-effectively.

With functional dependencies, the only class of database schemes that is proven to be bounded is the class of independent schemes [AtC][C1][IIK][S3]. Since γ-acyclic

BCNF database schemes are not independent in general, our result enlarges the class of known bounded database schemes.

The set of total tuples can be considered as the information content of a database [GMV][M][MUV][NG][S1]. We derived a simple and an efficient algorithm to generate the X-total projection for this class of schemes. This demonstrates that relationships among attributes are simple and answers to many queries can be computed very efficiently. Moreover, if a γ-acyclic BCNF scheme is lossless, then it is also ctf. Hence the class of γ-acyclic BCNF schemes is highly desirable with respect to query answering.

The problem of how to enforce constraints efficiently is a major problem in data management. In the context of the weak instance model, if we can find a cost-effective way to determine whether an updated state is consistent with the constraints, then this problem can be solved adequately. So far, the only class of database schemes that allows such enforcement of constraints is the class of independent schemes [GY][IIK][S1][S2]. In this paper, we showed that for γ-acyclic BCNF schemes, there is a simple and cost-effective way of determining if an updated state satisfies the set of fds embodied in the relation schemes. Unlike the incremental approach in [C2], our approach only needs to create indices on keys and no other data structure is required. Since relational systems allow indices to be created on keys, enforcement of fds can be carried out cost-effectively. γ-acyclic BCNF schemes are not independent schemes in general, hence our result extends the class of database schemes that allows efficient enforcement of constraints. This shows the desirability of this class of schemes with respect to updates.

Apparently to determine if a class of schemes is bounded or not is fundamental to the analysis of the behavior of the schemes with respect to query processing and updates. On the other hand, proving a class of database schemes is bounded seems to be very difficult, even in our restricted case of γ-acyclic BCNF schemes. To resolve this problem, we might need to develop other techniques for characterizing the bounded database schemes. An alternative approach is investigated in a forthcoming paper.

Acknowledgements

The first author's work was supported by the Natural Sciences and Engineering Research Council of Canada. The second author's work was supported by a Ph.D. Research Award from the Department of Computing Science, University of Alberta, and by the National Council of Science and Technology of Mexico (CONACYT).

References

[ABU] Aho, A.V., Beeri, C., Ullman, J.D. "The Theory of Joins in Relational Databases." *ACM TODS 4*, 3, September 1979, pp. 297-314.

[AtC] Atzeni, P., Chan E.P.F. "Efficient Query Answering in the Representative Instance Approach." *Proc. ACM PODS 1985*, pp. 181-188.

[B] Berge, C. *Graphs and Hypergraphs*. North-Holland, Amsterdam, The Netherlands, 1973.

[BB] Beeri, C., Bernstein, P.A. "Computational Problems Related to the Design of Normal Form Relational Schemas." *ACM TODS 4*, 1, March 1979, pp. 30-59.

[BBC] Bernstein, P.A., Blaustein, B.T., Clarke, E.M. "Fast Maintenance of Semantic Integrity Assertions using Redundant Aggregate Data." *Proc. VLDB 1980*, pp. 126-136.

[BBG] Beeri, C., Bernstein, P.A., and Goodman, N. "A Sophisticate's Introduction to Database Normalization Theory." *Proc. VLDB 1978*, pp. 113-124.

[BDB] Biskup, J., Dayal, U., and Bernstein, P.A. "Synthesizing Independent Database Schemas." *Proc. ACM-SIGMOD 1979*, Boston, Ma., pp. 143-151.

[BG] Bernstein, P.A., Goodman, N. "What Does Boyce-Codd Normal Form Do?" *Proc. VLDB 1980*, pp. 245-259.

[BV] Beeri, C., Vardi, M.Y. "A Proof Procedure for Data Dependencies." *JACM 31*, 4, October 1984, pp. 718-741.

[C1] Chan, E.P.F. "Optimal Computation of Total Projections with Unions of Simple Chase Join Expressions." *Proc. ACM-SIGMOD 1984*, Boston, Ma., pp. 149-163.

[C2] Chan, E.P.F. "An Incremental Approach to Testing Satisfaction of Functional Dependencies." Unpublished manuscript, University of Toronto, 1981.

[CA] Chan, E.P.F., Atzeni, P. "On the Properties and Characterization of Connection-trap-free Schemes." *Proc. PODS 1986*, pp. 140-147.

[CH] Chan, E.P.F., Hernańdez, H.J. "On the Desirability of γ-acyclic BCNF Database Schemes." Submitted to *Theoretical Computer Science*.

[CM] Chan, E.P.F., Mendelzon, A.O. "Answering Queries on the Embedded-complete Database Schemes." Unpublished manuscript, 1984.

[Co] Codd, E.F. "A Relational Model for Large Shared Data Banks." *CACM 13*, 6 (June 1970), pp. 377-387.

[Da] Date, C.J. *An Introduction to Database Systems*. 3rd. edition, Reading, Ma., Addison-Wesley, 1981.

[DM] D'Atri, A., Moscarini, M. "Acyclic Hypergraphs: Their Recognition and Top-down vs. Bottom-up Generation." *IASI-CNR, R.29*, Rome, Italy, 1982.

[F] Fagin, R. "Hypergraphs and Relational Database Schemes." *JACM 30*, 3, July 1983, pp. 514-550.

[GM] Graham, M.H., Mendelzon, A.O. "On Total Projections Computable by Relational Algebra." Unpublished manuscript, Department of Computer Science, University of Toronto, August 1982.

[GMV] Graham, M.H., Mendelzon, A.O., and Vardi, M.Y. "Notions of Dependency Satisfaction." *JACM 33*, 1, January 1986, pp. 105-129.

[GY] Graham, M.H., Yannakakis, M. "Independent Database Schemas." *JCSS* 28, pp. 121-141 (1984).

[H1] Honeyman, P. "Extension Joins." *Proc. VLDB 1980*, pp. 239-244.

[H2] Honeyman, P. "Testing Satisfaction of Functional Dependencies." *JACM 29*, 3, July 1982, pp. 668-677.

[IIK] Ito, M., Iwasaki, M., Kasami, T. "Some Results on the Representative Instance in Relational Databases." *SIAM J. of Computing 14*, 2 (1985), pp. 334-354.

[LeP] LeDoux, C.H., Parker, D.S. "Reflections on Boyce-Codd Normal Form." *Proc. VLDB 1982*, pp. 131-141.

[LO] Lucchesi, C.L., Osborn, S.L. "Candidate Keys for Relations." *JCSS 17*, 2, October 1978, pp. 270-279.

[M] Mendelzon, A.O. "Database States and their Tableaux." *ACM TODS 9*, 2, June 1984, pp. 264-282.

[Ma] Maier, D. *The Theory of Relational Databases.* Computer Science Press, 1983.

[MMS] Maier, D., Mendelzon, A.O., and Sagiv, Y. "Testing Implications of Data Dependencies." *ACM TODS 4*, 4, December 1979, pp. 455-469.

[MRW] Maier, D., Rozenshtein, D., Warren, D.S. "Windows On the World." *Proc. ACM-SIGMOD 1983*, pp. 68-78.

[MUV] Maier, D., Ullman, J.D., and Vardi, M.Y. "On the Foundations of the Universal Relation Model." *ACM TODS 9*, 2, June 1984, pp. 283-308.

[NG] Nicholas, J-M, Gallaire, H. "Data Bases: Theory vs Interpretation." *Logic and Data Bases*, Plenum Press, pp. 33-54.

[O] Osborn, S.L. "Testing for Existence of a Covering Boyce-Codd Normal Form." *IPL 8*, 1, January 1979, pp. 11-14.

[S1] Sagiv, Y. "Can We Use the Universal Instance Assumption Without Using Nulls?" *Proc. ACM-SIGMOD 1981*, pp. 108-120.

[S2] Sagiv, Y. "A Characterization of Globally Consistent Databases and their Correct Access Paths." *ACM TODS 8*, 2, June 1983, pp. 266-286.

[S3] Sagiv, Y. "Evaluation of Queries in Independent Database Schemes." Unpublished manuscript, 1984.

[St] Stonebraker, M.R. "Implementation of Integrity Constraints and Views by Query Modification." *Proc. ACM-SIGMOD 1975*, pp. 65-78.

[U] Ullman, J.D. *Principles of Database Systems.* 2nd. edition, Computer Science Press, 1982.

[V] Vassiliou, Y. "A Formal Treatment of Imperfect Information in Data Management." *CSRG TR-123*, University of Toronto, Nov. 1980.

[Y] Yannakakis, M. "Algorithms for Acyclic Database Schemes." *Proc. VLDB 1981*, pp. 82-94.

UPDATE SEMANTICS UNDER THE DOMAIN CLOSURE ASSUMPTION(*)

Laurence CHOLVY
ONERA-CERT-DERI
2, avenue Edouard Belin
B.P. 4025
31055 - TOULOUSE CEDEX (FRANCE)

ABSTRACT

The problem addressed in this paper is the characterization of the database state which results from an update. To reach this goal, we suppose that some transition constraints may be expressed.

We also assume that the set of objects which are manipulated in the database is finite, and the considered operation is not a domain modification.

Finally, we aim to define the update semantics in such a way that an update on two equivalent states leads to two equivalent resulting states.

The operations we consider are not restricted to facts, and may concern more general information.

1. INTRODUCTION

The problem addressed in this paper is the characterization of the database state which results from an update. This problem is generally called "update semantics".

We suppose that the information stored in the database is general, and not only factual [NIYA1][GMN]. From a formal point of view, this information is represented by first order formulas [CHLE]. We assume that the updates which are performed, concern any kind of formulas. So we place ourselves in the same context as [KUV][FUV] : considering the database under a formal representation (set of first

---

(*) This work was supported by the DRET under contract n° 86002.08.

order formulas), how to define an update, i.e. addition or deletion of a formula, or more complicated operation, and how to characterize the next database state ? We will consider that a formula is added if it can be deduced from the next state and if this state is consistent ; a formula is deleted if it can't be deduced from the next state and if this state is consistent.

However, our hypothesis differ on many points.

First, we are interested in determinism. The state following an update must be unique. Indeed, as it is shown in [FUV], there may be many possible states which satisfy the previous conditions. [FUV] [KUV] defined two ways to represent these possible states. [CHYA] suggested an integrated approach, using a temporal language for expressing this non determinism. Presently, we want a choice to be made among the different possible next states. To reach this goal, we assume that transition constraints [NICO] [CCF] may be expressed to choose the unique following state. If there is still non determinism (because no constraint is expressed, or because the constraints are not sufficient to characterize an unique state) then we will define the next state by the initial one, i.e. we will not take the update into account.

Secondly, we aim to define update semantics in such a way that the same update on two equivalent database states leads to two equivalent states (two sets of formulas are equivalent if they have the same models). This requirement is reasonable for any user who only knows the database by the answers of the queries he addresses. This user doesn't know how the data are stored, i.e. he hasn't have a syntactical view of the database and he is not able to distinguish two equivalent states. Suppose now that this user performs the same update on two equivalent states. He surely expects not to distinguish the resulting states, and he will be surprised if he obtains different answers to the same query. This is the reason why we want that the updates preserve the equivalence relation. Thus, in this paper, the update semantics is defined from a "semantical" point of view, and not from a syntactical point of view, as it is done in [FUV] [KUV], and in [CHOL]. In order to reach this goal, we consider the database under a normal form. This normal form is defined so that two equivalent sets have the same normal form. The update is then defined on this normal form. The same update on two equivalent sets thus leads to two equivalent (in fact identical) sets.

The following figure sums up this idea :

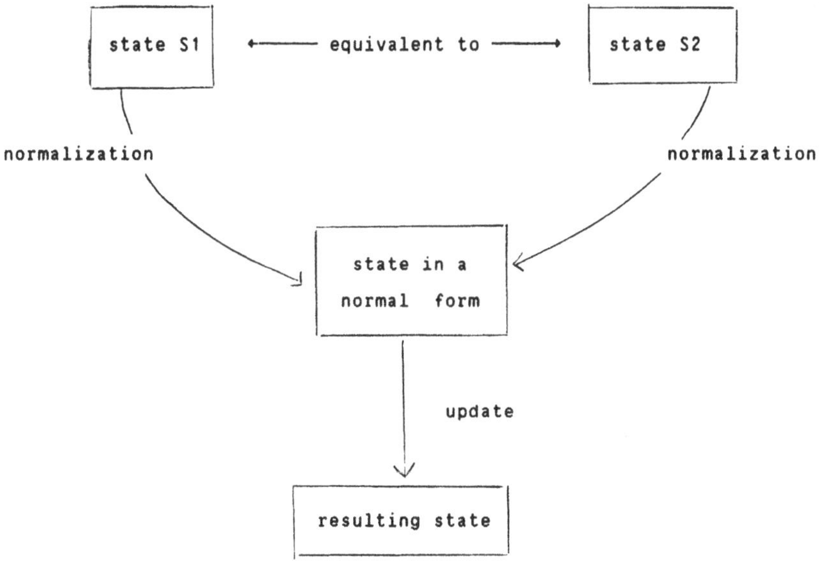

Finally, we suppose that the set of objects which are manipulated in the database is finite and that the considered operation is not a domain modification, i.e. is not the addition or deletion of a constant (closed domain). So we will assume that the same domain closure axiom [REIT] defines the manipulated objects in both the initial and next database states.

With regard to transition constraints, we restrict them in this paper, to formulas of a special modal language (with the "next" operator). In order to simplify the frame problem [CAHA] from a computational point of view, we assume they can't allow to deduce information about the initial state. So the constraints which are presently considered are not as general as the ones in [CCF] and [ELG]. However, this allows to give a constructive definition of the next state.

Furthermore, unlike [CCF][ELG], our approach is a proof-theoretic approach in the sense that the database is modelized by a set of formulas and the operations are not restricted to operations on facts.

The main subproblems we faced are :

- to find a suitable formalism to express the transition constraints,
- to take the frame problem into account, i.e. to determine the information which was available in the initial database state, and which remains available in the next state,

- to define formally the next database state, and define it constructivelly too.

Our idea is to find a formalism such that, we can express in the same language the knowledge available in the initial database state, the knowledge expressed by the constraints, the knowledge expressed by the update, and such that we can use the same inference rules to reason about these different kinds of knowledge. Furthermore, the main notion we want to deal with is "such formula will be theorem in the next state" which comes to indirectly manipulate sets of models. This can't be easily done in classical logic. And this is the reason why we turn to a modal formalism [HUCR]. Indeed, formalisms of this type have an appropriate semantics, in term of possible worlds (Kripke semantics) : an interpretation is a set of related worlds which can be seen as first order interpretations. The modal system we choose is such that its interpretation allows to represent the temporal relation between the set of models of the initial database state, and the set of models of the database state after the update. This formalism is described in section 2.

In section 3, we define the normal form of a set of formulas expressed in the previous language.

Section 4 addresses the update semantics problem. We first formally define the resulting state and then we show an algorithm to construct it. We consider elementary operations and more general ones as well.

2. THE FORMALISM

The formalism we use to represent the knowledge stored in the database, the operations, and the constraints as well, is a restriction of the first order modal theory Q [FARI1]. In this section, we quickly describe the syntax and the semantics of this system we will note Q' in this paper.

The language of Q is defined by the symbols of classical logic : constant symbols, variable symbols, predicate symbols, equality symbols, and one modal operator, that we will note "o" and call "next". (In general, Q is defined by two modal operators, usually noted by $\Box$ and $\Diamond$, but the second one is function of the first one : $\Diamond \equiv \neg\Box\neg$. So considering only one operator, $\Box$, is enough. Furthermore, we prefer to note it "o" because the semantics we attach to it in our particular case is almost the same that the one given in [MAPN] to operator "o". The rules which construct formulas of Q are the classical ones, and the following one : if A is a formula then oA is a formula.

As far as we are concerned, in system Q', we only consider a restriction of this language, and the formulas are defined by the following rules :

- an atomic first order formula is a first order formula,
- if A is a first order formula then $\neg A$ and $\forall x\ A$ are first order formulas,
- if A and B are both first order formulas then $A \wedge B$ is a first order formula,
- if A is a first order formula then oA is a modal formula,
- if A is a modal formula then $\neg A$ and $\forall x\ A$ are modal formulas,
- if A and B are both modal formulas then $A \wedge B$ is a modal formula,
- a first order formula is a formula,
- a modal formula is a formula.
- some other formulas $A \vee B$, $A \rightarrow B$, $A \leftrightarrow B$, $\exists x\ A$ are defined in the usual way.

So, in Q' formulas, an "o" occurrence is never governed by another one, and subformulas are exclusively first order, or exclusively modal. The first condition is intuitively explained by the fact that we don't want the transition constraints to concern the future states in general, but the immediate one. So they only constrain the transition between two states. The second condition is added in order to simplify the frame problem. And we don't want to deduce, with a transition constraint, information about the initial state, For example, we will not consider the constraint which expresses that if in the next state, we know that somebody is divorced, and in the initial state, we know that he was not divorced, then we can deduce that he was married in the initial state. (This is an interpretation of formula $\forall x\ (o\ d(x) \wedge \neg d(x) \longrightarrow m(x))$).

The axioms of modal theory Q are the classical logical axioms and

$$\begin{cases} o\neg A \rightarrow \neg oA \\ o(A \rightarrow B) \rightarrow (oA \rightarrow oB) \end{cases}$$

where A and B are formulas of Q.

The derivation rules are the classical ones (Modus Ponens, Generalization) and

(necessitation) $\dfrac{A}{oA}$ if A is a formula of Q

The axiomatisation of Q' is defined from the previous one, taking the limited form of Q' formulas into account, and taking into account the domain closure assumption. The axioms of Q' are then :

the logical axioms of predicate calculus with equality

$\forall x\ (x=a_1 \vee \ldots \vee x=a_n)$

$\neg a_1=a_2 \ \ldots \ \neg a_{n-1}=a_n$

$o(\neg A) \longrightarrow \neg oA$ where A and B are first order formulas

$o(A \rightarrow B) \longrightarrow (oA \rightarrow oB)$

The derivation rules are Modus Ponens, Generalization, and (necessitation) $\frac{A}{oA}$ where A is a first order formula.

Because of the necessitation rule, and because $\forall x\ x=a_1 \vee \ldots \vee x=a_n$ is a logical axiom of Q', $o(\forall x\ x=a_1 \vee \ldots\ x=a_n)$ is theorem of Q'. This expresses the domain closure assumption. The same remark holds for $o(\neg a_i = a_j)$ which express the preservation of the unique name axioms. Notice also that the Barcan formula $\forall x\ oA(x) \rightarrow o(\forall x\ A(x))$ holds in Q'.

The semantics of Q' is defined in terms of Kripke models. An interpretation is defined by $I=\langle D,w_o,W,F\rangle$ where :

- D is a set of n individuals, $a'_1 \ldots a'_n$
- wo is a world, (the initial one)
- W is a set of worlds
- F is an interpretation function :
  . for every constant symbol a : F(a) = a', where a' is an individual of D, and if a and b are two different constant symbols then $F(a) \neq F(b)$
  . for every m-ary predicate symbol P, but equality :
    $F(P) = \{\langle w,a'1,\ldots,a'm\rangle\} \subset (\{wo\} \cup W) \times D^m$
  . for equality : $F(=) = (\{wo\} \cup W) \times \text{diag}\ (D^2)$
  where $\text{diag}(D^2)$ denotes the diagonal of D x D.

An assignation AS is a function from the set of variables symbols to D.

The valuation of formulas under interpretation I, and assignation AS is defined by :

$V(P(t1,\ldots,tn),w) = 1 \iff \langle w,V(t1),\ldots,V(tn)\rangle \in F(P)$

where V(ti) = F(ti) if ti is a constant symbol

V(ti) = AS(ti) if ti is a variable symbol

$V(F1 \wedge F2,w) = 1 \iff V(F1,w) = 1$ and $V(F2,w) = 1$

$V(\neg F,w) = 1 \iff V(F,w) = 0$

$V(\forall x\ F(x),w) \iff \forall d \in \{a1...an\}\ V(F(d),w) = 1$

$V(oF,wo) = 1 \iff \forall w \in W \quad V(F,w) = 1$

($V(oF,w)$ is not defined for $w \in W$ because of the limited form of Q' formulas).

An interpretation I = <D,wo,W,F> is a model (or Q'-model) of a formula F iff V(F,wo) = 1, for every assignation. We will note M_F the set of Q'-models of F.

A formula F is Q'-valid iff every interpretation is one of its model.

The system Q' is sound and complete. The first property is proved by showing that every axiom of Q' is Q'-valid and that the derivation rules preserve this characteristic. The second property is proved by showing that every consistent formula is Q'-valid. Indeed, any formula of Q' may be associated to a modal propositional formula of system Q (see section 3). We can show that this transformation preserves the consistency. So, any consistant formula $\alpha_{Q'}$ of Q' may be associated to a modal propositional consistant formula α_Q of Q. Because Q is complete, there is a Q model of α_Q. From it, one can construct a Q' model of $\alpha_{Q'}$.

One must also notice that the axiomatization of Q' preserve the special form of Q' formulas, i.e. every formula which can be derived by derivation rules, belongs to the restricted language of Q'.

3. DEFINITIONS

In this section, we first define a normal form of a set of first order formulas. We show that this normal form is representative of an equivalence class of sets of formulas (according to the equivalence relation between sets of formulas). We then define a function which associates to any set of modal formulas of Q' a set of modal propositional formulas of Q.

3.1 - AN EQUIVALENT SET OF GROUND CLAUSES

Let us first consider the following function NO, which associates a first order formula of Q' to an equivalent propositional formula.

$NO(\forall x\ F(x)) = NO(F(a1) \wedge ... \wedge F(an))$

$NO(\neg F) = \neg NO(F)$

$NO((ai=aj) \wedge F) = \Lambda$

$NO(\neg(ai=ai) \wedge F) = \Lambda$

] where Λ is the empty formula

$NO(ai=ai \wedge F) = NO(F)$

$NO(\neg ai=aj \wedge F) = NO(F)$

$NO(F \wedge G) = NO(F) \wedge NO(G)$ if neither F nor G is $ai=ai$, $\neg ai=aj$, $ai=aj$, $\neg ai=ai$.

$NO(Fp)=Fp$ if Fp is an atomic formula with no variable symbol

Proposition : For any first order formula F, NO(F) is equivalent to F.

The proof is obtained by induction on the depth of a formula, and by noting that, since $\forall x\ (x=a1 \vee \ldots \vee x=an)$ is a domain closure axiom, $\forall x\ F(x) \longleftrightarrow F(a1) \wedge \ldots \wedge F(an)$ is a theorem of Q'.

At the end of the recursive application of NO, on a first order formula F, we obtain a formula whose elementary (atomic) formulas don't contain variable symbol nor equality symbol. After renaming its atomic formulas, this formula can be considered as a propositional one. So, the transformation ensures that every first order formula can be transformed in an equivalent propositional formula. (If we suppose that a propositional formula, obtained after renaming a first order formula with no variable symbol, is equivalent to it).

Let us note N1(F) the set of ground clauses obtained from NO(F) by writing it under a conjonctive form.

Proposition :

. for any first order formula F : N1(F) is equivalent to F.

. let F1 and F2 be two equivalent formulas. Then N1(F1) and N1(F2) are equivalent.

For example, let $(\forall x\ x=john \vee x=peter \vee x=phil)$ be one of the closure domain axioms of Q'. Then the formula $(\exists x\ father(x\ john))$ is equivalent to the set $\{(A \vee B \vee C)\}$, if A,B,C denote respectively father(john,john), father(peter,john), father(phil,john).

3.2 - A NORMAL FORM OF A GROUND CLAUSES SET

Let us consider now a finite set S of ground clauses. Let $S^{(1)}$ be the saturated set obtained from S by a recursive application of the rule (R1) : $S \cup \{A \vee B, \neg A \vee C\} \Rightarrow S \cup \{A \vee B, \neg A \vee C, B \vee C\}$ (where A is a literal, and B and C are clauses). $S^{(1)}$ is finite [LOVE]. Let N2(S) be the set obtained from $S^{(1)}$ by deleting the tautologies, and the subsumed clauses (these process are decidable since clauses are propositional). N2(S) is of course finite.

Proposition : Let S1 and S2 two equivalent sets of propositional clauses.
Then N2(S1) = N2(S2)

Proof :

To prove this theorem, we should note that N2(S) could also be defined by the following non constructive way :

First, construct $S^{(1)}$, the saturated set obtained from S by applying (R1).

Then consider $S^{(2)}$, the saturated set obtained from $S^{(1)}$ by applying (R1) extended with the condition $A=\phi$ (i.e. with the rule S U {B}, => S U {B,BVC}). $S^{(2)}$ is infinite.

Then add to $S^{(2)}$ all the propositional tautologies. Let $S^{(3)}$ be the resulting infinite set.

Finally, remove from $S^{(3)}$ all the tautologies and the subsumed clauses. Let $S^{(4)}$ be this set.

It is obvious that $S^{(4)}$ = N2(S).

Furthermore $S^{(3)}$ is the set of all the clauses which are theorems of S.

Indeed, let C be a clause which is theorem of S.

a) C is a tautology. Then $C \in S^{(3)}$.

b) C is not a tautology. Let us note C = C1 V...V Cn where Ci are litterals (positive or not).

S U {¬C1...¬Cn} is inconsistent

=> ∃ p≤n, S U {¬C1...¬Cp} is refutable by (R1) (completness of ground resolution [LOVE])

=> there is a R1-derivation which leads to C1 V...V Cp as a resolvent

=> C1 V...V Cp $\in S^{(2)}$

=> C1 V...V Cn $\in S^{(3)}$.

Let S1 and S2 be two equivalent sets of ground clauses. Then :

$S_1^{(3)} = S_2^{(3)}$. Thus $S_1^{(4)} = S_2^{(4)}$ i.e. N2(S1) = N2(S2)

3.3 - A NORMAL FORM OF A FIRST ORDER FORMULA SET

We define the normal form N(F) of a first order formula by the set of ground clauses N(F) = N2(N1(F)).

Proposition : two equivalent formulas have the same normal form.

Proof : Let F1 and F2 be equivalent formulas. Then N1(F1) and N1(F2) are equivalent (cf. § 3.1). So $N2(N1(F_1)) = N2(N1(F_2))$ (cf. § 3.2). This property justifies the term "normal form".

In the same way we define the normal forme N(S) of a finite set S of first order formulas, by $N(S) = N(\bigwedge_{F \in S} F)$

Proposition : two equivalent sets have the same normal form.

Example :

Let (∀x x=john V x=peter V x=phil) be one of the domain closure axioms of Q'. Let S = {∃x father(x,john), ∀x ∀y father(x,y) → ¬x=y} , N1(S) = {A V B V C, ¬A, D, E} where A, B, C, D, E respectively represent father(john,john), father(peter,john), father(phil,john), ¬father(peter,peter), ¬father(phil,phil). Then N(S) = (B V C, ¬A, D, E}.

3.4 - AN EQUIVALENT MODAL PROPOSITIONAL CLAUSES SET

In this section, we extend the definition of function N0, to modal formulas of Q' by N0(oF) = o(N0(F)), where F is a first order formula.

Then N0(F) is still equivalent to F in Q'. The proof is completed by induction of the depth of a formula F under the o operator, and by noting that o(∀x F(x)) ⟷ oF(a1) Λ... oF(an) is a theorem in Q'.

So a set S of modal formulas of Q' can be transformed in a set of modal propositional formulas, N0(S). Furthermore this set can be normalized in an equivalent set of clauses of the form oC1 V...V oCn V ¬o¬(D1 Λ...Λ Dp), where Ci and Di are propositional clauses [FARI1]. Let us call N1(S), this set of modal ground clauses.

For example, if ∀x (x=john V x=peter V x=phil) is the domain closure axiom, the formula ∀x (o married(x) → ¬o bachelor(x)) is equivalent to the set of clauses {¬o(A1 Λ A2), ¬o(B1 Λ B2), ¬o(C1 Λ C2)} where Ai,Bi,Ci denote respectively bachelor(john), married(john), bachelor(peter), married(peter), bachelor(phil), married (phil).

4. UPDATE SEMANTICS

In this section, we intend to give a formal definition of the state which results from an update on an initial database state. We will first restrict the operation to an elementary one. That is, if a database state is formally represented by a set of first order formulas, we first consider the addition of a formula to this set, or the deletion of a formula from this set. At the end of the section, we extend our results to non elementary operation which consist in many elementary ones.

4.1 - FORMAL DEFINITION OF THE RESULTING STATE

Let $\mathcal{T}o$ be the consistent finite set of first order closed formulas representing the initial state of the database.

Let $\mathcal{C}$ be the consistent finite set of modal closed formulas of Q', representing the transition constraints which must be satisfied when the database is updated.

Let σ be the formula which is added to (or deleted from) $\mathcal{T}o$.

Let us note :

TO=N($\mathcal{T}o$) the normal form set of $\mathcal{T}o$

OP=N1(oσ) in the addition case

OP=N1($\neg$oσ) in the deletion case

C=N1($\mathcal{C}$)

res(**OP**,$\mathcal{T}$**o**) the resulting database state, we want to construct.

We define the intermediate theory

$$T' = \mathbf{TO} \cup \mathbf{C} \cup \mathbf{OP} \cup \{oF : F \in \mathbf{TO} \text{ and } \mathbf{C} \cup \mathbf{OP} \not\vdash \neg oF\}$$

Notice that this definition is constructive : the subproblem consisting in testing if a formula $\neg$oF is not a theorem of **C** U **OP** is decidable [FARI1][FARI2].

Proposition : $\mathcal{M}_{TO} = \mathcal{M}_{\{F\ :\ F \text{ is first order and } T' \vdash F\}}$

The proof is obvious by noting that the first order theorems of T' are the theorems of **TO**. Indeed, formulas of **C** U **OP**, have no non-modal subformulas.

This property means that, as far as the initial database state is concerned, T' represents exactly the same knowledge that **TO**.

T' also represents information about the update ((oσ) or ($\neg$oσ)), constraints (**C**), and information which was available in the initial database state and whose availability in the next state is not inconsistent with the update and the constraints. This last condition expresses a kind of a frame problem [CAHA].

T' can be inconsistent for many reasons :

a) T' is inconsistent because (oσ), or (¬oσ), is inconsistent in Q'. This case happens when one wants to add a contradiction, or delete a tautology.

b) T' is inconsistent because **C** ∪ **OP** is inconsistent. This means that the operation contradicts the constraints.

c) T' is inconsistent although **C** ∪ **OP** is consistent. This means that, in **C** ∪ **OP**, one can derive a formula ¬oF1 V...V ¬oFn, and oF1,...,oFn have been added because ∀i i=1...n, Fi ∈ **TO** and **C** ∪ **OP** ⊬ ¬oFi. The fact that ¬oF1 V...V ¬oFn is a theorem of **C** ∪ **OP**, but no ¬oFi is a theorem, means that one of the formulas F1...Fn must be deleted from **TO**, but the choice is not fixed.

For example, let (∀x x=john V x=peter) be the domain closure axiom. Let *To* = {∀x (bachelor(x) V married(x)), ¬married(john), ¬married (peter)}, *C* = ∅, and consider the deletion of the formula ∀x bachelor (x).

TO = {bachelor(john), bachelor(peter),¬married(john), ¬married(peter)}

OP = {¬o(bachelor(john) Λ bachelor(peter)}

We can prove that **OP** ⊬ ¬o bachelor(john)

OP ⊬ ¬o bachelor(peter)

OP ⊬ ¬o¬married(john)

OP ⊬ ¬o¬married(peter)

So T' = **TO** ∪ **OP** ∪ {o bachelor(john), o bachelor(peter), o ¬married(john), o¬married(peter)}

T' is inconsistent because its subset {¬o (bachelor(john) Λ bachelor (peter)), o bachelor(john), o bachelor(peter)} is inconsistent. Intuitively, this means that the information bachelor(john) Λ bachelor(peter) can't be valid in the next state, i.e. bachelor (john) and bachelor(peter) can't be both valid in the next state. One of these formulas must be deleted but we don't know which one.

If T' is inconsistent, we consider that the operation is forbidden. And we define the resulting state res(**OP**,**TO**) = **TO**.

Let us now consider that T' is consistent.

Because of the semantics of "o" operator, the set of formulas F such that $\vdash_{Q'}$ (T' → oF) (i.e. such that oF is a thesis of T') represents the information which is supposed to be true in the next state, according to the information of the initial state, the constraints and the operation. So it is logical to require that the resulting state res(**OP**,**TO**) satisfies the following condition :

$$\mathcal{M}_{res(\mathbf{OP},\mathbf{TO})} = \mathcal{M}_{\{F,\ T' \vdash oF\}}$$

One can notice that this condition doesn't characterize an unique set of formulas but a theory. It doesn't provide a constructive definition of the resulting state.

In the next section we define an algorithm which constructs a finite set res(**OP**,**TO**) equivalent to {F : T' ⊢oF} and in normal form.

4.2 - CONSTRUCTIVE DEFINITION OF THE RESULTING THEORY

We first define a finite set T" equivalent to T' obtained from T' by saturating it with the following rules [FARI1] :

Let A be a literal
B1,B3 be propositional clauses
B5 be a conjunction of propositional clauses
B2,B4 be modal clauses

(R'1) : S U {o(A V B1) V B2 ; o(¬A V B3) V B4} =>
S U {o(A V B1) V B2 ; o(¬A V B3) V B4 ; o(B1 V B3) V B2 V B4}
with the particular case
S U {oA V B2 ; o¬A V B4} => S U {oA V B2, o¬A V B4, B2 V B4}

(R'2) : S U {o(A V B1) V B2 ; ¬o¬((¬A V B3) Λ B5) V B4)} =>
S U {o(A V B1) V B2 ; ¬o¬((¬A V B3) Λ B5) V B4 ; ¬o¬((B1 V B3) Λ B5) V B2 V B4}
with the particular case
S U {oA V B2 ; ¬o¬(¬A Λ B5) V B4} => S U {oA V B2 ; ¬o¬(¬A Λ B5) V B4; B2 V B4}

(R'3) : S U {¬o¬((A V B1) Λ (¬A V B3) Λ B5) V B2} =>
S U {¬o¬((A V B1) Λ (¬A V B3) Λ B5) V B2 ; ¬o¬((B1 V B3) Λ B5) V B2}
with the particular case
S U{¬o¬(A Λ ¬A Λ B5) V B2} => S U {¬o¬(A Λ ¬A Λ B5) V B2 ; B2}

(R'4) : S U {o(A V A V B1) V B2 } => S U {o(A V A V B1) V B2, o(A V B1) V B2}
S U {B1 V B1 V B2} => S U {B1 V B1 V B2, B1 V B2}

T" is finite (indeed, the initial set of litterals is finite, the rules don't generate new literals, so the set of all possible clauses defined with these literals, is finite).

Proposition : $\mathcal{M}_{T''} = \mathcal{M}_{T'}$

The proof is obvious since the saturation introduces only logical consequences.

We then define res(**OP**,**TO**) from {F : oF ∈ T"} by deleting the tautologies and the subsumed clauses. The following proposition ensures that res(**OP**,**TO**) satisfies the condition expressed at the end of § 4.).

Proposition : $\mathcal{M}_{res(\mathbf{OP},\mathbf{TO})} = \mathcal{M}_{\{F\ :\ T' \vdash oF\}}$

Proof :

a) Let F res(**OP**,**TO**)

=> oF ∈ T"

=> T" ⊢ oF

=> T' ⊢ oF (because of the previous proposition)

=> res(**OP**,**TO**) C {F : T' ⊢ OF}

=> $\mathcal{M}${F : T' ⊢ oF} ⊂ $\mathcal{M}$ res(**OP**,**TO**)

b) Let F such that T' ⊢ oF. We show that res(**OP**,**TO**) ⊢ F.
Let us suppose that F is not a tautology, and note oF = o(F1 V...V Fn) (this is the elementary case because any formula oF is equivalent to a set of formulas o(F1 V...V Fn)

Let F1 V... Fp a minimal subformula of F1 V... Fn such that T' ⊢ o(F1 V... Fp)
=> T" ⊢ o(F1 V... Fp)
=> T" U {¬o(F1 V... Fp)} is inconsistent
=> T" U {¬o(F1 V... Fp)} is refutable by the rules R'1, R'2, R'3.

(This result comes from an adaptation in our case of the result of [FARI1]. In this paper, Farinas presents a complete resolution method for modal logic (system Q). We adapted the resolution rules considering the particular form of the formulas we manipulate).

Thus there is a derivation which products o(F1 V... Fp) as a resolvent
=> o(F1 V...V Fp) ∈ T"
And because F1 V...V Fp is a minimal formula such that T' ⊢ o(F1 V...V Fp), it is not subsumed in {F : oF ∈ T"}. Thus it belongs to res(OP,TO)
=> res(**OP**,**TO**) ⊢ (F1 V...V Fn)

This proves that $M_{res(\mathbf{OP},\mathbf{TO})} \subset M_{\{F\ :\ T' \vdash OF\}}$

Example :

Let us take again the example defined in § 4.1, and consider the constraint "when one deletes the fact that everybody is bachelor, then, for everybody, one must delete the fact that he is bachelor" :

$C = \{\neg o(\forall x\ bachelor(x)) \rightarrow \forall x\ (\neg o\ bachelor(x))\}$

T' = {bachelor(john), bachelor(peter), ¬married(john), ¬married(peter)
¬o(bachelor(john) ∧ bachelor(peter))
¬o bachelor(john) ∨ o bachelor(peter)
¬o bachelor(peter) ∨ o bachelor(john)
o¬married(john), o¬married(peter)}

Indeed, because of the constraint, **C** U **OP** $\vdash$ ¬o bachelor(john) and
C U **OP** $\vdash$ ¬o bachelor(peter).
Thus T" = T' U {¬o bachelor(john), ¬o bachelor(peter)}
and res(**OP**,**TO**) = {married(john), married(peter)}.

4.3 - EXTENSIONS : NON ELEMENTARY OPERATIONS

In the previous sections, we focused on elementary operations by limiting an update to the addition or the deletion of a first order formula. The results can easily be extended in the case when the operation is not elementary but composed by several additions, and/or deletions. Notice that the notion of batch operation presented in [KUV] is a particular case since a batch operation is defined by several simultaneous additions, or by several simultaneous deletions.

Let $o\sigma 1 \wedge \ldots \wedge o\sigma n \wedge \neg o\sigma n{+}1 \wedge \ldots \neg o\sigma n{+}m$ be the modal formula representing the extended operation "addition of σ1 and... addition of σn and deletion of σn+1... and deletion of σn+m", and (**OP**) be the set of propositional modal formulas which is equivalent to this formula. The definition of T' and the process which has been adopted in the previous section remains valid.

Proposition :
Let **OP** be the propositional set equivalent to $o\tau 1 \wedge \ldots \wedge o\tau n$ in the case of the non elementary operation which consists in additions of formulas τ1...τn.
Let **OP'** be the propositional set equivalent to $o(\tau 1 \wedge \ldots \wedge \tau n)$ in the case of elementary operation which consists in the addition of formula $\tau 1 \wedge \ldots \tau n$.
Then res(**OP**,**TO**) = res(**OP'**,**TO**).

The proof is obvious since $o(F \wedge G) \leftrightarrow (oF \wedge oG)$ is a theorem of Q.

This property means that simultaneous additions of formulas is equivalent to addition of their conjunction.

However, a similar property for deletion is not true.

Proposition :
Let **OP** = $\neg o\tau1\wedge...\wedge\neg o\tau n$ in the case of the non elementary operation which consists in deletions of formulas $\tau1,...,\tau n$.
Let **OP'** = $\neg o(\tau1\vee...\vee\tau n)$ in the case of the elementary operation which consists in deletion of formula $\tau1\vee...\vee\tau n$. Then one can't affirm that

res(**OP**,**TO**) ⊂ res (**OP'**,**TO**) or res (**OP'**,**TO**) ⊂ res(**OP**,**TO**)

res(**OP**,**TO**) ⊄ res(**OP'**,**TO**) is proved by the example : **TO** = {p(a) V p(b)}, C = ∅, **OP** = {¬o p(a),¬o p(b)} and **OP'** = {¬o(p(a) V p(b))}. In this case : res(**OP**,**TO**) = {p(a) V p(b)} and res(**OP'**,**TO**) = ∅.

res(**OP'**,**TO**) ⊄ res(**OP**,**TO**) is proved by the example : **TO** = {p(a),p(b)}, C = ∅, **OP** = {¬o p(a), ¬o p(b)} and **OP'** = {¬o(p(a) V p(b))}. In this case : res(**OP**,**TO**) = ∅ and res(**OP'**,**TO**) = {p(a),p(b)}.

4.4 - REMARKS

The algorithm we presented is not optimized in the sense that T" is constructed without taking the formulas which are added or deleted, into account. In most case, considering the entire database state, and all the transition constraints, is not necessary. So in an optimized approach, the construction of T" (thus the construction of **TO** and **C**) would be minimal. This problem that we did not examine, here, is a well known problem of constraints verification optimization [NICO], and must of course be solved.

CONCLUSION

We present an algorithm to construct the database state which results from an update on an initial database state. This algorithm comes from a formal study of the problem, in a proof theoretic approach, which is to our opinion, attractive. Indeed, up to now, transition constraints have been studied in a model theoretic approach, and on another hand, the studies of database from a proof theoretic point of view didn't care about the transition constraints.

Furthermore, because the updates are defined on normal forms of the database states, we insure that the same update on two equivalent states leads to two equivalent (identical) states, which is an interesting property.

Concerning the hypothesis on which our work is based, although the closed domain is a realistic condition, it would be interesting to take more general constraints into account, and in particular constraints referring to the initial state. But this broadening will set the frame problem up, in a new way.

Acknowledgements : I'd like to thank Luis FARINAS DEL CERRO who helpfully advised me, and Pascal OSTERMANN for his comments.

BIBLIOGRAPHY

[CAHA] J. Mc CARTHY, P. HAYES : "Some philosophical problems from the standpoint or artificial intelligence", Machine Intelligence, n° 4, 1969, The University Press

[CCF] CASTILHO, CASANOVA, FURTADO : "A temporal frameworks for database specifications", Proc. VLDB, 1982

[CHLE] C. CHANG, R. LEE : "Symbolic logic and mechanical theorem proving", Academic Press

[CHOL] L. CHOLVY : "A modal approach to update semantics problem", Submitted to DS2

[CHYA] L. CHOLVY, K. YAZDANIAN : "Bases de données relationnelles et modélisation des actions", Rapport DERI n° 2/3245, 1986

[ELG] H.D. EHRICH, U.W. LIPECK, M. GOGELLA : "Specification, semantics and enforcement of dynamic database constraints", Proc. VLDB 1984

[FARI1] L. FARINAS DEL CERRO : "A simple deduction method for modal logic", Information Processing Letters, vol. 14 n° 2, april 1982

[FARI2] L. FARINAS DEL CERRO : "MOLOG : a system that extends PROLOG with modal logic"

[FARI3] L. FARINAS DEL CERRO : "Resolution modal logic", Logique et analyse, Juin-septembre 1985.

[FUV] R. FAGIN, J.D. ULLMAN, M.Y. VARDI : "On the semantics of updates in databases", Proc. ACM RODS 1983

[GMN] H. GALLAIRE, J. MINKER, J.-M. NICOLAS : "Logic and databases : a deductive approach", Computer Surveys, vol. 16 n° 2

[HUCR] G.E. HUGHES, M.J. CRESSWELL : "An introduction to modal logic", Methren London and New York

[KUV] G.M. KUPPER, J.D. ULLMAN, M.Y. VARDI : "On the equivalence of logical databases", Internal Report

[LOVE] D.W. LOVELAND : "Automated theorem proving. A logical basis", North Holland, 1978

[MAPN] Z. MANNA, A. PNUELI : "The modal logic of programs", Lecture notes in Computer Science n° 71, 1979

[NICO] J.-M. NICOLAS : "Contributions à l'étude théorique des bases de données : apports de la logique mathématique", Thèse ENSAE, Toulouse, 1979

[NIYA1] J.-M. NICOLAS, K. YAZDANIAN : "An outline of BDGEN", Proc. of IFIP 1983

[REIT] R. REITER : "Towards a logical reconstruction of relational database theory on conceptual modelling", Springer Verlag

Unsolvable Problems Related To The View Integration Approach*

Bernhard Convent

Universität Dortmund
Informatik VI
Postfach 500 500
4600 Dortmund 50
Federal Republic of Germany

Abstract. View integration is a method that should help to manage the complexity of design problems for extensive database applications with many different user groups. For each such user group the requirements and expectations are separately specified as simple view database schemes, which are subsequently integrated into a global scheme that is able to support all views.
In this paper we present a simple, formal specification method for view integration, which is used as a theoretical basis to show some severe computational limits of computer-aided view integration. Particularly, we prove that conflictfreeness of a set of views is undecidable and furthermore, we show that finite logical implication is undecidable for a simple class of integrity and integration constraints, which we believe to be essential to any reasonable integration method.

1. INTRODUCTION

One of the most difficult tasks in usual database applications is the design of an appropriate database scheme. So, according to a generally accepted methodology the complicated and time-consuming database design process is divided into several design steps [YNW], [Lum], [TeFr], [Nava].

In the first step, called requirements analysis, the information and processing requirements of each user group are analysed, collected and formally specified.

In the second step, these specified requirements are used to construct a small (view) database scheme for each user group, representing its appropriate view of the whole application. In this step, called view modelling, a conceptual data model is used, which should be independent of any concrete database management system.

The task of the next step is to construct a global database scheme that can support all different views. This global database scheme makes it possible to maintain all the

---

* This research was supported by the Deutsche Forschungsgemeinschaft under grant number Bi 311/1-1.

needed information within a single, global, centralized database, instead of having several independent small view databases, which would cause severe redundancy and inconsistency problems. So, in the view integration step all user views are analysed and merged, in order to construct such a global database scheme for the centralized, common database.

The above three steps, often referred to as conceptual design, cover the machine-independent, application-near parts of the design process, whereas the next two steps depend on the database management system chosen for the application.

In the next step, called implementation design, the global database scheme is refined and reconstructed to become a processible scheme of the target database management system.

In the last step, the physical design, an appropriate storage structure is chosen on the physical level of the target database management system to guarantee an efficient implementation of the whole application.

In the last years, many attempts based on the above methodology have been made to support the whole design process or single steps by computer-aided design tools (see e.g. DATAID [Ceri,AAL], TAXIS [MBGW] and DDEW [ReBr]). In this paper, we focus on the view integration step [NaGa], [BLM], [CaVi], [NEL], [BiCo].

View integration can itself be divided into two phases:

- Analysis and Specification: All the given user views are analysed in order to specify the connections and relationships between them and to detect possible conflicts.
- Integration: Considering the specified connections and relationships, all views are integrated into a global scheme for the centralized database that should be able to support all the different user groups.

We will consider two problems any computer-aided view integration tool will probably have to face. One is related to the analysis and specification phase whereas the other corresponds to the integration phase. First, given a specification consisting of several view schemes and their connections and relationships, it is an essential task to support the designer in detecting possible conflicts between the views. Second, when merging the views, it is often necessary to test whether a given set of integrity constraints and integration constraints, which specify the connections between the views, logically imply another given set of constraints.

As the main results, we will show that both problems in general are unsolvable under some natural assumptions, concerning the possibilities to specify integrity constraints within single views and to specify the connections between several views. Our results point out very clearly the computational limits of any reasonable computer-aided view integration support.

The paper is organized as follows. In Section 2, we carefully develop and motivate a formal specification method for view integration which forms the theoretical basis, needed for the formal unsolvability proofs. In Section 3, we show that finite logical implication is undecidable for the used class of integrity and integration constraints, and in Section 4, we reduce the decision problem of finite logical implication to the decision problem of conflictfreeness, showing that conflictfreeness is undecidable, too. Section 5 concludes this paper by pointing out some open problems and directions for further research.

2. A FORMAL SPECIFICATION METHOD FOR VIEW INTEGRATION

2.1. PRELIMINARIES

In the following, we first present some basic definitions and notational conventions, used throughout the paper.

Let **U** be a fixed finite set of attributes. An ordered subset X={A1,...,An}⊂**U** will be represented as X=A1...An, i.e., as a word over **U**. For two ordered subsets X,Y⊂**U** the assertion X⊂Y, respectively X∩Y=∅, will hold, if the same assertion holds for the corresponding unordered sets. Furthermore, we abbreviate the ordered union of two such disjoint sets X,Y⊂**U** by XY with the obvious new order in X∪Y, where the attributes of X come first, followed by the elements of Y. For convenience, we assume that all attributes correspond to the same domain **DOM**, a countable set of values.

Let X⊂**U** be an ordered set of attributes. A tuple t over X is an element t∈$\mathbf{DOM}^{|X|}$, where the i-th attribute of X is associated with the i-th value of t. A relation scheme R[X] consists of the relation name R and an ordered set X⊂**U** of attributes. A relation r over X is a finite set of tuples over X. A database scheme D=<**R**|**C**> consists of the name D, a finite set of relation schemes **R**={R1[X1],...,Rn[Xn]} and a finite set **C** of integrity constraints over **R**. A database d=(r1,...,rn) over **R** associates each relation scheme Ri[Xi] with a relation ri over Xi.

Integrity constraints are a formal means to distinguish between meaningful and meaningless databases with respect to the real world. They are used to specify time-invariable properties of the real world that any meaningful database must satisfy. Here, we concentrate on the probably most natural classes of integrity constraints, namely functional and inclusion dependencies. A functional dependency over **R** [Codd2] is an expression of the form Ri:Y->Z, where Y,Z⊂Xi. Such a dependency is satisfied by a database d=(r1,...,rn) over **R**, iff for all t,t'∈ri: t[Y]=t'[Y] ==> t[Z]=t'[Z]. This is denoted by d∈sat(Ri:Y->Z). An inclusion dependency over **R** [CFP] is of the form Ri[Y]⊂Rj[Z], where Y⊂Xi, Z⊂Xj and |Y|=|Z|. A database d=(r1,...,rn) over **R** satisfies such a dependency, denoted by d∈sat(Ri[Y]⊂Rj[Z]), iff ri[Y]⊂rj[Z].

Now, let D=<**R**|**C**> be a database scheme. A database d over **R** that satisfies all integrity constraints in **C** (i.e., d∈sat(**C**):=$\bigcap_{c \in \mathbf{C}}$ sat(c)) is called an instance or a valid database of D. The set of all valid databases of D is denoted by I(D).

Beyond these notational conventions and fundamental definitions, we assume a basic knowledge of database theory, as for instance can be found in [Ullm] and [Maie].

2.2. VIEW SCHEMES AND INTEGRATION CONSTRAINTS

In this paragraph, we present a formal method for specifying view database schemes and their connections and relationships. The here presented approach is only a proper subset of the specification method developed by Biskup/Convent [BiCo] and hence, it is rather simple and most likely not expressive enough to be used in all real world applications.

However, our goal in this paper is somewhat different. We do not want to present an in detail elaborated specification method, but instead, we try to collect and formalize those notions which we believe to be most natural and essential to any such approach. Then the unsolvability results, to be presented in Section 3 and 4, will apply to any integration approach, having at least the expressiveness of our simple, straightforward version. For a more detailed specification and integration method, extending this simple approach, the reader is referred to [BiCo].

First, we present what we believe to be most important for modelling views. Any reasonable specification method should allow specifying objects (entities or relationships) of the real world, each identified by a unique key. Furthermore, the specification of inclusion relationships that are going via keys should be allowed, which are for instance needed to describe IS-A hierarchies.

As already indicated, our specification method is based on the relational data model [Codd1], additionally using functional and inclusion dependencies (FDs and INDs). We restrict the use of these integrity constraints to the most essential cases where only one key dependency can be specified for each relation and only 'key-respecting inclusion dependencies' are allowed. This leads to the following definition of what we call 'proper database schemes'.

Definition 2.1. Let $D=\langle \mathbf{R}|\mathbf{C}\rangle$ be a database scheme. D is called a proper database scheme, iff for all relation schemes $Ri[Xi]\in\mathbf{R}$ there is a pair (Ki,Pi) of identifying attributes Ki and property attributes Pi, where $Ki\cap Pi=\emptyset$, KiPi=Xi such that

- for all $Rj[Xj]\in\mathbf{R}$:
  Rj:Kj->Pj is the only FD in **C** corresponding to Rj;
- for all $Rj[Y]\subset Rl[Z]\in\mathbf{C}$:
  $j\neq l$ and ($(Y=Kj$ and $(Z\subset Kl$ or $Z\subset Pl))$ or $(Z=Kl$ and $(Y\subset Kj$ or $Y\subset Pj))$).

Example 2.2. Assume, a trading company is selling a number of articles to its customers. A proper database scheme specifying its basic information needs might be $D=\langle \mathbf{R}|\mathbf{C}\rangle$, defined by

R: Articles: | *Article | Name | Price

Customers: | *Customer | Address

Orders: | *Order | *Customer | Delivery-date

Order-contents: | *Order | *Article | Qty

C: Articles: *Article->Name Price
Customers: *Customer->Address
Orders: *Order->*Customer Delivery-date
Order-contents: *Order *Article->Qty

Orders[*Order]⊂Order-contents[*Order]
Orders[*Customer]⊂Customers[*Customer]
Order-contents[*Order]⊂Orders[*Order]
Order-contents[*Article]⊂Articles[*Article] .

Now suppose a set of proper database schemes is given, each representing a special user group's view of the same real world application. Of course, there are many kinds of possible relationships and connections between those views that have to be analysed and specified before integration. Statements, describing such time-invariable connections are called integration constraints.

What we believe to be most natural, is that two such views see the same information on some real world object. This will formally be described by an identity constraint. Of course, identity constraints alone cannot be sufficient to capture all possible relationships between a set of views, but again, we solely concentrate on this most important case and will show that already simple identity constraints, as a restricted special type of integration constraints, in general will cause computational problems in detecting conflicts between the views.

First, we describe the formal syntax of identity constraints.

Definition 2.3. Let V1, ..., Vn be a set of proper database schemes, each representing a different view.
An identity constraint over V1, ..., Vn is a statement of the form 'Ri id Rj', where Ri and Rj belong to different views, |Xi|=|Xj| and additionally |Ki|=|Kj|.

To give the semantics of identity constraints, we introduce the notion of a combination of views with respect to a set **I** of identity constraints.

Definition 2.4. Let V1=<**R1**|**C1**>, ..., Vn=<**Rn**|**Cn**> be a set of proper database schemes with pairwise disjoint sets of relation schemes. Furthermore, let **I** be a finite set of identity constraints over V1, ..., Vn.
The combination of V1, ..., Vn with respect to **I** is the extended database scheme Comb(V1,...,Vn,**I**):=<**R**|**C**|**I**>, where

$\mathbf{R} := \bigcup_{i=1..n} \mathbf{Ri}$ and $\mathbf{C} := \bigcup_{i=1..n} \mathbf{Ci}$.

A database d over **R** is an instance of the extended scheme Comb(V1,...,Vn,**I**), iff d∈sat(**C**)∩sat(**I**), where

$\mathrm{sat}(Ri\ \mathrm{id}\ Rj) := \mathrm{sat}(Ri[Xi] \subset Rj[Xj]) \cap \mathrm{sat}(Rj[Xj] \subset Ri[Xi])$ and

$\mathrm{sat}(\mathbf{I}) := \bigcap_{i \in \mathbf{I}} \mathrm{sat}(i)$.

Again, the set of all instances of Comb(V1,...,Vn,**I**) is denoted by I(Comb).

Usually, the set **I** of the extended database scheme Comb(V1,...,Vn,**I**) contains all the specified integration constraints. Although we restrict ourselves to identity constraints, we will, from now on, always use the more general term 'integration constraint' instead. Furthermore, we often write 'Comb' instead of 'Comb(V1,...,Vn,**I**)', whenever V1, ..., Vn and **I** are understood.

Instances of Comb are often called 'valid global situations'. Intuitively, a valid global situation is a combination of valid local view databases that additionally satisfy all the integration constraints.

2.3. CONFLICTFREENESS OF VIEWS

Given a set of proper view database schemes and a set **I** of corresponding integration constraints, specifying which information is simultaneously seen in different views, we now ask, how to formalize the notion of conflicts between the views.

Often, the notion of conflicts between different views of the same application is simply reduced to naming conventions. But as in our approach each user group is allowed to choose its own appropriate names, our formal definition of conflicts or conflictfreeness should rather depend on structural connections between the views, as specified by the set **I** of integration constraints, than on simple naming conventions.

Naturally, a user of a specific view will expect that any of his possible view instances is reachable, in the sense that it is part of at least one valid global situation. Otherwise, there exists a view instance that cannot be combined with others to form a valid global situation because the structural inter-view connections, given by the set of integration constraints, cannot be satisfied. Surely, this indicates a conflict between the views.

Definition 2.5. Let $Comb=\langle \mathbf{R}|\mathbf{C}|\mathbf{I}\rangle$ be the combination of V1, ..., Vn with respect to **I** and let $d=(r11,\ldots,r1l_1,\ldots,\ldots,rn1,\ldots,rnl_n)$ be an instance of Comb, where $ri1, \ldots, ril_i$ are associated to the relation schemes of Vi.

For $1 \leq i \leq n$, the projection of d onto Vi is defined by $d[Vi]:=(ri1,\ldots,ril_i)$, and the projection of I(Comb) to Vi is defined by

$$I(Comb)[Vi]:=\{d[Vi] \mid d \in I(Comb)\}.$$

The views V1, ..., Vn are conflictfree with respect to **I**, iff

$$\forall\ i \in \{1,\ldots,n\}:\ I(Comb)[Vi]=I(Vi).$$

Definition 2.6. A decision problem of conflictfreeness is a pair **(V,I)**, where $\mathbf{V}=\{V1,\ldots,Vn\}$ is a finite set of proper database schemes and **I** is a finite set of integration constraints over V1, ..., Vn. One has to decide, whether or not V1, ..., Vn are conflictfree with respect to **I**.

Theorem 2.7. Conflictfreeness is undecidable.
Proof. see Section 4.

2.4. IMPLICATION PROBLEMS FOR CONSTRAINTS

Now, we consider another, rather natural problem related to the view integration approach. It directly corresponds to the integration method developed in [BiCo] using equivalence preserving scheme transformations, but it will probably occur in other formal methods, too.

For instance, assume the following situation: in the set **V** there are some views $V1=\langle \mathbf{R1}|\mathbf{C1}\rangle$, $V2=\langle \mathbf{R2}|\mathbf{C2}\rangle$ which are claimed to 'be identical' by some of the integration constraints in **I**. Nevertheless, as there are various possibilities to formulate integrity constraints within a view, **C1** and **C2** need not 'be identical'. So, when integrating those views, one has to be sure that **C1** and **C2** are equivalent, in the sense that **C1**∪**I** logically imply **C2** and **C2**∪**I** imply **C1**. More generally, during integration of the views one often has to decide whether a given set of integrity and integration constraints logically implies a single constraint.

From our practical point of view, only finite logical implication is of interest, i.e., only relations having a finite number of tuples have to be considered.

Definition 2.8. Let Comb=<**R**|**C**|**I**> be the combination of a set of views with respect to a set of integration constraints **I**.
A decision problem of finite logical implication is a pair (**B**,b), where **B**⊂**C**∪**I** and b∈**C**∪**I**. One has to decide, whether or not **B** logically implies b:
$\mathbf{B} \models_f b$:<==> for all databases d over **R**: d∈sat(**B**) ==> d∈sat(b).

Implication problems are known to be computationally rather difficult [Mitc], [FaVa], [ChVa], [Vard]. Indeed, in the next section, we will show that the above decision problems in general are undecidable. More precisely, we even prove a stronger result for a more restricted subclass of constraints which is of interest in itself. In this simple subclass, integration constraints are excluded and only integrity constraints of proper database schemes are considered.

Definition 2.9. Let **R** be a finite set of relation schemes. A decision problem of finite logical implication for proper database schemes is a pair (**B**,b), where **B** is a set of integrity constraints over **R** and b is a single integrity constraint over **R** such that <**R**|**B**∪{b}> is a proper database scheme. One has to decide, whether or not **B** logically implies b:
$\mathbf{B} \models_f b$:<==> for all databases d over **R**: d∈sat(**B**) ==> d∈sat(b).

Theorem 2.10. Finite logical implication for proper database schemes is undecidable.
Proof. see Section 3.

From the above theorem it simply follows that the more general implication problem which is of interest during view integration is undecidable, too.

Corollary 2.11. Finite logical implication is undecidable.

3. FINITE IMPLICATION IS UNDECIDABLE

In this section, we reduce the word problem for finite semigroups to the decision problem of finite logical implication for proper database schemes. We make use of proof methods provided by Mitchell [Mitc], who showed that finite and general implication is undecidable for general functional and inclusion dependencies. This was independently shown by Chandra/Vardi [ChVa]. For the finite case we sharpen their results to the more restricted dependency class which is allowed in proper database schemes, namely key dependencies and key-respecting inclusion dependencies. This result is of interest in itself.

First, we recall the word problem for semigroups and develop a convenient version of it. Let **V** be a finite set of variables, $\mathbf{E}=\{\alpha 1=\beta 1,\dots,\alpha n=\beta n\}$ a finite set of equations and let $e\equiv\alpha=\beta$ be a single equation, where $\alpha i,\beta i,\alpha,\beta\in \mathbf{V}^+$. The word problem for (finite) semigroups is to decide, whether or not e holds in every (finite) semigroup in which **E** holds, i.e.,

$$\mathbf{E} \models_{(f)} e :\Longleftrightarrow \forall \text{ (finite) semigroup } S: \forall \text{ homomorphism } h:\mathbf{V}^+ \dashrightarrow S:$$
$$(\forall i\in\{1,\dots,n\}: h(\alpha i)=h(\beta i)) \Longrightarrow h(\alpha)=h(\beta).$$

By standard methods, it can be shown that w.l.o.g. we can restrict equations to the form `x=z' or `x=yz', where $x,y,z\in\mathbf{V}$ and $x\neq z$. Furthermore, we recall that every semigroup is isomorphic to a transformation semigroup of functions from a set S to itself, and that the homomorphism h is uniquely determined by its image on the elements of **V** (see e.g. [Lall]). This leads to the following definitions.

Definition 3.1. Let **V** be a finite set of variables. A <u>(finite) interpretation I of **V**</u> is a pair I=(S,h), where S is a (finite) set and $h:\mathbf{V}\dashrightarrow\{f \mid f:S\dashrightarrow S \text{ function}\}$ associates to each $v\in\mathbf{V}$ a function $h_v:S\dashrightarrow S$.

An <u>identity equation over **V**</u> is of the form `x=z', where $x,z\in\mathbf{V}$ and $x\neq z$. An interpretation I satisfies an identity equation `x=z',

$I\in sat(x=z) :\Longleftrightarrow h_x=h_z$ (i.e., $\forall s\in S: h_x(s)=h_z(s)$).

A <u>composition equation over **V**</u> is of the form `x=yz', where $x,y,z\in\mathbf{V}$ and $x\neq z$. An interpretation I satisfies a composition equation `x=yz',

$I\in sat(x=yz) :\Longleftrightarrow h_x=h_y\circ h_z$ (i.e., $\forall s\in S: h_x(s)=h_y(h_z(s))$).

For a set **E** of equations, we define $I\in sat(\mathbf{E}) :\Longleftrightarrow \forall e\in\mathbf{E}: I\in sat(e)$.

Definiton 3.2. A <u>word problem for (finite) semigroups</u> is a pair (**E**,e), where

- **E** is a finite set of (identity or composition) equations and
- e is a single (identity or composition) equation.

One has to decide, whether or not **E** logically implies e:

$\mathbf{E} \models_{(f)} e :\Longleftrightarrow \forall$ (finite) interpretations I: $I\in sat(\mathbf{E}) \Longrightarrow I\in sat(e)$.

Both problems, for finite and general semigroups, are well known to be undecidable [Post], [Gure,GuLe]. For the rest of the paper, we only consider word problems for finite semigroups and will show, that given a fixed word problem P for finite semigroups, we can construct an equivalent implication problem for proper database schemes. The main idea is to mimic finite interpretations of P by valid databases of a corresponding proper database scheme $D_P=\langle \mathbf{R}_P | \mathbf{C}_P \rangle$. Furthermore, equations of P will be mimicked by inclusion dependencies over $\mathbf{R}_P$.

Now, let us fix some word problem for finite semigroups P=(**E**,e) and let **V**={v1,...,vn} be the set of variables occuring in **E**∪{e}. Assume, the subset of composition equations occuring in **E**∪{e} is {e1,e2,...,em}, where ei≡xi=yizi for i=1,...,m.

We define the corresponding proper database scheme $D_P=\langle \mathbf{R}_P | \mathbf{C}_P \rangle$ by

$\mathbf{R}_P$:={B[S], H[S'SV1...Vn],
R_{v1}[SV1], ..., R_{vn}[SVn],
R_{e1}[Z1X1], ..., R_{em}[ZmXm]},
$\mathbf{C}_P$:={H:S'->SV1...Vn,
H[S']=B[S], H[S]=B[S],
H[V1]⊂B[S], ..., H[Vn]⊂B[S],
R_{v1}[SV1]=H[SV1], ..., R_{vn}[SVn]=H[SVn],
R_{e1}[Z1X1]=H[Z1X1], ..., R_{em}[ZmXm]=H[ZmXm]}.

Remarks.

- Above, we use S', S, V1, ..., Vn as attributes to define the relation schemes.
- The intended correspondence between a finite interpretation I=(S,h) and a valid database of D_P is the following: (see transformation τ below)
  the base set S will be stored in B;
  the graph of h will be represented by H, where the two columns S',S additionally represent the identity function on S;
  R_{vi} will represent the graph of h_{vi} and
  R_{ei} will be used to mimic the composition equation ei.
- We have only specified the nontrivial key dependencies, i.e., the key of B is S, the key of R_{vi} is SVi and the key of R_{ei} is ZiXi.
- In $\mathbf{C}_P$ we use '=' as an abbreviation for two INDs, i.e., 'H[S']=B[S]' stands for 'H[S']⊂B[S], B[S]⊂H[S']'.
- Obviously, D_P is a proper database scheme.

Before we show how finite interpretations of **V** are transformed into valid databases, we prove some basic properties of D_P, which will be needed later on.

Lemma 3.3.

a) $\mathbf{C_P} \models_f$ H:S->S'V1...Vn.

b) $\mathbf{C_P} \models_f R_{Vj}$:S->Vj $\quad \forall j \in \{1,...,n\}$.

Proof.

a) For $d=(b,h,r_{V1},...,r_{Vn},r_{e1},...,r_{em}) \in sat(\mathbf{C_P})$ we have to show that $d \in sat$(H:S->S'V1...Vn).

Since $d \in sat(\mathbf{C_P})$, we have: $|h[S']| = (|b[S]| =)\ |h[S]|$. Additionally, this cardinal number is finite, and so from H:S'->S it follows that also H:S->S' holds.Therefore, we have H:S->S'V1...Vn.

b) follows directly form a) and $R_{Vj}[SVj]$=H[SVj]$\in \mathbf{C_P}\ \forall j \in \{1,...,n\}$. ■

Remark. It is easily shown that for the infinite case $\mathbf{C_P} \not\models$ H:S->S'V1...Vn, i.e., for proper database schemes finite and general implication do not coincide.

In the later proof, we need the following function 'ident', transforming any database $d=(b,h,r_{V1},...,r_{Vn},r_{e1},...,r_{em})$ over $\mathbf{R_P}$, such that afterwards for all tuples $t \in h$, we have $t[S']=t[S]$.

Definition 3.4. Let t be a tuple over S'SV1...Vn. Then, we define the <u>function 'ident'</u> by

$$\textbf{ident(t)(A)} := \begin{cases} t(A) & \text{for } A \in \{S,V1, ..., Vn\}\ ; \\ t(S) & \text{for } A=S'\ . \end{cases}$$

'ident' is canonically extended to relations over S'SV1...Vn, databases over $\mathbf{R_P}$ and finally to sets of databases over $\mathbf{R_P}$.

Lemma 3.5. $\forall\ d \in I(D_P)$: $\ ident(d) \in I(D_P)$.

Proof. follows directly by Lemma 3.3.a) and the form of $\mathbf{C_P}$. ■

Now, we describe the intended connection between the word problem P and the proper database scheme D_P by defining a transformation τ, which transforms finite interpretations of **V** into valid databases of D_P.

τ:{I | I=(S,h) finite interpretation of **V**} --> $I(D_P)$

I --> $\tau(I):=(b,h,r_{V1},...,r_{Vn},r_{e1},...,r_{em})$, where

b:=S,

$h:=\{(s,s,h_{V1}(s),...,h_{Vn}(s)) \mid s \in S\}$,

$r_{Vj}:=\{(s,h_{Vj}(s)) \mid s \in S\} \quad \forall j \in \{1,...,n\}$,

$r_{ej}:=\{(h_{zj}(s),h_{xj}(s)) \mid s \in S\} \quad \forall j \in \{1,...,m\}$.

Lemma 3.6.

a) τ is one-to-one.

b) The image of τ is ident(I(D_P)).

c) τ^{-1} associates exactly one interpretation of **V** to each database in ident(I(D_P)).

Proof. straightforward. ■

Another transformation γ is used to describe the connections between equations in E∪{e} and integrity constraints over $\mathbf{R}_P$.

$$\gamma(e') := \begin{cases} \{Rx[SX]=Ry[SY]\} & \text{for } e' \equiv x=y \in E\cup\{e\} \\ \{Re'[ZX] \subset H[SY]\} & \text{for } e' \equiv x=yz \in E\cup\{e\}. \end{cases}$$

As usual, we extend γ to sets of equations by $\gamma(E) := \bigcup_{e \in E} \gamma(e)$.

Lemma 3.7. Let I be a finite interpretation of **V**, and let e´ be an equation in E∪{e}. Then we have: I∈sat(e´) <==> τ(I)∈sat(γ(e´)). (see Figure 1.)

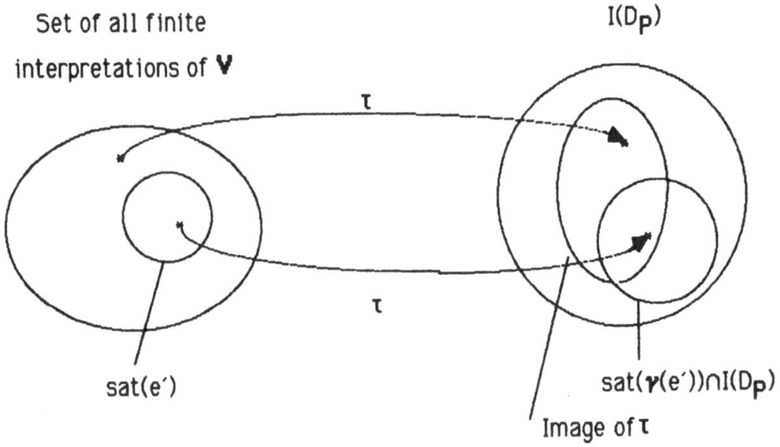

Figure 1.

Proof. Let I be a finite interpretation and $d := \tau(I) = (b,h,r_{v1},\ldots,r_{vn},r_{e1},\ldots,r_{em})$.

<u>Case 1:</u> e´≡x=y is an identity equation in E∪{e}, i.e., $\gamma(e') = \{R_x[SX]=R_y[SY]\}$.

According to the definition of τ we have:

$r_x = \{(s,h_x(s)) \mid s \in S\}$ and $r_y = \{(s,h_y(s)) \mid s \in S\}$. So, easily it follows:

I∈sat(e´) <==> $h_x = h_y$ <==> $r_x = r_y$ <==> τ(I)∈sat(γ(e´)).

Case 2: $e' \equiv x = yz$ is a composition equation in $E \cup \{e\}$, i.e., $\gamma(e') = \{R_{e'}[ZX] \subset H[SY]\}$.

"==>" For $I \in sat(x=yz)$, we show that $\tau(I) \in sat(R_{e'}[ZX] \subset H[SY])$. So, let t be a tuple in $r_{e'}$. According to the definition of τ there exists an element $s \in S$, such that $t[ZX] = (h_z(s), h_x(s))$. Since $h_z(s) \in S$, there exists another tuple t' in h with $t'[SY] = (h_z(s), h_y(h_z(s)))$. Since $I \in sat(x=yz)$, we can conclude that $h_x(s) = h_y(h_z(s))$, and thus we have $t[ZX] = t'[SY] \in h[SY]$.

"<==" For $I \notin sat(x=yz)$, we show that $\tau(I) \notin sat(R_{e'}[ZX] \subset H[SY])$. Since $I \notin sat(x=yz)$, there exists an element $s \in S$ such that $h_x(s) \neq h_y(h_z(s))$. So, according to the definition of τ there is a tuple $t \in r_{e'}$ with $t[ZX] = (h_z(s), h_x(s))$ and furthermore there is exactly one tuple $t' \in h$ with $t'[S] = h_z(s)$ $(= t[Z])$. But for this tuple t', we have $t'[Y] = h_y(h_z(s)) \neq h_x(s) = t[X]$ and thus $t[ZX] = (h_z(s), h_x(s)) \notin h[SY]$. ■

Given our word problem $P = (E, e)$ for finite semigroups, we are now able to define an equivalent decision problem of finite logical implication for proper databases.

Proposition 3.8. $E \models_f e \iff C_P \cup \gamma(E) \models_f \gamma(e)$.

Proof.

"<==" Assume $E \not\models_f e$. Then there exists a finite interpretation I of **V**, such that $I \in sat(E) \backslash sat(e)$. For the corresponding database $\tau(I)$, we conclude with Lemma 3.7. $\tau(I) \in sat(C_P \cup \gamma(E)) \backslash sat(\gamma(e))$, i.e., $C_P \cup \gamma(E) \not\models_f \gamma(e)$.

"==>" Assume $C_P \cup \gamma(E) \not\models_f \gamma(e)$. Then there exists a database $d \in sat(C_P \cup \gamma(E)) \backslash sat(\gamma(e))$. d is not necessarily in the image of τ, but according to Lemma 3.6.b) $d' := ident(d)$ lies in the image of τ $(\subset sat(C_P))$, and so there is a finite interpretation I, such that $\tau(I) = d'$. It is easily shown that also $d' \in sat(C_P \cup \gamma(E)) \backslash sat(\gamma(e))$ and with Lemma 3.7. we conclude: $I \in sat(E) \backslash sat(e)$, i.e., $E \not\models_f e$. ■

To sum up, we have reduced the word problem for finite semigroups to the decision problem of finite logical implication for proper database schemes. Thus, we have proved Theorem 2.10.

Remark. From a theoretical point of view also general logical implication for key dependencies and key-preserving inclusion dependencies might be of interest. However, it is still an open problem, whether it is decidable or not. We cannot use the same proof methods for the general case exactly because Lemma 3.3. strictly depends on the finiteness of relations.

4. CONFLICTFREENESS IS UNDECIDABLE

In this short section, we show that also the second interesting problem related to the view integration approach is undecidable. More precisely, we reduce the decision problem of finite logical implication for proper database schemes to the decision problem of conflictfreeness.

Now, let $P=(\mathbf{B},b)$ be a fixed decision problem of finite logical implication for proper database schemes over a set of relation schemes $\mathbf{R}=\{R1[X1],\ldots,Rn[Xn]\}$. Furthermore, let $\mathbf{R}':=\{R1'[X1],\ldots,Rn'[Xn]\}$ be an 'isomorphic' copy of $\mathbf{R}$ with new relation names $R1', \ldots, Rn'$. Analogously, we get $\mathbf{B}'$ by the same simple renaming out of $\mathbf{B}$.

We define the following corresponding decision problem of conflictfreeness $(\{V1,V2\},\mathbf{I})$, where $V1:=\langle \mathbf{R} | \mathbf{B}\cup\{b\}\rangle$, $V2:=\langle \mathbf{R}' | \mathbf{B}'\rangle$ and $\mathbf{I}:=\{Ri \text{ id } Ri' \mid i=1,\ldots,n\}$.

Proposition 4.1. $\mathbf{B} \models_f b \Longleftrightarrow$ V1 and V2 are conflictfree with respect to $\mathbf{I}$.

Proof. V1 and V2 are conflictfree with respect to $\mathbf{I}$

$\Longleftrightarrow I(Comb)[V1]=I(V1) \wedge I(Comb)[V2]=I(V2)$ (definition of conflictfreeness)

$\Longleftrightarrow \forall\, v1\in I(V1)\colon \exists\, v2\in I(V2)\colon (v1,v2)\in sat(\mathbf{I}) \wedge$
$\quad \forall\, v2\in I(V2)\colon \exists\, v1\in I(V1)\colon (v1,v2)\in sat(\mathbf{I})$

$\Longleftrightarrow \forall\, v1\in I(V1)\colon v1\in I(V2) \wedge \forall\, v2\in I(V2)\colon v2\in I(V1)$ (special form of $\mathbf{I}$)

$\Longleftrightarrow I(V1)=I(V2)$

$\Longleftrightarrow sat(\mathbf{B}\cup\{b\})=sat(\mathbf{B}')$

$\Longleftrightarrow sat(\mathbf{B}\cup\{b\})=sat(\mathbf{B})$ $(sat(\mathbf{B})=sat(\mathbf{B}'))$

$\Longleftrightarrow \mathbf{B} \models_f b$ ■

Since finite logical implication is undecidable, we have proved Theorem 2.7.

5. CONCLUSION

In our paper, we have developed a formalized version of what we believe to be the minimum expressiveness any practical specification method for view integration should possess. Then, we have given formal definitions of two natural problems, related to the view integration approach, which probably will have to be faced by any computer-aided integration tool.

On this formal basis we have developed our main results, showing both problems, finite implication and conflictfreeness, to be undecidable. More precisely, we have reduced finite implication to conflictfreeness, which additionally shows how both problems are related to each other.

In summary, our results clarify the computational limits of the view integration approach and show once more that view integration, or database design in general, is unlikely to be fully automated.

So, in a practical interactive, computer-aided integration tool appropriate heuristics have to be used, first, to support designers in detecting conflicts between the views, and second, to show logical implication at least for simple and often occuring special cases. This will be investigated in some further research.

Acknowledgements. I would like to thank Joachim Biskup, Egon Börger, Jimmy Brüggemann and Uwe Räsch for many helpful discussions.

REFERENCES.

[AAL] A. Albano, V. De Antonellis, A. Di Leva (eds.), 'Computer-aided database design: the DATAID project', North-Holland, 1985.

[BiCo] J. Biskup, B. Convent, 'A formal view integration method', ACM-Sigmod International Conference on Management of Data, 1986, 398-407.

[BLM] C. Batini, M. Lenzerini, M. Moscarini, 'Views integration', in [Ceri], 1983, 57-84.

[CaVi] M.A. Casanova, V.M.P. Vidal, 'Towards a sound view integration methodology', 2nd ACM-Sigact-Sigmod Symposium on Principles of Database Systems, 1983, 36-47.

[Ceri] S. Ceri (ed.), 'Methodology and tools for data base design', North-Holland, 1983.

[CFP] M.A. Casanova, R. Fagin, C.H. Papadimitriou, 'Inclusion dependencies and their interaction with functional dependencies', 1st ACM-Sigact-Sigmod Symposium on Principles of Database Systems, 1982, 171-176.

[ChVa] A.K. Chandra, M.Y. Vardi, 'The implication problem for functional and inclusion dependencies is undecidable', SIAM J. Comput., Vol. 14, No. 3, 671-677, 1985.

[Codd1] E.F. Codd, 'A relational model of data for large shared data banks', Comm. ACM 13 (6), 1970, 377-387.

[Codd2] E.F. Codd, 'Further normalization of the data base relational model', in 'Data base systems', R. Rustin (ed.), Courant Computer Science Symposia 6, Englewood Cliffs, N.J., Prentice-Hall, 1972, 33-64.

[FaVa] R. Fagin, M.Y. Vardi, 'The theory of data dependencies - a survey', IBM Research Report RJ 4321, IBM Research Laboratory, San Jose, 1984.

[GuLe] Y. Gurevich, H.R. Lewis, 'The word problem for cancellation semigroups with zero', Journal of Symbolic Logic, Vol. 49, No. 1, 1984, 184-191.

[Gure] Y. Gurevich, 'The word problem for certain classes of semigroups', Algebra and Logic, Vol. 5, 1966, 25-35. (in Russian)

[Lall] G. Lallement, 'Semigroups and combinatorial applications', John Wiley & Sons, 1979.

[Lum] V.Y. Lum et. al., '1978 New Orleans data base design workshop report', 5th VLDB, 1979, 328-339.

[Maie] D. Maier, 'The theory of relational databases', Computer Science Press, 1983.

[MBGW] J. Mylopoulos, A. Borgida, S. Greenspan, H.K.T. Wong, 'Information system design at the conceptual level - the TAXIS project', IEEE Database Engineering, Vol. 7, No. 4, 1984, 4-9.

[Mitc] J.C. Mitchell, 'The implication problem for functional and inclusion dependencies', Information and Control 56, 1983, 154-173.

[NaGa] S.B. Navathe, S.G. Gadgil, 'A methodology for view integration in logical database design', 8th VLDB, 1982, 142-164.

[Nava] S.B. Navathe, 'Important issues in database design methodologies and tools', in [AAL], 1985, 199-212.

[NEL] S.B. Navathe, R. Elmasri, J. Larson, 'Integrating user views in database design', IEEE COMPUTER, Jan. 1986, 50-62.

[Post] E.L. Post, 'Recursive unsolvability of a problem of Thue', Journal of Symbolic Logic, Vol. 12, 1947, 1-11.

[ReBr] D. Reiner, M. Brodie et al., 'The database design and evaluation workbench (DDEW) project at CCA', IEEE Database Engineering, Vol. 7, No. 4, 1984, 10-15.

[TeFr] T.J. Teorey, J.P. Fry, 'Design of database structures', Prentice-Hall, 1982.

[Ullm] J.D. Ullman, 'Principles of database systems', 2nd ed., Computer Science Press, 1982.

[Vard] M.Y. Vardi, 'Fundamentals of dependency theory', in 'Current trends in theoretical computer science', E. Börger (ed.), Computer Science Press, to appear.

[YNW] S.B. Yao, S.B. Navathe, J.-L. Weldon, 'An integrated approach to database design', Data Base Design Techniques I, Requirements and logical Structures, NYU Symposium New York, 1978, 1-30.

HORIZONTAL DECOMPOSITIONS BASED ON FUNCTIONAL-DEPENDENCY-SET-IMPLICATIONS

P. De Bra*

Department of Mathematics
University of Antwerp, U.I.A.
Universiteitsplein 1, 2610 Antwerp
Belgium

*Research assistant of the N.F.W.O.

Abstract

A new approach towards horizontal decompositions in the Relational Database Model is given. It is based on partial implications between sets of *functional dependencies*. This horizontal decomposition theory is especially useful for databases which must represent "real world" situations, in which there always are exceptions to rather severe constraints like *functional dependencies (fd's)*.

The *functional-dependency-set-implication (fsi)* generalizes all previous work on horizontal decompositions using partial implications between (single) fd's.

The exceptions to a set of fd's are formalized using another new constraint, the *anti-functional-dependency-set (afs)*. The membership problem is solved for mixed fsi's and afs', and a complete set of inference rules is given. The inheritance problem, i.e. which dependencies hold in the (two) subrelations generated by the horizontal decomposition) is shown to be solvable in polynomial time.

§1 Introduction

The *vertical decomposition* of relations into projections of these relations, based on *functional dependencies (fd's)*, was introduced with the *Relational Database Model* by Codd [Co], and has been exhaustively studied and generalized since. However, it relies on the assumption that the part of the real world, represented by the database, satisfies some rather severe constraints.

Because this assumption is highly unrealistic some mechanism for handling exceptions to these constraints is necessary. In [De1, De2, Pa, De3, De4, De5] a theory has been established that uses a ***horizontal decomposition*** of relations into restrictions (often called selections) of these relations, to put the "exceptions" in a well defined subrelation. This theory is based on "partial implications" between functional dependencies, given different names in each paper, as the class of these constraints became bigger and bigger.

In this paper we generalize the constraints of [De5] to include implications between sets of fd's instead of single fd's. The new constraint is called a *functional-dependency-set-implication (fsi)*. It means that if a (part of a) relation satisfies a set of fd's, then it must also satisfy some other set of fd's, which is said to be implied by the first set. Note that this is an ad-hoc implication, based on the observation of the real world, not just a "logical" deduction (which has been studied exhaustively already [Ul]).

The exceptions to a set of fd's are formalized using another new constraint: the *anti-functional-dependency-set (afs)*, a generalization of the *anti-functional dependency (afd)* of [De5].

In Section 2 we define the horizontal decomposition, based on fsi's. We also recall two theoretical tools, that are used throughout the horizontal decomposition theory: the *Armstrong relation* and the *conflict concept*. In Section 3 the membership problem is solved for mixed fsi's and afs' and a complete set of inference rules is given. A complicated construction of a relation instance is recalled from [De5], which also leads to the solution of the inheritance problem in Section 4. Both the membership and the inheritance problem are shown to be solvable in polynomial time.

We suppose the reader is aware of the basic definitions and notations of the Relational Database theory [Ul].

§2 Horizontal Decompositions

The traditional vertical decomposition, based on *functional dependencies (fd's)*, can only be applied to relations in which some fd's hold. Since fd's are rather restrictive they do not occur frequently in the "real world", at least not if no exceptions to any fd can be tolerated. For this reason a large number of weaker constraints have been defined in literature [Ul], which have a better chance of being satisfied, and which still lead to vertical decompositions. However, these constraints are less natural and do not all have the theoretical simplicity of fd's.

In [De1, De2, Pa] a method for handling exceptions to fd's is presented, using horizontal decompositions. The exceptions to an fd are put in a separate subrelation (obtained by taking a restriction of the relation), inducing the fd in the remaining (and main) part of the relation. Because the fd holds in this main part, it can be used to apply the classical vertical decomposition to this part.

Although an fd may not hold in the real world, the part that satisfies the fd may satisfy some other fd's too, which cannot be logically deduced from the first fd. Such "partial implications" between fd's have been studied in [De3, De4, De5], and have been shown to lead to the same horizontal decompositions as those of [De1, De2, Pa]. The drawback of all these horizontal decompositions is that they generate an awful lot of subrelations, exponential in the number of constraints.

In this paper we consider a more general class of constraints, using implications between sets of fd's. This enables the database designer to combine several implications between fd's into one implication between sets of fd's, reducing the number of constraints, and hence the number of generated subrelations.

We first illustrate the horizontal decomposition with the following example:

Example 2.1. Consider a large company with several divisions (e.g. factories) each having (several) departments (each) treating one or more jobs. Employees work in one or more departments (of one or more divisions). They have salaries and managers.

Although this may seem a rather unconstrained database, it may obviously obey the following constraint:

If in a *div*ision every *dep*artment treats only one *job*, every *emp*loyee has only one *job* and every *man*ager supervises only one *job* (for this division), then (the division is so large that) every *emp*loyee works in only one *dep*artment and has only one *sal*ary, and every *man*ager supervises (employees) in only one *dep*artment (for that division).

This constraint will be written as:

$$\{div, dep \rightarrow job; div, emp \rightarrow job; div, man \rightarrow job\} \overset{div}{\supset\!\!-} \{div, emp \rightarrow dep, sal; div, man \rightarrow dep\}$$

Note that none of the fd's of the second (or "implied") set are logical consequences of the first set of fd's. they are said to be implied by the first set of fd's by observing the real world.

□

We now define this constraint, and the horizontal decomposition induced by it, more formally.

Definition 2.2. Let X be a set of attributes.

A set of tuples S in a relation instance is called *X-complete* iff the tuples not belonging to S all have other X-projections than those belonging to S. Formally, if $t_1 \in S$, $t_2 \notin S$ then $t_1[X] \neq t_2[X]$.

A set of tuples S is called *X-unique* iff all the tuples of S have the same X-projection. Formally, if $t_1, t_2 \in S$ then $t_1[X] = t_2[X]$.

Definition 2.3. Let Z be a set of attributes, $\mathcal{F}_1$ and $\mathcal{F}_2$ be sets of fd's, such that $\forall X \rightarrow Y \in \mathcal{F}_1 \cup \mathcal{F}_2 : Z \subseteq X$.

The *functional-dependency-set-implication (fsi)* $\mathcal{F}_1 \overset{Z}{\supset\!\!-} \mathcal{F}_2$, means that in every Z-complete set of tuples (in every instance) in which all the fd's of $\mathcal{F}_1$ hold, all the fd's $\mathcal{F}_2$ must hold too.

The sets of tuples which are both X-complete and X-unique play an important role in the horizontal decomposition theory. In the sequel we shall use the term *"X-value"* to refer to such a set of tuples, as well as for the X-projection of the tuples of that set.

The requirement that all "left hand sides" of the fd's of $\mathcal{F}_1$ and $\mathcal{F}_2$ must include Z is not a severe restriction. In Section 5 we shall show that eliminating this restriction does not necessarily lead to a bigger class of constraints.

The *functional-dependency-implications (fdi's)* of [De5] are special fsi's where $\mathcal{F}_1$ and $\mathcal{F}_2$ each contain only one fd. Since all previously defined constraints of [De1, De2, Pa, De3, De4] are special fdi's they are fsi's too.

In particular fd's can be expressed in many ways as fsi's, some of which are fdi's. $X \rightarrow Y$ is equivalent to $\{X \rightarrow X\} \overset{X}{\supset\!\!-} \{X \rightarrow Y\}$ for instance, which is an fdi (in fact even a "cfd" of [De3]). But $X \rightarrow Y$ is also equivalent to $\emptyset \overset{X}{\supset\!\!-} \{X \rightarrow Y\}$ for instance, which is not an fdi.

Example 2.2. Consider the relation of Example 2.1. The horizontal decomposition separates the divisions in which every employee, every department and every manager have only one job, from the other divisions. If one assumes that most large divisions have enough work to distribute the jobs in this way, a major part of the database may consist of information about such large divisions, hence the exceptions to these fd's only have a minor influence on the cost of solving queries or making updates. However, if no horizontal decomposition was applied to the database, the few exceptions would have a great influence on the efficiency of the database system, since they would prevent the classical vertical decomposition that speeds up the system and reduces redundancy.

The "user" need not know about this horizontal decomposition. If an update (in a "large" division) causes one of the fd's ($div, dep \rightarrow job$; $div, emp \rightarrow job$ or $div, man \rightarrow job$) to be violated, all tuples with that *div*-value are moved to the subrelation for the exceptions. If an update causes the three fd's to become satisfied the tuples with that *div*-value have to move to the other subrelation automatically. Hence the user need not know about the horizontal decomposition. However, it may also be useful to let some users access the subrelations and some other users only the "union". By doing this one can easily allow some users to create or remove exceptions, while preventing other users from doing so.

□

The restriction operator for separating the "large" divisions from the "small" ones is defined as follows:

Definition 2.4. Let $\mathcal{R}$ be a relation scheme, Z be a set of attributes, $\mathcal{F}$ a set of fd's such that $\forall X \rightarrow Y \in \mathcal{F} : Z \subseteq X$.

For every instance R of $\mathcal{R}$, the ***restriction for*** $\mathcal{F}_Z$ ***of*** R, $\sigma_{\mathcal{F}_Z}(R)$, is the largest Z-complete subset (of tuples) of R in which all fd's of $\mathcal{F}$ hold.

The ***restriction for*** $\mathcal{F}_Z$ ***of*** $\mathcal{R}$, $\sigma_{\mathcal{F}_Z}(\mathcal{R})$, is a scheme $\mathcal{R}_1$, (with the same attributes as $\mathcal{R}$,) of which the instances are exactly the restrictions for $\mathcal{F}_Z$ of the instances of $\mathcal{R}$.

We require $Z \subseteq X$ for all $X \rightarrow Y \in \mathcal{F}$ to make sure that X-values of R are not split up by taking a restriction for $\mathcal{F}_Z$.

Definition 2.5. The ***horizontal decomposition of a scheme*** $\mathcal{R}$***, according to the fsi*** $\mathcal{F}_1 \overset{Z}{\supset\!-} \mathcal{F}_2$, is the couple $(\mathcal{R}_1, \mathcal{R}_2)$, where $\mathcal{R}_1 = \sigma_{\mathcal{F}_Z}(\mathcal{R})$ and $\mathcal{R}_2 = \mathcal{R} - \mathcal{R}_1$.

Note from Definition 2.5 that the horizontal decomposition of a scheme, according to $\mathcal{F}_1 \overset{Z}{\supset\!-} \mathcal{F}_2$ does not depend on $\mathcal{F}_2$, but it induces the $\mathcal{F}_2$ in $\mathcal{R}_1$. Hence one can always perform a horizontal decomposition to generate a subrelation with a "desirable" set of fd's $\mathcal{F}_1$, by using the "trivial" fsi $\mathcal{F}_1 \overset{Z}{\supset\!-} \emptyset$.

In $\mathcal{R}_2$, which contains the exceptions, for every X-value at least one of the fd's of $\mathcal{F}_1$ must not hold. In Example 2.1 this means that in such a division at least one department of employee or manager must have more than one job. (In these divisions nothing is known about the number of departments an employee or a manager works for, nor about an employee's salary).

The following constraint formalizes the notion of "exception".

Definition 2.6. Let $\mathcal{F}$ be a set of fd's, such that $\forall X \rightarrow Y \in \mathcal{F} : Z \subseteq X$.

The ***anti-functional dependency set (afs)*** $\not\mathcal{F}_Z$ means that in every nonempty Z-complete set of tuples, in every instance, at least one fd of $\mathcal{F}$ does not hold.

The ***restriction for*** $\not\mathcal{F}_Z$ ***of*** R, $\sigma_{\not\mathcal{F}_Z}(R)$, is the largest Z-complete set of tuples in which $\not\mathcal{F}_Z$ holds.

The ***restriction for*** $\not\mathcal{F}_Z$ ***of a scheme*** $\mathcal{R}$, $\sigma_{\not\mathcal{F}_Z}(\mathcal{R})$ is the scheme of which the instances are the restrictions for $\not\mathcal{F}_Z$ of the instances of $\mathcal{R}$.

One can easily see that $\mathcal{R} - \sigma_{\mathcal{F}_Z}(\mathcal{R}) = \sigma_{\not\mathcal{F}_Z}(\mathcal{R})$, hence the horizontal decomposition of $\mathcal{R}$ according to $\mathcal{F}_1 \overset{Z}{\supset\!-} \mathcal{F}_2$ is the couple of schemes $(\sigma_{\mathcal{F}_Z}(\mathcal{R}), \sigma_{\not\mathcal{F}_Z}(\mathcal{R}))$.

The ***anti-functional dependency (afd)*** introduced in [De5] is an afs $\not\mathcal{F}_Z$ for which $\mathcal{F}$ contains only one fd.

From now on we let a relation scheme $\mathcal{R}$ have a set $\mathcal{I}$ of fsi's and a set $\mathcal{A}$ of afs'. (Note that $\mathcal{I}$ also contains the fd's).

Having more than one fsi means that after the (horizontal) decomposition according to one fsi of $\mathcal{I}$ one may want to decompose the (two) subrelations again, using some other fsi of $\mathcal{I}$. Therefore one must (first) determine which fsi's hold in these subrelations. This is described in Section 4. Also, since decomposing a relation according to an fsi creates two subrelations which may sometimes both be decomposed further on, one obtains an exponential number of final subrelations. Therefore the designer must choose his fsi's carefully, putting many fd's in one fsi, to reduce the number of subrelations. This is the main advantage of fsi's over fdi's [De5], in which all the fd's are treated separately, leading to more fdi's, and hence exponentially more subrelations.

The presence of both fsi's and afs' in a relation scheme may induce a situation of "internal conflict" between the fsi's and the afs'. The easiest example of conflict is an fd $X \to Y$, which is a special fsi, and the afd $X \not\xrightarrow{X} Y$, which is a special afs.

Definition 2.7. A set $\mathcal{I} \cup \mathcal{A}$ of fsi's ($\mathcal{I}$) and afs' ($\mathcal{A}$) is *in conflict* iff the empty set of tuples is the only instance in which all dependencies of $\mathcal{I} \cup \mathcal{A}$ hold.

In Section 3 the membership problem for mixed fsi's and afs' is reduced to the conflict concept, which itself is reduced to the membership problem for fd's. So the conflict concept is an important theoretical tool.

In the proofs of Sections 3 and 4 a special instance is used, which is an *Armstrong relation for fd's* [Ar, De1]. It has a special property, also satisfied by the "direct product construction" of [Fa], but not by every (so called) Armstrong relation for fd's:

Theorem 2.8. *Let $Arm(\mathcal{F})$ denote the Armstrong relation for a set $\mathcal{F}$ of fd's [Ar, De1]. In $Arm(\mathcal{F})$ every fd, which is a consequence of $\mathcal{F}$, holds, and for every other fd $X \to Y$, the "corresponding" afd $X \not\xrightarrow{X} Y$ holds (which is an afs).*

□

§3 The Membership Problem for fsi's and afs'

In this section we reduce the membership problem for fsi's and afs' to a sequence of membership tests for fd's, for which many solutions are well known [Be, Ber].

We use the symbol $\models$ to denote the (logical) implication of a dependency by a set of dependencies, and the symbol $\vdash$ to denote the deduction of a dependency from a set of dependencies using the inference rules, given below. We shall prove the equivalence of $\models$ and $\vdash$, i.e. the completeness of the inference rules.

We denote the set of all the fd's which are consequences of a set $\mathcal{F}$ of fd's by $\mathcal{F}^*$. The set of all fd's $X \to Y$ of $\mathcal{F}^*$ for which $Z \subseteq X$ is denoted by $\mathcal{F}^{*Z}$.

$(F1)$: if $Y \subseteq X$ then $X \to Y$.
$(F2)$: if $X \to Y$ and $V \subseteq W$ then $XW \to YV$.
$(F3)$: if $X \to Y$ and $Y \to Z$ then $X \to Z$.
$(FS1)$: if $\mathcal{F}_2 \subseteq \mathcal{F}_1^{*Z}$ and $\forall X \to Y \in \mathcal{F}_1 : Z \subseteq X$ then $\mathcal{F}_1 \stackrel{Z}{\supset\!-} \mathcal{F}_2$.
$(FS2)$: if $\mathcal{F}_1 \stackrel{Z}{\supset\!-} \mathcal{F}_2$ and $\mathcal{F}_1 \stackrel{Z}{\supset\!-} \mathcal{F}_3$ then $\mathcal{F}_1 \stackrel{Z}{\supset\!-} \mathcal{F}_2 \cup \mathcal{F}_3$.
$(FS3)$: if $\mathcal{F}_1 \stackrel{Z}{\supset\!-} \mathcal{F}_2$ and $\mathcal{F}_2 \stackrel{Z}{\supset\!-} \mathcal{F}_3$ then $\mathcal{F}_1 \stackrel{Z}{\supset\!-} \mathcal{F}_3$.
$(FS4)$: if $\mathcal{F}_1 \stackrel{Z}{\supset\!-} \mathcal{F}_2$ and $Z \to Z'$ then $\mathcal{F}_1^{*Z'} \stackrel{Z'}{\supset\!-} \mathcal{F}_2^{*Z'}$.

$(FS5)$: if $\mathcal{F}_1$ holds and $\mathcal{F}_1 \overset{Z}{\supset\!\!-} \mathcal{F}_2$ then $\mathcal{F}_2$ holds and if $\mathcal{F}_2$ holds and $\forall X \to Y \in \mathcal{F}_1 \cup \mathcal{F}_2 : Z \subseteq X$ then $\mathcal{F}_1 \overset{Z}{\supset\!\!-} \mathcal{F}_2$ holds.

$(FA1)$: if $\mathcal{F}_1 \overset{Z}{\supset\!\!-} \mathcal{F}_2$ and $\not\mathcal{F}_{2Z}$ then $\not\mathcal{F}_{1Z}$.

$(FA2)$: if $\not\mathcal{F}_{1Z}$ and $\forall X \to Y \in \mathcal{F}_2 : Z \subseteq X$ then $\mathcal{F}_1 \overset{Z}{\supset\!\!-} \mathcal{F}_2$.

$(FA3)$: if $\not\mathcal{F}_Z$ and $Z \to Z'$ then $\not\mathcal{F}^{*Z'}_{Z'}$.

$(FA4)$: if $\not\mathcal{F}_{1Z}$ and $\mathcal{F}_1^{*Z} \subseteq \mathcal{F}_2^{*Z}$ and $\forall X \to Y \in \mathcal{F}_2 : Z \subseteq X$ then $\not\mathcal{F}_{2Z}$.

As fd's are special fsi's the use of fd's in these rules is allowed. In fact $FS5$ shows all representations of fd's as fsi's.

Theorem 3.1. *The rules $F1 \ldots F3$, $FS1 \ldots FS5$, $FA1 \ldots FA4$ are sound.*

Proof. This is very similar to the proof for fdi's and afd's [De5]. We give the proof for $FA3$ as an example.

One can easily see that the fd $Z \to Z'$ means that every Z'-complete set of tuples is also Z-complete.

Suppose $\not\mathcal{F}^{*Z'}_{Z'}$ does not hold. Hence in some Z'-complete set of tuples S all fd's of $\mathcal{F}^{*Z'}$ hold. Since S is also Z-complete it remains to prove that all fd's of $\mathcal{F}$ hold in S.

Let $X \to Y \in \mathcal{F}$, then $XZ' \to Y \in \mathcal{F}^{*Z'}$. $Z \to Z'$ and $Z \subseteq X$ induce $X \to XZ'$ by augmentation $(F2)$. By transitivity $(F3)$ we infer that $X \to Y$ holds in S.

□

The proof of the completeness of the inference rules consists of the following steps: first we prove that $F1 \ldots F3$, $FS1 \ldots FS5$ are complete for the deduction of fd's from a set of fsi's. Then we show that they are also complete for the deduction of fsi's. From this proof one can easily derive a membership algorithm for fsi's, which is essentially a sequence of fd-membership tests. Finally we prove that $F1 \ldots F3$, $FS1 \ldots FS5$, $FA1 \ldots FA4$ are complete for mixed fsi's and afs' by reducing this problem to the membership problem for fsi's only.

Throughout the proofs of this and the next section, we use the following set of fd's:

Definition 3.2. $FSAT_{\mathcal{I}}(\mathcal{F})$ is the smallest possible set of fd's, such that:

1. $\mathcal{F} \subseteq FSAT_{\mathcal{I}}(\mathcal{F})$.
2. If $\mathcal{F}_{i_1} \subseteq FSAT_{\mathcal{I}}(\mathcal{F})$ and $\mathcal{F}_{i_1} \overset{Z_i}{\supset\!\!-} \mathcal{F}_{i_2} \in \mathcal{I}$ then $\mathcal{F}_{i_2} \subseteq FSAT(\mathcal{F})$.
3. If $FSAT_{\mathcal{I}}(\mathcal{F}) = (FSAT_{\mathcal{I}}(\mathcal{F}))^*$.

□

$FSAT_{\mathcal{I}}(\mathcal{F})$ can be constructed starting from $\mathcal{F}$ and by repeatedly trying to satisfy 2) and 3) of the definition. However, the construction will never be useful in a membership algorithm since taking the closure (step 3) of a set of fd's is very costly. Fortunately one can quite easily construct an efficient algorithm for verifying whether an fd is in $FSAT_{\mathcal{I}}(\mathcal{F})$. A similar algorithm is given for cfd's in the extended version of [De3].

Note that $FSAT_{\mathcal{I}}(\mathcal{F}) = FSAT_{\mathcal{I} \cup \mathcal{F}}(\emptyset)$. This equality will be used several times without further notice.

Lemma 3.3. $FSAT_{\mathcal{I}}(\mathcal{F}) = \{P \to Q : \mathcal{I} \cup \mathcal{F} \models P \to Q\}$.

Proof. Consider $Arm(FSAT_{\mathcal{I}}(\mathcal{F}))$. By Definition 3.2 and Theorem 2.8 it is clear that $\mathcal{I} \cup \mathcal{F}$ holds in $Arm(FSAT_{\mathcal{I}}(\mathcal{F}))$. Hence all the fd-consequences of $\mathcal{I} \cup \mathcal{F}$ also hold. By Theorem 2.8 this implies that all these fd's are in $(FSAT_{\mathcal{I}}(\mathcal{F}))^*$. Step 3 of Definition 3.2 implies that these fd's are in $FSAT_{\mathcal{I}}(\mathcal{F})$.

The opposite inclusion is obvious from Definition 3.2.

□

The above lemma shows how to detect whether an fd is a consequence of a set of fsi's.

Lemma 3.4. $FSAT_{\mathcal{I}}(\mathcal{F}) = \{P \to Q : \mathcal{I} \cup \mathcal{F} \vdash P \to Q\}$.

Proof. From Theorem 3.1 and Lemma 3.3 we know that: $\{P \to Q : \mathcal{I} \cup \mathcal{F} \vdash P \to Q\} \subseteq FSAT_{\mathcal{I}}(\mathcal{F})$.

For the opposite inclusion we show that the property, that all elements of $FSAT_{\mathcal{I}}(\mathcal{F})$ can be deduced from $\mathcal{I} \cup \mathcal{F}$, remains valid throughout the construction of $FSAT_{\mathcal{I}}(\mathcal{F})$.

- If $P \to Q \in \mathcal{F}$ then the property is trivial.
- If $P \to Q$ is added to $FSAT_{\mathcal{I}}(X, Y)$ in step 2 of Definition 3.2 then $P \to Q \in \mathcal{F}_{i_2}$ for some $\mathcal{F}_{i_1} \overset{Z_i}{\succ} \mathcal{F}_{i_2} \in \mathcal{I}$. By induction all fd's of $\mathcal{F}_{i_1}$ can be inferred from $\mathcal{I} \cup \mathcal{F}$. Hence by rule $FS5$ $\mathcal{I} \cup \mathcal{F} \vdash \mathcal{F}_{i_2}$. Rule $FS5$ applied to $\mathcal{F}_{i_2}$ and $\mathcal{F}_{i_2} \overset{Z_i}{\succ} \{P \to Q\}$ (holding by $FS1$) gives $\mathcal{I} \cup \mathcal{F} \vdash P \to Q$.
- If $P \to Q$ is added in step 3 of Definition 3.2 then it can be deduced from fd's for which the property holds, by using $F1 \ldots F3$, which are the classical inference rules for fd's [Ul]. Hence $\mathcal{I} \cup \mathcal{F} \vdash P \to Q$.

□

If one chooses $\mathcal{F} = \emptyset$ then the following result becomes obvious:

Corollary 3.5. *$F1 \ldots F3$, $FS1 \ldots FS5$ are complete for the inference of fd's from a set of fsi's.*

□

In the construction of $FSAT_{\mathcal{I}}(\emptyset)$ only those fsi's $\mathcal{F}_{i_1} \overset{Z_i}{\succ} \mathcal{F}_{i_2}$ of $\mathcal{I}$ are used (in step 2) for which $\mathcal{I} \models \mathcal{F}_{i_1}$ (and hence also $\mathcal{I} \models \mathcal{F}_{i_2}$).

This leads to the following lemma:

Lemma 3.6. *Let* $\mathcal{I}_Z = \{\mathcal{F}_{i_1} \overset{Z_i}{\succ} \mathcal{F}_{i_2} \in \mathcal{I} : \mathcal{I} \models Z_i \to Z$ or $\mathcal{I} \models \mathcal{F}_{i_1}\}$.

$\mathcal{I} \models P \to Q$ iff $\mathcal{I}_Z \models P \to Q$ (for any Z).

□

In the sequel we will also need the following remark, which can be easily deduced from the inference rules for fd's:

Remark 3.7 *If $Z \to Z'$ and $\forall X \to Y \in \mathcal{F} : Z \subseteq X$ then $\mathcal{F}$ and $\mathcal{F}^{*Z'}$ are equivalent (i. e. $\mathcal{F}^* = (\mathcal{F}^{*Z'})^*$). In general however, (if $Z \not\to Z'$) $\mathcal{F}$ is more powerful than $\mathcal{F}^{*Z'}$.*

□

The following lemma shows an important property of $FSAT_{\mathcal{I}_Z}(\mathcal{F})$.

Lemma 3.8. *Let $\mathcal{I}_Z$ be as in Lemma 3.6. Let $\mathcal{F}$ be such that $\forall X \to Y \in \mathcal{F} : Z \subseteq X$.*

If $P \to Q \in FSAT_{\mathcal{I}_Z}(\mathcal{F})$ then $\mathcal{I} \models P \to Q$ or $\mathcal{I} \models P \to Z$.

Proof. We prove that the property remains valid throughout the construction of $FSAT_{\mathcal{I}_Z}(\mathcal{F})$.

- If $P \to Q \in \mathcal{F}$ then $P \to Z$ is trivial.
- If $P \to Q$ is added in step 2 of Definition 3.2 then $P \to Q \in \mathcal{F}_{i_2}$ for some $\mathcal{F}_{i_1} \overset{Z_i}{\succ} \mathcal{F}_{i_2} \in \mathcal{I}_Z$. There are two possibilities (by the definition of $\mathcal{I}_Z$): $\mathcal{I} \models \mathcal{F}_{i_1}$ or $\mathcal{I} \models Z_i \to Z$.
  - If $\mathcal{I} \models \mathcal{F}_{i_1}$ then $\mathcal{I} \models \mathcal{F}_2$ by $FS5$, hence obviously $\mathcal{I} \models P \to Q \in \mathcal{F}_{i_2}$.

- If $I \models Z_i \to Z$ then $I \models P \to Z$ by augmentation (since $Z_i \subseteq P$ if $P \to Q \in \mathcal{F}_{i_2}$).

- If $P \to Q$ is added in step 3 then it is derived from other fd's (already in $FSAT_{I_Z}(\mathcal{F})$) by reflexivity, augmentation or transitivity [Ul].
  - If $Q \subseteq P$ then $P \to Q$ is trivial.
  - If $P = P'P''$, $Q = Q'Q''$, with $P' \to Q'$ already in $FSAT_{I_Z}(\mathcal{F})$ and $Q'' \subseteq P''$, then $P \to Q$ or $P \to Z$ is deduced from $P' \to Q'$ or $P' \to Z$ by augmentation.
  - If $P \to O$ and $O \to Q$ already are in $FSAT_{I_Z}(\mathcal{F})$ then $P \to Q$ or $P \to Z$ is deduced from $P \to O$ or $P \to Z$ and $O \to Q$ or $O \to Z$ by transitivity.

□

The following lemma partially solves the membership problem for fsi's:

Lemma 3.9. *Let I_Z be as in Lemma 3.6. Let $\mathcal{F}_1$ be such that $\forall X \to Y \in \mathcal{F}_1 : Z \subseteq X$, $\mathcal{F}_2$ such that $\forall X \to Y \in \mathcal{F}_2 : Z' \subseteq X$, and let $I \models Z' \to Z$.*

Then $I_Z \models \mathcal{F}_1 \overset{Z}{\supset\!\!-} \mathcal{F}_2^{*Z}$ iff $\mathcal{F}_2 \subseteq FSAT_{I_Z}(\mathcal{F}_1)$.

Proof. If $I_Z \models \mathcal{F}_1 \overset{Z}{\supset\!\!-} \mathcal{F}_2^{*Z}$ then obviously $\mathcal{F}_2^{*Z} \subseteq FSAT_{I_Z}(\mathcal{F}_1)$. Since $I \models Z' \to Z$ $\mathcal{F}_2^{*Z}$ is equivalent to $\mathcal{F}_2$ by Remark 3.7. Hence also $\mathcal{F}_2 \subseteq FSAT_{I_Z}(\mathcal{F}_1)$ by step 3 of Definition 3.2.

For the converse we proceed as in Lemma's 3.4 and 3.8, by proving that the property remains valid throughout the construction of $FSAT_{I_Z}(\mathcal{F}_1)$.

- If $\mathcal{F}_2 = \mathcal{F}_1$ then rule $FS1$ gives $\mathcal{F}_1 \overset{Z}{\supset\!\!-} \mathcal{F}_2^{*Z}$.
- If $\mathcal{F}_2$ is added to $FSAT_{I_Z}(\mathcal{F})$ in step 2 of Definition 3.2 then $\mathcal{F}_2 = \mathcal{F}_{i_2}$ for some $\mathcal{F}_{i_1} \overset{Z}{\supset\!\!-} \mathcal{F}_{i_2} \in I_Z$. There are 2 possibilities (by the definition of I_Z):
  - If $I \models \mathcal{F}_{i_1}$ then $I_Z \models \mathcal{F}_{i_1}$ by Lemma 3.6. Hence $I_Z \models \mathcal{F}_{i_2}$ by rule $FS5$. Hence also $I_Z \models \mathcal{F}_{i_2}^{*Z}$ since $\mathcal{F}_{i_2}$ induces $\mathcal{F}_{i_2}^{*Z}$. $\mathcal{F}_1 \overset{Z}{\supset\!\!-} \emptyset$ (holding by $FS1$) and $\emptyset \overset{Z}{\supset\!\!-} \mathcal{F}_{i_2}^{*Z}$ (a representation for fd's, by $FS5$) induce $\mathcal{F}_1 \overset{Z}{\supset\!\!-} \mathcal{F}_{i_2}^{*Z} = \mathcal{F}_1 \overset{Z}{\supset\!\!-} \mathcal{F}_2^{*Z}$ by rule $FS3$.
  - If $I \models Z_i \to Z$ then we have that $\mathcal{F}_1 \overset{Z}{\supset\!\!-} \mathcal{F}_{i_1}^{*Z}$ by induction. Since $Z_i \to Z$, $\mathcal{F}_{i_1} \overset{Z_i}{\supset\!\!-} \mathcal{F}_{i_2}$ induces $\mathcal{F}_{i_1}^{*Z} \overset{Z}{\supset\!\!-} \mathcal{F}_{i_2}^{*Z}$ by $FS4$. Hence $\mathcal{F}_1 \overset{Z}{\supset\!\!-} \mathcal{F}_{i_2}^{*Z} = \mathcal{F}_1 \overset{Z}{\supset\!\!-} \mathcal{F}_2^{*Z}$.
- If $\mathcal{F}_2$ is added to $FSAT_{I_Z}(\mathcal{F}_1)$ in step 3 of Definition 3.2 then $\mathcal{F}_2 \subseteq \mathcal{F}^*$ for some $\mathcal{F}$ that was a part of $FSAT_{I_Z}(\mathcal{F}_1)$ already.
  From Lemma 3.8 we know that for all $X \to Y \in \mathcal{F} : I_Z \vdash X \to Y$ or $I_Z \vdash X \to Z$.
  - If $I_Z \vdash X \to Y$ then $I_Z \vdash XZ \to Y$ (by $F2$), hence $I_Z \vdash \mathcal{F}_1 \overset{Z}{\supset\!\!-} \{XZ \to Y\}$ by $FS3$ on $\mathcal{F}_1 \overset{Z}{\supset\!\!-} \emptyset$ and $\emptyset \overset{Z}{\supset\!\!-} XZ \to Y$ ($FS5$).
  - If $I_Z \vdash X \to Z$ then $I_Z \vdash \mathcal{F}_1 \overset{Z}{\supset\!\!-} \{XZ \to Y\}$ holds by induction (since $XZ \to Y \in \{X \to Y\}^{*Z}$).

  Let $\mathcal{F}' = \{XZ \to Y \in \mathcal{F} : I_Z \vdash X \to Z$ or $I_Z \vdash X \to Y\}$, then by $FS2$ $I_Z \vdash \mathcal{F}_1 \overset{Z}{\supset\!\!-} \mathcal{F}'$. One can easily see that $\mathcal{F}^{*Z} = \mathcal{F}'^{*Z}$ (using $F1 \ldots F3$), hence $I_Z \vdash \mathcal{F}_1 \overset{Z}{\supset\!\!-} \mathcal{F}^{*Z}$ by $FS3$ on $\mathcal{F}_1 \overset{Z}{\supset\!\!-} \mathcal{F}'$ and $\mathcal{F}' \overset{Z}{\supset\!\!-} \mathcal{F}'^{*Z} = \mathcal{F}^{*Z}$ ($FS1$). Hence by $FS3$ and $FS1$ one infers $I_Z \vdash \mathcal{F}_1 \overset{Z}{\supset\!\!-} \mathcal{F}_2$.

□

From the proof of Lemma 3.9 one can see that:

Corollary 3.10. *Let I_Z be as in Lemma 3.6, let $\mathcal{F}_1$ and $\mathcal{F}_2$ be such that $\forall X \to Y \in \mathcal{F}_1 \cup \mathcal{F}_2$, $Z \subseteq X$, then $I_Z \vdash \mathcal{F}_1 \overset{Z}{\supset\!\!-} \mathcal{F}_2$ iff $\mathcal{F}_2 \subseteq FSAT_{I_Z}(\mathcal{F}_1)$.*

□

To complete the proof of the completeness of $F1 \ldots F3$, $FS1 \ldots FS5$ for fsi's it remains to show that the fsi's of $I - I_Z$ have no influence on $I \models \mathcal{F}_1 \overset{Z}{\supset\!\!-} \mathcal{F}_2$. To prove this we need a complicated construction of an instance, similar to that of [De5], which we shall also be needing to prove the completeness for mixed fsi's and afs'. Therefore we include the properties of this instance, related to afs', in the following lemma:

Lemma 3.11. *Let $I \cup \mathcal{A}$ be not in conflict. Let I_Z be as in Lemma 3.6. Let $\mathcal{A}_Z = \{\mathfrak{F}_{Z_i} \in \mathcal{A} : I \models Z_i \rightarrow Z\}$. Let $I_Z \cup \mathcal{A}_Z \not\models \mathcal{F}_1 \overset{Z}{\supset\!\!-} \mathcal{F}_2$ (or let $I_Z \cup \mathcal{A}_Z \not\models \mathfrak{F}_{1Z}$).*

Then we can construct an instance in which $I \cup \mathcal{A}$ holds but in which $\mathcal{F}_1 \overset{Z}{\supset\!\!-} \mathcal{F}_2$ (resp. $\mathfrak{F}_{1Z}$) does not hold.

Proof. Suppose $I_Z \cup \mathcal{A}_Z \not\models \mathcal{F}_1 \overset{Z}{\supset\!\!-} \mathcal{F}_2$. We shall see later that in $R_1 = Arm(FSAT_{I_Z}(\mathcal{F}_1))$ $\mathcal{A}_Z$ holds. By Lemma 3.9 $\mathcal{F}_2 \not\subset FSAT_{I_Z}(\mathcal{F}_1)$, hence $\mathcal{F}_2$ does not hold in R_1. From Theorem 2.8 we can easily deduce that this means that for some $X \rightarrow Y \in \mathcal{F}_2$ $X \overset{X}{\not\rightarrowtail} Y$ holds in R_1, hence $X \overset{Z}{\not\rightarrowtail} Y$ holds (by $F1$ and $FA3$). We also know (from rule $FA2$) that $\mathfrak{F}_{1Z}$ cannot hold in R_1.

In R_1 a number of fsi's of $I - I_Z$ and a number of afs' of $\mathcal{A} - \mathcal{A}_Z$ may not hold. This will be solved by "adding" copies of $S = Arm(FSAT_I(\emptyset))$. In S $I \cup \mathcal{A}$ holds, as one can easily see.

Let some $\mathcal{F}_{i_1} \overset{Z_i}{\supset\!\!-} \mathcal{F}_{i_2} \in I - I_Z$ not hold in R_1. Then (Theorem 2.8) all fd's of $\mathcal{F}_{i_1}$ hold and some fd's of $\mathcal{F}_{i_2}$ do not hold. Since $\mathcal{F}_{i_1} \overset{Z_i}{\supset\!\!-} \mathcal{F}_{i_2} \notin I_Z$ for some fd $T \rightarrow U \in \mathcal{F}_{i_1} : I \not\models T \rightarrow U$.

Let the values that occur in S be renamed such that they all become different from the values of R_1, except that for some $t_1 \in R_1$, $t_2 \in S : t_1[\overline{Z_i}] = t_2[\overline{Z_i}]$, where $\overline{Z_i} = \{attribute\ A : I \models Z_i \rightarrow A\}$. The "modified" union of R_1 and S satisfies the following properties:

- In $R_1 \cup S$ I_Z still holds: let $\mathcal{F}_{j_1} \overset{Z_j}{\supset\!\!-} \mathcal{F}_{j_2} \in I_Z$ not hold. Then there are two cases:
  - either $I \models \mathcal{F}_{j_1}$, hence $I \models \mathcal{F}_{j_2}$ by $FS5$, and if $\mathcal{F}_{i_2}$ no longer holds then $\exists s_1 \in R_1, \exists s_2 \in S, \exists T_j \rightarrow U_j \in \mathcal{F}_{j_2}$: $s_1[T_j] = s_2[T_j]$ and $s_1[U_j] \neq s_2[U_j]$, and hence $T_j \subseteq \overline{Z_i}$ and $s_1[T_j] = s_2[t_j] = t_1[T_j]$, but then also $U_j \subseteq \overline{Z_i}$ since $I \models T_j \rightarrow U_j$, hence $s_1[U_j] = s_2[U_j] = t_1[U_j]$, a contradiction.
  - or $I \models Z_i \rightarrow Z$, but then $T_j \subseteq \overline{Z_i}$ (which holds for some $T_j \rightarrow U_j \in \mathcal{F}_{j_2}$ that does not hold in $R_1 \cup S$) and $Z_j \rightarrow Z$ would induce $Z \subseteq \overline{Z_i}$, a contradiction with $\mathcal{F}_{i_1} \overset{Z_i}{\supset\!\!-} \mathcal{F}_{i_2} \notin I_Z$.
- In $R_1 \cup S$ $\mathcal{A}_Z$ still holds since it is impossible to violate an afs by taking a union of two instances in which that afs holds.
- In $R_1 \cup S$ every fsi of $I - I_Z$ and every afs of $\mathcal{A} - \mathcal{A}_Z$ which already holds in R_1 (and also in S of course) still holds. For the afs' the reason is the same as for those of $\mathcal{A}_Z$. For the fsi's we have that if $\mathcal{F}_{k_1} \overset{Z_k}{\supset\!\!-} \mathcal{F}_{k_2} \in I - I_Z$ holds in R_1 then $\mathfrak{F}_{k_1 Z_k}$ holds in R_1 and S, and such an afs is not violated by the union. $FA2$ shows that this afs implies $\mathcal{F}_{k_1} \overset{Z_k}{\supset\!\!-} \mathcal{F}_{k_2}$.
- In $R_1 \cup S$ $\mathfrak{F}_{1Z}$ still does not hold, since it does not hold in R_1 and since (as explained above) R_1 and R_2 do not "share" a common Z-value which could influence $\mathfrak{F}_{1Z}$ in R_1 (otherwise $Z \subseteq \overline{Z_i}$).
- In $R_1 \cup S$ $\mathfrak{F}_{2Z}$ may no longer hold, because it may not hold in S. But in the "R_1-part" of $R_1 \cup S$ $\mathcal{F}_2^Z$ still holds, since R_1 and S do not share a Z-value (and hence also no T-value for any $T \rightarrow U \in \mathcal{F}_2$).
- But in $R_1 \cup S$ the number of Z_i-values for which all $X_{i_n} \rightarrow Y_{i_n} \in \mathcal{F}_1$ hold (and for which some $T_{i_n} \rightarrow U_{i_n} \in \mathcal{F}_2$ does not hold) is decreased by one, since the Z_i-value containing t_1 collapses with the Z_i-value of S, containing t_2, (in which $\mathfrak{F}_{1 Z_i}$ holds), and since S has no Z_i-values for which all $X_{i_n} \rightarrow Y_{i_n} \in \mathcal{F}_{i_1}$ hold.

By repeating the above construction for all other Z_i-values for which $\mathcal{F}_{i_1}$ holds one can generate a relation in which $\mathcal{F}_{i_1} \overset{Z_i}{\supset\!-} \mathcal{F}_{i_2}$ holds (since $\not\mathcal{F}_{i_1 Z_i}$ holds).

By then repeating the above construction for all fsi's of $I - I_Z$ which do not hold in $Arm(FSAT_{I_Z}(\mathcal{F}_1))$ one generates a relation in which I holds (and $\mathcal{F}_1 \overset{Z}{\supset\!-} \mathcal{F}_2$ still does not hold).

For the afs' of $\mathcal{A} - \mathcal{A}_Z$ the construction proceeds in a similar way.

If $I_Z \cup \mathcal{A}_Z \not\models \not\mathcal{F}_Z$ then we shall see later that in $Arm(FSAT_{I_Z}(\mathcal{F}))$ $\mathcal{A}_Z$ holds, as well as $I_Z \cup \{\mathcal{F}\}$.

The same construction as above leads to an instance in which $I \cup \mathcal{A}$ holds, and in which $\not\mathcal{F}_Z$ does not hold.

□

Theorem 3.12. *$F1 \ldots F3$, $FS1 \ldots FS5$ are complete for fdi's.*

Furthermore, let $\mathcal{F}_1$ and $\mathcal{F}_2$ be such that $\forall X \to Y \in \mathcal{F}_2 \cup \mathcal{F}_2 : Z \subseteq X$, then $I \vdash \mathcal{F}_1 \overset{Z}{\supset\!-} \mathcal{F}_2$ iff $\mathcal{F}_2 \subseteq FSAT_{I_Z}(\mathcal{F}_1)$.

Proof. If $I \models \mathcal{F}_1 \overset{Z}{\supset\!-} \mathcal{F}_2$ then by Lemma 3.11 $I_Z \models \mathcal{F}_1 \overset{Z}{\supset\!-} \mathcal{F}_2$. Lemma 3.9 yields $\mathcal{F}_2 \in FSAT_{I_Z}(\mathcal{F}_1)$, while Corollary 3.10 implies $I_Z \vdash \mathcal{F}_1 \overset{Z}{\supset\!-} \mathcal{F}_2$.

The converse is trivial.

□

Before we prove the completeness of our rules for mixed fsi's and afs', we take a closer look at the conflict concept.

Lemma 3.13. *$I \cup \mathcal{A}$ is in conflict iff for some $\not\mathcal{F}_Z \in \mathcal{A}$ $I \models \mathcal{F}$ holds.*

Proof. The if-part is trivial.

For the only-if-part consider $Arm(FSAT_I(\emptyset))$. In $Arm(FSAT_I(\emptyset))$ I holds, hence if $I \cup \mathcal{A}$ is in conflict some $\not\mathcal{F}_Z \in \mathcal{A}$ does not hold. If for some fd $X \to Y \in \mathcal{F}$ $X \to Y$ does not hold in $Arm(FSAT_I(\emptyset))$ then by Theorem 2.8 $X \overset{X}{\not\to} Y$ must hold. With rules $FS1, FA3$ and $FA4$ one can easily deduce that $X \overset{X}{\not\to} Y$ induces $\not\mathcal{F}_Z$. Hence for no $X \to Y \in \mathcal{F}$ $X \overset{X}{\not\to} Y$ can hold. Theorem 2.8 then induces that for all $X \to Y \in \mathcal{F}$ $X \to Y$ holds, hence $\mathcal{F}$ holds and must be a consequence of $FSAT_I(\emptyset)$. Step 3 of Definition 3.2 implies that $\mathcal{F} \subseteq FSAT_I(\emptyset, \emptyset)$, hence $I \models \mathcal{F}$ by Lemma 3.3.

□

Lemma 3.14. *Let $I \cup \mathcal{A}$ be not in conflict.*

$I \cup \mathcal{A} \models \not\mathcal{F}_Z$ iff $I_Z \cup \mathcal{A}_Z \vdash \not\mathcal{F}_Z$.

Proof. The if-part is trivial.

For the only-if-part, suppose $I_Z \cup \mathcal{A}_Z \nvdash \not\mathcal{F}_Z$. We first show that $I_Z \cup \mathcal{A}_Z \not\models \not\mathcal{F}_Z$.

Suppose $I_Z \cup \mathcal{A}_Z \models \not\mathcal{F}_Z$, hence $I_Z \cup \mathcal{A}_Z \cup \mathcal{F}$ is clearly in conflict. Then in $Arm(FSAT_{I_Z}(\mathcal{F}))$ for some afs $\not\mathcal{F}'_V$ of $\mathcal{A}_Z$ $\mathcal{F}'$ holds (by Lemma 3.13 and Theorem 2.8). Hence (Theorem 2.8) $I_Z \cup \mathcal{F} \models \mathcal{F}'$. Since $I_Z \models V \to Z$ Lemma 3.9 yields $I_Z \models \mathcal{F} \overset{Z}{\supset\!-} \mathcal{F}'^{*Z}$.

$\not\mathcal{F}'_V$ induces $\not\mathcal{F}'^{*Z}_Z$ by rule $FA3$. Rule $FA1$ (with $\mathcal{F} \overset{Z}{\supset\!-} \mathcal{F}'^{*Z}$ induces $\not\mathcal{F}_Z$, a contradiction with $I_Z \cup \mathcal{A}_Z \nvdash \not\mathcal{F}_Z$.

Hence $I_Z \cup \mathcal{A}_Z \not\models \not\mathcal{F}_Z$ and $\mathcal{A}_Z$ holds in $Arm(FSAT_{I_Z}(\mathcal{F}))$ (this was used in Lemma 3.11, considering that $FA2$ deduces $\mathcal{F}_1 \overset{Z}{\supset\!-} \mathcal{F}_2$ from $\not\mathcal{F}_{1Z}$. Lemma 3.11 then says that there exists an instance in which $I \cup \mathcal{A}$ holds and in which $\not\mathcal{F}_Z$ does not hold. Hence $I \cup \mathcal{A} \not\models \not\mathcal{F}_Z$.

□

Lemma 3.15 *Let $\mathcal{I} \cup \mathcal{A}$ be not in conflict.*
$\mathcal{I} \cup \mathcal{A} \models \mathcal{F}_1 \overset{Z}{\supset\!\!-} \mathcal{F}_2$ *iff* $\mathcal{I}_Z \vdash \mathcal{F}_1 \overset{Z}{\supset\!\!-} \mathcal{F}_2$ *or* $\mathcal{I}_Z \cup \mathcal{A}_Z \vdash \not{\mathcal{F}}_{1Z}$.

Proof. The if part is trivial (using $FA2$ if $\mathcal{I}_Z \cup \mathcal{A}_Z \vdash \not{\mathcal{F}}_{1Z}$).

For the only-if-part, assume that $\mathcal{I}_Z \not\vdash \mathcal{F}_1 \overset{Z}{\supset\!\!-} \mathcal{F}_2$ and $\mathcal{I}_Z \cup \mathcal{A}_Z \not\vdash \not{\mathcal{F}}_{1Z}$. By the proof of Lemma 3.14 $\mathcal{I}_Z \cup \mathcal{A}_Z \not\models \not{\mathcal{F}}_{1Z}$. Hence by Lemma 3.11 there exists an instance in which $\mathcal{I} \cup \mathcal{A}$ holds and in which $\mathcal{F}_1 \overset{Z}{\supset\!\!-} \mathcal{F}_2$ does not hold. Hence $\mathcal{I} \cup \mathcal{A} \not\models \mathcal{F}_1 \overset{Z}{\supset\!\!-} \mathcal{F}_2$.

□

The above lemmas prove:

Theorem 3.16 *$F1 \ldots F3, FS1 \ldots FS5$ and $FA1 \ldots FA4$ are complete for mixed fsi's and afs'.*

□

The following property shows how to solve the membership problem (and is easy to prove):

Corollary 3.17 *Let $\mathcal{I} \cup \mathcal{A}$ be not in conflict.*
Let $\mathcal{I}_Z = \{\mathcal{F}_{i_1} \overset{Z_i}{\supset\!\!-} \mathcal{F}_{i_2} \in \mathcal{I} : \mathcal{F}_{i_1} \subseteq FSAT_{\mathcal{I}}(\emptyset)$ *or* $Z_i \rightarrow Z \in FSAT_{\mathcal{I}}(\emptyset)\}$.
Let $\mathcal{A}_Z = \{\not{\mathcal{F}}'_{V_i} \in \mathcal{A} : V_i \rightarrow Z \in FSAT_{\mathcal{I}}(\emptyset)\}$.
$\mathcal{I} \cup \mathcal{A} \models \not{\mathcal{F}}_Z$ *iff for some afs* $\not{\mathcal{F}}'_{V_i}$ *of* $\mathcal{A}_Z$ *we have* $\mathcal{F}' \subseteq FSAT_{\mathcal{I}_Z}(\mathcal{F})$.
$\mathcal{I} \cup \mathcal{A} \models \mathcal{F}_1 \overset{Z}{\supset\!\!-} \mathcal{F}_2$ *iff* $\mathcal{I} \cup \mathcal{A} \models \not{\mathcal{F}}_{1Z}$ *or* $\mathcal{F}_2 \in FSAT_{\mathcal{I}_Z}(\mathcal{F}_1)$.

□

Using Corollary 3.17 and a membership test for *FSAT*, a polynomial time membership algorithm for mixed fsi's and afs' can be easily constructed. The major factor in the time complexity is the calculation of $\mathcal{I}_Z$ and $\mathcal{A}_Z$.

§4 The Inheritance of Dependencies

In Example 2.1 the relation scheme contains only one fsi. In general however a scheme may have several fsi's and afs'. So after decomposing it according to one of its fsi's, we want to decompose the subschemes further on, using other fsi's. But not all fsi's (and afs') still hold in the subschemes. In this section we describe how to decide which dependencies hold in the subschemes. This is called the *inheritance problem*.

Notation 4.1. In the sequel we always treat the horizontal decomposition of a scheme $\mathcal{R}$, with fsi's $\mathcal{I}$ and afs' $\mathcal{A}$, according to $\mathcal{F}_1 \overset{Z}{\supset\!\!-} \mathcal{F}_2 \in \mathcal{I}$, into the subschemes $\mathcal{R}_1 = \sigma_{\mathcal{F}_{1Z}}(\mathcal{R})$ with fsi's $\mathcal{I}_1$ and afs' $\mathcal{A}_1$, and $\mathcal{R}_2 = \sigma_{\not{\mathcal{F}}_{1Z}}(\mathcal{R})$ with fsi's $\mathcal{I}_2$ and afs' $\mathcal{A}_2$. We assume that $\mathcal{I} \cup \mathcal{A}$ is not in conflict, and also that $\mathcal{I} \cup \mathcal{A} \not\models \mathcal{F}_1$ and $\mathcal{I} \cup \mathcal{A} \not\models \not{\mathcal{F}}_{1Z}$ (otherwise $\mathcal{R}_1$ resp. $\mathcal{R}_2$ would always be empty). We only require $\mathcal{I}_1 \cup \mathcal{A}_1$ and $\mathcal{I}_2 \cup \mathcal{A}_2$ to be generating for the sets of all dependencies which hold in $\mathcal{R}_1$ and $\mathcal{R}_2$.

Remark 4.2. *Since fd's cannot be violated by taking a restriction, all the fd's which hold in $\mathcal{R}$ also hold in $\mathcal{R}_1$ and $\mathcal{R}_2$.*

□

The following inclusions are easy to prove:

Lemma 4.3.

$\mathcal{I}_1 \subseteq \{\mathcal{F}_1' \overset{Z'}{\supset\!-} \mathcal{F}_2' : \mathcal{I} \cup \mathcal{A} \cup \mathcal{F}_1 \models \mathcal{F}_1' \overset{Z'}{\supset\!-} \mathcal{F}_2'\}$.

$\mathcal{I}_2 \subseteq \{\mathcal{F}_1' \overset{Z'}{\supset\!-} \mathcal{F}_2' : \mathcal{I} \cup \mathcal{A} \cup \mathfrak{F}_{1Z} \models \mathcal{F}_1' \overset{Z'}{\supset\!-} \mathcal{F}_2'\}$.

$\mathcal{A}_1 \subseteq \{\mathfrak{F}_{Z'}' : \mathcal{I} \cup \mathcal{A} \cup \mathcal{F}_1 \models \mathfrak{F}_{Z'}'\}$.

$\mathcal{A}_2 \subseteq \{\mathfrak{F}_{Z'}' : \mathcal{I} \cup \mathcal{A} \cup \mathfrak{F}_{1Z} \models \mathfrak{F}_{Z'}'\}$.

Theorem 4.4. *An fsi or afs must hold in $\mathcal{R}_1$ (resp. $\mathcal{R}_2$) iff it is a consequence of $\mathcal{I}_Z \cup \mathcal{A}_Z \cup \mathcal{F}_1$ (resp. $\mathcal{I}_Z \cup \mathcal{A}_Z \cup \mathfrak{F}_{1Z}$).*

Proof. From Lemma 4.3 it follows that $(\mathcal{I}_Z \cup \mathcal{A}_Z \cup \mathcal{F}_1)^* \subseteq (\mathcal{I}_1 \cup \mathcal{A}_1)^* \subseteq (\mathcal{I} \cup \mathcal{A} \cup \mathcal{F}_1)^*$ and also that $(\mathcal{I}_Z \cup \mathcal{A}_Z \cup \mathfrak{F}_{1Z})^* \subseteq (\mathcal{I}_2 \cup \mathcal{A}_2)^* \subseteq (\mathcal{I} \cup \mathcal{A} \cup \mathfrak{F}_{1Z})^*$, where $*$ means the "closure" operator, i. e. taking all the consequences of a set of dependencies (as we already did for fd's in Section 3). We prove that the first inclusions are equalities.

Let $\mathcal{I} \cup \mathcal{A} \cup \mathcal{F}_1 \models \mathfrak{F}_{Z'}'$, but $\mathcal{I}_Z \cup \mathcal{A}_Z \cup \mathcal{F}_1 \not\models \mathfrak{F}_{Z'}'$. We prove that $\mathfrak{F}_{Z'}'$ does not hold in $\mathcal{R}_1$.

$\mathcal{I}_Z \cup \mathcal{A}_Z \cup \mathcal{F}_1 \not\models \mathfrak{F}_{Z'}'$ implies that $\mathcal{I}_Z \cup \mathcal{A}_Z \cup \mathcal{F}_1 \cup \mathcal{F}_1'$ is not in conflict, by the proof of Lemma 3.14. By the proof of Lemma 3.11 one can construct an instance R in which $\mathcal{I} \cup \mathcal{A}$ holds but in which $\mathfrak{F}_{Z'}'$ does not hold. One starts with $R_1 = Arm(FSAT_{\mathcal{I}_Z \cup \mathcal{F}_1}(\mathcal{F}'))$ this time, and adds copies of $Arm(FSAT_{\mathcal{I}}(\emptyset, \emptyset))$ to obtain R. From the construction, used in the proof of Lemma 3.11 one can easily see that $R_1 = \sigma_{\mathcal{F}_{1Z}}(R)$, since the copies of $Arm(FSAT_{\mathcal{I}}(\emptyset, \emptyset))$ have $\mathfrak{F}_{1Z}$ and have different Z-values than those occurring in R_1. Hence we obtain an instance in which $\mathcal{I} \cup \mathcal{A}$ holds, and such that $\mathfrak{F}_{Z'}'$ does not hold in R_1. Hence $\mathfrak{F}_{Z'}' \notin (\mathcal{I}_1 \cup \mathcal{A}_1)^*$.

The proof of the other three cases (an fsi in R_1, an afs in R_2 and an fsi in R_2) is similar and therefore left to the reader.

□

From Theorem 4.4 one can easily deduce an algorithm which calculates the inherited dependencies in the same time as a membership algorithm.

A decomposition algorithm can be easily constructed for the following normal form:

Definition 4.8. A scheme $\mathcal{R}$ is said to be in *FSI-Normal Form, (FSINF)* iff for all fsi's $\mathcal{F}_1 \overset{Z}{\supset\!-} \mathcal{F}_2$ of $\mathcal{I}$ either $\mathcal{F}_1$ or $\mathfrak{F}_{1Z}$ holds in $\mathcal{R}$.

A decomposition $\{\mathcal{R}_1, \ldots, \mathcal{R}_n\}$ is in *FSINF* iff all the $\mathcal{R}_i, i = 1 \ldots n$ are in *FSINF*.

Note that in the "final" subschemes there are no "real" fsi's any more, only fd's and afs'.

Note also that if only fdi's are given, (i. e. $\mathcal{F}_1$ and $\mathcal{F}_2$ each contain only one fd) then the decomposition algorithm generates a decomposition into the *FDI-Normal Form* of [De5]. If the fdi is trivial (i. e. the "left" fd is trivial) then the decomposition algorithm generates a decomposition into the *Clean Normal Form* of [De2]. If all trivial fdi's are explicitly said to be inherited (from $\mathcal{I}$ to $\mathcal{I}_1$ and $\mathcal{I}_2$) then we obtain the decomposition into the *Inherited Normal Form* of [De2].

§5 Possible extensions

The fsi's $\mathcal{F}_1 \overset{Z}{\supset\!-} \mathcal{F}_2$ still have a rather severe restriction: $\forall X \rightarrow Y \in \mathcal{F}_1 \cup \mathcal{F}_2 : Z \subseteq X$. In this section we shall show how far this restriction can be removed, without seriously affecting the semantics of the constraint.

If one changes the restriction to $X \rightarrow Z$ instead of $Z \subseteq X$, one can easily prove the following remark:

Remark 5.1 *Let $\mathcal{F}_1'$ (resp. $\mathcal{F}_2$)$= \{X' \rightarrow Y : X' = XZ$ and $X \rightarrow Y \in \mathcal{F}_1$ (resp. $\mathcal{F}_2$)$\}$.*

The fsi $\mathcal{F}_1' \overset{Z}{\supset\!-} \mathcal{F}_2'$ plus the set of all fd's $XZ \rightarrow Y : X \rightarrow Y \in \mathcal{F}_1 \cup \mathcal{F}_2$ are equivalent to the "generalized" fsi $\mathcal{F}_1 \overset{Z}{\supset\!-} \mathcal{F}_2$.

□

One cannot remove the restriction that $X \rightarrow Z$ must hold as well. The class of constraints would certainly become bigger, but in the subrelation $\mathcal{R}_1$, generated by the "generalized" fsi $\mathcal{F}_1 \overset{Z}{\supset\!-} \mathcal{F}_2$ the set of fd's $\mathcal{F}_1$ does not hold any more, as one can easily see from the following example:

Suppose we have the "unconstrained" fsi $Emp \rightarrow Job \overset{Dep}{\supset\!-} Emp \rightarrow Sal, Man$, meaning that if an employee has only one job in some department, then he has only one salary and one manager for that department. There is something peculiar about this constraint: if for two departments the constraint holds, then (since the two departments together form a *Dep*-complete set of tuples) every employee who works in both departments must have the same job, the same salary and the same manager in both departments! To avoid this altered semantics one can change the definition of the constraint, replacing the phrase "X-complete set" by "X-value" (i.e. X-complete and X-unique set). The definition then becomes:

Definition 5.2 The *"generalized" functional-dependency-set-implication (gfsi)* $\mathcal{F}_1 \overset{Z}{\supset\!-} \mathcal{F}_2$, means that in every Z-unique, Z-complete set of tuples (in every instance) in which all the fd's of $\mathcal{F}_1$ hold, all the fd's of $\mathcal{F}_2$ must hold too.

There is no restriction on X any more. However one can easily prove that such a gfsi is again equivalent to a normal fsi:

Remark 5.3 *Let $\mathcal{F}_1'$ (resp. $\mathcal{F}_2$)$= \{X' \rightarrow Y : X' = XZ$ and $X \rightarrow Y \in \mathcal{F}_1$ (resp. $\mathcal{F}_2$)$\}$.*

The fsi $\mathcal{F}_1' \overset{Z}{\supset\!-} \mathcal{F}_2'$ is equivalent to the gfsi $\mathcal{F}_1 \overset{Z}{\supset\!-} \mathcal{F}_2$.

□

The constraint from Example 2.1 now can be written as the gfsi

$$\{dep \rightarrow job; emp \rightarrow job; man \rightarrow job\} \overset{div}{\supset\!-} \{emp \rightarrow dep, sal; man \rightarrow dep\}$$

The meaning now reflects the formal description of the constraint more closely than in Example 2.1.

In future research a similar theory should be established for handling exceptions to other constraints, such as multivalued dependencies or inclusion dependencies.

References

[Ar] Armstrong W., Dependency structures of database relationships, *Proc. IFIP 74*, North Holland, pp. 580–583, 1974.

[Be] Beeri C., Bernstein P.A., Computational Problems related to the Design of Normal Form Relation Schemes, *ACM TODS*, vol. **4.1**, pp. 30–59, 1979.

[Ber] Bernstein P.A., Normalization and Functional Dependencies in the Relational Database Model, *CSRG-60*, 1975.

[Co] Codd E., Further normalizations of the database relational model, In *Data Base Systems* (R. Rustin, ed.) Prentice Hall, N.J., pp. 33–64, 1972.

[De1] De Bra P., Paredaens J., The membership and the inheritance of functional and afunctional dependencies, Proc. of the Colloquium on Algebra, Combinatorics and Logic in Computer Science, Gyor, Hungary.

[De2] De Bra P., Paredaens J., Horizontal Decompositions for Handling Exceptions to Functional Dependencies, in "Advances in Database Theory", Vol. II, pp. 123–144, 1983.

[De3] De Bra P., Paredaens J., Conditional Dependencies for Horizontal Decompositions, in "Lecture Notes in Computer Science", Vol. **154**, pp. 67–82, (10-th *ICALP*), Springer-Verlag, 1983.

[De4] De Bra P., Imposed-Functional Dependencies Inducing Horizontal Decompositions, in "Lecture Notes in Computer Science", Vol. **194**, pp. 158–170, (12-th *ICALP*), Springer-Verlag, 1985.

[De5] De Bra P., Functional Dependency Implications, Inducing Horizontal Decompositions, UIA-report 85-30, 1985.

[Fa] Fagin R., Armstrong Databases, *IBM RJ 3440*, 1982.

[Pa] Paredaens J., De Bra P., On Horizontal Decompositions, *XP2-Congress*, State Univ. of Pennsylvania, 1981.

[Ul] Ullman J., Principles of Database Systems, Pitman, 1980.

UPDATE SERIALIZABILITY IN LOCKING

R. C. Hansdah and L. M. Patnaik
Department of Computer Science and Automation
Indian Institute of Science
Bangalore 560 012
INDIA

Abstract.

There are many concurrency control algorithms that use weak consistency of read-only transactions to enhance concurrency in database systems[3,8,18]. We identify these schedules (which become serializable when the weakly consistent read-only transactions are deleted from them) as update serializable schedules. In this paper, we study how update serializable schedules can be produced using locking and the advantages of allowing update serializable schedules in locking protocols. We show that if a locking protocol P which uses exclusive mode locks only is made heterogeneous, then the new locking protocol, called the heterogeneous locking protocol P, ensures update serializability. In addition, we also show that if the original locking protocol is deadlock-free , then a deadlock cycle in the heterogeneous locking protocol involves at least two read-only transactions. We also discuss the advantages that one gets when the guard locking protocol is made heterogeneous. The heterogeneous two phase locking protocol operates on general databases and ensures serializability. We present a simple non-two phase locking protocol on general databases that produces update serializable schedules which are not serializable. This protocol allows the read-only transactions to be non-two phase and restricts the update transactions to access exactly one data item.

1. Introduction

A database is a set **V** of data items together with a domain of values for each data item. A state of a database is an assignment of values to the data items of the database. The state of a database is said to be consistent if the values of the data items satisfy certain consistency constraints so that the values of the data items of the database may represent a real world situation. In essence , a database consists of a set **V** of data items together with a set **C** of consistency constraints.

A database management system should ensure the consistency of the database when it is accessed concurrently by several asynchronously running programs. In addition , it must ensure that each such program sees a consistent view of the database. A common approach to this problem is to group the actions of the programs so that each such group of actions when executed alone preserves the consistency of the database. Each such group of actions is called a transaction. An action is an atomic step of a transaction. A schedule s over a set **T** of transactions is the concurrent execution of the transactions. When a database is accessed concurrently by several transactions , another common problem that arises is the lost update problem. This can be best illustrated by an example.

Example 1.1. Consider the schedule shown below.

$$R_1[x]R_2[x]W_2[x]W_1[x],$$

where $R_i[x]$ and $W_i[x]$ denote read and write actions respectively on data item x , by the transaction T_i. In the above schedule,the effect of T_2 on the database is lost.

The execution of an arbitrary schedule may not preserve the consistency of the database or some transactions may not see a consistent view of the database. It is the task of the scheduler or concurrency control algorithm to intercept the actions of the transactions and reorder them so that the resulting schedule preserves the consistency of the database. A serial schedule is one in wich the transactions are executed one after another. A serial schedule preserves the consistency of the database and each transaction in the serial schedule sees a consistent database. Hence , a schedule output by a scheduler must be "equivalent" to some serial schedule. So we say that a schedule is correct if it is equivalent to some serial schedule. There are various definitions of correctness of schedules depending on the meaning attached to the equivalence of schedules. The correctness criterion most commonly used in practice is view serializability defined in [20]. The other correctness criterion less commonly used in practice is state serializability defined in [15,20]. A view serializable schedule is always state serializable.

The aim of most common concurrecy control algorithms based on techniques such as locking and timestamping is to achieve view serializability. One of the measures of concurrency provided by a scheduler is the size of the set of correct schedules that can be output by the scheduler[11]. It is believed that the larger the size of the set of correct schedules that can be output by a scheduler , the higher the concurrency provided by it. So various researchers have devised concurrency control algorithms that can produce schedules which are not view serializable but are correct in the sense that they either are state serializable or at least preserve the consistency of the database. To achieve this , some concurrency control algorithms use both the the semantics of the transactions and the database[3,7,8,12].

Another common approach adopted to enhance concurrency is to reduce the interval of time during which a particular transaction , say T , prevents other transactions from accessing a data item x. We call this interval of time the hold time of the transaction T on the data item x. For example , when a transaction holds an exclusive lock on a data item x , the hold time of the transaction on the data item x is the interval of time during which the transaction holds the lock on the data item x. In other concurrency control algorithms , the hold time of a transaction on a data item may not be defined so easily as in the case of locking protocols; however it can be defined in any concurrency control algorithms. Intuitively , it appeals that the smaller the hold time of a transaction on a data item , the higher the concurrency that can be achieved. Since two phase locking protocol[6] does not permit the release of locks till all the locks have been acquired , non-two phase locking protocols have been proposed on structured databases[2,9,13,16,17] and on general databases[5]. In a non-two phase locking protocol , locks can be released before all the locks are acquired. This characteristics of a non-two phase locking protocol helps to reduce the hold time of a transaction on a data item.

The concurrency control algorithms in centralized databases based on locking have aimed to achieve view serializability only[6,9,16,17]. The wait-for list centralized algorithm(WLCA) for distributed databases reported in [8] produces weakly consistent schedules. Using multiversion database, the implementation of read-only transactions for distributed databases allows weak consistency of read-only transactions in the concurrency control algorithms presented in [3]. We say that a schedule is update serializable if it is serializable after deleting the weakly consistent read-only transactions from the schedule and a formal definition of update serializability is given in section 2. An update serializable schedule is not necessarily view serializable but it satisfies the following three conditions most commonly accepted by the users and proposed in [4].

(1) The database after the schedule has been executed is consistent.

(2) Each transaction sees a consistent database.

(3) No updates are lost.

The concurrency control algorithms that allow update serializable schedules use the semantics of the database that is evident from the concurrently executing update transactions and the fact that the read-only transactions do not modify the database.In this paper , we show that if a locking protocol P which uses exclusive mode locks only is made heterogeneous by allowing two types of transactions , viz., update transactions that can request locks in exclusive mode only and read-only transactions that can request locks in share mode only , and both types of transactions follow the locking protocol P, then the schedules produced by the modified locking protocol are update serializable. This is expected to enhance concurrency in the locking protocols, as the size of the set of schedules output by a lock manager is increased. The modified locking protocol is said to be a heterogeneous locking protocol. A heterogeneous locking protocol need not be deadlock-free. However , if the original locking protocol is deadlock-free , then a deadlock cycle in the heterogenous locking protocol always involves at least two read-only transactions. It is known that the heterogeneous two phase locking protocol ensures serializability [10,13] and hence it does not produce update serializable schedules which are not serializable. We propose a simple non-two phase locking protocol on general databases that ensures update serializability and allows read-only transactions to be non-two phase. This protocol uses the restriction that update transactions can access exactly one data item.

The rest of the paper is organised as follows. In section 2 , we define update serializability. In section 3 , we review the relevant locking protocols. In section 4 , we show that a heterogenous locking protocol ensures update serializability. We also discuss the advantages that one gets when the guard locking protocol is made heterogeneous in section 4. We propose a simple non-two phase locking protocol on general databases in section 5 and prove that it ensures update serializability. The environments under which this new protocol is advantegeous are also discussed in section 5. Section 6 concludes this paper.

2. Definitions

In the following , we define a series of terms leading to the definition of update serializability. A transaction is a finite sequence of steps $T_i = (T_{i1}, \ldots, T_{in})$, where each step T_{ij} is either a read action or a write action on some data item x. A read action $R_i[x]$ on a data item x by a transaction T_i reads the current value of the data item x. A write action $W_i[x]$ on a data item x by a transaction T_i changes the value of the data item x to a new value computed by the transaction or supplied by the user. We assume that each transaction reads and/or writes each data item at most once and that a transaction does not read a data item after it has written it. The value written by a transaction is a fuction of the values of the data items read by it so far. A transaction is an update transaction if it contains at least one write action ; otherwise it is a read-only transaction. A schedule s over a set **T** of transactions is the merging of the actions of the transactions in **T** such that if T_{ij} precedes T_{ik} in s, then j<k. A schedule is serial if the actions of the differrent transactions are not interleaved, i.e., an action of a transaction T_i does not lie between two actions of some other transaction T_j in s. A schedule s of a set **T** of transactions is view serializable (VSR) if there is a serial schedule s' of **T** such that for every initial state of the database and for every interpretation of the various fuctions computed by the transactions each transaction of **T** receives the same view of the database in s and s' and the execution of s or s' will leave the database in the same final state[20]. A schedule s of a set **T** of transactions is state serializable if there is a serial schedule s' of **T** that produces the same final state as that produced by s, for every interpretation of the various fuctions computed by the transactions[15,20].

Definition 2.1. A schedule s over a set **T** of transactions is update serializable (USR) iff each schedule s' obtained from s after deleting all but one read-only transaction is view serializable. If there are no read-only transactions , then no transactions need be deleted.

The notion of update serializable schedule is the same as the notion of weakly consistent schedule defined in [3,8,18] and only for the sake of convenience and clarity we have redefined it. An update serializable schedule is not neccessarily view serializable and it is always state serializable. In addition , there are schedules which are state serializable but are not update serializable. This is illustrated in the following examples.

Example 2.1. Consider the schedule shown below.

$R_1[a]R_1[b]R_2[a]W_2[a]R_3[a]R_3[b]R_3[c]R_4[c]W_4[c]R_1[c]$.

This schedule is update serializable. The state of the database after the schedule is executed is the one produced by the execution of the serial schedule T_2T_4 or T_4T_2 of the update transactions only. The read-only transaction T_1 sees the consistent database state obtained from the initial database state by the execution of T_4 and the schedule which T_1 perceives is $T_4T_1T_2$. Similarly, T_3 sees the consistent database state obtained from the initial database state by the execution of T_2 and the schedule which T_3 perceives is $T_2T_3T_4$. However , there is no single serial schedule view-equivalent to the given schedule.

Example 2.2. Consider the schedule shown below.

$R_1[x]R_2[y]W_2[x]W_1[y]W_3[x]$.

This schedule is state equivalent to $T_1T_2T_3$ and it is SSR. However, the schedule is not VSR. As there are no read-only transactions, the schedule is also not USR.

From now on , by a serializable schedule , we mean a view serializable schedule.

3. Review of Locking Protocols

A transaction locks a data item before accessing it and can access the data item as long as it holds the lock on the data item. The transaction locks the data item in exclusive (X) mode if it reads and writes or only writes the data item. The transaction locks the data item in share (S) mode if it just reads the data item. The transaction unlocks the data item after reading and/or writing it. We say that a lock mode A is compatible with another lock mode B if a transaction T can lock a data item(which is locked by some other transaction in mode B) in mode A. An X mode lock is neither compatible with itself nor with an S mode lock. However, an S mode lock is compatible with itself. A transaction is well-formed if it locks every data item it accesses , and unlocks only those data items which it has previously locked. The definition of a schedule over a set **T** of locked transactions is identical to that of the unlocked transactions. However, in the case of the set **T** of well-formed locked transactions, a schedule s is legal if two incompatible locks are not requested on the same data item at the same time. From now on , by a transaction, we mean a well-formed locked transaction unless otherwise stated.

In a locking protocol, there is a restriction on the transaction to lock and unlock data items so that every legal schedule of a set **T** of locked transactions results in a serializable schedule. The two phase locking protocol (2PL) which uses X mode locks only is one such protocol[6]. The generalization of 2PL to allow S mode locks and lock conversion is proposed in [10,13]. The generalized 2PL (G2PL) ensures serializability. A heterogeneous locking protocol (HTLP) allows two types of transactions, viz., update transactions which can request locks in X mode only and read-only transactions which can request locks in S mode only, and both types of transactions follow the same rules. Thus, a locking protocol which uses X mode locks only can be made heterogeneous by allowing both the update transactions and the read-only transactions. Both the update and the read-only transactions follow the rules of the original locking protocol. The heterogeneous 2PL protocol (HT2PL) is a special case of the G2PL protocol. Hence it ensures serializability. In 2PL protocol, a transaction cannot release locks until all the locks required by the transaction have been acquired. This restricts the amount of concurrency as the transaction holds the data items for more time than it is necessary. To reduce the hold time of a transaction on a data item, several non-two phase locking protocols have been proposed. In a N2PL protocol, locks can be released by a transaction even if all the locks required by the transaction have not been acquired. A N2PL protocol, called the tree protocol, is proposed in [16] using X mode locks only on data items that are organised as a rooted directed tree. The tree protocol is extended to a case in which the data items are organised as a directed acyclic graph (DAG). This protocol, called the guard locking protocol (GLP) [17] uses X mode locks only. A more general locking protocol, called the hypergraph policy[21] (HP) covers both the 2PL protocol and the GLP protocol. The entry point protocol proposed in [2] is applicable to arbitrarily structured databases. A N2PL protocol, called the five color protocol, on general databases is presented in [5]. The GLP protocol is extended to include S mode locks in [9]. The GLP protocol is stated below as it is used to illustrate the advantages acrueing from the introduction of update serializability.

In the GLP protocol, the database is organised as a DAG **G** =(**V**,**E**), where **V** is the set of vertices and **E** is the set of arcs. Data items in the database are in 1:1 correspondence with vertices; so we use the terms data item and vertex interchangebly. The arcs represents the relationship between the data items (logical or physical). We say that a DAG **G** is a guarded graph iff with each $v \in V$ there is associated a (possibly empty) set of pairs:

$$\text{guard}(v)=\{\langle A_1^v,B_1^v\rangle,\langle A_2^v,B_2^v\rangle,\ldots,\langle A_k^v,B_k^v\rangle\}$$

satisfying the conditions:

(1) $\emptyset \neq B_i^v \subseteq A_i^v \subseteq \mathbf{V}$, for $1 \leqslant i \leqslant k$.

(2) $\forall x \in A_i^v$, x is a parent of v and $1 \leq i \leq k$.

(3) If $A_i^v \cap B_i^v = \emptyset$, then there is no biconnected component[1] of G including the vertices from both A_i^v and B_i^v .

Each pair $<A_i^v, B_i^v>$ is called a subguard of v. We say that the subguard $<A_i^v, B_i^v>$ is <u>satisfied</u> in lock mode M by a transaction T if T currently holds a lock in mode M on all the vertices in B_i^v and it has locked (and possibly unlocked) all the vertices in $A_i^v - B_i^v$ in mode M. The rules of the GLP protocol on a guarded graph using X mode locks only are [17]:

(1) A transaction T may lock any vertex first.

(2) A transaction T may lock a subsequent vertex v only if T has not previously locked it and there exists a subguard $<A_i^v, B_i^v>$ satisfied in mode X by T.

(3) A transaction may unlock a vertex any time.

The GLP protocol ensures serializability and is deadlock-free[17].

The GLP protocol has been generalized to heterogeneous GLP(HTGLP) in [1,9]; however in the HTGLP protocol the DAG is restricted to rooted DAG and the update transactions must lock the root vertex first. The HTGLP protocol ensures serializability and is deadlock-free[1,9]. We denote the GLP protocol generalized to heterogeneous GLP without the above restrictions by HTGLP'.

4. Heterogeneous Locking Protocol

In this section, we prove that a HTLP protocol always ensures update serializabilty if the original locking protocol ensures serializability. Moreover, we also show that if the original locking protocol is deadlock-free, then a deadlock cycle in the HTLP protocol would involve at least two read-only transactions.

Before stating the result in a theorem, we introduce a few definitions required to prove the theorem and to clarify the concepts.

A <u>partial</u> schedule s' of a set T of transactions is a legal schedule of those actions of the transactions which have been processed by the scheduler. The actions of the transactions in s' maintain the order of the actions present in each transaction.

---

[1] A biconnected component of a graph consists of maximal collections of vertices $u_1, u_2, \ldots, u_p$ such that either p>3 and for each pair (u_i, u_j) there exists two or more disjoint chains between u_i and u_j or p=2 and u_1 and u_2 share an arc.

Let s be a schedule of a set **T** of transactions and $\mathbf{T'} \subseteq \mathbf{T}$. A subschedule s' of s consisting of the transactions in **T'** is obtained by deleting the transactions in **T-T'** from s.

We denote by $\langle T_i, A_i, e_j \rangle$ the action A_i performed by the transaction T_i on the data item e_j at the jth step of the transaction T_i. An action may be a read, write, lock, or unlock action. The share lock, exclusive lock, and unlock action of a transaction T_i on a data item e are denoted by $\langle T_i, LS, e \rangle$, $\langle T_i, LX, e \rangle$, and $\langle T_i, UN, e \rangle$ respecttively.

We define the "waits-for" relations $>$ and $>_e$ at some point in time in a set **T** of transactions which are executing as follows:

$T_i >_e T_j \iff T_j$ holds a lock on a data item e in mode L and T_i waits to lock e in a mode which conflicts with the mode L.

$T_i > T_j \iff \exists e[T_i >_e T_j]$.

We define the "precedes" relations $<-$ and $<-_e$ in a legal schedule s of a set **T** of transactions as follows:

$T_i <-_e T_j \iff T_i$ locks the data item e before T_j locks it in s and one of the lock requests is in mode X.

$T_i <- T_j \iff \exists e[T_i <-_e T_j]$.

PROPOSITION 4.1. A locking protocol ensures serializability if for all legal schedules s of a set **T** of transactions obeying the locking protocol, the associated "precedes" relation $<-$ is acyclic.

PROOF. See[19,theorem 11.3].

It is not necessary that every locking protocol when generalized to HTLP protocol produces update serializable schedules which are not serializable. For example, the HT2PL protocol produces only serializable schedules. The following example illustrate a HTLP protocol that produces update serializable schedules which are not serializable. The schedule of example 2.1 is one such schedule and in the example below we produce this schedule by the heterogeneous tree protocol.

Fig.1. A rooted directed tree

<u>Example</u> 4.1. Consider the database graph consisting of three data items a,b,c as shown in fig.1. The read-only transactions T_1 and T_3 and the update transactions T_2 and T_4 obeying the heterogeneous tree protocol and operating in the database organised as a rooted tree and shown in fig.1 produces the following schedule which is update serializable but is not serializable.

$<T_1,LS,a><T_1,LS,b><T_1,UN,a><T_2,LX,a><T_2,UN,a>$
$<T_3,LS,a><T_3,LS,b><T_3,LS,c><T_3,UN,a><T_3,UN,b>$
$<T_3,UN,c><T_4,LX,c><T_4,UN,c><T_1,LS,c><T_1,UN,b>$
$<T_1,UN,c>$.

The schedule is not serializable as we have the following cycle in $<-$.

$$T_1 <-_a T_2 <-_a T_3 <-_c T_4 <-_c T_1 .$$

If we assume that a transaction holding an X mode lock on a data item reads and then writes the data item, then the above schedule produces the schedule of example 2.1.

If the original locking protocol is deadlock-free, then a deadlock cycle in the HTLP protocol involves at least two read-only transactions. The following example illustrates that the deadlock-freeness of a locking protocol may not be preserved when it is generalized to HTLP protocol.

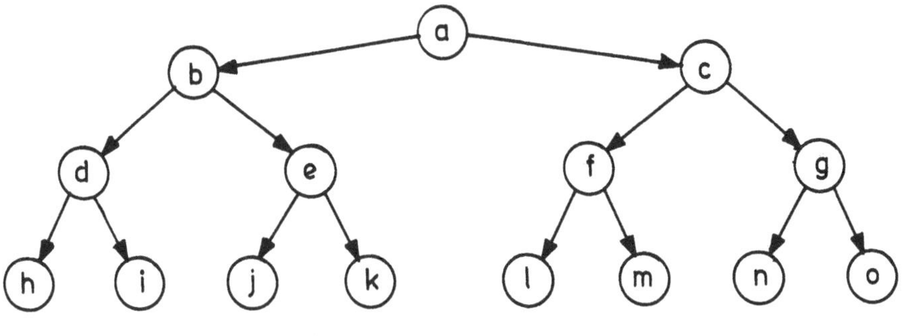

Fig.2. A rooted directed tree

<u>Example</u> 4.2. The tree protocol is deadlock-free[16]. When the read-only transactions T_1 and T_3 ,and the update transactions T_2 and T_4 following the heterogeneous tree protocol operates on a database(organised as rooted tree) shown in fig.2 according to the following schedule, they develop the deadlock cycle shown below.

$<T_1,LS,a><T_1,LS,b><T_1,LS,c><T_1,LS,d><T_1,UN,a>$
$<T_1,UN,b><T_2,LX,b><T_2,LX,d><T_3,LS,a><T_3,LS,c>$
$<T_3,LS,f><T_3,LS,l><T_3,UN,c><T_3,UN,f><T_3,LS,b>$
$<T_4,LX,f><T_4,LX,l><T_1,LS,f>$...

This schedule develops the deadlock cycle

$$T_1 >_f T_4 >_1 T_3 >_b T_2 >_d T_1 .$$

Now we state the result in a theorem.

THEOREM 4.1. Let **T** be a set of update transactions and each transaction in **T** obeys a locking protocol P which ensures serializability. Let **T'** be a set of read-only and update transactions and each transactions in **T'** obeys the same locking protocol P. Then the following holds:

(a) Any legal schedule of the transactions in **T'** ensures update serializability.

(b) If the locking protocol P is deadlock-free, then a deadlock cycle in the heterogeneous locking protocol P involves at least two read only transactions.

PROOF. (a) Consider a legal schedule s of the transactions in **T'** . If there are no read-only transactions or there is only one read-only transaction in s, then the lone read-only transaction(if present) in s can be treated as an update transaction. Hence, the schedule s is serializable, as it is a legal schedule of update transactions which follow the protocol P. However, if there are more than one read-only transactions in s, the schedule s may not be serializable. Obtain a schedule s' from s by dropping all but one read-only transaction from s. The schedule s' is legal and it is serializable since there is only one read-only transaction in s' and each transaction in s' obeys the locking protocol P. Hence,the schedule s is update serializable. This follows from the defintion of update serializability. This proves the part (a) of the theorem.

(b) Assume that there arises a deadlock cycle of the form

$$T_0 >_{a_1} T_1 >_{a_2} T_2 >_{a_3} \ldots >_{a_n} T_n >_{a_0} T_0 ,$$

when the transactions of **T'** are executing.Now abort all transactions which are not in the deadlock cycle. No transactions in the deadlock cycle will be affected. That is, the partial schedule s' of the transactions in the deadlock cycle has been obtained without violating the protocol P. In the deadlock cycle, no two consecutive transactions can be read-only transactions, as a read-only transaction will not wait for another read-only transaction. If there are no read-only transaction or there is one read-only transaction in the deadlock cycle, then the deadlock cycle should not have occured as the protocol P prohibits it. Hence, a deadlock cycle in a HTLP protocol must involve at least two read-only transactions if the original locking protocol is deadlock-free. Hence, the part (b) of the theorem is proved.

In the following, we show by qualitative arguments how the HTGLP' protocol performs better compared to the HTGLP protocol and an improved version of the HTGLP protocol, called the super guard protocol(SGP) [14]. Thus the introduction of update serializability is not only important from the theoretical point of view, since it increases the fixpoint set of the scheduler, but also useful for practical applications. The SGP protocol uses the INV lock mode. A transaction holding an INV mode lock on a data item can neither read nor write the data item. An INV mode lock is compatible with itself and with an X mode lock but it is not compatible with an S mode lock.

The HTGLP' protocol has the following advantages over the HTGLP protocol and the SGP protocol.

(1) The HTGLP' protocol is more general than the HTGLP protocol and the SGP protocol, since the former operates on a DAG while the latter operate on a rooted DAG.

(2) The HTGLP' protocol ensures update serializability, while the HTGLP protocol and the SGP protocol ensure serializability. Hence, the former provides more concurrency than the latter in terms of the fixpoint set of a scheduler.

(3) In the SGP protocol, the update transactions have to lock the root vertex first either in INV or in X mode. In the HTGLP protocol, an update transaction locks the root vertex first in mode X. Since an INV mode lock and an X mode lock are not compatible with an S mode lock, the problem of root vertex becoming bottleneck to achieving a higher concurrency is only partially solved in the SGP protocol. In the HTGLP' protocol, both the update transactions and the read-only transactions can lock any vertex first; hence, the problem of root vertex becoming a bottleneck to achieving higher concurrency does not arise.

(4) Suppose an update transaction wants to update a few data items in the leaves of a rooted DAG. Following SGP protocol, it has to start locking the vertices from the root vertex till it acquires the first X mode lock. Since an INV mode lock is not compatible with an S mode lock, it can be blocked on the way by read-only transactions. With the HTGLP' protocol, this problem does not arise.

(5) The HTGLP' protocol is not deadlock-free. However, since the GLP protocol is deadlock-free, a deadlock cycle in the HTGLP' protocol involves at least two read-only transactions. Hence, a deadlock cycle in the HTGLP' protocol can be broken by aborting some of the read-only transactions. The abortion of read-only transactions does not require undoing the actions of the read-only transactions on the database.

5. A Simple Non-Two Phase Locking Protocol(SN2PL) on General Databases

It is known that G2PL ensures serializability, and hence, it does not produce any schedule which is update serializable but is not serializable. Hence, only non-two phase locking protocols can produce schedules which are update serializable but are not serializable. In this section, we dsrcribe a simple non-two phase locking protocol(SN2PL) on general databases that ensures update serializability. This is achieved by restricting the access of each update transaction to exactly one data item. This protocol allows read-only transactions to be non-two phase and hence, it provides more concurrency. The SN2PL protocol is described below.

Each transaction obeying the SN2PL protocol must obey the following the rules:

(1) A read-only transaction may lock a data item any time and may also unlock a data item any time. This implies that a read-only transaction may also be two phase.

(2) An update transaction may lock exactly one data item. This ensures that each update transaction is two phase.

(3) Each transaction may lock a data item at most once.

By an example, we show that the SN2PL protocol produces a schedule which is update serializable but is not serializable.

Example 5.1. The schedule of example 4.1 is one such schedule.

THEOREM 5.1. The SN2PL protocol ensures update serializability.
PROOF. Simple.

THEOREM 5.2. The SN2PL protocol is deadlock-free.
PROOF. Simple.

THEOREM 5.3. Let **T** be a set of transactions obeying the SN2PL protocol. $\mathbf{T}' \subseteq \mathbf{T}$ such that every transaction in **T'** is two phase. Let s be a legal schedule of **T** and s' be a subschedule of s consisting of the transactions in **T'** . Then the schedule s' is serializable.

PROOF. From s drop all the transactions which are not in **T'** . Then the schedule s' obtained in this way is legal and consists of transactions which are two phase. Hence, s' is serializable.

There are many examples where update transactions need to access only one data item. For example, in case of making reservation on a specific flight, the reservation database for this flight can be considered as a single data item. For booking a seat on this flight, one needs to access only one data item. Moreover, the read-only transactions have the option of remaining two phase and thereby any two read-only transactions which are two phase would agree on a common serial order of the update transactions according to theorem 5.3.

6. Conclusions

The notion of update serializability is useful in situations where the read-only transactions are generally much larger than the update transactions. We have shown that when a locking protocol is made heterogeneous, any legal schedule of a set **T** of transactions obeying the heterogeneous locking protocol is update serializable. The heterogeneous two phase locking protocol ensures serializability. Hence, in order that a heterogeneous locking protocol produces schedules which are update serializable but are not serializable, the original locking protocol must be non-two phase. However, one would like to know under what condition a non-two phase locking protocol,when made heterogeneous, would produce schedules which are update serializable but are not serializable. We have also presented a simple non-two phase locking protocol on general databases that can produce update serializable schedules which are not serializable. The SN2PL protocol allows the read-only transactions to be non-two phase and restricts the update transactions to access exactly one data item. Since, in general, the update transactions need to access more than one data item, the SN2PL protocol needs to be extended for update transactions which can access more than one data item. Work is in progress in this direction. The results of this work will be reported in a forthcoming paper.

References

1. Buckley,G.N., Silberschatz, A. On the heterogeneous guard locking protocol. The Computer Journal,27,1(1984), pp.86-87.
2. Buckley,G.N., and Silberschatz, A. Beyond two phase locking. J. ACM, 32,2(Apr. 1985),314-326.
3. Chan, A., and Gray, R. Implementing distributed read-only transactions. IEEE Trans. Soft. Eng. SE-11, 2(Feb. 1985),205-212.
4. Casanova,M.A. The concurrency control problem for database systems. Lecture Notes in Computer Science, vol. 116,Berlin-Heidelberg-New York, Springer 1981.
5. Dasgupta,P., and Kedem,Z.M. A non-2-phase locking protocol for general databases. Proc. of the 8th Int. Conference on Very Large Databases, Oct. 1983, 92-96.

6. Eswaran,K.P., Gray,J.N., Lorie,R.A.,and Traiger,I.L. The notions of consistency and predicate locks in a database system. Comm. ACM, 19,11(Nov. 1976),624-633.
7. Garcia-Molina,H. Using semantic knowledge for transaction processing in distributed databases. ACM Trans. Database Syst., 8, 2(1983),186-213.
8. Garcia-Molina,H. Read-only transactions in distributed databases. ACM Trans. Database Syst., 7, 2(Jun. 1982),209-234.
9. Kedem,Z.M., and Silberschatz,A. Locking protocols from exclusive to shared locks. J. ACM, 30, 4(Oct.1983),787-804.
10. Korth,H. Locking protocols: general lock classes and deadlock freedom. Ph.D. Thesis, Princeton University, Jun. 1981.
11. Kung,H.T., and Papadimitriou,C.H. An optimality theory of concurrency control in databases. Acta Informatica, 19, 1(1983), 1-12.
12. Lamport,L. Towards a theory of correctness for multi-user database systems. Technical Report CA 7610-0712, Masachussetts Computer Associates Inc., Oct. 1976.
13. Mohan,C. Strategies for enhancing concurrency and managing deadlocks in database locking protocols. Ph.D. Thesis, Dept. of Computer Science, University of Texas at Austin, 1981.
14. Mohan,C., Fussel,D., and Silberschatz,A. Compatibility and commutativity of lock modes. Information and control,61,1(April 1984), 38-64.
15. Papadimitriou,C.H. The serializability of concurrent database updates. J. ACM, 29,4(Oct. 1979), 631-653.
16. Silberschatz,A., and Kedem,Z.M. Consistency in hierarchical database systems. J. ACM, 27,1(Jan. 1980), 72-80.
17. Silberschatz,A., and Kedem,Z.M. A family of locking protocols for database systems that are modeled by directed graphs. IEEE Trans. Soft. Engg., SE-8,6(Nov. 1982), 558-602.
18. Stearns,R.E., Lewis,P.M. II, and Rosenkrantz,D.Z. Concurrency control for database systems. Proc. 17th Symp. on Foundations of Computer Science, Oct.1976, 19-32.
19. Ullman,J.D. Principles of database systems. Computer Science Press Inc., Potomac, Md., 1982.
20. Yannakakis,M. Serializability by locking. J. ACM, 31, 2(Apr. 1984), 227-244.
21. Yannakakis,M. A theory of safe locking policies in database systems. J. ACM, 29,3(July 1982), 718-740.

Filtering Data Flow in Deductive Databases

Michael Kifer
Department of Computer Science
SUNY at Stony Brook
Stony Brook, NY 11794, USA

Eliezer L. Lozinskii
Department of Computer Science
The Hebrew University
Jerusalem 91904, Israel

ABSTRACT

We investigate the question of how query optimization strategies devised for relational databases can be used for deductive databases. In particular, we show how the well known method of moving selections and projections down the parse trees of relational algebra expressions can be generalized to the case of deductive databases. The optimization is achieved by means of filtering data flow in the system.

1. Introduction

One of the query optimization methods widely used in relational databases is "pushing" selections and projections, determined by the query, closer to the sources of data. But the relational model does not include recursion. Overcoming this drawback, Aho and Ullman [AhU79] introduced the least fixed point operator (which is equivalent to recursion) and presented a method of pushing selections through that operator.

In this paper we show how algebraic manipulations with relational expressions, and the result of [AhU79] can be extended for general recursion in deductive databases. The ideas presented here originate in the recent works on PROD and APEX [Loz85b, Loz86]. Query evaluation is represented by the *system graph* which is an analog of relational expression parse trees in ordinary databases. This analogy enables a generalization of the relational algebra optimization techniques to recursive Horn databases.

We have chosen system graphs as a concise representation of data flow in the course of bottom-up query evaluation. Our main goal is to restrict this data flow while preserving soundness and completeness of the system. This is achieved by imposing special restrictions, called *filters*, on the arcs of the system graph. This approach proved fruitful in handling of a wide range of aspects of deductive databases, such as run-time query optimization, incorporating function symbols, etc. [KiL86b, KiL86c]. The present paper describes just one aspect of the approach, namely compile-time optimization by means of *static filtering*.

Some aspects of our approach are related to the works of McKay and Shapiro [McS81, ShM80], which present one of the earliest methods based on graph representation of the data flow in the course of bottom-up query evaluation. However, these works show no attempts to optimize query evaluation, while the latter is the main concern of the present paper.

Research of M. Kifer was supported in part by the National Science Foundation grant DCR-8603676 and by the summer award from the NYS/UUP Professional Development and Quality of Working Life Committee. The work of E.L. Lozinskii was supported in part by the Israel National Council for Research and Development under the grant 2454-85 and by the NSF grant DCR-8603676; it has been partially performed at SUNY @ Stony Brook while on a sabbatical leave from the Hebrew University.

2. Preliminaries

2.1. Deductive Databases

A *deductive database* consists of a collection of relations (represented by predicate names) and logical axioms (represented by first-order formulas). Relations can be represented *extensionally*, i.e., by a set of (positive) ground atoms, and *intentionally*, i.e., by logical axioms, which for the purpose of this paper will be universally quantified function-free[1] Horn clauses with nonempty premises and consequent. *Base relations* are allowed to have an extensional component, i.e. some of the tuples may be explicitly stored in the database, and others can be derived using the axioms. Nonbase relations are assumed to be purely intentional.

2.2. AC-Notation for Axioms

We shall use a special notation for axioms (cf. [Loz86]), called *AC-notation*. In this notation terms are taken out of literals and placed into certain conditions attached to each axiom. Inside each literal terms are replaced by *distinct* variables associated with the predicate name of that literal, so that different predicates do not share variables. These variables are related to each other by a condition attached to the axiom (which suggests the name AC-notation). This makes the AC-notation more suitable for the data flow approach described in the sequel. Thus, axioms will be represented as follows:

$$\alpha \; : \; R(\overline{\mathbf{r}}) \leftarrow Q_1(\overline{\mathbf{q}}_1/1), \ldots, Q_n(\overline{\mathbf{q}}_n/n), \; Cond_{\alpha} \, , \qquad (1)$$

i) where $\overline{\mathbf{r}}$, $\overline{\mathbf{q}}_1, \ldots, \overline{\mathbf{q}}_n$ are vectors of variables associated with $R, Q_1, \ldots, Q_n$, respectively. A predicate name can appear several times in an axiom α, so we use $\overline{\mathbf{p}}/i$ to denote the vector of variables of a predicate, P, that occupies the i-th position within the body of α.

ii) $Cond_{\alpha}$ is the *attached condition* of α of the form $(u1 \,\theta_1\, v1) \wedge (u2 \,\theta_2\, v2) \wedge \ldots$, where $u1$, $v1$, $u2$, $v2$,..., are variables appearing in $\overline{\mathbf{r}}$, $\overline{\mathbf{q}}_1/1, \ldots, \overline{\mathbf{q}}_n/n$, and θ_i's stand for elementary comparisons $=, >, <, \geq, \leq$.

For instance, axiom $A(x,y) \leftarrow A(x,z), B(z,w), A(w,y)$ will be represented as

$$A(a1, a2) \leftarrow A(a1/1, a2/1), B(b1/2, b2/2), (a1/3, a2/3),$$
$$a1 = a1/1, \; a2/1 = b1/2, \; b2/2 = a1/3, \; a2 = a2/3 \, .$$

The last line shows the attached condition of the axiom.

It is important to emphasize that users need not write queries in the AC-notation. Translation from a conventional notation can be done automatically. The AC-notation is just a convenient formalism for describing data flow during query evaluation.

---

[1] A way to extend this method to allow function symbols is reported in [KiL86c].

3. Simplistic Query Evaluation

3.1. System Graphs and Queries

Let **S** be a collection of axioms. *System graph for* **S**, denoted *SG* (**S**) (or just *SG*, when **S** is obvious), is a directed bipartite AND/OR graph whose node set consists of *rel-nodes* and *ax-nodes*. *SG* (**S**) contains exactly one rel-node (resp., ax-node) corresponding to each relation name (resp., axiom) appearing in **S**. In figures rel-nodes are depicted as rectangles, while ax-nodes are depicted as ovals enclosing the corresponding attached conditions.

Let α be an axiom of the form $R(\overline{\mathbf{r}}) \leftarrow Q_1(\overline{\mathbf{q}}_1),\ldots,Q_n(\overline{\mathbf{q}}_n)$, $Cond_\alpha$. Let P be the predicate name of a literal Q_i. Then there is an arc labeled i_α going from the rel-node P to the ax-node α. Also, a single unlabeled arc goes from α to the rel-node representing R. Fig. 1 shows a system graph corresponding to a set of clauses defining the transitive closure of a relation, P, followed by selection on the second argument and projection on the first.

Without loss of generality we will consider only queries of the form $\{ \overline{\mathbf{x}} \mid \boldsymbol{Ans}_{\mathbf{q}}(\overline{\mathbf{x}}) \}$, where $\boldsymbol{Ans}_{\mathbf{q}}$ is a special *query predicate* (one per each query, **q**) defined by the following set

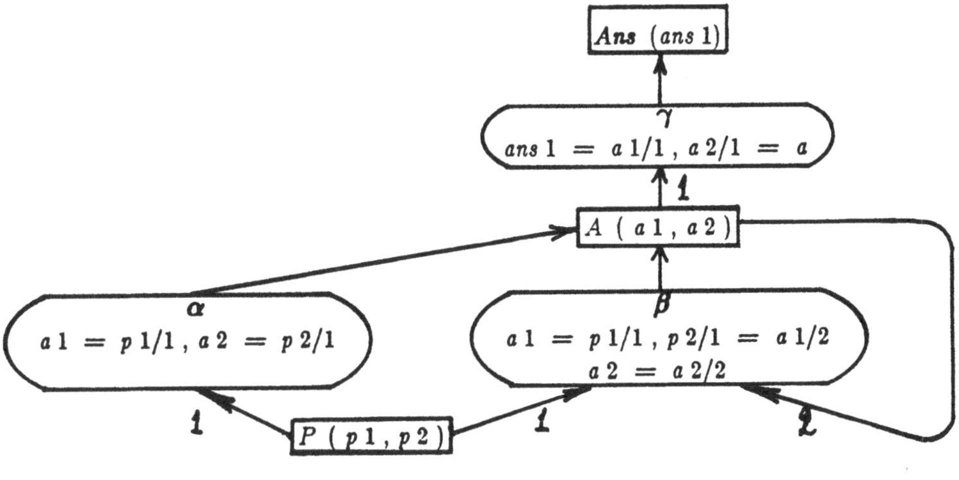

α : $A(a\,1, a\,2) \leftarrow P(p\,1/1\,,\,p\,2/1)\,,\ a\,1{=}p\,1/1\,,\ a\,2{=}p\,2/1$
β : $A(a\,1, a\,2) \leftarrow P(p\,1/1\,,\,p\,2/1)\,,\ A(a\,1/2\,,\,a\,2/2)$
γ : $\boldsymbol{Ans}(ans\,1) \leftarrow A(a\,1/1\,,\,a\,2/1)\,,\ ans\,1 = a\,1/1\,,\ a\,2/1 = a\,,$
$a\,1{=}p\,1/1\,,\ p\,2/1 = a\,1/2\,,\ a\,2{=}a\,2/2$

Fig. 1.

S′ of axioms (represented in the conventional notation):

$$S' \begin{cases} Ans_q(\bar{x}) \leftarrow Q_{11}(\bar{x},\bar{y}), \ldots, Q_{1 n_1}(\bar{x},\bar{y}) \\ \ldots \quad \ldots \quad \ldots \\ Ans_q(\bar{x}) \leftarrow Q_{k1}(\bar{x},\bar{y}), \ldots, Q_{k n_k}(\bar{x},\bar{y}), \end{cases}$$

where Q_{ij} are some database predicates. Let **S** denote the set of axioms of the intentional database. Then $SG(\mathbf{S} \cup \mathbf{S}')$ is called the *system graph for query* **q**.

With this definition, we can consider the third axiom of Fig. 1 as a query to the database whose intentional part is given by the first pair of axioms. The graph of Fig. 1 can then be viewed as an SG of that query, while the lower part of the graph corresponds to the SG of the intentional database.

3.2. Data Flow in System Graphs and Query Evaluation

System graphs represent flow of data among the rel- and ax-nodes, and are used in our approach as a tool for query evaluation. With this intention in mind the arcs will be usually referred to as *ports*. An ax-node has exactly one *output port* and one or more *input ports*. A rel-node may have zero or more input and output ports. Rel-nodes without input ports are base relations. We denote the i-th input port of an ax-node α by i_α.

Data is sent along the ports only in the directions indicated by the arrows. For instance, rel-node $P(p1,p2)$ in Fig. 1 may send a tuple $<b,e>$ to ax-node α along the port 1_α. Variables $p1/1_\alpha$ and $p2/1_\alpha$ of α will receive the values of variables $p1$ and $p2$ of $P(p1, p2)$, respectively (where it is necessary to denote that a variable, say $p1/1$, appears in a certain axiom, e.g. α, we specify a subscript, $p1/1_\alpha$). Node α further sends tuple $<b,e>$ to the rel-node $A(a1,a2)$ so, that $a1$ will receive the value b of $p1/1_\alpha$, and $a2$ will get the value e of $p2/1_\alpha$, as indicated by the equations in α.

Next, $A(a1,a2)$ can send $<b,e>$ to β along the port 2_β. In β the variables $a1/2_\beta$ and $a2/2_\beta$, associated with port 2_β, will get the values of $a1$ and $a2$, respectively. At that point $P(p1,p2)$ may have sent a tuple, $<c,b>$, to β via 1_β, which assigns value c to $p1/1_\beta$ and b to $p2/1_\beta$. The two tuples, $<c, b>$ and $<b, e>$, satisfy the condition of β, so $<c,e>$ is generated, and sent to $A(a1,a2)$, etc.

"Slashed" variables $p1/1_\alpha$, $p2/1_\alpha$, $a1/2_\beta$ etc. are *input variables* receiving their values via input ports from the corresponding variables associated with the preceding rel-nodes. For instance, $p1/1_\alpha$ gets its values via port 1_α from variable $p1$ of $P(p1,p2)$. "Non-slashed" variables of axioms (e.g., $a1$, $a2$ of α) are *output variables*. When the condition of an axiom, α, is satisfied then its output variables are instantiated, and a tuple of output values is sent out via the single output port of α. For simplicity we assume that variables of the head predicate of an axiom also appear in its body. That is, in the ax-nodes each output variable is bound to an input variable.

Now we can think of the following *simplistic query evaluation*. Computation starts when all the base rel-nodes send out all their tuples (or appropriate projections thereof, see [KiL85]) via all their *relevant* output ports. A port is *relevant* to a query, **q**, if it is a part of a directed path to the query node Ans_q. Ax-nodes store tuples that they receive from each input port in a local file associated with this port. As soon as an ax-node discovers that some sets of tuples in its local files can be joined (more precisely, θ-joined, where $\overline{u}\theta\overline{v}$ is the attached condition of the axiom) to produce *new* output tuples that were not produced before, it performs the join and sends the set of new tuples through the output port. Rel-nodes accumulate all tuples they receive. When a file of tuples arrives at a rel-node, the tuples are checked against the information stored at that rel-node. New tuples that are not yet stored are saved (at that rel-node) and then sent out via all relevant output ports of that rel-node. Computation terminates when no more new tuples can be generated by the system.

It should be emphasized that the simplistic query evaluation just described is actually set-oriented, i.e., each rel-node sends its new tuples as a file, and ax-nodes can join files in any suitable way (nested loops, sort-merge, etc.), depending on characteristics of the files being joined. Distributed termination of this process is based on the algorithm described in [Loz85a]. It can be shown [KiL85, vaK76] that the simplistic evaluation is *sound* and *complete.* It is important to understand that the query evaluation just described works for any kind of Horn databases (e.g., mutually recursive, nonlinear, etc.).

4. Optimization of System Graphs

4.1. Motivation

It is known that syntactic structure of queries and database axioms can be utilized to reduce the amount of data flow needed to compute queries. The common idea is to apply selections, found in the attached conditions of ax-nodes, as close as possible to the sources of data, since this obviously will cut down the amount of data exchanged in the system. This idea is extensively used in optimizing relational algebra expressions. For instance, in expression $\sigma_{T\,=\,a}(R(X,Y) \underset{Y=Z}{\bowtie} Q(Z,T))$ we will be better off applying selection directly to the second relation: $R(X,Y) \underset{Y=Z}{\bowtie} \sigma_{T\,=\,a}\, Q(Z,T)$ [Ull82].

Example 1. Consider the transitive closure example of Fig. 1 again. In a similar situation in relational algebra, it is recommended to push selection condition $a\,2/1{=}a$ of γ down the SG which will result in imposing restrictions $p\,2{=}a$ on port 1_α and $a\,2 = a$ on ports 1_γ and 2_β as shown in Fig. 2. It is easily verified that the SGs of Fig. 1 and 2 compute the same relation ***Ans***. However, the graph depicted in Fig. 2 represents a more economical computation, since tuples violating the restrictions on ports are now cut off. []

Example 1 suggests a slight modification to the notion of SG which permits restrictions on ports, to cut off irrelevant data. These restrictions are called *filters.* Our goal consists in imposing of most restrictive filters on ports while preserving query equivalence. For the needs of this paper we adopt the following notion of equivalence: Two SGs for a query, that differ only in the values of filters on ports, are *equivalent w.r.t. the query* if the corresponding query evaluations store identical sets of tuples in the query nodes ***Ans*** of both SGs.

The analogy between the SG optimization demonstrated in Example 1 and the relational algebra optimization is not accidental. In fact, SG is a program (with loops) in the language of relational algebra operators such as Cartesian product, selection and projection. Indeed, at each ax-node tuples arrived at input ports are first θ-joined (joins are specified by the attached

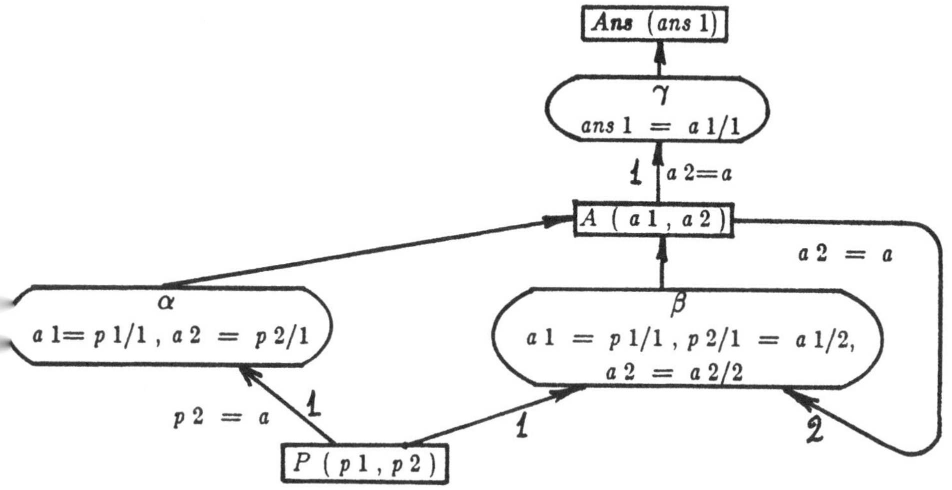

Fig. 2.

condition), and then projected on the output variables of that ax-node. Ways of translating recursive queries into such iterative programs were studied by Chang [Cha81] and Henschen and Naqvi [HeN84]. However, the Chang's result is restricted to the case of regular axioms, while the method of Henschen and Naqvi faces difficulties in handling complex cases of mutual recursion. As noted earlier, system graphs are not subject to any of those restrictions.

The major difficulty in performing optimization stems, of course, from the recursion. First, since SG may have cycles, one has to decide at which point selections need not be pushed down any more. Second, pushing selections in the recursive environment is not so straightforward as it may seem: some "obvious" approaches may result in loss of answers to the query.

Example 2. Let the SG be as in Example 1, but this time let the selection in the query be applied to the first argument of A. The SG is depicted in Fig. 3. Intuitively, pushing $a\,1/1 = b$ down the graph should impose filter $p\,1{=}b$ on ports 1_α and 1_β. However, it is easy to see, that with these filters the SG of Fig. 3 will compute the transitive closure of $\sigma_{a1=b}\, A(a\,1, a\,2)$ while the SG of Fig. 3 (without filters) computes $\sigma_{a1=b}$ applied to the transitive closure of $A(a\,1, a\,2)$, which is not the same thing. ▯

Example 2 shows that applying relational optimization methods to recursive databases requires special care. We now describe the general idea of how selections can be pushed safely.

Till the end of Section 4.2 let δ denote an axiom of the form $R(\bar{r}) \leftarrow Q_1(\bar{q}_1/1_\delta), \ldots, Q_n(\bar{q}_n/n_\delta), Cond_\delta$. Suppose R has k output ports with filters $F_1, \ldots, F_k$. Ax-node δ has n input ports coming from rel-nodes $Q_1, \ldots, Q_n$. We want to restrict data flow through the input ports of δ by imposing on them filters $\bar{F}_{1_\delta}, \ldots, \bar{F}_{n_\delta}$. At

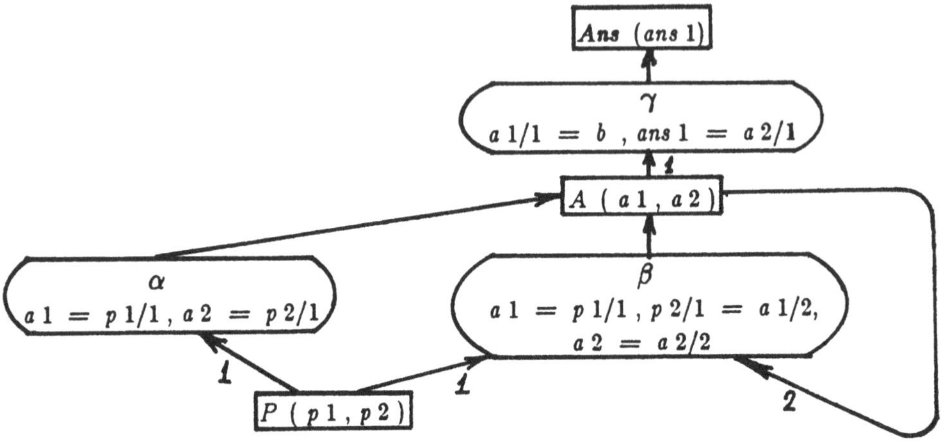

Fig. 3.

the same time it is necessary to preserve the data flow through all output ports of R. That is, tuples that will be cut off by these filters (i.e., $\overline{F}_{1_\delta}$, ..., $\overline{F}_{n_\delta}$) must not affect data flow from R.

Indeed, since tuples produced by δ flow through R, it is wasteful for δ to produce tuples which are then cut off by the output filters of R. Hence, to produce a new tuple that has a chance to pass through, at least one of the output filters of R, the inputs of δ must satisfy condition $\overline{C} = Cond_\delta \wedge (F_1 \vee \ldots \vee F_k)$. We would like to cut useless tuples before they enter δ. For this we need to know how $\overline{C}$ can be projected on the input ports of δ. Let *projection* of $\overline{C}$ on port i_δ, denoted $\overline{C}[i_\delta]$, be defined as follows.

- o First take the strongest consequence of $\overline{C}$ which can be expressed purely in terms of the components of $\overline{\mathrm{q}}_i/i_\delta$, constants appearing in $\overline{C}$, and in terms of comparisons $=$, $>$, etc. A naive way to obtain such strongest consequence is to take a conjunction of all consequences of $\overline{C}$ expressed in those terms (there may be only a finite number of them).
- o Then replace each "slashed" variable from the vector $\overline{\mathrm{q}}_i/i_\delta$ by the corresponding nonslashed variable from $\overline{\mathrm{q}}_i$. The result is $\overline{C}[i_\delta]$.

Thus, $\overline{C}[i_\delta]$ is a condition expressed in terms of constants and variables of $\overline{\mathrm{q}}_i$, associated with the rel-node Q_i (which is connected to δ via port i_δ). An efficient method to compute $\overline{C}[i_\delta]$ is based on the work of Rozenkrantz and Hunt [RoH80], and will be presented elsewhere. Now, $C[i_\delta]$ can be imposed on the port i_δ to reduce the amount of data that will be sent by Q_i to δ. The following example shows how it works.

Example 3. For the fragment of a system graph depicted in Fig. 4(a), C is $(r1 = q1/2) \wedge (q1/2 > p1/1) \wedge (r2 = p2/1)$, F_1 is $(r1 = a) \wedge (r2 > b)$ and F_2 is $(r1 = c) \wedge (r2 < d)$. Thus, $C \wedge (F_1 \vee F_2)$ is equivalent to

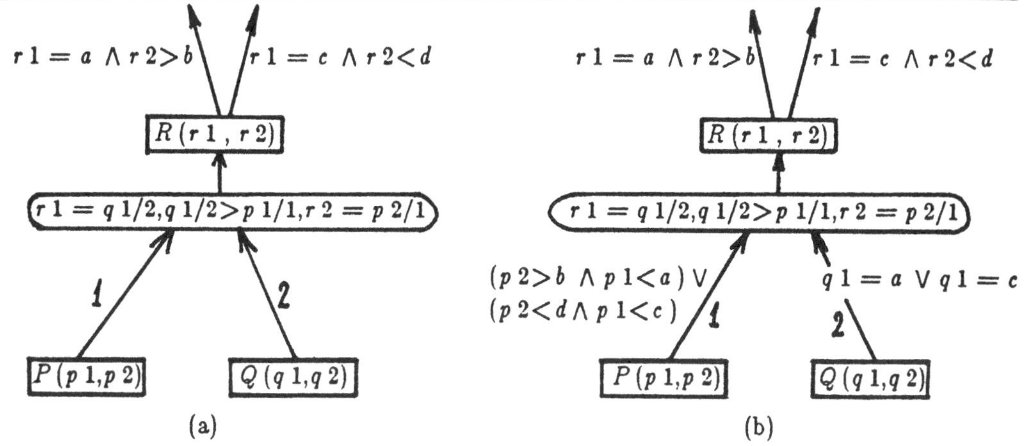

Fig. 4.

$$\begin{aligned}&[(r1 = q1/2) \wedge (q1/2 > p1/1) \wedge (r2 = p2/1) \wedge (r1 = a) \wedge (r2 > b)]\\ \vee\ &[(r1 = q1/2) \wedge (q1/2 > p1/1) \wedge (r2 = p2/1) \wedge (r1 = c) \wedge (r2 < d)].\end{aligned} \tag{2}$$

It is easily verified that the strongest condition implied by (2) in terms of variables $p1$, $p2$ of port 1 is $(p2>b \wedge p1<a) \vee (p2<d \wedge p1<c)$. Similarly, the strongest condition implied by (2) in terms of variables $q1$, $q2$ of port 2 is $q1 = a \vee q1 = c$. Therefore, these are the strongest restrictions one can impose on ports 1 and 2 without affecting the data flow out of the rel-node $R(r1, r2)$. Thus, replacing fragment (a) of Fig. 4 by fragment (b) results in an equivalent, but better SG. []

As follows from the previous discussion, if the filters on all output ports of a rel-node are already known, then it is worthwhile pushing them farther past that node. However, sometimes certain output filters of a rel-node, A, cannot be evaluated before applying some **push**-operations to A. Indeed, this is typical for cyclic SGs which correspond to recursive databases. For instance, at the very beginning in Example 1 we would have filter $a2=a$ on port 1_γ, but the filter on port 2_β is yet unknown. Thus, it may seem that pushing filters, as described above, is useless. Nevertheless, we will see that one can still use pushing to build filters incrementally: At the very beginning all filters are set to **false**, which means that the corresponding ports are blocked. Pushing selections down makes filters less and less restrictive until the moment when their values stabilize.

Now we define the **push**-operation formally. Let R and δ be as before and let $\mathbf{S}$ denote a system graph containing rel- and ax-nodes corresponding to R and δ. Let F be a restriction imposed on the output ports of R. Then F is expressed in terms of the variables of $\overline{\mathbf{r}}$ and constants. Define the effect of pushing F through R and δ in $\mathbf{S}$ as follows: **push**($\mathbf{S}$; $F \rightarrow R \rightarrow \delta$) $=$ $\mathbf{S}'$, where $\mathbf{S}'$ is an SG which differs from $\mathbf{S}$ only in the values of filters on the ports connecting rel-nodes $Q_1, \ldots, Q_n$ with δ. Suppose that before performing the **push**-operation there have already been filters, $F_{i_\delta}(\mathbf{S})$, imposed on ports i_δ,

$i=1,...,n$, respectively. Then **push** will change these filters to $F_{i_\delta}(\mathbf{S}') \equiv F_{i_\delta}(\mathbf{S}) \vee (Cond_\delta \wedge F)[i_\delta]$, for $i=1,...,n$. The rest of the filters of $\mathbf{S}'$ are identical to the corresponding filters of $\mathbf{S}$. In what follows the specific SG to which **push** is applied will be clear from the context and will be omitted.

The following lemma ensures that approximation of input filters of δ can be incrementally improved by the backward propagation of changes made to the output filters of R.

LEMMA 1. Let R and δ be as before. Let F_1 and F_2 be conditions on output ports of R. Then $(Cond_\delta \wedge (F_1 \vee F_2))[i_\delta] \equiv (Cond_\delta \wedge F_1)[i_\delta] \vee (Cond_\delta \wedge F_2)[i_\delta]$. []

By Lemma 1, **push**($F_1 \vee ... \vee F_n \rightarrow R \rightarrow \delta$) can be obtained by a sequence of simpler operations **push**($F_i \rightarrow R \rightarrow \delta$) in any order. This property enables us to approximate filters. Indeed, suppose that an old value F of the filter on an output port of R is refined by a new disjunct F' (so that the new approximation becomes $F \vee F'$). If F has been already pushed, then in order to refine filters on the input ports of δ we need only push F', i.e., to perform **push**($F' \rightarrow R \rightarrow \delta$), and not (the more costly operation) **push**($F \vee F' \rightarrow R \rightarrow \delta$).

4.2. The Optimization Algorithm

Let, as before, F ($\equiv F_1 \vee ... \vee F_n$, where the F_i are conjunctions of elementary comparisons) be a condition expressed purely in terms of $\overline{\mathbf{F}}$ and constants, and let F_{i_δ} be the filter on port i_δ. Finally, let $C_1 \vee ... \vee C_k$ be a disjunctive normal form of $(Cond_\delta \wedge F)[i_\delta]$. Then, for $i = 1,...,n$, **push**($F \rightarrow R \rightarrow \delta$) changes F_{i_δ} to $F_{i_\delta} \vee C_1 \vee ... \vee C_k$.

Since the number of constants, variables, and nodes employed in any SG is finite, it can be easily seen that in any infinite series of **push**-operations there must be a point after which pushings have no effect on the system graph. Thus filters cannot "grow" indefinitely. After a certain point all filters have to stabilize, and any subsequent **push** makes no change to F_{i_δ} (which means that $C_1 \vee ... \vee C_k$ implies F_{i_δ}). We say that after that point **push** *no longer affects* F_{i_δ}. The filter is *affected* by **push**, if its states before and after **push** are not equivalent.

We distinguish between two kinds of disjuncts in filters: those that have already been pushed down and those that have not. The former disjuncts are called **used** and the latter are referred to as **fresh**. We assume that the **push**-operation does all the book-keeping: whenever **push**($F_1 \vee \cdots \vee F_m \rightarrow R \rightarrow \delta$) is encountered in the algorithm, $F_1, ..., F_m$ are assumed to be **fresh** disjuncts in the appropriate output filters of R. After completing of the operation these disjuncts are marked as **used**. Furthermore, whenever **push** attempts to add a new disjunct to an input filter of δ, it checks whether this disjunct implies the already existing filter. If it does, the disjunct is ignored (in that filter), because adding it will not change the filter. Otherwise, it is added to the filter as a **fresh** disjunct.

The Optimization Algorithm.

Input : Original SG for a query.

Output : Optimized equivalent SG.

```
1.  Initialize all filters to false
2.  for each axiom δ defining Ans do
        push(true→Ans → δ )
        for each antecedent Q of δ s.t. at least one of its output filters
                was affected by the above push-operation do
            mark Q
        endfor
    endfor
3.  while there are marked rel-nodes do
        /* Let R be a marked rel-node and let FRESH be a disjunction
                of all the fresh elements in the output filters of R.   */
        unmark R
3.1     for each axiom β defining R do
            push(FRESH →R → β )
3.2         for each antecedent Q of β s.t. at least one of its output filters
                    was affected by the above push-operation do
                mark Q
            endfor
        endfor
    endwhile
```

Because of the space limitation we state the following properties of the Optimization Algorithm without proofs. The proofs and additional details can be found in [KiL85].

THEOREM 1. The Optimization Algorithm eventually terminates. []

THEOREM 2. Suppose that the Optimization Algorithm is applied to a SG, **G**, producing another SG, $\overline{\mathbf{G}}$. Then **G** and $\overline{\mathbf{G}}$ are equivalent. []

In what follows we will refer to this method as *static filtering*, because filters are established here at compile time. It should not be confused with *dynamic filtering* described in [KiL86b], where filters are computed also at run time to account for the "sideways information passing".

Being computed at compile time, and making no use of a run-time information, static filters provide in certain cases no optimization. It is instructive at this point to make another look at the situation of Example 2 (Fig. 3), where it has been shown that an intuitive method of pushing selections is not sound. One can easily verify that applying the optimization algorithm to the SG of Fig. 3 results in a SG, which is almost identical to the original graph of Fig. 3, apart from the filter $a1 = b$ on port 1_γ. Particularly, the optimization algorithm does not impose any filters on ports 1_α and 1_β, in contrast to what has been conjectured in the example. Hence, in Example 2 static filtering is of no help, as it degenerates to the simplistic query evaluation.

5. Complexity of Static Filtering

The complexity of the method depend on the following three factors:

1. complexity of a single **push**-operation;
2. number of **push**-operations needed to compute all filters;
3. complexity of the fact generation stage that follows filter computation.

Each **push**-operation through an ax-node α can be performed in polynomial time in the size of the attached condition of α. Details of the algorithm will appear elsewhere. However, the number of **push**-operations may be exponential in the size of the system graph (not of the database!). This exponential complexity comes at no surprise, since it can be shown [KiL86a] that each **push**-operation corresponds to a step in the SLD-resolution, which is known to have an exponential complexity. It should be noted, however, that static filtering develops only a relatively small (and finite) part of the search tree that would have been developed by the SLD-resolution. Particularly, static filtering does not develop those subtrees of the full SLD-tree that grow from goals obtained by at least one resolution with a database fact.

Complexity of the data generation stage is polynomial in the number of individual constants in the database. Although reduced by filters, the number of facts produced at this stage may become huge. However, this worst case complexity pertains also to other known methods (e.g. [BMS86, SaZ86a], etc), which employ ingenious means for reducing the amount of generated facts.

6. Distributing Selections Through the Least Fixed Point Operator

One of the earliest attempts to optimize queries in recursive databases was undertaken by Aho and Ullman [AhU79], who considered the problem of commuting selections and the Least Fixed Point (abbr. LFP) operator. Let $f(X)$ be a function which has the form of a monotonic relational expression involving a relational argument, X, and, possibly, some other (nonvariable) relations. Then the least fixed point of f, $\mathbf{Y}(f)$, is such a relation R that (1) $R = f(R)$, and (2) R is the minimal relation satisfying (1) ($\mathbf{Y}(f)$ is unique, if f is monotonic). The problem solved by Aho and Ullman may be stated as follows. Given a condition, ϕ, find another condition, ψ, s.t. $\sigma_\phi(\mathbf{Y}(f)) = \sigma_\phi(\mathbf{Y}(f \circ \sigma_\psi))$. In [AhU79] this problem was solved for a class of relational expressions, f, where X has at most one occurrence in $f(X)$. Recently Devanbu and Agrawal [DeA86] proposed a method that slightly improves the result of [AhU79]. However, this method is also restricted to the case of only one occurrence of X in $f(X)$.

Any system graph, **S**, computes a LFP of some relational expression, f_S. To see that, let **H** be a set of definite Horn clauses corresponding to **S**, and let $A_1, ..., A_n$ be all predicates mentioned in **H**. It has been shown in [vaK76] that for each such **H** there is a monotonic function, T_H, mapping $r_1 \times ... \times r_n$ to $r_1' \times ... \times r_n'$, where $r_1, r_1', ..., r_n, r_n'$ are relations over $A_1, ..., A_n$ respectively. An easy (but tiresome) exercise should convince the reader that T_H can be represented as a relational expression involving $A_1, ..., A_n$. It is now a simple matter to construct f_S from T_H. A simple way (although not the best one) to do this is to take a "long" predicate, R, of the arity equal to the sum of the arities of all the A_i, and replace each occurrence of each A_i in T_H by an appropriate projection of R. Then $f_S(R) = T_H(A_1,...,A_n)$.

Conversely, for any relational expression, $f(R)$, there is an SG, $\mathbf{S}_f$, that computes $\mathbf{Y}(f)$. Indeed, let $f = f_1 \bigcup \cdots \bigcup f_k$, where each f_i is constructed of selections, projections and Cartesian products. Then $\mathbf{Y}(f)$ is the LFP of the following Horn program:

$$\begin{array}{l} \alpha_{f_1}: R(\bar{\mathbf{r}}) \leftarrow A_{11}(\bar{\mathbf{a}}_{11}), ..., A_{1n_1}(\bar{\mathbf{a}}_{1n_1}), Cond_{f_1} \\ \cdots \qquad \cdots \qquad \cdots \\ \alpha_{f_k}: R(\bar{\mathbf{r}}) \leftarrow A_{k1}(\bar{\mathbf{a}}_{k1}), ..., A_{kn_k}(\bar{\mathbf{a}}_{kn_k}), Cond_{f_k} \end{array} \tag{3}$$

where $A_{i1}, ..., A_{in_i}$ are relation names mentioned in f_i, $i=1,...,k$, and $Cond_{f_i}$ is a condition expressing relationships among the arguments of α_{f_i}, as specified by f_i. Now, applying selection σ_ϕ to $\mathbf{Y}(f)$ corresponds to posing the following query to the database (3)

$$\boldsymbol{Ans}(\overline{\mathbf{ans}}) \leftarrow R(\bar{\mathbf{r}}), Cond_\phi, \tag{4}$$

where $Cond_\phi$ is an attached condition constructed from ϕ. It is easily seen that distributing σ_ϕ through $\mathbf{Y}$ (and getting $\sigma_\phi(\mathbf{Y}(f \circ \sigma_\psi))$ as a result) corresponds to placing the filter ψ on *each* of the ports connecting the rel-node R with axioms $\alpha_{f_1}, ..., \alpha_{f_k}$, (in the SG constructed from (3) and (4)). Therefore, it is interesting to compare static filtering with the optimization achieved by [AhU79, DeA86].

First observe that since system graphs can encode any Horn database, the filtering method imposes no restrictions on relational expressions, and it may achieve optimization when the other methods [AhU79, DeA86] cannot. An example to that effect is given in [BaR86]. As another illustration consider the following example:

$\alpha : R(x,y) \leftarrow A(x,y)$
$\beta : P(x,y) \leftarrow B(x,y)$
$\gamma : R(x,y) \leftarrow A(x,z), P(z,y)$
$\delta : P(x,y) \leftarrow B(x,z), R(z,y)$
$\eta : \boldsymbol{Ans}(x) \leftarrow R(x,c)$

The corresponding relational expression, $f(X)$, can be constructed as follows. Let $X(r1,r2,p1,p2)$ be a new predicate (intuitively, X is a concatenation of R and P), and $D(a1,a2,b1,b2)$ be an auxiliary predicate used in construction of f (D is a concatenation of A and B). Then

$$f(X) = D \bigcup (\pi_{1,4}(\pi_{1,2}(D) \bowtie \pi_{3,4}(X)) \times \pi_{1,4}(\pi_{3,4}(D) \bowtie \pi_{1,2}(X))),$$

and the corresponding query is $\sigma_{2=c}(\pi_{1,2}(\mathbf{Y}(f)))$. This expression has two occurrences of X, so the methods [AhU79, DeA86] do not handle this case. In contrast, the static filtering will restrict ports 1_α, 1_β, 2_γ, 2_δ and 1_η allowing only tuples with the second component c to pass through. The resulting SG computes the query $\sigma_{2=c}(\pi_{1,2}(\mathbf{Y}(f')))$, where f' is as follows:

$$f'(X) = \sigma_{2=c \vee 4=c}(D) \bigcup (\pi_{1,4}(\pi_{1,2}(D) \bowtie \pi_{3,4}(\sigma_{4=c}(X))) \times \pi_{1,4}(\pi_{3,4}(D) \bowtie \pi_{1,2}(\sigma_{2=c}(X)))).$$

Second, although in some cases static filtering provides no optimization (Example 2), it follows from the next theorem, that whenever $f(X)$ has only one occurrence of X, and distributing selection through the least fixed point operator is at all possible, our optimization algorithm will do it.

THEOREM 3. ([KiL86a]) Let $f(X)$ be a monotone relational expression with at most one occurrence of X. Suppose $\sigma_{\phi}\mathbf{Y}(f) = \sigma_{\phi}\mathbf{Y}(f \circ \sigma_{\psi})$. Then static filtering restricts each output port of the rel-node representing X by a condition that is at least as strong as ψ. []

7. Some Comparison With Other Methods

A number of elegant query evaluation techniques for deductive databases has been proposed during the past decade (see [BaR86, GMN84] for a comprehensive survey). In this section we compare our method with SNIP of McKay and Shapiro [McS81], the method of Henschen and Naqvi [HeN84], Magic Sets of Bancilhon, Maier, Sagiv and Ullman [BMS86], and the Counting method [BMS86, SaZ86a, SaZ86b].

7.1. SNIP

SNIP uses active connection graphs (ACG) to represent data flow during query evaluation. An ACG has one *rule-node* per axiom, which corresponds to ax-nodes of SG. It also has *goal nodes* that play a role similar to our rel-nodes. But, unlike SG, ACG may have more than one goal node per predicate, as illustrated by the following example.

Example 4. Let the database be

$T(y) \leftarrow R(a, y)$
$T(y) \leftarrow R(b, y)$
$R(x, y) \leftarrow Q(x, y)$
... ...

Suppose the query is $\{ y \mid T(y) \}$. Then SNIP creates a goal node for $T(y)$, and then two separate goal nodes for $R(a, y)$ and $R(b, y)$, since the two latter literals are nonunifiable. In comparison, SGs always have only one rel-node per predicate. Thus, an SG may be more compact than the corresponding ACG, which is an advantage, especially if one thinks of a multiprocessor implementation of the system. []

Furthermore, it has been shown [BaR86] that query evaluation in SNIP corresponds to semi-naive evaluation. The simplistic evaluation, described in Section 3.2, is essentially an implementation of the semi-naive evaluation. Hence in terms of the data flow the filtering method does at least as well as SNIP, and, when static filtering does not degenerate to the simplistic query evaluation, it does better.

7.2. Henschen-Naqvi, Magic Sets, Counting

The method of Henschen and Naqvi (abbr. H-N) compiles queries into iterative programs involving relational algebra expressions. Compilation succeeds if a "repeated pattern" of relational expressions emerges during the compilation, which provides basis for the iterative program. This dependence on a repeated pattern severely restricts the applicability of the method, and it is believed [BaR86, BMS86] that the application domain of H-N does not extend beyond linear axioms (it will be shown shortly, that H-N cannot also handle some complex sets of linear axioms).

The idea behind Magic Sets is to determine sets of facts relevant to the query, and then use these facts to reduce the amount of data used in the course of query evaluation. As noted by the authors of the method, it is applicable mainly to databases with linear axioms.

Counting method was first described in [BMS86], and then further developed and generalized by Sacca and Zaniolo [SaZ86a, SaZ86b]. The idea is similar to Magic Sets, but while constructing magic sets for a query, Counting computes the "distance" from each tuple in a magic set to the tuple of bindings specified in the query. Such magic sets with the distance attached to each tuple are called *counting sets.* Counting sets allow to do more precise selections while computing the query, which is an advantage over the Magic Sets method. On the other hand, the "distance" between tuples of the magic set and the query binding may not be uniquely defined. In this case Counting tends to do some extra work w.r.t. to Magic Sets. Another, more serious problem, is that magic sets may be, in a sense, cyclic. In such a case the corresponding counting sets become infinite, and query evaluation under the Counting method does not terminate.

We compare static filtering with the three approaches on a number of examples, that show that neither is always the best. This, once again, supports the conclusion suggested by [BaR86, BMS86] that there, probably, does not exist a single method which is always better than the others.

Although in certain cases static filtering is not better than even the simplistic evaluation (Example 2), it is capable of handling some nonlinear rules to which H-N, Magic Sets and Counting do not apply. Consider the following rules:

α : $R(x,y,z) \leftarrow B(x,y,z)$
β : $R(x,y,z) \leftarrow A(x,u,v), R(u,y,z), R(v,z,y)$

Let the query be $\{ <x,y> \mid R(x,y,a) \}$. Here H-N fails to compile the rules into an iterative program, and Magic Sets does not work because the two occurrences of the recursive predicate, R, in β mutually bind one another (and this is a kind of rules that Magic Sets cannot handle). Counting (as described in [SaZ86b]) does not work either, because computation of the counting sets does not stop. In contrast, static filtering will correctly determine (by establishing appropriate filters) that the only useful tuples of R and B, that have to be considered in the query evaluation, are those with the second or third component equal to a.

Let us now consider some examples of linear rules. In Example 2, as we noted, static filtering degenerates to the simplistic query evaluation, and is not very useful. Magic Sets, although succeeding in finding relevant facts, repeats essentially the same work twice. Indeed, the magic set of relevant facts is defined here by the rules

magic (b)
magic $(z) \leftarrow$ *magic* (x), $A(x,z)$

So, just computing *magic* (z) is equivalent to solving the query. Counting has a similar problem, and, in addition, should the binary relation P in the example be cyclic, the method does not terminate. In contrast, H-N works perfectly here, as that example happens to be "tailored" for that method.

The next example shows that H-N cannot deal with certain sets of linear axioms[2].

$P(x,y) \leftarrow A(x,y)$
$P(x,y) \leftarrow B(x,z),\ P(z,y)$
$P(x,y) \leftarrow C(x,z),\ P(z,y)$

Here the compilation process of Henschen and Naqvi will generate sequences of joins of the form $B^{k_1} \bowtie C^{k_2} \bowtie B^{k_3} \bowtie C^{k_4} \bowtie \ldots \bowtie A$, for arbitrary $k_i \geq 0$, which do not contain a repeated pattern on which an iterative program can be built[3]. In this example static filtering and Magic Sets do equally well for the query $\{ x \mid P(x,a) \}$. Counting, again, runs into trouble, since computing of the counting sets never stops. In addition, Magic Sets alsos work reasonably well for the query $\{ y \mid P(b,y) \}$, while static filtering degenerates to the simplistic query evaluation (like in Example 2). Counting also works well for that query, unless B or C is a cyclic relation.

As an example where H-N, Counting and static filtering all do better than Magic Sets consider the following database.

Example 5. Let $A(x,y,z)$ denote that y is a parent of x descending from z ($y=z$ is possible).

$A(des,anc,anc) \leftarrow P(des,anc)$
$A(des,par,anc) \leftarrow P(des,par),\ A(par,grandpar,anc)$

Suppose the query is $\{ par \mid A(a,par,b) \}$ asking for all parents of a descending from b. Here H-N first computes all ancestors of a, and then applies selection $\sigma_{3=b}$. Counting will do essentially the same work as H-N (unless P is cyclic, in which case Counting does not terminate). Static filters start from the other end: first all descendants of b are computed, and then selection $\sigma_{1=a}$ is applied. All three methods perform in this case comparably.

However, Magic Sets exhibits a somewhat irrational behaviour. Indeed, it rewrites the original set of rules as follows:

$magic(a,b)$
$magic(par,anc) \leftarrow magic(des,anc),\ P(des,par)$
$A(des,anc,anc) \leftarrow magic(des,anc),\ P(des,anc)$
$A(des,par,anc) \leftarrow magic(des,anc),\ P(des,par),\ A(par,grandpar,anc)$

It is easily seen that the magic set computed by the first two rules consists of all pairs $<c,b>$, where c is some ancestor of a, not necessarily descending from b. At this point Magic Sets has done almost all the job that H-N would have done (except for the final selection). But it goes on to the second stage, and, using the last pair of rules, finds all the descendants of b who are also ancestors of a. Note that the amount of work performed at this stage is essentially the same as that done by static filtering. □

8. Conclusions

We have shown that the well-known algebraic manipulations used to optimize relational algebra expressions [Ull82] can be transferred to the deductive database soil. The optimization

[2] As shown in [ChH82] every linear mutual recursion can be reduced to a set of linear rules with only one recursive predicate. Hence, inability of H-N to deal with this case is not at all surprising, because mutual recursion was known as a difficult nut for that method (see [HeN84]).

[3] Interestingly, these axioms are *regular* [Cha81], therefore Chang's method can successfully treat this case.

is performed in a top-down manner, and is accomplished at the query compile time. The method presented here can be extended to push projections as well [KiL85].

Other optimization strategies commonly used in relational databases also fit in our framework. First, as a fringe benefit of the approach, ***common subexpressions*** [Ull82] are identified at the time of construction of SG. Each subexpression corresponds to a part of SG. Since identical subexpressions correspond to the same part of SG, they never are evaluated twice. ***Query decomposition*** is another well-known strategy commonly used in relational databases [WoY76]. It can be incorporated in our framework in several different ways. Two such examples are provided in [Loz85b, Loz86]. A more efficient way to do so is through the use of *dynamic filtering* [KiL86b].

It should be emphasized that the static filtering described in this paper is only one aspect of an approach, called SYGRAF (for SYstem GRAph Filtering), which is a truly comprehensive system, able to deal in one framework with a wide class of deductive databases, including those with function symbols [KiL86a, KiL86b, KiL86c].

Another interesting feature of SYGRAF is that it can easily integrate many other methods. For instance, an appropriate rule rewriting technique (e.g., [BMS86, SaZ86b]) can be used as a preprocessor for constructing an efficient SG, which will then be used by SYGRAF for query evaluation.

ACKNOWLEDGEMENTS We thank Suzanne Wagner Dietrich and David Scott Warren for the very helpful comments on an earlier draft of this paper. We also thank Rakesh Agrawal and Prem Devanbu for sending us a draft of their work [DeA86].

9. References

[AhU79] A. V. Aho and J. D. Ullman, "Universality of Data Retrieval Languages", *Proc. Sixth ACM Symp. on Prin. of Programming Languages*, 1979, 110 - 120.

[BaR86] F. Bancilhon and R. Ramakrishnan, "An Amateur's Introduction to Recursive Query Processing Strategies", *ACM Proc. of the ACM-SIGMOD Intl. Conf. on Management of Data*, 1986.

[BMS86] F. Bancilhon, D. Maier, Y. Sagiv and J. D. Ullman, "Magic Sets and Other Strange Ways to Implement Logic Programs", *Proc. of the ACM SIGACT-SIGMOD Symp. on Prin. of Database Systems*, Cambridge, MA, March, 1986.

[ChH82] A. K. Chandra and D. Harel, "Horn Clauses and the Fixed Point Hierarchy", *Proc. of the ACM SIGACT-SIGMOD Symp. on Prin. of Database Systems*, 1982, 158 - 163.

[Cha81] C. Chang, "On Evaluation of Queries Containing Derived Relations in a Relational Database", in *Advances in Databases*, vol. 1, H. Gallaire, J. Minker and J. M. Nicolas, (eds.), Plenum Press, 1981, 235-260.

[DeA86] P. Devanbu and R. Agrawal, "Moving Selections into Fixpoint Queries", unpablished manuscript, 1986.

[GMN84] H. Gallaire, J. Minker and J. Nicolas, "Logic and Databases: A Deductive Approach", *Computing Surveys*, **16**, 2 (June 1984), 153-185.

[HeN84] L. J. Henschen and S. A. Naqvi, "Compiling Queries in Relational First-Order Databases", *J. ACM*, **31**, 1 (1984), 47-85.

[KiL85] M. Kifer and E. L. Lozinskii, "Query Optimization in Deductive Databases", Tech. Rep.# 85/16, Dept. of Computer Science, SUNY at Stony Brook, June 1985.

[KiL86a] M. Kifer and E. L. Lozinskii, "On Compile-Time Query Optimization in Deductive Databases", submitted, 1986.

[KiL86b] M. Kifer and E. L. Lozinskii, "A Framework for an Efficient Implementation of Deductive Database Systems", *Proceedings of the 6-th Advanced Database Symposium*, Tokyo, Japan, Aug. 1986.

[KiL86c] M. Kifer and E. L. Lozinskii, "Can We Implement Logic as a Database System? ", Tech. Rep.# 86/16, Dept. of Comp. Sci., SUNY @ Stony Brook, March 1986.

[Loz85a] E. L. Lozinskii, "A Remark on Distributed Termination", *Proc. of the 5-th IEEE Intern. Conf. on Distributed Computing*, Denver, Colorado, May, 1985.

[Loz85b] E. L. Lozinskii, "Evaluating Queries in Deductive Databases by Generating", *Proc. of IJCAI*, 1985, 173-177.

[Loz86] E. L. Lozinskii, "A Problem-Oriented Inferential Database System", *ACM Trans. Database Systems*, 1986. To appear.

[McS81] D. P. McKay and S. C. Shapiro, "Using Active Connection Graphs for Reasoning with Recursive Rules", *IJCAI*, 1981, 368-374.

[RoH80] D. J. Rosenkrantz and H. B. Hunt, "Processing Conjunctive Predicates and Queries", *Proc. of the ACM Intl. Conf. on Very Large Data Bases*, 1980, 64-72.

[SaZ86a] D. Sacca and C. Zaniolo, "On the Implementation of the Simple Class of Logic Queries for Databases", *Proc. of the ACM SIGACT-SIGMOD Symp. on Prin. of Database Systems*, 1986, 16-23.

[SaZ86b] D. Sacca and C. Zaniolo, "Implementing Recursive Logic Queries with Function Symbols", Tech. Rep.# DB-065-86, MCC, Austin, Tx, Feb 1986.

[ShM80] S. C. Shapiro and D. P. McKay, "Inference with Recursive Rules", *Proc. First Annual National Conf. On Artificial Intelligence*, Stanford, 1980, 151-153.

[Ull82] J. D. Ullman, *Principles of Database Systems*, Computer Science Press, Rockville, MD, 1982.

[vaK76] M. H. vanEmden and R. A. Kowalski, "The Semantics of Predicate Logic as a Programming Language", *J. ACM*, **23**, 4 (Oct. 1976), 733-742.

[WoY76] E. Wong and K. Youssefi, "Decomposition - A Strategy for Query Processing", *ACM ACM Trans. Database Systems*, **1**, 3 (Sept. 1976), 223-241.

Multidimensional Order Preserving Linear Hashing with Partial Expansions

Hans-Peter Kriegel
Lehrstuhl fuer Informatik I
Universitaet Wuerzburg
D-8700 Wuerzburg
West Germany

Bernhard Seeger
Institut fuer Informatik II
Universitaet Karlsruhe
D-7500 Karlsruhe 1
West Germany

Abstract

We present a new multidimensional dynamic hashing scheme without directory intended for files which grow and shrink dynamically. For previous schemes, the retrieval performance either suffers from a superlinearly growing directory or from an uneven distribution of the records over the pages of a file even for uniform record distribution. Our scheme is a multidimensional order preserving extension of (one-dimensional) linear hashing with partial expansions and thus overcomes these disadvantages. For uniform distribution our scheme performs better than its competitors which is underligned by experimental runs with an implementation of our scheme. In the last section we give a brief outline of the quantile method which guarantees that our scheme performs for a non-uniform distribution practically as well as for a uniform distribution. In addition to its excellent performance, our scheme fulfills all the necessary requirements to be used in an engineering database system: it is dynamic, is suitable for secondary storage devices, supports point data and spatial data objects and supports spatial clustering (proximity queries).

1. Introduction

Concerning database systems for standard applications, e.g. commercial applications, there is a large variety of index structures at the disposal of the database designer for the implementation of the physical level of a database system. As demonstrated in [Kri 84] there are efficient tree-based index stuctures such as multidimensional B-trees, in particular kB-trees.

For non-standard databases, also called engineering databases, used in applications such as image processing, design and manufacturing (CAD/CAM) etc. none of the tree-based index structures is suitable, since they cluster records according to the lexicographical ordering. Hash-based index structures cluster records which are close together in the key space. This is the type of clustering which we need in engineering databases.

However, multidimensional hashing schemes suffer from two shortcomings. In most engineering applications, objects are nonuniformly distributed in space. First, there is no multidimensional hashing scheme which exhibits practically the same retrieval performance for nonuniform distribution as for uniform distribution. Second, even for uniform distribution, the retrieval performance of all known multidimensional hashing schemes suffers from two shortcomings which will be elaborated in the following paragraph.

Thus we will proceed in two steps. In this paper we will design a multidimensional dynamic hashing scheme which will perform better than its competitors for uniform distribution. For nonuniform distribution all hashing schemes degenerate performancewise. In the last section we will outline a method which applied to our scheme guarantees for nonuniform distributions practically the same performance as for uniform distribution. None of the previous schemes for multidimensional data achieves this performance. In this paper we will primarily focus on uniform distributions, which is the explicit or implicit assumption in all publications dealing with multidimensional hashing.

Multidimensional hashing schemes fall into one of two broad categories: those that do not use a directory and those that use a directory. Typical representatives of the second category are the grid file [NHS 84] and multidimensional extendible hashing (MEH) [Oto 84]. Unfortunately, all methods with directory which a) guarantee two disk accesses for an exact match query and b) are dynamic (in the sense that there is no upper bound for the number of records) exhibit a superlinear growth of the directory in the number of records, even when the records are uniformly distributed in the key space. In case of nonuniform distributions the directory may require exponential space.

Since last year a series of variants either of the grid file or of multidimensional extendible hashing have been suggested all distributing the directory on several levels and accomodating as much as possible of the directory in central memory: the 2-level grid file [Hin 85], the multilevel grid file [KW 85], the balanced multidimensional extendible hash tree [Oto 86] and the interpolation-based grid file [Ouk 85]. As indicated by the name, in [Ouk 85] the concepts of the grid file and interpolation-based index maintenance [Bur 83] are integrated. As shown in the paper [Ouk 85] the interpolation-based grid file grows ***linear in the number of data pages*** . However, as not even mentioned in this paper, the directory may grow ***exponential in the number of records*** , since a split of a directory page may propagate recursively. In [KW 85] and [Oto 86] the directory is partitioned using the K-D-B-tree concept [Rob 81]. However, for large files, the two-disk-access-guarantee for exact match queries does not hold any more. Depending on the file sizes three or four disk accesses may be necessary to answer an exact match query. Summarizing we can say that none of the structures with directory and no overflow records guarantees linear growth of the directory in the number of records and guarantees two disk accesses for an exact match query at the same time.

For most applications a linearly growing directory is a must. This was the basic motivation for the Symmetric Dynamic Index Maintenance (SDIM) scheme suggested by Otoo [Oto 85]. In contrast to the grid file and MEH, SDIM uses a control function that allows overflow records and guarantees the linear growth of the directory. The SDIM organization is comprised of two levels: a first level of a directory, and a second level of data pages which hold the records. Using the storage mapping function G_{SDIM} each record is mapped onto a directory entry containing a pointer to the header page of a short chain of data pages. By its design, SDIM avoids the performance penalty due to a superlinearly growing directory. However, there still remains a major performance penalty in SDIM which is not mentioned in [Oto 85]. Even in the case of a uniform distribution, SDIM may produce chains with relative load factor 1, 1/2,.., $1/2^d$, where d is the number of attributes. Obviously, this large variance of the load factors leads to poor performance of retrieval and update algorithms.

Another very important drawback of a directory based hashing scheme is its undynamic behavior in case of insertions and deletions. If an insert operation requires introducing a new partitioning hyperplane, this will necessitate O($n^{1-1/d}$) accesses to secondary storage.

Our goal is the design of an efficient multidimensional dynamic hashing scheme which uses no directory and creates chains with relative load factors distributed between 0.5 and 1. Using no directory we have to allow overflow records which are organized by bucket chaining. We consider a page to be a chain of blocks, where the first block, the primary block, is put in a primary file and the other blocks, the secondary blocks, are put in a secondary file.

Looking at the development of onedimensional hashing schemes, we see that the problem of largely varying relative load factors already deteriorates performance of linear hashing [Lit 80]. Larson suggested a very efficient solution of the problem: linear hashing with partial expansions (LHPE) [Lar 80]. The major difference compared with linear hashing is that doubling the file size is done in p partial expansions, where p=2 turned out to be the best compromise. The expected number of page accesses for a successful search is very close to 1. Thus our goal is to suggest a multidimensional order preserving extension of linear hashing with partial expansions.

In the following, we consider a file of d-attribute composite keys $K = (K_1,..,K_d)$. We assume the domain of the keys to be the unit d-dimensional cube $[0, 1)^d$. Obviously, this requirement can easily fulfilled for an arbitrary domain by simple transformation. Our scheme should support the following operations efficiently: insertion and deletion, exact match query, range query and other proximity queries.

This paper is organized as follows. In section 2 we give a brief description of linear hashing with partial expansions and suggest an order preserving variant. In the third section we present our scheme, multidimensional order preserving linear hashing with partial expansions (MOLHPE). In particular, we introduce the address function of our scheme and show how partial expansions are performed. A precise description of the algorithms for exact match and range query in a modula 2 - like formulation follows in section 4. In the fifth section, we report on the performance of an implementation of our scheme. In section 6 we give a short outline of the quantile method which guarantees for non-uniform distributions practically the same ideal behavior of our scheme as for uniform distributions. Section 7 concludes this paper.

2. Linear Hashing with partial expansions

In this section we are dealing with hashing schemes for one dimensional keys. All multidimensional schemes are a generalization of a onedimensional scheme.

The original linear hashing scheme proposed by Litwin [Lit 80] considers a file of N pages with addresses 0,1,..,N-1 at the beginning . When the page j is split, the file will be extended by one page with adress N+j, j = 0,..,N-1. The predetermind sequence of splitting is given by 0,1,..,N-1, i.e. first page 0 is split into page 0 and page N, then page 1 is split, etc.. A pointer p keeps track of the page, which will be split next. If all N pages are split, the file size has doubled, the pointer p is reset to 0 and the splitting process starts over again. After doubling the file size a full expansion is finished.

There are two important remarks for constructing an access algorithm. First the decision, whether a record remains in the old page or moves to the new page depends only on the key of the record. Second, the old and the new page should be filled uniformly, i.e. half of the records should remain in the old page. It follows from the second remark that the record load over the file is non - uniform, because the load of split pages can only be half of the load of non - split pages. To achieve a more even load distribution we must partition the pages into groups. If a new page is added to the file, one group of pages will be expanded by one page. Let us consider a group size of two pages at the beginning. If every group is expanded by one page, we will say the first partial expansion is finished, i.e. the file size increases to 1.5 times of the orginal size. After expanding all groups one more time the file size has doubled and a full expansion has been finished.

Assuming two partial expansions per full expansion, we start from a file of 2N pages divided into N groups of two pages. Group j consists of pages (j, j + N), j = 0,1,..,N-1. The file will be expanded by group 0, group 1, etc. until the first expansion will be finished. If we expand the j-th group, one third of the records from page j and from page j+N should be relocated in the new page 2N+j. Then we consider N groups of three pages (j, j+N, j+2N), j = 0,..,N-1, and we start the second partial expansion. During the second partial expansion new pages will be created with addresses 3N+j, j = 0,..,N-1.

Example 2.1

(i) Splitting during the first partial expansion (p = 0)

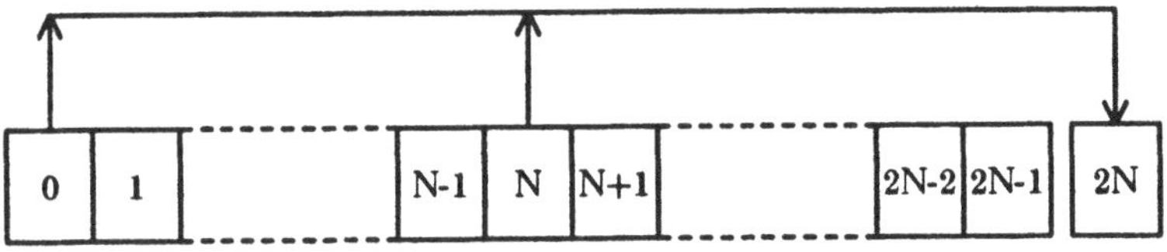

(ii) Splitting during the second partial expansion (p = 0)

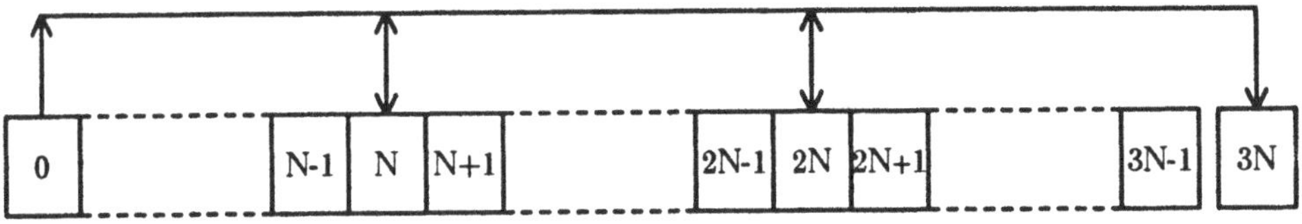

The choice of the hashing function is very important for the sequential access to the records. We propose an order preserving hashing function, i.e we can sort the pages p_i, i = 0,..,M in such a way that the keys of all records in page p_{i-1} are smaller than the keys of records in page p_i, i = 1,..,M.

In particular, we choose the following hashing function

$$h(K, L, p) = \begin{cases} \sum_{j=0}^{L-1} b_{j+1} 2^j \text{ , if } \sum_{j=0}^{L-1} b_{j+1} 2^j < 2^{L-1} + p \\ \sum_{j=0}^{L-2} b_{j+1} 2^j \text{ } otherwise \end{cases}$$

where key K $\in$ [0, 1) has the binary representation $\sum_{j \geq 1} b_j 2^{-j}$.

In the above hashing function the level L of the file indicates, how often the file size has doubled and p points to the first page in the group of pages to be expanded next. The following algorithm which is applicable only for two partial expansions is similar to other proposals.

2.2 Algorithm Hash(K, L, p, ex)

```
(* K = Σ_{j≥1} b_j 2^-j *)

BEGIN
    group:= Σ_{j=1}^{L-2} b_{j+1} 2^j;        edge:= Σ_{j=1}^{L-2} b_j 2^-j;
    IF group ≥ p THEN
        q:=ex + 1
    ELSE
        q:=ex + 2
    END;
    (2b_1 + b_0 ):= TRUNC(q * 2^(L-1) * ( K - edge ) );
    (* b_0, b_1 ∈ { 0,1 } *)
    IF q = 2 THEN
        buddy := b_0
    ELSE
        buddy := 2*b_0 + b_1
    END;
    RETURN ( 2^(L-1) * buddy + group)
END Hash.
```

Algorithm 2.2 uses the following variables: K is the key, L is the level of the file, p points to the first page in the group of pages to be expanded next, ex $\in \{1,2\}$ indicates which of the two partial expansion is presently performed, group gives the group of pages and buddy the page of that group, in which the record with key K resides, and edge gives the left edge of the interval corresponding to the group.

We will generalize order preserving linear hashing with partial expansions to the multidimensional case in the next section. For further considerations of partial expansions the reader is referred to [Lar 80] and [RL 82] and for order preserving hashing schemes we refer to [Ore 83].

3. The address function

We want to present an address function G which is well known from multidimensional extendible hashing (MEH) [Oto 84]. MEH is a directory based hashing scheme, in which the directory is organized as a multidimensional dynamic array addressed by the function G. In the components of the array there are pointers referencing the data pages. In our approach, we will use the function G to address pages, more exactly chains of blocks (since we allow overflow records) without a directory.

The address function G of level L computes addresses $0,..,2^L-1$, where each dimension is treated equally. Each dimension j has an own level L_j, $j = 0,..,d$, which is given by

(3.1) $L_j = L \text{ DIV } d + 1 \qquad j \in \{1,..,L \text{ MOD } d\}$

$L_j = L \text{ DIV } d \qquad L \text{ MOD } d < j \leq d$

First we evaluate by a special application of algorithm (2.2) an index array $I = (i_1,..,i_d)$.

(3.2) $\quad i_j = \text{Hash}(K_j, L_j, 0, 1) \qquad j = 1,..,d$

The function G is given by

(3.3)

$$G(i_1,..,i_d) = \begin{cases} i_z * \prod_{j \in M} J_i + \sum_{j \in M} c_j * i_j & \text{, if } \max\{i_1,..,i_d\} \neq 0 \\ 0 & \textit{otherwise} \end{cases}$$

where z, M, t, J_i, c_i are given as follow:

$z = \max \{ j \in \{1,..,d\} \mid \text{TRUNC}(\log_2 i_j) = \max \{\text{TRUNC}(\log_2 i_k) \mid k \in \{1,..,d\} \} \}$

$M = \{ 1,..,d \} \setminus \{ z \}$

$t = \text{TRUNC}(\log_2 i_z)$

$$J_i = \begin{cases} 2^{t+1} & \textit{, if } i < z \\ 2^t & \textit{otherwise} \end{cases} \quad , i \in M$$

$$c_i = \prod_{\substack{r=j+1 \\ r \neq z}}^{d} J_i \quad , i \in M$$

Example 3.4

File of level L = 4 addressed by G (d = 2).

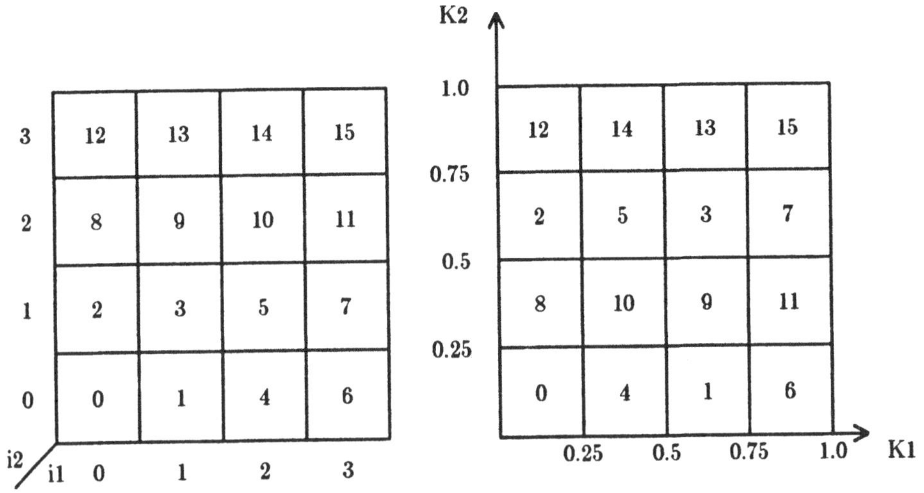

On the left side of the illustration we depict the addresses produced by the function G dependent on the Index I = (i_1, i_2). On the right side we illustrate the addresses dependent on the domain of the keys. Every address corresponds to a rectangle, for example address 5 corresponds to rectangle [0.25, 0.5) × [0.5, 0.75).

Our goal is to double the file size not in one step, but to expand the file page by page using an expansion pointer ep $= (ep_1,..,ep_d)$. Similar as in one dimensional LHPE, we consider groups of pages, which will be expanded by one page in order to improve retrieval performance. Up to now we have considered two partial expansions. All the following algorithms are given for this case. Nevertheless we can generalize the algorithms to an arbitrary number of partial expansions. However, two partial expansions turned out to be a good compromise between the cost for inserting and searching a record [Lar 80].

Let us consider a file of size 2^L pages, $L \geq d$. We will designate the dimension $s = L \text{ MOD } d + 1$ as the dimension, in which the expansion will be carried out. During the first partial expansion, we consider groups of two pages addressed by

$$(G(i_1,..,i_s,..,i_d), G(i_1,..,i_s + 2^{L_s - 1} ,..,i_d))$$

$$0 \leq i_j < 2^{L_j} \quad j \in \{1,..,d\} \setminus \{ s \}$$
$$0 \leq i_s < 2^{L_s - 1}$$

This group of pages will be expanded by one page with address

$$G(i_1,..,i_s + 2^{L_s},..,i_d)$$

One third of the records of the old pages should be relocated in the new page.

The expansion pointer ep $= (ep_1,..,ep_d)$ refers to the group of pages, which will be expanded next. The address of the first page in the group is given by G(ep). At the beginning of a partial expansion the pointer is initialized to

ep := (0,..,0)

If a group is expanded during a partial expansion, the pointer ep will be updated by the algorithm NextPointer.

3.5 Algorithm NextPointer (ep, L)

```
BEGIN
    IF s ≠ 1 THEN i:=1 ELSE i:=2 END;
    LOOP
        ep_i := ep_i + 1;
        IF ep_i = 2^L_i THEN
            p_i := 0;
            i:=Next(i)
            (* IF i = k THEN i:=s END *)
            (* IF i = s - 1 THEN i:=s+1 ELSE i:=i+1 END *)
        ELSE
            EXIT
        END
    END (* LOOP *)
END NextPointer.
```

After the first partial expansion has been completed, the file size has increased by the factor 1.5. Then the second partial expansion is started considering groups of three pages addressed by

$$(\ G(i_1,..,i_s,..,i_d), G(i_1,..,i_s + 2^{L_s - 1},..,i_d), G(i_1,..,i_s + 2^{L_s},..,i_d) \ )$$

This group of pages will be expanded by one page with the address

$$G(i_1,..,i_s + 2^{L_s-1} + 2^{L_s},..,i_d)$$
$$0 \leq i_j < 2^{L_j} \qquad j \in \{1,..,d\} \setminus \{ s \}$$
$$0 \leq i_s < 2^{L_s-1}$$

The splitting process of the second partial expansion proceeds in a way analgous to the first partial expansion and therefore will not described here. The following example 3.6 demonstrates the growth of the file during both partial expansions. The addresses of the pages depend on the domain of the keys.

Example 3.6

(i) Let us consider a file of level L = 4 (see example 3.2). At the beginning of the first partial expansion, the pages are divided into groups as follows :

(0, 4), (1, 6), (8, 10), (9, 11), (2, 5), (3, 7), (12, 14), (13, 15)

(ii) after the 1st expansion of the group G(ep), ep = (0, 0)

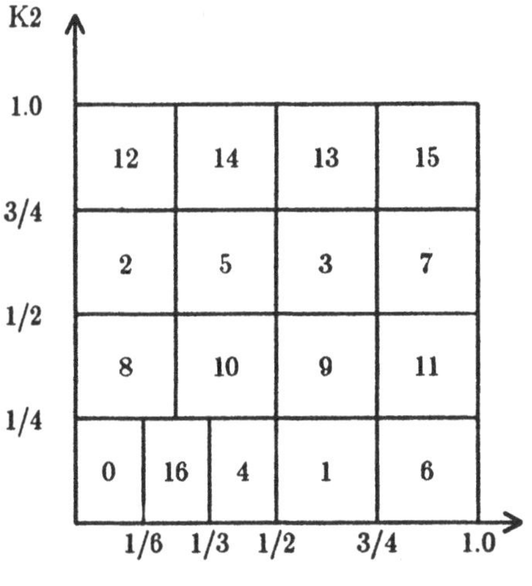

(iii) after the 2nd expansion of of the group G(ep), ep = (0, 1)

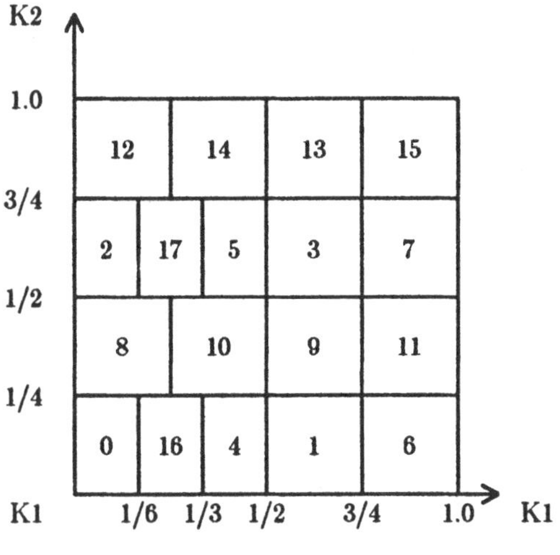

(iv) after the 1st partial expansion has been completely finished

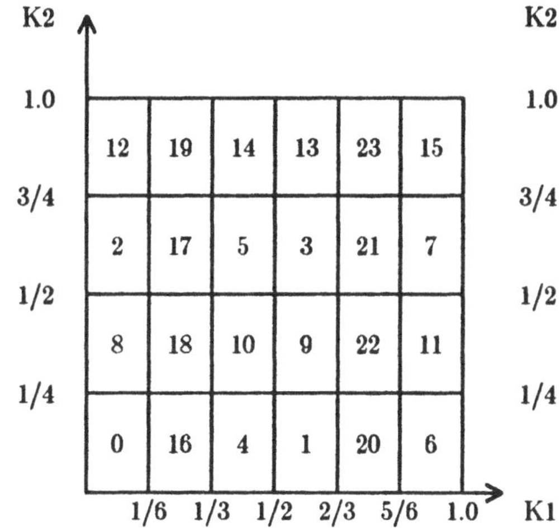

(v) one more expansion during the second partial expansion of the group G(ep), ep = (0, 0)

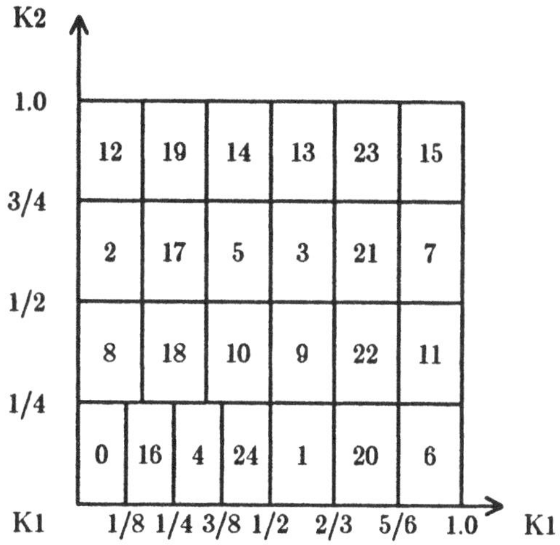

4. Queries

Let us first present the address computation algorithm for multidimensional order preserving linear hashing with partial expansions (MOLHPE). It can be used to answer exact match queries. This algorithm is based on the algorithm Hash (2.2) and additionally incorporates the address function G proposed in the last section. Let us emphasize that the retrieval algorithms presented in this section assume two partial expansions per full expansion.

4.1 Algorithm MultiHash (K, L, ep, ex)

(* $K = (K_1,..,K_d)$ mit $K_j = \sum_{i \geq 1} b_i^j \, 2^{-i}$ *)

BEGIN

  group[j] := $\sum_{i=0}^{L_s - 1} b_{i+1}^j \, 2^i$ $j \in \{1,..,d\} \setminus \{ s \}$;

  group[s] := $\sum_{i=0}^{L_s - 2} b_{i+1}^s \, 2^i$;

  edge := $\sum_{i=0}^{L_s - 2} b_i^s \, 2^{-i}$;

  IF (group[s], group) $\geq^L$ (ep[s], ep) THEN

    (* group of pages isn't expand *)

    q := ex + 1

  ELSE

    q := ex + 2

  END;

  $(2 * b_1 + b_0)$:= TRUNC ($q * 2^{L_s - 1} * (K_s - edge)$);

```
    IF q = 2 THEN
        buddy := b0
    ELSE
        buddy := 2 * b0 + b1
    END;
    RETURN G ( group[1],..,group[s] + buddy * 2^(Ls-1),..,group[d] )
END MultiHash.
```

Algorithm 4.1 uses the following variables : K is the multidimensional key, L is the level of the file, ep is the expansion pointer, ex $\in$ {1,2} indicates which of the two partial expansions is presently performed, group gives the address G(group) of the group of pages in which the wanted record resides and buddy determines the page within the group. The operator $\geq$ denotes of lexicographical ordering.

Let us remark that in the case d = 1 the algorithm MultiHash is identical to the algorithm Hash. Furthermore the description complexity of the algorithm is practically not increased by the concept of partial expansions.

Example 4.2

Let us consider the situation of example 3.4 (iii). The invocation of the procedure

MultiHash((0.25, 0.66), 4, (0, 2), 1)

results in the following situation :

group = 0, edge = 0, q = ex + 2 = 3, buddy = 2

G (4, 1) = 17, RETURN(17)

Now let us consider range queries where we specify a pair of bounds, Klow, Khigh $\in [0, 1)^d$ such that $Klow_j \leq Khigh_j$, $j \in \{1,..,d\}$, is fulfilled. Then we ask for all the records with key K in the d - dimensional rectangle R(Klow, Khigh) = $\bigtimes_{i=1}^{d} [Klow_j, Khigh_j)$. In the following we present the algorithm RangeQuery, which produces a range query.

4.3 Algorithm RangeQuery (Klow, Khigh, L, ep, ex)

1. Evaluate the index grouplow, grouphigh of the group and the left limit of the interval edgelow, edgehigh correspondending to the keys Klow and Khigh.
2.
```
actgroup := grouplow;
FOR i = 1,2 DO
    q_i := ex + i;
    low_i := TRUNC( q_i * 2^(Ls-1) * (Klow_s - edgelow) );
    high_i := TRUNC( q_i * 2^(Ls-1) * (Khigh_s - edgehigh) );
END;
```
3.
```
REPEAT
    IF (actgroup[s], group) ≥ ( ep[s], ep) THEN
        j := 1
```

```
        ELSE
            j := 2
        END;
        IF grouplow[s] = grouphigh[s] THEN
            from := low_j; to := high_j
        ELSIF actgroup[s] = grouplow[s] THEN
            from := low_j; to := q_j - 1
        ELSIF actgroup[s] = grouphigh[s] THEN
            from := 0; to := high_j
        ELSE
            from := 0; to := q_j - 1
        END;
        FOR i := from TO to DO
            actpage := actgroup;
            ( 2 * b_1 + b_0 ) := i ;          (* b_1, b_0 ∈ { 0, 1} *)
            IF q_j = 2 THEN
                buddy :=b_0
            ELSE
                buddy := 2 * b̄_0 + b_1
            END; actpage[s] := actpage[s] + 2^(L_s-1) * buddy;
            adr := G( actpage )
            (* Now we can fetch the page with address adr into core and prove the records,
            wether they lay in the region of the query. *)
            end := actgroup = grouphigh;
        END;
        Update the variable actgroup ;
    UNTIL end;
END RangeQuery.
```

We want to emphasize that the algorithm evaluates only addresses of pages, which intersect the region R(Klow, Khigh) of the range query. Even every group of pages we access only to those pages of the group which intersect the region of the query. This is taken care of in the IF - statement at the beginning of the REPEAT - statement. The variable actgroup indicates the actual group intersecting the region of the query.

Since records which are close together in data space reside most likely in one page (if not then in neighboring pages) we can answer proximity queries, such as near neighbor queries very efficiently. This is as well due to the fact that given a page we can easily compute the adresses of all neighbor pages.

5. Performance of MOLHPE

In order to demonstrate the performance of our scheme, we have implemented MOLHPE for one, two and four partial expansions in Modula 2 on an Olivetti M24 PC under MSDOS. Let us mention that MOLHPE using one partial expansion has the same performance as the interpolation based scheme [Bur 83]. The results from all our experiments can be summarized in the statement that for uniform distribution MOLHPE has the same performance as LHPE and thus is superior to its competitors. Introducing order preserving hashing functions and extending LHPE to the multidimensional case does not cost any performance penalty.

In our experimental set-up we consider only the case of the growing file, i.e. we insert records into the file, but do not delete them. Furthermore, we will assume that each record will be accessed with equal probability. The parameter which is fixed in all our experiments is the capacity of a primary block containing 31 records. From all our experiments, we will present the following selection:

Experiment 5.1:
This experiment was performed for uniform distibution of 2-dimensional records. The maximum file size was 30000 records corresponding to level L = 10. The following parameters were varied within this experiment: the control function for the expansion of the file and the capacity of a secondary block. Although the number of partial expansion were varied from one to four, we present only the results for two partial expansions in this paper.

5.1.1:
i) expansion after c = 28 insertions
ii) capacity s of a secondary block is s = 7 records
Figures 5.2 and 5.3 depict the average number of successfull and unsuccessfull exact match query during the full expansion of the file from level L = 9 to L = 10, corresponding to a doubling of the file from 15000 to 30000 records.

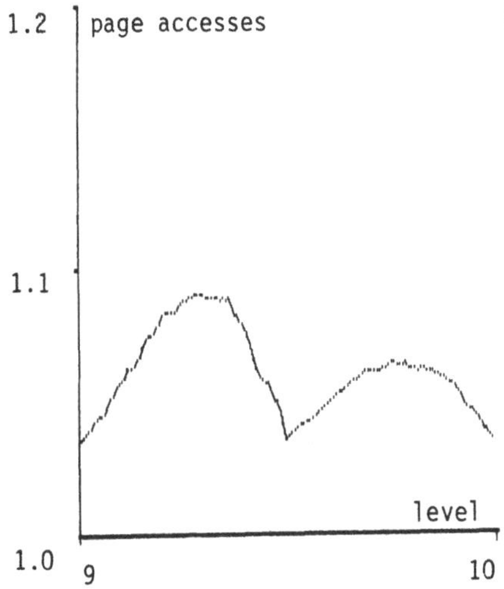

figure 5.2

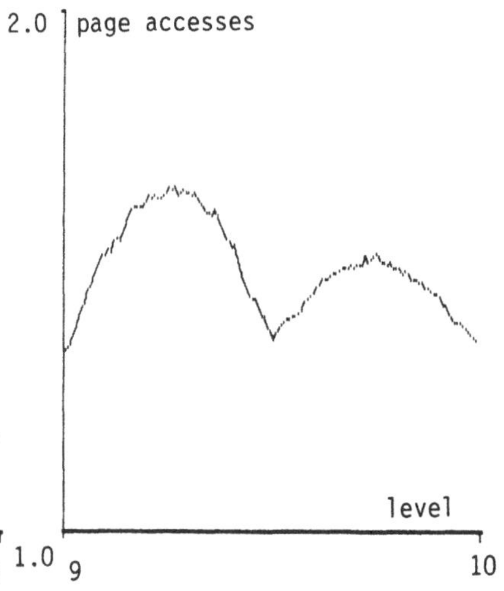

figure 5.3

For the number of page accesses in an exact match query and for the storage utilization, table 5.9 lists the maximum value, the minimum value and the average over a full expansion. Table 5.9 is shown after presentation of all experiments. Furthermore, the maximum number of blocks in a chain, denoted by maxblock, is listed in this table. If maxblock is not more than two we have a two-disk-access-guarantee for successful and unsuccessful exact match query like for the grid file.

5.1.2:

i) expansion after c = 28 insertions

ii) capacity s of a secondary block is s = 31 records

In this experiment the capacity of the secondary block is increased in order to fulfill the two-disk-access-guarantee (maxblock = 2 in this experiment). Again we depict the average number of page accesses in a successfull and unsuccessfull exact match query during the full expansion of the file in figure 5.4 and 5.5. Comparing table 5.9 it turns out that in this set-up which give the two-disk-access-guarantee at the expense of sacrificing storage utilization (whith an average of 70% will not worse than the grid file) and a slight improvement in exact match performance compared with experiment 5.1.1. Compared with the grid file we have considerably improved average exact match performanace. The improvement in range query performance compared with the grid file will be more drastic.

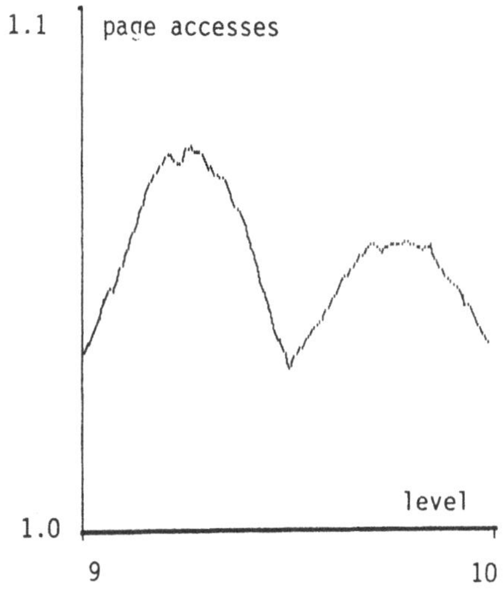

figure 5.4

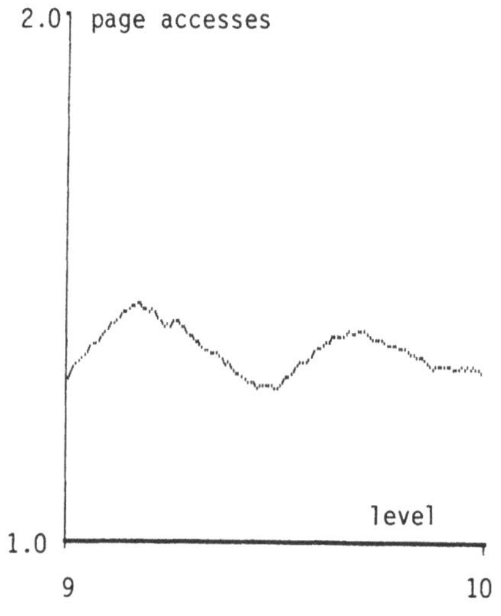

figure 5.5

5.1.3:

i) expansion after c = 21 insertions

ii) capacity s of secondary block is s = 7 records

In this experiment, the expansion is performed already after 21 insertions. This will improve average exact match performance to practically ideal values, in case of successfull exact match queries to 1.005 page accesses, for unsuccessfull ones to 1.065 page accesses. Average storage utilization with 67% is in the grid file range.

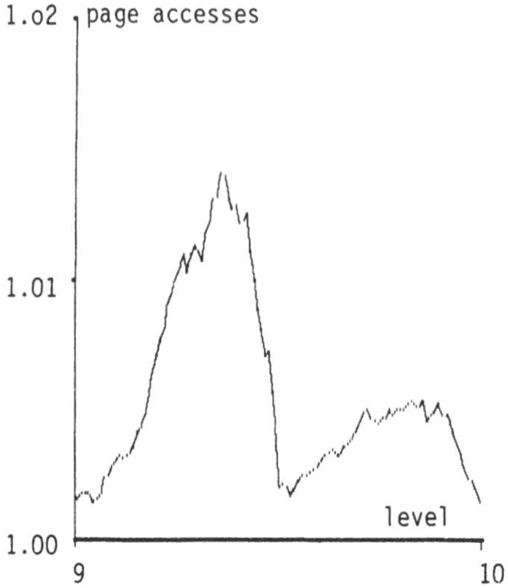

figure 5.6

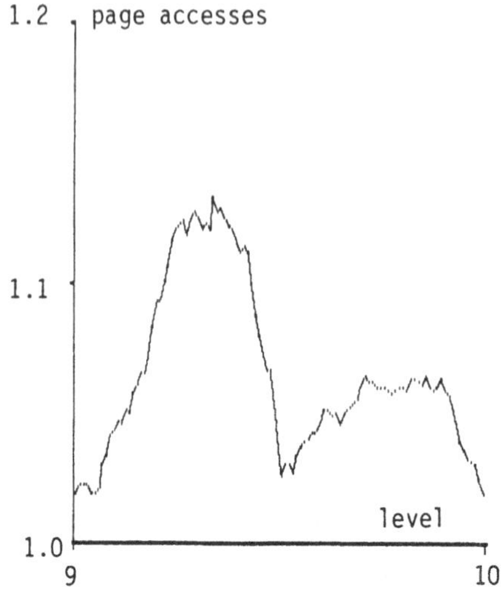

figure 5.7

Experiment 5.8:
This experiment was performed for a non - uniform distribution, where objects are concentrated in the left lower coner (south-west coner) of the unit square $[0, 1)^2$. More exactly, for $K_i \in [0, 1)$, $i = 1,2$, we have:

$Pb(K_i < 1/4) = 9/16$

$Pb(K_i < 1/2) = 5/16$

where Pb denotes the probability with which K_i is in the specified intervall, $i = 1,2$. Howver we accept component keys K_i which f;;ow the distribution and are not in [0.6, 0.7]. Table 5.9 shows that for such a non - uniform distribution retrieval performance degenerates. Even the maximum number of page accesses in a successfull exact match query of 4.36 is still bad enough. In this respect MOLHPE is not better than any other multidimensional dynamic hashing scheme. Considering the grid file, such a non - uniform distribution will blow up the grid directory, which will result for example in very bad range query performance. Summarizing we can say that MOLHPE turned out to be superior to other schemes for uniform record distributions.

experiment		successful emq	unsuccessful emq	storage utilization	maxblock
5.1.1	maximum	1.090	1.658	0.8498	5
	minimum	1.035	1.340	0.8188	
	average	1.060	1.503	0.8339	
5.1.2	maximum	1.074	1.454	0.7362	2
	minimum	1.031	1.290	0.6677	
	average	1.052	1.366	0.7023	
5.1.3	maximum	1.014	1.132	0.6737	4
	minimum	1.001	1.018	0.6633	
	average	1.006	1.065	0.6693	
5.8	maximum	4.356	9.915	0.6093	26
	minimum	3.728	8.627	0.6019	
	average	3.992	9.193	0.6053	

table 5.9

6. Handling non - uniform record distributions

In the last section, we have seen how the performance of MOLHPE may degenerate for non-uniformly distributed records. In this section we want to give a short outline of the quantile method which guarantees that MOLHPE performs for a non - uniform distribution practically as well as for a uniform distribution.

MOLHPE partitions the key space using equidistant partitioning hyperplanes and thus exhibits optimal performance for uniform record distribution. The more the distribution of records differs from uniform, the worse MOLHPE will perform. We will overcome this disadvantage by selecting the partitioning points depending on the distribution of objects.

Let us demonstrate our method considering a 2-dimensional distribution function F with marginal distribution functions f_1 and f_2. We assume that the stochastic variables K_1 and K_2 are independent, i.e.

$$F(K_1, K_2) = f_1(K_1) * f_2(K_2)$$

For $a \in [\,0,\, 1]$ the a-quantile of the 1st (2nd) attribute is the domain value x_a (y_a) such that

$$f_1(x_a) = a \qquad (f_2(y_a) = a)$$

Now let us assume that starting from an empty file we have to partition the key space for the first time and we decide to partition the first dimension (axis). If f_1 is a non-uniform distribution function, we will not partition the first dimension in the middle, but we will choose the 1/2-quantile as the partitioning point. This guarantees that a new record will be stored with equal probability in the page corresponding to the rectangle $[0\,,\, x_{0.5}) \times [0\,,\, 1)$ or in the page corresponding to the rectangle $[x_{0.5}\,,\, 1) \times [0\,,\, 1)$, see figure 6.1. During the next expansion we will partition the second dimension (axis) and we will choose the partitioning point $y_{1/2}$, see figure 6.2.

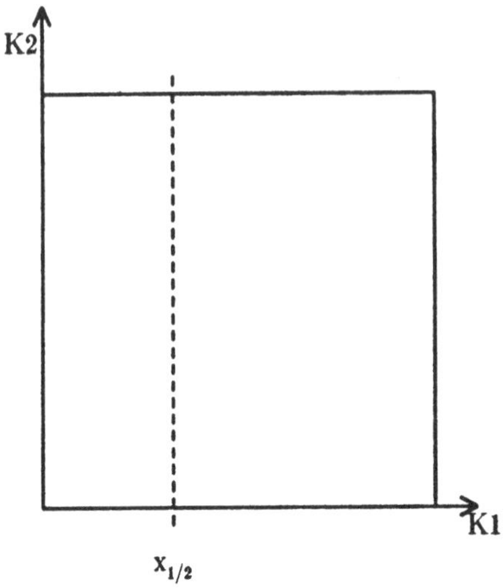

figure 6.1

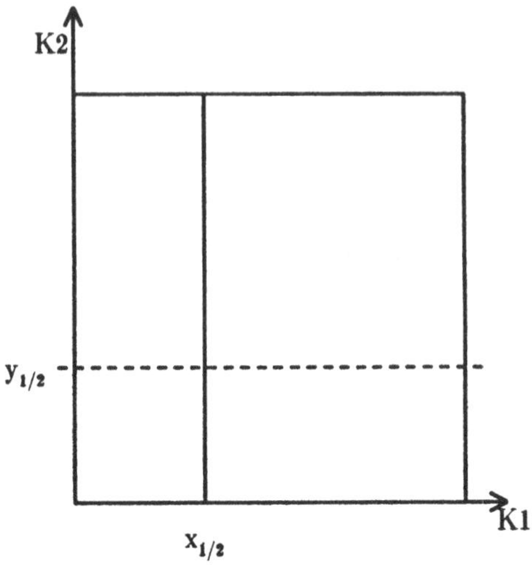

figure 6.2

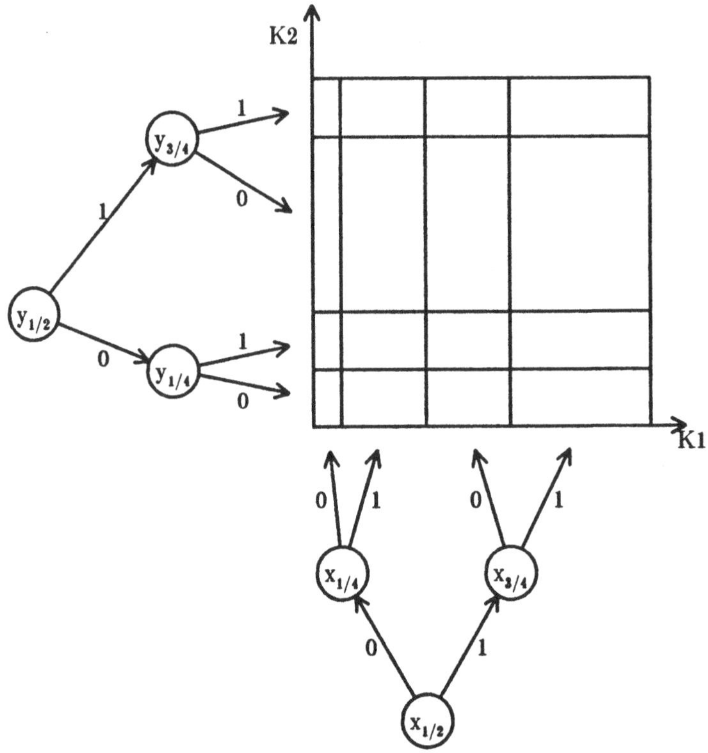

figure 6.3

Figure 6.3 shows the file at level L = 4 and ep = (0, 0), where each axis has been partitioned at the 1/4, 1/2 and 3/4 quantile. As depicted in figure 6.3, the partitioning points are stored in binary trees which can easily be stored in main memory. The ***most important property*** of these binary trees of partitioning points is the following : for each type of operation a nonuniformly distributed query value K_j, j = 1,2 , is transformed into a uniformly distributed a $\in$ [0, 1) by searching the corresponding binary tree of partitioning points. This uniformly distributed a $\in$ [0, 1) is then used as an input to the retrieval and update algorithms of MOLHPE.

In most practical applications the distribution of objects is not known in advance and therefore we will approximate the partitioning points based on the records presently in the file using a stochastic approximation process. Since we do not know the exact partitioning point (a-quantile) we are dealing with estimates, instead. Now, when the approximation process yields a new estimate we have to shift the corresponding partitioning line and reorganize the file. If this is done in one step, it requires O($n^{1-1/d}$) page accesses and thus our method would not be dynamic any more. At this point we refer to the paper [KS 86] which deals with all the problems of the quantile method. Concerning the above problem we can assure the reader that reorganization of the file can be performed stepwise requiring only a constant number of page accesses. This is due to the fact that MOLHPE uses no directory. The interested reader is referred to [KS 86]. For the non - interested reader we can summarize this paper in the following statement : the quantile method applied to MOLHPE exhibits for non-uniform record distributions practically the same ideal performance as MOLHPE for uniform distributions. This emphasizes once more the importance of a multidimensional hashing scheme which performs optimally for uniform distributions. For a non-uniform distribution the quantile method can at best exhibit the performance which the underlying scheme has for a uniform distribution.

7. Conclusions

For uniform record distributions we intended to suggest a multidimensional dynamic hashing scheme with no directory which exhibits best possible retrieval performance. The retrieval performance of all known multidimensional hashing schemes either suffers from a superlinearly growing directory or from a very uneven distribution of the records over the pages of the file. By using no directory and applying the concept of linear hashing with partial expansions to the multidimensional case we have overcome both performance penalties. Furthermore, our scheme is order preserving and therefore suitable for engineering database systems. Considering all the ingredients from which our scheme is composed we call it multidimensional order preserving linear hashing with partial expansions (MOLHPE). First experimental runs of an implementation of MOLHPE show that our scheme performs better than its competitors for uniform distribution.

However, as its competitors MOLHPE performs rather poorly for non-uniform record distributions. In the last section we have given a brief introduction to the quantile method which guarantees that MOLHPE with the quantile method exhibits for non - uniform distributions practically the same ideal performance as MOLHPE for uniform distributions.

References

[Bur 83] Burkhard, W.A.:'Interpolation - based index maintenance', BIT 23, 274 - 294 (1983)

[Hin 85] Hinrichs, K.:'The grid file system: implementation and case studies of applications',Ph.D. Dissertation, Swiss Federal Institute of Technology, Zürich (1985)

[Kri 84] Kriegel, H.P.: 'Performance comparison of index structures for multi-key retrieval', Proc. 1984 ACM/SIGMOD Int. Conf. on Management of Data, 186 - 196

[KS 86] Kriegel, H.P., Seeger, B.: 'Multidimensional dynamic quantile hashing is very efficient for non - uniform record distributions', submitted for publication

[KW 85] Krishnamurthy, R., Whang, K.-Y.: 'Multilevel grid files', Draft Report, IBM Research Lab., Yorktown Heights (1985)

[Lar 80] Larson, P.-A.: 'Linear hashing with partial expansions', Proc. 6th Int. Conf. on VLDB, 224 - 232 (1980)

[Lit 80] Litwin, W.: 'Linear hashing: a new tool for file and table addressing', Proc. 6th Int. Conf. on VLDB, 212 - 223 (1980)

[NHS 84] Nievergelt, J., Hinterberger, H., Sevcik, K.C.: 'The grid file: an adaptable, symmetric multikey file structure', ACM TODS, 9, 1, 38 - 71 (1984)

[Oto 84] Otoo, E.J.: 'A mapping function for the directory of a multidimensional extendible hashing', Proc. 10th Int. Conf. on VLDB, 491 - 506 (1984)

[Oto 85] Otoo, E.J.: 'Symmetric dynamic index maintenance scheme', Proc. of Int. Conf. on Foundations of Data Org., 283 - 296 (1985)

[Oto 86] Otoo, E.J.: 'Balanced multidimensional extendible hash tree', Proc. 5th ACM SIGACT/SIGMOD Symp. on PoDS, (1986)

[Ouk 85] Ouksel, M.: 'The interpolation based grid file', Proc. 4th ACM SIGACT/SIGMOD Symp. on PoDS, 20 - 27 (1985)

[Rob 81] Robinson, J.T.: 'The K-D-B-tree: a search structure for large multidimensional dynamic indexes', Proc. 1981 ACM/SIGMOD Int. Conf. on Management of Data, 10 - 18 (1981)

[RL 82] Romamohanarao, W., Lloyd, J.: 'Dynamic hashing schemes', Comp. J., 25, 4, 478 - 485 (1982)

SPLIT-FREEDOM AND MVD-INTERSECTION : A NEW CHARACTERIZATION OF MULTIVALUED DEPENDENCIES HAVING CONFLICT-FREE COVERS

V.S. Lakshmanan
Department of Computer Science and Automation
Indian Institute of Science
Bangalore 560012, India

Abstract

Sets of multivalued dependencies (MVDs) having conflict-free covers are important to the theory and design of relational databases [Li, Sc1, Sc2, BFMY]. Their desirable properties motivate the problem of testing a set M of MVDs for the existence of a conflict-free cover. In [GT1] Goodman and Tay have proposed an approach based on the possible equivalence of M to a single (acyclic) join dependency (JD). We remark that their characterization does not lend an insight into the nature of such sets of MVDs. Here, we use notions that are intrinsic to MVDs to develop a new characterization. Our approach proceeds in two stages. In the first stage, we use the notion of "split-free" sets of MVDs and obtain a characterization of sets M of MVDs having split-free covers. In the second, we use the notion of "intersection" of MVDs to arrive at a necessary and sufficient condition for a split-free set of MVDs to be conflict-free. Based on our characterizations, we also give polynomial time algorithms for testing whether M has split-free and conflict-free covers. The highlight of our approach is the clear insight it provides into the nature of sets of MVDs having conflict-free covers. Less emphasis is given in this paper to the actual efficiency of the algorithms. Finally, as a bonus, we derive a desirable property of split-free sets of MVDs, thereby showing that they are interesting in their own right.

1. INTRODUCTION

Conflict-free sets of multivalued dependencies, first introduced by Lien [Li], are of considerable interest in the theory and design of relational databases because of their desirable properties [Sc1, Sc2, BFMY, Ja]. For instance, they admit a unique 4NF [Fa] decomposition. Besides, all MVDs in a given conflict-free set of MVDs participate in the decomposition process. Recent results connect such sets of MVDs with acyclic database schemes [BFMY, FMU]. It is shown that a set M of MVDs is equivalent to a single (acyclic) JD if and only if M has a conflict-free cover. This further enriches the desirable properties of such sets of MVDs. The foregoing considerations motivate the problem of testing a given set M of MVDs for the existence of a conflict-free cover. The bruteforce approach of testing equivalence of M to conflict-free sets of MVDs is of course exponential in the worst case. Recently, Goodman and Tay [GT1] proposed a better approach based on the possible equivalence of M to a single (acyclic) JD. Though simple, the characterization in [GT1] does not lend an insight into the nature of such sets of MVDs.

In this paper, we use certain notions that are intrinsic to MVDs to obtain a new characterization of sets of MVDs having conflict-free covers. We introduce the notions of "split-free" sets of MVDs and "intersection" of MVDs. We show that a set M of MVDs has a conflict-free cover if and only if M has a split-free cover, say N, and further N satisfies a property we term "MVD-intersection property". Our method then naturally divides into two stages. In the first stage, we obtain a characterization of sets M of MVDs having split-free covers. In the second, we derive a necessary and sufficient condition for a split-free set of MVDs to be conflict-free. We show that split-free sets of MVDs are quite interesting in their own right. Thus, we establish that they always "generate" acyclic database schemes.

The highlight of the approach we present here is the clear insight it provides into the exact nature of sets of MVDs having conflict-free covers. Less emphasis is given here to the efficiency of the algorithms, which will be investigated in a future work.

Finally, we observe that Goodman and Tay [GT1] remark that conflict-freedom is irrelevant to deciding equivalence of M to a single JD. Our result here leads to a "dual" viewpoint that acyclicity (actually, equivalence to a single acyclic JD) is irrelevant to testing whether M has a conflict-free cover. This is because, our approach only uses notions intrinsic to sets of MVDs and is independent of the notion of equivalence of M to (acyclic) JDs.

2. PRELIMINARIES

For the definitions of the relational model, MVDs and JDs, hypergraph models of database schemes, etc. we refer the reader to [BFMY, GS, Ma, Ul]. We use the following notations. A database scheme is a set $\mathbf{D} = \{R_1, ..., R_m\}$ of relation schemes such that $\bigcup \mathbf{D} = U$, where U is the universal relation scheme. A database scheme $\mathbf{D}$ can be represented by a hypergraph $H = (U, \mathbf{D})$ with U as the set of nodes and **D** as the set of edges. A **qual graph** for a database scheme **D** = $\{ R_1, ..., R_m \}$ is a connected graph G on the nodes $R_1, ..., R_m$ with the property that between any two nodes R_i and R_j, G contains a path such that each node R_k lying on this path includes the attributes in $R_i \cap R_j$. A database scheme **D** is said to be **acyclic** if some qual graph for **D** is a tree; otherwise, **D** is said to be **cyclic.**

For an attribute set $X \subset U$, $\bar{X}$ denotes the complement U - X of X. For an MVD d: $X \rightarrow\rightarrow Y$, define LHS(d) = X to be the **key** of d, and RHS(d) = Y to be the **right-hand-side** of d. For a set M of MVDs, LHS(M) = $\{ LHS(d) : d \in M \}$ is called the **set of keys** of M. An MVD $X \rightarrow\rightarrow Y$ is called **trivial** if either XY = X, or XY = U. The **dependency basis** DEP(X) of an attribute set $X \subset U$ w.r.t. a set M of MVDs is the unique partition of $\bar{X}$ such that for any nontrivial MVD $X \rightarrow\rightarrow Y$ with $X \cap Y = \phi$, $M \models X \rightarrow\rightarrow Y$ if and only if Y is the union of some blocks in DEP(X). Note that since we consider only nontrivial MVDs, we adopt the convention that DEP(X) is a partition of $\bar{X}$ rather than of U. Furthermore, an MVD $X \rightarrow\rightarrow Y$ is equivalent to the MVD $X \rightarrow\rightarrow Y - X$ [Ma, Ul], so we assume without loss of generality that the MVDs we consider have disjoint LHS and RHS. An MVD $X \rightarrow\rightarrow Y$ **splits** an attribute set W if $W \cap Y \neq \phi$ and $W \cap Z \neq \phi$, where Z = U - XY. A set M of MVDs **splits** W if some MVD in M splits W. The set of all logical consequences of M is called the **closure** of M, and is denoted by M*. Two sets of MVDs are said to be **covers** of each other if their closures are the same. For two logically equivalent sets M_1, M_2, of MVDs and an attribute set X, M_1 splits X if and only if M_2 splits X [BFMY].

Definition 2.1 A set M of MVDs is said to be **split-free** if M does not split any of its keys.

□

Definition 2.2 A set M of MVDs is said to be **conflict-free** if M is split-free and further M is hypergraph generated, that is, for any two keys X, Y of M,

$$DEP(X) \cap DEP(Y) \subset DEP(X \cap Y).$$

□

Given an MVD $X \rightarrow\rightarrow Y$ and a relation scheme R such that $X \subset R$, $R \cap Y \neq \phi$, and $R - XY \neq \phi$, R can be losslessly decomposed into the relation schemes $R \cap XY$ and $R \cap XZ$, where Z = U - XY [Ma, Ul]. Given a set M of MVDs, a **decomposition algorithm** [Fa, Li, BFMY] produces relation schemes by successive decomposition starting with U, using MVDs in M. If **D** is a database scheme produced by a decomposition algorithm using some (possibly all) MVDs in M, then we say that M **generates** the database scheme **D** by decomposition. It is clear in such a case that M logically implies the JD $\bowtie$**D.**

We notice that for two logically equivalent sets M_1, M_2 of MVDs M_1 is hypergraph generated if and only if M_2 is. Thus, the problem of determining whether M has a conflict-free cover reduces to finding if M has a split-free cover which is hypergraph generated. In this spirit, we first give in Section 3 a characterization of sets of MVDs having split-free covers. We also derive a desirable property of split-free sets of MVDs relating to database design. Next, we obtain in Section 4 a necessary and sufficient condition for a split-free set of MVDs to be hypergraph generated. In Section 5 we present the algorithms.

3. A CHARACTERIZATION OF SETS OF MVDs HAVING SPLIT-FREE COVERS

In this section we study split-free sets of MVDs as well as sets of MVDs having split-free covers. Let M be any set of MVDs. We say that M is **nonredundant** if no proper subset of M is a cover for M. In general, M may split its keys. We define $K_s(M) = \{ X \in LHS(M) : M \text{ splits } X \}$ to be the set of keys split by M, and we let $K_u(M) = LHS(M) - K_s(M)$ be the set of keys not split by M. For an attribute set X, we let MAX(X) denote the set of maximal subsets of X that are not split by M.

Let M be any set of MVDs. Suppose that the MVDs in M are used in a decomposition algorithm to design a 4NF database scheme. In general, a cyclic database scheme might result. For instance consider the set $M = \{ AB \twoheadrightarrow CEF, CD \twoheadrightarrow ABG \}$ of MVDs, where $U = \{ A, ..., H \}$. Suppose that the second MVD is used first to produce the database scheme $\{ ABCDG, CDEFH \}$. The first MVD applied on ABCDG leads to the database scheme $\{ ABC, ABDG, CDEFH \}$ which is clearly cyclic. This is an undesirable phenomenon. Are there sets of MVDs satisfying suitable properties such that they always generate acyclic database schemes? Of course, conflict-free sets of MVDs are one such type. But, we show that the above property holds for a larger class of sets of MVDs, namely split-free sets of MVDs.

Theorem 3.1 Let M be a split-free set of MVDs and **D** a database scheme generated by M. Then **D** is acyclic.

Proof Without loss of generality, assume that all MVDs in M are used in the decomposition algorithm producing the database scheme **D**. We prove the result by inducing on $|M|$, the number of MVDs in M. The basis case of $|M| = 1$ is trivial. Assume the result for $|M| = k - 1$ and suppose that $|M| = k$. Let $X \twoheadrightarrow Y$ be the MVD in M that was applied last in the decomposition algorithm. Let $M' = M - \{ X \twoheadrightarrow Y \}$ and let **D'** be the database scheme generated by

M' such that the scheme **D** is obtained from **D'** by decomposing appropriate relation schemes using the MVD $X \rightarrow\rightarrow Y$. By the inductive hypothesis, **D'** is acyclic. Let T' be a qual tree for **D'**. We now modify T' into a qual tree T for the database scheme **D**, thus showing that **D** is acyclic. Suppose that some relation scheme R in **D'** is decomposed into the relation schemes R_1, R_2 using the MVD $X \rightarrow\rightarrow Y$. Then, since M does not split its keys, for each node S in T' which is adjacent to R, either $R \cap S \subset R_1$ or $R \cap S \subset R_2$. For each such relation scheme R we do the following:

> Delete the node R (from T') and add the nodes R_1, R_2 and the edge (R_1, R_2). For each node S in T' adjacent to R, if $R \cap S \subset R_1$, then replace the edge (R, S) with the new edge (R_1, S); otherwise replace (R, S) with the new edge (R_2, S).

Once this is done, it is easy to verify that the resulting graph T is a qual tree for **D**. Hence **D** is acyclic.

□

Thus, split-free sets of MVDs have the nice property that they always lead to the design of acyclic database schemes. In addition, all MVDs in a given split-free set of MVDs can participate in the decomposition process. These desirable properties show that split-free sets of MVDs are rather interesting in their own right. Now, suppose that M is a set of MVDs and that M has a split-free cover N. Then M can "inherit" the nice properties above through its cover N, even when M itself is not split-free. Our next task is thus to obtain a characterization of sets of MVDs having split-free covers. Intuitively, it is clear that M can have a split-free cover if and only if we can replace each MVD in M whose key is split by M, with a set of MVDs with keys not split by M, such that the closure of M is preserved. The crux of the problem is in determining for each MVD $X \rightarrow\rightarrow Y$ in M with X split by M, this associated set of MVDs which exactly "makes up" for $X \rightarrow\rightarrow Y$ in M (see condition C of Theorem 3.2 below). Note that if M is redundant, then it could turn out that $M - \{X \rightarrow\rightarrow Y\} \models X \rightarrow\rightarrow Y$. Since, given M we can always obtain a nonredundant subset M' which is a cover for M, without loss of generality, we consider only nonredundant M in what follows.

We now describe informally the ideas involved in the main theorem. Suppose that M is nonredundant, $X \rightarrow\rightarrow Y \in M$, and M splits X. Let $M_o = M - \{X \rightarrow\rightarrow Y\}$. We first determine the minimal attribute set Y_1 such that (a) $Y \subset Y_1$ and (b) $M_o \models X \rightarrow\rightarrow Y_1$. Since $Y_1 \neq Y$, we form a new set N_1 of MVDs such that $M \models N_1$ and $M_o \cup N_1 \models X \rightarrow\rightarrow Y_2$ for some Y_2 with

$Y \subset Y_2 \subsetneq Y_1$. We also make sure that M does not split the keys of N_1. In general, at the ith stage, we determine the minimal Y_i such that (a) $Y \subset Y_i$ and (b) $M_o \cup N_1 \cup \dots \cup N_{i-1} \models X \twoheadrightarrow Y_i$, and we agree that $N_o = \phi$. If $Y_i \neq Y$, we form a new set N_i of MVDs whose keys are not split by M, such that $M \models N_i$ and $M_o \cup N_1 \cup \dots \cup N_i \models X \twoheadrightarrow Y_{i+1}$, for some Y_{i+1} with $Y \subset Y_{i+1} \subsetneq Y_i$. We proceed in this manner until at some stage k, we find that we cannot refine Y_k any further, satisfying $Y \subset Y_k$. If for each such MVD $X \twoheadrightarrow Y$, we are able to derive $X \twoheadrightarrow Y$ from the MVDs in $M_o \cup N_1 \cup \dots \cup N_k$, (in this case $Y_k = Y$), for some k, then we say that this method succeeds. The theorem that follows formally proves that this method succeeds precisely when M has a split-free cover. In Section 5, we give a polynomial time algorithm which uses this method to test M for the existence of a split-free cover.

The notations used in the following theorem are as in the preceding discussion.

Theorem 3.2 Let M be a nonredundant set of MVDs. Then M has a split-free cover if and only if for each MVD $X \twoheadrightarrow Y$ in M with X split by M, the following condition C is satisfied.

C : there exist sets of MVDs

$N_i = \{ W \twoheadrightarrow Z : W \in MAX(\bar{Y}_i), \quad Y \subset Z \}$, $i = 1, \dots, k$, for some k, such that

(i) $M \models N_i$, $i = 1, \dots, k$, and

(ii) $(M - \{X \twoheadrightarrow Y\}) \cup N_1 \cup \dots \cup N_k \models X \twoheadrightarrow Y$. □

Note that in the theorem above Y_i is the minimal attribute set such that (a) $Y \subset Y_i$ and (b) $(M - \{X \twoheadrightarrow Y\}) \cup N_1 \cup \dots \cup N_{i-1} \models X \twoheadrightarrow Y_i$, $i = 1, \dots, k$. We observe that the MVDs in the union of the sets N_i of MVDs, $i = 1, \dots, k$, above precisely "make up" for the MVD $X \twoheadrightarrow Y$ in M.

Before proving Theorem 3.2, we make some observations concerning derivations of MVDs [Ma, Ul]. The following is a complete axiom system for MVDs[BV].

MVD0 (complementation axiom) : $X \twoheadrightarrow \bar{X}$, for any attribute set $X \subset U$.

MVD1 (augmentation rule) : If $X \twoheadrightarrow Y$ and $W \supseteq Z$, then $XW \twoheadrightarrow YZ$.

MVD2 (subset rule) : If $X \twoheadrightarrow Y$, $W \twoheadrightarrow Z$, and $W \cap Y = \phi$, then $X \twoheadrightarrow Y \cap Z$ and $X \twoheadrightarrow Y - Z$.

Using this axiom system, one can prove the **complementation rule** that an MVD $X \twoheadrightarrow Y$ is logically equivalent to the MVD $X \twoheadrightarrow Z$, where $Z = U - XY$ [Ma, Ul]. For convenience we refer to this MVD $X \twoheadrightarrow Z$ as the **complement** of the MVD $X \twoheadrightarrow Y$.

Now, from the results of Beeri [B], Sagiv [Sa], and Galil [Ga], we can infer the following property of derivations of MVDs. Suppose that there is a derivation of an MVD $X \twoheadrightarrow Y$ from a set M of MVDs. Then there is a derivation of $X \twoheadrightarrow Y$ from M satisfying the following conditions.

(i) The augmentation rule is always applied to an MVD in M with a key that is included in X, or the complement of such an MVD. Further, suppose that $X' \twoheadrightarrow Y' \in M$ and that $X' \subset X$. When this MVD is augmented to get $X \twoheadrightarrow Y'$, in general, it might turn out that $X \cap Y' \neq \phi$. Then, since this MVD is equivalent to the MVD $X \twoheadrightarrow Y$, where $Y = Y' \cap \bar{X}$, we assume without loss of generality that in such a case $\dot{X} \cap Y' = \phi$, in our proofs, to reduce the detail.

(ii) The subset rule is always applied to an MVD in M* with key X. The other MVD that is used in this rule is either the axiom $X \twoheadrightarrow \bar{X}$, a member of M, or an MVD in M* with key X.

We now prove Theorem 3.2.

Proof of Theorem 3.2

(If) : Suppose that for each MVD $X \twoheadrightarrow Y$ in M with X split by M, condition C given in the theorem is satisfied. For each such MVD $X \twoheadrightarrow Y$ replace $X \twoheadrightarrow Y$ with the MVDs in $N_1 \cup \ldots \cup N_k$, where N_i, $i = 1, \ldots, k$, are the sets of MVDs specified in condition C. Notice that M and hence M* does not split the keys of the MVDs in $(N_1 \cup \ldots \cup N_k)$. Condition C then guarantees that the resulting set of MVDs is a split-free cover for M.

(Only If) : Suppose that M has a split-free cover. We prove this part by actually proving the following stronger result : for each nontrivial MVD $X \twoheadrightarrow Y$ in M* with X split by M, the condition C' is satisfied where

C' : there exist sets of MVDs $N_i = \{ W \twoheadrightarrow Z : W \in MAX(\bar{Y}_i), Y \subset Z \}$, $i=1, \ldots, k$, for some k, such that

(i) $M \models N_i$, $i = 1, \ldots, k$, and

(ii) $(M - \{P \twoheadrightarrow Q \in M : P \in K_s(M), \ P \subset X\}) \cup N_1 \cup \ldots \cup N_k \models X \twoheadrightarrow Y$.

Here, Y_i is the minimal attribute set such that (a) $Y \subset Y_i$ and (b) $M_o \cup N_1 \cup \dots \cup N_{i-1} \models X \twoheadrightarrow Y_i$, $i = 1, \dots, k$, where $M_o = M - \{P \twoheadrightarrow Q \in M : P \subset X, P \in K_s(M)\}$. We of course agree that $N_o = \phi$. Note that each Y_i is unique because of the subset rule.

Suppose that N is a split-free cover for M. Let $X \twoheadrightarrow Y \in M^*$ be such that M splits X. We shall prove the required result by inducing on the length p of a derivation of $X \twoheadrightarrow Y$ from N.

<u>Basis</u> p = 1. Two cases arise.

<u>Case 1</u> $X \twoheadrightarrow Y$ is derived from the MVD $X' \twoheadrightarrow Y'$ in N, by augmentation using $W \supseteq Z$, where $X' \subset X$. Since $X \cap Y = X' \cap Y' = \phi$, we have $Z = \phi$ and hence $Y' = Y$. Now, $M \models X' \twoheadrightarrow Y$. M does not split X' since $X' \in LHS(N)$. Obviously, $X \cap Y_1 = \phi$ and hence $X' \cap Y_1 = \phi$, where Y_1 is as defined above. We immediately see that there is a set $W \in MAX(\bar{Y}_1)$ such that $X' \subset W$ and $W \twoheadrightarrow Y \in N_1$, and hence that $M_o \cup N_1 \models X \twoheadrightarrow Y$.

<u>Case 2</u> $X \twoheadrightarrow Y$ is derived from the axiom $X \twoheadrightarrow \bar{X}$ and the MVD $S \twoheadrightarrow T$ in N, using the subset rule. Then clearly, $S \subset X$, and $Y \subset T$ or $Y \subset (U - ST)$. For both cases, we can complete the proof in a manner identical to that for case 1.

<u>Induction</u> Assume the condition C' with respect to all nontrivial MVDs $X \twoheadrightarrow Y$ in M* with X split by M, such that $X \twoheadrightarrow Y$ has a derivation from N of length $p \leq n-1$. Suppose now that $X \twoheadrightarrow Y \in M^*$ is nontrivial, X is split by M, and $X \twoheadrightarrow Y$ has a derivation from N of length $n > 1$. From our observations concerning derivations of MVDs, we see that the following cases arise.

<u>Case 1</u> $X \twoheadrightarrow Y$ is obtained by augmentation from some MVD $X' \twoheadrightarrow Y'$ in N. This case is similar to case 1 of the basis case.

<u>Case 2</u> $X \twoheadrightarrow Y$ is obtained using the subset rule. Suppose now that $X \twoheadrightarrow Y$ is derived from the MVD $X \twoheadrightarrow Y'$ (obtained in the derivation), using the subset rule. Since $X \twoheadrightarrow Y'$ then has a derivation from N of length n-1 or less, by inductive hypothesis the condition C' holds for the MVD $X \twoheadrightarrow Y'$. So, there are sets of MVDs $N_i' = \{W' \twoheadrightarrow Z' : W' \in MAX(\bar{Y}_i'), Y' \subset Z'\}$, $i = 1, \dots, k$, for some k, such that

(i) $M \models N_i'$, $i = 1, \dots, k$, and

(ii) $M_o \cup N_1' \cup \dots \cup N_k' \models X \twoheadrightarrow Y'$.

Here, Y_i' is the minimal set such that (a) $Y' \subset Y_i'$ and (b) $(M_o \cup N_1' \cup \ldots \cup N_{i-1}') \models X \twoheadrightarrow Y_i'$, $i = 1, \ldots, k$. We shall show that condition C' holds for the MVD $X \twoheadrightarrow Y$, for each of the following cases.

Case 2.1 $X \twoheadrightarrow Y$ is obtained using the subset rule from $X \twoheadrightarrow Y'$ and the axiom $X \twoheadrightarrow \bar{X}$. If $Y = Y' \cap \bar{X}$, then since $X \cap Y' = \phi$, we have $Y = Y'$ and we are trivially done. If $Y = Y' - \bar{X} = \phi$ then the MVD $X \twoheadrightarrow Y$ becomes trivial, which is a contradiction. So suppose that $Y = \bar{X} - Y'$. Now, by inductive hypothesis there are sets $N_1', \ldots, N_k'$ of MVDs such that

$$M \models N_i', \ i = 1, \ldots, k, \text{ and}$$

$$M_o \cup N_1' \cup \ldots \cup N_k' \models X \twoheadrightarrow Y'.$$

From $X \twoheadrightarrow Y'$, we can then infer the MVD $X \twoheadrightarrow \bar{X} - Y'$ by the complementation rule. It can then be easily shown that condition C' holds for $X \twoheadrightarrow Y$.

Case 2.2 $X \twoheadrightarrow Y$ is obtained from the MVD $X \twoheadrightarrow Y'$ in M* and the MVD $S \twoheadrightarrow T$ in N. Either $Y = Y' \cap T$ or $Y = Y' - T$. We shall only prove for the case $Y = Y' \cap T$. The other case has an analogous proof.

We now construct sets N_i of MVDs, for $i = 1, \ldots, k$, as $N_i = \{W \twoheadrightarrow Z: W \in MAX(\bar{Y}_i)$, Z minimal s.t. $Y \subset Z$ and $M \models W \twoheadrightarrow Z\}$. Here, for $i = 1, \ldots, k$, Y_i is the minimal set such that $Y \subset Y_i$ and $(M_o \cup N_1 \cup \ldots \cup N_{i-1}) \models X \twoheadrightarrow Y_i$. From the definitions of Y_1' and Y_1, it is easy to see that $Y_1 \subset Y_1'$. From the set-forming predicates of N_i' and N_i, it follows by an easy induction that $Y_i \subset Y_i'$, $i = 1, \ldots, k$. Let Y_{k+1} be the minimal set such that (a) $Y \subset Y_{k+1}$ and (b) $M_o \cup N_1 \cup \ldots \cup N_k \models X \twoheadrightarrow Y_{k+1}$. It is clear that $Y_{k+1} \subset Y'$. If $Y_{k+1} = Y$, we are done. Otherwise, since $S \cap Y' = \phi$, we have $S \cap Y_{k+1} = \phi$. Now, form the set $N_{k+1} = \{W \twoheadrightarrow Z : W \in MAX(\bar{Y}_{k+1})$, Z minimal s.t. $Y \subset Z$ and $M \models W \twoheadrightarrow Z\}$ of MVDs. Then N_{k+1} contains an MVD, say $W \twoheadrightarrow Z$, such that $Y \subset Z \subset T$ and $W \cap Y_{k+1} = \phi$. Then $M_o \cup N_1 \cup \ldots \cup N_{k+1} \models X \twoheadrightarrow Y$, since $Y' \cap T = Y$ implies $Y_{k+1} \cap Z = Y$. Thus, condition C' holds for the MVD $X \twoheadrightarrow Y$, where $N_1, \ldots, N_{k+1}$ are the sets of MVDs required in the condition.

Case 2.3 $X \twoheadrightarrow Y$ is obtained from $X \twoheadrightarrow Y'$ and $X \twoheadrightarrow Y''$ in M* using the subset rule. Again, we only consider the case $Y = Y' \cap Y''$. The cases $Y = Y' - Y''$, $Y = Y'' - Y'$ are similar. Then by inductive hypothesis, there are sets of MVDs N_i'', $i = 1, \ldots, p$, for some p, such that

$M \models N''_i, \quad i = 1, \ldots, p$, and

$M_o \cup N''_1 \cup \ldots \cup N''_p \models X \twoheadrightarrow Y''$.

Without loss of generality, let $k \geqslant p$, and define $N''_j = N''_p$ and $Y''_j = Y''$, for $j = p+1, \ldots, k$. Now, construct the sets of MVDs N_i, $i = 1, \ldots, k$ in a manner identical to that in case 2.2 above. Then by an argument similar to the one advanced there, we can prove that $Y_i \subset Y'_i \cap Y''_i$, where Y''_i corresponds to N''_i, for $i = 1, \ldots, k$, and Y_i, Y'_i are as defined above. Determine the minimal set Y_{k+1} as in case 2.2 such that (a) $Y \subset Y_{k+1}$ and (b) $M_o \cup N_1 \cup \ldots \cup N_k \models X \twoheadrightarrow Y_{k+1}$. Again similar to case 2.2 we have $Y_{k+1} \subset Y'$ and $Y_{k+1} \subset Y''$ and hence $Y_{k+1} \subset Y' \cap Y''$. This implies that $Y_{k+1} = Y$, since $Y = Y' \cap Y'' \subseteq Y_{k+1}$. Thus, condition C' clearly holds for the MVD $X \twoheadrightarrow Y$ where $N_1, \ldots, N_k$ are the sets of MVDs required in the condition.

The induction is now complete. In particular, condition C' holds for each MVD $X \twoheadrightarrow Y$ in M with X split by M. Now, it is easy to see that condition C' implies condition C. That completes the proof. □

Let us consider an example to help bring out the import of the theorem. Suppose that $U = \{A, \ldots, K\}$ and $M = \{AB \twoheadrightarrow CEF, CDI \twoheadrightarrow ABE, C \twoheadrightarrow ABDEFIJK, GH \twoheadrightarrow ABEFIJK, G \twoheadrightarrow ABEJ\}$. M can be easily verified to be nonredundant. Now, the key X = CDI is split by M. Let $M_o = M - \{CDI \twoheadrightarrow ABE\}$. The minimal Y_1 such that $Y = ABE \subset Y_1$ and $M_o \models X \twoheadrightarrow Y_1$ can be determined to be $Y_1 = ABEJ$. $\bar{Y}_1 = CDFGHIK$. $MAX(\bar{Y}_1) = \{C, F, GH, D, IK\}$. Consider $N_1 = \{C \twoheadrightarrow ABE\}$. It is easy to see that $M \models N_1$ and $M_o \cup N_1 \models CDI \twoheadrightarrow ABE$. Now, the set $M' = \{AB \twoheadrightarrow CEF, C \twoheadrightarrow ABE, C \twoheadrightarrow ABDEFIJK, GH \twoheadrightarrow ABEFIJK, G \twoheadrightarrow ABEJ\}$ is a split-free cover for M.

In general, a few more steps of this iteration would be needed to determine a split-free cover for a given M, if it exists. We now move on to the second stage of our approach.

4. A CHARACTERIZATION OF CONFLICT-FREEDOM

In this section we derive a necessary and sufficient condition for a given split-free set M of MVDs to be hypergraph generated and hence conflict-free. We show that when M is split-free, M is hypergraph generated if and only if a simple property called "MVD-intersection property" holds for M.

Suppose that M is a split-free set of MVDs and let $X_p \twoheadrightarrow Y_p$, $X_q \twoheadrightarrow Y_q \in M$. Then, since M is split-free, either $X_p \subset X_qY_q$ or $X_p \cap Y_q = \phi$, and similarly either $X_q \subset X_pY_p$ or $X_q \cap Y_p = \phi$. Suppose without loss of generality that $X_p \cap Y_q \neq \phi$ and $X_q \subset X_pY_p$. Then we call the MVD $X_p \cap X_q \twoheadrightarrow Y_p \cap Z_q$ the **intersection** of the MVDs $X_p \twoheadrightarrow Y_p$ and $X_q \twoheadrightarrow Y_q$, where $Z_q = U - X_qY_q$. The idea is that for two MVDs $X_1 \twoheadrightarrow Y_1$, $X_2 \twoheadrightarrow Y_2$ such that each does not split the key of the other, we first check if $X_1 \cap Y_2 = \phi$ and $X_2 \cap Y_1 = \phi$. If $X_i \cap Y_j \neq \phi$, then we obtain the complement MVD $X_j \twoheadrightarrow Z_j$ of $X_j \twoheadrightarrow Y_j$, where $Z_j = U - X_jY_j$, $1 \leqslant i \neq j \leqslant 2$. (See Section 3). Otherwise, we retain the original MVD $X_j \twoheadrightarrow Y_j$. Suppose that $X_1 \twoheadrightarrow W_1$, $X_2 \twoheadrightarrow W_2$ are the resulting MVDs, where W_i is Y_i or Z_i, as the case may be, for i = 1,2. Then the MVD $X_1 \cap X_2 \twoheadrightarrow W_1 \cap W_2$ is called the intersection of the MVDs $X_1 \twoheadrightarrow Y_1$ and $X_2 \twoheadrightarrow Y_2$.

<u>Definition 4.1</u> Let M be a split-free set of MVDs. Then we say that M satisfies the **MVD-intersection property** whenever M logically implies the intersection of every pair of MVDs in M.

□

Our next theorem establishes a result on split-free sets of MVDs satisfying the MVD-intersection property.

<u>Theorem 4.1</u> Let M be a split-free set of MVDs and suppose that M satisfies the MVD-intersection property. Then for each MVD $d_i : X_i \twoheadrightarrow Y_i$ in M, and for each MVD $d : X \twoheadrightarrow Y$ in M* with $X \in$ LHS(M), M logically implies the intersection of d_i and d.

<u>Proof</u> First, notice that since M is split-free and X_i, $X \in$ LHS(M), M* does not split X, X_i. Hence the intersection of d_i and d is always well defined. We prove the result by inducing on the length p of a derivation of $X \twoheadrightarrow Y$ from M. The basis case of p = 0 is trivial. Assume the result w.r.t. each MVD $X \twoheadrightarrow Y$ in M* that has a derivation from M of length $p \leqslant n-1$. Suppose that $X \twoheadrightarrow Y$ has derivation from M of length $n > 0$. Consider an MVD $X_i \twoheadrightarrow Y_i$ in M. Suppose without loss of generality that $X_i \cap Y = \phi$ and $X \cap Y_i = \phi$. From our observations in Section 3 on derivations of MVDs, we see that the following cases arise.

<u>Case 1</u> $X \twoheadrightarrow Y$ is obtained by augmentation from $X' \twoheadrightarrow Y' \in M$ using $W \supseteq Z$ where $X' \subset X$. Since $X \cap Y = X' \cap Y' = \phi$, we have $Z = \phi$ and hence

$Y' = Y$. We then trivially have $M \models X_i \cap X' \twoheadrightarrow Y \cap Y_i$, and by augmentation, we get $M \models X_i \cap X \twoheadrightarrow Y \cap Y_i$.

Case 2 $X \twoheadrightarrow Y$ is derived using the subset rule, from the MVD $X \twoheadrightarrow Y'$ in M^*. We have the following subcases.

Case 2.1 $X \twoheadrightarrow Y$ is obtained from the axiom $X \twoheadrightarrow \bar{X}$ using the subset rule. The other MVD used in the subset rule is either some $X' \twoheadrightarrow Y' \in M$, with $X' \subset X$ and possibly $Y \subset Y' \subset YX$, or some MVD $X \twoheadrightarrow Y'$ in M^*.

For the first case, if $X_i \cap Y' = \phi$, then the result immediately follows. So suppose that $X_i \cap Y' \neq \phi$. Then, by split-freedom, $X_i \cap Z' = \phi$, where $Z' = U - X'Y'$. Now, $X \cap Y_i = \phi$ implies $X' \cap Y_i = \phi$. Since $X' \twoheadrightarrow Y'$ has a derivation from M of length n-1 or less, by inductive hypothesis,

$$M \models X' \cap X_i \twoheadrightarrow Y_i \cap Z'.$$

By the complementation rule,

$$M \models X' \cap X_i \twoheadrightarrow Z_iY'.$$

By augmentation,

$$M \models X \cap X_i \twoheadrightarrow Z_iY'.$$

Removing all attributes in Z_iY' that are also in $X \cap X_i$,

$$M \models X \cap X_i \twoheadrightarrow Z_iY.$$

Now, $X_i \cap Z_iY = \phi$. Hence, using the subset rule, we get

$M \models X \cap X_i \twoheadrightarrow Y \cap Y_i$, as required.

For the second case, note that $Y = \bar{X} - Y'$ is the only nontrivial case. In this case, the result follows from the inductive hypothesis, using the definition of intersection of MVDs.

Case 2.2 $X \twoheadrightarrow Y$ is obtained from $X \twoheadrightarrow Y'$ in M^* and an MVD $X_p \twoheadrightarrow Y_p$ in M using the subset rule. Then, clearly $X_p \cap Y' = \phi$. We only consider the case $Y = Y' \cap Y_p$, the case $Y = Y' - Y_p$ being similar. Now, if $X_i \cap Y' = \phi$, then since $X \twoheadrightarrow Y'$ has a derivation of length n-1 or less, by inductive hypothesis, $M \models X \cap X_i \twoheadrightarrow Y' \cap Y_i$. Using this with $X_p \twoheadrightarrow Y_p$ and applying the subset rule, we get $M \models X \cap X_i \twoheadrightarrow Y' \cap Y_i \cap Y_p$, i.e., $M \models X \cap X_i \twoheadrightarrow Y \cap Y_i$, as required. So, assume that $X_i \cap Y' \neq \phi$. Since M is split-free, we have $X_i \cap Z' = \phi$, where $Z' = U - XY'$. By inductive hypothesis, then $M \models X \cap X_i \twoheadrightarrow Y_i \cap Z'$, and by the complementation rule,

$$M \models X \cap X_i \twoheadrightarrow Z_iY', \text{ where } Z_i = U - X_iY_i. \qquad (1)$$

Now, $X_i \cap Y' \neq \phi$ and $X_i \cap Y = \phi$. Since $Y = Y' \cap Y_p$, this implies that $X_i \cap Y' \subset Y' \cap Z_p$ and hence that $X_i \cap Z_p \neq \phi$. Since M is split-free, $X_i \cap Y_p = \phi$.

<u>Case 2.2.1</u> $X_p \cap Y_i = \phi$.

Then by the hypothesis of the theorem,

$$M \models X_i \cap X_p \twoheadrightarrow Y_i \cap Y_p, \text{ where } Z_p = U - X_pY_p. \qquad (2)$$

Now, $(X_i \cap X_p) \cap (Z_iY') = \phi$. Hence from (1) and (2), by the subset rule,

$$M \models X \cap X_i \twoheadrightarrow (Y_i \cap Y_p) \cap (Z_iY'),$$

i.e.,

$$M \models X \cap X_i \twoheadrightarrow Y_i \cap Y_p \cap Y',$$

i.e.,

$$M \models X \cap X_i \twoheadrightarrow Y_i \cap Y, \text{ as required.}$$

<u>Case 2.2.2</u> $X_p \cap Y_i \neq \phi$.

By split-freedom, $X_p \cap Z_i = \phi$. Then by the hypothesis of the theorem,

$$M \models X_i \cap X_p \twoheadrightarrow Z_i \cap Y_p.$$

By the complementation rule,

$$M \models X_i \cap X_p \twoheadrightarrow Z_p\, Y_i. \qquad (3)$$

Case 2.2.2.1 $\quad X \cap Y_p = \phi.$

By inductive hypothesis,

$$M \models X \cap X_p \twoheadrightarrow Y' \cap Y_p,$$

i.e.,
$$M \models X \cap X_p \twoheadrightarrow Y. \qquad (4)$$

Now, $(X \cap X_p) \cap Z_iY' = \phi$. Hence, from (1) and (4), using the subset rule, we have

$$M \models X \cap X_i \twoheadrightarrow (Z_iY') \cap Y,$$

i.e.,
$$M \models X \cap X_i \twoheadrightarrow Y, \text{ since } Y \subset Y'.$$

Since $X_i \cap Y = \phi$, we then get

$$M \models X \cap X_i \twoheadrightarrow Y \cap Y_i, \text{ by the subset rule.}$$

Case 2.2.2.2 $\quad X \cap Y_p = \phi.$

Since X is not split, we have $X \cap Z_p = \phi$.

By inductive hypothesis, since $X_p \cap Y' = \phi$, we have

$$M \models X \cap X_p \twoheadrightarrow Y' \cap Z_p.$$

Using the complementation rule,

$$M \models X \cap X_p \twoheadrightarrow Z'Y_p. \qquad (5)$$

Note that $(X \cap X_p) \cap Z_iY' = \phi$. Then, using (1) and (5) and applying the subset rule, we have

$$M \models X \cap X_i \twoheadrightarrow (Z'Y_p) \cap (Z_iY'),$$

i.e.,
$$M \models X \cap X_i \twoheadrightarrow Y(Z_i \cap (Z'Y_p)). \qquad (6)$$

Further, $X_i \cap [Y(Z_i \cap (Z'Y_p))] = \phi$. Hence, using (6) and the MVD $X_i \twoheadrightarrow Y_i$ in M, and applying the subset rule, we get

$$M \models X \cap X_i \twoheadrightarrow Y \cap Y_i, \text{ as required.}$$

Case 2.3 $X \twoheadrightarrow Y$ is derived from the MVDs $X \twoheadrightarrow Y'$ and $X \twoheadrightarrow Y''$ in M*, using the subset rule. Then the MVDs $X \twoheadrightarrow Y'$, $X \twoheadrightarrow Y''$ each have a derivation of length n-1 or less. We shall only consider the case $Y = Y' \cap Y''$, the other cases, namely $Y = Y' - Y''$, $Y = Y'' - Y'$, being similar. Now, if $X_i \cap Y' = \phi$, then by inductive hypothesis, $M \models X \cap X_i \twoheadrightarrow Y' \cap Y_i$. Since $X \cap (Y' \cap Y_i) = \phi$, using the subset rule, we then obtain

$$M \models X \cap X_i \twoheadrightarrow Y' \cap Y_i \cap Y'',$$

i.e.,
$$M \models X \cap X_i \twoheadrightarrow Y \cap Y_i, \text{ as required.}$$

A similar argument applies to the case $X_i \cap Y'' = \phi$. So, suppose that $X_i \cap Y' \neq \phi \neq X_i \cap Y''$. In this case, since X_i is not split, we obtain $X_i \cap Z' = \phi = X_i \cap Z''$, where $Z' = U - XY'$ and $Z'' = U - XY''$.

By inductive hypothesis,

$$M \models X \cap X_i \twoheadrightarrow Y_i \cap Z'.$$

By the complementation rule,

$$M \models X \cap X_i \twoheadrightarrow Z_iY'. \tag{7}$$

Similarly, we can show that

$$M \models X \cap X_i \twoheadrightarrow Z_iY''. \tag{8}$$

Using (7) and (8), and applying the subset rule, we have

$$M \models X \cap X_i \twoheadrightarrow Z_i(Y' \cap Y''),$$

i.e.,
$$M \models X \cap X_i \twoheadrightarrow Z_iY. \tag{9}$$

Now, $X_i \cap (Z_i Y) = \phi$. Hence, using (9) and the MVD $X_i \twoheadrightarrow Y_i$ in M, and applying the subset rule, we get

$$M \models X \cap X_i \twoheadrightarrow Y \cap Y_i, \text{ as required.}$$

That completes the induction and the proof. □

Theorem 4.1 essentially says that by its very nature, the MVD-intersection property of a set M of MVDs naturally extends to the MVDs in the closure M* of M whose keys belong to LHS(M). Using this we prove the MVD-intersection property necessary and sufficient for a split-free set M of MVDs to be conflict-free.

Theorem 4.2 Let M be a split-free set of MVDs. Then M is conflict-free if and only if M satisfies the MVD-intersection property.

Proof Note that since M is split-free, M is conflict-free if and only if it is hypergraph generated, that is, for each X_i, X_j in LHS(M),

$$DEP(X_i) \cap DEP(X_j) \subset DEP(X_i \cap X_j).$$

(Only If) : Suppose that M is hypergraph generated. Let $X_i \twoheadrightarrow Y_i$, $X_j \twoheadrightarrow Y_j$ be any two MVDs in M. Let $X_i \cap W_j = X_j \cap W_i = \phi$, where W_p is Y_p or Z_p, as the case may be, for p = i, j. Then, since $M \models \{X_i \twoheadrightarrow W_i, X_j \twoheadrightarrow W_j\}$ we have

$$M \models X_i \twoheadrightarrow W_i \cap W_j \tag{1}$$

and

$$M \models X_j \twoheadrightarrow W_i \cap W_j. \tag{2}$$

For each W in $DEP(X_i)$ such that $W \subset W_i \cap W_j$, since $X_i \cap (W_i \cap W_j) = \phi$, we have $M \models X_j \twoheadrightarrow W$. It can be seen then that $W \in DEP(X_j)$. Since M is hypergraph generated, each such W is in $DEP(X_i \cap X_j)$. It then easily follows that $M \models X_i \cap X_j \twoheadrightarrow W_i \cap W_j$. Thus, M satisfies the MVD-intersection property.

(If) : Suppose that M satisfies the MVD-intersection property. We shall show that M is hypergraph generated. Let X_i, X_j be any two keys of M and consider any $W \in DEP(X_i) \cap DEP(X_j)$. Let $X_i \twoheadrightarrow Y_i$, $X_j \twoheadrightarrow Y_j \in M$ and suppose that

$W \subset W_p$, where W_p is Y_p or Z_p, as the case may be, for $p = i, j$. Note that W has to be disjoint with exactly one of Y_p, Z_p. Consider the MVDs $X_i \twoheadrightarrow W_i$ in M and $X_j \twoheadrightarrow W$ in M*. By Theorem 4.1, it follows that $M \models X_i \cap X_j \twoheadrightarrow W \cap W_i$, i.e., $M \models X_i \cap X_j \twoheadrightarrow W$.

Now, if $M \models X_i \cap X_j \twoheadrightarrow W'$, for some $W' \subsetneq W$, then $M \models X_i$ —— W' which is clearly impossible. That shows that $W \in DEP(X_i \cap X_j)$. Hence, M is hypergraph generated. This was to be shown.

□

Thus, for sets of MVDs, given split-freedom, conflict-freedom is exactly captured by the otherwise weaker notion of MVD-intersection property.

Given a nonredundant set M of MVDs, we carry out the following. For each MVD $X \twoheadrightarrow Y$ in M with X split by M, replace $X \twoheadrightarrow Y$ with a set of MVDs that exactly "makes up" for the MVD $X \twoheadrightarrow Y$ in M, if such a set exists. Otherwise, retain the MVD $X \twoheadrightarrow Y$ in M. The set N of MVDs that finally results is called the **resolved version** of M. Note that N is then a cover for M. We have the following

Theorem 4.3 Let M be a nonredundant set of MVDs and let N be the resolved version of M. Then M has a conflict-free cover if and only if N is split-free and N satisfies the MVD-intersection property.

Proof Follows from Theorems 3.2 and 4.2 and the fact that M is hypergraph generated if and only if N is hypergraph generated.

□

We observe that a set M of MVDs is equivalent to a single JD if and only if M has a conflict-free cover [BFMY]. Further, a JD ⋈ **D** is equivalent to a set of MVDs if and only if **D** is acyclic [FMU]. From these results it follows that our characterization can also be used to test whether M is equivalent to a single (acyclic) JD.

Finally, as we remarked in Section 1, our characterization of sets M of MVDs having conflict-free covers is independent of equivalence of M to a single JD, whereas the approach of Goodman and Tay [GT1] is based on this equivalence. Just as they remark that conflict-freedom is irrelevant to testing M for equivalence to a single JD, we take the "dual" viewpoint that the notion of equivalence to a single (acyclic) JD is irrelevant to testing M for the existence of a conflict-free cover, in view of our results. In the next section, we give the algorithms.

5. ALGORITHMS

We shall give the algorithms only in a schematic form. The issues of efficient implementations will not be considered here. The notations used in the following are as in Sections 3 and 4. First, we give an algorithm for testing whether a given nonredundant set of MVDs has a split-free cover.

Algorithm **SPLIT-FREE COVER ;**

Input : A nonredundant set M of MVDs.

Output : A decision as to whether M has a split-free cover, and such a cover if M has one.

begin

N := ϕ ; /* Initialize the prospective split-free cover for M */

for each MVD $X \rightarrow\!\!\rightarrow Y$ in M **do**

if M splits X **then**

begin

$M_o := M - \{X \rightarrow\!\!\rightarrow Y\}$; i := 0 ;

N' := ϕ ; Y_o := U;

repeat

N' := N' u $\{W \rightarrow\!\!\rightarrow Z$: $W \in MAX(\bar{Y}_i)$, Z minimal s.t. $Y \subset Z$ and $M \models W \rightarrow\!\!\rightarrow Z\}$;

/* N' is the set of MVDs that could make up for $X \rightarrow\!\!\rightarrow Y$ in M */

i := i+1; find Y_i minimal s.t. $Y \subset Y_i$ and M_o u N' $\models X \rightarrow\!\!\rightarrow Y_i$

until $(Y_i = Y_{i-1})$;

if $Y_i \neq Y$ **then return** ('No'); N := N u N';

end

else N := N u $\{X \rightarrow\!\!\rightarrow Y\}$

rof;

print ('Yes'); **return** (N)

end.

The algorithm is self-explanatory. The termination and correctness of this algorithm follow from Theorem 3.2 and the discussions. Note that MAX(P) for a set P can be determined by a method similar to Algorithm SPLIT of Goodman and Tay [GT1]. (See also [GT2].) From their remarks on Algorithm SPLIT and our observations on derivations of MVDs, we see that Algorithm SPLIT-FREE COVER takes time polynomial in $|M| + ||M|| + |U|$, where $||M||$ is the size of the description of M. Notice that whenever M has a split-free cover, our algorithm produces such a cover N. We observe that a variant of this algorithm can be used to obtain the resolved version of M.

We now give an algorithm to test M for the existence of a conflict-free cover. Given M, we can always construct a nonredundant cover for M [Ma, Ul]. Hence, we assume without loss of generality that M is nonredundant.

Algorithm CONFLICT-FREE COVER ;

Input : A nonredundant set M of MVDs.

Output : A decision as to whether M has a conflict-free cover, and such a cover if M has one.

begin

(1) Obtain the resolved version, say N, of M, using Algorithm SPLIT-FREE COVER (variant);

(2) **If** N is not split-free **then return** ('No');

(3) **for each** d_i, $d_j \in N$ **do**
  if $M \not\models$ the intersection of d_i and d_j
  then return ('No')

  rof;

  print ('Yes'); **return** (N)

end.

It is easy to see how Algorithm CONFLICT-FREE COVER works. This algorithm clearly takes time polynomial in $|M| + |U| + ||M||$. Termination is obvious. Correctness follows from Theorem 4.3.

It will be noticed that both the algorithms are easy to understand because of their intuitive nature. It is certainly possible to make each of the above algorithms much more efficient. This will be pursued in a future work.

Before closing this section let us consider some examples. Let U = $\{A, ..., F\}$ and let M = $\{AC \twoheadrightarrow BD, AE \twoheadrightarrow CD\}$. Clearly, M is split-free. The intersection of the two MVDs in M is $AC \cap AE \twoheadrightarrow BD \cap BF$, i.e., the MVD $A \twoheadrightarrow B$. Obviously, $M \not\models A \twoheadrightarrow B$. From Theorem 4.2, we then conclude that M is not hypergraph generated and hence not conflict-free. Next, consider $M = \{AB \twoheadrightarrow CEF, CD \twoheadrightarrow ABE\}$, where $U = \{A, ..., H\}$. It is easy to see that M does not even have a split-free cover and hence does not have a conflict-free cover either. Finally, consider $M = \{AB \twoheadrightarrow D, AC \twoheadrightarrow F, BC \twoheadrightarrow E\}$ with $U = \{A, ..., F\}$. M is split-free. Since the intersection of every pair of MVDs in M is trivial, M is hypergraph generated and hence conflict-free.

6. CONCLUSIONS

Using new notions of split-freedom and MVD-intersection property we developed a characterization of sets of MVDs having conflict-free covers. We also gave polynomial time algorithms to test a set of MVDs for the existence of split-free and conflict-free covers. Our characterization is significant for the clear insight it provides into the nature of conflict-free sets of MVDs. In addition, we also established an interesting property of split-free sets of MVDs.

REFERENCES

[B] C. BEERI, "On the membership problem for functional and multivalued dependencies", **ACM TODS** 5,3 (Sept. 1980), 241-259.

[BFMY] C. BEERI, R. FAGIN, D. MAIER, and M. YANNAKAKIS, "On the desirability of acyclic database schemes", **J. ACM** 30, 3 (July 1983), 479-513.

[BV] C. BEERI and M.Y. VARDI, "On the properties of join dependencies", In : **Advances in Database Theory** (H. Gallaire, J. Minker, and J.M. Nicolas, Eds.), Plenum Press, 1981, 25-72.

[Fa] R. FAGIN, "Multivalued dependencies and a new normal form for relational databases", **ACM TODS** 2,3 (Sept. 1977), 262-278.

[FMU] R. FAGIN, A.O. MENDELZON, and J.D. ULLMAN, "A simplified universal relation assumption and its properties", **ACM TODS 7,3** (Sept. 1982), 343-360.

[Ga] Z. GALIL, "An almost linear-time algorithm for computing a dependency basis in a relational database", **J. ACM** 29, 1 (Jan. 1982), 96-102.

[GS] N. GOODMAN and O. SCHMUELI, "Syntactic characterization of tree database schemas", **J. ACM** 30, 4 (Oct. 1983), 767-786.

[GT1] N. GOODMAN and Y.C. TAY, "Synthesizing fourth normal form relations using multivalued dependencies", Tech. Rep. TR-17-83, Aiken Computation Lab, Harvard Univ., 1983.

[GT2] N. GOODMAN and Y.C. TAY, "A characterization of multivalued dependencies equivalent to a join dependency", **Inform. Proc. Letters,** 18 (1984), 261-266.

[Ja] S. JAJODIA, "On the equivalence of relational and network models", **Inform. Proc. Letters,** 20 (1985), 51-54.

[Li] Y.E. LIEN, "On the equivalence of database models", **J. ACM** 29, 2 (April 1982), 333-363.

[Ma] D. MAIER, **The Theory of Relational Databases,** Comp. Sci. Press., Maryland, 1983.

[Sa] Y. SAGIV, "An algorithm for inferring multivalued dependencies with an application to propositional logic", **J. ACM** 27, 2 (April 1980), 250-262.

[Sc1] E. SCIORE, "Some observations of real-world data dependencies", **Proc. XP1 Workshop,** Stony Brook, N.Y., June 1980.

[Sc2] E. SCIORE, "Real-world MVDs", In: **Proc. Int. Conf. on Management of Data** (April 1981), ACM N.Y., 1981, pp. 121-132.

[Ul] J.D. ULLMAN, **Principles of Database Systems,** Comp. Sci. Press, Maryland, 1980.

Towards Online Schedulers Based on Pre–Analysis Locking

Georg Lausen
Institut für Programm- und Informationssysteme
Technische Hochschule Darmstadt, D-6100 Darmstadt, West-Germany

Eljas Soisalon-Soininen†
Department of Computer Science,
University of Helsinki, SF-00250 Helsinki 25, Finland

Peter Widmayer
Institut für Angewandte Informatik und Formale Beschreibungsverfahren,
Universität Karlsruhe (TH), D-7500 Karlsruhe, West-Germany

Abstract

Locking is one familiar mechanism for a database concurrency control to achieve safe transaction systems. Pre–Analysis Locking bases on an algorithm which analyses a set of transactions to determine the conflicting actions. Different to known locking policies, e.g. 2–Phase Locking, the position of lock operations depends only on the location of the conflicting actions within the transactions. Therefore, depending on the structure of the transactions, Pre–Analysis Locking allows for a higher potential degree of concurrency than 2–Phase Locking. Until now Pre–Analysis Locking requires the knowledge of the complete set of transactions to be executed in advance. In this paper, iterative Pre–Analysis Locking is proposed, which manages the case of previously unknown transactions. Further, dynamic Pre–Analysis Locking is introduced, which additionally is able to forget finished transactions and therefore is an appealing new approach to online scheduling. Safety of the policies is proven and the issue of deadlock freedom is discussed.

1. Introduction

Locking is one familiar mechanism for a database concurrency control to achieve safe transaction systems. Locking has been studied by many authors in the past. In Eswaran et al. (1976) the 2-Phase Locking policy (2PL) has been introduced which achieves safety by not allowing a transaction to lock a variable after having already unlocked one. In the work of Kedem and Silberschatz (1980), Silberschatz and Kedem (1980), and Yannakakis (1982) it is shown that this fixed lock/unlock rule can be weakened if the order of lock and unlock operations is controlled by a structure on the database variables. Bayer et al. (1980) studies locking

† The work of this author was supported by the Alexander von Humboldt Foundation.

in a multiversion database environment, and Korth (1983) investigates the impact of different lock modes on the allowed interleavings of transactions running concurrently. Our approach to locking is an algorithmic continuation of the geometric characterization of locking introduced by Papadimitriou (1983). In Lausen et al. (1985,1986) we introduce the Pre–Analysis Locking algorithm PAL which first analyses a set of transactions to determine the conflicting actions of different transactions. Conflicts are represented as (conflict) points in the coordinate plane of the respective transaction pair. Based on the geometric pattern of the points lock/unlock operations are inserted into the transactions in a way which guarantees safety and freedom from deadlock. In contrast to 2PL, where locking is done according to conflicts and the lock/unlock rule, PAL locks only according to the position of conflict points, which are a–priori known as the result of the pre–analysis. Whether 2PL or PAL allows for a higher degree of potential concurrency depends therefore on the position of conflicting actions of the transactions forming the transaction system being analyzed.

Until now PAL policies require the knowledge of the complete set of transactions to be executed in advance. In this paper, iterative PAL is proposed, which manages the case of previously unknown transactions. Further, dynamic PAL is introduced, which additionally is able to forget finished transactions and therefore is an appealing new approach to online scheduling. Safety of the policies is proven and the issue of deadlock freedom is discussed.

The structure of the paper is as follows. In Section 2 we introduce basic definitions and a geometric characterization of concurrency. Section 3 shows how locking relates to the geometric approach. To raise interest for investigating PAL policies, we discuss in Section 4 a scenario which characterizes transactions, for which a PAL policy allows a higher degree of potential concurrency than a 2PL policy. Section 5 then introduces iterative PAL, and Section 6 dynamic PAL. Finally, in Section 7 we sketch polynomial time bounds of the algorithms presented in this paper.

2. Basic Definitions and Geometric Characterization

A **transaction system** $\tau = \{T_1, \ldots, T_d\}$ is a set of **transactions**. A transaction $T_i = (A_{i1}, \ldots, A_{im_i})$, $m_i \geq 1$, is a sequence of **actions**. Each action A_{ij} has associated with it an **entity** $x_{ij} \in E$, where E is a set of entities forming the database. We distinguish read and write actions, $A_{ij} = R_{ij}$ meaning **read** x_{ij} and $A_{ij} = W_{ij}$ meaning **write** x_{ij}. Each transaction reads each entity at most once and writes each entity at most once, and it is not allowed to read an entity after it has written it. A **schedule** s of τ is a permutation of all actions of τ such that for any transaction T_i, $1 \leq j < k \leq m_i$ implies $s(A_{ij}) < s(A_{ik})$.

Two actions of two different transactions **conflict**, if they involve the same entity, and at least one of them is a write action. With each schedule s we associate a directed graph $D(s)$ called **conflict graph** having as nodes the transactions of τ and an edge $T_i \rightarrow T_j$ if an action of T_i precedes in s a conflicting action of T_j. A schedule is called **conflict–serializable** if $D(s) = D(s')$ for some serial schedule s' of τ, or, equivalently, if $D(s)$ is acyclic. A transaction system τ is called **conflict–safe** if every schedule of τ is conflict–serializable. Whenever we refer to serializability or safety in the following, we always will mean conflict–serializability and conflict–safety.

For testing serializability and safety, conflicts between transactions must be considered. We define a binary relation on the set of actions of the transaction system in the following way. We say $P = (A_{ip}, A_{jq})$ is a **direct conflict point** between T_i and $T_j, i \neq j$, if A_{ip} and A_{jq} conflict. Point $P = (A_{ip}, A_{jq})$ is called a **conflict point** between T_i and T_j, $i \neq j$, if there exists a set of transactions $\{T_{k_l} | 1 \leq l \leq n\} \subseteq (\tau - \{T_i, T_j\})$ for some n, such that for all l, $1 \leq l \leq n-1$, there exist $p_l \leq m_{k_l}$ and $q_{l+1} \leq m_{k_{l+1}}$ such that $(A_{k_l p_l}, A_{k_{l+1} q_{l+1}})$ is a direct conflict point between T_{k_l} and $T_{k_{l+1}}$, and $(A_{ip}, A_{k_1 q_1})$ and $(A_{k_n p_n}, A_{jq})$ are direct conflict points between T_i and T_{k_1}, T_{k_n} and T_j, respectively. The sequence $(A_{ip}, A_{k_1 q_1})$, $(A_{k_1 p_1}, A_{k_2 q_2})$, $\ldots$, $(A_{k_{n-1} p_{n-1}}, A_{k_n q_n})$, $(A_{k_n p_n}, A_{jq})$ is called a **conflict point path** for P. The number n of intermediate transactions is called the **length** of the path. In the case of $n = 0$, P is a direct conflict point; otherwise, i.e., for $n \geq 1, P$ is called an **indirect conflict point**.

We will characterize concurrency geometrically in the same spirit as it is done in the context of locking by Papadimitriou (1983). In a coordinate plane each axe corresponds to one transaction, the integer points on the axe are the respective actions. Conflict points then are grid points in the plane. Let $T_i = (A_{i1}, \ldots, A_{im_i})$, $T_j = (A_{j1}, \ldots, A_{jm_j})$ be two transactions. Any nondecreasing curve in the (T_i, T_j) plane from point $(0,0)$ to point $(m_i + 1, m_j + 1)$ not passing through any other grid point represents a schedule of $\{T_i, T_j\}$. The actions are in the order the curve passes the corresponding grid lines. For example, in Figure 1 in the (T_1, T_2) plane the schedule $W_1 a\ W_2 a\ W_2 b\ W_1 c$ is represented.

In the case of transaction systems containing two transactions the geometric representation relates to serializability very intuitively:

Fact 2.1 (cf. Papadimitriou, 1983): Let $\tau = \{T_1, T_2\}$, and let s be a schedule of τ. s is not serializable iff the curve of s separates two (direct) conflict points in the plane (T_1, T_2).

■

However, for arbitrary transaction systems things are a bit more involved. Let s be a schedule of a transaction system $\tau = \{T_1, T_2, \ldots, T_d\}$. For any pair $i, j \in \{1, \ldots, d\}, i \neq j$, the schedule s_{ij} is a schedule of the transaction system $\tau_{ij} = \{T_i, T_j\}$, and s_{ij} is derived as a projection from s by deleting all actions of transactions not in τ_{ij}.

Corollary 2.2: Let $\tau = \{T_1, \ldots, T_d\}$, and let s be a schedule of τ. s is not serializable if there exist transactions $T_i, T_j \in \tau, i \neq j$, such that the curve of s_{ij} separates two direct conflict points in the plane (T_i, T_j).

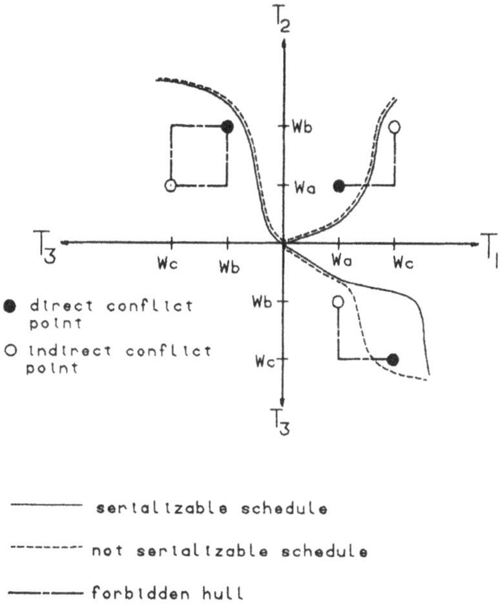

Figure 1

■

Fact 2.3 (Lausen et al. (1985)): Let $\tau = \{T_1, T_2, \ldots, T_d\}$, and let s be a schedule of τ which is not serializable. Then there exist transactions $T_i, T_j \in \tau, i \neq j$, such that the curve of s_{ij} separates two conflict points in the plane (T_i, T_j) , at least one of which is a direct conflict point.

■

The opposite directions do not hold as counterexamples show in Figure 1.

3. Locking

Fact 2.3 shows how safe transaction systems can be achieved by a pairwise consideration of the transactions. What has to be done is to forbid all schedules s whose projected curve s_{ij} separates conflict points in the (T_i, T_j) plane; $T_i, T_j \in \tau, i \neq j$. We will forbid these schedules by means of connected forbidden regions containing all conflict points of a given plane. The exact boundary of a forbidden region is irrelevant because a schedule can be represented by a set of curves. Therefore, we restrict the subsequent discussion to rectilinear polygons, i.e. polygons with sides parallel to the coordinate axes, for the forbidden regions.

Rectilinear connected regions can be constructed from a set of conflict points in a plane by the algorithm of Ottmann et al. (1984). Such a region will be called the **forbidden hull** of the corresponding set of conflict points. In Figure 1 the according forbidden hulls are indicated by dashed lines. The hulls computed by the algorithm have the following closure property. If for any two points $(x_1, y_1), (x_2, y_2)$ in the hull there holds $x_1 < x_2$ and $y_1 > y_2$, then also the points $(x_1, y_2), (x_2, y_1)$ are contained in the hull. For example look at the forbidden hull in plane (T_2, T_3) of Figure 1. The motivation for such **northeast–southwest** closed hulls can be found in Papadimitriou (1983). We call a forbidden hull **southeast** closed, if for any two points $(x_1, y_1), (x_2, y_2)$ in the hull, $x_1 < x_2$ and $y_1 < y_2$ implies that the point (x_2, y_1) is contained in the hull. Moreover, the hulls computed by the algorithm are smallest connected regions containing all conflict points which fulfill the closure property.

Locking is a means to guarantee that transactions do not enter a forbidden hull (Papadimitriou, 1983). To this end, for each plane one first computes a set of rectangles covering the hull. Then, according to the position of the corner points of each rectangle, the transactions are augmented by lock/unlock operations. This procedure is described in detail in Lipski and Papadimitriou (1981); Figure 2 can be used for illustration.

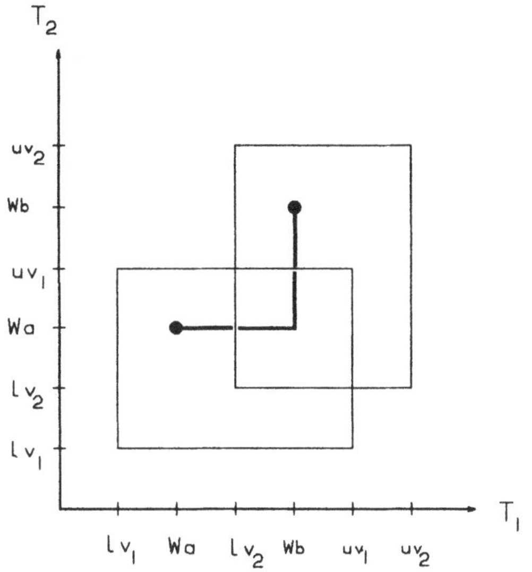

Figure 2

A **locked transaction system** L_T then is a set of **locked transactions**, $L_T = \{LT_1, LT_2, \ldots, LT_d\}$, where each locked transaction is a transaction containing **lock** v (lv) and **unlock** v (uv) operations besides the read and write actions, for $v \in LV$. LV is the set of **locking variables**; it is independent of the set of entities. For any $v \in LV$ and any locked transaction, there is at most one lock v and one unlock v operation in the transaction; lock v must be followed by unlock

v, and unlock v must be preceded by lock v. Further, each locking variable v is used in at most two transactions. We say, v **acts** in the corresponding plane. We say that a locked schedule Ls of L_T is **legal**, if in Ls each lock v operation is followed first by an unlock v operation before the next lock v operation.

In Lausen et al. (1985, 1986) we have introduced an algorithm called **Pre–Analysis Locking (PAL)** which transforms a given transaction system into a safe and deadlock free locked transaction system in polynomial time. Safety is achieved according to Fact 2.3 by inserting lock/unlock operations into the transactions according to a forbidden hull of each plane in which there is at least one direct conflict point.

4. Pre–Analysis Locking and 2–Phase Locking

It is shown in Lausen et al. (1985) that PAL and 2–Phase Locking (2PL) do not dominate each other with respect to the set of allowed schedules. To raise interest for investigating PAL policies, we will discuss an example in the following which points out more general situations, in which PAL policies allow for a higher potential degree of concurrency than 2PL policies.

Using a 2PL policy, a transaction must lock every entity before it accesses it, but, after some entity is unlocked, no succeeding lock is allowed any more. For each entity there exists one locking variable which is used by any transaction to lock the corresponding entity. We denote 2PL* the policy which locks an entity immediately before the corresponding action is performed and unlocks as early as possible. We denote p2PL the preclaiming policy, i.e. one lock operation locking all entities accessed by the transaction is executed as the transaction's first step. We again assume that unlocking is done as early as possible. It is well known that 2PL* is not free from deadlocks, but p2PL is.

Figure 3 illustrates the differences between PAL, 2PL* and p2PL. PAL bases lock/unlock operations on the position of direct and indirect conflict points. On the other hand side, 2PL* and p2PL lock only direct conflict points. However, 2PL* can start unlocking not before the last but one action, and p2PL must perform locking before the first action. Hence, the locked region in each plane also depends on the length of the transaction. In Figure 3 we see a transaction system, in which PAL allows more schedules than p2PL or 2PL*, even though the locked regions of PAL are not contained in any of the locked regions of the other policies.

Since in PAL and 2PL policies direct conflict points are contained in the forbidden region, PAL policies basically loose concurrency due to the location of indirect conflict points. Thus, indirect conflict points are the main problem with PAL. In Figure 4 we show a transaction system which would be safely locked if PAL were applied only to direct conflict points. So to develop improved PAL policies we should try to avoid indirect conflict points.

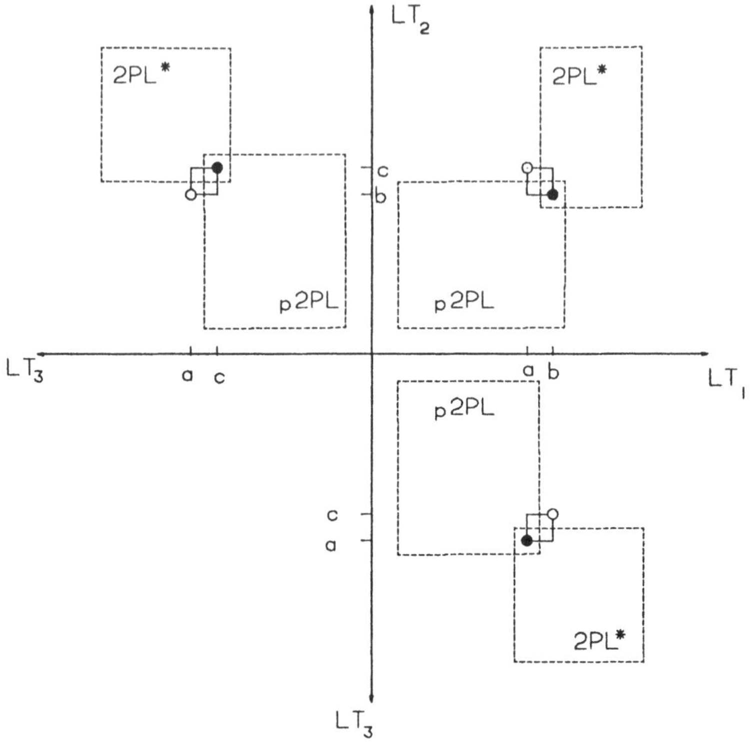

Figure 3

5. The Iterative Pre–Analysis Locking Policy

PAL analyzes a complete transaction system at once; the set of all conflict points is computed in one step. **Iterative Pre–Analysis Locking (iPAL)** is a different policy. The transaction system still is assumed to be given in advance. However, the locked transaction system is computed by iterating the following step:

> Let $L\tau = \{LT_1, \ldots, LT_l\}$ be a safe locked transaction system. Let T_{l+1} be a new transaction. Apply iPAL on $L\tau$ and T_{l+1} to construct a new locked transaction system $L\tau' = \{L'T_1, \ldots, L'T_l, LT_{l+1}\}$.

The surprising property of iPAL is that to obtain safe $L\tau'$, we only have to compute the indirect conflict points of each plane $(T_i, T_{l+1}), 1 \leq i \leq l$; planes $(T_i, T_j), 1 \leq i,j \leq l, i \neq j$ can be left unchanged. Thus, iPAL is a step towards an online situation, where new transactions are issued by the users dynamically.

Algorithm iPAL

Let $\tau = \{T_1, \ldots, T_d\}$ be a transaction system.

1. Let $L\tau = \{LT_1\}$, where $LT_1 = T_1$.

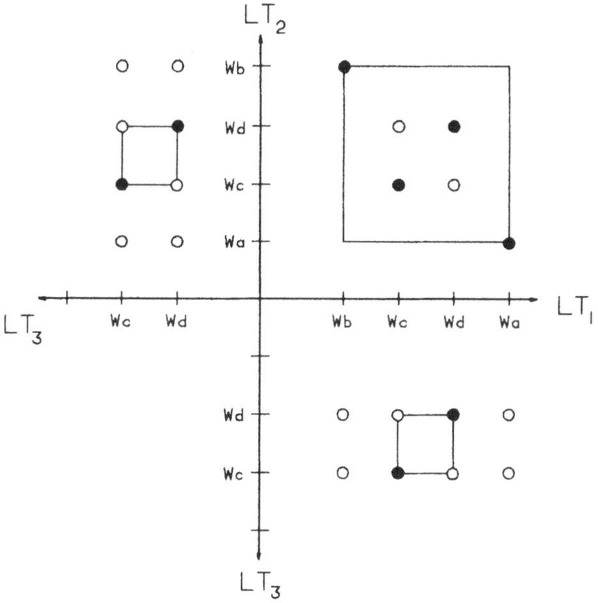

Figure 4

2. For $i = 2$ to d perform

   2.1 Determine the set of direct and indirect conflict points with respect to $\{T_1, \ldots, T_i\}$ between all pairs $(T_k, T_i), 1 \leq k \leq i-1$.

   2.2 For each pair $(T_k, T_i), 1 \leq k \leq i-1$, whose plane (T_k, T_i) contains at least two conflict points, construct a southeast–closed forbidden hull of all conflict points in the plane (T_k, T_i).

   2.3 Augment each locked transaction $LT_k, 1 \leq k \leq i-1$, by lock and unlock operations derived from the southeast–closed forbidden hull of the conflict points in the plane (T_k, T_i).

   2.4 Regard T_i as a locked transaction LT_i with no lock and unlock operations.

   For each locked transaction $LT_k, 1 \leq k \leq i-1$, augment LT_i by lock and unlock operations derived from the southeast–closed forbidden hull of the conflict points in the plane (T_k, T_i).

   2.5 Let $L_{\mathcal{T}} = \{LT_1, \ldots, LT_i\}$.

End of Algorithm iPAL

Next we prove safety of iPAL.

Lemma 5.1: Let $\tau = \{T_1, \ldots, T_d\}$, and let s be a schedule of τ which is not serializable. Then there exists a plane $(T_i, T_j), T_i, T_j \in \tau, i \neq j$, containing a direct conflict point $P = (A_{ip_i}, A_{jq_j})$ and a conflict point $Q = (A_{iq_i}, A_{jp_j})$ with path $(A_{iq_i}, A_{k_1p_1})$, $(A_{k_1q_1}, A_{k_2p_2}), \ldots$, $(A_{k_nq_n}, A_{jp_j}), n \geq 0$, such that s_{ij} separates P and Q and there holds

$$s(A_{ip_i}) < s(A_{jq_j}) \text{ and } s(A_{iq_i}) > s(A_{k_1p_1}),\ s(A_{k_1q_1}) > s(A_{k_2p_2}), \ldots,\ s(A_{k_nq_n}) > s(A_{jp_j}).$$

Proof: Because s is not serializable, $D(s)$ has a cycle, say $T_1 \rightarrow T_2 \rightarrow \ldots \rightarrow T_k \rightarrow T_1, k \geq 2$. It follows from the proof of Fact 2.3 that for some transactions contained in the cycle, say T_1, T_2, the projected schedule s_{12} separates a direct conflict point and a conflict point in plane (T_1, T_2). Let the direct conflict point be $P = (A_{1p_1}, A_{2q_2})$ and let the conflict point be $Q = (A_{1q_1}, A_{2p_2})$ with conflict point path $(A_{2p_2}, A_{3q_3}), (A_{3p_3}, A_{4q_4}), \ldots, (A_{kp_k}, A_{1q_1})$ following from the cycle in $D(s)$. Further, from the direction of the cycle follows $s(A_{1p_1}) < s(A_{2q_2})$ and $s(A_{1q_1}) > s(A_{kp_k})$, $s(A_{k-1q_{k-1}}) > s(A_{k-2p_{k-2}}), \ldots, s(A_{3q_3}) > s(A_{2p_2})$.

■

Let $LT_i, LT_j \in L\tau$. $LT_i|_j$ means the deletion of all lock/unlock operations in LT_i which do not act in plane (LT_i, LT_j).

Lemma 5.2: Let $L\tau = \{LT_1, \ldots, LT_{d-1}\}$ be any safe locked transaction system, and let $T_d \notin \tau$ be a transaction. Let $L\tau' = \{L'T_1, \ldots, L'T_{d-1}, LT_d\}$ be a locked transaction system for which holds:

(1) $L'T_i|_j = LT_i|_j, 1 \leq i, j \leq d-1, i \neq j$.

(2) Let each plane $(T_i, T_d), 1 \leq i \leq d-1$, contain all conflict points with respect to $\{T_1, \ldots, T_d\}$.

   (a) $L'T_i, 1 \leq i \leq d-1$, is derived from LT_i by augmentation by lock/unlock operations derived from the southeast–closed forbidden hull of all conflict points in plane (T_i, T_d).

   (b) LT_d is derived by augmenting T_d by lock/unlock operations derived from the southeast–closed forbidden hulls of all conflict points in planes (T_i, T_d), $1 \leq i \leq d-1$.

Then $L\tau'$ is safe.

Proof: Assume there exists a schedule Ls of $L\tau'$ and s is not serializable. Since we only ignored conflict points in planes $(T_i, T_j), 1 \leq i, j \leq d-1, i \neq j$, Ls must separate some indirect conflict point Q and some direct conflict point P in such a plane (T_i, T_j) according to Lemma 5.1. Moreover, since $L\tau$ is safe, each cycle in the conflict graph $D(s)$ must contain T_d. Hence, since the condition of Lemma 5.1 implies a cycle in $D(s)$, the conflict point path of Q must also contain T_d.

Let $P = (A_{ip_i}, A_{jq_j})$, $Q = (A_{iq_i}, A_{jp_j})$ and let the conflict point path of Q be $(A_{iq_i}, A_{k_1p_1})$, $(A_{k_1q_1}, A_{k_2p_2}), \ldots, (A_{k_rq_r}, A_{dp_d}), (A_{dq_d}, A_{k_{r+1}p_{r+1}}), \ldots, (A_{k_nq_n}, A_{jp_j}), n \geq 0$. We then can infer indirect conflict points (A_{jq_j}, A_{dp_d}), (A_{jp_j}, A_{dq_d}), and (A_{ip_i}, A_{dq_d}), (A_{iq_i}, A_{dp_d}). Further, since in the planes $(T_i, T_d), (T_j, T_d)$ conflict points are contained in forbidden hulls, we can follow one of the following cases:

(i) $s = \ldots\ A_{dq_d} \ldots\ A_{ip_i} \ldots$, and $s = \ldots\ A_{dp_d} \ldots\ A_{iq_i} \ldots$,

(ii) $s = \ldots\ A_{iq_i} \ldots\ A_{dp_d}\ \ldots$, and $s = \ldots\ A_{ip_i} \ldots\ A_{dq_d}\ \ldots$.

Assume case (i) occurred. Since $D(s)$ contains a cycle implied by the conflicts of P and Q, the cycle contains a path $T_i \rightarrow \ldots \rightarrow T_d$. However, we have $s(A_{dq_d}) < s(A_{ip_i})$ and $s(A_{dp_d}) < s(A_{iq_i})$. It follows, there must exist some transactions contained in the cycle, which 'carry a conflict' from T_i 'back' to T_d. For one such transaction, say $T_{k_l}, 1 \leq l \leq n$, with actions $A_{k_l p_l}, A_{k_l q_l}$, these actions must be interleaved in s with actions A_{dp_d}, A_{dq_d} of T_d in one of the following ways:

(i.1) $s = \ldots\ A_{k_l p_l} \ldots A_{dq_d} \ldots A_{k_l q_l} \ldots$,

(i.2) $s = \ldots\ A_{k_l q_l} \ldots A_{dp_d} \ldots A_{k_l p_l} \ldots$.

Since we also can conclude the indirect conflict points $(A_{dq_d}, A_{k_l p_l})$, $(A_{dp_d}, A_{k_l q_l})$ in plane (T_{k_l}, T_d), there follows one of the situations shown in Figure 5, what contradicts condition (2)(b). Observe, that in Figure 5(b), (c) we have no separation of conflict points. It follows, that we need southeast–closed forbidden hulls to ensure safety.

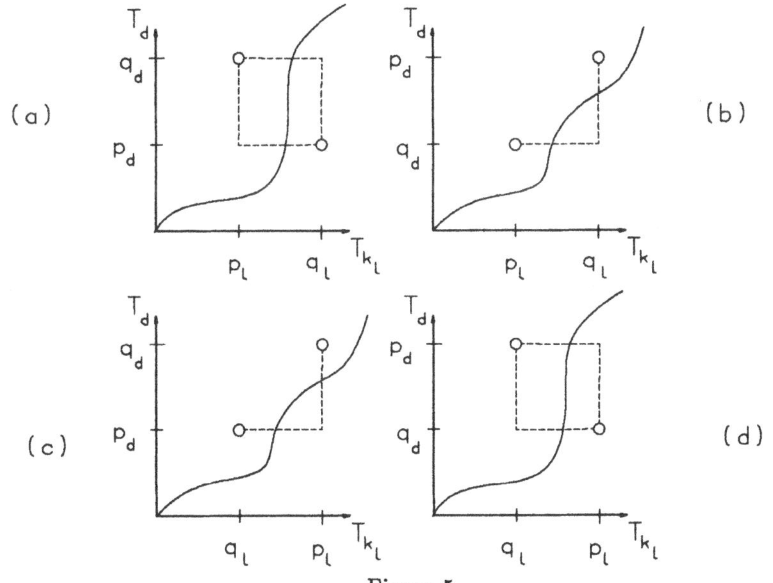

Figure 5

Assume case (ii) occurred. Since $T_d \rightarrow \ldots \rightarrow T_i$ is contained in the cycle, there must exist some transactions contained in the cycle, which 'carry a conflict' from T_d 'back' to T_i. For one such transaction, say T_{k_l} as above, one of the following holds:

(ii.1) $s = \ldots\ A_{k_l p_l} \ldots A_{d p_d} \ldots A_{k_l q_l} \ldots,$

(ii.2) $s = \ldots\ A_{k_l q_l} \ldots A_{d q_d} \ldots A_{k_l p_l} \ldots.$

A contradiction follows as shown in Figure 6.

■

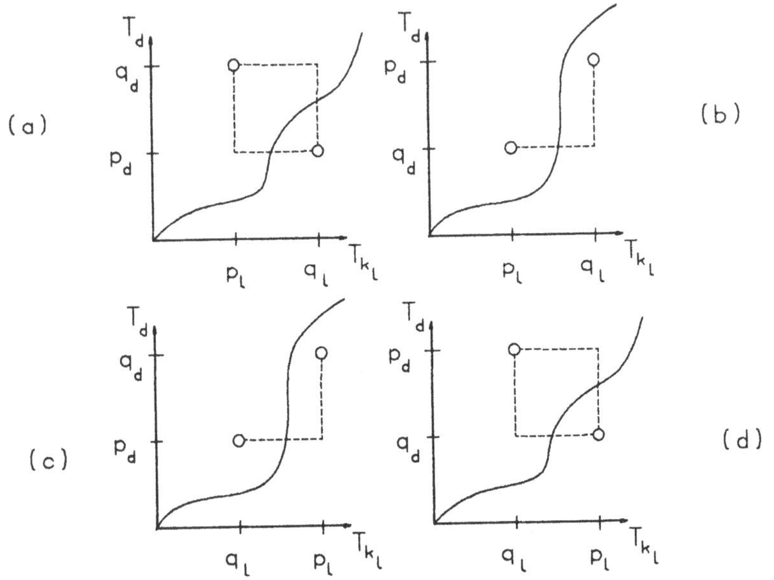

Figure 6

Theorem 5.3: iPAL is safe.

Proof: Each iteration of iPAL fulfills the conditions of Lemma 5.2.

■

We will point out the differences between PAL and iPAL by discussing the scenario in Figure 7. We assume that iPAL processes the transactions in ascending order. The forbidden hulls resulting from PAL and the indirect conflict points not being considered by iPAL for constructing a forbidden hull are dashed.

We have to lock under PAL in one plane more than under iPAL. It is easy to verify, that whenever a transaction system of d transactions can only cause a cycle of length d as it is in Figure 7, PAL will lock in d planes and iPAL in $d-1$. It is worth to point out that if only transaction $T_1, \ldots, T_4$ in Figure 7 are run concurrently, no locking is done under iPAL, since the indirect conflict points are not considered for constructing the forbidden hulls. What is not nice with iPAL is that we have to use southeast–closed forbidden hulls, i.e., sometimes we have

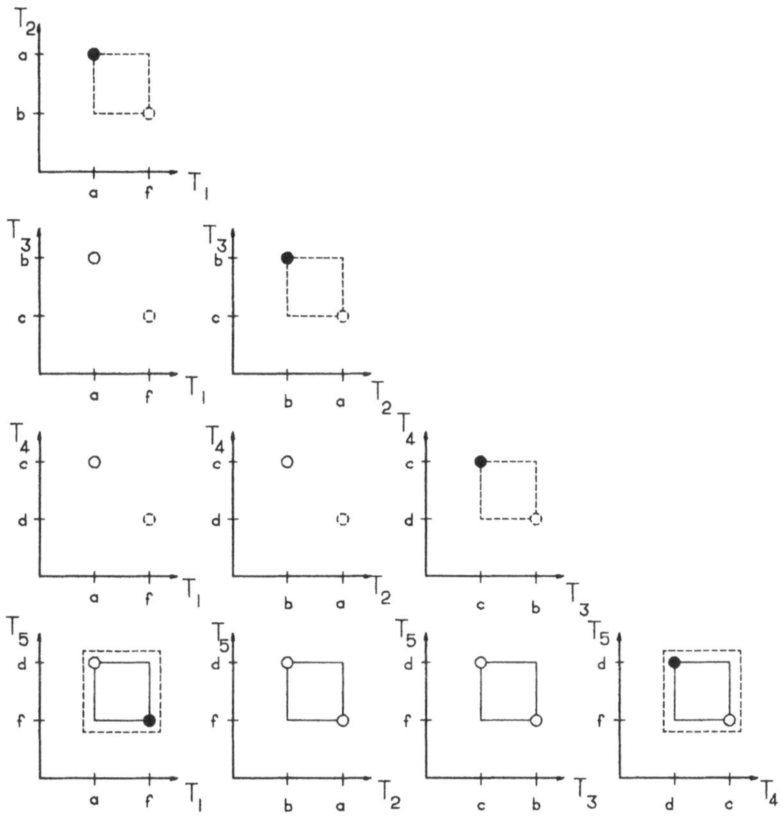

Figure 7

to lock larger regions than it would be necessary under PAL. The reason for this property is that there may exist not serializable schedules which separate conflict points only in one plane. If this is a plane not being considered by iPAL, the schedule must be forbidden in planes not having a separation of conflict points. Note, that we do not need Northwest–closed hulls in these cases. This follows from the proof of Lemma 5.2 and the order the transactions are assigned to the coordinate axes.

PAL is free from deadlock. The interesting question now is, whether iPAL has the same property. Unfortunately, iPAL is not free from deadlock. Figure 8 characterizes a locked transaction system resulting from iPAL with a deadlock situation. The forbidden hull results from processing the transactions in the order T_1, T_2, T_3. However, having a closer look at the figure, we can recognize, that if we shift lock operation lv_1 in LT_1 to the left of lv_3, the resulting locked transaction system is free from deadlock. This stems from the fact, that now lock operations in each transaction are executed in the global order of the locking variables. This technique can be generalized for any locked transaction system constructed by iPAL. Hence there exists a deadlock free variant of iPAL (with a lower degree of concurrency), which is easy to achieve starting from a locked transaction system under iPAL.

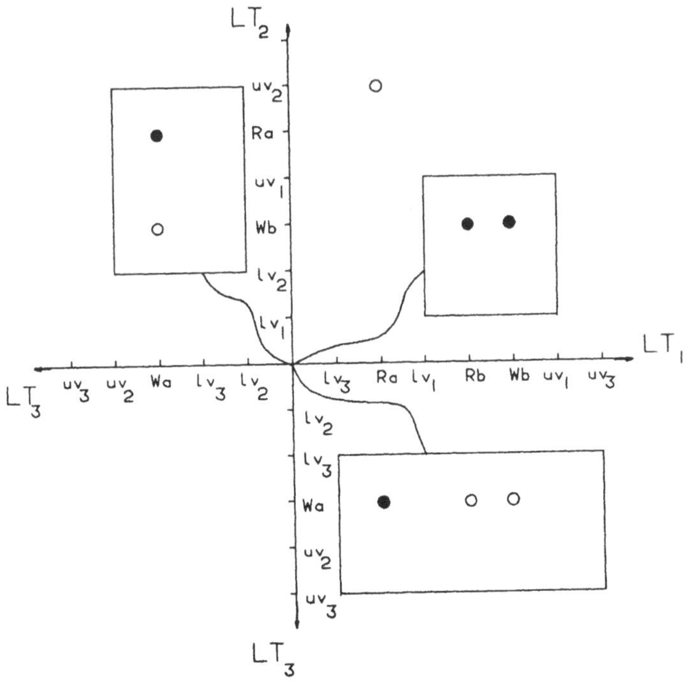

Figure 8

6. Online Scheduling Based on Pre–Analysis Locking

The component of a database management system which is responsible for concurrency control is called **scheduler**. We call a scheduler **online**, if the transaction system need not be known in advance. However, we require for the following, whenever a new transaction is issued by an user, then the complete (action sequence of the) transaction is made known to the scheduler. This assumption holds for many commercial online systems, e.g. accounting or reservation; it is applicable for general transactions if a superset of the actions to be executed can be assumed. Recently, multilevel concurrency control techniques have been introduced (Beeri et al. (1983), Weikum (1986)). In this kind of framework transactions may generate subtransactions, which are executed on the next lower level and which may again generate subtransactions. It is shown, that for each level within this architecture we can use a scheduler optimal with respect to the specific requirements. For example, a complex query, which is an action of a highlevel transaction, is translated into several more primitive queries. If we treat the original query as lowerlevel transaction with actions the primitive queries, then for this lower level our predeclaration assumption will be satisfied.

Can we base an online scheduler on PAL? That means, whenever a new transaction is issued, we recompute conflict points and lock/unlock operations for all pairs of transactions. In Figure 9 we show an example which clearly demonstrates that PAL is not appropriate for online scheduling. In Figure 9(a) transactions T_1, T_2 have been processed by PAL and some actions have been executed. Since there is only one (direct) conflict point, no lock/unlock operations have been introduced. Now assume a new transaction T_3 is issued and PAL is performed again. Then there follows for each plane a forbidden region as indicated in Figure 9(b). Moreover, in the (T_1, T_2) plane, the projected schedule s_{12} intersects the forbidden region. Hence, we cannot find a legal prefix Ls according to PAL.

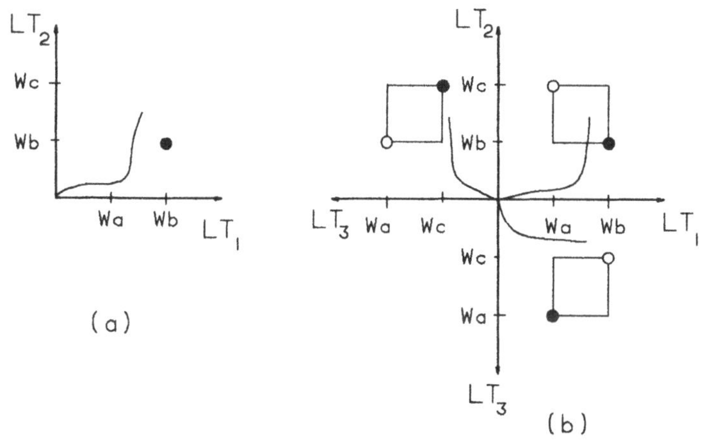

Figure 9

However, iPAL is appropriate for online scheduling, since planes of transactions which already have started their execution need not be considered later again. If we use iPAL instead of PAL in the situation shown in Figure 9, then a situation as shown in Figure 10 follows. The plane (T_1, T_2) is left unchanged. Therefore, the above problem is avoided and iPAL can be used for online scheduling.

But now consider the serializable schedule $s = W_1aW_2bW_2cW_3cW_3aW_1b$ of the transaction system shown in Figure 10. It follows from the figure, that this schedule is not allowed by iPAL. Next we will introduce a criterion which will allow a scheduler to forget transactions whenever we can be sure that no not serializable situation can occur. This leads to **dynamic Pre–Analysis Locking (dPAL)**, which will also allow the above schedule s.

Forgetting a transaction increases the potential degree of concurrency for a PAL policy, since the number of (indirect) conflict points decreases. It is a standard result of concurrency control theory, that a scheduler can forget a finished transaction whenever each predecessor in the

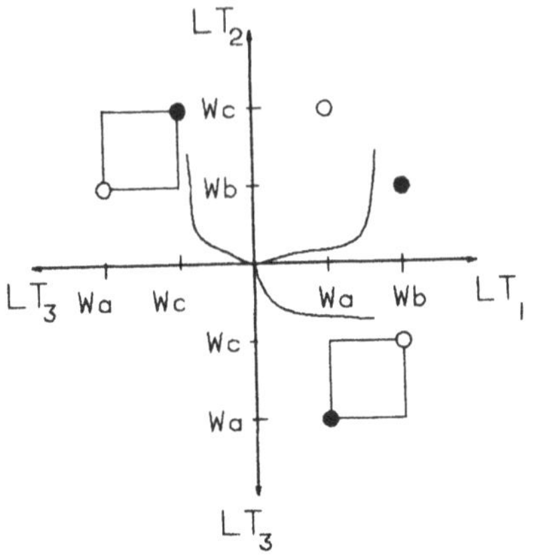

Figure 10

conflict graph of the respective transaction also is finished (e.g. Schlageter (1978)). We will introduce a similar criterion which bases on a pairwise consideration of the transactions.

Let us consider the following dynamic scenario. Let $\tau^\star$ be the dynamically growing transaction system containing all transactions which have been or are currently known to the scheduler. Let $\tau \subseteq \tau^\star$ be the subset of transactions which are currently known to the scheduler. A transaction T_i is called **forgotten**, if $T_i \in \tau^\star \setminus \tau$. Each schedule we will consider then is a prefix of a schedule of $\tau^\star$; let $s^\star$ be such a current prefix. A transaction T_i is called **finished**, if $T_i \in \tau$ and all actions of T_i are contained in $s^\star$. A transaction $T_i \in \tau$ can be forgotten, i.e. T_i is deleted from τ, if T_i is finished and for each other transaction $T_j \in \tau$ there holds:

> if there is a direct conflict point (A_{ip}, A_{jq}) in plane (T_i, T_j), then either A_{ip} has been executed before A_{jq}, i.e. $s^\star = \ldots A_{ip} \ldots A_{jq} \ldots$, or A_{jq} has not been executed up to the current moment.

Algorithm dPAL

Let $\tau = \{T_1, \ldots, T_{d-1}\}$ be the set of currently known transactions.

Whenever there is a new transaction (issued by a user) $T_d \notin \tau$, perform the following steps:

(1) As long as there exists a transaction $T_i \in \tau$ which can be forgotten, erase T_i from τ.

(2) Add T_d to $L\tau$ using one iteration of step (2) of iPAL.

End of Algorithm dPAL

dPAL contains a problem which could not occur under iPAL: we have to augment transactions which might have already started their execution by lock operations. However, we introduce only lock operations acting in the plane of the new transaction T_d that has not been started yet. Hence, we can position lock/unlock operations anywhere in transactions $LT_i, i \neq d$, without violating legality of the schedule s^*.

Theorem 6.1: dPAL is safe.

Proof: Assume dPAL is not safe. Then there exists a schedule s^* such that $D(s^*)$ contains a cycle, say $T_1 \rightarrow T_2 \rightarrow \ldots \rightarrow T_k \rightarrow T_1$. Consider the moment the arc $T_i \rightarrow T_j$ causing the cycle has to be introduced since an action A_{jx} is to be executed. Then, since iPAL is safe (with respect to the transactions in τ), at that moment the cycle contains a transaction T_l which was already forgotten. Hence, the cycle contains a path $T_i \rightarrow T_j \rightarrow \ldots \rightarrow T_l$. But this is a contradiction, since T_l already is forgotten.

■

Let us return to the discussion of Figure 10. We claimed that the serializable schedule s, which could not be allowed by iPAL, is allowed by dPAL. The reason is that after processing W_2c T_2 is finished and since W_2b has already been executed but W_1b has not, T_2 can be forgotten. If then T_3 is issued and iPAL is performed on T_1 and T_3, plane (T_1, T_3) will contain only one (direct) conflict point. Thus, no locks are introduced and the schedule s is allowed.

Finally, can dPAL be modified in the same way to become free from deadlock as iPAL? The answer is no. Assume the situation shown in Figure 8 occurs during runtime, i.e. schedule s_{12} has already reached the indicated position in plane (T_1, T_2). Then clearly, after having processed T_3, we cannot shift operation lv_1 in LT_1 to the left any more. Hence, we can run into the deadlock situation characterized in the figure.

7. Conclusion

In this paper we have shown that the approach of Pre–Analysis Locking is feasible for online scheduling, as well. If transactions have conflicting actions as characterized in section 4, the potential degree of concurrency under dPAL will be higher than under a 2PL policy. However, further work in comparing the PAL and 2PL families of locking policies including simulation studies surely is necessary.

Online scheduler must have efficient time bounds. In Lausen et al. (1986) we have derived the rough upper time bound $O(n^2 \log n + e^2)$ for PAL, where n is the total number of actions of the transactions of the given transaction system, and e is the number of edges of the so called conflict point graph, which is the undirected graph constructed from the direct conflict points between the transactions of the transaction system. By applying similar arguments we can derive the rough upper bound of iPAL $O(n^2 \log n + d^2 e)$. The difference stems from the iterative approach used by iPAL, however in the worst case, $d^2 = e$. Thus PAL and iPAL both are polynomial algorithms having the same upper time bound.

For online scheduling we are interested in the time amound needed for processing one transactions by dPAL. Since dPAL containes only one iteration of iPAL for locking the current transaction, we conjecture that for processing one transaction $O(m_d \log n + de)$ is an upper time bound of dPAL, where m_d is the number of actions of the current transaction. We emphazise that this time amount is needed only once for each transaction before the transaction starts its execution. Therefore we believe, that efficient implementations of dPAL are possible by using the power of current multiprocessor computer systems.

References

Bayer, R., Heller, H., Reiser, A. (1980), "Parallelism and recovery in database systems," *ACM Trans. Database Syst.* **5**, 139–156.

Beeri, C., Bernstein, P.A., Goodman, N., Lai, M.Y., Shasha, D.E. (1983), "A concurrency control theory for nested transactions," Proc. 2nd ACM SIGACT–SIGOPS Symp. on Principles of Distributed Computing

Eswaran, K.P., Gray, J.N., Lorie, R.A., and Traiger, I.L. (1976), "The notions of consistency and predicate locks in a database system," *Comm. Assoc. Comput. Mach.* **19**, 624–633.

Kedem, Z., and Silberschatz, A. (1980), "Non–two phase locking protocols with shared and exclusive locks," Proc. Int. Conf. Very Large Databases.

Korth, H.F. (1983), "Locking primitives in a database system," *J. Assoc. Comput. Mach.* bf 30, 55–79.

Lausen, G., Soisalon-Soininen, E., and Widmayer, P. (1985), "Pre–Analysis Locking: a safe and deadlock free locking policy," Proc. Int. Conf. Very Large Databases.

Lausen, G., Soisalon-Soininen, E., and Widmayer, P. (1986), "Pre–Analysis Locking," *Information and Control* to appear 1986.

Lipski, W., and Papadimitriou, C.H. (1981), "A fast algorithm for testing for safety and detecting deadlocks in locked transaction systems," *Journal of Algorithms* **2**, 211–226.

Ottmann, Th., Soisalon-Soininen, E., and Wood, D. (1984), "On the definition and computation of rectilinear convex hulls," *Information Sciences* **33**, 157–171.

Papadimitriou, C.H. (1979), "Serializability of concurrent database updates," *J. Assoc. Comput. Mach.* **26**, 631–653.

Papadimitriou, C.H. (1983), "Concurrency control by locking," *SIAM J. Comput.* **12**, 215–226.

Schlageter, G. (1978), "Process synchronization in database systems," *ACM Trans. Database Syst.* **3**, 248–271.

Silberschatz, A., and Kedem, Z. (1980), "Consistency in hierarchical database systems," *J. Assoc. Comput. Mach.* **27**), 72–80.

Weikum, G. (1986), "A theoretical foundation of multilevel concurrency control," ACM SIGACT–SIGMOD Symp. on Principles of Database Systems.

Yannakakis, M. (1982), "A theory of safe locking policies," *J. Assoc. Comput. Mach.* **29**, 718–740.

QUERY PROCESSING IN INCOMPLETE LOGICAL DATABASES

Nadine Lerat.
Laboratoire de Recherche en Informatique
U.A. 410 du C.N.R.S. "Al Khowarizmi"
Université de Paris-Sud, Centre d'Orsay
Bât. 490, 91405 Orsay Cédex, France

Abstract

An incomplete database T combines two types of information about the real world modeled by the database : (a) the relational database with null values ("value not known") represented by axioms of a First Order Theory T_0 and (b) the data dependencies that are known to be satisfied in the real world. For a given set of dependencies (functional and inclusion dependencies), a chase process transforms in two steps ("forward" and "backward" chase) type (b) information into an equivalent type (a) form. This yields a new first order theory T_1 ; for a class Γ of queries (subclass of monotone queries) the evaluation on T and on T_1 are equivalent. A technique involving both algebraic and theorem-proving methods provides for a sound and complete evaluation of the query.

INTRODUCTION

Logic provides a sound basis for a proper treatment and understanding of incomplete information and a ***uniform framework*** for databases since it can be used for query languages, performing deductive searches, handling negative information...etc... Hence, in section 1, we consider the formalization of relational databases with null values by a first ordér theory T_0 as in [Rei3] (i.e. a theory containing axioms of specific types). This theory T_0 models the extensional data which reflects the current state of the world.

However, we may consider another kind of information about the real world such as integrity constraints or data dependencies. This intentional data describes general properties of the real world.
For instance, functional and inclusion dependencies can be taken into account by adding to the theory the sentences of first order logic expressing them. In this situation, data dependencies are inference rules and they have an influence on the process of query answering.

Yet, seeking for efficiency when large amount of data is involved, we would like to avoid applying directly costly theorem proving techniques. Therefore, since intentional data has a completely different format than tuples and will require an inference mechanism for query processing, we transform the data given in extensional and intentional form into extensional form only.

This is performed by adapting the usual chase procedure described in [Ull] to our logical approach. This transformation does not preserve all the information of the original data but correct evaluation is ensured for a class of queries to specify. That is to say that the corruption of information introduced by the transformation cannot be discovered if we restrict ourselves to such queries.

In section 2, we describe the usual chase process in our proof-theoretic approach. A new first order theory $chase_{\Sigma}(T_0)$ belonging to the type specified in [Rei3] is constructed. Positive queries are correctly evaluated over this theory and we can "forget" about data dependencies as far as positive queries are concerned. The answer can be computed either by automated theorem proving techniques [Rei4] or (which usually proves more efficient) by algebraic bottom-up methods [Imi].

In section 3, we construct the first order theory T_1 that approximates the original information in the best possible way without entailing any inference mechanism within the theory Although no extra complexity is added for query processing, the class of queries correctly evaluated is extended (some negative selection conditions are permitted). We describe a practical way of evaluating these queries that combines algebraic and theorem-proving tools. Such a mixed method does not contradict our previous remarks since theorem proving tehniques are not used straightforwardly : first an algebraic evaluation retrieves a set of candidate answers and in a second step theorem proving tools are used on this restricted set for discarding some of these answers.

The proofs of the theorems quoted here will be given in the full paper.

1. REITER'S PROOF-THEORETIC APPROACH

Whenever some information for a given tuple of a relation is missing, a special symbol called a ***null value*** is introduced. This symbol can be interpreted in several ways (value *does not exist* —[LL] proposes a proper treatment of this kind of null —, value *exists* but is *unknown*...). In this paper, a null value will be interpreted as "value exists but is presently unknown".

In Reiter's proof-theoretic approach, a relational database with null values is represented by a theory T whose axioms are expressed in the first order predicate calculus language (A, W) whose alphabet A contains Skolem constants $\alpha, \beta, \gamma, \ldots$ A Skolem constant α models the concept of a null value since information of the type $\exists x\ P(x)$ will be represented in the theory by $P(\alpha)$ (Skolemization process). A *distinguished binary predicate* E stands for equality.

The theory $T \subseteq W$ contains only the following axioms :

1/ Let $c_1,..,c_n$ be the constants and $\alpha_1,..,\alpha_p$ the Skolem constants of A. Then, T contains the *domain closure axiom* :

$$(\forall x)\ [\ E(x,c_1) \vee .. \vee E(x,c_n) \vee E(x,\alpha_1) \vee .. \vee E(x,\alpha_p)]$$

2/ T contains the *unique name axioms* $\neg\ E(c_i,c_j)\ \ \forall\ 1 \leq i < j \leq n$

T *may* contain some additional information of the type

$$\neg E(c_i,\alpha_j) \quad 1\leq i\leq n,\ 1\leq j\leq p \quad \text{or} \quad \neg E(\alpha_i,\alpha_j) \quad 1\leq i<j\leq p$$

3/ T contains the ***axioms of equality*** : reflexivity, commutativity, transitivity and Leibniz' substitution principle.

4/ For each predicate P of arity n of A distinct from E, T contains exactly one formula, called the ***extension axiom*** of P :

$$(\forall x)P(x) \equiv [E(x,t_1)\vee..\vee E(x,t_r)]$$

where t_i are n-tuples of constants or Skolem constants of A.

Such a theory will be said to be "friendly" since queries can be evaluated easily by the algorithm defined in [Rei4]. No unique name axiom involves any Skolem constant α so that α should model a completely or partially (depending whether additional information of the type $\neg E(\alpha,c_i)$ or $\neg E(\alpha,\alpha_i)$ is given in the theory) unknown value. In what follows, for a theory T we will only specify the extension axioms of its predicates and the additional information it may contain about Skolem constants (represented by greek letters), the other axioms will be understood.

A query is any expression of the form $< x \mid W(x) >$ where x denotes the set $x_1,..,x_n$ of variables of A and $W(x)\in W$ is a wff whose free variables are among $x_1,..,x_n$. The answer for a query,as in [Imi], specifies ***what is known*** about Q(x), *i.e.* if the database consists of the formula $R(a,b)\vee R(c,d)$ and the query is $Q(x) \equiv \{ x \mid (\exists y)\ R(x,y)\}$ then, in our approach the answer will be $Q(a)\vee Q(c)$. Therefore, if L(Q) denotes a set of formulas in which Q appears as a predicate symbol, the answer for a query $Q(x)=<x \mid W(x)>$ is given by :

Definition : A wff of L(Q), φ, is an answer to the query Q(x) if $\varphi = \bigvee_{i=1}^{i=p} Q(c^i)$

$$\text{and} \quad T \vdash \bigvee_{i=1}^{i=p} W(c^i)$$

2. INCORPORATING KNOWLEDGE GIVEN BY A SET OF DEPENDENCIES

Let's consider T_0 a theory, as defined in section 1, formalizing a database with null values and Σ a set of data dependencies. For the moment, we restrict ourselves to a set Σ of functional dependencies.

A FD $X \to Y$ holding on predicate P is denoted $P: X \to Y$.
As noticed in [Nic], this FD can be written as a sentence of first order logic $(\forall t)(\forall s)\ (P(t) \wedge P(s) \wedge E(t[X],s[X]) \implies E(t[Y],s[Y]))$

We denote $Sent(\Sigma)$ the set of sentences of first order logic representing the functional dependencies of Σ.

Definition : If $T = T_0 \cup Sent(\Sigma)$ is consistent, then we say that the initial theory T_0 **satisfies** the set of dependencies Σ.

The theory T has no longer the "friendly structure" defined in section 1 and the FDs of Σ must be used as inference rules for query processing. Therefore, we define a chase process yielding a theory $chase_\Sigma(T_0)$ which has this "friendly structure". On this "chased" theory, some queries (positive queries) can be algebraically evaluated disregarding the set of dependencies Σ, which is of particular interest when large amount of data is involved.
Let's consider, for instance, the theory T_0 in which the extension of predicate P is represented by the following instance :

NAME	ADDRESS	AGE
Dupont	Paris	α
Dupont	β	26
γ	London	32

and the dependency $\Sigma = \{ NAME \to AGE \}$
Consider the query $Q = \{ x, y : P(x,y,26) \}$ which retrieves in the database the name and address of 26 year old people.
No relational algebra expression f correctly evaluates this query on the theory T_0 since the information α=26 is induced by the FD.

The chase process incorporates this information within the extension of predicate P by replacing every occurrence of α by '26' in the axioms of the theory and by removing α from the domain.

Then, in $chase_\Sigma(T_0)$ the extension of P is represented by :

NAME	ADDRESS	AGE
Dupont	Paris	26
Dupont	β	26
γ	London	32

and the answer for Q is correctly computed on this theory by the relational algebra expression $f = \Pi_{[NAME,ADDRESS]}(\sigma_{AGE=26})$
i.e. $\| Q \|_{T_0 \cup Sent(\Sigma)} = \| Q \|_{chase_\Sigma(T_0)} = f(\, chase_\Sigma(T_0)\,)$

Hence, the chase procedure is performed as follows. All the equalities between symbols induced by the FDs on the original theory T_0 are derived. Two elements x and y of the domain D of T_0 are equivalent if the equality x=y has been derived from $T_0 \cup Sent(\Sigma)$. It determines a set of equivalence classes on D ; a unique representative x_i is selected in each class C_i and in all the axioms of T_0 every occurrence of the element x of C_i will be replaced by an occurrence of x_i. It yields a theory $chase_\Sigma(T_0)$ whose domain D' contains only the x_i's ($D' \subseteq D$).
In order to choose x_i in C_i, we proceed as follows :

- if there exists exactly one constant c in C_i, then x_i=c. (if there are at least two constants c and c' in C_i, then $T_0 \cup Sent(\Sigma)$ is inconsistent).
- otherwise, we define a partial function $p(x) = 1 - [\, not(x) \div N \,]$ for Skolem constants, where N is the number of elements of the domain of the theory (constants *and* Skolem constants) and $0 \leq not(x) \leq N\text{-}1$ is the number of distinct inequality axioms of T_0 involving x (not(x) is all the smaller as x is better specified).

To minimize the number of modifications of the axioms of the theory, we choose x_i such that $p(x_i)$ is minimal. Moreover, we assume that a total order relation R has been initially defined over the set of Skolem constants. Thus, if for two elements x and y of C_i p(x)=p(y) is the minimal value of p on C_i, we will keep x_i=x if x R y. This assumption simply ensures that the chase procedure described above has the Church-Rosser property ; i.e. all methods of performing the chase terminate with the same result.

Besides, during the chase we keep in a set called T_G all the equalities $x=x_i$ that have been used to decrease the domain (x is an element of C_i which is no longer in D'). This set of formulae works as an historic of all the operations performed over the initial theory.

Chase Algorithm $\quad chase_{\Sigma}(T_0) := T_0$;

Consider $L = \{ x : T_0 \not\vdash E(x,y)$ and $T_0 \cup Sent(\Sigma) \vdash E(x,y)$ for some $y\}$

Let $x_1 = inf(L)$ be the element of L, minimal for the partial function p and for the total order. We denote $L(x_1)$ the subset of the domain of the theory T_0 $\quad L(x_1) = \{ y ; T_0 \cup \Sigma \vdash E(x_1,y) \} - \{x_1\}$

$L(x_1)$ is the equivalence class of x_1. Let $\varphi(x_1) = inf(L(x_1))$.

- if x_1 and $\varphi(x_1)$ are both constants, we add $E(x_1,\varphi(x_1))$ as an axiom of $chase_{\Sigma}(T_0)$. Since $\neg E(x_1,\varphi(x_1))$ is already an axiom of $chase_{\Sigma}(T_0)$, $chase_{\Sigma}(T_0)$ will be inconsistent.
- if either x_1 or $\varphi(x_1)$ are Skolem constants, every y in $L(x_1)$ is replaced by the minimal element of $L(x_1)$ —i.e. x_1 —as follows :

a/ * in every extension axiom of a predicate P of T_0, each occurrence of y is replaced by an occurrence of x_1.

* the term involving y is deleted from the domain closure axiom.

b/ if $T_0 \vdash \neg E(y,z)$ and $T_0 \not\vdash \neg E(x_1,z)$, then we add $\neg E(x_1,z)$ to the set of unique name axioms and if x_1 is a Skolem constant $p(x_1)$ is modified ($p(x_1)$ can only decrease, thus it remains minimal).

c/ $T_G = T_G \cup \{E(x_1,y)\}$.

(T_G is assumed to be empty at the beginning of the chase).

d/ when all the equalities in $L(x_1)$ have been considered :

$$L = L - L(x_1)$$

We iterate the process, with $x_2 = inf(L)$.

Eventually, we have constructed two sets of formulae :

- $\text{chase}_\Sigma(T_0)$: the new theory where all the null values of T_0 redundant w.r.t. the set of dependencies Σ have been deleted.
- T_G : it keeps track of a null value which has been eliminated from the domain and tells us to which element of the reduced domain it has been equated.

Theorem 1 : $T_0 \cup \text{Sent}(\Sigma) \vdash \square \iff \text{chase}_\Sigma(T_0) \vdash \square$
(if the original theory T_0 is inconsistent with the set of dependencies SIGMA, the chased theory will also be inconsistent).

Church-Rosser-ness and complexity analysis

The chase procedure that we described is a finite Church-Rosser replacement system, that is, all methods of performing the chase terminate with the same result.

Theorem ([Hon]) : If k is the number of tuples in the extension of predicate P of T_0 (assuming that P is the only predicate of T_0 distinct from the equality predicate) and q the number of FDs of Σ (holding on P), then the chased structure can be computed in O(kq log kq) —i.e. in O(klogk), since in practice q is insignificant in comparison to k.

As underlined in [Gra], Honeyman extends the usual chase on tableaux to T-maps (variant of a tableau containing constants instead of distinguished symbols). The chase computes equivalence classes and the resulting T-map is obtained as follows : an equivalence class is represented by its minimal element when defined and by the symbol † otherwise (i. e. when the class contains two distinct constants). Hence, the origin of inconsistency —if any —is lost in the T-map resulting from the chase whereas in our process it actually remains within the theory. However, this slight difference does not affect the complexity result above which is still relevant for our chase process.

Answering a query on the new structure $\text{chase}_\Sigma(T_0)$, T_G

We have to handle a more complex structure composed of an "extended relational theory" as defined in [Rei2] [$\text{chase}_\Sigma(T_0)$] and of a set of general statements [T_G]. Henceforth, a question arises : **what kind of answer does the user expect ?**

Unlike in the model-theoretic approach where nulls are artificially introduced *à postériori* to store incomplete information provided by the user, in our setting the user ***knows about*** all the elements of the initial domain. Therefore, we believe that it is not enough to provide as an answer for a query the set of tuples of $chase_\Sigma(T_0)$ that satisfy the query. Indeed, the answer should also contain the subset of all the equalities of T_G involving elements appearing in these tuples.

Definition The answer for a query in $chase_\Sigma(T_0)$, T_G will be a set of sentences, where each sentence is the conjunction of two first order logic subformulas :

* the answer for the query in $chase_\Sigma(T_0)$ as defined in section 1.
* the conjunction of all the equality statements of T_G concerning elements appearing in the tuples of the first part.

e.g. To illustrate this definition, let's consider the theory containing the following facts : $\{ R(a,b) \vee R(c,d),\ R(a',b'),\ R(a',\alpha) \}$ and satisfying the dependency $\Sigma = \{ R : A \rightarrow B \}$. The chased database contains the axioms $\{ R(a,b) \vee R(c,d),\ R(a',b') \}$ and the set of equalities is $T_G = \{ E(\alpha,b') \}$.

Then, the answer for the query $Q(x) = \{ y \mid \exists x\ R(x,y) \}$ is the set of sentences $\{ Q(b) \vee Q(d),\ Q(b') \wedge E(\alpha,b') \}$. Hence, the second sentence not only provides the answer $Q(b')$ but it also tells the user that the element α he introduced at the beginning turned out to be redundant with b' w.r.t. the set of dependencies Σ. The type of answer defined above allows more informative answers (see [Jan]).

Correct evaluation of queries

As the chase process integrates only a part of the information given by the dependencies, the following theorem determines a class of queries for which $T_0 \cup Sent(\Sigma)$ on the one hand, and $chase_\Sigma(T_0), T_G$ in the other hand provide equivalent answers.

A query $Q(x) = < x \mid W(x) >$ is positive if the formula $W(x)$ is a wff built from logical connectives and quantifiers $\wedge$, $\vee$, $\exists$, $\forall$. That is to say that in the relational algebra expression evaluating the query no difference operator nor negation within a selection operator is allowed.

Theorem 2: The class of positive queries is correctly evaluated on the theory $chase_{\Sigma}(T_0)$

As $chase_{\Sigma}(T_0)$ is an extended relational theory, we can use Reiter's query evaluation algorithm proposed in [Rei2]. This algorithm is sound and complete in the case of positive queries. Henceforth, as far as positive queries are concerned, we can forget about the data dependencies of Σ ; i.e. we may evaluate these queries directly over the "chased" structure $chase_{\Sigma}(T_0),T_G$ having equivalent correct answers guaranteed.

Efficient query evaluation

Reiter's algorithm provides for a **top-down** method —at the level of description —for evaluating a query Q, i.e. the evaluation is performed inductively on the complexity of Q. This finds an algebraic expression equivalent to Q *during* the query evaluation process and elements of the answer for the query are retrieved **one-at-a-time** by resolution based techniques (such as PROLOG).

Yet, as in Data Bases Management Systems we usually deal with a large amount of data stored on external memory devices, algebraic **bottom-up** techniques like relational algebra turn out to be easier to control and optimize than theorem-proving tools. It consists in finding first an algebraic expression f_Q equivalent to Q, and then in evaluating it over tables representing the extensions of the predicates of the theory. The following theorem provides for a **practical** and **efficient** way of evaluating some positive queries.

Theorem Let T_V be the set of V-tables. A V-table ([IL1]) allows to represent incomplete information given as null values : it consists in tuples containing variables (or Skolem constants) —playing the part of null values —and constants.

As the theory T_0 contains no disjunctive data of the form $P(a,b) \vee P(c,d)$, the algebra $< T_V , PCS^+ >$ correctly computes answers for the class of positive queries.

P, C, S^+ stand respectively for the operators of projection, cartesian product and positive condition. A positive condition is a wff built up from equality statements, conjunction and disjunction.

This theorem is another expression of theorem 1 of [Imi] and we refer to this paper for a proof.

3. COMPLETE EVALUATION OF A LARGER SET OF QUERIES

Up to now, the functional dependencies have only been applied in a "forward manner" for deriving the equality of symbols. They may however be applied in a "backward manner", which produces (a disjunction of) inequalities between symbols. For instance, if the axioms P(Dupont,Paris), P(α,London) satisfy the functional dependency P : NAME $\rightarrow$ ADDRESS, from the unique name axiom $\neg$ E(Paris,London) we can infer the additional "negative" information $\neg$ E(α,Dupont) on the Skolem constant α. In a model-theoretic setting, this additional (negative) knowledge cannot be represented in the chase process (unless you consider sophisticated tables such as conditional tables... but then, the complexity of query evaluation is highly increased, especially when large amount of data is considered). Indeed, our proof-theoretic approach constitutes a more adequate frame for taking this kind of information into account and entails minor extra complexity for query processing.

Consider the extension of predicate P in theory T_0 represented by

NAME	ADDRESS
α	Paris
Smith	London
Smith	β

and the dependency P : NAME $\rightarrow$ ADDRESS .

Executing the chase, we get T_G = { E(β,London)} and in the new theory

$chase_\Sigma(T_0)$, the extension of P is represented by

NAME	ADDRESS
α	Paris
Smith	London

Yet, as $\neg E(\alpha,Smith) \vee E(Paris,London)$ is one of the sentences of $Sent(\Sigma)$ and as $T_0 \vdash \neg E(Paris,London)$, we infer :

$$T_0 \cup Sent(\Sigma) \vdash \neg E(\alpha,Smith).$$

Therefore, we integrate this negative statement to yield a new theory T_1, hoping that T_1 will provide for a better approximation of $T_0 \cup Sent(\Sigma)$ (meaning that it will support a larger set of queries) without entailing too much extra computational complexity. For instance, for the query $Q(x) = \{ x : \exists z\ P(x,z) \wedge x \neq Smith \}$ we get for each theory : $ANS_{T_0 \cup Sent(\Sigma)}(Q) = \{ Q(\alpha)\}$, $ANS_{chase_\Sigma(T_0),T_G}(Q) = \{\}$ and $ANS_{T_1,T_G}(Q) = \{ Q(\alpha)\}$.

where $ANS_T(Q)$ denotes the answer for query Q in the theory T.

Definition : The theory T_1 (that we could also denote $chase_\Sigma^{-1}(chase_\Sigma(T_0))$) contains all the axioms of $chase_\Sigma(T_0)$ and :

if $T_0 \cup Sent(\Sigma) \vdash \neg E(\alpha,\beta)$ then $T_1 := T_1 \cup \{ \neg E(\alpha,\beta)\}$.

Naturally, whenever an axiom of the type $\neg E(\alpha,\beta)$ is added to T_1 the partial functions of α and β are updated.

We stress here that strictly disjunctive information of the type $\neg E(\alpha,\beta) \vee E(\gamma,\delta)$ (this disjunction cannot be reduced since $T_0 \cup Sent(\Sigma) \nvdash \neg E(\gamma,\delta)$) has not been taken into account in T_1. However, since for evaluating queries this kind of information would entail a inference mechanism within the theory, the definition of T_1 above limits the complexity of query evaluation on this theory.

Although the transformation of $T_0 \cup Sent(\Sigma)$ into T_1 is not

information preserving, we look for a class of queries that would be correctly evaluated on T_1. We provide for an efficient query evaluation process for a query in that class.
Let's consider the class Γ of queries $Q(x) = <x \mid W(x)>$ with $W(x) = W_1(x) \wedge C(x)$, where $Q_1(x)=<x \mid W_1(x)>$ is a positive query and where $C(x)$ is a condition only involving free variables of Q such that

$$C(x) = \wedge (\vee \neg E(x_i,x_j) \vee \vee \neg E(x_i,c_i))$$

where x_i, x_j are variables of x and c_i is an element of the domain.

Intuitively, the condition $C(x)$ enables us to select from the tuples on NAME and ADDRESS that satisfy the positive query Q_1 ('retrieve the names and addresses of all the people in the database') people whose name is not Smith (or whose address is not Paris). Hence, negation is now allowed in the selection operator and Γ is a significant subclass of the set of monotonous queries (queries defined as Q above but where the condition $C(x)$ is arbitrary).

Theorem 3 : Any query Q belonging to the class Γ defined above is correctly evaluated on the theory T_1.

For evaluating efficiently a query $Q(x) = <x \mid W_1(x) \wedge C(x)>$ of class Γ, let $Q_1(x)$ correspond to the query $<x \mid W_1(x)>$ and $Q_2(x)$ to $<x \mid C(x)>$.

$$\| Q(x) \| = \| Q_1(x) \| \cap \| Q_2(x) \|$$

As stated in [Imi], we are able to approximate the real value of the answer to the query Q from both sides, using V-tables, constructing lower and upper approximations

$$\| Q(x) \|_L \subseteq \| Q(x) \| \subseteq \| Q(x) \|_U = \| Q_1(x) \|$$

where $\| Q(x) \|_L$ is the result of computing the arbitrary PCUS-expression f_Q, corresponding to the query, on the V-table(s) corresponding to the theory $chase_\Sigma(T_0)$ when all the elements of the domain D' of $chase_\Sigma(T_0)$ are treated as pairwise uncomparable elements (i.e. $\neg E(a,b)$ is assumed to be false, for any two elements a, b of D'). Besides, there exists an algebraic expression f_{Q_1} which correctly computes $\| Q_1(x) \|$.

The only formulas that need to be tested are those which represent

$\| Q \|_U \setminus \| Q \|_L$. For every $Q_1(c)$in this set, we examine whether $T_1 \vdash C(c)$ using a theorem-proving technique. If so, the answer is kept in $\| Q(x) \|$ and we eventually obtain a correct evaluation of query Q.

This technique reduces the accesses to external devices. Moreover, we can extend it to queries involving arbitrary conditions C(x). In that case, the theory T_1 provides for a *sound* but no longer *complete* evaluation of the query.

i.e.

$$ANS_{T_1,T_G}(Q) \subseteq ANS_{T_0 \cup Sent(\Sigma)}(Q) \subseteq ANS_{T_1,T_G}(Q_1)$$

That is, for every $Q_1(c)$ in $\| Q \|_U \setminus \| Q \|_L$: if $T_1 \vdash C(c)$ then $Q(c) \in \| Q(x) \|$, if $T_1 \vdash \neg C(c)$ the tuple c is discarded from the answer, otherwise we examine whether $T_0 \cup Sent(\Sigma) \vdash C(c)$ and keep Q(c) in the answer if it is true.

In order to illustrate the method proposed above, let's consider the theory T_0 in which the extension of predicate P is represented by the following instance :

NAME	ADDRESS	AGE
Smith	London	γ
α	Paris	γ
α	β	γ'
Smith	β'	γ''
α'	Paris	29

and the dependencies $\Sigma = \{$ NAME $\rightarrow$ ADDRESS , NAME $\rightarrow$ AGE $\}$
The chased theory is represented by the table

NAME	ADDRESS	AGE
Smith	London	γ
α	Paris	γ
α'	Paris	29

and $T_G = \{ E(\beta,\text{Paris}), E(\beta',\text{London}), E(\gamma',\gamma), E(\gamma'',\gamma) \}$

Moreover, the theory T_1 contains the additional information : $\neg E(\alpha,Smith)$ and $\neg E(\alpha',Smith)$.

Let $Q = \{x,y,z : P(x,y,z) \wedge (\neg E(x,Smith) \vee E(y,\beta')) \wedge E(z,\gamma)\}$ be the query. As β' is not in D' (i.e. β' is not in the domain of T_1), to evaluate the query we replace β' by its representative in D' i.e. London. The corresponding positive query is $Q_1 = \{x,y,z : P(x,y,z) \wedge E(z,\gamma)\}$ and $f_{Q_1}(P) = \sigma_{AGE=\gamma}(P)$.

i.e. $ANS_{T_1,T_G}(Q_1) = \{Q_1(Smith,London,\gamma), Q_1(x,Paris,\gamma)\}$

$\| Q \|_L = \| x,y,z : P(x,y,z) \wedge E(y,London)) \wedge E(z,\gamma) \| = Q(Smith,London,\gamma)$

We now examine whether $T_1 \vdash \neg E(\alpha,Smith) \vee E(Paris,London)$ (since the answer $(Smith,London,\gamma)$ is already represented in $\| Q \|_L$, we have only to examine the second tuple). As $T_1 \vdash \neg E(\alpha,Smith)$, the tuple $(\alpha,Paris,\gamma)$ also belongs to the response.

Hence, although the query Q does not belong to the class Γ, Q is correctly evaluated on the theory T_1 and the sentences

$$Q(Smith,London,\gamma) \wedge E(\beta',London) \wedge E(\gamma',\gamma) \wedge E(\gamma'',\gamma)$$
$$\text{and} \quad Q(\alpha,Paris,\gamma) \wedge E(\beta,Paris) \wedge E(\gamma',\gamma) \wedge E(\gamma'',\gamma)$$

correspond to $\| Q \|$.

also belongs to the response.

Hence, although the query Q does not belong to the class Γ, Q is correctly evaluated on the theory T_1 and the sentences

$$Q(Smith,London,\gamma) \wedge E(\beta',London) \wedge E(\gamma',\gamma) \wedge E(\gamma'',\gamma)$$
$$\text{and} \quad Q(\alpha,Paris,\gamma) \wedge E(\beta,Paris) \wedge E(\gamma',\gamma) \wedge E(\gamma'',\gamma)$$

In fact, with the method described here T_1 correctly evaluates a larger class than the class Γ stated above but no characterisation of this class independant of the set of dependencies Σ can be given.

Generalization to a set of functional and inclusion dependencies

Inclusion dependencies (INDs) are of great interest for database design. An IND can state, for instance, that every MANAGER entry of the instance of predicate P appears as an EMPLOYEE entry of the instance of

predicate Q (every manager is an employee).
This inclusion dependency is denoted P[MANAGER] $\subseteq$ Q[EMPLOYEE] and it can be expressed in first order logic by $\forall x \; P(x) \Rightarrow \exists y \; Q(x, y)$ if Q is a predicate on { EMPLOYEE, SALARY}.

The chase procedure for a set of INDs, described in [JK], simply consist in applying recursively the following rule :

For each IND of Σ $R[A_1,..,A_m] \subseteq S[B_1,..,B_m]$

Let r and s be the relations over R and S respectively.

Then for every tuple t of r we add to relation s the tuple t' such that the components of t' are $t[A_1],..,t[A_m]$ on $B_1,..,B_m$ and new undistinguished variables on the other attributes over which predicate S ranges.

For more simplicity we choose the chase described as the 0-chase in [JK], i.e. we always add a new tuple to relation s even if we already had t' in s satisfying $t'[B_1,..,B_m]=t[A_1,..,A_m]$.

We will now try to give a characterization of a set Σ of INDs which entails no infinite generation while performing the chase described above.

Definition : Let Σ be a set of INDs and D the database scheme.
We call Σ-representation the graph G whose nodes are the relation schemes and which contains the oriented arc $R \rightarrow S$ if there exists in Σ an inclusion dependency $R[A_1,..,A_m] \subseteq S[B_1,..,B_m]$.

Theorem Let D=<R,S,..> be a database scheme

Let Σ be a set of INDs and G be the Σ-representation

Then the database resulting from the chase is *finite* if and only if G is *acyclic*.

Hence, for a set Σ of functional and inclusion dependencies, provided that the criteria of acyclicity given above is satisfied, the chase procedure terminates. Since inclusion dependencies are only tuple-generating dependencies the results of theorems 2 and 3 are still relevant in this case.

CONCLUSION

The chase process described here transforms a large amount of logically heterogenous data (facts reflecting the current state of the real world [extensional data] and data dependencies expressing time invariant properties of that world [intensional data]) into extensional form only. Although these two forms of information are not logically equivalent, there are undistinguishable for some subclass of queries. However, whereas theorem proving techniques —known to be inefficient when large knowledge bases are considered — are compulsory for processing the original data (the dependencies are used as inference rules), we have showed that data in the second form could be processed efficiently. Hence, we gain in efficiency what has formerly been lost in power of expression.

Our purpose is the same as in [Im85] ; yet, Imielinski studied this problem from a model-theoretic point of view. Thus, chasing V-tables he cannot perform the "backward" chase that we described in section 3. Hence, our proof-theoretic approach allows us to transform more intentional data into extensional form without entailing any inference mechanism. Indeed, the first order theory formalizing the database captures more information than V-tables without reaching the complexity of conditional tables for query evaluation. A large subclass of monotonous queries (negative conditions are allowed) can be evaluated without having to refer to the dependencies.

This chase procedure is likely to be generalisable to more general data dependencies (equality and tuple-generating dependencies). It provides for a balance between expressive power and complexity of query processing. We wish to study how these results modify when other cases of information incompleteness, such as disjunctive information, occur in the database.

REFERENCES

[Gra] M. H. Graham, A new proof that the chase is a Church-Rosser replacement system, June 1980.

[Grh] G. Grahne, Dependency satisfaction in databases with incomplete information. *Proc. 10th Symp. on Very Large Data Bases*, Singapore, Aug. 1984, 37-47.

[Hon] P. Honeyman, Testing Satisfaction of Functional Dependencies. *J. Assoc. Comput. Mach. 29*, 3(July 1982), 668-677.

[IL1] T. Imielinski, W. Lipski, Incomplete information in Relational Databases. *J. Assoc. Comput. Mach. 31*, 4(Oct. 1984), 761-791.

[IL2] T. Imielinski, W. Lipski, Dependencies in relational databases with incomplete information. To appear.

[Imi] T. Imielinski, On algebraic query processing in logical databases. In *Advances in Data Base Theory, vol 2* (H. Gallaire, J. Minker, J.-M. Nicolas, eds), Plenum Press, New York, 1984, 285-318.

[Im85] T. Imielinski, Abstraction in Query Processing. 1985.

[Jan] J. Janas, On the feasibility of informative answers. In *Advances in Database Theory, vol. 1* (H. Gallaire, J. Minker and J. M. Nicolas, eds), Plenum Press, New York, 1981, pp. 397-414.

[JK] D. S. Johnson and A. Klug, Testing Containment of Conjunctive Queries under Functional and Inclusion Dependencies. *J. Computer Syst. Sci. 28*, 167-189 (1984).

[LL] N. Lerat, W. Lipski, Non-applicable nulls. To appear in Theoretical Computer Science.

[Nic] J.-M. Nicolas, First order logic formalization for functional, multivalued, and mutual dependencies. *Proc. ACM SIGMOD Symp. on Management of Data*, 1978, 40-46.

[Rei1] R. Reiter, Towards a logical reconstruction of relational database theory. In *Conceptual Modelling : Perspectives from Artificial Intelligence, Databases and Programming Languages* (M. L. Brodie, J. Mylopoulos and J. Schmidt, eds), Springer-Verlag, to appear.

[Rei2] R. Reiter, A sound and sometimes complete query evaluation algorithm for relational databases with null values. *Techn. Rep.*, Dept. of Computer Science, Univ. of British Columbia, Vancouver, BC, June 1983.

Introduction to the Theory of Nested Transactions

Nancy Lynch
Massachusetts Institute of Technology
Cambridge, Mass.

Michael Merritt
A. T. and T. Bell Laboratories
Murray Hill, New Jersey

July 21, 1986

1. Introduction

This paper develops the foundation for a general theory of nested transactions. We present a simple formal model for studying concurrency and resiliency in a nested environment. This model has distinct advantages over the many alternatives, the greatest of which is the unification of a subject replete with formalisms, correctness conditions and proof techniques. The authors are presently engaged in an ambitious project to recast the substantial amount of work in nested transactions within this single intuitive framework. These pages contain the preliminary results of that project – a description of the model, and its use in stating and proving correctness conditions for two variations of a well-known algorithm.

The model is based on *I/O automata*, a simple formalization of communicating automata. It is not complex – it is easily presented in a few pages, and easy to understand, given a minimal background in automata theory. Each nested transaction and data object is modelled by a separate I/O automaton. These automata, the system *primitives*, issue requests to and receive replies from some *scheduler*, which is simply another I/O automaton. Simple syntactic constraints on the interactions of these automata ensure, for example, that no transaction requests the creation of the same child more than once. One scheduler, in this case the "serial scheduler", interacts with the transactions and objects in a particularly constrained way. The "serial schedules" of the primitives and the serial scheduler are the basis of our correctness conditions. Specifically, alternative schedulers are required to ensure that nested transaction automata individually have local schedules which they could have in a serial schedule. In essence, each scheduler must "fool" the transactions into believing that the system is executing in conjunction with the serial scheduler.

In the past ten years, an important and substantial body of work has appeared on the design and analysis of algorithms for implementing concurrency control and resiliency in database transaction systems [EGLT,RLS,BG,KS,Gr,LaS, etc.]. Among this has been a number of results dealing with nested transactions [R,Mo,LiS,LHJLSW,AM,BBGLS,BBG, etc.]. The present work does not replace these other contributions, but augments them by providing a unifying and mathematically tractable framework for posing and exploring a variety of questions. This previous work uses behavioral specifications of nested transactions, focusing on what nested transactions do, rather than what they are. By answering the question "What is a nested transaction?", I/O automata provide a powerful tool for understanding and reasoning about them.

Some unification is vitally important to further development in this field. The plethora and complexity of existing formalizations is a challenge to the most seasoned researcher. More critically, it belies the argument that nested transactions provide a clean and intuitive tool for organizing distributed databases and more general distributed applications. It is particularly important to provide an intuitive and precise description of nested transactions themselves, as in typical systems, these are the components which the application programmer must implement!

The remainder of this paper is organized as follows. The I/O automaton model is described in Section 2. The rest of the paper contains an extended example, which establishes correctness properties for two related lock-based concurrent schedulers.

Section 3 contains simple definitions for naming nested transactions and objects, and for specifying the operations (interactions) of these components. Simple syntactic restrictions on the orders of these operations are presented, and then a particular system of I/O automata is presented, describing the interactions of nested transactions and objects with a serial scheduler. The interface between the serial scheduler and the transactions provides a basis for the specification of correctness conditions for alternative schedulers. These schedulers would presumably be more efficient than the serial scheduler. The strongest correctness condition, "serial correctness," requires that *all* non-access transactions see serial behavior at their interface with the system. The second condition, "correctness for T_0," only requires that this serial interface be maintained at the interface of the system and the external world. These interfaces also provide simple descriptions of the environment in which nested transactions can be assumed to execute. A particular contribution is the clear and concise semantics of ABORT operations which arises naturally from this formalization. The section closes with some lemmas describing useful properties of serial systems.

Next, a lock-based concurrent system is presented. Section 4 contains a description of a special type of object, called a "resilient object", which is used in the concurrent system. Section 5 describes the remainder of the concurrent system, the "concurrent scheduler." This concurrent scheduler includes "lock manager" modules for all the objects; lock managers coordinate concurrent accesses.

Section 6 defines a system which is closely related to the concurrent system, the "weak concurrent system." This system preserves serial correctness for those transactions whose ancestors do not abort (i.e.. those that are not "orphans"). Since the root of the transaction tree, T_0, has no ancestor, weak concurrent systems are correct for T_0. Section 7 contains correctness theorems for concurrent and weak concurrent sytems; concurrent systems are serially correct, and weak concurrent systems are correct for T_0. The stronger condition is obtained for concurrent systems as a corollary to a result about weak concurrent systems.

It is interesting that the concurrent system algorithms are described in complete detail (essentially, in "pseudocode"), yet significant formal claims about their behavior can be stated clearly and easily. Despite the detailed level of presentation, the underlying model is general enough that the results apply to a wide range of implementations.

The style of the correctness proof is also noteworthy. It is a constructive proof, in that for each step of the weak concurrent system and each non-orphan transaction, an execution of the serial system is explicitly constructed. The transaction's local "view" in the constructed execution is identical to that in the original weak concurrent execution, establishing the correctness of the weak concurrent system. One may think of the weak concurrent system as maintaining consistent, parallel "world views" within which concurrent siblings execute. As siblings return to their parent, these parallel worlds are "merged" to form a single consistent view. The locking policy prevents collisions between different views at the shared data. This intuition is strongly supported and clarified by the correctness proof, which constructs the parallel views as different serial schedules consistent with each sibling's local history. Lemmas illustrate how these serial schedules can be merged as siblings return or abort to their parent.

Section 8 contains a discussion of the relationship of this work to previous results, and Section 9 contains an indication of the work that lies ahead.

This paper is a shortened version of a complete paper with the same title, available as a technical report from MIT or AT&T Bell Labs [LM]. Whereas the present paper omits many easy lemmas and straightforward proofs, the longer paper contains completely detailed proofs of all results.

2. Basic Model

In this section, we present the basic I/O automaton model, which is used to describe all components of our systems. This model consists of rather standard, possibly infinite-state, nondeterministic automata that have operation names associated with their state transitions. Communication among automata is described by identifying their operations. This model is very similar to models used by Milner, Hoare [Mi,Ho] and others. There are a few differences: first, we find it important to classify operations of any automaton or system of automata as either "input" or "output" operations, of that automaton or system, and we treat these two cases differently. Also, we allow identification of arbitrary numbers of operations from different automata, rather than just pairwise identification as considered in [Mi].

This paper is not intended to develop the basic model. For the general theory of I/O automata, including a unified treatment of finite and infinite behavior, we refer the reader to [LT]. In the present treatment of concurrent transaction systems, we only prove properties of finite behavior, so we only require a simple special case of the general model.

2.1. I/O Automata

All components in our systems, transactions, objects and schedulers, will be modelled by *I/O automata.* An I/O automaton $\mathcal{A}$ has components *states*($\mathcal{A}$), *start*($\mathcal{A}$), *out*($\mathcal{A}$), *in*($\mathcal{A}$), and *steps*($\mathcal{A}$). Here, *states*($\mathcal{A}$) is a set of states, of which a subset *start*($\mathcal{A}$) is designated as the set of start states. The next two components are disjoint sets: *out*($\mathcal{A}$) is the set of *output operations*, and *in*($\mathcal{A}$) is the set of *input operations.* The union of these two sets is the set of *operations* of the automaton. Finally, *steps*($\mathcal{A}$) is the transition relation of $\mathcal{A}$, which is a set of triples of the form (s',π,s), where s' and s are states, and π is an operation. This triple means that in state s', the automaton can atomically do operation π and change to state s. An element of the transition relation is called a *step* of $\mathcal{A}$.

The output operations are intended to model the actions that are triggered by the automaton itself, while the input operations model the actions that are triggered by the environment of the automaton. Our partitioning of operations into input and output indicates that each operation is only triggered in one place. We require the following condition.

Input Condition: For each input operation π and each state s', there exist a state s and a step (s',π,s).

This condition says that an I/O automaton must be prepared to receive any input operation at any time. This condition makes intuitive sense if we think of the input operations as being triggered externally. (In this paper, this condition serves mainly as a technical convenience, but in [LT], where infinite behavior is considered, it is critical.)

An *execution* of $\mathcal{A}$ is an alternating sequence $s_0,\pi_1, s_1,\pi_2,...$ of states and operations of $\mathcal{A}$; the sequence may be infinite, but if it is finite, it ends with a state. Furthermore, s_0 is in start($\mathcal{A}$), and each triple (s',π,s) which occurs as a consecutive subsequence is a step of $\mathcal{A}$. From any execution, we can extract the *schedule*, which is the subsequence of the execution consisting of operations only. Because transitions to different states may have the same operation, different executions may have the same schedule.

If S is any set of schedules (or property of schedules), then $\mathcal{A}$ is said to *preserve* S provided that the following holds. If $\alpha = \alpha'\pi$ is any schedule of $\mathcal{A}$, where π is an output operation, and α' is in S, then α is in S. That is, the automaton is not the first to violate the property described by S.

2.2. Composition of Automata

We describe systems as consisting of interacting components, each of which is an I/O automaton. It is convenient and natural to view systems as I/O automata, also. Thus, we define a composition operation for I/O automata, to yield a new I/O automaton.

A set of I/O automata may be composed to create a *system* $\mathcal{S}$, if all of the output operations are disjoint. (Thus, every output operation in $\mathcal{S}$ will be triggered by exactly one component.) The system $\mathcal{S}$ is itself an I/O automaton. A state of the composed automaton is a tuple of states, one for each component, and the start states are tuples consisting of start states of the components. The set of *operations* of $\mathcal{S}$, *ops*($\mathcal{S}$), is exactly the union of the sets of operations of the component automata. The set of *output operations* of $\mathcal{S}$, *out*($\mathcal{S}$), is likewise the union of the sets of output operations of the component automata. Finally, the set of *input operations* of $\mathcal{S}$, *in*($\mathcal{S}$), is *ops*($\mathcal{S}$) - *out*($\mathcal{S}$), the set of operations of $\mathcal{S}$ that are not output operations of $\mathcal{S}$. The output operations of a system are intended to be exactly those that are triggered by components of the system, while the input operations of a system are those that are triggered by the system's environment.

The triple (s',π,s) is in the transition relation of $\mathcal{S}$ if and only if for each component automaton $\mathcal{A}$, one of the following two conditions holds. Either π is an operation of $\mathcal{A}$, and the projection of the step onto $\mathcal{A}$ is a step of $\mathcal{A}$, or else π is not an operation of $\mathcal{A}$, and the states corresponding to $\mathcal{A}$ in the two tuples s' and s are identical. Thus, each operation of the composed automaton is an operation of a subset of the component automata. During an operation π of $\mathcal{S}$, each of the components which has operation π carries out the operation, while the remainder stay in the same state. Again, the operation π is an output operation of the composition if it is the output operation of a component – otherwise, π is an input operation of the composition.[1] An *execution* of a system is defined to be an execution of the automaton composed of the individual automata of the system. If α is a schedule of a system with component $\mathcal{A}$, then we denote by $\alpha|\mathcal{A}$ the subsequence of α containing all the operations of $\mathcal{A}$. Clearly, $\alpha|\mathcal{A}$ is a schedule of $\mathcal{A}$.

Lemma 1: Let α' be a schedule of a system $\mathcal{S}$, and let $\alpha = \alpha'\pi$, where π is an output operation of component $\mathcal{A}$. If $\alpha|\mathcal{A}$ is a schedule of $\mathcal{A}$, then α is a schedule of $\mathcal{S}$.

---

[1]Note that our model has chosen a particular convention for identifying operations of different components in a system: we simply identify those with the same name. This convention is simple, and sufficient for what we do in this paper. However, when this work is extended to more complicated systems, it may be expedient to generalize the convention for identifying operations, to permit reuse of the same operation name internally to different components. This will require introducing a renaming operator for operations, or else defining composition with respect to a designated equivalence relation on operations. We leave this for later work.

3. Serial Systems

In this paper, we define three kinds of systems: "serial systems" and two types of "concurrent systems". Serial systems describe serial execution of transactions. Serial systems are defined for the purpose of providing a correctness condition for other systems: that the schedules of the other systems should "look like" schedules of the serial system to the transactions. As with serial schedules of single-level transaction systems, our serial schedules are too inefficient to use in practice. Thus, we define systems which allow concurrency, and which permit the abort of transactions after they have performed some work. We then prove that the schedules permitted by concurrent systems are correct.

In this section, we define "serial systems". Serial systems consist of "transactions" and "basic objects" communicating with a "serial scheduler". Transactions and basic objects describe user programs and data, respectively. The serial scheduler controls communication between the other components, and thereby defines the allowable orders in which the transactions may take steps. All three types of system components are modelled as I/O automata.

We begin by defining a structure which describes the nesting of transactions. Namely, a *system type* is a four-tuple ($\mathcal{T}$,parent,$\mathcal{O}$,V), where $\mathcal{T}$, the set of transaction names, is organized into a tree by the mapping parent:$\mathcal{T} \rightarrow \mathcal{T}$, with T_0 as the root. In referring to this tree, we use traditional terminology, such as child, leaf, least common ancestor (lca), ancestor and descendant. (A transaction is its own ancestor and descendant.) The leaves of this tree are called *accesses.* The set $\mathcal{O}$ denotes the set of objects; formally, $\mathcal{O}$ is a partition of the set of accesses, where each element of the partition contains the accesses to a particular object. The set V is a set of *values,* to be used as return values of transactions.

The tree structure can be thought of as a predefined naming scheme for all possible transactions that might ever be invoked. In any particular execution, however, only some of these transactions will actually take steps. We imagine that the tree structure is known in advance by all components of a system. The tree will, in general, be an infinite structure.

The classical transactions of concurrency control theory (without nesting) appear in our model as the children of a "mythical" transaction, T_0, the root of the transaction tree. (In work on nested transactions, such as ARGUS [LiS,LHJLSW], the children of T_0 are often called "top-level" transactions.) It is very convenient to introduce the new root transaction to model the environment in which the rest of the transaction system runs. Transaction T_0 has operations that describe the invocation and return of the classical transactions. It is natural to reason about T_0 in much the same way as about all of the other transactions, although it is distinguished from the other transactions by having no parent transaction. Since committing and aborting are operations which take place at the parent of each transaction (see below), T_0 can neither commit nor abort.

Thus, a commit or abort of a top-level transaction to T_0 is an irreversible step.

The internal nodes of the tree model transactions whose function is to create and manage subtransactions, but not to access data directly. The only transactions which actually access data are the leaves of the transaction tree, and thus they are distinguished as "accesses". The partition $\mathcal{O}$ simply identifies those transactions which access the same object.

A serial system of a given system type is the composition of a set of I/O automata. This set contains a transaction for each *internal* (i.e. non-leaf, non-access) node of the transaction tree, a basic object for each element of $\mathcal{O}$ and a serial scheduler. These automata are described below. (If X is a basic object associated with an element $\mathcal{X}$ of the partition $\mathcal{O}$, and T is an access in $\mathcal{X}$, we write $T \in accesses(X)$ and say that "T is an access to X".)

3.1. Transactions

This paper differs from earlier work such as [Ly,Go,We] in that we model the transactions explicitly, as I/O automata. In modelling transactions, we consider it very important not to constrain them unnecessarily; thus, we do not want to require that they be expressible as programs in any particular high-level programming language. Modelling the transactions as I/O automata allows us to state exactly the properties that are needed, without introducing unnecessary restrictions or complicated semantics.

A non-access *transaction* T is modelled as an I/O automaton, with the following operations.

Input operations:
- CREATE(T)
- COMMIT(T',v), for $T' \in$ children(T) and $v \in V$
- ABORT(T'), for $T' \in$ children(T)

Output operations:
- REQUEST−CREATE(T'), for $T' \in$ children(T)
- REQUEST−COMMIT(T,v), for $v \in V$

The CREATE input operation "wakes up" the transaction. The REQUEST−CREATE output operation is a request by T to create a particular child transaction.[2] The COMMIT input operation reports to T the successful completion of one of its children, and returns a value recording the results of that child's execution. The ABORT input operation reports to T the unsuccessful completion of one of its children, without returning any other information. We call COMMIT(T',v), for any v, and ABORT(T') *return* operations for

[2] Note that there is no provision for T to pass information to its child in this request. In a programming language, T might be permitted to pass parameter values to a subtransaction. Although this may be a convenient descriptive aid, it is not necessary to include in it the underlying formal model. Instead, we consider transactions that have different input parameters to be different transactions.

transaction T'. The REQUEST−COMMIT operation is an announcement by T that it has finished its work, and includes a value recording the results of that work.

It is convenient to use two separate operations, REQUEST−CREATE and CREATE, to describe what takes place when a subtransaction is activated. The REQUEST−CREATE is an operation of the transaction's parent, while the actual CREATE takes place at the subtransaction itself. In actual systems such as ARGUS, this separation does occur, and the distinction will be important in our results and proofs. Similar remarks hold for the REQUEST−COMMIT and COMMIT operations.[3] We leave the executions of particular transaction automata largely unspecified; the choice of which children to create, and what value to return, will depend on the particular implementation. For the purposes of the schedulers studied here, the transactions (and in large part, the objects) are "black boxes." Nevertheless, it is convenient to assume that schedules of transaction automata obey certain syntactic constraints. Thus, transaction automata are required to preserve well-formedness, as defined below.

We recursively define *well-formedness* for sequences of operations of transaction T. Namely, the empty schedule is well-formed. Also, if $\alpha = \alpha'\pi$ is a sequence of operations of T, where π is a single operation, then α is well-formed provided that α' is well-formed, and the following hold.

- If π is CREATE(T), then
  (i) there is no CREATE(T) in α'.

- If π is COMMIT(T',v) or ABORT(T') for a child T' of T, then
  (i) REQUEST−CREATE(T') appears in α' and
  (ii) there is no return operation for T' in α'.

- If π is REQUEST−CREATE(T') for a child T' of T, then
  (i) there is no REQUEST−CREATE(T') in α'
  (ii) there is no REQUEST−COMMIT(T) in α' and
  (iii) CREATE(T) appears in α'.

- If π is a REQUEST−COMMIT for T, then
  (i) there is no REQUEST−COMMIT for T in α' and
  (ii) CREATE(T) appears in α'.

These restrictions are very basic; they simply say that a transaction does not get created more than once, does not receive repeated notification of the fates of its children, does not receive conflicting information

[3] Note that we do not include a REQUEST−ABORT operation for a transaction: we do not model the situation in which a transaction decides that its own existence is a mistake. Rather, we assign decisions to abort transactions to another component of the system, the scheduler. In practice, the scheduler must have some power to decide to abort transactions, as when it detects deadlocks or failures. In ARGUS, transactions are permitted to request to abort; we regard this request simply as a "hint" to the scheduler, to restrict its allowable executions in a particular way. This operation could be made explicit, constraining the scheduler to abort the requesting transaction, without substantively changing the model or results.

about the fates of its children, and does not receive information about the fate of any child whose creation it has not requested; also, a transaction does not perform any output operations before it has been created or after it has requested to commit, and does not request the creation of the same child more than once. Except for these minimal conditions, there are no restrictions on allowable transaction behavior. For example, the model allows a transaction to request to commit without discovering the fate of all subtransactions whose creation it has requested. Also, a transaction can request creation of new subtransactions at any time, without regard to its state of knowledge about subtransactions whose creation it has previously requested. Particular programming languages may choose to impose additional restrictions on transaction behavior. (An example is ARGUS, which suspends activity in transactions until subtransactions complete.) However, our results do not require such restrictions.

3.2. Basic Objects

Recall that I/O automata are associated with non-access transactions only. Since access transactions model abstract operations on shared data objects, we associate a single I/O automaton with each object, rather than one for each access. The operations for each object are just the CREATE and REQUEST−COMMIT operations for all the corresponding access transactions. Although we give these operations the same names as the operations of non-access transactions, it is helpful to think of the operations of access transactions in other terms also: a CREATE corresponds to an invocation of an operation on the object, while a REQUEST−COMMIT corresponds to a response by the object to an invocation. Actually, these CREATE and REQUEST−COMMIT operations generalize the usual invocations and responses in that our operations carry with them a designation of the position of the access in the transaction tree. We depart from the traditional notational distinction between creation of subtransactions and invocations on objects, since the common terminology for access and non-access transactions is of great benefit in unifying the statements and proofs of our results. Thus, a *basic object* X is modelled as an automaton, with the following operations.

Input operations:
    CREATE(T), for T in accesses(X)

Output operations:
    REQUEST−COMMIT(T,v), for T in accesses(X)

The CREATE operation is an invocation of an access to the object, while the REQUEST−COMMIT is a return of a value in response to such an invocation.

As with transactions, while specific objects are left largely unspecified, it is convenient to require that schedules of basic objects satisfy certain syntactic conditions. Thus, each basic object is required to preserve well-formedness, defined below.

Let α be a sequence of operations of basic object X. Then an access T to X is said to be *pending* in α provided that there is a CREATE(T), but no REQUEST−COMMIT for T, in α. We define *well-formedness* for sequences of operations of basic objects recursively. Namely, the empty schedule is well-formed. Also, if $\alpha = \alpha'\pi$ is a sequence of operations of basic object X, where π is a single operation, then α is well-formed provided that α' is well-formed, and the following hold.

- If π is CREATE(T), then
  (i) there is no CREATE(T) in α', and
  (ii) there are no pending accesses in α'.

- If π is REQUEST−COMMIT for T, then
  (i) there is no REQUEST−COMMIT for T in α', and
  (ii) CREATE(T) appears in α'.

These restrictions simply say that the same access does not get created more than once, nor does a creation of a new access occur at a basic object before the previous access has completed (i.e. requested to commit); also, a basic object does not respond more than once to any access. and only responds to accesses that have previously been created.

3.3. Serial Scheduler

The third kind of component in a serial system is the serial scheduler. The serial scheduler is also modelled as an automaton. The transactions and basic objects have been specified to be any I/O automata whose operations and behavior satisfy simple syntactic restrictions. The serial scheduler, however, is a fully specified automaton, particular to each system type. It runs transactions according to a depth-first traversal of the transaction tree. The serial scheduler can choose nondeterministically to abort any transaction after its parent has requested its creation, as long as the transaction has not actually been created. In the context of this scheduler, the "semantics" of an ABORT(T) operation are that transaction T was never created. The operations of the serial scheduler are as follows.

Input Operations:
REQUEST−CREATE(T)
REQUEST−COMMIT(T,v)

Output Operations:
CREATE(T)
COMMIT(T,v)
ABORT(T)

The REQUEST−CREATE and REQUEST−COMMIT inputs are intended to be identified with the corresponding outputs of transaction and object automata, and correspondingly for the CREATE, COMMIT and ABORT output operations. Each state s of the serial scheduler consists of four sets:

create−requested(s), created(s), commit−requested(s), and returned(s). The set commit−requested(s) is a set of (transaction,value) pairs. The others are sets of transactions. There is exactly one initial state, in which the set create−requested is $\{T_0\}$, and the other sets are empty.

The transition relation consists of exactly those triples (s',π,s) satisfying the pre- and postconditions below, where π is the indicated operation. For brevity, we include in the postconditions only those conditions on the state s which may change with the operation. If a component of s is not mentioned in the postcondition, (such as returned(s) in the postcondition for REQUEST−CREATE(T)), it is implicit that the set is the same in s' and s (that returned(s') = returned(s), in this example). Note that here, as elsewhere, we have tried to specify the component as nondeterministically as possible, in order to achieve the greatest possible generality for our results.

- REQUEST−CREATE(T)
  Postcondition:
  create−requested(s) = create−requested(s') $\cup$ {T}

- REQUEST−COMMIT(T,v)
  Postcondition:
  commit−requested(s) = commit−requested(s') $\cup$ {(T,v)}

- CREATE(T)
  Precondition:
  T $\in$ create−requested(s') - created(s')
  siblings(T) $\cap$ created(s') $\subseteq$ returned(s')
  Postcondition:
  created(s) = created(s') $\cup$ {T}

- COMMIT(T,v)
  Precondition:
  (T,v) $\in$ commit−requested(s')
  T $\notin$ returned(s')
  children(T) $\cap$ create−requested(s') $\subseteq$ returned(s')
  Postcondition:
  returned(s) = returned(s') $\cup$ {T}

- ABORT(T)
  Precondition:
  T $\in$ create−requested(s') - created(s')
  siblings(T) $\cap$ created(s') $\subseteq$ returned(s')
  Postcondition:
  created(s) = created(s') $\cup$ {T}
  returned(s) = returned(s') $\cup$ {T}

The input operations, REQUEST−CREATE and REQUEST−COMMIT, simply result in the request being recorded. A CREATE operation can only occur if a corresponding REQUEST−CREATE has occurred and the CREATE has not already occurred. The second precondiition on the CREATE operation says that the serial scheduler does not create a transaction until all its previously created sibling transactions have returned. That is, siblings are run sequentially. The precondition on the COMMIT operation says that the scheduler does not allow a transaction to commit to its parent until its children have returned. The precondition on the ABORT operation says that the scheduler does not abort a transaction while there is activity going on on behalf of any of its siblings. That is, aborted transactions are run sequentially with respect to their siblings.

3.4. Serial Systems and Serial Schedules

In this subsection, we define serial systems precisely and provide some useful terminology for talking about them.

The composition of transactions with basic objects and the serial scheduler for a given system type is called a *serial system*. Define the *serial operations* to be those operations which occur in the serial system: REQUEST−CREATES, REQUEST−COMMITS, CREATES, COMMITS and ABORTS. The schedules of a serial system are called *serial schedules*. The non-access transactions and basic objects are called the system *primitives*. (Recall that each basic object is an automaton corresponding to a set of access transactions. Thus, individual access transactions are not considered to be primitives.)

Recall that the operations of the basic objects have the same syntax as transaction operations. It is convenient to refer to CREATE(T) and REQUEST−COMMIT(T), when T is an access to basic object X, both as operations of transaction T and of object X. To avoid confusion, it is important to remember that there is no transaction automaton associated with any access operation.

For any serial operation π, we define *transaction*(π) to be the transaction at which the operation occurs. (For CREATE(T) operations and REQUEST−COMMIT operations for T, the transaction is T, while for REQUEST−CREATE(T) operations, and COMMIT and ABORT operations for T, the transaction is parent(T).) For a sequence α of serial operations, transaction(α) is the set of transactions of the operations in α.

Two sequences of serial operations, α and α', are said to be *equivalent* provided that they consist of the same operations, and $\alpha|P = \alpha'|P$ for each primitive P. Obviously, this yields an equivalence relation on sequences of serial operations.

We let $\alpha|T$ denote the subsequence of α consisting of operations whose transaction is T, even if T is an access. (This is an extension of the previous definition of $\alpha|T$, as accesses are not component automata of the serial system.)

Let α be a sequence of serial operations. We say that a transaction T is *live* in α provided that a CREATE(T), but no COMMIT(T,v) or ABORT(T), occurs in α. We say that transaction T' is *visible* to T in α provided that for each ancestor T" of T' which is a proper descendant of lca(T,T'), some COMMIT(T",v) occurs in α. (In particular, any ancestor of T is visible to T in α.) For sequence α and transaction T, let *visible*(α,*T*) be the subsequence of α consisting of operations whose transactions are visible to T in α. (These include access transactions T'.) We say that transaction T *sees everything* in α provided that visible(α,T) = α.

This is the same definition of visibility as appears, in a different model, in [Ly]. Visibility captures an intuitive notion suggested by the name: the transactions visible to a transaction T in α are those whose effects T is permitted to "see" in α. If transaction T' is visible to transaction T in α, it means that descendants of T may have passed to T information about T', obtained by accessing objects that were previously accessed by descendants of T'.

If α is a sequence of operations, not necessarily all serial, then define serial(α) to be the subsequence of α consisting of the serial operations. We say that T is *live* in α provided that it is live in serial(α). We say that T' is *visible* to T in α if T' is visible to T in serial(α), and define visible(α,T) to be visible(serial(α),T). Also, T *sees everything* in α provided that T sees everything in serial(α). Similarly, define transaction(α) = transaction(serial(α)).

3.5. Correctness Condition

We use serial schedules as the basis of our correctness definitions. Namely, we say that a sequence of operations is *serially correct for a primitive P* provided that its projection on P is identical to the projection on P of some serial schedule. We say that any sequence of operations is *serially correct* if it is serially correct for every non-access transaction. That is, α "looks like" a serial schedule to every non-access transaction.

In the remainder of this paper, we define two systems: concurrent systems and weak concurrent systems. We show that schedules of concurrent systems are serially correct, and that schedules of weak concurrent systems are serially correct for T_0. Thus, we use the serial scheduler as a way of describing desirable behavior, just as serial schedules describe desirable behavior in more classical concurrency control settings (those without nesting). Then serial correctness plays the role in our theory that serializability plays in classical settings.

Note that our correctness conditions are defined at the transaction interface only, and do not constrain the object interface. We believe that this makes the conditions more meaningful to users, and more likely to suffice for a large variety of algorithms, which may use a variety of back-out, locking or version schemes to implement objects. Previous work has focussed on correctness conditions at the object interface [EGLT, etc.]. While we believe that object interface conditions are important, their proper role in the theory is not to serve as the basic correctness condition. Rather, they are useful as intermediate conditions for proving correctness of particular implementations.

The serial correctness condition says that a schedule α must look like a serial schedule to each non-access transaction; this allows for the possibility that α might look like *different* serial schedules to different non-access transactions. This condition may at first seem to be too weak. It may seem that we should require that all transactions see a projection of the *same* serial schedule. But this stronger condition is not satisfied by most of the known concurrency control algorithms. Also, the serial correctness condition is really not as weak as it may seem at first because T_0, the root transaction, is included among the transactions to which α must appear serial. As discussed above, transaction T_0 can be thought of as modelling the environment in which the rest of the transaction system runs. Its REQUEST−CREATE operations correspond to the invocation of top-level transactions, while its COMMIT and ABORT operations correspond to return values and external effects of those transactions. Since α's projection on T_0 must be serial, the environment of the transaction system will see only results that could arise in a serial execution.

3.6. Properties of Serial Systems

In this subsection, we give a pair of lemmas which describe ways in which serial schedules can be "cut and pasted" to yield other serial schedules. These lemmas are used in the proof of the main theorem, in Section 7. The proofs are omitted from this paper, but appear in [LM]. [LM] also contains many additional interesting properties of the behavior of serial systems.

Lemma 2: Let $\alpha\beta_1$COMMIT(T',u) and $\alpha\beta_2$ be two serial schedules and T, T' and T'' three transactions such that the following conditions hold:
(1) T' is a child of T'' and T is a descendant of T'' but not of T',
(2) T' sees everything in $\alpha\beta_1$,
(3) T sees everything in $\alpha\beta_2$,
(4) α = visible($\alpha\beta_1$,T'') = visible($\alpha\beta_2$,T'') and
(5) no basic object has operations in both β_1 and β_2.
Then $\alpha\beta_1$COMMIT(T',u)β_2 is a serial schedule.

Lemma 3: Let αABORT(T') and $\alpha\beta$ be two serial schedules, and let T, T' and T'' be transactions, such that the following conditions hold:
(1) T' is a child of T'' and T is a descendant of T'' but not of T',
(2) T sees everything in $\alpha\beta$, and
(3) α = visible(α,T'') = visible($\alpha\beta$,T'').
Then αABORT(T')β is a serial schedule.

4. Resilient Objects

Having stated our correctness conditions, we are now ready to begin describing implementations and proving that they meet the requirements. This section and the next are devoted to the description of a concurrent system which permits the abort of transactions that have performed steps. An important component of a concurrent system is a new kind of object called a "resilient object," which we introduce in this section. A resilient object is similar to a basic object, but it has the additional capability to undo operations of transactions that it discovers have aborted.

Resilient objects have no capabilities for managing concurrency: rather, they assume that concurrency control is handled externally (by lock manager components of the scheduler). This section defines resilient objects. The complete paper [LM] presents some of their properties, and also describes and proves correct a particular implementation of resilient objects, constructed by keeping multiple versions of corresponding basic objects.

4.1. Definitions

Resilient object R(X) mimics the behavior of basic object X, but has two additional input operations, INFORM−COMMIT−AT(X)OF(T) and INFORM−ABORT−AT(X)OF(T), for every transaction T. Upon receiving an INFORM−ABORT−AT(X)OF(T), R(X) erases any effects of accesses which are descendants of T. This property is made formal as the "Resiliency Condition" below.

R(X) has the following operations, which we call *R(X)-operations.*

Input Operations:
CREATE(T), T an access to X
INFORM−COMMIT−AT(X)OF(T)
INFORM−ABORT−AT(X)OF(T)

Output Operations:
REQUEST−COMMIT(T,v), T an access to X

In order to describe well-formedness for resilient objects, we require a technical definition for the set of transactions which are *active* after a sequence of R(X)-operations. Roughly speaking, the transactions which are active are those on whose behalf the object has carried out some activity, but whose fate the object does not know.

The definition is recursive on the length of the sequence of R(X) operations. Namely, only T_0 is active after the empty sequence. Let $\alpha = \beta\pi$, where π is a single operation, and let A and B denote the sets of active transactions after α and β, respectively. If π is CREATE(T), then $A = B \cup \{T\}$. If π is a

REQUEST−COMMIT for T, then A = B. If π is INFORM−COMMIT−AT(X)OF(T), and if T is in B, then A = (B - {T}) ∪ {parent(T)}; if T is not in B, then A = B. If π is INFORM−ABORT−AT(X)OF(T), then A = B - descendants(T).

Now we define *well-formedness* for sequences of R(X) operations. Again, the definition is recursive. Namely, the empty schedule is well-formed. Also, if $\alpha = \alpha'\pi$ is a sequence of R(X)-operations, then α is well-formed provided that α' is well-formed, and the following hold.

- If π is CREATE(T), then
  (i) there is no CREATE(T) in α',
  (ii) all the transactions which are active after α' are ancestors of T.

- If π is a REQUEST−COMMIT for T, then
  (i) there is no REQUEST−COMMIT for T in α', and
  (ii) T is active after α'.

- If π is INFORM−COMMIT−AT(X)OF(T), then
  (i) there is no INFORM−ABORT−AT(X)OF(T) in α', and
  (ii) if T is an access to X, then a REQUEST−COMMIT for T occurs in α'.

- If π is INFORM−ABORT−AT(X)OF(T), then
  (i) there is no INFORM−COMMIT−AT(X)OF(T) in α'.

An immediate consequence of these definitions is that the transactions active after any well-formed sequence of R(X)-operations α are a subset of the ancestors of a single active transaction, which we denote least(α).

For α a sequence of R(X)-operations, define *undo(α)* recursively as follows. Define undo(λ) = λ, where λ is the empty sequence. Let $\alpha = \beta\pi$, where π is a single operation. If π is a serial operation (a CREATE or a REQUEST−COMMIT), then undo(α) = undo(β)π. If π is INFORM−COMMIT−AT(X)OF(T), then undo(α) = undo(β). If π is INFORM−ABORT−AT(X)OF(T), then undo(α) is the result of eliminating, from undo(β), all operations whose transactions are descendants of T. Note that undo(α) contains only serial operations.

Let α be any sequence of R(X)-operations, and let π be an operation in α of the form INFORM−ABORT−AT(X)OF(T). Then the *scope* of π in α is the subsequence γ of α consisting of operations eliminated by π.

Resiliency Condition

Resilient object R(X) *satisfies the resiliency condition* if for every well-formed schedule α of R(X), undo(α) is schedule of basic object X.

We require that resilient object R(X) preserve well-formedness and satisfy the resiliency condition.

The resiliency condition is the correctness condition required by the concurrent schedulers at the object interface. The well-formedness requirement is a syntactic restriction, and the condition that undo(α) be a schedule of basic object X expresses the required semantic relationship between the resilient object and the basic object it incorporates; specifically, that the resilient object "backs out" operations in the scope of INFORM−ABORTS.

5. Concurrent Systems

As with serial schedules in classical settings, our serial schedules contain no concurrency or resiliency and thus are too inefficient to use in practice. Their importance is solely for defining correctness for transaction systems. In this section, we define a new kind of system called a *concurrent system*. The new system consists of the same transactions as in a serial system, a resilient object R(X) for every basic object X of the serial system, and a concurrent scheduler.

Concurrent systems describe computations in which transactions run concurrently and can be aborted after they have performed some work. The concurrent scheduler has the joint responsibility of controlling concurrency and of seeing that the effects of aborted transactions (and their descendants) become undone. Concurrent systems make use of the roll-back capabilities of resilient objects to make sure that ABORT operations in concurrent systems have the same semantics (so far as the transactions can tell) as they do in serial systems.

Concurrent systems are defined in this section. In the next section, the more permissive "weak concurrent systems" are defined. In Section 7, we prove that the schedules of concurrent systems are serially correct, as a corollary of a weaker correctness property for the weak concurrent system.

5.1. Lock Managers

The scheduler we define is called the *concurrent scheduler*. It is composed of several automata: a *lock manager* for every object X, and a single *concurrent controller*. The job of the lock managers is to insure that the associated object receives no CREATES until the lock manager has received abort or commit information for all necessary preceding transactions. This lock manager models an exclusive locking protocol derived from Moss' algorithm [Mo]. The lock manager has the following operations.

Input Operations:
- INTERNAL−CREATE(T), where T is an access to X
- INFORM−COMMIT−AT(X)OF(T), for T any transaction
- INFORM−ABORT−AT(X)OF(T), for T any transaction

Output Operations:
CREATE(T), where T is an access to X

The input operations INTERNAL−CREATE, INFORM−COMMIT and INFORM−ABORT will compose with corresponding output operations of the concurrent scheduler which we will construct in this subsection. The output CREATE operation composes with the CREATE input operation of the resilient object R(X). The lock manager receives and manages requests to access object X, using a hierarchical locking scheme. It uses information about the commit and abort of transactions to decide when to release locks.

Each state s of the lock manager consists of the following three sets of transactions: lock−holders(s), create−requested(s), and created(s). Initially, lock−holders = $\{T_0\}$, and the other sets are empty. The operations work as follows.

- INTERNAL−CREATE(T)
  Postcondition:
  create−requested(s) = create−requested(s') ∪ {T}

- INFORM−COMMIT−AT(X)OF(T)
  Postcondition:
  if T ∈ lock−holders(s') then lock−holders(s) = (lock−holders(s') - {T}) ∪ {parent(T)}

- INFORM−ABORT−AT(X)OF(T)
  Postcondition:
  lock−holders(s) = lock−holders(s') - descendants(T)

- CREATE(T)
  Precondition:
  T ∈ create−requested(s') - created(s')
  lock−holders(s') ⊆ ancestors(T)
  Postcondition:
  lock−holders(s) = lock−holders(s') ∪ {T}
  created(s) = created(s') ∪ {T}

Note that resilient object R(X) and the lock manager for X share the INFORM−ABORT and INFORM−COMMIT input operations. These compose with the output from the concurrent controller defined below.

Thus, the lock manager only sends a CREATE(T) operation on to the object in case all the current lock−holders are ancestors of T. When the lock manager learns about the commit of a transaction T for which it holds a lock, it releases the lock to T's parent. When the lock manager learns about the abort of a transaction T for which it holds a lock, it simply releases all locks held by that transaction and its descendants. Our model provides an exceptionally simple and clear way of describing this important algorithm.

5.2. The Concurrent Controller

The concurrent controller is similar to the serial scheduler, but it allows siblings to proceed concurrently. In order to manage this properly, it interacts with "concurrent objects" (lock managers and resilient objects) instead of just basic objects. The operations are as follows.

Input Operations:
REQUEST−CREATE(T)
REQUEST−COMMIT(T,v)

Output Operations:
CREATE(T), T a non-access transaction
INTERNAL−CREATE(T), T an access transaction
COMMIT(T,v)
ABORT(T)
INFORM−COMMIT−AT(X)OF(T)
INFORM−ABORT−AT(X)OF(T)

Each state s of the concurrent controller consists of five sets: create−requested(s), created(s), commit−requested(s), committed(s), and aborted(s). The set commit−requested(s) is a set of (transaction,value) pairs, and the others are sets of transactions. (As before, we will occasionally write T ∈ commit−requested(s) for (T,v) ∈ commit−requested(s) for some v.) All sets are initially empty except for create−requested, which is $\{T_0\}$. Define returned(s) = committed(s) ∪ aborted(s). The operations are as follows.

- REQUEST−CREATE(T)
  Postcondition:
  create−requested(s) = create−requested(s') ∪ {T}

- REQUEST−COMMIT(T,v)
  Postcondition:
  commit−requested(s) = commit−requested(s') ∪ {(T,v)}

- CREATE(T), T a non-access transaction
  Precondition:
  T ∈ create−requested(s') - created(s')
  Postcondition:
  created(s) = created(s') ∪ {T}

- INTERNAL−CREATE(T), T an access transaction
  Precondition:
  T ∈ create−requested(s') - created(s')
  Postcondition:
  created(s) = created(s') ∪ {T}

- COMMIT(T,v)
  Precondition:

(T,v) ∈ commit−requested(s')
T ∉ returned(s')
children(T) ∩ create−requested(s') ⊆ returned(s')
Postcondition:
committed(s) = committed(s') ∪ {T}

- ABORT(T)
  Precondition:
  T ∈ (create-requested(s') - created(s')) ∪ (commit−requested(s') - returned(s'))
  children(T) ∩ create−requested(s') ⊆ returned(s')
  Postcondition:
  created(s) = created(s') ∪ {T}
  aborted(s) = aborted(s') ∪ {T}

- INFORM−COMMIT−AT(X)OF(T):
  Precondition:
  T ∈ committed(s')

- INFORM−ABORT−AT(X)OF(T):
  Precondition:
  T ∈ aborted(s')

The concurrent controller is closely related to the serial scheduler. In place of the serial scheduler's CREATE operations, the concurrent controller has two kinds of operations, CREATE operations and INTERNAL−CREATE operations. The former is used for interaction with non-access transactions, while the latter is used for interaction with access transactions. From the concurrent controller's viewpoint, the two operations are the same; however, our naming convention for operations requires us to assign them different names, since the INTERNAL−CREATE operations are intended to be identified with INTERNAL−CREATE operations of the lock managers (which also have CREATE operations, for interaction with the resilient objects). The precondition on the serial scheduler's CREATE operation which insures serial processing of sibling transactions, does not appear in the concurrent controller. Thus, the concurrent controller may run any number of sibling transactions concurrently, provided their parent has requested their creation.

The concurrent controller's COMMIT operation is the same as the serial scheduler's COMMIT operation (except for a minor difference in bookkeeping). The concurrent controller's ABORT operation is different, however; in addition to aborting a transaction in the way that the serial scheduler does, the concurrent controller has the additional capability to abort a transaction that has actually been created and has carried out some steps. In this particular formulation, aborts occur if the transaction was not created (as with the serial scheduler), or if the transaction has previously requested to commit, and its children have returned. Together with the requirements on the COMMIT operation, this condition insures that all transaction completion occurs bottom-up. In the weak concurrent system to be considered in Section 6, a different, "weak", concurrent controller will be used; it differs from the concurrent controller of this section precisely in not requiring ABORT operations to wait for their transactions (and subtransactions) to complete.

The concurrent controller also has two additional operations not present in the serial scheduler. These operations allow the concurrent controller to forward necessary abort and commit information to the lock managers and resilient objects.

5.3. Concurrent Systems

The composition of transactions, resilient objects and the concurrent scheduler (lock managers and concurrent controller) is the *concurrent system*. A schedule of the concurrent system is a *concurrent schedule*, and the operations of a concurrent system are *concurrent operations*.

A main result of this paper is that every concurrent schedule is serially correct. This will be proved as a corollary of another result, in Section 7.

6. Weak Concurrent Systems

In this section, we define "weak concurrent systems", which are exactly the same as concurrent systems, except that they have a more permissive controller, the "weak concurrent controller". The weak concurrent controller reports aborts to a transaction's parent while there is still activity going on in the aborted transaction's subtree. In this paper, weak concurrent systems are used primarily to provide an intermediate step in proving the correctness of concurrent systems: proving a weaker condition for weak concurrent systems allows us to infer the stronger correctness condition for concurrent systems. However, weak concurrent systems are also of interest in themselves. In a distributed implementation of a nested transaction system, performance considerations may make it important for the system to allow a transaction to abort without waiting for activity in the transaction's subtree to subside. In this case, a weak concurrent system might be an appropriate choice, even though the correctness conditions which they satisfy are weaker. Weak concurrent systems also appears to have further technical use, for example in providing simple explanations of the ideas used in "orphan detection" algorithms [HLMW].

6.1. The Weak Concurrent Controller

In this subsection, we define the weak concurrent controller. As we have already said, it is identical to the concurrent controller except that it has a more permissive ABORT operation. For convenience, we describe the controller here in its entirety. It has the same operations as the concurrent controller:

Input Operations:

REQUEST−CREATE(T)
REQUEST−COMMIT(T,v)

Output Operations:
CREATE(T), T a non-access transaction
INTERNAL−CREATE(T), T an access transaction
COMMIT(T,v)
ABORT(T)
INFORM−COMMIT−AT(X)OF(T)
INFORM−ABORT−AT(X)OF(T)

Each state s of the concurrent controller consists of five sets: create−requested(s), created(s), commit−requested(s), committed(s), and aborted(s). The set commit−requested(s) is a set of (transaction,value) pairs, and the others are sets of transactions. (As before, we will occasionally write T ∈ commit−requested(s) for (T,v) ∈ commit−requested(s) for some v.) All are empty initially except for create−requested, which is $\{T_0\}$. Define returned(s) = committed(s) ∪ aborted(s). The operations are as follows.

- REQUEST−CREATE(T)
  Postcondition:
  create−requested(s) = create−requested(s') ∪ {T}

- REQUEST−COMMIT(T,v)
  Postcondition:
  commit−requested(s) = commit−requested(s') ∪ {(T,v)}

- CREATE(T), T a non-access transaction
  Precondition:
  T ∈ create−requested(s') - created(s')
  Postcondition:
  created(s) = created(s') ∪ {T}

- INTERNAL−CREATE(T), T an access transaction
  Precondition:
  T ∈ create−requested(s') - created(s')
  Postcondition:
  created(s) = created(s') ∪ {T}

- COMMIT(T,v)
  Precondition:
  (T,v) ∈ commit−requested(s')
  T ∉ returned(s')
  children(T) ∩ create−requested(s') ⊆ returned(s')
  Postcondition:
  committed(s) = committed(s') ∪ {T}

- ABORT(T)

Precondition:
T ∈ create-requested(s') - returned(s')
Postcondition:
created(s) = created(s') ∪ {T}
aborted(s) = aborted(s') ∪ {T}

- INFORM−COMMIT−AT(X)OF(T):
  Precondition:
  T ∈ committed(s')

- INFORM−ABORT−AT(X)OF(T):
  Precondition:
  T ∈ aborted(s')

Thus, the weak concurrent controller is permitted to abort any transaction that has had its creation requested, and which has not yet returned.

6.2. Weak Concurrent Systems

The composition of transactions, resilient objects and the weak concurrent scheduler (lock managers and weak concurrent controller) is the *weak concurrent system*. A schedule of the weak concurrent system is a *weak concurrent schedule.*

Weak concurrent systems exhibit nice behavior to transactions except possibly to those which are descendants of aborted transactions. Thus, we say that a transaction T is an *orphan* in any sequence α of operations provided that an ancestor of T is aborted in α. In many of the properties we prove for weak concurrent systems, we will have to specify that the transactions involved are not orphans. Orphans have been studied in [Go,Wa,HM].

6.3. Properties of Weak Concurrent Systems

We here give some useful basic properties for weak concurrent schedules. As before, complete proofs and additional results appear in [LM].

Lemma 4: Let α be a weak concurrent schedule. Let R(X) be a resilient object, let T and T' be accesses to R(X), and suppose that T' is not an orphan in α. If an operation π of T precedes an operation π' of T' in α, and π is not in the scope of an INFORM−ABORT in α, then T is visible to T' in α.

Proof: By lock manager properties. ∎

The following is a key lemma.

Lemma 5: Let α be a weak concurrent schedule, and let T be live and not an orphan in α.

1. If T' is a transaction, then visible(α,T)|T' is a prefix of α|T' and a schedule of T'.

2. If R(X) is a resilient object, then visible(α,T)|R(X) is a prefix of undo(α|R(X)) and a schedule of basic object X.

Proof: 1. Immediate from the fact that visible(α,T)|T" is either equal to α|T" or is the empty sequence.

2. By Lemma 4 and properties of visibility. ∎

Finally, we show that, in a weak concurrent schedule, concurrently executing transactions access disjoint sets of resilient objects.

Lemma 6: Let α be a weak concurrent schedule, with transactions T and T' live and not orphans in α. Let T" = lca(T,T'). Let β = visible(α,T) - visible(α,T") and β' = visible(α,T') - visible(α,T"). Then no resilient object has operations in both β and β'.

Proof: By lock manager properties. ∎

7. Simulation of Serial Systems by Concurrent Systems

In this section, we prove the main results of this paper, that concurrent schedules are serially correct, and that weak concurrent schedules are correct at T_0. Both these results follow from an interesting theorem about weak concurrent schedules, which says that the portion of any weak concurrent schedule which is visible to a live non-orphan transaction is equivalent to (i.e. looks the same at *all* primitives as) a serial schedule.

The proof of this theorem is quite interesting, as it provides considerable insight into the scheduling algorithm. The proof shows not only that a transaction's view of a weak concurrent schedule is equivalent to *some* serial schedule, but by a recursive construction, it actually produces such a schedule. It is interesting and instructive to observe how the views that different transactions have of the system execution get passed up and down the transaction tree, as CREATES, COMMITS and ABORTS occur.

Theorem 7: Let α be a weak concurrent schedule, and T any transaction which is live and not an orphan in α. Then there is a serial schedule β which is equivalent to visible(α,T).

Proof: We proceed by induction on the length of α. The basis, length 0, is trivial. Fix α of length at least 1, and assume that the claim is true for all shorter weak concurrent schedules. Let π be the last operation of α, and let $\alpha = \alpha'\pi$. Fix T which is live and not an orphan in α. We must show that there is a serial schedule β which is equivalent to visible(α,T).

If π is not a serial operation, then visible(α',T) = visible(serial(α'),T) = visible(serial(α),T) = visible(α,T), and the result is immediate by induction. So we can assume that π is a serial operation. Also, if transaction(π) is not visible to T in α, then visible(α,T) = visible(α',T), and the result is again immediate by induction. Thus, we can assume that transaction(π) is visible to T in α. Also, T is not an orphan in α'.

There are four cases.

(1) π is an output operation of a transaction or resilient object.

Then the inductive hypothesis implies the existence of a serial schedule β' which is equivalent to visible(α',T). Let $\beta = \beta'\pi$. We must show that β is equivalent to visible(α,T) and serial.

Let P be any primitive. Then $\beta|P = \beta'\pi|P$ = visible(α',T)$\pi|P$ by inductive hypothesis, = visible(α,T)$|P$. Therefore, β is equivalent to visible(α,T).

Let π be an output of primitive P. Then $\beta|P$ = visible(α,T)$|P$ by equivalence, which is a schedule of P by Lemma 5. Lemma 1 implies that β is serial.

(2) π is a CREATE(T') operation.

Then transaction(π) = T', and so T' is visible to T in α. Then π is the first operation in α whose transaction is a descendant of T'. By the definition of visibility, it must be that T' = T. Then parent(T) is live in α'. Since parent(T) is not an orphan in α, the inductive hypothesis implies the existence of a serial schedule β' which is equivalent to visible(α',parent(T)). Let $\beta = \beta'\pi$. We must show that β is equivalent to visible(α,T) and serial.

Let P be any primitive. Then $\beta|P = \beta'\pi|P$, = visible(α',parent(T))$\pi|P$ by inductive hypothesis, = visible(α,T)$|P$. Thus, β is equivalent to visible(α,T).

Consider any execution of the serial system having β' as its operation sequence, and let s' be the state of the serial scheduler after β'. Also consider any execution of the weak concurrent system having α as its operation sequence, and let s be the state of the weak concurrent scheduler after α'. Since π is enabled in s, it is easy to show that it is also enabled in s'.

(3) π is a COMMIT(T',v) operation.

Then T" = parent(T') = transaction(π) is visible to T and not an orphan in α. Also, T' is not an orphan in α'. Then T' is live in α', and so T" is live in α' and so in α. Since T" is live and visible to T, T" is an ancestor of T. Since T is live in α, T is not a descendant of T'. The inductive hypothesis yields two serial schedules, β' and β'', which are equivalent to visible(α',T') and visible(α',T), respectively. Let γ = visible(β',T"). Let $\beta_1 = \beta' - \gamma$ and $\beta_2 = \beta'' - \gamma$. We must show that $\beta = \gamma\beta_1\pi\beta_2$ is equivalent to visible(α,T) and serial.

Equivalence is straightforward. We show that β is serial. This follows from Lemma 2, provided we can show that:
(3.a) $\gamma\beta_1\pi$ is a serial schedule,
(3.b) T' sees everything in $\gamma\beta_1$,
(3.c) T sees everything in $\gamma\beta_2$,
(3.d) γ = visible($\gamma\beta_1$,T") = visible($\gamma\beta_2$,T") and
(3.e) no basic object has operations in both β_1 and β_2.
But (3.a) - (3.d) are straightforward, while (3.e) is immediate from Lemma 6.

(4) π is an ABORT(T') operation.

Then T" = parent(T') = transaction(π) is visible to T in α, and so is not an orphan in α. Then T' is live in α', and T" is live in α' and so in α. Since T" is live and visible to T in α, T is a descendant of T". Since T is not an orphan in α, T is not a descendant of T'. The inductive hypothesis yields two serial schedules, β' and β'', which are equivalent to visible(α',T'') and visible(α',T), respectively. Let $\beta_1 = \beta'' - \beta'$. We must show that $\beta = \beta'\pi\beta_1$ is equivalent to visible(α,T) and serial.

Equivalence is straightforward. We show that β is serial. This follows from Lemma 3, provided we can show that:
(4.a) $\beta'\pi$ is a serial schedule,
(4.b) T sees everything in $\beta'\beta$, and
(4.c) β' = visible(β',T'') = visible($\beta'\beta$,T'').
But this is straightforward. ∎

Corollary 8: Every weak concurrent schedule is serially correct for every non-orphan non-access transaction.

Corollary 9: Every weak concurrent schedule is serially correct for T_0.

Corollary 10: Every concurrent schedule is serially correct.

8. Acknowledgments

We thank Bill Weihl for many, many comments and questions, and much encouragement, during the course of this project. We also thank all the other members of the ARGUS design and implementation group at MIT, for providing a concrete model for us to try to abstract and generalize. Also, we thank Yehuda Afek for his comments on an early draft, and Sharon Perl for her comments on later drafts.

9. References

[AM] Allchin, J. E., and McKendry, M. S., "Synchronization and Recovery of Actions," *Proc. 1983 Second Annual ACM Symposium on Principles of Distributed Computing*, Montreal, Quebec, Canada, August 17-19, 1982, pp. 31-44.

[BBG] Beeri, C., Bernstein, P. A., and Goodman, N., "A Model for Concurrency in Nested Transaction Systems," Manuscript.

[BBGLS] Beeri, C., Bernstein, P. A., Goodman, N., Lai, M. Y., and Shasha, D. E., "A Concurrency Control Theory for Nested Transactions," *Proc. 1983 Second Annual ACM Symposium on Principles of Distributed Computing*, Montreal, Quebec, Canada, August 17-19, 1983, pp. 45-62.

[BG] Bernstein, P. A., and Goodman, N., "Concurrency Control in Distributed Database Systems," *ACM Computing Surveys* 13,2 (June 1981), pp. 185-221.

[EGLT] Eswaren, K. P., Gray, J. N., Lorie, R. A., and Traiger, I. L., "The Notions of Consistency and Predicate Locks in a Database Systems," *Communications of the ACM*, Vol. 19, No. 11, November 1976, pp. 624-633.

[Go] Goree, Jr., John A., "Internal Consistency of a Distributed Transaction System With Orphan Detection," MS Thesis, Technical Report MIT/LCS/TR-286, MIT Laboratory for Computer Science, Cambridge, MA., January 1983.

[Gr] Gray, J., "Notes on Database Operating Systems," in Bayer, R.,. Graham, R. and Seegmuller, G. (eds), Operating Systems: an Advanced Course, Lecture Notes in Computer Science, Vol. 60, Springer-Verlag, 1978.

[HM] Herlihy, M., and McKendry, M., "Time-Driven Orphan Elimination", in *Proc. of the 5th Symposium on Reliability in Distributed Software and Database Systems*, Los Angeles, CA., January 1986, pp. 42-48.

[Ho] Hoare, C.A.R., "Communicating Sequential Processes", Prentice Hall International Englewood Cliffs, NJ, 1985.

[KS] Kedem, Z., and Silberschatz, A., "A Characterization of Database Graphs Admitting a Simple Locking Protocol", *Acta Informatica* 16 (1981) pp. 1-13.

[LaS] Lampson, B. W., and Sturgis, H. E., "Crash Recovery in a Distributed Data Storage System," Tech. Rep., Computer Science Lab., Xerox Palo Alto Research Center, Palo Alto, Calif., 1979.

[LHJLSW] Liskov, B., Herlihy, M., Johnson, P., Leavens, G., Scheifler, R., and Weihl, W., "Preliminary Argus Reference Manual," Programming Methodology Group Memo 39, October 1983.

[LiS] Liskov, B., and Scheifler, R., "Guardians and Actions: Linguistic Support for Robust, Distributed Programs", *ACM Transactions on Programming Languages and Systems* 5, 3, (July 1983), pp. 381-404.

[LM] Lynch, N., and Merritt, M., "Introduction to the Theory of Nested Transactions", MIT Technical Report, AT&T Bell Labs Technical Report.

[LT] Lynch, N., and Tuttle, M., "Correctness Proofs for Distributed Algorithms", in progress.

[Ly] Lynch, N. A., "Concurrency Control For Resilient Nested Transactions," *Advances in Computing Research* 3, 1986, pp. 335-373.

[Mi] Milner, R., "A Calculus of Communicating Systems", *Lecture Notes in Computer Science*, #92, Springer-Verlag, Berlin, 1980.

[Mo] Moss, J. E. B., "Nested Transactions: An Approach To Reliable Distributed Computing," Ph.D. Thesis, Technical Report MIT/LCS/TR-260, MIT Laboratory for Computer Science, Cambridge, MA., April 1981. Also, published by MIT Press, March 1985.

[R] Reed, D. P., "Naming and Synchronization in a Decentralized Computer System," Ph.D Thesis, Technical Report MIT/LCS/TR-205, MIT Laboratory for Computer Science, Cambridge, MA 1978.

[RLS] Rosenkrantz, D. J., Lewis, P. M., and Stearns, R. E., "System Level Concurrency Control for Distributed Database Systems," *ACM Transactions on Database Systems*, Vol. 3, No. 2, June 1978, pp. 178-198.

[Wa] Walker, E. F., "Orphan Detection in the Argus System," M.S. Thesis, Technical Report/MIT/LCS/TR-326, MIT Laboratory for Computer Science, Cambridge, MA., June 1984.

[We] Weihl, W. E., "Specification and Implementation of Atomic Data Types," Ph.D Thesis, Technical Report/MIT/LCS/TR-314, MIT Laboratory for Computer Science, Cambridge, MA., March 1984.

This work was supported in part by the Office of Naval Research under Contract N00014-85-K-0168, by the Office of Army Research under Contract DAAG29-84-K-0058, by the National Science Foundation under Grant DCR-83-02391, and by the Defense Advanced Research Projects Agency (DARPA) under Grant N00014-83-K-0125.

ENTITY-RELATIONSHIP CONSISTENCY FOR RELATIONAL SCHEMAS

Johann A. Makowsky, Victor M. Markowitz and Nimrod Rotics
Computer Science Department, Technion
Israel Institute of Technology, Haifa 32000

ABSTRACT

We investigate the significance of requiring from a relational schema to comply with an entity-relationship structure. Relational database schemas here consist of traditional relational schemas together with key and inclusion dependencies. Such schemas are said to be entity-relationship (ER) consistent, either if they are the translate of, or if it is possible to translate them into, entity-relationship diagrams. An algorithm is presented which decides if a schema is ER-consistent and its complexity is discussed. ER-consistency expresses information structure normalization just as relational normal forms represent data representation normalization. For ER-consistent relational schemas we propose an Entity-Relationship Normal Form, and present the corresponding normalization procedure. ER-consistency expresses the capability of relational schemas to model information oriented systems. ER-consistent relational schemas allow the direct use of ER oriented query and update languages within the relational model.

I. INTRODUCTION.

One of the main objectives of the relational model is communicability [4], which means offering the user a data model which is easy to understand, use and communicate about. Regretfully, this objective is only partially fulfilled by the relational model since it conceals much of the semantic structure of the real world. Consequently, *semantic models* have been developed, with the entity-relationship (ER model [2] emerging as the most popular. The ER concepts reflects a natural, although limited, view of the world: entities are qualified by their attributes and interactions between entities are expressed by relationships. Because it lacks both a well defined instance level and, consequently, a well defined data manipulation language, the ER model has been mostly accepted as an early stage data base design tool. Once the design stage ends, the entity-relationship schema, represented by an entity-relationship diagram (ERD) is translated into a relational schema and its role is therewith ended (cf. [14]).

We propose to take this translation more seriously and try to capture all the information about the database design contained in the original ER diagram. This leads us to relational schemas involving key and inclusion dependencies. Relational schemas obtained by this translation are said to be trivially entity-relationship consistent. Conversely, a relational schema translatable to an ER diagram is said to be ER-consistent. For ER-consistent relational schemas we propose an *Entity-Relationship Normal Form*.

Our work emerged from, and is a continuation of, [11]. Prior to [11], ER to relational structure mappings were presented in numerous papers, starting with [2]; all these mappings are informal and do not attempt to characterize anyhow the relational translates of ER diagrams. The absence of such a characterization makes the reverse mappings presented in [6] and [8] partial and mostly informal. Our approach is graph oriented, allowing both an accurate and concise graph characterization of ER diagrams, and to relate ER diagrams to relational based graphs. Following [11], we give precedence to the structural information provided by the keys over the inclusion dependencies. Unlike [6], [8], and [11], we attempt not to rely on any convenient well behavior of relational schemas, in order to encompass an, as large as possible, class of relational schemas. Note that the Entity-Relationship Normal Form defined in [6] corresponds to our concept of ER-consistency, and not to the homonym normal form introduced by us.

A design methodology for relational schemas based on functional and inclusion dependencies is presented in [9]. The inclusion dependency set acyclicity and key basing, pursued by the methodology, are immediate results of the ER diagram to relational schema mapping presented by us. Furthermore, the flatness of the pure relational environment of [9] defeats any intention of a simple and natural design.

ER-consistency expresses the capability of relational schemas to model information oriented systems. We propose the ER-consistency based schema design as the, information oriented, alternative to the, syntactically oriented, relational normalization, as suggested in [1]. ER-consistent relational schemas allow the direct use of ER oriented query and update languages within the relational model.

The 2nd section of the paper reviews concepts of the relational model necessary to our presentation. Next, in section 3, we introduce the graph oriented definition of ER diagrams. In section 4 we present the mapping of ER diagrams to relational schemas and the characterization of the translate relational schemas. In section 5 we discuss the significance of ER consistency and how it relates to relational normal forms. In section 6 we propose a reverse mapping, from relational schemas to ER diagrams, and investigate when and whether this mapping is possible. In section 7, for ER-consistent relational schemas, we propose an Entity-Relationship Normal Form, and present the corresponding normalization procedure. We close the paper by summarizing the results and drawing some conclusions.

II. THE RELATIONAL MODEL.

A *relational schema (RS)* is a pair (R, D) where R is a set of relational schemes, $R=(R_1,...,R_k)$, and D is a set of dependencies over R. A *relational scheme* is a named set of attributes, $R_i(A_i)$. On the semantic level, every attribute is assigned a domain. A *database state* of R is defined as $r = <D_1,...,D_m, r_1...r_k>$, where r_i is assigned a subset of the cartesian product of the domains corresponding to its attributes.

In the present paper we are concerned with two kinds of dependencies, one inner relational, and one inter relational. A *functional dependency (FD)* over $R_i(A_i)$, is a statement of the form $X \rightarrow Y$, where both X and Y are subsets of A_i; an FD $X \rightarrow Y$ is valid in a state r iff for any two tuples of r_i, t and t', $t[Y]=t'[Y]$, whenever $t[X]=t'[X]$. A *key dependency (KD)* over R_i, is the functional dependency $K_i \rightarrow A_i$, where $K_i \subseteq A_i$ and there is no subset of K_i with this property; K_i is called *key*. An *inclusion dependency (IND)* is a statement of the form $R_i[X] \subseteq R_j[Y]$, where X and Y are subsets of A_i and A_j, respectively, and $|X|=|Y|$. An IND $R_i[X] \subseteq R_j[Y]$, is valid in a state r, iff $r_i[X] \subseteq r_j[Y]$. The sets of KDs and INDs associated with some relational schema, are denoted K and I, respectively.

Provided the domains are sets of interpreted values which are restricted conceptually and operationally, two attributes are said to be *compatible* if they are associated with a same domain. Compatible attributes with different names express, generally, different *roles* played by a domain within a database. Two sets of attributes, A_i and A_j, are said to be *compatible* iff there is a one-to-one correspondence of compatible attributes between A_i and A_j.
The *attribute compatibility graph* is the graph $G_{AC}=(V,E)$, where $V=A$ and (A_{i_1},A_{i_2}) is an edge of E iff A_{i_1} and A_{i_2} are compatible; then, two attributes are said to be compatible if they belong to a same connected component of the associated attribute compatibility graph. If the domains are sets of *uninterpreted* values, an alternative way of defining attribute compatibility is either by explicitly specifying the attribute compatibility graph or by using the set of specified INDs as follows: given a set of INDs, I, over R, the attribute compatibility graph is defined as above, but (A_{i_1},A_{i_2}) is an edge of E iff there is some IND in I, $R_1[X_{j_1}...X_{j_m}] \subseteq R_2[Y_{j_1}...Y_{j_m}]$ s.t. $A_{i_1}=X_{j_k}$ and $A_{i_2}=Y_{j_k}$.

Given a relation scheme R_i, a *correlation key (CK)* in R_i is a subset of A_i, CK_{i_j}, appearing as a key in some relation, other than R_i. For a relation scheme R_i, $CK_i = \bigcup_j CK_{i_j}$.

For a set of KDs, K, over R, the associated *key correlation graph (KG)* is a digraph $G_K=(V,E)$, where $V=R$ and $R_1 \rightarrow R_2$ is an edge of E iff (i) $CK_1=K_1=K_2$; or (ii) $K_2 \underset{\neq}{\subset} CK_1$ and there is no R_3 s.t. $K_2 \underset{\neq}{\subset} CK_3$ and $K_3 \underset{\neq}{\subset} CK_1$.

An IND $R_1[X] \subseteq R_2[Y]$, is said to be

(i) *key-based* [12], if $Y=K_2$; and

(ii) *typed* [7], if $X=Y$.

A set of INDs, I, is said to be

(i) *bounded* [12], if whenever $R_1[X_1] \subseteq R_2[X_2]$, and $R_1[X_1] \subseteq R_3[X_3]$, then there is R_4 s.t. $R_2[X_2] \subseteq R_4[X_4]$, and $R_3[X_3] \subseteq R_4[X_4]$, are implied by I; and

(i) *cyclic* if either $R_i[X] \subseteq R_i[Y]$ for $X \neq Y$, or there are $R_1...R_n$ s.t. $R_1[X_1] \subseteq R_2[Y_2]$, $R_2[X_2] \subseteq R_3[Y_3]$, ..., $R_n[X_n] \subseteq R_1[Y_1]$.

For a set of INDs, I, over R, the associated *IND graph (IG)* is the digraph $G_I=(V,E)$, where $V=R$ and $R_1 \rightarrow R_2$ is an edge of E iff $R_1[X] \subseteq R_2[Y]$ is in I.

Proposition 1.1 (Theorem 1 [12]). A set of INDs, I, is acyclic iff the associated IG digraph is a dag.

Proposition 1.2 (Theorem 5.1 [7]). Given a set of typed INDs, I, every IND $R_i[X] \subseteq R_j[Y]$ is implied by I iff either it is trivial, or $X=Y$ and there is a path from R_i to R_j in the associated IG digraph, corresponding to a sequence of INDs of I, $R_i[W] \subseteq \cdots \subseteq R_j[W]$, s.t. $X \subseteq W$.

Proposition 1.3 (Theorem 5.3 [7]). Let I and K be sets of INDs and KDs, respectively, in a relation schema (R,K,I); then $(I \cup K)^+ = I^+ \cup K^+$.

III. THE ENTITY-RELATIONSHIP DIAGRAM.

An Entity-Relationship Schema, called the *Entity-Relationship Diagram (ERD)* , is a finite labeled digraph $G_{ER}=(V,H)$, where

- V is the disjoint union of four sets of vertices:

  (i) s-vertices (S); (ii) a-vertices (A); (iii) e-vertices (E); and (iv) r-vertices (R);

- H is the set of directed edges, where an edge can be of one of the following forms:

  (i) $E_i \rightarrow A_j$; (ii) $R_i \rightarrow A_j$; (iii)$R_i \rightarrow E_j$; (iv) $E_i \rightarrow E_j$; (v) $A_i \rightarrow S_j$.

The *reduced ERD, ErRD,* is the digraph $G'_{ER} = (V',H')$, $V'=E \cup R$, and $H'=H-\{X_i \rightarrow A_j \mid X_i \rightarrow A_j \in H\}$.

Graphically s-vertices and e-vertices are represented by rectangles, a-vertices and r-vertices are represented graphically by circles and diamonds, respectively. A self-explanatory example of an ERD is given in figure 1.

Intuitively, s-vertices, e-vertices, a-vertices and r-vertices represent value-sets, entity-sets, attributes of entity-sets or relationship-sets, and relationship-sets, respectively. An *entity-set* groups entities of a same type, where the entity-type is perceived as the sharing of a same set of attributes. A *value-set* is a special kind of entity-set, without attributes, and grouping atomic values of a certain type. A relationship represents the interaction between several entities, and relationships of the same type are grouped in a *relationship-set.* A relationship-set can have attributes, just like an entity-set. An attribute is associated with one or several value-sets and provides an interpretation for that combination of value-sets in the context of an entity-set or relationship-set. A subset of the attributes associated with an entity-set may be specified as the, not necessarily unique, *entity-identifier*. An entity-set in a relationship-set may have a *role,* expressing the function it plays in the relationship.

Every ERD vertex is labeled by the name of the associated value-set, entity-set, relationship-set, or attribute name; e-vertices, r-vertices and s-vertices are uniquely identified by their labels globally, while a-vertices are uniquely identified by their labels only locally, within the set of a-vertices connected to some e-vertex/r-vertex. Generally value-sets are not represented in ERD and, alternatively, every edge $E_i \rightarrow A_j$ or $R_i \rightarrow A_j$, may be labeled by the combined type of the value-sets associated with A_j. In the present paper we omit the specification of value-sets for the sake of conciseness.

We shall use the following notations:

- X_i denotes either E_i or R_i;
- $Atr(X_i) = \{A_j \mid X_i \rightarrow A_j \in H\}$;
- $Id(E_i) \subseteq Atr(E_i)$, denotes the *entity-identifier* specified for E_i;

- $Ent(X_i) = \{E_j | X_i \rightarrow E_j \in H\}$;
- $X_i \rightarrow\rightarrow X_j$ denotes a directed path from X_i to X_j.

ERD edges specify existence constraints:

$(X_i \rightarrow A_j)$ where X_i is either an e-vertex or an r-vertex, express the fact that an attribute value is meaningful only as characterizing an entity or relationship;

$(E_i \rightarrow E_j)$ an entity may be contingent on the existence of other entities, through ISA or ID relationships:

- the ISA relationship expresses a subset relationship between two entity-sets; the corresponding edge is labeled by an *ISA* label and is called ISA-edge;
- the ID relationship expresses an identification relationship between an entity-set, called weak entity-set, which cannot be identified by its own attributes, but has to be identified by its relationship(s) with other entity-sets; the corresponding edge is labeled by an *ID* label and is called ID-edge;

$(R_i \rightarrow E_j)$ a relationship can exist only when the related entities also exist.

Cardinality constraints [13] are restrictions on the minimum and maximum number of entities from a given entity-set, that can be related, in the context of some relationship-set, to a specific combination of entities from other entity-sets. Every edge $R_i \rightarrow E_j$ is labeled as follows: if it corresponds to a maximum cardinality of one, it is labeled with *1* , and is called *one-labeled* ; if it corresponds to a maximum cardinality greater than one, it is labeled with *m, n* ..., and is called *many-labeled* ; we shall assume that at least one outgoing edge of every r-vertex is many labeled.

Identifiers are underlined

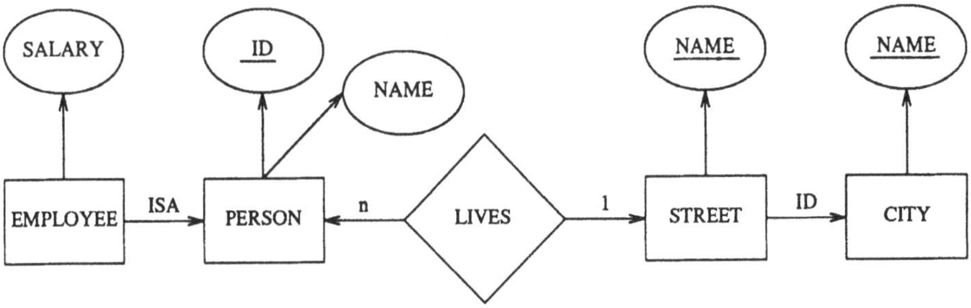

Fig.1 Entity-Relationship Diagram example.

A directed path in an ERD is called an *ISA-path* if all the edges on the path are ISA-edges; a directed path in an ERD is called an *ID-path* if at least one edge on the path is an ID-edge. An ISA-path (ID-path) from E_i to E_j, is denoted $E_i\text{–}ISA \rightarrow\rightarrow E_j$ ($E_i\text{–}ID \rightarrow\rightarrow E_j$).

The entity-set, relationship-set and attribute *compatibility*, whose intuition is straightforward, have the following ERD based definitions:

(i) two attributes, A_i and A_j, are said to be compatible iff the a-vertices representing them are connected to the same s-vertices, that is, are of the same type;

(ii) two entity-sets, E_i and E_j, are said to be compatible iff either they are directly connected by an ISA-path, or there is some e-vertex E_k such that $E_i\text{–}ISA \rightarrow\rightarrow E_k$ and $E_j\text{–}ISA \rightarrow\rightarrow E_k$; and

(iii) two relationship-sets, R_i and R_j, are said to be compatible iff there is a one-to-one correspondence of compatible entity-sets between $Ent(R_i)$ and $Ent(R_j)$.

Definition. An ERD is said to be *well-formed* iff it obeys the following constraints:

(ER0) every *a-vertex* A_i, has $indegree(A_i)=1$;

(ER1) every *e-vertex* E_i,

(ER1.i) cannot have both ISA and ID outgoing edges;

(ER1.ii) $Id(E_i) \neq \emptyset$, whenever it has either outgoing ID-edges, or $Ent(E_i)=0$;

(ER1.iii) $Id(E_i)=\emptyset$, whenever it has outgoing ISA-edges;

(ER1.iv) there are no attributes connected to a same set of value-sets, that is of a same type, neither within an entity-identifier, nor in different entity-identifiers;

(ER2) every *r-vertex* R_i, has $indegree(R_i)=0$ and $Ent(R_i) \geq 2$;

(ER3) ERD is a connected dag;

(ER4) there are no parallel or unlabeled edges;

(ER5) two ISA paths having a common start e-vertex, E_i, must end in a same e-vertex, E_j, $j \neq i$;

(ER6) let two ID/directed paths start in the e-vertex/r-vertex, X_i, and let E_j, $j \neq i$, be their common end e-vertex;

(ER6.i) every edge, $X_k \rightarrow E_j$, belonging to these paths, must be labeled by the corresponding role of E_j; or

(ER6.ii) if roles are not used, two ID/directed paths having the same start e-vertex/r-vertex, must never meet.

Constraints (ER0) to (ER6) define proper ER structures. An attribute characterizes a single entity-set or relationship-set, therefore an a-vertex is connected by a single edge to a single e-vertex or r-vertex, as expressed by constraint (ER0). Note that directed cycles could consist only of ISA and ID edges. Constraint (ER3) above guarantees that such cycles do not exist; the meaning of this constraint is that an entity-set will neither be defined as depending on identification on itself, nor be defined as a proper subset of itself. Constraint (ER5) above guarantees entity-set compatibility. Constraint (ER6) expresses the minimal role labeling requirement, namely, whenever an entity-set is involved, with different functions, in some entity or relationship, set. In order to avoid the use of roles, we shall assume that two ID/directed paths having the same start e-vertex/r-vertex, do not meet (ER6.ii).

IV. MAPPING ER DIAGRAMS INTO RELATIONAL SCHEMAS.

The mapping shown in figure 2 is an extension of the known ER to relational schema mapping (cf. [2]). An exemplification of this mapping is given in figure 3, for the ERD of figure 1, section III.

Input: $G_{ER}=(V,H)$, an ERD;

Output: the relational schema (R,K,I) interpreting G_{ER};

(0) initially R,K,I, are empty;

(1) assure *global uniqueness* for labels of a-vertices belonging to entity-identifiers: prefix the labels of the a-vertices belonging to entity-identifiers by the label of the corresponding e-vertex;

(2) compute the following sets of a-vertices:

(2.i) for every e-vertex, E_i:

$$Key(E_i)=Id(E_i) \cup \{Key(E_j) \mid E_i \rightarrow\rightarrow E_j\};$$

$$TotAtr(E_i)=Atr(E_i) \cup Key(E_i);$$

(2.ii) for every r-vertex, R_i:

$$Key(R_i)=\bigcup \{Key(E_j) \mid R_i \rightarrow E_j \text{ is many-labeled }\};$$

$$TotAtr(R_i)=Atr(R_i) \cup \{Key(E_j) \mid R_i \rightarrow E_j \};$$

Note: ERD acyclicity guarantees the finiteness of this step;

(3) for every e-vertex/r-vertex X_i, define relation-scheme R_i:

$$A_i := TotAtr(X_i); \quad R := R \cup R_i(A_i);$$

$$K_i := Key(X_i); \quad K := K \cup (K_i \rightarrow A_i);$$

(4) for every edge $X_i \rightarrow E_j$, where X_i is an e-vertex/r-vertex and E_j is an e-vertex, corresponding to relational schemes R_i and R_j, respectively:

$$I := I \cup (R_i[K_j] \subseteq R_j[K_j]);$$

(5) build the attribute compatibility graph, G_{AC}, following the ERD based definition of compatibility.
Note: only the ERD attribute compatibility has a relational correspondent, and accordingly, the entity-set and relationship-set compatibility is lost by the mapping.

Fig. 2 Mapping ER Diagram into Relational Schema Procedure (T_s).

Lemma 4.1.

Let (R, K, I) be the relational schema translate of the ERD G_{ER}; the IG digraph G_I associated with (R, K, I), and the corresponding ERrD G'_{ER}, are isomorphic.

Proof:

(i) a vertex of G'_{ER} is either an e-vertex or an r-vertex; by translation T_s (step 3), to every such vertex corresponds exactly one relation scheme which, in G_I, is associated, by definition, with exactly one vertex;

(ii) let $X_i \rightarrow X_j$ be an edge of G'_{ER}, such that X_i and X_j correspond, by translation T_s, to relation schemes R_i and R_j respectively; by translation T_s (step 4), $X_i \rightarrow X_j$ iff $R_i[K_j] \subseteq R_j[K_j]$, which is associated in G_I with the edge $R_i \rightarrow R_j$.

The following proposition provides the characterization of the relation-scheme translates of r-vertices and e-vertices.

Proposition 4.2.

Let (R, K, I) be a relational schema translate of an ERD G_{ER}. An IND of I, $R_i[K_j] \subseteq R_j[K_j]$, corresponds to an edge of G_{ER} which is:

ID-labeled	iff K_i is not included in CK_i;
ISA-labeled	iff $K_i = CK_i = K_j$;
many-labeled	iff $K_i \subsetneq CK_i$, and $K_j \subseteq K_i$;
one-labeled	iff $K_i \subseteq CK_i$, K_j not included in K_i and $K_j \subsetneq CK_i$.

The proof of the above proposition is based directly on the mapping T_s. An illustration of the above proposition is given in figure 4.

---

relation-schemes (keys are underlined):

CITY(CITY.NAME)
STREET(STREET.NAME,CITY.NAME)
PERSON(PERSON.ID,NAME)
EMPLOYEE(PERSON.ID,SALARY)
LIVES(PERSON.ID,STREET.NAME,CITY.NAME)

inclusion dependencies:

STREET[CITY.NAME] ⊆ CITY[CITY.NAME]
LIVES[STREET.NAME,CITY.NAME] ⊆ STREET[STREET.NAME,CITY.NAME]
LIVES[PERSON.ID] ⊆ PERSON[PERSON.ID]
EMPLOYEE[PERSON.ID] ⊆ PERSON[PERSON.ID]

Fig.3 Relational Schema Translate of the ERD of Fig.1.

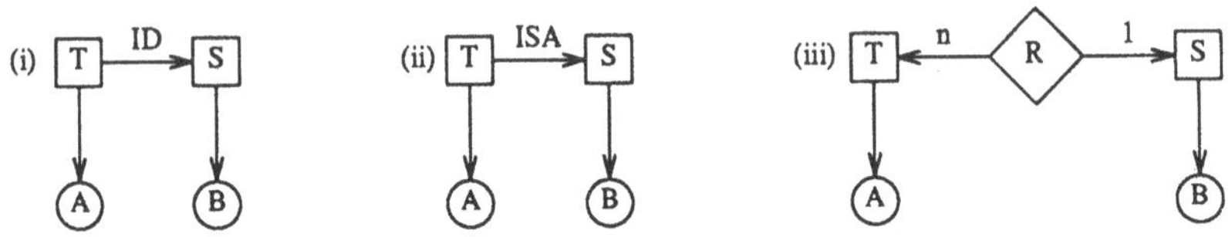

(i) S(B), key B; T(AB), key AB, correlation key B; and T[B] $\subseteq$ S[B];

(ii) S(B), key B; T(AB), key B, correlation key B; and T[B] $\subseteq$ S[B];

(iii) S(B), key B; T(A), key A; R(AB), key A, correlation key AB; and R[A] $\subseteq$ T[A], R[B] $\subseteq$ S[B].

Fig.4 Exemplification for Proposition 4.2

Proposition 4.3.
Let (R, K, I) be the relational schema translate of an ERD G_{ER}. The corresponding IND set, I, is typed, key-based, acyclic and bounded.
Proof:

(i) the translation T_s generates only key-based and typed INDs;

(ii) since the IG graph associated with the relational schema translate and the corresponding ERrD are isomorphic (lemma 4.1), the IG graph inherits the acyclicity property (ER3) of the ERD; consequently, the IND set I is acyclic (Proposition 1.1);

(iii) suppose $R_1[A] \subseteq R_2[A]$ and $R_1[A] \subseteq R_3[A]$; by (ER0) and (ER6), it can be shown that R_1 can be the translate only of an e-vertex, and both INDs correspond to ISA edges; as above, the IG graph inherits the property (ER5) of the corresponding ERD, which expresses the boundness property for the involved, typed and key-based, INDs.

Definition. The relational schema translate of an ERD is said to be trivially *Entity-Relationship (ER) consistent.*

V. ER-CONSISTENCY vs RELATIONAL NORMALIZATION.

The relational model has intended to achieve data independence by separating the logical and physical aspects of database management [4]. ER-consistency carries out the same objective on a higher level by making independent the actual information from its logical data representation.

Relational normal forms (cf. [14]) have been developed in order to decrease both the impact of the side effects when changing relations and the data redundancy in relations. The main cause of lack of normalization is the embedding of data about independent real-world facts into one relation. Real-world facts are described by natural language sentences. We shall call a fact *elementary* if it is described by a single-verb declarative natural language sentence. The ER-oriented schema design, together with the principle that a relationship-type always models an elementary fact, ensure a certain degree of *information normalization*. ER-consistent schemas favor the realization of many of the relational normalization objectives. An example should make this clear. Let DEPARTMENT(DN, SN, FLOOR) be a relation-scheme with DN, SN and FLOOR denoting department number, supplier number and department floor, respectively; let DN,SN be the designated key, and DN → FLOOR be an FD. The scheme is not normalized ,namely not in 2NF, because of the partial functional dependency of attribute FLOOR on a key subset. Suppose that the associated key is only SN; then the scheme is still not normalized, now not in 3NF, because of the transitive dependency of attribute FLOOR on key SN. In both situations the relational scheme represents the *embedding of independent relationships*, among DN and FLOOR, and DN and SN, respectively.

Relational normal forms are *data representation* normalizations, while ER-consistency is an expression of information normalization. Therefore, ER-consistency is not equivalent to any of the normal forms, such as 2NF, 3NF, etc. Thus, DEPARTMENT in the above example becomes normalized if DN is the designated key, but remains *not* ER-consistent (figure 5). As another example, take the step of collapsing relations with equivalent keys in the normalization procedures (cf. [14]). The equivalence of keys could represent a one-to-one relationship, such as an ISA relationship, therefore the merging of such relations might lead to the embedding of independent facts, precisely what normal forms try to avoid. By achieving a certain level of semantic separation, the relational normal forms overlap with ER-consistency, but do not ensure it. Similarly, ER-consistency does not ensure relational normalization as illustrated by the following example: let SUPPLY(DN,IN,SN), with key DN,IN, be the translate of the

---

Identifiers and keys are underlined

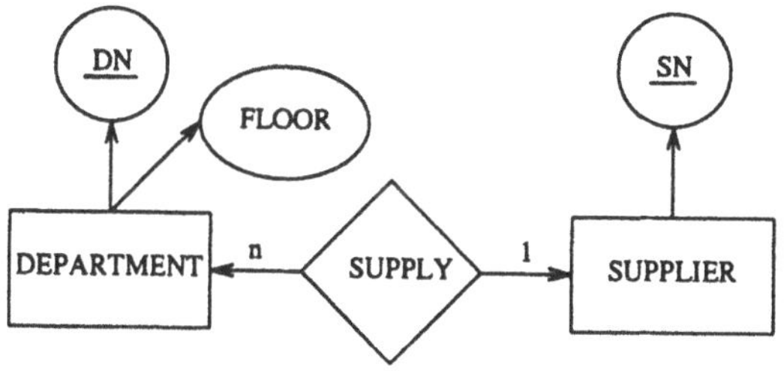

ER-consistent relational schema:

DEPARTMENT(DN, FLOOR), SUPPLIER(SN) SUPPLY(DN,SN)

SUPPLY[DN] ⊆ DEPARTMENT[DN], SUPPLY[SN] ⊆ SUPPLIER[SN]

3NF relational schema:

DEPARTMENT(DN,SN,FLOOR), SUPPLIER(SN)

Fig.5 ER-Consistent vs 3NF Relational Schema.

SUPPLY r-vertex below:

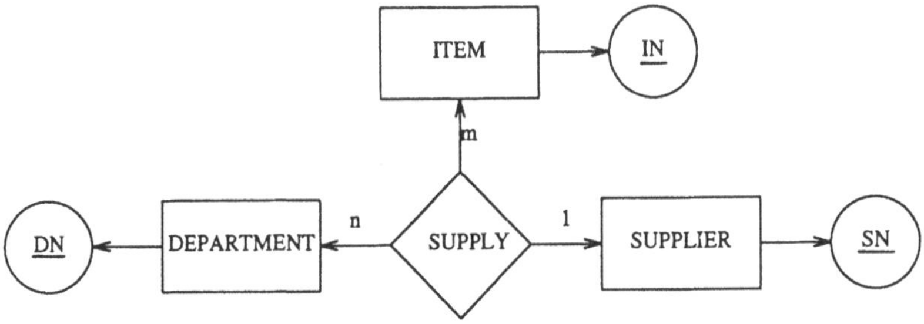

The additional FD constraint IN $\rightarrow$ SN, causes the relation scheme not to be in 2NF. Regarding the ER-consistency, it does not matter whether some relation scheme can be further normalized. In the example above, for instance, only from a data representation point of view is important to decompose the SUPPLY relation, in order to reduce the data redundancy; on the information level, only the representation of the elementary fact "supplier supplies items to departments", is relevant.

The acyclicity, boundness and key-basing properties imposed on the set of INDs have been proposed in [12] in order to restrict the excessive, and possibly harmful, power of INDs. These properties, considered in [12] as necessary characteristics of well-designing, are captured in a precise manner by ER-consistency. Moreover, ER-oriented schema design makes possible the expression of the *explicit* inclusion dependencies as ERD *inherent* constraints, that is, constraints that are part of the schema structure, which considerably simplifies their use.

A design methodology for relational schemas based on functional and inclusion dependencies has been investigated in [9]. Unlike traditional normalization procedures, the proposed methodology is interactive, leading to an *Inclusion Dependency Normal Form.* The inclusion dependency set acyclicity and key basing pursued by the methodology are immediate results of mapping ER diagrams into relational schemas. Furthermore, the flatness of the pure relational environment defeats the declared intention of a simple and natural design.

VI. MAPPING RELATIONAL SCHEMAS INTO ER DIAGRAMS.

Now we shall investigate the question of the range of the translation T_s, and when and whether a reverse translation T_s^R is defined.

Let (R,K,I) be the translate relational schema of ERD G_{ER}. We have seen above that the INDs generated by translation T_s are key-based, and that the corresponding IG digraph G_I and the source ERrD G'_{ER} are isomorphic. Moreover, for a translate relational schema, G_I is a subgraph of G_K: both have the same set of vertices; and the set of edges of G_I is a subset of the set of edges of G_K. These observations suggest to base the reverse translation from relational schemas to ERDs, T_s^R, on the structural information provided by the key set. Given a relational schema (R,K,I), our procedure derives a *candidate* ERD from G_K, and verifies whether it is *well-formed.*

Mapping Relational Schemas into ER Diagrams (T_s^R).

Input: relational schema (R, K, I) and the associated attribute compatibility graph G_{AC}, where I is acyclic and in any key of K, there are no two compatible attributes.

Output: either an ERD G_{ER}, or a fail message;

(0) rename to a common name all the key attributes associated with vertices belonging to a same connected component of G_{AC};

(1) construct the digraph G_K associated with the input relational schema;

(2) derive candidate ERrD $G'_{ER} = (V'_{ER}, H'_{ER})$, from G_K:

(2.1) $V'_{ER} := V_K$, and $H'_{ER} := H_K$;

(2.2) label every edge in H'_{ER}, $X_i \rightarrow Y_j$, corresponding to edge $R_i \rightarrow R_j$ in G_K, as follows:

(ID-label) K_i not included in CK_i;

(ISA-label) $K_i = K_j = CK_i$;

(many-label) $K_i \subsetneq CK_i$, and $K_j \subseteq K_i$;

(one-label) $K_i \subseteq CK_i$, K_j not included in K_i and $K_j \subsetneq CK_i$.

(2.3) split V'_{ER} into two disjunctive sets of e-vertices and r-vertices, where vertex X_i is an r-vertex iff every outgoing edge is either many- or one-labeled;

(3) for every edge $X_i \rightarrow X_j \in G'_{ER}$, of one of the following forms, corresponding to edge $R_i \rightarrow R_j \in G_K$, verify:

(E_i–$ID \rightarrow E_j$) if $R_i[K_j] \subseteq R_j[K_j]$ is not logically implied by (K, I), then *mark* missing IND;

(E_i–$ISA \rightarrow E_j$) if $R_i[K_j] \subseteq R_j[K_j]$ is not logically implied by (K, I), then:

remove E_i–$ISA \rightarrow E_j$ from G'_{ER}, whenever E_j–$ISA \rightarrow E_i \in H'_{ER}$;

mark missing IND, whenever E_j–$ISA \rightarrow E_i \notin H'_{ER}$;

($R_i \rightarrow E_j$) if $R_i[K_j] \subseteq R_j[K_j]$ is not logically implied by (K, I), then:

remove $R_i \rightarrow E_j$ from G'_{ER}, whenever there is E_k s.t. both $R_i \rightarrow E_k \in H'_{ER}$ and E_j–$ISA \rightarrow E_k \in H'_{ER}$;

if there is no E_k s.t. both $R_i \rightarrow E_k \in H'_{ER}$ and E_j–$ISA \rightarrow E_k \in H'_{ER}$, then *mark* missing IND;

(4) remove extraneous edges from G'_{ER}:

(E_i–$ISA \rightarrow E_j$) remove E_i–$ISA \rightarrow E_j$ from G'_{ER} whenever there is an ISA-path, other than E_i–$ISA \rightarrow E_j$, from E_i to E_j;

($R_i \rightarrow E_j$) remove $R_i \rightarrow E_j$ from G'_{ER} whenever there is an e-vertex E_k s.t. both $R_i \rightarrow E_k \in H'_{ER}$ and E_k–$ISA \rightarrow\rightarrow E_j \in H'_{ER}$;

(5) complete ERrD to a full ERD:

for every e-vertex E_i corresponding to relation scheme $R_i(A_i)$:

$Id(E_i) = K_i - \{A_j \mid A_j \in Id(E_j)$, where $E_i \rightarrow\rightarrow E_j\}$; $Atr(E_i) = Id(E_i) \cup (A_i - K_i)$;

for every r-vertex R_i corresponding to relation scheme $R_i(A_i)$:

$$Atr(R_i) = A_i - \{A_j \mid A_j \in Id(E_j), \text{ where } R_i \to\to E_j\};$$

(6) verify that the resulting ERD, G_{ER}, is *well-formed*, that is, constraints (ER0) to (ER6) hold.

Several remarks concerning T_s^R are in order:

(i) since implication for unrestricted sets of INDs and FDs is undecidable [10], we must require the input set of INDs to be acyclic; implication for acyclic INDs and FDs has exponential lower bound [5], therefore step (3) of T_s^R is, generally, highly complex; by further restricting the set of input INDs to typed and key-based INDs, which we know to be the only ones we are interested in, the complexity of this step could be reduced to polynomial (Propositions 1.2 and 1.3);

(ii) step (2) of T_s^R is based on lemma 4.1 and proposition 4.2;

(iii) in step (3) apparently missing INDs are *marked*; this feature of T_s^R highlights the precedence given in T_s^R to the keys over the inclusion dependencies: we assume that the choice of the key for a relational scheme is not arbitrary, but it represents either an entity or a relationship; accordingly, an attribute set A_j compatible with some key K_i, refers to the same entity-set or relationship-set which is represented by K_i and we shall *expect* that either $R_j[A_j] \subseteq R_i[K_i]$ or $R_i[K_i] \subseteq R_j[A_j]$ will hold;

(iv) the failure of T_s^R does not mean necessarily that the relational schema has no associated ERD, but could be the result of a specific key choosing; such failures could be limited by extending the input set of keys with several, rather than one, candidate keys for every relational scheme;

(v) the restriction put on the input set of keys is analogous to the constraints (ER1.iv) and (ER6.ii) (when roles are not considered); the following example illustrates the significance of constraint (ER6); let E(A), F(AB), G(AC) and R(ABC) be relational schemes with keys A, AB, AC and ABC, respectively, and let R[AB] $\subseteq$ F[AB], R[AC] $\subseteq$ G[AC], F[A] $\subseteq$ E[A] and G[A] $\subseteq$ E[A] be the associated set of INDs; the candidate ERD, which does not obey (ER6), would be

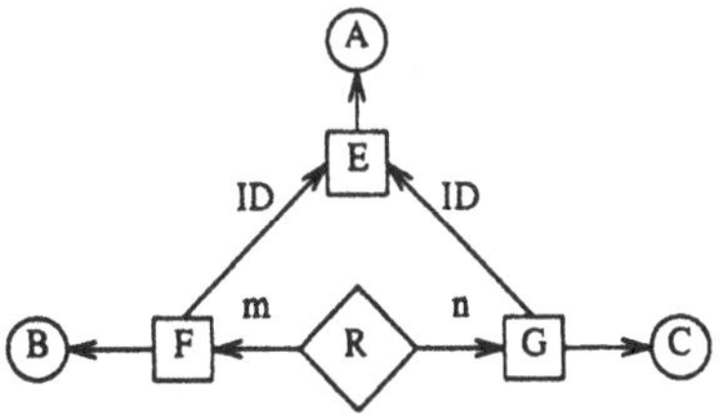

but the relationship key for R should be ABAC!; an extension of T_s^R in the sense of [11] could cope with the removal of these restrictions; the extension is straightforward but tedious;

(vi) note that $T_s^R o T_s (G_{ER}) \equiv G_{ER}$, but $T_s o T_s^R (R,K,I) \neq (R,K,I)$, that is, T_s^R is only the *left inverse* of T_s:

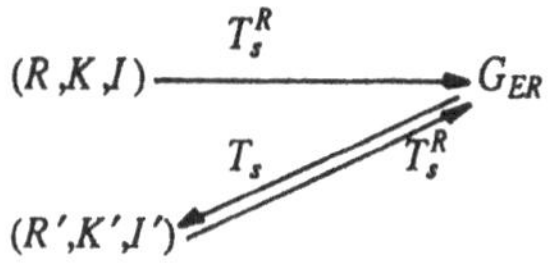

Definition. Entity-Relationship Consistency for relational schemas is defined as follows:

A relational schema (R,K,I) is said to be *ER-consistent* if there is a mapping S from the set of relational schemas to the set of ERDs, such that $T_s oS (R,K,I)$ and (R,K,I) are related in the following way:

(i) attributes are the same, up to a renaming for compatible key attributes;

(ii) relation schemes are the same, up to the renaming of compatible key attributes;

(iii) $T_s oS (I)$ is a consequence of (K,I).

Theorem.

Let (R,K,I) be a relation schema. Procedure T_s^R, taking (R,K,I) as input, succeeds iff (R,K,I) is ER-consistent.

Sketch of the proof: The if direction follows from the specification (Input/Output of T_s^R) and correctness of T_s^R (whose proof is out of the scope of this paper). For the other direction, it suffices to show that T_s^R succeeds on $T_s oS (R,K,I)$ rather than on (R,K,I). The latter is true because $S(R,K,I)$ is an ERD and therefore satisfies constraints (ER0) to (ER6).

VII. THE ENTITY-RELATIONSHIP NORMAL FORM.

We propose for the ER-consistent relational schemas a normal form called *Entity-Relationship Normal Form (ERNF)*. ERNF relation schemas are *key invariant*, thus representing the independence of the information structure from entity-identifier specifications. Note that the Entity-Relationship Normal Form defined in [6] corresponds to our concept of ER-consistency, and not to the homonym normal form introduced by us.

The mapping of ERDs into ERNF relational schemas, Tn_s, presented in figure 6, is an extension of the mapping T_s of section IV. Given an ERD digraph G_{ER}, we associate with every e-vertex E_i having $Id(E_i) \neq \emptyset$, a dummy a-vertex denoted $\%E_i$. The relational schema is of the form (R,K,I,J) where (R,K,I) is as before and J is a set of pairs $(\%E_i, Id(E_i))$, such that every pair corresponds to the relational scheme translate of an e-vertex E_i with $Id(E_i) \neq \emptyset$. An exemplification of the Tn_s mapping is given in figure 7, for the ERD of figure 1, section III.

Several remarks concerning this mapping are in order:

(i) we do not have to rename, as we did T_s (step 1), the labels of the a-vertices belonging to entity-identifiers in order to make them globally unique within the ERD digraph;

(ii) the dummy attribute acts almost like the surrogate attribute; recall that a surrogate is intended to represent an aggregated object, that is an entity, within a given database state [3]; a surrogate is information free and the

---

Input: $G_{ER}=(V,H)$, an ERD;

Output: the ERNF relational schema (R,K,I,J);

(0) initially R,K,I,J are empty;

(1) for every e-vertex E_i compute the set of a-vertices:

$$Key(E_i) = [\%E_i] \cup \{Key(E_j) | E_i \rightarrow\rightarrow E_j\}; \quad TotAtr(E_i) = Atr(E_i) \cup Key(E_i);$$

(2) for every e-vertex E_i with $Id(E_i) \neq \emptyset$;

$$J := J \cup (\%E_i, Id(E_i))$$

(3-6) : steps 2.ii-5 of T_s of section IV.

Fig.6 Mapping ER Diagram into ERNF Relational Schema Procedure (Tn_s).

---

user can do no more than cause its deletion or generation; for a given entity-set E_i, $Key(E_i)$, which is a set of dummy attributes, corresponds to the surrogate attribute and $Key(E_i)$ consists of more than one dummy attribute only for entity-sets which are ID related to other entity-sets;

(iii) extending Tn_s to handle several, rather than one, identifiers per entity-set, is straightforward;

(iv) T_s^R can be easily extended in order to obtain $T_s^R \; o \; Tn_s(G_{ER}) \equiv G_{ER}$.

The *normalization procedure* for an ER-consistent relational schema is $T_s^R \; o \; Tn_s$. The following proposition characterizes the relationship between an ER-consistent relational schema and its corresponding ER Normal Form.

---

relation-schemes (keys are underlined):

CITY(<u>%CITY</u>,NAME)
STREET(<u>%STREET</u>,%CITY,NAME)
PERSON(<u>%PERSON</u>,ID,NAME)
EMPLOYEE(<u>%PERSON</u>,SALARY)
LIVES(<u>%PERSON</u>,%STREET,%CITY)

inclusion dependencies:

STREET[%CITY] $\subseteq$ CITY[%CITY]
LIVES[%STREET,%CITY] $\subseteq$ STREET[%STREET,%CITY]
LIVES[%PERSON] $\subseteq$ PERSON[%PERSON]
EMPLOYEE[%PERSON] $\subseteq$ PERSON[%PERSON]

J={ (%COUNTRY,NAME), (%CITY,NAME), (%STREET,NAME), (%PERSON,ID) }.

Fig.7 ERNF Relational Schema Corresponding to the ERD of Fig.1.

Proposition 6.1

Let (R,K,I) be an ER-consistent relational schema, $(R^*,K^*,I^*,J^*) = T_s^R \circ Tn_s(R,K,I)$, its corresponding ERNF schema and let (R',K',I') be the result of mapping Td_s applied on (R^*,K^*,I^*,J^*):

(i)   the attributes of J^* are renamed in order to become globally unique within the relational schema;

(ii)   for every $(\%E_i,Id(E_i)) \in J^*$, replace $\%E_i$ by $Id(E_i)$ in:

(ii.R)   every relational scheme R_i of R^*;

(ii.K)   every key K_i of K^*; and

(ii.I)   every IND of J^*.

Then (R,K,I) and (R',K',I') are related in the following way:

(i)   attributes are the same, up to a renaming for compatible key attributes;

(ii)   relation schemes are the same, up to the renaming of compatible key attributes;

(iii) I' is a consequence of (K,I).

The proposition, whose proof is straightforward, expresses the following extension of the diagram of the preceding section:

$$
\begin{array}{ccc}
& T_s^R & \\
(R,K,I) & \xrightarrow{\hspace{2cm}} & G_{ER} \\
& T_s \nearrow \quad \nwarrow T_s^R \quad \downarrow Tn_s & \\
(R',K',I') & \xleftarrow{\hspace{2cm}} & (R^*,K^*,I^*,J^*) \\
& Td_s &
\end{array}
$$

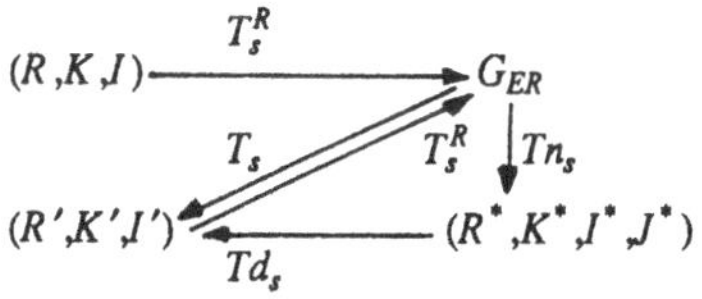

VIII. CONCLUSION.

We have introduced the concept of ER-consistency for relational schemas. ER oriented design, embodied by ER-consistency, simplifies and makes natural the task of keeping independent facts separated, and assures a greater adaptability to changes not concerning the structure of the modeled information, such as the cardinality of relationships. As such the ER-consistency based schema design is the, information structure oriented, alternative to the, syntactically oriented, relational normalization.

We have presented two mappings; the first defines the relational interpretation of ERDs; the second attempts to find the ERD correspondent of a relational schema. The ERD edges represent only a part of the INDs that could belong to some set I in a relation schema. Generally this restriction is useful in keeping the set of INDs manageable. However, some INDs are not representable because of the limitations of the ERD, such as the impossibility of connecting two r-vertices. An extension of the mappings T_s and T_s^R, over ERDs relaxing these restrictions is presented elsewhere. The range of both mappings can be also extended in the sense of [11], by using roles in order to loosen constraint (ER6.ii).

For the ER-consistent relational schemas we have proposed an *Entity-Relationship Normal Form (ERNF)*, and we have presented the corresponding normalization procedure. ERNF reflects the independence of the information structure from entity-identifier specifications.

ER-consistency expresses the capability of relational schemas to model information oriented systems. ER-consistent relational schemas allow the direct use of ER oriented query and update languages within the relational model.

REFERENCES.

[1] C.Beeri and M.Y.Vardi, "A note on decompositions of relations databases", *ACM SIGMOD Record* 12,1, Oct. 1981, pp. 33-37.

[2] P.P. Chen, "The entity-relationship model- towards a unified view of data", *ACM Trans. on Database Systems* 1,1 (March 1976), pp. 9-36.

[3] E.F. Codd, "Extending the relational database model to capture more meaning", *ACM Trans. on Database Systems* 4,4 (Dec 1979), pp. 397-434.

[4] E.F. Codd, "Relational databases: A practical foundation for productivity", *Comm. ACM* 25,2 (Feb 1982), pp. 109-117.

[5] S.S. Cosmadakis and P.C. Kanellakis, "Equational Theories and Database Constraints", in *Proc 17th ACM Symposium on Theory of Computing,* 1985, pp. 273-284.

[6] M.A. Casanova and J.E. Amaral de Sa, "Mapping uninterpreted schemes into entity-relationship diagrams: two applications to conceptual schema design", *IBM Journal of Research and Development* **28,** 1 (Jan 1984), pp. 82-94.

[7] M.A. Casanova and V.M.P. Vidal, "Towards a sound view integration methodology", *Proc of Second ACM Symposium on Principles of Database Systems* , 1983, pp. 36-47.

[8] A. Klug, "Entity-relationship views over uninterpreted enterprise schemas", *Entity-Relationship Approach to Systems Analysis and Design* , Chen, P.P.(ed), North-Holland, 1980, pp. 39-59.

[9] H. Mannila and K-J. Raiha, "Inclusion dependencies in database design", *Proc of Second Conf. on Data Engineering* , 1986, pp. 713-718.

[10] J.C. Mitchell, "The implication problem for functional and inclusion dependencies", *Information and Control* **56**,3 (March 1983), pp. 154-173.

[11] N. Rotics, *A unifying approach to the entity-relationship and relational data models,* M.Sc. Thesis, Computer Science Dept, Technion, Israel, June 1985.

[12] E. Sciore, "Inclusion dependencies and the universal instance", in *Proc. 1983 ACM Symposium on Principles of Database Systems* , 1983, pp. 48-57.

[13] D.C. Tsichritzis and F.H. Lochovsky, *Data models.* Prentice-Hall , 1982.

[14] J.D. Ullman, *Principles of database systems* (second edition), Computer Science Press, 1982.

Modelling Large Bases of Categorical Data with Acyclic Schemes

F. M. Malvestuto

(Studi: Documentazione e Informazione, ENEA - Italy)

ABSTRACT

The design and the implementation of a large base of categorical data raise several problems: storage requirements, performance of the query-processing system, consistency ... Most problems find a simple and efficient solution if and only if the database has an acyclic scheme.

1 . Introduction

Many existing databases contain "categorical data" [4], that is, counts of inividuals who within a categorical framework have the same description. Typical examples are: census data, demographic data, medical data, inventory data. Also the "distribution model" of a relational database [14] can be regarded as a categorical database.

Essentially, a categorical database is a collection of "contingency tables" [4], resulting from the categorization of the same population of individuals according several classification schemata.

By its nature, a categorical database is quasi-static, in that the updatings of its information content are done with considerable time intervals. So, the interrogation is the major operation on a categorical database. A query normally consists in the retrieval of some statistical information. However, a user may wish categorical data (referred to as "cross-classified categorical data"), that are not in the database but can be "estimated" starting from the stored data. In this case, we need an estimation procedure (equivalent to the join for relations), which is known as "iterative proportional fitting procedure" (IPFP) [4].

Typically, there are two ways where a categorical database can be built.

Top-down approach. A categorical database is the result of a decomposition of a single table that has such a high number of category attributes (this is the case of census data) that instead of storing the universal table the data base administrator decides to store a suitable set of its marginals in order to reduce both the storage requirement and the response time.

Bottom-up approach. A categorical database is formed by a number of tables coming from distinct data sources.

In both cases, we encounter more or less serious problems.
In the first case, we have to select the "best" decomposition with respect to a certain performance parameters, which take into account both the storage saving and the accuracy of the estimation procedure.
In the second case, the categorical data base should be globally compatible to combine the information contents of distinct tables. This is a crucial aspect of most categorical databases, which "do not represent a homogeneous collection of data, but can be thought of as multiple databases" [16] .

In this paper we show that acyclic database schemes, known from the relational database theory, enjoy the following desirable properties.

* The overhead introduced by the estimation procedure (IPFP) reduces practically to zero if anf only if the categorical database has an acyclic scheme.

* The top-down design of a categorical database is programmable if and only if it has an acyclic scheme.

* The pairwise compatibility of a categorical database is sufficient for its global compatibility if and only if it has an acyclic scheme.

The paper is organized as follows. Section 2 contains basic definitions and terminology. In Section 3 the notions of stochastic extension and model are introduced. In Section 4 and Section 5 desirable properties of acyclic schemes for categorical databases are stated. Section 6 deals with the implementation of a view.

2. Basic definitions and terminology

We are concerned with the situation where people or things are classified simultaneously by two or more category attributes. For example, we might categorize people simultaneously by sex, age, amount of schooling, region (see Example 1). The results of such a *multiple classification* can be conveniently arranged as a table of counts known as a *contingency table* [4].

EXAMPLE 1. *Distribution of Soviet Population in 1959 (000 individuals).*

		Urban Region				Rural region			
		Years of schooling				Years of schooling			
Sex	*Age*	< 4	4-7	8-10	>10	< 4	4-7	8-10	>10
Male	16-29	632	4381	7557	915	1719	5266	5719	154
	30-49	1177	4175	5384	1056	2387	4293	3051	317
	> 49	2376	1808	1188	502	5379	1862	376	69
Female	16-29	664	2844	9180	1275	2536	4247	5887	232
	30-49	3826	4482	6873	1071	7181	4653	3090	242
	> 49	7433	1889	1313	276	13090	1071	207	24

Source [4]

A contingency table is "complete" if it does not contain zero entries (see Example 1); otherwise, it is "incomplete" (see Example 2).

EXAMPLE 2. *Distribution of Soviet Population in 1959 (000 individuals)*

	Years of schooling			
Party Membership	< 4	4-7	8-10	>10
Yes	0	2290	4580	1368
No	48398	38685	45244	4764

Source [4]

The presence of zero entries in a table may be accidental *(random zero entries)* or may be due to conceptual relationships *(dependencies)* between category attributes that make certain category combinations logically impossible *(structural zero entries)* .

For example, given a set of category attributes, X , let Y and Z be two subsets of X . If Y is a classification that is a refinement of the classification Z , then it is not logically possible that two category combinations, or X-tuples, that agree on Y but disagree on Z have both a nonzero entry. Such a dependency is the analogue of a *functional dependency* for relational attributes. It is easy to see that all relational database dependencies (multivalued, first-order hierarchical, join dependencies) can be translated in a categorical context [11].

Dependencies derive from the semantical interpretation given to the category attributes concerned in a table. To specify a semantics, we have to specify the set of all possible X-tuples.

Formally, a *(contingency) table* T is defined by:

i) a finite set X of category attributes, according to which the individuals of a given population are classified (X is called the *classification schema*)

ii) a set Ω of X-tuples, called *cells* : a cell is defined by a combination of (logically) possible choices of a category for each attribute in X

iii) a frequency distribution $n(x)$ over the cells in Ω, normalized to the size N of the given population.

In the following, we limit ourselves to consider only "factorial" tables [4]. For these tables the set of cells Ω is the Cartesian product of the value sets associated with the attributes of the classification schema (see Example 1 and 2). This implies no dependencies are assumed to hold in factorial tables.

Given a (factorial) table T, the subset R of Ω defined as

$$R = \{x \textit{ in } \Omega : n(x) > 0\}$$

will be called the *characteristic relation* of the table. By definition, if T contains random zero entries, they are in $\Omega - R$.
Now, let Y be a subset of X . The marginal count $n(y)$ is the number of individuals in the marginal cell y, obtained as the sum of the $n(x)$ for all the cells x that agree with y on the attributes in Y:

$$n(y) = \sum n(x)$$

In other words, the distribution $n(y)$ gives the counts in the marginal table, $T[Y]$, where the individuals only are classified according to the category attributes in Y . The cell set of the resulting marginal table is the projection of Ω onto Y .

A *categorical database scheme* (abbr. *database scheme*) $S = \{X_1, \ldots, X_k\}$ is a collection of sets of category attributes. If $T_1, \ldots, T_k$ are contingency tables with classification schemata $X_1, \ldots, X_k$ over the same population of individuals, then we call $\mathcal{T} = \{T_1, \ldots, T_k\}$ a *categorical database* over S . We say that $\mathcal{T} = \{T_1, \ldots, T_k\}$ is:

pairwise compatible if the marginals of T_i and T_j onto the set of their common attributes are the same, for each i and j;

globally compatible if there is a "universal table" T with classification schema $X = U_i X_i$ (that we may call the *universal schema*) such that the marginal of T with classification schema X_i coincides with T_i, for each i.

With every categorical database we may associate a *relational database* .
If $\mathcal{T} = \{T_1,...,T_k\}$ is a categorical database with $T_i = < X_i, \Omega_i, n_i(x_i) >$, let us define the *characteristic relation* of the table T_i as follows

$$R_i = \{x_i \textit{ in } \Omega_i : n_i(x_i) > 0\}.$$

The set $\mathcal{R} = \{R_1,...,R_k\}$ defines a relational database over S . It will be called the *relational database associated with* $\mathcal{T}$.
Recall that a relational database, $\mathcal{R} = \{R_1,...,R_k\}$, is:

pairwise consistent if the projections of any two relations R_i and R_j onto the set of the common attributes are the same;

globally consistent if there exists a "universal relation" , R , such that each relation R_i is a projection of R.

The pairwise (global) compatibility of a categorical database is closely connected with the pairwise (global) consistency of its associated relational database.
We shall come back to the compatibility of a categorical database in Section 5.

3. Join of relations and stochastic extension

In this section, we are concerned with the problem of combining the information contents of two or more data sets, no matter whether relations or contingency tables. We present a general inference method based on the *entropy principle,* which states that *of all extensions of given data sets, we should choose the one with the largest entropy* (extensions and entropy will be defined in a moment). Compared with other methods of inductive inference, the entropy principle proves to be the uniquely "correct" method [15].

We begin to consider a globally consistent relational database $\mathcal{R} = \{R_1,...,R_k\}$

over $S = \{X_1,\ldots,X_k\}$. By an *extension* of $\mathcal{R}$ we mean a relation over the universal schema $X = \cup_i X_i$ that has $R_1,\ldots,R_k$ as its projections.
The *join* of $R_1,\ldots,R_k$ is the extension R^* defined as

$$R^* = \{x \textit{ with } X_i\textit{-component in } R_i \ (i=1,\ldots,k)\} .$$

The importance of the join in the relational database theory is due to the fact that, if $S = \{X_1,\ldots,X_k\}$ defines a "join dependency", any relation R over X , where that join dependency holds, can be recovered without loss of information by joining its projections $R_1,\ldots,R_k$ onto $X_1,\ldots,X_k$.
But, if little is known about the relationship among the category attributes, a question raises in a natural way: if a user wishes cross-referenced relational data, how to compose the relations of a relational database ?
Indeed, there are as many ways to combine given relations as their extensions. For example, consider the following two relations with binary attributes:

AB	AC
00	00
01	01
10	10
	11

They admit 7 extensions, of which two contain 4 tuples, four contain 5 tuples and one contains 6 tuples.

ABC	ABC	ABC	ABC	ABC	ABC	ABC
001	000	001	000	000	000	000
010	011	010	010	001	001	001
100	100	011	011	011	010	010
101	101	100	100	100	100	011
		101	101	101	101	100
						101

All existing database systems allow to compute the join R^* , only. Of all the extensions, R^* is the one with the largest number of tuples and, therefore, it maximizes the *qualitative entropy*

$$H_0(R) = \log |R| ,$$

which will be taken as a measure of the amount of information contained in R.
So, recalling the uniqueness of the entropy principle as an inference method, we can answer the above question: entropy maximization (that is, the join) is the only correct inference procedure.

More precisely, any inference procedure that uses an objective function but qualitative entropy will lead to inconsistency unless the new objective function and qualitative entropy have identical solutions. To clarify this point, let us decide to follow a clustering approach, for example. Then, from among all extensions we should choose the relation that most "separates" the "clusters" $X_1,\ldots,X_k$. Now, a suitable measure of the "separation" (or "interdependence") of $X_1,\ldots,X_k$ is given by the so-called *qualitative mutual information* [19]

$$I_o(R_1,\ldots,R_k) = \Sigma_i H_o(R_i) - H_o(R) ,$$

which is a nonnnegative quantity that vanishes if and only if R has the same number of tuples as the Cartesian product of $R_1,\ldots,R_k$. If this is the case, $X_1,\ldots,X_k$ are called *algebraically independent*.
But, minimizing I_o is equivalent to maximizing H_o and, therefore, the clustering solution coincides with R^*.

By the way, it is convenient to decompose I_o as follows

$$I_o(R_1,\ldots,R_k) = [\Sigma_i H_o(R_i) - H_o(R^*)] + [H_o(R^*) - H_o(R)] ,$$

where the two square brackets distinguish the different contributions to the interdependence of $X_1,\ldots,X_k$ separately given by what we call the "redundancy" of the database scheme S and the "interaction" of $R_1,\ldots,R_k$ in R . The contribution of the redundancy,

$$\Sigma_i H_o(R_i) - H_o(R^*) ,$$

vanishes if and only if R^* coincides with the Cartesian product of $R_1,\ldots,R_k$, that is, if and only if $S = \{X_1,\ldots,X_k\}$ is a partition of X (provided singleton relations are not met).
The contribution of the interaction,

$$H_o(R^*) - H_o(R) ,$$

is a nonnegative quantity and vanishes if and only if $R = R^*$.
Summarizing, we can say that the join of $R_1,\ldots,R_k$ selects the extension where there is no interaction among $X_1,\ldots,X_k$ and all their interdependence is due only to the redundancy of the database scheme S.

The problem of getting cross-classified categorical data from different tables of a categorical database is exactly the equivalent of the problem of joining relations and can be solved by applying the entropy principle again.

Consider a globally compatible categorical database $\mathcal{T} = \{T_1,\dots,T_k\}$ with $T_i = < X_i, \Omega_i, n_i(x_i) >$. By an *extension* of $T_1,\dots,T_k$ we mean a table T over the universal schema $X = U_i X_i$ that has $T_1,\dots,T_k$ as its marginals. The *stochastic extension*, T^*, is defined as the extension with the largest *entropy*

$$H(T) = \log N - (1/N) \sum n(x) \log n(x) ,$$

where N is the size of the population of individuals under examination.
The stochastic extension might be defined in an equivalent way as the extension that minimizes the *mutual information*

$$I(T_1,\dots,T_k) = \Sigma_i H(T_i) - H(T) .$$

Mutual information is a nonnegative quantity that vanishes if and only if $X_1,\dots,X_k$ are *(statistically) independent*, that is, if and only if

$$n(x) = n_1(x_1) \cdot \dots \cdot n_k(x_k) .$$

It should be noted that for independence the database scheme S is required to be a partition.
The following decomposition of the mutual information

$$I(T_1,\dots,T_k) = [\Sigma_i H(T_i) - H(T^*)] + [H(T^*) - H(T)]$$

singles out the two contributions given to the mutual information by the redundancy and by the interaction.
So, the join of relations as well as the stochastic extension are uniquely determined by a condition of no interaction.
However, there is a direct relationship between join of relations and stochastic extension. In fact, given a categorical database $\mathcal{T} = \{T_1,\dots,T_k\}$ consider its associated relational database $\mathcal{R} = \{R_1,\dots,R_k\}$ it is possible to prove that the characteristic relation of the stochastic extension of $\mathcal{T}$ is the join of the relations in $\mathcal{R}$.

The stochastic extension $n^*(x)$ can be calculated using an iterative proportional fitting procedure, commonly referred to as IPFP. If a categorical database is the result of the decomposition of a single table, T ,we can measure the closeness of the stochastic extension T^* to T by the so-called *divergence* [11]

$$D(n : n^*) = \Sigma\, n(x)\ \log n(x)/n^*(x)\ ,$$

which is a nonnegative quantity that vanishes if and only if $n(x) = n^*(x)$.
In general, when we assign the procedure to obtain cross-classified categorical data from the contingency tables of a categorical database, we specify a *model*.
In some models $n^*(x)$ has a closed-form expression. Let us see two examples of closed-form expressions.
If $S = \{X_1,\ldots,X_k\}$ is a partition of X, then without resorting to the IPFP we can write

$$n^*(x) = n_1(x_1)\ \ldots\ n_k(x_k)\ .$$

Such a model is said to be an "independence model" because it is based on the hypothesis that $X_1,\ldots,X_k$ are independent.
If $S = \{X_1,\ldots,X_k\}$ is a "rooted" covering of X with root Y (that is, $X_i \cap X_j = Y$, for each couple i and j), then we can write

$$n^*(x) = n_1(x_1) \cdot \ldots \cdot n_k(x_k)\ /\ n_o(y)^{\ k-1}\ ,$$

where $n_o(y)$ is the common restriction of $n_1(x_1),\ldots,n_k(x_k)$ to the root Y.
Such a model is said to be a "conditional independence model" because it is based on the hypothesis that $X_1,\ldots,X_k$ are *conditionally independent given* Y.
As an example of model, consider the categorical database consisting of the two tables of Example 1 and Example 2. This is a case of a bottom-up definition of a categorical database.
We meet a conditional independence model:

$$n^*(S, A, Y, R, P) = n_1(S, A, Y, R)\ n_2(P, Y)\ /\ n_o(Y)$$

where S, A, Y, R, P stand for Sex, Age, Years of schooling, Region and Party membership.
The model allows to answer a database user who whishes cross-classified categorical data, for example, the number of the party members who live in the rural region.

4. Acyclic Schemes and Decomposable Models

There is a natural correspondence between database schemes and hypergraphs. In fact, a database scheme $S = \{X_1,\ldots,X_k\}$ can be interpreted as the "edge" set

of a hypergraph, which has as its "node" set the universal schema $X = U_i\ X_i$.
Let us introduce some basic definitions, most of which belong to the standard database terminology of hypergraph theory [2,3] .
A node is "pendant" ("insulated" in [2]) if it belongs to exactly one edge.
An edge is "redundant" if it is a (proper or improper) subset of another edge.
A hypergraph is "singular" if it contains redundant edges; otherwise, it is "regular" ("reduced" in [2]).
A "path" is a sequence of edges, such that any two edges in succession have a nonempty intersection.
Two edges are "connected" if there is a path that contains both of them. Two nodes are connected, if they belong to connected edges. A "connected component" is a maximal connected set of nodes.
The "subhypergraph" generated by a subset, Y , of the node set X of a hypergraph is obtained by intersecting the edges of the hypergraph with Y .
Given a connected, regular hypergraph, (X, S), let X_i and X_j be two edges.
The set $Y = X_i \cap X_j$ is said to be an "articulation set" if the subhypergraph generated by $X\text{-}Y$ is not connected.
A hypergraph with no articulation sets is called "biconnected".
A "block" of a regular hypergraph is a maximal biconnected subhypergraph. A block is "multiple" if it is composed of two or more edges; otherwise, it is "simple".
A regular hypergraph is *acyclic* if all its blocks are simple.

Testing acyclicity is a problem having a polynomial complexity (a linear-time algorithm has been given by Tarjan et al. [17]). A simple way to test acyclicity consists in applying the following two rules recursively:

Delete all pendant nodes.

Delete all redundant edges.

The algorithm, usually called "reduction procedure" or "Graham's algorithm", is said to *terminate with success* if it terminates with an empty set. It is well-known that the reduction procedure terminates with success if and only if the hypergraph is acyclic.

A number of "nice" properties of acyclic hypergraphs are known from the relational database theory, where a database scheme is called acyclic if its representative hypergraph is acyclic [2].

Abstract properties:

(A1) (*Running intersection*) A database scheme S is acyclic if there is an ordering $X_1,\dots,X_k$ of S such that for $2 \le i \le k$ there exists an integer $j < i$ such that

$$X_i \cap (X_1 \cup \dots \cup X_{i-1}) \subset X_j$$

(A2) We premise the following definition of a "join graph".
A *join graph* associated with a database scheme S is a graph with node set such that

(i) each edge (X_i, X_j) is labelled by the set of the attributes $X_i \cap X_j$

(ii) for every pair X_i and X_j $(i \neq j)$, for every A in $X_i \cap X_j$, each edge along a path between X_i and X_j includes label A (possibly among others).

A database scheme S is acyclic if and only if it has a join graph that is a forest.

Relational properties:

(R1) (*Sufficiency*) Every pairwise consistent relational database is globally consistent.

(R2) An acyclic join dependency is equivalent to a set of multivalued dependencies.

About ten years before acyclic database schemes were formally defined, *decomposable models* were formally introduced in the theory of maximum likelihood estimation [7,8,9,10].
After Haberman [9], the model generated by a database scheme $S = \{X_i : i=1,\dots,k\}$ is called *decomposable* if S consists of one element ($k=1$), or if it is the union of two decomposable models generated by the schemes $S' = \{X_{i'}\}$ and $S'' = \{X_{i''}\}$ such that for some $X_{j'}$ in S' and $X_{j''}$ in S''

$$(\cup_{i'} X_{i'}) \cap (\cup_{i''} X_{i''}) = X_{j'} \cap X_{j''} \quad .$$

As shown by Haberman [9] a decomposable model has two fundamental properties:

(S1) the stochastic extension has an explicit closed-form expression
(S2) the model can be interpreted in terms of conditional independence

The property (S1) says that a decomposable model can be directly calculated without resorting to the IPFP. The property (S2) echoes (R2).
Additional properties of decomposable models can be found in Andersen [1], Darroch et al. [6], Darroch [5]. Haberman [9] showed that a model is decomposable if and only if its scheme enjoys the running intersection property. Goodman [8] showed that a model is decomposable if and only if the reduction procedure terminates with success.
These latter two facts prove that acyclicity and decomposability are equivalent concepts.

So, we can extend to decomposable models all properties of acyclic database schemes and vice versa. For example, we can state that a decomposable model is generated by a scheme that has a join forest. The usefulness of the notion of join forest for decomposable models is stressed by the following result, proven by the author in a recent paper [12]: the expression of the stochastic extension $n^*(x)$ for a decomposable model is

$$n^*(x) = \Pi_i \, n_i(x_i) \,/\, \Pi_g \, n_g(u_g)$$

where $\{U_g : g \in G\}$ are the edge set of a join forest associated to S.
Note that $G \subset \{1,\dots,k\}$.
So, to determine the closed form of a decomposable model we have to find a join forest.
The following algorithm is a new edition of the reduction procedure, intended to determine a join forest associated in the case of acyclic hypergraph.

Step 1. Create a list *INPUT*, where initially the edge set $S = \{X_1,\dots,X_k\}$ of the hypergraph is loaded.

Step 2. Create a list *OUTPUT*, initially empty.

Step 3. If the list *INPUT* is empty, then exit with *success*; otherwise continue.

Step 4. Apply the following two operations:
- (4a) Delete all the nodes that appear in exactly one edge in the list *INPUT*;
- (4b) Move all redundant edges in the list *INPUT* to the list *OUPUT*.

If neither can be applied, exit with *failure*; otherwise go to step 3.

If the algorithm terminates with success, the elements in the list *OUTPUT* form the edge set of a join forest associated with that acyclic hypergraph and, consequently, the closed form of the corresponding decomposable model can be derived.
Now, we are able to evaluate the storage saving obtained using acyclic database schemes. Consider a contingency table with s q.ary category attributes. The storage of such a table requires the use of q^s registers. However, if we employ an acyclic database scheme with p connected components and with all X_i of the same order, say $r \geq 2$, then the required storage quantity amounts to $q^r \cdot k$ registers. The number k of components is easily seen to obey the following limitations:

$$[(s-p) / (r-1)] \leq k \leq s - p\,(r-1) \qquad ,$$

where the square brackets are used to denote the smallest integer greater than or equal to the argument. (This formula returns the well-known value $k = s-1$ for ordinary trees: $p = 1$, $r = 2$).
The storage reduction rate is measured by the ratio

$$q^{r-s} \cdot k \leq q^{r-s} [s-p(r-1)] ,$$

which decreases exponentially to $s-r$. This is the evidence that generally the storage saving is remarkable.
Another important property of acyclic schemes is that the "cost" of a model $n^*(x)$, measured by the divergence D , takes a linear form

$$D = \Sigma_i H(X_i) - \Sigma_g H(U_g) - H(X) .$$

Linearity is very important in that it is a necessary qualification for optimization. So, the problem of determining the optimum decomposable model of a given table can be solved using informed research strategies [13].

5. Global compatibility

As the pairwise consistency of a relational database is not sufficient for its global consistency, so the pairwise compatibility of a categorical database is not sufficient for its global compatibility (see Example 3).

EXAMPLE 3 . Let A , B and C be binary attributes according to which a set of 100 objects are classified. Consider the database scheme $S = \{AB, AC, BC\}$ and the following categorical database:

AB	n_1
00	50
01	0
10	0
11	50

AC	n_2
00	0
01	50
10	50
11	0

BC	n_3
00	50
01	0
10	0
11	50

This categorical database turns out to be pairwise compatible, but it is not globally compatible. In fact, the existence of a universal frequency distribution $n(abc)$ would give rise to the following contradiction:

$$\begin{aligned} 50 &= n_2(01) = n(001) + n(011) \leq \\ &\leq [n(001) + n(101)] + [n(011) + n(010)] = \\ &= n_3(01) + n_1(01) = 0 . \end{aligned}$$

Another necessary (but not sufficient) condition for the global compatibility of a categorical database is the global consistency of its associated relational database, as it is stated by the following theorem.

THEOREM 1 . If a categorical database is globally compatible, then its associated relational database is globally consistent.
PROOF . Let $\{n_1(x_1),...,n_k(x_k)\}$ be the set of the frequency distributions in a given globally compatible categorical database and let $R_1,...,R_k$ be their characteristic relations. If $n(x)$ is an extension, its characteristic relation R turns out to be an extension of $R_1,...,R_k$.

In Example 4 we have a categorical database which is pairwise compatible and has the associated relational database globally consistent, but it is not globally compatible.

EXAMPLE 4. Let A , B and C be binary attributes according to which a set of 100 objects are classified. Consider the database scheme $S = \{AB, AC, BC\}$ and the following categorical database:

AB	n_1
00	10
01	40
10	40
11	10

AC	n_2
00	30
01	20
10	20
11	30

BC	n_3
00	40
01	10
10	10
11	40

It is easy to see that this categorical database is not globally compatible. In fact, the existence of a universal frequency distribution $n(abc)$ would give rise to the following contradiction:

$$\begin{aligned} 40 &= n_1(01) = n(010) + n(011) \leq \\ &\leq [\, n(010) + n(110)\,] + [\, n(001) + n(011)\,] = \\ &= n_3(10) + n_2(01) = 30 \quad . \end{aligned}$$

At present, the existence of necessary and sufficient conditions for global compatibility is an open problem (see the multi-index transportation problem [18]).
A computational consequence of Theorem 1 is that, since deciding whether a relational database is a NP-problem, then deciding whethe a categorical database is globally compatible is a NP-hard problem.
On the other hand, testing pairwise compatibility is far less difficult. This makes us understand how desirable are acyclic database schemes, for which pairwise compatibility is sufficient to global compatibility.

THEOREM 2. The pairwise compatibility of any categorical database is sufficient for its global compatibility if and only if its scheme is acyclic.
PROOF. (*if*) The global compatibility of a categorical database $\mathcal{T} = \{T_1,\ldots,T_k\}$ follows from the observation that the pairwise compatibility of $\mathcal{T}$ is enough to make the form

$$n^*(x) = \Pi_i\, n_i(x_i) \,/\, \Pi_g\, n_g(u_g)$$

an extension of $n_1(x_1),\ldots,n_k(x_k)$.
(*only if*) Acyclicity is proven by contradiction. Assume there exists a cyclic database scheme $S = \{X_1,\ldots,X_k\}$ such that any categorical database over S is globally compatible. Now, since S is cyclic, by virtue of the property (R1) of acyclic schemes there exists a set of relations $\{R_1,\ldots,R_k\}$, that is pairwise consistent but <u>not globally consistent</u>.
Let $\{n_1(x_1),\ldots,n_k(x_k)\}$ be a family of pairwise compatible distributions having as their characteristic relations $R_1,\ldots,R_k$. The part (if) assures the existence of an extension. From Theorem1 it follows that $\{R_1,\ldots,R_k\}$ is <u>globally consistent</u>. This contradiction shows that the sufficiency of pairwise compatibility for global compatibility cannot be extended to cyclic decompositions.

6. Views

In this section we present an algorithm optimizing the implementation of a view, under the assumption that the underlying categorical database has an acyclic scheme.
Consider the conjunctive query $V = v$ (where V is a subset of the universal schema X and v is a V-cell) intended to estimate the number $n^*(v)$ of individuals with the same V-description. Then, we must proceed as follows:

(1) compute $n^*(x)$ by using the product form associated with the acyclic scheme $S = \{X_1,\ldots,X_k\}$
(2) restrict $n^*(x)$ to V .

It should be noticed that this is the only correct way to compute $n^*(v)$ when $n_1(x_1),\ldots,n_k(x_k)$ are given. For example, it should be wrong to work out the maximum-entropy extension of the set $\{n_i(v_i) : V_i = V \cap X_i\}$.
Let s be the size of X and r be the size of V . If the category attributes are q.ary, in order to calculate $n^*(v)$ we have to sum q^{s-r} values of $n^*(x)$
To reduce the cost of implementation, we propose the following algorithm, inspired by the reduction procedure.

The input is given by the view V and by the set $\{(X_i, U_g)\}$ computed as shown in the previous section. Then, we start by setting $W = X - V$. Hence, we apply the following two rules until neither can be further applied.

(a) If A is an attribute in W such that it appears in exactly one X_i, then delete A from both W and X_i.
(b) Delete one X_i if there is an X_j with $j \neq i$ such that X_i is a subset of X_j. If X_i is deleted because $X_i \subseteq X_j$ and $j \notin G$, then delete i from G.

Let W', $S' = \{Y_h\}$ and G' be what remains of W, $S = \{X_i\}$ and G. Then, if we put $Z_h = X_h - Y_h$, then $n^*(v)$ may be written as

$$n^*(v) = \Sigma_{W'} \left[\Pi_h \, n_h(y_h) / \Pi_{g'} \, n_{g'}(u_{g'}) \right]$$
$$= \Sigma_{W'} \left[\Pi_h \, \Sigma_{Zh} \, n_h(x_h) / \Pi_{g'} \, n_{g'}(u_{g'}) \right]$$

EXAMPLE 5 . Consider the following acyclic scheme: $X_1 = ABQ$, $X_2 = AM$, $X_3 = BN$, $X_4 = BS$, $X_5 = BCDR$, $X_6 = CDT$, $X_7 = CEF$, $X_8 = DG$, $X_9 = DH$, $X_{10} = EL$. Suppose that the result of the application of the reduction procedure be the following:

$X_1 = ABQ$		$X_6 = CDT$	$U_6 = CD$
$X_2 = AM$	$U_2 = A$	$X_7 = CEF$	$U_7 = C$
$X_3 = BN$	$U_3 = B$	$X_8 = DG$	$U_8 = D$
$X_4 = BS$	$U_4 = B$	$X_9 = DH$	$U_9 = D$
$X_5 = BCDR$	$U_5 = B$	$X_{10} = EL$	$U_{10} = E$

Consider the view $V = CERST$. To implement it, $q^{s-r} = q^{10}$ values are to be summed:

$$n^*(CERST) = \Sigma_{ABDFGHLMNQ} \; n^*(ABCDEFGHLMNQRST)$$

Instead, apply our algorithm with the input

$$W = ABDFGHLMNQ, \quad S = \{X_i : i = 1,\ldots,10\}, \qquad \{U_g : g = 2,\ldots,10\} .$$

The output is

$$W' = BD \qquad G' = \{5, 6, 7\} \text{ and } S' = \{Y_h : h = 4, 5, 6, 7\},$$

with

$Y_4 = BS \qquad Y_5 = BCDR \qquad Y_6 = CDT \qquad Y_7 = CE$

So, we have

$$n^*(CERST) = \Sigma_{BD} \left[n_4(BS)\, n_5(BCDR)\, n_6(CDT)\, n_7(CE) / n_5(B)\, n_6(CD)\, n_7(C) \right]$$
$$= \left[\Sigma_{BD}\, n_4(BS)\, n_5(BCDR)\, n_6(CDT) / n_5(B)\, n_6(CD)\right] \left[\Sigma_F\, n_7(ECF) / n_7(CE)\right]$$

It follows that $n^*(CERST)$ can be computed by summing just q^2+q terms instead of q^{10}.

7. Conclusions

A relational approach to categorical databases has been presented and the major issues connected with their conceptual design are discussed by pointing out the analogies with the relational case.
It has been shown that simple and efficient solutions can be found if we model categorical databases with acyclic schemes, according to the well-known definition given in the relational database theory.
Indeed, acyclic schemes of categorical databases are the same as decomposable models, an older acquaintance of the statistical estimation theory.

REFERENCES

1. A.H. Andersen, Multidimensional contingency tables, *Scand. J. Stat.* **1** (1974) 115-127
2. C. Beeri, R. Fagin, D. Maier and M. Yannakakis, On the desirability of acyclic database schemes, *J. ACM* **30** (1983) 479-513
3. C. Berge, *Graphs and hypergraphs*. NORTH HOLLAND, 1973.
4. Y. Bishop et al., *Discrete multivariate analysis: theory and practice*. MIT PRESS, 1978.
5. J.N. Darroch, Interaction models, *Encyclopedia of statistical sciences*, **4** (1983) 182-187
6. J.N. Darroch et al., Markov fields and log-linear interaction models for contingency tables, *The Ann. of Statist.* **8**:3 (1980) 522-539
7. L.A. Goodman, The multivariate analysis of qualitative data: interactions among multiple classifications, *J. Amer.Stat. Assoc.* **65** (1070) 226-256
8. L.A. Goodman, Partitioning of chi-square, analysis of marginal contingency tables and estimation of extected frequencies in multidimensional contingency tables, *J. Amer. Statist. Assoc.* **66** (1971) 339-344
9. S.J. Haberman, The general log-linear model. Ph. D. thesis. Dept. Statist. Univ. Chicago.
10. S.J. Haberman, *The analysis of frequency data*. Un.Chicago PRESS, 1974
11. F.M. Malvestuto, Statistical treatment of the information content of a database, *Inf. Systems* **11**:3 (1986)
12. F.M. Malvestuto, Decomposing complex contingency tables to reduce storage requirements, *Proc. Conf. on "Computational Statistics"* (1986)
13. F.M. Malvestuto, La Ricerca Operativa nella progettazione delle vasi di dati statistici, *Atti delle Giornate AIRO su "Informatica e RIcerca Operativa"* (1986)
14. T.H. Merret et al., Distribution model of relations, *Proc. 5th Conf. on Very Large Data Bases*, Rio de Janeiro.
15. J.E. Shore et al., Axiomatic derivation of the principle of maximum entropy and the principle of minimum cross-entropy, *IEEE Trans. Inf. Theory* **26** (1980) 26-37
16. A. Shoshani et al., Statistical and scientific database issues, *IEEE Trans. Soft. Eng.* **11** (1985) 1040-1047
17. R.E. Tarjan et al., Simple linear-time algorithm to test chordality of graphs, test acyclicity of hypergraphs, and selectively reduce acyclic hypergraphs, *SIAM J. Comput.* **13**:3 (1984)
18. M. Vlach, Conditions for the existence of solutions of the three-dimensional planar transportation problem, *Discr. Appl. Math.* **13** (1986) 61-78
19. S. Watanabe, A unified view of clustering algorithms, *IFIP Congress on "Foundations of information processing"*, 1971

Some Extensions to the Closed World Assumption in Databases

Shamim A. Naqvi

MCC
9430 Research Blvd.,
Austin, Texas 78759

1. Motivation

Reiter's Closed World Assumption (CWA) [Reiter 78b] allows one to assume a ground negative atomic formula in Horn databases. Minker generalizes this result to allow the assumption of ground negative atomic formulas in first-order databases. We extend Minker's results in two different directions; firstly, to allow the assumption of a non-atomic and ground formula, and secondly for non-ground (and non-atomic) formulas. The CWA is a form of non-monotonic reasoning and also provides a basis for negation in logic programming and logic based systems. We expect our extensions to be of theoretical interest to researchers in these areas.

2. Preamble

A database (DB) is a finite set of closed (first-order) formulas in which all variables are universally quantified. Reiter [1978a,1978b] has studied such databases and introduced the terms *open and closed world databases.* An open world database is one in which all information, i.e., all those statements that are known to be true or false about the domain, are explicitly represented. To answer a query, one uses the provability relation to show that the query follows logically from the database.

A problem with an open DB is that the amount of negative information that needs to be represented about some domain may be prohibitively large. An alternative to the open world DB is a closed world DB which contains no negative data; to prove a negative fact, one attempts to prove the corresponding positive fact first. If unsuccessful then one can assume that the negative fact is true. Thus certain answers are admitted from an inability to find a proof. Reiter's Closed World Assumption (CWA)[1978a, 1978b], namely, that *the information given about a predicate is all and only the relevant information about that predicate,* serves as the intuition behind a closed DB. The THNOT operator of PLANNER (Hewitt [1972]) was related to this idea. Reiter [1982] has also shown that the CWA is related to McCarthy's circumscription schema for non-monotonic reasoning[1980]. This style of reasoning appears as a central research topic in artificial intelligence thus increasing the importance of the CWA for further investigation.

In this paper we focus on an extension of the CWA, called the Generalized Closed World Assumption (GCWA), by Minker [1982]. We extend Minker's result in two directions. In section

2 the CWA and GCWA are examined in more detail and we list the results of previous research in this area. Sections 3 and 4 present our extensions, followed by a brief summary in section 5.

The Closed World and Generalized Closed World Assumptions

Definition (1.0): A database is a set of closed first-order formulas in which all variables are universally quantified.

Usually when writing formulas we shall omit the universal quantifier. When all the formulas in DB are Horn (defined later) DB is said to be a **Horn database.** A *literal* is a positive or negative atomic formula. A *clause* is a disjunction of literals. *A clause is said to be Horn* if it contains at most one positive literal. The symbol |– stands for the provability relation, i.e., S |– K is read as "K is derivable from the set of formulas S". A formula is *ground* if it contains no variables. The *Herbrand universe of DB* is the set of constants in DB (note that under our assumption of no function signs in DB, this set is finite). For all the predicate symbols P in DB, the set of all ground atomic formulas $P(t_1,...,tn)$ where the t_i belong to the Herbrand universe of DB is called the *Herbrand base, H,* of DB. A *Herbrand Interpretation,* I, is a subset of H. The semantics of clauses are defined as follows:

a ground positive literal, P, is true iff $P \in I$.

a ground negative literal, ¬P, is true iff P is not in I.

a ground clause is true in I iff at least one of its elements is true in I.

a clause is true in I iff all its ground instances are true in I.

a set of clauses is true in I iff every clause in the set is true in I.

A *model* of DB is a Herbrand Interpretation I such that every clause of DB is true in I. A Herbrand Interpretation I that forms a model of DB such that no proper subset of I is a model is termed a *minimal model* of DB, MM(DB). Bossu and Siegel [1985] have shown that databases, as per definition (1.0), have a minimal model.

Syntactic Definition of CWA (2.0): $\overline{DB}$={¬Pa| P is some predicate in DB, a is a tuple of constants from the Herbrand universe, and Pa is not provable from DB}.

Semantic Definition of CWA (2.1): A negative ground literal ¬Pa can be assumed in a Horn DB iff Pa does not belong to the unique minimal model of DB.

Marten van Emden and Kowalski[1976] show the equivalence of (2.0) and (2.1). Reiter [1978b] shows that for a Horn DB, DB ∪ $\overline{DB}$ is consistent. The CWA cannot be used when the database does not have the Horn property. For example, consider the database DB={Pa∨Pb} Using the CWA we can assume ¬Pa, and similarly ¬Pb making DB ∪ $\overline{DB}$ inconsistent. The question then is to figure out how to apply the CWA to such databases. Minker [1982] proposes an extension of the CWA, called the Generalized Closed World Assumption (GCWA), which is based upon the notion of minimal models:

Semantic Definition of GCWA (2.2): A ground negative literal ¬Pa,can be assumed in DB iff Pa does not occur in any minimal model of DB.

Syntactic Definition of GCWA (2.3): Let E={Pa | DB |-Pa∨K, K is a positive (possibly null) clause, and K is not provable from DB} (thus E consists of all those atoms which are contained in minimal positive clauses derivable from DB). A negative ground atom, ¬Pa, can be assumed in DB iff its positive counterpart, Pa, is not in E.

Equivalence of the Semantic and Syntactic Definitions (2.4): Definitions (2.2) and (2.3) are equivalent.

Example (2.5): Let DB be the non-Horn DB {Pa∨Pb}. Then the minimal models are {Pa} and {Pb}. Thus we can not assume ¬Pa, nor can we assume ¬Pb. If DB={Qa, Pa∨Pb} then the minimal models are {Qa,Pa} and {Qa,Pb}. As Qb does not exist in any minimal model we can assume ¬Qb.

In the next two sections we present our extensions to Minker's GCWA.

3. Extending GCWA to Non-atomic Ground Formulas

We show when a negative ground clause, not necessarily atomic, can be assumed to be true in a non-Horn database. Let MM(DB) denote the set of minimal models of DB and let C=¬L1∨¬.....∨¬Ln.

Semantic Definition (3.1): C may not be assumed if all atoms of C belong to some minimal model M, M∈MM(DB).

Syntactic Definition (3.2): C may not be assumed if there exists a positive or null clause K such that for all i

1. DB |-L_i ∨K,

2. ¬(DB |-K)

Example (3.3): Let DB={Pa,Mb,¬Pa∨Ma∨Mc}. The minimal models are {Pa,Mb,Ma} and {Pa,Mb,Mc}. Since Pb and Pc do not exist in any minimal model we can assume ¬Pb∨¬Pc.

We now must show the equivalence of the semantic and syntactic definitions given above. The proof is patterned after Minker [1982].

Theorem (3.4): Definition 3.1 ≡ Definition 3.2[1].

Proof: Recall that DB has a minimal model [Bossu and Siegel 85].

(←)If 3.2 then 3.1:

Condition 1 states that for all i ($1 \leq i \leq n$) DB |- L_i ∨K where K is null or positive. If K is null then DB |- L_i and hence L_i ∈ some MM(DB). If K is not null then DB |- L_i ∨K. This implies that every minimal model of DB contains a literal of L_i ∨K. But condition 2 says that (¬DB |- K). So

[1] A different proof of this theorem has been independently given by Yahya and Henschen [1985].

there exists some minimal model of DB, say M, that does not contain K. Hence M must contain each L_i

($\rightarrow$)If 3.1 then 3.2:

Let $M_1, M_2, \ldots, M_m$,M be all the minimal models of DB.

Case 1: $(M_i - M) = \phi$. In this case there is only minimal model, say M, and for null K and consistent DB, both conditions 1 and 2 hold.

Case 2: $(Mi-M) \neq \phi$. Let Q1,....,Qm be chosen from $\{M_i - M\}$, and let K=Q1v....vQm. Then DB $|-L_i \vee K$ since an atom of $L_i \vee K$ is in all the elements of MM(DB). Also K is not derivable from DB since none of the Qi are in M.

4. Extending GCWA to Non-ground Formulas

Notice that all the results so far show how a negative ground clause (atomic or non-atomic) can be assumed in a database. We now extend this result to non-ground clauses. Before doing so, we need to define the concepts of Π-*clauses* and Π-*representation* from Fishman and Minker [1975].

Recall that a *substitution* σ is a set of variable-constant pairs $\{x_1/c_1, x_2/c_2, \ldots, xn/cn\}$ such that no two x_i are the same. The application of σ to a literal L, written as Lσ, replaces the variables in L that are in σ by the corresponding constants. Two literals L_1 and L_2 are said to be unifiable if there exists a substitution such that $L_1\sigma = L_2\sigma$.

We now define Fishman's idea of Π-representations using examples from Fishman [1975]. A Π-representation consists of two parts: a clause without constant symbols which serves as a template, and substitution sets in which variables occurring in the template clause range over sets of constants. The set of clauses represented by such a pair is obtained by universal instantiation of the variables in the template clause by the constants contained in the corresponding substitution sets.

Definition (4.0): A Π-substitution component is an expression of the form v/S where v is a variable, and S is a non-empty set of constants.

Definition (4.1): A Π-substitution σ is a possibly empty set of Π-substitution components. ε denotes the empty substitution. If σ={v1/S1,v2/S2,...,vn/Sn} then σ may be interpreted as all possible combinations of substitutions. Given a clause C and a Π-substitution σ, the application of σ to C, denoted by Cσ, will be called a Π-instance of C. If σ=ε then Cσ=C. If σ1,...,σn are all possible combinations of substitutions in σ then Cσ is the set of n clauses Cσ1,...,Cσn.

Example (4.2): Let σ={x/[a,b],y/[b,c,d]}. Then σ may be interpreted as representing the six substitutions

{x/a,y/b},{x/a,y/c},{x/a,y/d},{x/b,y/b},{x/b,y/c},{x/b,y/d}

Definition (4.3): A Π-set is a non-empty set of Π-substitutions.

Definition (4.4): A Π-clause is a pair (C,σ) where C is a clause containing no constants, and σ is a Π-set.

Example (4.5): Using σ from example 4.2, the Π-clause (P(x,f(z))∨Q(x,y),σ) represents the six clauses

P(a,f(z))∨Q(a,b), P(b,f(z))∨Q(b,b)

P(a,f(z))∨Q(a,c), P(b,f(z))∨Q(b,c)

P(a,f(z))∨Q(a,d), P(b,f(z))∨Q(b,d)

The idea of unification is to find a substitution that makes two literals identical. Fishman used this notion for Π-clauses: Two Π-clauses (P(x),{x/S1}) and (P(y),{y/S2}) should not unify if S1∩S2=φ. Fishman presents a unification algorithm for Π-clauses and defines Π-resolution. Let the provability relation over Π-clauses be denoted by $|-_\Pi$.

We now return to the question of assuming non-ground formulas by using the GCWA.

Definition (4.6): Given the set of minimal models of DB, MM(DB), and M∈MM(DB), a Π-clause set for M is the set of Π-clauses "Px{x/a}" for every atomic formula Pa in M.

Semantic Definition (4.7): Let Q1,...,Qn be the Π-clause sets corresponding to the minimal models M1,...,Mn of DB. A negative atomic formula, ¬Px{σ} can not be assumed in DB iff, for some Qi, Px{σ} unifies with a Π-clause in Qi.

Syntactic Definition (4.8): A negative atomic formula, ¬Px{σ1}, can not be assumed in DB iff there exists a positive or null Π-clause (K,σ2) such that

DB $|-_\Pi$ {Px∨K,(σ1,σ2)}, and

(K,σ2) is not Π-provable from DB; (K,σ2) is a positive (possibly null) clause set.

Example (4.9): Let DB={Qa,Pa∨Pb}. Then MM(DB)={{Qa,Pa},{Qa,Pb}}. The Π-clause sets are {Qx{x/a},Px{x/a}} and {Qx{x/a},Px{x/b}}. So we can not assume ¬Px{x/a}. Some clauses that can be assumed are ¬Qx{x/[b,c]}.

Example (4.10): Here is a less abstract example; let the set of formulas be

Person(joe)

Mammal(peter)

∀xPerson(x)⊃Mammal(x)

Then DB={Person(joe),Mammal(peter),¬Person(x)∨Mammal(x)}. The minimal model is {Person(joe),Mammal(peter),Mammal(joe)}. The Π-clause sets are {Person(x){x/joe}, and Mammal(x){x/[joe,peter]}. Thus, one may assume (¬Person(x){x/peter}) in this DB. In general, one may assume ¬Person(x) as long as "x" is different from "joe", and one may assume ¬Mammal(x) as long as "x" is neither "joe" nor "peter". Notice that DB is Horn.

Example (4.11): Finally, an example involving a non-Horn set of formulas:

Human(socrates)

Fallible(turing)

Wrong(aristotle)

$\forall$xHuman(x)$\supset$Fallible(x)$\vee$Wrong(x)

Then

DB={Human(socrates),Fallible(turing),Wrong(aristotle),

¬Human(x)$\vee$Fallible(x)$\vee$Wrong(x)}

The minimal models are

{Human(socrates),Fallible(turing),Wrong(aristotle),Fallible(socrates)}

and

{Human(socrates),Fallible(turing),Wrong(aristotle),Wrong(socrates)}.

So one may not assume

¬Human(x){x/socrates}

However, one can assume

(¬ Human(x){x/[aristotle,turing]})

Theorem (4.12): Definition 4.7 $\equiv$ Definition 4.8.

Proof: follows from Theorem 3.4 and from the definition of π–clauses and π–substitutions.

It can be easily seen that the above definitions include the case when the assumed clauses are ground, for in such a situation the conditional clauses become simple clauses with null conditional components.

Finally, we show that if $\overline{DB}$ is the set of negative clauses assumed according to 4.7 (or 4.8) from DB then DB $\cup$ $\overline{DB}$ is consistent in the following sense. We extend the concept of maximal consistency first introduced by Minker [1982].

Definition (4.13): A set of π–clauses in DB is *maximally consistent* with the GCWA if the addition of a negative Π-clause, say (¬ Px,σ) to DB such that (¬Px,σ) is not subsumed by DB satisfies the following conditions:

DB $\cup${¬Px,σ} is inconsistent, or

DB $\cup${¬Px,σ} $\vdash_{\Pi}$ L where L is a positive Π–clause such that L is not Π–provable from DB.

What this definition says is that no new negative information can be added to DB ∪ $\overline{DB}$ without either making DB inconsistent or making it possible to derive a positive clause L that was not derivable from DB before.

Theorem (4.14): DB ∪ $\overline{DB}$ is maximally consistent.

Proof: Let (¬Px,σ1) not belong to DB. Then from definition 4.8, there must exist a clause (Py∨K,{σ2}) (K is positive or null) such that DB $|-_{\Pi}$ (Py∨K,{σ2}). Now (Py∨K,{σ2}) can be rewritten as (¬Py⊃K,{σ2}); this together with (¬Px,{σ1}) implies (K,{σ1,σ2}). But this violates the second condition of (4.8). Hence (¬Px,{σ1}) can not be added to DB ∪ $\overline{DB}$.

5. Summary

Minker has shown how the CWA can be generalized to non-Horn domains. However, his results hold for assuming ground atomic formulas only. We have shown extensions by which non-ground and non-atomic formulas can be assumed in non-Horn databases.

6. Acknowledgement

Larry Henschen and Francois Bancilhon helped by reading several drafts of this report. In addition, Francois made several comments on the font sizes on the *Interleaf* version of this paper. Thanks to both of them.

7. References

G. Bossu, P. Siegel 1985: Saturation, Non-monotonic Reasoning, and the Closed World Assumption, **Artificial Intelligence 25**, No. 1, Jan 1985.

C. Hewitt 1972: Description and Theoretical Analysis (Using Schemata) of PLANNER: A Language for Proving Theorems and Manipulating Models in a Robot, **AI Memo No. 251,** MIT Project MAC, Cambridge, MA 1980.

D. Fishman, J. Minker 1975: P-Representation: A Clause Representation for Parallel Search, **Artificial Intelligence 6**, 1975.

R. Kowalski 1978: Logic for Data Description, In **Logic and Data Bases**, (H. Gallaire and J. Minker,eds.), Plenum Press, NY 1978.

J. McCarthy 1980: Circumscription-A Form of non-Monotonic Reasoning, **Artificial Intelligence 13**, 1 1980.

J. Minker 1982: On Indefinite Data Bases and the Closed World Assumption, **Springer-Verlag Lecture Notes in Computer Science**, (ed. D. Loveland), no. 138, NY 1982.

R. Reiter 1978a:Deductive Q-A on Relational Data Bases, In **Logic and Data Bases**,(H. Gallaire and J. Minker, eds.), Plenum Press, NY 1978.

R.Reiter 1978b: On Closed World Data Bases, In **Logic and Data Bases**, (H. Gallaire and J. Minker, eds.), Plenum Press, NY 1978.

R.Reiter 1982: Circumscription Implies Predicate Completion(Sometimes), Proc. of NCAI, Pittsburgh, PA, 1982.

M. van Emden,R.Kowalski 1976: The Semantics of Predicate Logic as a Programming Language, **J. of the ACM 23**, 4, 1976.

A. Yahya, L. Henschen1985: Deduction in non-Horn Databases, **Journal of Automated Reasoning**, 1, No. 2, 1985.

EXPEDIENT STOCHASTIC MOVE-TO-FRONT AND OPTIMAL STOCHASTIC MOVE-TO-REAR LIST ORGANIZING STRATEGIES*

B. John Oommen
School of Computer Science
Carleton University
Ottawa, Ontario Canada, K1S 5B6

E.R. Hansen
Lockheed Missiles and Space Co. Inc.
Sunnyvale, California
94086 USA

ABSTRACT

Consider a list of elements $\{R_1,\ldots,R_N\}$ in which the element R_i is accessed with an (unknown) probability s_i. If the cost of accessing R_i is proportional to i (as in sequently search) then it is advantageous if each access is accompanied by a simple reordering operation. This operation is chosen so that ultimately the list will be sorted in the descending order of the access probabilities.

In this paper we present two list organizing schemes -- the first of which uses bounded memory and the second which uses memory proportional to number of elements in the list. Both of the schemes reorder the list by moving only the accessed element. However, as opposed to the schemes discussed in the literature the move operation is performed stochastically in such a way that ultimately no more move operations are performed. When this occurs we say that the scheme has converged. We shall show that:

(i) The bounded memory stochastic move-to-front algorithm is expedient, but is always worse than the deterministic move-to-front algorithm.

(ii) The linear-memory stochastic move-to-rear scheme is optimal, independent of the distribution of the access probabilities. By this we mean that although the list could converge to one of its N! configurations, by suitably updating the probability of performing the move-to-rear operation, the probability of converging to the right arrangement can be made as close to unity as desired.

INTRODUCTION

Suppose we are given a set of elements $\{R_1,\ldots,R_N\}$. At every time instant one of these elements is accessed. Further, the element R_j is accessed with an unknown access probability s_j. We assume that the accesses are made independently. Whenever an element R_j is accessed, a sequential search is performed on the list. To minimize the cost of accessing, it is desirable that the records are ordered in the descending order of their access probabilities. We shall refer to a file ordered in this way as a completely organized file.

McCabe [11, pp.398-399; 12] was the first to propose a solution to this problem.

---

* Partially supported by the Natural Sciences and Engineering Research Council of Canada.

Keywords: Dynamic list ordering, move to front rule, adaptive learning, self-organizing lists, stochastic list operations.

His solution rendered the list dynamically self-organizing and it involved moving an element to the front of the list every time is was accessed. Using this rule, the Move-to-Front (MTF) rule, the limiting average value of the number of probes done per access has the value C_{MTF}, where,

$$C_{MTF} = 0.5 + \sum_{i,j} (s_i \, s_j)/(s_i + s_j)$$

Many other researchers [3,6-9,14] have also extensively studied the MTF rule and various properties of its limiting convergence characteristics are available in the literature.

McCabe [11, pp.398-399, 12] also introduced a scheme which is called the transposition rule. This rule requires that an accessed element is interchanged with its preceding element in the list, unless, of course, it is at the front of the list. Much literature is available on the transposition rule [1,2,4,11,12,13] but particularly important is the work of Rivest [13] and Tenenbaum et al. [1,15] who extensively studied this rule and suggested its generalizations - the Move-k-Ahead rule and the POS(k) rule. In the former, the accessed element is moved k-positions forward to the front of the list unless it is found in the first k positions - in which case it is moved to the front. The POS(k) rule moves the accessed element to position k of the list if it is in positions k+1 through n. It transposes it with the preceding element if it is in positions 2 through k. If it is the first element it is left unchanged.

Rivest [13] showed that the limiting behaviour of the transposition rule (quantified in terms of the average number of probes) was never worse than that of the MTF rule. He conjectured that the transposition rule has lower expected cost than any other reorganization scheme. He also conjectured that the move-k-ahead rule was superior to the move-k+1-ahead rule; but as yet this is unproven. Tenenbaum and Nemes [15] proved various results for the POS(k) rule primarily involving a distribution in which $s_2 = s_3 = \ldots = s_N = (1-s_1)/(N-1)$. Their results seem to strengthen Rivest's conjecture.

All of the schemes discussed in the literature are represented by Markov chains which are ergodic. By virtue of this fact, the list can be in any one of its N! configurations - even in the limit. Thus, for example, a list which was completely organized can be thoroughly disorganized by the MTF rule by a single request for the element which is accessed most infrequently. Observe that after this unfortunate occurrence, it will take a long time for the list to be organized again - i.e., for this element to dribble its way to the tail of the list.

In this paper we propose two learning algorithms in which the elements of the list adaptively learn to find their place. The first algorithm is essentially a move-to-the front algorithm with the exception that on the nth access, the accessed element is moved to the front of the list with a probability f(n). This probability is systematically decreased every time an element is accessed. Ultimately on being accessed, each element tends to stay in the place where it is (as opposed to moving to the front of the list). In other words, the Markovian representation of the procedure is absorbing, as opposed to ergodic. The organization of the list gets "absorbed" into one of the N! orderings. But, we shall show that the scheme is expedient, i.e., if $s_i > s_j$, then the probability of absorption into an arrangement in which R_i precedes R_j is always greater than 0.5.

The second algorithm which we present is far more powerful. In this case, the algorithm is a move-to-rear scheme in which the accessed element R_j is moved to the rear of the list with a probability q_j. This quantity q_j is progressively decremented every time the element is accessed. As before, ultimately there is no move operation performed on the list. Thus this scheme too is absorbing in its Markovian representation and so could converge into any one of its N! arrangements. However, in this case, we shall show that the probability of converging to the optimal arrangement can be made as close to unity as desired.

The techniques introduced here require more workspace than the traditionally used methods. However, apart from the latter algorithm being much more accurate than all the algorithms reported in the literature, it is also computationally more efficient. This is because the access of an element requires the update of exactly one probability (namely the probability q_j associated with the accessed element R_j). Further, unlike the contemporary algorithms, since the list operations are essentially stochastic, a list operation is not necessarily performed on every access. Finally, since the Markovian representation of the scheme is absorbing, the number of list operations performed asymptotically decreases to zero.

As in the literature concerning the theory of adaptive learning, we shall use the terms algorithm, rule and scheme interchangeably. Further, for the sake of simplicity we shall assume that the access probabilities of the records are distinct. The cases when they are nondistinct are those when there are many optimal configurations. A remark about these cases will be made appropriately in the body of the paper.

BOUNDED MEMORY PROBABILISTIC MOVE-TO-FRONT OPERATIONS

The concept of performing probabilistic move operations on an accessed element is not entirely new. Kan and Ross [9] suggested a probabilistic transposition scheme and showed that no advantage was obtained by rendering the scheme probabilistic. Their scheme, however, required that the probability of performing the operation, be time invariant. As opposed to this, we shall define move operations which as essentially probabilistic, but the probabilities associated with the move operations are dynamically varied.

Let f(n) be the probability (at time 'n') of any element being moved to the front of the list on being accessed. Observe that this implies than an element, on being accessed, stays where it is with probability (1-f(n)). For an initial condition we define,

$$f(0) = a \tag{2.1}$$

The probability f(n) is updated every time any record is accessed. The updating scheme is given by (2.2) below, for $0<a<1$.

$$f(n+1) = a.f(n) \quad \text{every time a record is accessed.} \tag{2.2}$$

The quantity 'a' is defined as the updating constant.

Let ${}_iP_j(n)$ be the expected probability of a record R_i succeeding R_j at the nth time instant. Clearly ${}_jP_i(n) = 1-{}_iP_j(n)$, for all n. We shall derive the transient and asymptotic properties of ${}_iP_j(n)$. To do this we need the following lemma.

LEMMA 1

Let A be any nxn matrix with distinct eigenvalues. Let K be the matrix which diagonalizes A. Let

$$B(n) = I+a^n A$$

Then, B(n) is diagonalizable by the same matrix K, for all n.

Proof

Since A has distinct eigenvalues, and K diagonalizes A,

$$K^{-1} A K = \text{Diag}(\theta_1,\ldots,\theta_N)$$

where $\text{Diag}(\theta_1,\ldots,\theta_N)$ is the diagonal matrix with the eigenvalues of A on its diagonal. Let $B(n) = I+a^n A$. Then,

$$\begin{aligned} K^{-1} B(n) K &= K^{-1} (I+a^n A) K \\ &= I+a^n K^{-1} A K \\ &= I+a^n \cdot \text{Diag}(\theta_1,\ldots,\theta_N) \end{aligned}$$

and the lemma is proved.

Using the above lemma and the theory of Markov's chains we prove the following theorems.

THEOREM I

Let ${}_iP_j(n)$ be the expected probability of R_i succeeding R_j at the nth time instant. Then, ${}_iP_j(n)$ and ${}_jP_i(n)$ obey the following time varying Markov equation:

$$\begin{bmatrix} {}_iP_j(n+1) \\ {}_jP_i(n+1) \end{bmatrix} = [B(n)] \begin{bmatrix} {}_iP_j(n) \\ {}_jP_i(n) \end{bmatrix}$$

where $B(n) = \begin{bmatrix} 1-a^n s_i & a^n s_i \\ a^n s_j & 1-a^n s_j \end{bmatrix}^T$

Proof

R_i succeeds R_j at time instant 'n+1' if and only if

(a) R_i succeeded R_j at time instant 'n' and no list operation was performed, or

(b) R_j was accessed and it was moved to the front of the list. Observe that R_i cannot succeed R_j if R_i was accessed and moved to the front.

Let ${}_ip_j(n)$ = Prob[R_i succeeds R_j at time 'n']. Clearly, $E[{}_ip_j(n)]={}_iP_j(n)$. The above leads to the following recursive definition of ${}_ip_j(n)$.

$$\begin{aligned} {}_ip_j(n+1) &= 0 && \text{if } R_i \text{ is accessed and MTF performed} \\ &= 1 && \text{if } R_j \text{ is accessed and MTF performed} \\ &= {}_ip_j(n) && \text{otherwise.} \end{aligned}$$

Observe that the probabilities of the events defined above are readily available in terms of the unknown access probabilities. Further, a MTF operation is performed at 'n' with a probability a^n. Thus,

$$\begin{aligned} {}_ip_j(n+1) &= 0 && \text{w.prob. } s_i \cdot a^n \\ &= 1 && \text{w.prob } s_j . a^n \\ &= {}_ip_j(n) && \text{w.prob } 1-(s_i+s_j). a^n \end{aligned} \tag{2.3}$$

Taking conditional expectations, we have,

$$E[{}_ip_j(n+1) | {}_ip_j(n)] = a^n s_j + {}_ip_j(n) - {}_ip_j(n) \cdot a^n (s_i+s_j)$$

Taking expectations again and observing that $E[{}_ip_j(n)]={}_iP_j(n)$, we get,

$${}_iP_j(n+1) = [1-a^n(s_i+s_j)]\ {}_iP_j(n) + s_j \cdot a^n$$

Since ${}_iP_j(n)+{}_jP_i(n)=1$, we expand the constant term as

$$s_j\ a^n = s_j\ a^n[{}_iP_j(n)+{}_jP_i(n)]$$

Thus,

$${}_iP_j(n+1) = [1-a^n\ s_i]\ {}_iP_j(n) + [a^n\ s_j]\ {}_jP_i(n)$$

This leads to the following matrix equation

$$\begin{bmatrix} {}_iP_j(n+1) \\ {}_jP_i(n+1) \end{bmatrix} = \begin{bmatrix} 1-a^n\ s_i & a^n\ s_j \\ a^n\ s_i & 1-a^n\ s_j \end{bmatrix} \begin{bmatrix} {}_iP_j(n) \\ {}_jP_i(n) \end{bmatrix}$$

and the theorem is proved.

THEOREM II

The constant matrix K, where

$$K = \begin{bmatrix} 1 & 1 \\ s_i/s_j & -1 \end{bmatrix}$$

diagonalizes B(n), for all values of n.

Proof

Observe that B(n) is of the form,

$$B(n) = I + a^n A$$

where

$$A = \begin{bmatrix} -s_i & s_j \\ s_i & -s_j \end{bmatrix}$$

Since B(n) is a stochastic matrix, we know that one of its eigenvalues is unity. Further, since the sum of the eigenvalues is equal to the trace of the matrix, the second eigenvalue is $1-a^n(s_i+s_j)$. Using Lemma I, we know that the matrix which diagonalizes B(0) also diagonalizes B(n) for all n. In this case, it is easy to see that the eigenvectors for B(0) are

(i) $[1 \; s_i/s_j]^T$ for the eigenvalue unity, and

(ii) $[1 \; -1]^T$ for the eigenvalue $1-(s_i+s_j)$

Thus, the constant matrix K, where,

$$K = \begin{bmatrix} 1 & 1 \\ s_i/s_j & -1 \end{bmatrix}$$

diagonalizes B(n) for all n. This proves the theorem.

Remark: By performing elementary operations, it is easy to see that K^{-1} has the form:

$$K^{-1} = \frac{1}{s_i+s_j} \begin{bmatrix} s_j & s_j \\ s_i & -s_j \end{bmatrix} \qquad (2.4)$$

One can trivially verify that,

$$K^{-1} B(n) K = \text{Diag}(1, 1-a^n(s_i+s_j)),$$

where

$$\text{Diag}(1, 1-a^n(s_i+s_j)) = \begin{bmatrix} 1 & 0 \\ 0 & 1-a^n(s_i+s_j) \end{bmatrix}$$

Similarly, $K \cdot \text{Diag}(1, 1-a^n(s_i+s_j)) \cdot K^{-1}$ is exactly B(n).

THEOREM III

The value of ${}_iP_j(n)$ for an updating constant 'a' obtained by solving the Markov equation given by Theorem I, has the form:

$$ {}_iP_j(n) = \frac{s_j}{s_i+s_j} Q_{a,n} + \frac{s_i}{s_i+s_j} (1-Q_{a,n}) $$

where

$$ Q_{a,n} = 0.5 \left[\prod_{k=0}^{n-1} (1-a^k(s_i+s_j)) \right] $$

Proof

From the results of Theorem I, we can see that

$$ \begin{bmatrix} {}_iP_j(n+1) \\ {}_jP_i(n+1) \end{bmatrix} = B(n) \begin{bmatrix} {}_iP_j(n) \\ {}_jP_i(n) \end{bmatrix} $$

Thus, the solution of the matrix difference equation yields,

$$ \begin{bmatrix} {}_iP_j(n) \\ {}_jP_i(n) \end{bmatrix} = \begin{bmatrix} B(n-1).B(n-2) \ \ldots \ B(0) \end{bmatrix} \begin{bmatrix} {}_iP_j(0) \\ {}_jP_i(0) \end{bmatrix} = \begin{bmatrix} \prod_{k=0}^{n-1} B(k) \end{bmatrix} \begin{bmatrix} {}_iP_j(0) \\ {}_jP_i(0) \end{bmatrix} $$

Rewriting each B(k) in terms of the diagonal matrix $\mathrm{Diag}(1,1-a^k(s_i+s_j))$,

$$ \begin{bmatrix} {}_iP_j(n) \\ {}_jP_i(n) \end{bmatrix} = \begin{bmatrix} \left(\prod_{k=0}^{n-1} K.[\mathrm{Diag}(1,1-a^k(s_i+s_j))] \cdot K^{-1} \right) \end{bmatrix} \cdot \begin{bmatrix} {}_iP_j(0) \\ {}_jP_i(0) \end{bmatrix} $$

Since the product of each consecutive pair $K \cdot K^{-1}$ yields the identity matrix, we write,

$$ \begin{bmatrix} {}_iP_j(n) \\ {}_jP_i(n) \end{bmatrix} = K\left[\prod_{k=0}^{n-1} \mathrm{Diag}(1,1-a^k(s_i+s_j)) \right] \cdot K^{-1} \cdot \begin{bmatrix} {}_iP_j(0) \\ {}_jP_i(0) \end{bmatrix} $$

$$ = K \begin{bmatrix} 1 & 0 \\ 0 & \prod_{k=0}^{n-1} (1-a^k(s_i+s_j)) \end{bmatrix} K^{-1} \begin{bmatrix} {}_iP_j(0) \\ {}_jP_i(0) \end{bmatrix} \qquad (2.5) $$

Let $Q_{a,n}=1/2 \prod_{k=0}^{n-1} (1-a^k(s_i+s_j))$. Since, with no loss of generality, ${}_iP_j(0)={}_jP_i(0)=0.5$, we expand (2.5) above to yield,

$$ \begin{bmatrix} {}_iP_j(n) \\ {}_jP_i(n) \end{bmatrix} = \frac{1}{s_i+s_j} \begin{bmatrix} 1 & 1 \\ \frac{s_i}{s_j} & -1 \end{bmatrix} \begin{bmatrix} 1 & 0 \\ 0 & 2 \cdot Q_{a,n} \end{bmatrix} \begin{bmatrix} s_j & s_j \\ s_i & -s_j \end{bmatrix} \begin{bmatrix} 0.5 \\ 0.5 \end{bmatrix} $$

After considerable simplification this results in

$$\begin{bmatrix} {}_iP_j(n) \\ \\ {}_jP_i(n) \end{bmatrix} = \frac{1}{s_i+s_j} \begin{bmatrix} s_j\ (1-Q_{a,n}) + s_i \quad Q_{a,n} \\ \\ s_i\ (1-Q_{a,n}) + s_j \quad Q_{a,n} \end{bmatrix} \tag{2.6}$$

and the theorem is proved.

Remark: Observe that ${}_iP_j(n)={}_jP_i(n)=0.5$ if $s_i=s_j$. This is intuitively satisfying.

To prove the asymptotic value of ${}_iP_j(n)$ we need the following lemma.

LEMMA II

The infinite product:

$$\prod_{k=1}^{\infty} (1+b_k) \qquad (\text{where } b_k \neq -1 \text{ for all } k)$$

tends to a non-zero finite limit if and only if the infinite sum,

$$\sum_{k=1}^{\infty} b_k$$

is convergent.

Proof

The lemma is proved in Titchmarsh [17, pp.13-15].

THEOREM IV

The stochastic bounded memory Move-to-Front Algorithm is asymptotically always less accurate than the deterministic Move-to-Front Algorithm.

Proof

Consider the term for ${}_iP_j(n)$ as

$${}_iP_j(n) = \frac{s_i}{s_i+s_j}(1-Q_{a,n}) + \frac{s_j}{s_i+s_j} Q_{a,n}$$

where $Q_{a,n}$ is defined in Theorem III.

Using Lemma II, it is clear that $Q_{a,n}>0$ as $0<a<1$, but tends to zero as a tends to unity. Differentiating with respect to a, we obtain,

$$\frac{\delta\, {}_iP_j(n)}{\delta a} = (s_j-s_i) \cdot Q_{a,n} \cdot \sum_{k=1}^{n-1} \frac{k \cdot a^{k-1}}{1-a^k(s_i+s_J)}$$

Since $0<a<1$, and $0<s_i+s_j<1$, we have,

$$0<1-a^k\ (s_i+s_j)<1 \qquad \text{for all } k \geq 1.$$

Assume that with no loss of generality that $s_i<s_j$. This tells us that,

$$\frac{\delta\, {}_iP_j(n)}{\delta a} > 0 \qquad (2.7)$$

In other words, ${}_iP_j(n)$ has no stationary point with respect to a in the interval $0<a<1$. Further, due to (2.7), the largest value of ${}_iP_j(n)$ occurs when a=1. Since (2.7) is true for finite and infinite values of n, the value of ${}_iP_j(\infty)$ is maximized at the largest acceptable value of a and the theorem is proved.

COROLLARY IV.I

The stochastic bounded memory Move-to-Front Algorithm is expedient independent of the access distribution of the records.

Proof

Due to the multiplying factor of 0.5, and the previous theorem, it is easy to see that for all a, $0<Q_{a,n}<0.5$. The result is now obvious since ${}_iP_j(n)$ is merely a convex combination of $s_i/(s_i+s_j)$ and $s_j/(s_i+s_j)$ weighted by $(1-Q_{a,n})$ and $Q_{a,n}$ respectively.

Remark: Throughout this discussion it was assumed that the single memory location that stores f(n) can contain an arbitrarily small positive real number. In practice, however, all that we need to store is an index, n, of the time that has lapsed since the file reorganization scheme was initiated. From this index, f(n) can be computed trivially, since,

$$f(n) = a^n$$

It is also appropriate to observe that the maximum number that this index should attain is governed by the uniform random number generator accessible to the system. If the smallest positive number yielded by the random number generator is x_{min}, then the memory location which stores n need not store numbers larger than n_{max}, where,

$$n_{max} = \left\lceil \log_a (x_{min}) \right\rceil$$

We now proceed to study the linear memory stochastic move-to-rear scheme.

LINEAR MEMORY PROBABILISTIC MOVE-TO-REAR OPERATIONS

In this section we shall show how a probabilistic scheme with an absorbing Markovian representation can indeed be made asymptotically optimal. The idea is essentially one of moving the accessed element R_j to the rear of the list with a probability q_j which is systematically updated so that, as in the previous case, in the limit, no list operations are performed. In this case, we shall show that the list converges to one of the N! possible arrangements, and the probability of converging to the optimal one can be made arbitrarily close to unity. Let $q_j(n)$ be the probability (at time 'n') of moving the element R_j to the rear of the list on being accessed. This implies that on being accessed, the element stays where it is with probability $(1-q_j(n))$.

Initially, we set $q_j(0)=1$ for all $j=1,\dots,N$. After this, the quantity $q_j(n)$ is decremented every time R_j is accessed as below:

$$q_j(n+1) = aq_j(n) \text{ if } R_j \text{ is accessed.}$$
$$= q_j(n) \text{ otherwise.} \tag{3.1}$$

Observe that the updating scheme is reiminiscent of the Linear Reward-Inaction scheme studied extensively in the area of adaptive learning.

We now derive the properties of $q_j(n)$. Unless explicitly stated q_j refers to $q_j(n)$.

THEOREM V

$E[q_i(n)]$ decreases monotonically with time. Further, for all $j\neq k$,

$$s_j>s_k \text{ if and only if } E[q_j(n)]<E[q_k(n)]. \tag{3.2}$$

Proof

Consider the random variable $q_i(n+1)$. By virtue of (3.2), the latter has the following distribution:

$$q_i(n+1) = aq_i \quad \text{, w. prob. } s_i$$
$$= q_i \quad \text{, w. prob. } (1-s_i) \tag{3.3}$$

Thus, $E[q_i(n+1)|q_i] = aq_is_i+q_i(1-s_i)$

$$= q_i(1-(1-a)s_i)$$
$$= e_iq_i, \qquad \text{where } e_i=1-(1-a)s_i \tag{3.4}$$

Note that since $0<a<1$, for all i, e_i obeys $0<e_i<1$. Taking expectations again, we obtain,

$$E[q_i(n+1)] = e_iE[q_i(n)] \ . \tag{3.5}$$

This difference equation subject to the initial condition $q_i(0)=1$, yields the solution,

$$E[q_i(n)] = e_i^{\,n}.$$

Clearly, $E[q_i(n)]$ is monotonically decreasing with n. Further,

$$s_j>s_k<=>e_j<e_k<=>e_j^{\,n}<e_k^{\,n},$$

and the theorem is proved.

COROLLARY V.1

For all i,

$$\lim_{n\to\infty} q_i(n) = 0 \qquad \text{w.prob 1.}$$

The result follows since the Markov process $\{q_i(n)\}$ has only one absorbing barrier, namely the probability 0 [10].

THEOREM VI

For $n>0$, $Var[q_i(n)]$ decreases monotonically with n and its limiting value is zero.

Proof

From the distribution of $q_i(n)$ given by (3.3), we obtain,

$$q_i^2(n+1) = a^2q_i^2 \quad \text{w. prob } s_i$$
$$= q_i^2 \quad \text{w. prob } (1-s_i).$$

Thus, $E[q_i^2(n+1)|q_i] = [1-(1-a^2)s_i]q_i^2.$ (3.6)

Taking expectations again we obtain the difference equation,

$$E[q_i^2(n+1)] = [1-(1-a^2)s_i]\ E[q_i^2(n)].$$

Since $E[q_i^2(0)] = 1$, we have,

$$E[q_i^2(n)] = [1-(1-a^2)s_i]^n. \quad (3.7)$$

Consider now the expression for $Var[q_i(n+1)|q_i]$. Using the form of $E[q_i(n+1)|q_i]$ from Theorem I, we obtain,

$$Var[q_i(n+1)|q_i] = E[q_i^2(n+1)|q_i] - E^2[q_i(n+1)|q_i]$$
$$= [1-(1-a^2)s_i]\ q_i^2 - [1-(1-a)]^2\ q_i^2$$
$$= (1-a)^2\ s_i(1-s_i)q_i^2\ .$$

Taking expectations again and using (3.7), we get

$$Var[q_i(n+1)] = (1-a)^2\ s_i(1-s_i)\ [1-(1-a^2)s_i]^n$$

which monotonically decreases with n and has a limiting value of zero.

Remark: The fact that the limiting value of $Var[q_i(n)]$ is zero is obvious from Theorem I, since $q_i(n)$ is a nonnegative random variable whose limiting mean is zero. However, the fact that it monotonically decreases to this limiting value is not necessarily obvious, and this is the main contribution of Theorem VI.

Summarizing the results of the above theorems we note that given two elements R_j and R_k, the probabilities of q_j and q_k converge w.p.1 to zero. Further, at any instant,

$$E[q_j(n)]>E[q_k(n)] \text{ if and only if } s_j<s_k.$$

Observe that this is true for all $0<a<1$. By appropriately choosing the value of the updating constant 'a', we shall now show that a stochastically stronger inequality exists - which not merely relates the expected values of q_j and q_k but the probabilities themselves.

THEOREM VII

For all j, k where $j \neq k$, if $s_j > s_k$, then, the quantity $Pr[q_j(n) < q_k(n)]$ can be made as close to unity as desired.

Proof

Assume with no loss of generality that $s_j > s_k$. Let,

$$x_{j,k}(n) = q_j(n)/q_k(n).$$

Clearly, $x_{j,k}(0)=1$, Further, $x_{j,k}(n)$ can only assume non-negative values. Consider the distribution of $x_{j,k}(n+1)$ given the values of $q_j(n)$ and $q_k(n)$. By virtue of (3.1),

$$\begin{aligned} x_{j,k}(n+1) &= (a\, q_j)/q_k && \text{w.prob.} s_j, \\ &= q_j/(a\, q_k) && \text{w.prob.} s_k, \\ &= q_j/q_k && \text{w.prob.} (1-s_j-s_k). \end{aligned}$$

$$\begin{aligned} \text{Thus, } x_{j,k}(n+1) &= a.\, x_{j,k}(n) && \text{w.prob.} s_j, \\ &= x_{j,k}(n)/a && \text{w.prob.} s_k, \\ &= x_{j,k}(n) && \text{w.prob.} (1-s_j-s_k) \,. \end{aligned} \tag{3.8}$$

Taking conditional expectations yields,

$$E[x_{j,k}(n+1)|x_{j,k}(n)] = 1/a\ [a^2 s_j + a(1-s_j-s_k)+s_k]\cdot x_{j,k}(n)$$

Whence on taking expectation again and observing that $x_{j,k}(0)=1$, we get,

$$E[x_{j,k}(n)] = (h_{j,k})^n, \text{ where } h_{j,k}=1/a\ [a^2 s_j + a(1-s_j-s_k)+s_k]. \tag{3.9}$$

Let a be any real number satisfying, $s_k < a\ s_j$. Then,

$$s_k/a < s_j$$

$$=> s_k(1-a)/a < s_j(1-a)$$

$$=> s_k(1/a-1) < s_j(1-a)$$

$$=> a s_j - s_j - s_k + (s_k/a) < 0$$

$$=> h_{j,k} < 1.$$

Thus $h_{j,k}$ can be made strictly less than unity by appropriately choosing 'a'. From (3.9), this implies that $E[x_{j,k}(n)]$ can be rendered monotonically <u>decreasing</u> with n, and further,

$$\lim_{n\to\infty} E[x_{j,k}(n)] = 0$$

But $x_{j,k}(n)$ is always nonnegative. This implies that

$$\lim_{n\to\infty} x_{j,k}(n) \to 0 \qquad \text{w.prob.1}$$

Thus, $\quad Pr[x_{j,k}(n)>0] \to 0 \quad$ w.prob.1, as n tends to ∞.

and the result follows.

Remark: Observe that although the values of $\{s_i\}$ are unknown, the above theorem says that by making 'a' sufficiently close to unity the asymptotic value $Pr[q_j(n)<q_k(n)]$

can be made as close to zero as desired.

We now prove the optimality of the scheme.

Let ${}_iY_j(n)$ be the expected probability that R_i succeeds R_j at the nth time instants. Clearly,

${}_jY_i(n) = 1-{}_iY_j(n)$ for all $i,j=1,\ldots,N$; $i\neq j$.

The properties of ${}_iY_j(n)$ are summarized by the following theorem.

THEOREM VIII

The asymptotic value of ${}_iY_j(n)$ is unity if and only if $s_i>s_j$.

Proof

The theorem follows in a manner analogous to that of Theorem I.

Note that R_i succeeds R_j at time 'n+1' if and only if:

(a) R_i succeeded R_j at time n and no list operation was performed, or

(b) R_i was accessed at time n and it was moved to the rear of the list.

Let ${}_iy_j$ = Prob[R_i succeeds R_j at time 'n']. Clearly, $E[{}_iy_j(n)]={}_iY_j(n)$. We thus have the following recursive definition of ${}_iy_j(n)$.

$$
\begin{aligned}
{}_iy_j(n+1) &= 0 \text{ if } R_j \text{ was accessed and MTR is performed.}\\
&= 1 \text{ if } R_i \text{ was accessed and MTR is performed.}\\
&= {}_iy_j(n) \text{ otherwise.}
\end{aligned}
$$

Let Z_i be the number of times R_i was accessed prior to and including the time instant 'n'. Clearly, Z_i is a random variable, with $\sum_{i=1}^{N} Z_i=n$. Further, the probability of moving R_i at the nth time instant (on being accessed) to the rear of the list is exactly a^{Z_i-1}. Thus, we rewrite ${}_iy_j(n)$ to obey the following equations:

$$
\begin{aligned}
{}_iy_j(n+1) &= 0 && \text{w.prob. } s_j \cdot a^{Z_j-1}\\
&= 1 && \text{w.prob. } s_i\, a^{Z_i-1}\\
&= {}_iy_j && \text{otherwise.}
\end{aligned}
$$

Taking expectations twice and observing that $E[{}_iy_j(n)]={}_iY_j$, we obtain,

$$
\begin{bmatrix} {}_iY_j(n+1) \\ {}_jY_i(n+1) \end{bmatrix} = \begin{bmatrix} 1 - a^{Z_j-1} s_j & a^{Z_j-1} s_j \\ a^{Z_i-1} s_i & 1-a^{Z_i-1} s_i \end{bmatrix} \begin{bmatrix} {}_iY_j(n) \\ {}_jY_i(n) \end{bmatrix}
$$

Unlike the case of Theorem II, this time varying difference equation cannot be solved directly using the theory of diagonalization. This is because there is no single constant matrix which diagonalizes the Markov matrix for every time instant. However, we consider the asymptotic value of ${}_iY_j(n)$. On converging,

$$ {}_iY_j(\infty) = a^{Z_i-1} s_i + (1 - a^{Z_i-1} s_i - a^{Z_j-1} s_j)\ {}_iY_j(\infty) $$

which yields:

$$ {}_iY_j(\infty) = \lim_{Z_i,Z_j\to\infty} a^{Z_i-1}\cdot s_i/(a^{Z_i-1}\cdot s_i + a^{Z_j-1}\cdot s_j) = \lim_{Z_i,Z_j\to\infty} \frac{a^{Z_i}s_i}{a^{Z_i}s_i + a^{Z_j}s_j} $$

Let $t=s_i/s_j$. Further, using the law of large numbers,

$$ Z_j = s_j/s_i \cdot Z_i = t\,Z_i $$

Thus, $ {}_iY_j(\infty) = \lim_{Z_i\to\infty} \dfrac{1}{1 + t\,a^{(t-1)Z_i}} $

Now, since we assume that $s_i<s_j$, t is strictly less than unity. Therefore,

$$ \lim_{Z_i\to\infty} a^{(t-1)Z_i} = 0 $$

and hence, $\lim_{Z_i\to\infty} {}_iY_j(\infty) = 1.$

Hence the theorem!

Remark: Observe that in this case too, ${}_iY_j(\infty)$ has a value of 0.5 if $s_i=s_j$, which is what we would expect.

A natural consequence of the above theorem is the corollary stated below. The corollary is obvious in as much as the above theorems are valid for every arbitrary pair of records R_i and R_j.

COROLLARY VIII.1

The probability of the list converging to the optimal arrangement (out of the N! possible arrangements) can be made as close to unity as desired.

Remarks: (1) Just as in the case of the stochastic MTF scheme, observe that we have assumed that the quantities $q_j(n)$ can be arbitrarily small positive real numbers. However, in practice, just as in the above case, it is sufficient to retain indices which remember the number of times a record is accessed. From these indices the quantities $q_j(n)$ can be trivially computed. Observe too that the maximum integer a memory location should contain need not exceed n_{max}, where,

$$ n_{max} = \lceil \log_a x_{min} \rceil + 1 $$

where x_{min} is the smallest positive real number yielded by the random number generator accessible to the user.

(2) In this connection, it is beneficial to compare the scheme we have proposed with the scheme which keeps the records sorted in the order of the number of times they have been accessed. First of all, observe that our scheme does not require any

"global" comparisons, as for example, comparing $q_i(n)$ with $q_j(n)$. Further consider the case when two records R_i and R_j have exactly the same access probabilities. If Z_i and Z_j respectively are the number of time these records are accessed, then, notice that if one keeps the list sorted on the basis of counters, Pr[Move Operation Performed $|Z_i=Z_j$; R_j succeeds R_i; R_j accessed] = 1. However, this probability will tend to <u>zero</u> in the stochastic MTR scheme which we have proposed essentially because of the absorbing Markovian representation of our scheme. One can easily extrapolate this situation to the case when many records have been accessed exactly the same number of times.

CONCLUSIONS

We have considered a list of elements $\{R_1,...,R_N\}$ in which the element R_i is accessed with a probability s_i, which is unknown apriori. Two stochastic list organizing schemes have been proposed both of which have absorbing Markovian representations. The first of these schemes requires bounded memory and is of a move-to-front flavour. It is expedient, but is always less optimal than the deterministic move-to-front algorithm. The second scheme performs a move to the rear operation on the accessed element R_j with a probability q_j which is systematically decreased. Ultimately, the list gets absorbed into one of the N! possible arrangements. We have shown that the asymptotic probability of converging to the optimal arrangement can be made as close to unity as desired.

ACKNOWLEDGEMENTS

We are greatly indebted to my colleague Nicola Santoro who introduced us to the problem and to the literature in the field. We are grateful to him and our colleague Mike Atkinson for their encouragement and comments during the course of the study. We are also grateful to Professor Ian Munroe, from the University of Waterloo who first conjectured, while in personal conversation, the result that the Stochastic MTF scheme was at its best expedient.

REFERENCES

[1] Arnow, D.M. and Tenebaum, A.M., "An Investigation of the Move-Ahead-K Rules", Congressus Numerantium, Proc. of the Thirteenth Southeastern Conference on Combinatorics, Graph Theory and Computing, Florida, February 1982, pp.47-65.

[2] Bitner, J.R., "Heuristics That Dynamically Organize Data Structures", SIAM J. Comput., Vol.8, 1979, pp.82-110.

[3] Burville, P.J. and Kingman, J.F.C., "On A Model for Storage and Search", J. Appl. Probability, Vol.10, 1973, pp.697-701.

[4] Cook, C.R., and Kim, D.J., "Best Sorting Algorithm for Nearly Sorted Lists", Comm. ACM, Vol.23, 1980, pp.620-624.

[5] Dijkstra, E.W., "Smoothsort, An Algorithm for Sorting in SITU", Science of Computer Programming, 1982, pp.223-233.

[6] Gonnet, G.H., Munro, J.I. and Suwanda, H., "Exegesis of Self Organizing Linear Search", SIAM J. Comput., Vol.10, 1981, pp.613-637.
[7] Hendricks, W.J., "The Stationary Distribution of an Interesting Markov Chain", J. Appl. Probability, Vol.9, 1972, pp.231-233.
[8] Hendricks, W.J., "An Extension of a Theorem Concerning an Interesting Markov Chain", J. App. Probability, Vol.10, 1973, pp.231-233.
[9] Kan, Y.C. and Ross, S.M., "Optimal List Order Under Partial Memory Constraints", J. App. Probability, Vol.17, 1980, 1004-1015.
[10] Karlin, S. and Taylor, H.M., "A First Course in Stochastic Processes", Academic Press, 1975.
[11] Knuth, D.E., "The Art of Computer Programming, Vol.3, Sorting and Searching", Addison-Wesley, Reading, Ma., 1973.
[12] McCabe, J., "On Serial Files With Relocatable Records", Operations Research, Vol.12, 1965, pp.609-618.
[13] Rivest, R.L., "On Self-Organizing Sequential Search Heuristics", Comm. ACM, Vol.19, 1976, pp.63-67.
[14] Sleator, D. and Tarjan, R., "Amortized Efficiency of List Update Rules", Proc. of the Sixteenth Annual ACM Symposium on Theory of Computing, April 1984, pp.488-492.
[15] Tenenbaum, A.M. and Nemes, R.M., "Two Spectra of Self-Organizing Sequential Search Algorithms", SIAM J. Comput., Vol.11, 1982, pp.557-566.
[16] Oommen, B.J., "On the Use of Smoothsort and Stochastic Move-to-Front Operations for Optimal List Organization", Proc. of the Twenty-Second Allerton Conference on Communication, Control and Computing, October 1984, pp.243-252.
[17] Titchmarsh, E.C., The Theory of Functions, Oxford University Press, 1964.

The Cost of Locking

Peter K. Rathmann
Stanford University

Abstract. Consider the problem of locking two transactions A and B, each a linear sequence of atomic database steps. Let a fixpoint H be a subset of all possible shuffles of the steps of A and B. [Papadimitriou-82] gave a necessary and sufficient condition for H to be realizable as the set of all sequences of steps "legal" under some locking program. This paper addresses two questions his work left unanswered. First, how many locks are required to realize a given fixpoint set? Second, what sets are realizable as fixpoints of a locking program in the case of three or more transactions? Here, in response to the first query, we demonstrate that for two transactions, any fixpoint set which satisfies this condition may be realized with $O(m^2n)$ locks, while for three or more transactions, we show the existence of realizable fixpoint sets which require a number of locks exponential in the number of transaction steps. We also give a partial response to the second query, by developing necessary conditions for the realization of fixpoints which involve three transactions.

Introduction

Concurrency control seeks to allow parallel access to a database, while maintaining database integrity. A user accesses and updates the database via *transactions,* which, if run in isolation, preserve the consistency of the database. However, if transactions run concurrently, inconsistencies may arise, so care must be taken to coordinate their execution. This coordination is effected by a *scheduler*, a mechanism which delays some requests and permits the immediate completion of others. Most schedulers in use today employ locking.

This paper is a direct extension of the work in [Papa-82] and follows the definitions and transaction model from that work. This model abstracts transactions a

---

This work supported by contract N39-84-C-0211 (the Knowledge Base Management Systems Project, Prof. Gio Wiederhold, Principal Investigator) from the Defense Advanced Research Projects Agency.

great deal. Under this model, a transaction $A = a_1, a_2, \ldots, a_m$ is a linear series of uninterpreted atomic database steps, each of which represents some action on the database. If we have two transactions $A = a_1, a_2, \ldots, a_m$ and $B = b_1, b_2, \ldots, b_n$ running at the same time, their steps may be interleaved. Such an interleaving is called a transaction *history*. The *shuffle* of A and B, $A * B$, is defined as the set of all possible histories of the steps of A and B. Some of the histories in the shuffle may lead to violations of the database integrity constraints. The goal of locking, or any method of concurrency control, is to allow only those histories of a shuffle which obey the integrity constraints. We introduce lock steps, where l_i and u_i stand for steps which involve locking or unlocking the ith lock variable. A *locked transaction* A' is formed by inserting distinct lock–unlock steps, $l_1, u_1, \ldots, l_k, u_k$ among the steps of A. A pair of such locked transactions (A', B') defines a *locking policy*. A history $h \in A * B$ is called *legal* with respect to a locking policy if there exists h', an element of the shuffle of the locked transactions A' and B', such that

1) between any two occurrences of a lock step l_i, there appears an unlock step u_i, and

2) h is the same as h' with h''s lock and unlock steps removed.

The set of all legal histories, H, is the *fixpoint* of the policy. The power of a concurrency control method may be measured by the richness of the class of fixpoints it realizes.

We will often deal with fragments of transaction histories, and use the notation steps(h) to indicate the set of all database steps taken within the fragment h. Two histories $h, g \in A * B$ are said to *cross* if $h = h_1 a_i h_2 a_j h_3$, and $g = g_1 b_l h_2 b_m g_3$ where $a_i, a_j \in$ steps(A), $b_l, b_m \in$ steps(B), and steps($h_1 a_i$) = steps($g_1 b_l$). [Papa 82] proved the following properties of all realizable fixpoint sets:

1) if $h = h_1 a_i h_2 a_j h_3$ and $g = g_1 b_l h_2 b_m g_3$ are two crossing histories in a fixpoint H, then the histories $h_1 a_i h_2 b_m g_3$, and $g_1 b_l h_2 a_j h_3$ are also in H, and

2) the serial histories are included in H. A serial history is one in which there is no interleaving, all the steps in A precede all the steps in B or vice versa.

These two conditions, when met, are also sufficient to insure that a set of histories is realizable as the fixpoint of some locking policy.

A geometric viewpoint is helpful in studying locking policies and fixpoints. A policy of two transactions may be mapped into the plane, where the two coordinates represent progress in completing each of the transactions. In this viewpoint the transaction history is a path in the plane. The path crosses the grid lines

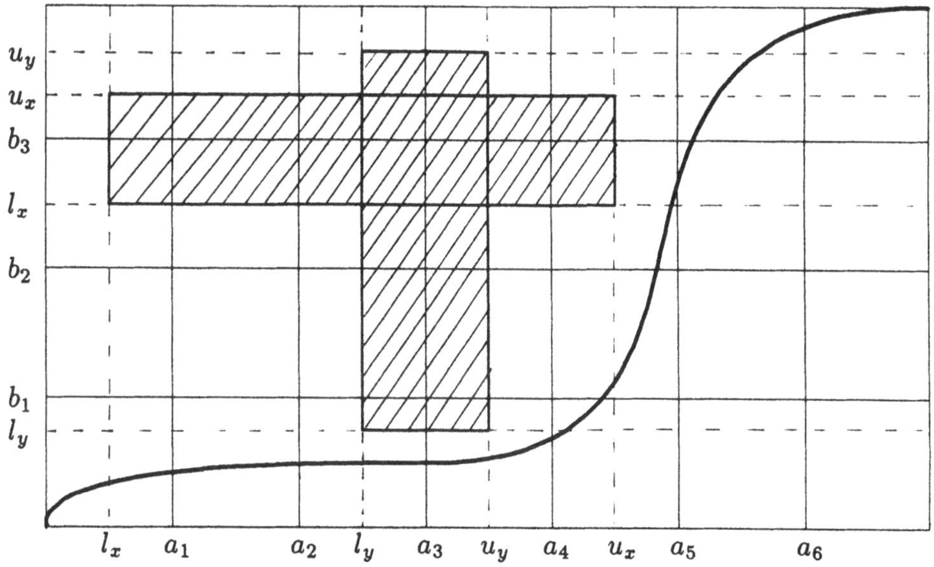

figure 1. A Geometric View of Locked Transactions

which represent transaction steps, in the same order as that in which those steps appear in the history. Lock and unlock steps are represented like transaction steps, as grid lines in the plane, where crossing the grid line indicates locking or unlocking the associated variable. The variable is locked while the path is in the strip between two such steps and the intersection of two strips with the same variable represents the illegal state of holding a lock variable twice. Such intersections appear as forbidden rectangles in the plane. A legal history, then, is one for which it is possible to find an increasing path which does not intersect any forbidden rectangles.

The geometric viewpoint also provides a plausibility argument for the crossing condition. If two histories cross, this means that one of the paths starts out below the other and eventually is above the other. By the intermediate value theorem, for two curves to do this in the plane, they must intersect. At this point of intersection, both histories are in exactly the same state. Being in the same states, they have the same options as to how to continue.

Number of locks

In the original 1982 JACM paper [Papa-82], Papadimitriou showed how to construct a locking program to realize any fixpoint which includes the serial histories and satisfies the crossing requirement. However, the number of locks needed for this realization was left as an open problem. Here I outline an argument which limits the number of locks required to $O(m^2n)$, where m and n are the number of steps in each of the two transactions locked. Let our transactions be $A = a_1, a_2, \ldots, a_m$ and $B = b_1, b_2, \ldots, b_n$ and let the desired fixpoint be $H \subseteq A * B$.

We shall achieve this bound in two steps. First, we shall describe a method which bounds the number of locks by $O(m^2n^2)$, and refine this method to achieve a bound of $O(m^2n)$.

The first method, which yields an $O(m^2n^2)$ bound on the total number of locks needed to realize a fixpoint shall have the following basic structure. The grid lines representing the transaction steps divide the locking diagram into $(m+1)(n+1)$ small squares. The construction [Papa-82] of a locking to realize a given set of histories proceeds square by square, by putting channels through each square. The number of locks needed at each square is at most linear in the number of channels which must pass through that square. Therefore, summing channels over all the squares will give a bound on the total number of locks needed to realize a fixpoint.

Consider one such square T of the locking diagram. This square is the region in the plane bounded between the grid lines for step a_i and a_{i+1}, in one dimension, and between the grid lines for steps b_j and $b_j + 1$ in the other. Each history which corresponds to a path that passes through T can be divided into two parts, a prefix and a suffix. The prefix represents those database steps the path takes before penetrating the interior of T, while the suffix represents those steps the path takes after exiting T. The prefixes and suffixes may be grouped into equivalence classes. Two suffixes s_1, and s_2 are said to be equivalent if they have the same set of prefixes, i.e., if for every prefix p, if ps_1 is a history in the fixpoint, then ps_2 is a history in the fixpoint and vice versa. The definition of equivalence classes for prefixes is symmetric. Both the incoming and outgoing equivalence classes have a natural linear order, based on the lexicographic order of the histories. Formally $s < s'$ if there exist h, h' and h'' such that $s = hah'$ and $s' = hbh''$. The equivalence classes are intervals of this linear order [Papa-82].

For equivalence classes of suffixes, define $<$ so that a class is less than another iff all its suffixes are less than those in the other class. Since the equivalence classes are disjoint intervals, this imposes a total order on the suffix equivalence classes

Now, let E_j and E_i be equivalence classes of the suffixes, such that $E_j > E_i$. Further, let $s' = \inf(E_j)$, and let $s = \sup(E_i)$. We know $s < s'$, and can find h, h' and h'' such that $s = hah'$ and $s' = hbh''$. Intuitively, this means that s and s' follow the same path initially but split at a grid point, with s' going above the grid point and s below it. Let us call this grid point the *upper bollard* of E_i. Conversely, we call it the *lower bollard* of E_j. This grid point marks a boundary between equivalence classes.

Lemma 1. *No suffix in E_i or any lower equivalence class passes above the upper bollard of E_i.*

An equivalent restatement of this condition is that no suffix which is less than s passes above the upper bollard of E_i. We start by assuming that l is a suffix which violates the above lemma, that is, $l < s$, but goes above the upper bollard of E_i.

We need some additional notation for this proof. Define $\text{BPROGRESS}(p, i)$ to be the highest numbered B step already completed when the path p crosses step a_i. Since $s < s'$, let $s = ha_kh'$ and $s' = hb_nh''$. This means that the two paths separate at the (k, n) grid point. This is the upper bollard of E_i. Consequently,

$$\text{BPROGRESS}(s, k) = n - 1.$$

Since l goes above this grid point,

$$\text{BPROGRESS}(l, k) \geq n.$$

Since $l < s$, let $l = ma_rm'$ and $s = mb_qm''$. This means

$$\text{BPROGRESS}(l, r) < \text{BPROGRESS}(s, r), \text{for some } r < k$$

Let w be the largest integer in the interval $[r, k]$ such that $\text{BPROGRESS}(l, w) < \text{BPROGRESS}(s, w)$ and let x be the smallest integer greater than w such that $\text{BPROGRESS}(l, x) > \text{BPROGRESS}(s, x)$. Also, let $y = \text{BPROGRESS}(s, w)$. Before path l crosses a_{w+1}, it must equal s in progress in the B direction. In particular, it must cross b_y. Then, if $\gamma_1 b_y$ is a prefix of l, and $\delta_1 a_w$ is a prefix of s, we know that $\text{steps}(\gamma_1 b_y) = \text{steps}(\delta_1 a_w)$. At this point, both histories may continue together for 0 or more steps, (call this fragment of a path γ_2), but when they reach a_x, l has crossed more B steps than s has. Then if $z = \text{BPROGRESS}(s, x)$ we have:

$$l = \gamma_1 b_y \gamma_2 b_{z+1} \gamma_3,$$

$$s = \delta_1 a_w \gamma_2 a_x \delta_3$$

This satisfies the crossing condition, and thus we can form the suffix $l' = \delta_1 a_w \gamma_2 b_{z+1} \gamma_3$. The suffix l' must have the same set of prefixes as s, and thus $l' \in E_i$. But, $l' > s$, yet s was defined to be the sup of E_i. This is a contradiction, and thus there can be no path l both less than s and going above the upper bollard. A symmetric argument demonstrates that no suffix higher in the order than s' can go below the upper bollard of E_i. □

We use these properties to get a bound on the total number of suffix equivalence classes. Every equivalence class except the greatest one has an upper bollard. This upper bollard is unique. To see why each is unique, assume E_i and E_j have the same upper bollard. WOLOG, $E_i > E_j$, and hence E_i must be entirely above E_j's upper bollard. But this is also E_i's upper bollard, which results in the conclusion that E_i is entirely above its own upper bollard. This is contradictory, since all paths in E_i must pass below the upper bollard. Since all equivalence classes, except the top one, have an upper bollard, there is a natural pairing which gives us:

Lemma 2. *The total number of suffix equivalence classes for any given square T is at most one greater than the number of grid points above and to the right of T.*
□

In order to construct a given fixpoint, the method used in [Papa-82] requires that for each square we use a number of locks linear in the total number of suffix equivalence classes passing through that square. Thus if we are locking transactions of length m and n, it will take $O(mn)$ locks to lock a given square. Since there are $(m+1)(n+1)$ squares, this means that any realizable fixpoint set can be realized with $O(m^2n^2)$ locks. □

To refine this result, we will build the locks a column at a time instead of a square at a time. The advantage of this method of construction is that we can then show there are at most O(mn) suffix or prefix equivalence classes for the entire column, rather than the first method which counted this many equivalence classes for a single square. A slight modification of the construction in [Papa-82] will then lock an entire column using a number of locks linear in the sum of the number of column suffix and prefix equivalence classes. Since there are m columns, each requiring $O(mn)$ locks, the total number of locks required will then be bounded by $O(m^2n)$.

We will consider a column made up of all the small squares between a_j and a_{j+1}. For each square, call a suffix an *A-suffix* if it leaves the square via a transaction step in A. We are interested in the suffixes of the paths as they cross a_{j+1}. The set of these suffixes is composed of the union of the sets of A-suffixes of the individual squares making up the column. This union is in effect the set of suffixes of the column.

Within any given square, the suffixes remain ordered by $<$. We extend this ordering across squares of the column so that a suffix from a square that is higher in the locking diagram is greater than one from a lower square, or more formally we say that $s < s'$ if the smallest numbered B step in s is less than the smallest in s', or if these are equal, if $s < s'$ in the usual lexicographic ordering.

We group these column suffixes into equivalence classes, with the understanding that suffixes leaving different squares are always in different equivalence classes. Our first goal is to show that there are, at most, $O(mn)$ of these equivalence classes. (We already know that there are, at most, $O(mn^2)$ — the total we get by summing up the numbers of equivalence classes from each of the small squares). A column analog of lemma 1 remains essentially unchanged. We let E_i be an interior equivalence class. By this we mean that it has both an upper and a lower bollard. The entire column can have at most $O(n)$ equivalence classes which are not interior.

Lemma 3. *If E_i is an interior equivalence class, no suffix in E_i or any lower equivalence class passes above the upper bollard of E_i.*

The proof for this lemma is a straightforward extension of that given for lemma 1. I will give an overview only. As before let $s = \sup(E_i)$, and let l be a candidate suffix, $l < s$, and l goes above the upper bollard of E_i. Since we already know from the proof of lemma 1 that l can not exit the same square as s, assume l is from a lower square. Therefore, as l is crossing a_{j+1} to leave the column, l has completed fewer B steps than s. Or,

$$\text{BPROGRESS}(l, j+1) < \text{BPROGRESS}(s, j+1).$$

On the other hand, l goes above the upper bollard of E_i. If this upper bollard is the (k, n) grid point, we have

$$\text{BPROGRESS}(l, k) > \text{BPROGRESS}(s, k) \text{ for some } k > j+1.$$

As in lemma 1, we can now construct a crossing of l and s, and therefore show the existence of a path which is both greater than s and an element of E_i. This is a contradiction, so there can be no such l, and the lemma is proved. □

Using lemma 3, we can now see that every interior equivalence class has a unique upper bollard. This implies that there can be at most $O(mn)$ interior equivalence classes for the entire column. Since interior equivalence classes account for all but $O(n)$ of the equivalence classes, we have an $O(mn)$ bound on the total number of column equivalence classes.

Now the problem is to lock a column with O(mn) locks. We can do this with a slight modification of the construction given in [Papa-82]. Within a small square, all but a maximum of two channels go from the left to the right, left to top, bottom to right, or bottom to top. (The exceptional channels are those which straddle a corner of the square.) By lemma 3, or its equivalent for prefixes, we know that, summing over the entire column, there can be at most $O(mn)$ channels which either exit to the right of their square or enter on the left of their square. The only case not counted in at least one of these categories are those channels which enter a square on the bottom, and exit it on the top. However, these channels can be constructed without adding any new locks at all. We merely extend the channel walls from the lower square all the way to the square above, increasing the extent of the old locks, rather than adding new ones. The only additional constraint this poses is that the intervals through which the channels flow must be in the same position at the top and bottom boundaries. Since it is only the relative order of the locks that matters, we can construct a locking program satisfying this constraint and we have:

Theorem 1. *If $A = a_1, a_2, \ldots, a_m$ and $B = b_1, b_2, \ldots, b_n$ are transactions wit m and n atomic database steps respectively, and $H \subset A * B$ is a set of histories o A and B, and H includes the serial histories and satisfies the crossing conditio (that is, H can be realized at all), then H may be realized as the fixpoint of locking policy containing $O(m^2n)$ locks.*

Thus, we have locked a column using $O(mn)$ locks. Since there are m suc columns, the entire fixpoint can be realized with $O(m^2n)$ locks. This adds ne insight to the characterization of realizable two transaction fixpoint sets. In som sense these sets have a complexity that is at most polynomial, since they can b generated by a program which has only a polynomial number of locks.

Three transactions

Now we look at the complexity (in terms of number of locks required) for realizing a fixpoint for three transactions. Unlike the two transaction case, for three transactions, the class of realizable fixpoints have not been fully characterized. While we do not provide such a characterization, we show that the class of realizable fixpoints is rich enough that simple counting arguments demonstrate that an exponential number of locks is sometimes needed.

The geometric model provided earlier can be extended in order to illustrate locking problems with three transactions. Instead of a region of a plane, the transactions are now mapped into a 3-cube. Position in the cube indicates the state of progress for each of the transactions. As before, a history is an increasing curve through the cube. Locks are interspersed with the transaction steps as before, but forbidden regions have a slightly different character. The region bounded by a lock–unlock pair is a slab in 3-space; forbidden regions are intersections of any two of these, or rectangular prisms.

The crossover A major change in moving from two to three dimensions affects the crossing condition. In two dimensions, if we are given certain starting and ending positions of a pair of paths, we can conclude that the paths must cross and hence that extra hybrid paths must be allowed. In three dimensions, if two paths actually intersect, then there will also be these additional hybrid paths. However, there is more room in three dimensions for paths to move past each other without intersecting. Despite the restricted nature of the forbidden regions, we shall see that it is possible to construct channels through space, such that the two allowed paths have projections which intersect, but the paths themselves do not.

Our actual construction of this behavior builds on an example due to Soisalon-Soininen and Yannakakis [Papa-85]. We have the three transactions $A = a_1a_2$, $B = b_1b_2$, and $C = c_1c_2$, and we lock them as follows: $l_xa_1l_yu_xa_2u_y$; $l_xb_1u_xb_2$; $l_yc_1u_yc_2$.

If we look at the geometric interpretation of this locking program (figure 2), we see that the forbidden region generated consists of two partially overlapping perpendicular prisms. The essential property here is that the path labeled α, starting at point P, going first in the C direction and then in the B direction, can get around the forbidden region without having to go as far in the A direction as the path labeled β, which starts at the same place, but goes in the C direction before going in the B direction. (This is why $a_1c_1c_2b_1b_2a_2$ is allowed in the example but

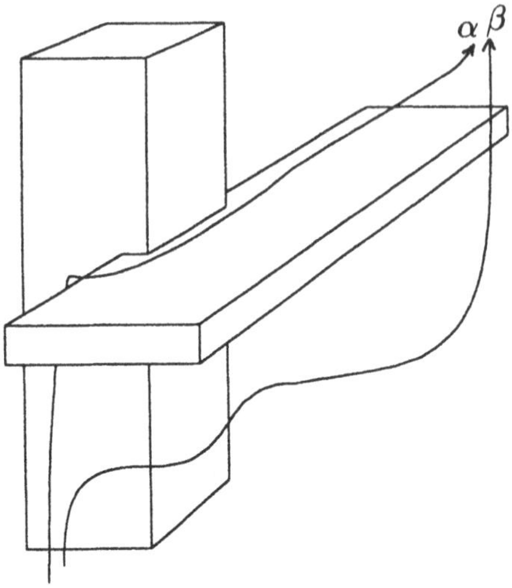

figure 2.

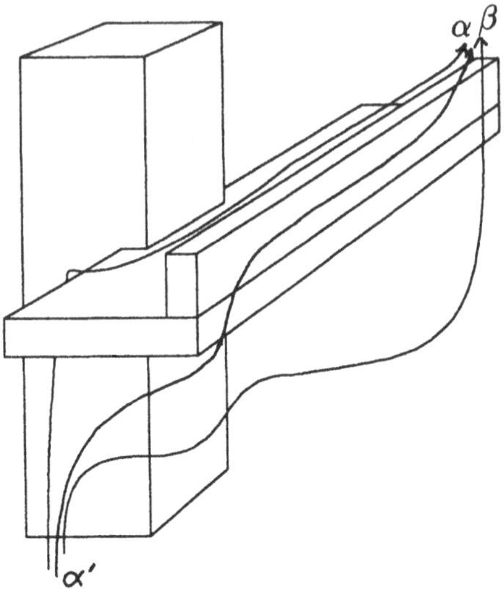

figure 3.

$a_1b_1b_2c_1c_2a_2$ is not.) In figure 3, we have added another prism in order to separate α and β. Note however, that this does not eliminate α', a path with the same BC projection as α, but which is not separated from β. To eliminate α', we add still a fourth prism, a vertical one [figures 4 & 5]. If α and β start slightly separated, and their movement in the BC plane is restricted to follow the pictured paths, then even though their projections cross, the paths themselves do not intersect. This is called a crossover, and it is the building block from which we can construct fixpoints far more general than those that are possible in the two dimensional case.

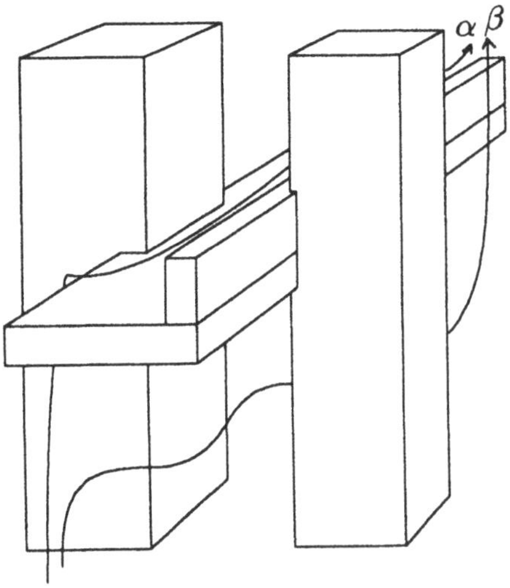

figure 4.

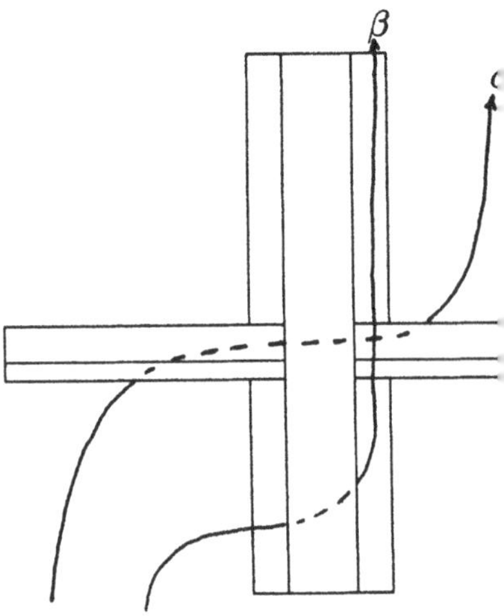

figure 5.

Using the crossover as a building block. Here I will outline informally how the crossover may be put into context so that it can be used to construct fixpoint sets. Assume we have a set of parallel channels, and we want two adjacent channels to cross over each other without intersecting. The way to do this with the crossover is shown in figure 6.

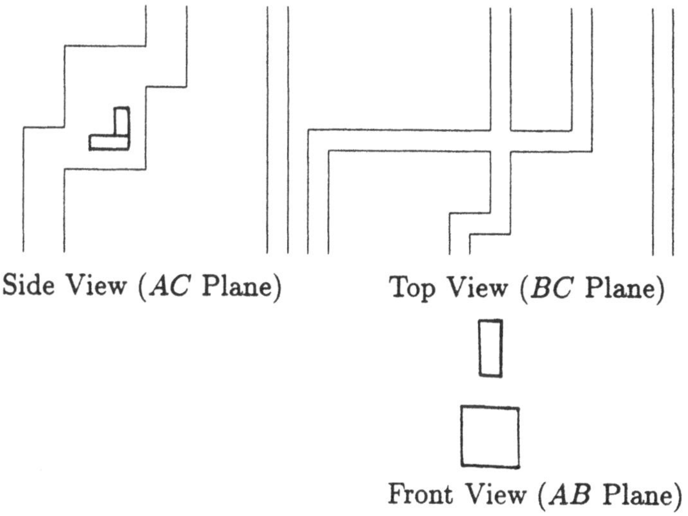

figure 6. Integrating the Crossover

In the top view, we see the channels are restricted by locks in the *BC* plane. As shown in the side view, the channels are also all restricted in the *A* direction by locks in the *AC* direction. In the region of the crossover, there is a widening in the *A* dimension, and all paths increase slightly in the *A* dimension. The island in this widening is formed by the union of the two horizontal prisms from figures 3 and 4, viewed end on. The increase in the *A* direction is necessary because both paths going through the crossover must advance in all three dimensions. We note that although the crossover requires the use of forbidden prisms in both the *B* and *C* direction, these prisms can be confined to a small space in the *A* dimension. If α and β are just two of many parallel channels, all the channels should make the small jump at this point, and then the prisms will not block them. Thus we can have multiple crossovers, and we can localize them to any needed extent, by making the jump in the *A* direction small. Thus, if we have n channels running in parallel, we can permute them arbitrarily, using $O(n^2)$ crossovers, and a method similar to a bubble sort.

From here, let us consider paths of the type $a_1a_2ha_3\dots a_n$, where h contains all the steps of B and C. Now, using crossovers, we would like to see how general we can make h. At the lower left corner, $\binom{2n}{n}$ channels are started. These channels will trace out all possible paths across the square. Whenever two such channels are forced to cross in the BC projection, we insert a crossover so that they don't actually intersect. These crossovers must be staggered, so that none overlap. Since the amount by which the crossovers are to be staggered can be made arbitrarily small this can be accomplished, although I omit the details here.

This construction allows all possible paths. This is an extremely complicated way to build up what could have been obtained with no locks at all, but now we can block any of these channels individually with a lock in the BC plane. The only paths which must remain unblocked are the serial ones, because we can never block a surface path without also blocking all inside paths. Thus we can realize any subset of $B * C$ as h, so long as that subset includes the serial paths.

The above construction is not efficient in terms of locks used, but only some of this excess is avoidable. There are $\binom{2n}{n}$ total paths in the layer and we may choose whether or not to include any of them independently, except for the two serial paths. Any scheme which names all the possible subsets uniquely must include at least some names of at least $\binom{2n}{n} - 2$ bits. Since a locking program is one way of naming a fixpoint, we see that some of the locking programs will have to be very long because $\binom{2n}{n}$ grows super–exponentially. This is an important difference from realizable fixpoints of two transactions where it is never necessary to use more than $O(n^3)$ locks, and we summarize it as:

Theorem 2. *If $A = a_1 \dots a_n$, $B = b_1 \dots b_n$, and $C = c_1 \dots c_n$ are three transactions, each with n atomic database steps, then there exists $H \subset A * B * C$, which is realizable as the fixpoint of a locking program, but for which even the smallest such locking program requires $\Omega(e^n)$ locks.*

Steps toward characterization. There is a simple characterization of realizable fixpoints for two transactions, but the question remains: Can we find such a characterization for three or more transactions? The above construction of an arbitrary layer is suggestive of a characterization. By modifying this argument, it should be possible to stack the layers, allow for interconnections between them and thus allow any subset of those paths which go through the interior of the cube. Although interesting, this is not a characterization. In order to get this generality of interior paths, the construction allows all exterior paths. This is because locks are monotonic; adding a lock can never make possible histories that were not possible before. Thus, if a path is possible through the interior of the cube, all of its projections onto the exterior of the cube must be possible as well. So the question is then, what fixpoints are possible when even the surface fixpoints are restricted? We divide the set of allowed paths into two types: surface and interior. Surface paths are those which could go entirely on the surface of the cube. Any history which is serial in a pair of its transactions has a surface path. An interior path is anything else, none of its pairwise projections is serial. Necessary conditions for a fixpoint to be realizable are:

1) The sets of surface paths are realizable in the sense of [Papa-82]
2) The fixpoint must be monotonic. This means that if we project all allowed paths onto a single face of the cube, the resulting set of paths must be a subset of the surface paths on that face.

It is not necessary to allow all paths that have allowed projections. Given three realizable two dimensional fixpoints, it is possible to construct a locking which allows the paths in these fixpoints as its three projections, but allows only surface paths and no interior paths. Consider the following example of this type of behavior. We have transactions $A = a_1 \ldots a_n$, $B = b_1 \ldots b_n$, and $C = c_1 \ldots c_n$, and we lock them as follows:

$$A' = l_x l_z l_w a_1 u_z u_w l_y u_x l_x u_y a_2 l_y u_x \ldots l_x u_y a_j l_y u_x \ldots a_n u_x$$

$$B' = l_z l_x l_w b_1 u_x u_w l_y u_z l_z u_y b_2 l_y u_z \ldots l_z u_y b_j l_y u_z \ldots b_n u_z$$

$$C' = l_w l_z l_x c_1 u_z u_x l_y u_w l_w u_y c_2 l_y u_w \ldots l_w u_y c_j l_y u_w \ldots c_n u_w$$

Note that we have only used four lock variables: x, z, w, and y, but that we have reused each many times. This locking program realizes a fixpoint which includes all surface paths, but no interior paths.

The above requirements are necessary, but not sufficient. Consider the following special case. We have two paths through the interior of the cube r and y. We shall look at the projections of r and y on each of the three faces of the cube. In all cases we shall require that the projections of the paths be separated, that is that they flow through separate channels on the three surfaces. We can ensure that this requirement is satisfied by requiring that none of the paths formed by

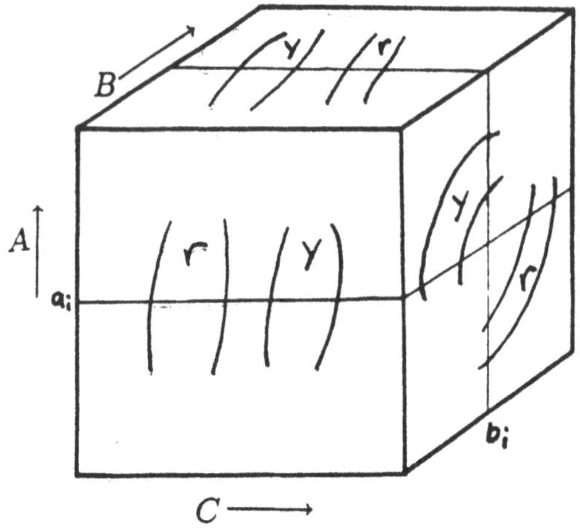

Figure 7. An Unrealizable Configuration

crossovers between the projections r and y are allowed in the fixpoint. In the AC plane, we require that at the points where the projections of r and y cross th transaction step a_i, the projection of r has made less progress in the C dimensio than the projection of y. In the BC plane, we require that as the projections o the paths cross the step b_j, that y have made less progress in the C dimension tha r. Finally, we require that in the AB plane, the projection of r passes through th step b_j before it passes through a_i, while y does the opposite; it passes throug a_i before it passes through b_j. There is nothing in this set of requirements whic contradicts either of the conditions above. Despite this, no set of histories whic contains r and y, and has the required restrictions on surface paths, is realizab as the fixpoint of a locking program.

To show this, we will need an additional concept. We define $\inf_y(a_i)$ t be the smallest C coordinate that a path through channel y could have as crosses transaction step a_i. Similarly define $\sup_y(a_i)$ to be the largest C coordinat possible for a path through channel y as it crosses transaction step a_i. Now, onl relative order of locks and channels matters, so we can not evaluate an actual re number for $\inf_y(a_i)$, but we can learn about the relative ordering of such quantitie For example, y crosses a_i before it crosses b_j. If $\inf_y(a_i) > \sup_y(b_j)$ then the pat would have to go backwards in the C direction. Therefore $\inf_y(a_i) \leq \sup_y(b_j$ Similarly the channel r crosses b_j before a_i, so by the same reasoning as for path we conclude that $\inf_r(b_j) \leq \sup_r(a_i)$. On the other hand, we have that as r cross

b_j, it is further in the C direction than y, and that the channel projections do not overlap, implying that $\inf_r(b_j) > \sup_y(b_j)$. Similarly, as y crosses a_i, it is further in the C direction than r, implying that $\inf_y(a_i) > \sup_r(a_i)$. We can summarize these inequalities as follows:

$$\sup_y(b_j) \geq \inf_y(a_i) > \sup_r(a_i) \geq \inf_r(b_j) > \sup_y(b_j)$$

This is a contradiction, since it implies $\sup_y(b_j) > \sup_y(b_j)$, and hence we see that no pair of paths satisfying all the above requirements can exist.

Conclusion. We have shown that the task of implementing a realizable fixpoint set may be accomplished with a polynomial number of locks if there are only two transactions, while if there are three or more transactions, we have shown that any implementation will sometimes require an exponential number of locks. We have also achieved a partial characterization of the class of realizable fixpoints for locking programs of three transactions and have described a case in which this characterization is incomplete.

Acknowledgements

Many thanks go to Christos Papadimitriou, who suggested the problem and provided consistently helpful input and guidance, and to Gio Wiederhold and Vaughan Pratt for useful discussions and to Georg Gottlob and Kate Bloch for substantive and stylistic comments.

References

[Papa-82] C. H. Papadimitriou "A Theorem in Database Concurrency Control", J. ACM, Vol. 29, No. 4, October 1982, pp. 998-1006.

[Papa-85] C. H. Papadimitriou "Correction to 'A Theorem in Database Concurrency Control'", J. ACM, Vol. 32, No. 3, July 1985, p. 750.

[YPK-79] Yannakakis, M., Papadimitriou, C.H., and Kung, H.T. "Locking policies: Safety and freedom from deadlock." Conf. Rec. 20th Ann. IEEE Symp. on Foundations of Computer Science, San Juan, Puerto Rico, 1979, pp. 283–287.

Theoretical Foundation of Algebraic Optimization Utilizing Unnormalized Relations

Marc H. Scholl

Technical University of Darmstadt
Department of Computer Science
Alexanderstrasse 24
D-6100 Darmstadt, West Germany

Abstract—Unnormalized (NF^2) relations, not conforming to the first normal form condition (1NF) of the relational model have been proposed recently for a variety of new applications. In this paper we extend NF^2 relational theory in a way that it becomes possible to use NF^2 relations as storage structures for conventional 1NF relational database interfaces. Physical clustering of precomputed joins can be achieved this way without introducing redundancy. However, applying transformation rules to internal relations straightforwardly, will still yield unnecessary join operations. With the equivalence rules introduced here we prove that efficient algebraic optimization can be performed using standard (1NF) techniques. Particularly, all redundant joins can be properly removed.

1. Introduction

A lot of recent research in relational databases has concentrated on unnormalized relations. Dropping the first normal form condition and allowing non-first-normal-form relations (NF^2 relations) has been recognized as a promising attempt to capture the requirements introduced by new ("nonstandard") applications of database systems. The areas of interest include textual [SP82], pictorial [BR84], geographical [MSW86], and office data [SLTC82] as well as knowledge representation techniques [SR86]. While experience with the feasibility of the model in these applications is not yet available, the theory of NF^2 relations is already in an advanced state. Formal definitions of the NF^2 relational model have been given by [AB84, FT83, Ja85, RKS85a, SS84] and most of these include operations on NF^2 relations in algebra and/or calculus style. Also design theory for NF^2 relations has already come up with results [AB84, FG85, FT83, Gu85, OY85, RKS85a].

The focus of this paper is different from the above work. As already mentioned in [AB84, FT83, SS83] we consider NF^2 relations to be a reasonable storage structure even for 1NF databases. The underlying idea is the following: the hierarchical structure of NF^2 relations can be utilized as an efficient possibility to store precomputed joins without introducing redundancy. "Denormalization" as a means of internally materializing the most frequent join operations was proposed in [SS80, SS81]. A physical database layout differing from the usual "1 relation—1 operating system file" choice was proven to dramatically reduce query processing costs. The most important but also expensive operation in relational systems is the join. Hence, significant performance enhancements can be achieved with this approach. Redundant storage of tuples from one relation with each matching tuple of the other relation can be avoided, if we use a hierachical storage scheme. Therefore, NF^2 relations were proposed in [SS83] as reasonable storage structures for 1NF databases. Besides the formal description of the internal database layout, as an additional benefit the transformations between conceptual (user) and internal (system) levels, C and I respectively, can be described within the model by the NF^2 relational algebra.

Three related problems with this approach are discussed and solved in this paper. The first one intuitively concerns the information contents of the conceptual and internal levels, which obviously must be identical. Formally, when the transformations are (algebraic) mappings, these must be *invertible*. Invertibility of relational algebra expressions has partly been studied in the past. "Lossless joins" [ASU79] are an example. We will use joins and nesting for the mapping $C \to I$ to obtain the hierarchical structures. In order to guarantee invertibility of this mapping, we use the outer join rather than natural join to avoid loosing "dangling" tuples. As a consequence of this, we have to deal with a special kind of *null value* introduced by the outer join. It should be clear, that these null values are a formal description of some "dummy" storage objects at an internal DBS layer. Therefore, this paper does not deal with null values in a general context. The interested reader is refered to [RKS85b] for a detailed discussion on several types of nulls in the NF^2 relational model. For our purposes only a few properties of the null value "ω" resulting from the outer join are discussed and the necessary formalism to manipulate these "dummy objects" is defined.

The second and more substantial problem is imposed by the need for algebraic optimization of queries. The algebraic expressions defining the mapping $I \to C$ can be substituted for the conceptual relations used in the expressions of the user queries. However, algebraic equivalences have to be applied in order to eliminate redundant joins, for instance. Consider two C-relations that are internally stored in one materialized join relation. The C-relations can be reobtained by projections. Thus substituting the projection expressions into user queries yields a join of two projections. Algebraic optimization techniques can be used to recognize the redundant join—according to [ASU79]—and eliminate it from the query. Without this optimization, the efficient internal structure could not be utilized.

Equivalence rules known from previous research [ASU79, Ul82, Ma83] for the 1NF case and also including NF^2 relations [AB84, FT83, JS82] are not sufficient to do the necessary transformations. Extended equivalences are presented in this paper. According to these, all materialized joins in user queries can be properly eliminated.

The third aspect captured by this paper, concerns the NF^2 queries resulting from the optimization step. Obviously, for our hierarchical internal DB layout there is a class of NF^2 queries that reflects this structure and therefore can be evaluated very efficiently. Our objective is to map a maximum of user queries to that kind of internal counterparts. In fact, we will see that select-project-join queries can be transformed to these "single pass processible" NF^2 queries, if all joins are internally materialized. It is exactly this class of NF^2 queries that will be available at the kernel interface of a prototype NF^2 relational database system developed at the University of Darmstadt [DOPSSW85, DPS86, SW86, Sche86].

As an introductory example consider two conceptual (4NF) relations

$$Dept(\underline{dno}, dname, budget)$$
$$Emp(\underline{eno}, ename, sal, dno)$$

If we internally store the NF^2 relation

$$Idept(\underline{dno}, dname, budget, Iemp(\underline{eno}, ename, sal))$$

we do not need to compute $Dept \bowtie Emp$ at runtime of user queries. For instance consider the user query $\pi_{dname,sal}\sigma_{ename=\text{'Smith'}}(Dept \bowtie Emp)$ which can be processed very efficiently by the following NF^2 algebraic expression (see section 2 for details).

$$\mu_{Iemp}(\pi[dname, \pi[sal](\sigma_{ename=\text{'Smith'}}(Iemp))](Idept))$$

The internal query contains only a simple NF^2 filter expression and unnesting but no join operation, thus it can be evaluated efficiently.

Section 2 shortly reviews the NF^2 relational model from [SS84] and introduces the notations used throughout the paper. The class of ***single pass processible*** queries is informally characterized and a subset of the algebra is claimed to be single pass processible. In section 3 we define the type of conceptual-to-internal mappings foreseen in this paper and deal with the problem of inverting the mapping. We present the necessary rules to deal with the special type of null value resulting from the outer joins.

Extended algebraic equivalence rules involving the null values as well as the nested algebra operators from [SS84] are presented in section 4. With these rules we prove that algebraic optimization can be done in our environment using essentially 1NF optimization and some simple transformation rules. Optimal "quasi 1NF" expressions are computed and then transformed to NF^2 expressions by an optimizer sketched in section 5. The paper concludes with an outline of further research in section 6.

2. The NF^2 Relational Model

Relations with relation valued attributes do not conform to the first-normal-form, because they allow decomposable attribute values, namely relations. Thus, formal definitions like [FT83, RKS85a, SS84] apply 1NF notations repeatedly to capture the nested relational structures. We do not give formal definitions in this paper, but shortly review the notations drawn from [SS84]. As in the 1NF case (cf. [Ma83]) we have a relation R as a pair $\langle d, v\rangle$ consisting of a description d and a value v. The description d is a pair $\langle n, s\rangle$, where n is the name of the relation drawn from some given set N of names. The schema s describes the components of R. Hence s is a set of descriptions d_i of the attributes of R. Atomic attributes have descriptions $\langle a_i, \emptyset\rangle$, i.e. the empty set serves as the schema of atomic attributes. Relation valued attributes have descriptions $\langle a_i, s_i\rangle$, where $s_i \neq \emptyset$ is the schema of the corresponding (sub-) relation. For a relation $R = \langle d, v\rangle$ with $d = \langle n, s\rangle$ we apply the following notation:

$\text{sch}(R) = \text{sch}(d) = s$	the schema
$\text{val}(R) = v$	the value and
$\text{attr}(R) = \{a_i \mid \langle a_i, s_i\rangle \in d\}$	the attributes (name components of sch(R)) of R.

The value of a relation val(R) is a set of tuples, each tuple can either be regarded as a mapping from an attribute set to a corresponding domain set or as an element of a Cartesian product of domains [SS84, Ja86]. We adopt the first interpretation here and use $t(a_i)$ to denote the a_i-value of a tuple t in val(R) where $a_i \in \text{attr}(R)$. Extending this notion canonically $t(A)$ is the A-value of t in val(R) for $A \subseteq \text{attr}(R)$. As usual we give the schema of an NF^2 relation in the following form:

$$R(a_1, \ldots, a_n, b_1(\ldots), \ldots, b_m(\ldots))$$

where the a_i are the names of atomic attributes of R and b_i the names of relation valued attributes. Between the parentheses after b_i we denote the schema of the b_i in exactly the same way.

The NF^2 relational algebra we use in the following has been presented in [SS83] and formally defined in [SS84]. Operators $\times, \cup, \cap, -, \bowtie$ are defined exactly as in the 1NF case, whereas π and σ (projection and selection) have been extended and two new operators ν and μ (nest and unnest) were introduced. The latter two are also used in [AB84, JS82, FT83, RKS85a, SS83, SS84]. Extended defintions for μ and ν will be given in section 3 of this paper, the extensions of π and σ shall be exemplified in the following.

For the scope of this paper, concerning extended selection we only need set comparisons allowed in selection formulae together with set-valued constants (especially $\emptyset$). Within projection lists, i.e. the set of attributes that are projected, we allow the application of algebraic expressions (especially again π and σ) to relation valued attributes. As an example consider a relation

$$Dept(dno, dname, Emp(eno, ename, sal, Course(cno, year)))$$

(with the obvious interpretation) then

$$Q_1 = \sigma[dname = \text{'research'} \wedge Emp \neq \emptyset](Dept)$$

yields 'established' research departments, i.e. those who already have employees,

$$Q_2 = \pi[dname, \pi[ename, sal](Emp)](Dept)$$

gives a list of department names each with a list of employee names and salaries, i.e. the schema of Q_2 is $Q_2(dname, Emp(ename, sal))$ and

$$Q_3 = \pi[dname, \sigma[sal > 10.000](Emp)](Dept)$$

yields a relation with schema $Q_2(dname, Emp(eno, ename, sal, Course(\ldots)))$—a list of "rich" employees grouped by *dname*. Details of the nested algebra are not important in this paper, the interested reader is referred to [SS84]. Nevertheless, we will shortly discuss our notion of ***single pass processible*** queries. By the term single pass processible we indicate, that this kind of queries can be evaluated efficiently by an NF^2 relational DBMS [DPS86, Sche85]. The results of these queries can be computed within one (hierarchical) scan over the tuples in val(R). The notion was influenced by so-called single-table queries in flat relational systems, i.e. queries that do not include joins. However, in our case of nested relations "single table" queries may well contain operations with join complexity (set comparisons, nested joins). Therefore we need a more sophisticated notion of "simplicity" of queries. A detailed discussion of what is single pass processible and what is not, is deferred to a forthcomming report. However, the following theorem describes a class of queries that surely belongs to this class.

THEOREM 2.1. *An NF^2 relational expression is* **single pass processible,** *if it is built according to the following recursive rule:*

$$\text{spe}(R) = \pi[L]\sigma[F]\begin{cases} R \\ \pi[L^*](R) \end{cases}$$

L *is a "1NF" projection list, i.e. without nested algebraic expressions*

F *is a simple selection formula, consisting of conjunctions of comparisons between attributes and constants ($\emptyset$ is the only constant permitted for relation valued attributes) and*

L^* *is a projection list containing single pass expressions applied to relation valued attributes, i.e.* spe(A) ∎

Like most results of this paper, due to limitations on space the above is stated without proof.

3. Transformation Between Conceptual and Internal Layer

In this section we will define conceptual schemata, the various choices of conceptual-to-internal mappings and study invertibility of these mappings. Extensions of nest and unnest operators—compared to [AB84, FT83, RKS85a, SS84]—are introduced to capture the null values resulting from outer joins. The latter are needed to guarantee invertibility of the denormalization, because natural joins would loose "dangling" tuples in general.

3.1 Conceptual Relations

We consider a given set "conceptual DB schema" $C = \{CR_1, \ldots, CR_n\}$ of (conceptual) relations CR_i. The schema C is in 4NF [Fa77], which means every valid MVD (and thus FD) is expressed as a key condition in one of the CR_i. Furthermore, we assume C to be free of null values. We denote with $\text{key}(CR_i) \subseteq \text{attr}(CR_i)$ the set of primary key attributes of CR_i. Without loss of generality we assume all attribute names in C distinct except foreign keys. $A \subseteq \text{attr}(CR_i)$ is a foreign key, iff $A = \text{key}(CR_j)$ for some $j \neq i$ and $CR_i, CR_j \in C$. We will sometimes use C_i as a short form for $\text{attr}(CR_i)$. For the following discussion of mappings it is useful to illustrate the conceptual schema by a directed (acyclic) graph.

DEFINITION 3.1. *Let C be a set of relations with known keys and foreign keys. The corresponding* **schema graph** *is* $\text{sg}(C) = (N, E)$, *where the set of nodes N contains one node per conceptual relation.* $N = \{\overline{CR_i} \mid CR_i \in C\}$ *and the set of edges E is obtained from the key-foreign key relationships in C:* $E = \{\overline{CR_i} \to \overline{CR_j} \mid \text{key}(CR_i) \subseteq \text{attr}(CR_j) \wedge i \neq j\}$

A similar schema graph with attribute nodes added is used in [FT83]. $\text{sg}(C)$ corresponds to the Bachman-diagram of the equivalent CODASYL database. In analogy to this, if $\overline{CR_i} \to \overline{CR_j}$ is in $\text{sg}(C)$ we will call CR_i the "owner relation" of the "member" CR_j in the following.

3.2 Conceptual to Internal Mappings

As claimed in the introduction and illustrated by an example our overall goal in choosing internal representations is improving performance. Two aspects of physical database design will be considered in this section: clustering and denormalization. Clustering means mapping data that is accessed together very frequently to the same block or at least adjacent blocks of secondary storage media thus reducing the costs of physical I/O. Denormalization was proposed in [SS80, SS81]. Whenever two relations are combined by (natural) joins in a considerable portion of user queries, it may be advantageous to internally precompute the join and store the result. Obviously, the decision for or against this "materialization" of the join depends on update frequencies for the involved relations. Whereas [SS80, SS81] decide to store the original relations in addition to the join sometimes, we can drop them if the join is materialized. The reason is twofold. First we use the outer join rather than a natural join to avoid loosing tuples and secondly we nest the "member" relation into the "owner" yielding a hierarchical structure. Therefore we do not introduce redundant storage of owner attributes with every matching member as in [SS80, SS81]. Moreover, nesting the members into the owner tuples yields a clustered storage structure. By the combination of join and nest we can establish both physical design objectives mentioned above. Considering the conceptual schema graph $\text{sg}(C)$ we can describe the possible internal NF^2 representations (that do not introduce redundancy) by the following definition.

DEFINITION 3.2. *Given a conceptual schema C with its graph* sg(C)*, the set* ir(C) *of all possible* **internal representations** *obtained by denormalization and nesting is described by the set* for(sg(C)) *of all forests that can be obtained by deleting some of the edges in* sg(C).

The set of internal NF^2 relations corresponding to $I \in \text{ir}(C)$ is intuitively clear. Every tree in for(I) is a relation, where the root denotes the top level relation and descendents denote subrelations. In general ir(C) will contain more than one alternative. It is the task of physical database design (optimization) to select one of them based upon an estimated transaction mix. An example is given in figure 3.1.

$$C = \{CR_1(\underline{A}, B, C),\ CR_2(\underline{D}, E, F),\ CR_3(\underline{A, D}, G)\}$$

sg(C) =

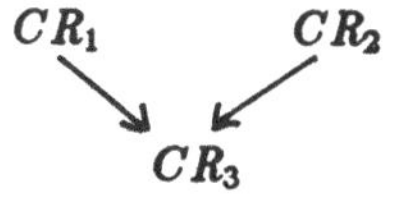

$$\text{ir}(C) = \{I_1, I_2, I_3\}$$

$\text{for}(I_1) = CR_1 \downarrow CR_3 \quad CR_2$ $\qquad$ $\text{for}(I_2) = CR_1 \quad CR_2 \downarrow CR_3$ $\qquad$ $\text{for}(I_3) = CR_1 \quad CR_2 \quad CR_3$

corresponding internal relations:

$I_1 = \{IR_1, IR_2\}$ $\qquad$ $I_2 = \{IR_1, IR_2\}$ $\qquad$ $I_3 = \{IR_1, IR_2, IR_3\}$

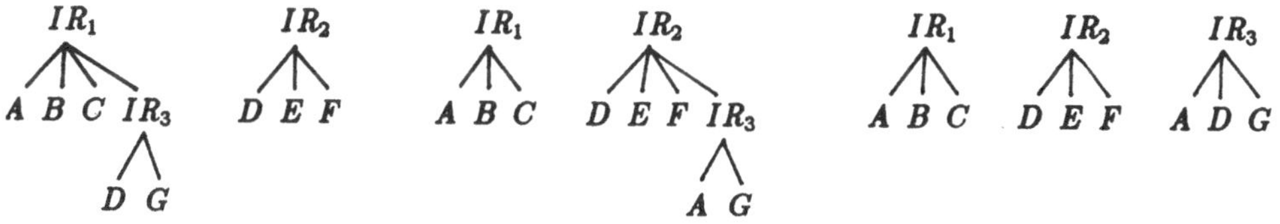

Figure 3.1: Choices for internal representations

DEFINITION 3.3. *The* **tree representation** *[SS84] of the internal* NF^2 *relations corresponding to* for(I) *is obtained by appending nodes* $\overline{a_i}$ *for* $a_i \in attr(CR_i)$ *to the nodes* $\overline{CR_i}$*, iff* $a_i \notin key(CR_j)$ *and* $\overline{CR_j} \rightarrow \overline{CR_i}$ *in* for(I)*. Finally* $\overline{CR_i}$ *is renamed to* $\overline{IR_i}$*. The internal schema I is the set of relations denoted by root nodes in* for(I).

Every edge in for(I) corresponds to an outer join between the owner and member relation followed by a nest operation. All attributes of the member except the foreign key are nested into a subrelation.

EXAMPLE 3.1.

$$\text{for}(I) = \begin{array}{c} CR_1 \\ \downarrow \\ CR_2 \end{array} \Longrightarrow \begin{array}{l} I = \{IR_1\} \\ \\ IR_1 = \nu_{IR_2=(C_2 \setminus C_1)}(CR_1 ⟗ CR_2) \end{array}$$

As we used the outer join operator (⟗) to produce null values for dangling tuples, we have to decide on how nest should behave on tuples containing nulls. One decision is obvious: if all attributes to be nested have a null value, then the resulting tuple should have an empty subrelation. However, a problem arises, if all attributes that are *not* nested have a null value. Especially, should several of such occurrences be regarded equal or not. In a more general context, this would lead to a discussion on equality of null values or the concept of "informativeness" of tuples containing nulls—see [RKS85b], for instance. Again we remind the reader, that this paper is not meant as an overall treatment of null values. As we introduced the null values as a formal tool of modelling "dummy objects", we can decide on equality from a pragmatic point of view. For our purpose of defining an internal schema it is appropriate to consider nulls equal in non-nesting attributes, i.e. all member tuples without owners are gathered in a subrelation of a single tuple containing only nulls in the owner attributes. Notice that this situation was excluded in our definition of conceptual schemata, because we did not allow nulls in C-relations. Nevertheless, we give a definition of ν that captures this case too. For instance, consider figure 3.2. Notice that all definitions that follow will not contain the *schema* part of the operations defined. Most of the definitions from [SS84] can be applied. In the other cases, the schema transforming effect of the operations should be obvious. A formal treatment would require additional notational conventions that were left out. The same applies for the proofs of equivalent algebraic expressions.

R			
A	B	C	D
a_1	b_1	ω	ω
a_2	b_2	c_1	d_1
a_2	b_2	c_2	d_2
ω	ω	c_3	d_3
ω	ω	c_4	d_3

$\Longrightarrow$

$\nu_{CD=(C,D)}(R)$			
A	B	CD	
		C	D
a_1	b_1	$\emptyset$	
a_2	b_2	c_1	d_1
		c_2	d_2
ω	ω	c_3	d_3
		c_4	d_3

Figure 3.2: Nesting tuples containing nulls

Here "ω" denotes a null meaning "not existent". (This "closed world assumption" is appropriate, because we want to store existent tuples from the C-relations !)

DEFINTION 3.4. *Let* $\text{attr}(R) = A, B \subseteq A$, *then*

$$\text{val}(\nu_{x=(B)}(R)) = \{t \mid t(A \setminus B) \in \text{val}(\pi_{A \setminus B} R) \wedge t(x) = \{t'(B) \mid t' \in \text{val}(R) \wedge t'(A \setminus B) = t(A \setminus B) \wedge \forall b \in B : t'(b) \neq \omega\}\}$$

Notice how the additional condition $t'(b) \neq \omega$ for all $b \in B$ produces the desired empty subrelations.

3.3 Inversion of the Mapping $C \rightarrow I$

Conversely, unnest should map empty subrelations to nulls rather than eliminating these tuples, as it does in the standard definitions [AB84, FT83, RKS85a, SS84], hence we introduce an unnest operator $\overline{\mu}$ that preserves tuples containing empty subrelations by mapping $\emptyset$ to ω.

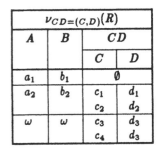

DEFINITION 3.5. *Let* attr$(R) = A$*,* $x \in A$ *and* attr$(x) = B$*, then*

$$\text{val}(\overline{\mu}_{x=(B)}(R)) = \{t \mid \exists t' \in \text{val}(R) : t(A \setminus B) = t'(A \setminus B) \wedge \\ \quad ((t(B) \in t'(x) \wedge t'(x) \neq \emptyset) \vee (\forall b \in B : t(b) = \omega \wedge t'(x) = \emptyset)) \}$$

The conceptual relations did not contain null values, hence we need an operation, to eliminate tuples containing nulls. Therefore, we introduce a reduction operator ρ_X, deleting all tuples from a relation, containing a null value in at least one of the attributes in X:

DEFINITION 3.6. *Let* R *be a relation with* $X \subseteq \text{attr}(R)$*, then*

$$\text{val}(\rho_X(R)) = \{t \mid t \in \text{val}(R) \wedge \forall a \in X : t(a) \neq w\}$$

$$\rho(R) = \rho_{\text{attr}(R)}(R)$$

Obviously, whether we unnest first and eliminate ω-tuples afterwards or delete tuples containing empty sets and then unnest yields the same result. Further, the standard unnest operator μ comprises ρ and $\overline{\mu}$.

LEMMA 3.1.

$$\rho_X \overline{\mu}_{C=(X)}(R) = \overline{\mu}_{C=(X)} \sigma_{C \neq \emptyset}(R) = \mu_{C=(X)}(R) \qquad \blacksquare$$

It is known from [FT83, JS82] that any nest operation can be undone by applying the corresponding unnest, i.e. $\mu_A \nu_A(R) = R$. Our simple extension of the nest operation, however, invalidates this property in general. Consider two tuples $t_1 = \langle a, \omega \rangle$ and $t_2 = \langle a, b \rangle$; nesting the second attribute produces $t' = \langle a, \{b\} \rangle$. A subsequent unnest will not reproduce tuple t_1. The reason is that there was another tuple (t_2) containing the same information in the attributes not nested, and thus nest did not map t_1 to $\langle a, \emptyset \rangle$ (t_2 is *more informative* than t_1). We could think about a more sophisticated definition of nest, but fortunately for our purpose the current definition is sufficient, because the above situation does not occur as we see from the following lemmas.

LEMMA 3.2. *Iff* $\forall t \in \text{val}(R) : (t(A) = \omega \Rightarrow \nexists t' \in \text{val}(R) : t'(\text{attr}(R) \setminus A) = t(\text{attr}(R) \setminus A))$ *then*

$$\overline{\mu}_A \nu_A(R) = R \qquad \blacksquare$$

LEMMA 3.3. *Let* $t \in \text{val}(R \boxtimes S)$ *and* $a, a' \in \text{attr}(R) \setminus \text{attr}(S)$*, then*

$$t(a) = \omega \Longleftrightarrow t(a') = \omega \qquad \blacksquare$$

COROLLARY 3.1.

$$R \boxtimes S = \overline{\mu}_X \nu_{X=(\text{attr}(R) \setminus \text{attr}(S))} R \boxtimes S \qquad \blacksquare$$

This means, nesting member tuples as a subrelation into the corresponding owner tuples is always invertible. The following lemma captures the well known fact that outer join is always invertible:

LEMMA 3.4.

$$R = \pi_{\text{attr}(R)}\, \rho_{\text{attr}(R)}\, (R \boxtimes S)$$ ■

With lemma 3.3 we further conclude that instead of checking all attributes of R against null values it is sufficient to check either one except the join attributes:

COROLLARY 3.2.

$$\forall a \in \text{attr}(R) \setminus \text{attr}(S): \; R = \pi_{\text{attr}(R)} \rho_a (R \boxtimes S)$$ ■

For our example 3.1 we can therefore define the inversion of the mapping $C \rightarrow I$ by:

EXAMPLE 3.1 (CONT'D).

$$IR_1 = \nu_{IR_2=(C_2 \setminus C_1)}(CR_1 \boxtimes CR_2) \implies \begin{array}{l} CR_1 = \pi_{C_1}\rho_{C_1}(IR_1) \\ CR_2 = \pi_{C_2}\rho_{C_2}\overline{\mu}_{IR_2}(IR_2) = \pi_{C_2}\mu_{IR_2}(IR_1) \end{array}$$

Notice that the simplification $CR_1 = \pi_{C_1}(IR_1)$ is valid, if the foreign key condition is maintained on level C, because in this case no "member" tuples would be accepted with a foreign key pointing to a nonexistent "owner". As we did not allow null values in C-relations, there is also no member without an owner. Further we see from example 3.1 that μ-operations are sufficient in the mapping $I \rightarrow C$, if we only unnest those subrelations of IR_i needed to reconstruct a certain CR_j.

Our basic idea for the optimization step described in sections 4 and 5 is the following: use a global unnest-operation, i.e. one that procudes the equivalent 1NF relation (e.g. UNNEST* in [FT83] = μ^* in [RKS85a]) in all of the equations for the mapping $I \rightarrow C$. This yields the same 1NF relation $\mu^*(IR_i)$ in all equations for conceptual relations that are contained in a common IR_j. The benefit is, that to eliminate redundant joins from queries involving such conceptual relations, we could then utilize 1NF techniques. The following consideration explains, why we introduced $\overline{\mu}$ and will use $\overline{\mu}^*$ in the sequel. Consider an owner relation CR_1 with two members CR_2, CR_3. A tuple in IR_1 (with both joins materialized, i.e. subrelations IR_2, IR_3) that has members in IR_2 but not in IR_3 would disappear, if we used μ^*. Hence, we use $\overline{\mu}^*$ preserving all tuples and decide on nulls afterwards using the ρ-operation.

In order to prepare for the next theorem we give a lemma, that allows to bring the equations defining $C \rightarrow I$ into a canonical form.

LEMMA 3.5. *Let* $X \subseteq \text{attr}(R) \setminus \text{attr}(S)$, *then*

$$\nu_{a=(X)}(R \boxtimes S) = \nu_{a=(X)} R \boxtimes S$$ ■

Any internal relation is obtained by a sequence of "outer join followed by nest"-operations, i.e.

$$IR_j = \nu_{IR_{j_1}=(CR_{j_1} \setminus CR_{j_2})}(CR_{j_2} \boxtimes (\nu_{\dots}(\cdots \boxtimes \cdots)))$$

According to lemma 3.5 this can be rewritten as $IR_j = \nu_{IR_{j_1}=(CR_{j_1} \setminus CR_{j_2})}(\nu_{\dots}(\nu \cdots (CR_{j_1} \boxtimes (\cdots \boxtimes \cdots (\cdots)))))$, i.e. a sequence of outer joins followed by a sequence of nest operations. Now it is easy to prove theorem 3.1, capturing the invertibility proposition of our conceptual to internal mapping. The inversion can be done by equations in a canonical form using global unnest:

THEOREM 3.1. *Given $C = \{CR_1, \ldots, CR_n\}$ a set of conceptual relations and I a corresponding internal representation $I \in \mathrm{ir}(C)$. For $1 \leq i \leq n$ let $\overline{IR_{j_i}}$ be the root of the tree in $\mathrm{for}(I)$ containing node $\overline{IR_i}$, then:*

$$CR_i = \pi_{C_i} \rho_{C_i} \overline{\mu}^* (IR_{j_i})$$

■

4. Algebraic Equivalences

For the classical relational model a large scale of algebraic equivalences have been studied, a summary of the results is contained e.g. in [Ul82]. [ABU79, ASU79] have given lossless join properties that can be used to eliminate redundant joins from queries expressed in 1NF algebra or the like. Concerning the NF^2 relational model [JS82] presented some first equivalence rules capturing inversion of nest by unnest and vice versa, commutativity of nest and unnest and a few other properties. The work of [FT83] gives a comprehensive overview of positive and negative results on commuting nest/unnest with the other algebraic operators. In case of an extended algebra for NF^2 relations like [AB84, SS84] first results have also been presented. Obviously, with an extended algebra we can prove some more properties than with a standard algebra enriched by nest and unnest only. Here we summarize the main equivalence rules that can be used to efficiently optimize and process select-project-join (SPJ-) queries on level C by NF^2 queries on level I.

As ρ-operations are contained in the expressions we need additional transformation rules for commuting ρ and the other algebraic operators. These are given in subsequent lemmas. We also need criteria for deciding whether the join of two projections equals the original relation (lossless join property) when reduction operations are involved. This can be regarded as an extension of the results from [ABU79]. Theorem 4.1 states the corresponding proposition. Using these results, we can further prove that neglecting the reductions ρ during the join elimination phase and inserting them in the right places afterwards yields correct results.

In the following we will use $X, Y, \ldots$ to denote sets of attributes and adopt the usual short notation XY for the union $X \cup Y$. First we state properties on commuting ρ with other algebra operations, notice that ρ is some special kind of selection.

LEMMA 4.1.

(1) $\rho_X \rho_Y R = \rho_{XY} R$

(2) $\rho_X \sigma_F R = \sigma_F \rho_X R$

(3) $\rho_X \pi_Y R = \pi_Y \rho_X R \iff X \subseteq Y$

(4) $\rho_{XY}(R \times S) = \rho_X R \times \rho_Y S \iff X \subseteq \mathrm{attr}(R) \wedge Y \subseteq \mathrm{attr}(S)$

(5) $\rho_{XY}(R \bowtie S) = \rho_X R \bowtie \rho_Y S \iff X \subseteq \mathrm{attr}(R) \wedge Y \subseteq \mathrm{attr}(S)$

(6) $\nu_{a=(X)} \rho_X R = \sigma_{a \neq \emptyset} \nu_{a=(X)} R$

(7) $\rho_X \overline{\mu}_{a=(X)} R = \overline{\mu}_{a=(X)} \sigma_{a \neq \emptyset} R = \mu_{a=(X)} R$ ■

LEMMA 4.2.

$$\pi_{XY}(R \bowtie S) = \pi_X R \bowtie \pi_Y S \iff X \cap Y = \mathrm{attr}(R) \cap \mathrm{attr}(S)$$

Proof: Substitute π, σ and $\times$ for $\bowtie$ and apply the equivalences known from [Ul82]. ■

Combining the two lemmas we derive the following theorem giving a lossless join criterion for project-join mappings containing ρ's:

THEOREM 4.1. *Let $X, X', Y, Y' \subseteq \mathrm{attr}(R)$, then*

$$\pi_X \rho_Y R \bowtie \pi_{X'} \rho_{Y'} R = \pi_{XX'} \rho_{YY'} R$$

$$\Longleftrightarrow$$

$$X \cap X' = XY \cap X'Y' \wedge (X \cap X' \twoheadrightarrow XY \vee X \cap X' \twoheadrightarrow X'Y')$$

Proof:

$$\begin{aligned}
\pi_X \rho_Y R \bowtie \pi_{X'} \rho_{Y'} R &= \pi_X(\pi_{XY} \rho_Y R) \bowtie \pi_{X'}(\pi_{X'Y'} \rho_{Y'} R) \\
&= \pi_{XX'}(\pi_{XY} \rho_Y R \bowtie \pi_{X'Y'} \rho_{Y'} R) \\
&\qquad \Longleftrightarrow X \cap X' = XY \cap X'Y' \text{ (Lemma 4.2)} \\
&= \pi_{XX'}(\rho_Y \pi_{XY} R \bowtie \rho_{Y'} \pi_{X'Y'} R) \\
&= \pi_{XX'} \rho_{YY'}(\pi_{XY} R \bowtie \pi_{X'Y'} R) \\
&= \pi_{XX'} \rho_{YY'} \pi_{XYX'Y'} R \\
&\qquad \Longleftrightarrow XY \cap X'Y' \twoheadrightarrow XY \text{ or } X'Y' \text{ ([ABU79])} \\
&= \pi_{XX'} \rho_{YY'} R
\end{aligned}$$

We applied lemma 4.1 in the 3rd, 4th and 6th equation. The preconditions for the 2nd and 5th equations conclude the proof. ■

Provided with the above equivalences we can transform user queries from the conceptual to the internal level by substituting the equations for CR_i (from $I \rightarrow C$) into the C-query. Optimization and join elimination can be performed by applying these results. In this "verbatim" approach, however, we have to deal with reduction operations (ρ). Thus we have to develop a new formula manipulation system, or whatever method else. Our claim in the beginning was, that *traditional 1NF* techniques would suffice. In order to prove this statement we give a variation of the lossless join condition in the following. Due to this new criterion we can rely on join elimination that does not consider ρ's. The only prerequisite is that we introduce the appropriate reductions into the optimized query expressions afterwards.

THEOREM 4.2. *For some conceptual relations CR_1, CR_2 internally stored in IR, with attribute sets C_1, C_2 respectively the following equivalence holds:*

(i) $$\pi_X(\pi_{C_1} \rho_{C_1} \overline{\mu}^* IR) \bowtie \pi_{X'}(\pi_{C_2} \rho_{C_2} \overline{\mu}^* IR) = \pi_{XX'} \pi_{C_1C_2} \rho_{C_1C_2} \overline{\mu}^* IR$$

$$\Longleftrightarrow$$

(ii) $$\pi_X \overline{\mu}^* IR \bowtie \pi_{X'} \overline{\mu}^* IR = \pi_{XX'} \overline{\mu}^* IR$$

Proof: $(i) \Rightarrow (ii)$: Easy (and not used in the following)

$(i) \Leftarrow (ii)$:

$$(ii) \Rightarrow X \cap X' \twoheadrightarrow X \text{ or } X \cap X' \twoheadrightarrow X' \text{ in } \overline{\mu}^* IR$$

The outer join does not introduce any MVDs, except the following:

$$R = R_1 \boxtimes R_2 \Longrightarrow R_1 \cap R_2 \twoheadrightarrow R_1 \text{ and } R_1 \cap R_2 \twoheadrightarrow R_2 \text{ in } R$$

Hence, $X \cap X' \rightarrow\!\!\rightarrow X$ or $X \cap X' \rightarrow\!\!\rightarrow X'$ must be valid MVDs in C. As C was claimed to be in 4NF there are no nontrivial MVDs except key conditions. Thus there must exist CR_1, CR_2 such that $X \subseteq C_1$, $X' \subseteq C_2$, with $X \cap X' = C_1 \cap C_2$ and $X \cap X' \rightarrow\!\!\rightarrow C_1$ or $X \cap X' \rightarrow\!\!\rightarrow C_2$. From this and theorem 4.1 we conclude $(ii) \Rightarrow (i)$ which completes the proof. ∎

5. An NF² Algebraic Query Optimizer

In this section we will emphasize the practical issues of our theory. The conclusion will be that in fact 1NF optimization is the essential part needed in our proposed environment. However, before we can outline a prototype implementation we have to state a few more algebraic equivalences involving the nested NF² algebra from [SS84].

From theorem 4.2 we conclude that substituting the expression from $I \rightarrow C$ and applying 1NF join elimination plus rules to move selections and projections down the expression tree (which reduces the size of intermediate results and is a standard algebraic optimization technique—see [Ul82]) yields an optimized "quasi-1NF" relational expression of the form

$$E = \pi\sigma(\bowtie(\pi\sigma(\rho\overline{\mu}^* IR_j)))$$

that does not contain redundant joins anymore. By the term "quasi-1NF" we indicate the fact, that the essential part of the expression uses only 1NF algebra. However, due to the presence of $\overline{\mu}^*$ we actually have an NF² expression.

The strategy now is to push the unnest operations up in the query's parse tree in order to utilize the power of the NF² algebra. In fact we will not apply $\overline{\mu}^*$, but rather the necessary $\overline{\mu}$'s only. As a result we will observe a single type of NF² expressions resulting from this process, namely *single pass processible queries* (or joins of those to be exact). For the scope of this paper we will only give the rules to commute $\overline{\mu}$ and the σ and π operations that follow in the above expression E. Some types of joins with subrelations can be performed within the NF² algebra, results on this topic will be presented in a forthcomming report. The transformation rules for ρ and π/σ are given in the following theorems, which are stated without proofs, because the formalism needed was left out in this paper.

THEOREM 5.1. *If $F = F_1 \wedge F_2$ where F_1 refers to attributes in* $\text{attr}(R) \setminus \{A\}$ *and F_2 refers to* $\text{attr}(A)$, *then*

$$\sigma[F]\,\overline{\mu}_A(R) = \overline{\mu}_A\,\sigma[F_1]\left(\pi[\text{attr}(R) \setminus A,\, \sigma[F_2](A)]\,(R)\right)$$ ∎

THEOREM 5.2. *If $L = L'L''$ where $L' \subseteq \text{attr}(R) \setminus A$, $L'' \subseteq \text{attr}(A)$, then*

$$\pi[L]\,\overline{\mu}_A(R) = \overline{\mu}_A\,\pi[L',\, \pi[L''](A)]\,(R)$$ ∎

We give example applications of these transformation rules in the following.

EXAMPLE 5.1. *Let $R = R(A_1(A_{11}(A_{111}, A_{112})), A_2)$ then*

$$\sigma_{A_{111}=5 \wedge A_2=3}\,\overline{\mu}_{A_{11}}\left(\overline{\mu}_{A_1}(R)\right)$$

$$\downarrow$$

$$\overline{\mu}_{A_{11}}\sigma_{A_2=3}\left(\pi[\ldots,\sigma_{A_{111}=5}(A_{11})]\,(\overline{\mu}_{A_1}(R))\right)$$

$$\downarrow$$

$$\overline{\mu}_{A_{11}}\sigma_{A_2=3}\left(\overline{\mu}_{A_1}\left(\pi\left[A_2,\pi[\sigma_{A_{111}=5}(A_{11})](A_1)\right](R)\right)\right)$$

$$\downarrow$$

$$\overline{\mu}_{A_{11}}\overline{\mu}_{A_1}\sigma_{A_2=3}\pi\left[A_2,\pi[\sigma_{A_{111}=5}(A_{11})](A_1)\right](R)$$

EXAMPLE 5.2. *Here we illustrate the treatment of the reductions ρ. Let* $\mathrm{sg}(C) = \{\overline{CR_1} \rightarrow \overline{CR_2}\}$ *and* $I = \{\,IR_1((\mathrm{attr}(CR_1)), IR_2(\mathrm{attr}(CR_2) \setminus \mathrm{attr}(CR_1)))\,\}$. *This means the join between the "owner" CR_1 and the "member" CR_2 is materialized. Consider the following user query:*

$$Q_C = \pi_{C_1}(CR_1 \bowtie CR_2)$$

Notice that $Q_C \neq CR_1$ in general! Following are the equations defining $C \rightarrow I$ and $I \rightarrow C$:

$$\begin{aligned} C \rightarrow I : IR_1 &= \nu_{IR_2=(C_2\setminus C_1)}(CR_1 \boxtimes CR_2) \\ I \rightarrow C : CR_1 &= \pi_{C_1}\rho_{C_2}\overline{\mu}^* IR_1 \\ CR_2 &= \pi_{C_2}\rho_{C_2}\overline{\mu}^* IR_1 \end{aligned}$$

Knowing $C_1 \cap C_2 \rightarrow C_1$, we conclude from theorem 5.1 that the join is redundant, and hence Q_C can be simplified to $\pi_{C_1}\rho_{C_1C_2}\overline{\mu}^* IR_1$. The following is a derivation of this result by application of the rules from section 4:

$$\begin{aligned} Q_C &= \pi_{C_1}(CR_1 \bowtie CR_2) \\ &= \pi_{C_1}(\pi_{C_1}\rho_{C_1}\overline{\mu}^* IR_1 \bowtie \pi_{C_2}\rho_{C_2}\overline{\mu}^* IR_1) \\ &= \pi_{C_1}\left(\rho_{C_1}(\pi_{C_1}\overline{\mu}^* IR_1) \bowtie \rho_{C_2}(\pi_{C_2}\overline{\mu}^* IR_1)\right) \\ &= \pi_{C_1}\rho_{C_1C_2}\left(\pi_{C_1}\overline{\mu}^* IR_1 \bowtie \pi_{C_2}\overline{\mu}^* IR_1\right) \\ &= \pi_{C_1}\rho_{C_1C_2}\pi_{C_1C_2}\overline{\mu}^* IR_1 \\ &= \pi_{C_1}\rho_{C_1C_2}\overline{\mu}^* IR_1 \\ &= \pi_{C_1}\rho_{C_1}\overline{\mu}^*\sigma_{C_2\neq\emptyset} IR_1 \\ &= \pi_{C_1}\rho_{C_1}\sigma_{C_2\neq\emptyset} IR_1 \\ &= \pi_{C_1}\sigma_{C_2\neq\emptyset} IR_1 \end{aligned}$$

the last equation holds if foreign key conditions are maintained, the fifth one is valid because of the FD given. Notice that without the ρ-operation we would have concluded $Q_C = \pi_{X_1}\pi_{C_1C_2}\overline{\mu}^* IR_1 = \pi_{C_1}\overline{\mu}^* IR_1 = CR_1$, which is not correct!

EXAMPLE 5.3. *Now we derive the result already presented in the introductory example. The equations defining the mappings between conceptual and internal mappings are:*

$$\begin{aligned} C \rightarrow I : Idept &= \nu_{eno,ename,sal:Iemp}(Dept \boxtimes Emp) \\ I \rightarrow C : Dept &= \pi_{dno,dname,budget}\rho_{dno,dname,budget}\overline{\mu}^* Idept \\ Emp &= \pi_{eno,ename,sal,dno}\rho_{eno,ename,sal,dno}\overline{\mu}^* Idept \end{aligned}$$

The transformation of the query can be done as follows:

$$\pi_{dname,sal}\sigma_{ename=\text{'Smith'}}(Dept \bowtie Emp)$$

$$= \pi_{dname,sal}\sigma_{ename=\text{'Smith'}}$$
$$(\pi_{dno,dname,budget}\rho_{dno,dname,budget}\overline{\mu}^{*} Idept \bowtie \pi_{eno,ename,sal,dno}\rho_{eno,ename,sal,dno}\overline{\mu}^{*} Idept)$$

$$= \pi_{dname,sal}\sigma_{ename=\text{'Smith'}}\rho_{dno,dname,budget,eno,ename,sal}$$
$$(\pi_{dno,dname,budget}\overline{\mu}^{*} Idept \bowtie \pi_{eno,ename,sal,dno}\overline{\mu}^{*} Idept)$$

$$= \pi_{dname,sal}\sigma_{ename=\text{'Smith'}}\rho_{dno,dname,budget,eno,ename,sal}(\pi_{dno,dname,budget,eno,ename,sal}\overline{\mu}^{*} Idept)$$

$$= \pi_{dname,sal}\sigma_{ename=\text{'Smith'}}\rho_{dno,dname,budget,eno,ename,sal}(\overline{\mu}^{*} Idept)$$

$$= \pi_{dname,sal}\sigma_{ename=\text{'Smith'}}\rho_{dname,sal}(\overline{\mu}^{*} Idept)$$

$$= \rho_{dname,sal}\pi_{dname,sal}\sigma_{ename=\text{'Smith'}}(\overline{\mu}^{*} Idept)$$

$$= \rho_{dname,sal}\pi_{dname,sal}\overline{\mu}^{*}\pi[dno, dname, budget, \sigma_{ename=\text{'Smith'}}(Iemp)](Idept)$$

$$= \rho_{dname,sal}\overline{\mu}^{*}\pi[dname, \pi[sal](Iemp)]\pi[dno, dname, budget, \sigma_{ename=\text{'Smith'}}(Iemp)](Idept)$$

$$= \rho_{dname,sal}\overline{\mu}^{*}\pi[dname, \pi[sal]\sigma_{ename=\text{'Smith'}}(Iemp)](Idept)$$

$$= \rho_{dname}\overline{\mu}^{*}\sigma_{Iemp\neq\emptyset}\pi[dname, \pi[sal]\sigma_{ename=\text{'Smith'}}(Iemp)](Idept)$$

Notice that we did not check against null values in the formulation given in the introduction, i.e. the reduction operation and the selection on Iemp were omitted there.

One of the last transformations in the above example combined two subsequent NF^2 projections into one. The following equivalence states the corresponding extension of the classical cascaded projections rule from [Ul82] for our case of nested projections:

LEMMA 5.1. *Let $expr_1, expr_2$ be algebraic expressions (operator sequences), then*

$$\pi[expr_1(A)](\pi[expr_2(A)](R)) = \pi[expr_1(expr_2(A))](R) \qquad \blacksquare$$

Now we are able to state the main result of our work contained in this paper. As claimed in the beginning, using NF^2 relations internally does not introduce additional complexity to the join elimination process and thus to algebraic optimization.

THEOREM 5.3. *Given C in 4NF, I as NF^2 relations obtained by denormalization and nesting according to definitions 3.2, 3.3. Any conjunctive SPJ (select-project-join) query on C can be optimized and transformed to I using only 1NF optimization techniques and additionally the rules in theorems 5.1, 5.2 and lemma 5.5. Whenever all joins contained in the conceptual query are materialized internally, this results in only* **one single pass processible** *NF^2 query.* ■

As the applications of the transformation rules from above are straightforward and can be realized efficiently, the complexity of the whole process is dominated by join elimination (i.e. the 1NF optimization). Hence, with the appropriate restrictions on conceptual queries one can for instance optimize in polynominal time using tableaux techniques [ASU79].

A prototype algebraic optimizer has already been implemented in PROLOG. The optimization algorithm can be sketched as follows:

Step 1 – Analyse the parse tree.
If there are two leaf nodes referring to the same internal relation, consider the projections that occur on the path from the leaves to their lowest common ancestor in the tree and find out, whether the join is redundant (applying knowledge about keys, FD's and MVD's).

Step 2 – Move π and σ as far down the tree as possible.

Step 3 – Consider the $\overline{\mu}^*$-operations: apply the necessary unnests and move $\overline{\mu}$ up the tree.

Implicitely, step 1 applies rules from [Ul82] to move selections up in the tree past joins— in order to check redundancy of the join according to [ASU79]. However, as selections can always be moved *up* (but not down), we do not actually transform the tree but simply ignore selections, when we decide whether a join is redundant. If a join is eliminated, the selections from both subtrees are conjunctively combined. In step 2 we perform the usual optimization, trying to move σ (and π) down the parse tree. Finally, step 3 transforms the optimized "quasi 1NF" query to nested NF^2 algebra. Step 3 is the only one using the rules for NF^2 algebra operations, whereas the others are standard 1NF techniques. In step 3 we also introduce the necessary ρ-operations, or apply the corresponding σ (eliminating empty subrelations before the unnest).

Allthough we used PROLOG in this first implementation and added some more equivalences than the ones presented here—concerning disjunctions in selection formulae—response times of the optimizer are fairly short (An adhoc test in a multi-user environment on a SIEMENS mainframe, optimizing the query from example 5.3—including dialogue handling—took about 1.7*sec* CPU-time and $< 5sec$ response time.) Of course it is known that in general optimization is NP-complete [ASU79]. Nevertheless computation time seems to be tolerable in all practical cases.

6. Conclusion

The use of unnormalized relations as a storage structure for 4NF relations has been proposed. As a consequence, the mapping between the differing conceptual and internal database layouts could be defined algebraically. A series of new equivalence rules among algebraic expressions containing unnest and reduction operators as well as NF^2 selections and projections were presented. Based on these equivalences we proved the applicability of our approach. Algebraic optimization needed for elimination of materialized, hence redundant joins can be performed utilizing only 1NF techniques with little additional information for the case of NF^2 relations. Moreover, whenever queries do not need any join operations internally, because all joins contained in the user query are materialized, a simple, efficiently evaluable type of NF^2 expressions results from the transformation. We also sketched a first implementation having proven practicability of the results presented.

From the above observation we also conclude some justification of the way our algebra was designed. Allthough [AB84] use a different type of algebra for their Verso model, they come to a similar result. [Bi85] also states that select-projection-join queries can be mapped to a single "Verso superselection" under some circumstances. While parts of the Verso model will be implemented in hardware (the Verso DB machine [BRS82, V86]), we are pursuing a software implementation. A database *kernel* system, called DASDBS—**DA**rm**S**tadt **D**ata**B**ase **S**ystem— is currently being implemented at the Technical University of Darmstadt [DOPSSW85, Sche86, SW86]. The architecture is partitioned into an application independent kernel, and several application specific front-ends ("DBS family"). All functions that are exspected to be common to the various application areas planned (conventional 4NF interface, geographic applications, knowledge representation support) will be implemented in the kernel. Currently the kernel will support NF^2 relations and single pass expressions. The application specific front-end for the conventional (flat) relational interface will be built on top of this kernel. The results presented in this paper are the theoretical foundation of the query optimizer contained in this "standard applications module".

Related work for the future includes treatment of disjunctive selection criteria, utilization of nested NF^2 joins and more sophisticated conceptual to internal mappings reflecting e.g. $n : m$-relationships. With little additional (foreign) key redundancy we could support access in a more symmetrical way than by splitting into disjoint hierarchies. The algebraic manipulations needed to optimize in the presence of the new internal structures can easily be added to our solution.

Acknowledgement

Thanks to Hans-Jörg Schek for initiating my work on this subject. Bernd Paul and Gerhard Weikum have contributed by clarifying discussions on the contents and presentation of this paper. Liz Klinger needed little TEXnical support to do the typing.

7. References

[AB84] S. Abiteboul, N. Bidoit: *Non First Normal Form Relations to Represent Hierarchically Organised Data*, Proc. 3rd ACM PODS, Waterloo, Ontario, Canada, 1984

[ABU79] A.V. Aho, C. Beeri, J.D. Ullman: *The Theory of Joins in Relational Databases*, ACM TODS, Vol. 4:3, 1979

[ASU79] A.V. Aho, Y. Sagiv, J.D. Ullman: *Equivalences Among Relational Expressions*, SIAM Journ. of Computing, Vol. 8:2, 1979

[Bi85] N. Bidoit: *Efficient Evaluation of Queries Using Nested Relations*, Techn. Report INRIA, 1985

[BR84] W. Benn, B. Radig: *Retrieval of Relational Structures for Image Sequence Analysis*, Proc. 10th VLDB Conference, Singapore, 1984

[BRS82] F. Bancilhon, P. Richard, M. Scholl: *On Line Processing of Compacted Relations*, Proc. 8th VLDB Conference, Mexico, 1982

[DOPSSW85] U. Deppisch, V. Obermeit, H.-B. Paul, H.-J. Schek, M.H. Scholl, G. Weikum: *The Storage Component of a Database Kernel System*, Techn. Rep. DVSI–1985–T1, TU Darmstadt,
Short German version in: Proc. GI Conf. on DBSs in Office, Technical and Scientific Applications, Karlsruhe, 1985, IFB 94, Springer, german title: *Ein Subsystem zur stabilen Speicherung versionenbehafteter, hierarchisch strukturierter Tupel*

[DPS86] U. Deppisch, H.-B. Paul, H.-J. Schek: *A Storage System for Complex Objects*, Proc. Int'l Workshop on Object-Oriented Database Systems, Pacific Grove, CA, 1986

[Fa77] R. Fagin: *Mulitvalued Dependencies and a New Normal Form for Relational Databases*, ACM TODS, Vol. 2:3, 1977

[FG85] P.C. Fischer, D. van Gucht: *Determining When a Structure is a Nested Relation*, Proc. 11th VLDB Conference, Stockholm, 1985

[FT83] P.C. Fischer, S.J. Thomas: *Operators for Non-First-Normal-Form Relations*, Proc. IEEE COMPSAC 1983

[Gu85] D. van Gucht: *Theory of Unnormalized Relational Structures*, Ph. D. Thesis, also available as Techn. Rep. CS–85–07, Vanderbilt University, Nashville, TN, 1985

[Ja85] G. Jaeschke: *Recursive Algebra for Relations with Relation Valued Attributes*, Techn. Rep. TR 85.03.002, IBM Heidelberg Scientific Centre, 1985

[Ja86] G. Jaeschke: *Algebraic Expressions for Higher Order Relational Databases*, unpublished manuscript

[JS82] G. Jaeschke, H.-J. Schek: *Remarks on the Algebra of Non-First-Normal-Form Relations*, Proc. 1st ACM PODS, Los Angeles, 1982

[Ma83] D. Maier: *The Theory of Relational Databases*, Pitman Publishing Ltd., London, 1983

[MSW86] F. Maher, H.-J. Schek, W. Waterfeld: *A Database Kernel System for Geoscientific Applications*, to appear in: Proc. 2nd Int'l Symp. on Spatial Data Handling, Seattle, 1986

[OY85] Z.M. Ozsoyoglu, L.Y. Yuan: *A Normal Form for Nested Relations*, Proc. 4th ACM PODS, 1985

[RKS85a] M.A. Roth, H.F. Korth, A. Silberschatz: *Extended Algebra and Calculus for ¬1NF Relational Databases*, Techn. Rep. TR–84–36, Revised Version, University of Texas at Austin, 1985

[RKS85b] M.A. Roth, H.F. Korth, A. Silberschatz: *Null Values in ¬1NF Relational Databases*, Techn. Rep. TR–85–32, University of Texas at Austin, 1985

[Sche85] H.-J. Schek: *Towards a Basic Relational NF^2 Algebra Processor*, Proc. Int'l Conf. on FODO, Kyoto, 1985

[Sche86] H.-J. Schek: *Research Activities of the DVSI-Group 1983–1985*, Techn. Rep. DVSI–1986–T2, TU Darmstadt, 1986

[SLTC82] N.C. Shu, V.Y. Lum, F.C. Tung, C.L. Chang: *Specification of Forms Processing and Business Procedures for Office Automation*, IEEE TOSE, Vol. SE–8:5, 1982

[SP82] H.-J. Schek, P. Pistor: *Data Structures for an Integrated Database Management and Information Retrieval System*, Proc. 8th VLDB Conference, Mexico, 1982

[SR86] H.-J. Schek, U. Reimer: *A Frame Representation Model and its Mapping to NF^2 Relations*, submitted for publication, 1986

[SS80] M. Schkolnik, P. Sorenson: *Denormalization: A Performance Oriented Database Design Technique*, Proc. AICA Conf., Bologna, Italy, 1980

[SS81] M. Schkolnik, P. Sorenson: *The Effects of Denormalization on Database Performance*, Res. Rep. RJ3082 (38128), IBM Res. Lab. San Jose, Ca., 1981

[SS83] H.-J. Schek, M.H. Scholl: *Die NF^2-Relationenalgebra zur einheitlichen Manipulation externer, konzeptueller und interner Datenstrukturen*, in: J.W. Schmidt (ed.): *Sprachen für Datenbanken*, IFB 72, Springer, 1983

[SS84] H.-J. Schek, M.H. Scholl: *The Relational Model with Relation–Valued Attributes*, Techn. Rep. DVSI–1984–T1, TU Darmstadt, published in: *Information Systems*, Vol. 11:2, 1986

[SW86] H.-J. Schek, G. Weikum: *DASDBS: Concepts and Architecture of a Database System for Advanced Applications*, Techn. Rep. DVSI–1986–T1, TU Darmstadt, 1986

[V86] Verso, J. (pen name for the Verso team): *Verso: A Database Machine Based on Non-First-Normal-Form Relations*, INRIA Report, 1986

[Ul82] J.D. Ullman: *Principles of Database Systems (2nd ed.)*, Computer Science Press Rockville, MD, 1982

A POLYNOMIAL-TIME JOIN DEPENDENCY IMPLICATION ALGORITHM FOR UNARY MULTI-VALUED DEPENDENCIES

P. Thanisch* and G. Loizou**

*Department of Computer Science, Heriot-Watt University,
79 Grassmarket, Edinburgh EH1 2HJ, Scotland

**Department of Computer Science, Birkbeck College, University of London,
Malet Street, London WC1E 7HX, England

1. Introduction

We assume that the reader is familiar with the relational model of databases [10] and, in particular, with the definitions of multi-valued dependency (MVD) [6] and join dependency (JD) [11].

Let $U = \{A_1, A_2, \ldots, A_n\}$, $n \geqslant 2$, be the universal attribute set. (All attribute sets are assumed to be subsets of U.) The JD implication problem is the problem of deciding whether a set, D, of MVDs implies a JD. In general, the JD implication problem is NP-hard [7]. An MVD, $X \twoheadrightarrow Y$, is a unary MVD (UMVD) if $|Y| = 1$. Given a set of UMVDs, the JD implication problem can be decided in polynomial time [5].

Herein we deal with this problem with respect to the set, Unary(D), of UMVDs that are implied by the set, D, of arbitrary MVDs. Although the size of Unary(D) is exponential in the size of U, we present a polynomial-time algorithm to determine whether Unary(D) implies a JD. We also describe a method whereby an instance of the JD implication problem can be transformed into an equivalent problem instance in which the MVDs are more unary.

2. Definitions and Preliminaries

Let d be a data dependency. SAT(d) denotes the set of relations over U that satisfy d. Correspondingly, SAT(D) is the set of relations that satisfy each of the data dependencies in D. D implies d, denoted by $D \models d$, if $SAT(D) \subseteq SAT(d)$. Where d is a JD, we use the notation $D \overset{?}{\models} d\ (U)$ to denote an instance of the JD implication problem.

Given the attribute set, X, we define DEP(X), the dependency basis of X with respect to the set, D, of MVDs thus: DEP(X) partitions the set U into the collection of attribute sets $\{Y_1, Y_2, \ldots, Y_h\}$ such that if $Z \subseteq U$ then $X \twoheadrightarrow Z \in D^+$, the closure of D, if and only if Z is the union of some of the Y_i's [10]. The elements of the dependency basis set are called blocks [8].

Lemma 1. Given a set, D, of MVDs and a pair, X_1 and X_2, of disjoint non-empty attribute sets, $DEP(X_1X_2)$ is at least as fine a partition of U as $DEP(X_1)$.

Proof. By the definition of dependency basis, for each block, $B \in DEP(X_1)$, $X_1 \twoheadrightarrow B \in D^+$. Since $X_1 \subset X_1X_2$, for any block, $C \in DEP(X_1X_2)$, such that $C \subseteq U - X_1X_2$, $X_1 \cap C = \emptyset$. Thus, if $C \cap B \neq \emptyset$ and $C - B \neq \emptyset$, then we can derive the MVD $X_1X_2 \twoheadrightarrow C - B$ by using the augmentation and projectivity axioms for MVDs [10]. By the definition of dependency basis, however, any MVD in D^+ with left-hand side X_1X_2 must have a right-hand side that is the union of some of the blocks in $DEP(X_1X_2)$, which is a contradiction. □

Let $R = \{R_1, R_2, \ldots, R_m\}$ be a decomposition scheme for U; when discussing the Chase algorithm, we refer to the usual tableau representation [11] for the decomposition scheme, R, in which each column of the tableau, say T, is associated with a particular attribute in U and each row, i, of T is associated with a particular relation scheme $R_i \in R$. We shall often use the name of the associated attribute in order to refer to a particular column. TABLE(R) denotes the tableau initialised from R by using the method described in [1], viz. for $1 \leqslant i \leqslant m$ and $1 \leqslant j \leqslant n$, if $A_j \in R_i$ then $T(i, j) = a_j$; otherwise, $T(i, j) = b_{ij}$.

Note that any particular symbol can only occur in one column of the tableau. We will need to refer to subsets of the set of symbols that occur in a row of the tableau. As in [7], we shall refer to such subsets as <u>strings</u>, even though the symbols in a string might not occur in consecutive columns.

Let $X \subseteq U$. $T(i, X)$ denotes the string of symbols in the columns of row i of T corresponding to the attributes in X. If $X = \emptyset$, then $T(i, X)$ is the empty string.

The Chase algorithm employs the following rules, which we shall refer to as the M-rules (cf. J-rules in [11]). There is one M-rule for each MVD.

The M-rules work as follows.

For each row, p, in T, the other rows are investigated. If there is another row, say s, such that, for some MVD $X \twoheadrightarrow Y \mid Z \in D$, $T(p, X) = T(s, X)$, then an additional row, g, is generated that agrees with p and s in the X-columns, agrees with p in the Y-columns and agrees with s in the Z-columns. We use the notation

$$g: T(p, X)\ T(p, Y)\ T(s, Z) \tag{1}$$

to represent the row thus generated. If T does not already contain a row with this string of symbols, then row g is added to T.

The M-rules are applied until no more new rows can be added to T.

We represent a particular M-rule application by the 4-tuple

$$< T', p, q, X \twoheadrightarrow Y \mid Z >,$$

where T' denotes the state of the tableau immediately prior to this M-rule application, rows p and q match in the X-columns of T' and $X \twoheadrightarrow Y \mid Z$ is the MVD used for this M-rule application.

We now introduce some more terminology. For two rows, i and h, in T and a singleton attribute set, B, we define the relatin '<' on the strings T(i, B) and T(h, B) as follows.

T(i, B) < T(h, B) iff T(h, B) contains a 'b' symbol and T(i, B) either contains an 'a' symbol or a 'b' symbol with a smaller row subscript than that of the 'b' symbol in T(h, B).

Similarly, T(i, B) $\leqslant$ T(h, B) if either T(i, B) = T(h, B) or T(i, B) < T(h, B).

Given, as arguments, a tableau T, a set comprising a pair of distinct row numbers, {h, i}, and a singleton attribute set, B, such that T(h, B) $\neq$ T(i, B), the function MIN(T, {h, i}, B) returns a row number, p ε {h, i}, such that, where q = {h, i} - {p}, T(p, B) < T(q, B).

We now define the following function, MATCH, for a tableau, T, and two of its rows, h and i.

$$\text{MATCH}(T, h, i) = \{A \mid T(h, \{A\}) = T(i, \{A\})\},$$

that is, X = MATCH(T, h, i) is the set of attributes associated with the columns of T in which rows h and i have identical symbols.

For any given column, say A, the set of symbols occurring in that column induces an equivalence relation on the set of row numbers of the rows in T such that two row numbers, h and i, are in the same equivalence class for the A-column if and only if T(h, {A}) = T(i, {A}). We let EC(T, h, {A}) = {i| T(h, {A}) = T(i, {A})}. In other words, EC(T, h, {A}) is the set of tableau row numbers in which the symbol T(h, {A}) occurs.

On termination of the Chase algorithm, we refer to the state of T as CHASE(T, D). The following lemma shows the relationship between CHASE(T, D) and the JD implication problem.

<u>Lemma 2</u>. ([11]). D $\models$ *[R] (*[R] is the JD induced by R) if and only if CHASE(TABLE(R), D) contains a row of all 'a' symbols.

We often refer to a tableau, T, being <u>interpreted as a relation</u>. By this, we mean a valuation [10] that maps tableau symbols to domain elements such that a symbol in the A_j-column of T is mapped to an element of Dom(A_j).

The following lemma shows the connection between CHASE(T, D) and the notion of dependency satisfaction.

<u>Lemma 3</u>. ([11]). CHASE(T, D) = T if and only if T, interpreted as a relation, is in SAT(D).

3. U-Rules and the Chase Algorithm

We now introduce U-rules for use with UMVDs in the Chase algorithm. For every UMVD, $X \twoheadrightarrow B \in D^+$, there is an associated U-rule. The U-rule for $X \twoheadrightarrow B$ represents a class of transformations that can be applied to a tableau, depending on which rows are chosen.

The U-Rules work as follows.

Let h and i be a pair of rows in T, and let X = MATCH(T, h, i). If there is a singleton set $B \in$ DEP(X) such that $B \not\subseteq X$, we apply the U-rule for $X \twoheadrightarrow B$ as follows. Let p = MIN(T, {h, i}, B) and let q = {h, i} - {p}. Then, for each $g \in$ EC(T, q, B), T(g, B) := T(p, B).

Let *[R] be a JD for U and let T = TABLE(R). The following procedure, UCHASE, decides whether or not Unary(D) $\models$ *[R].

```
procedure UCHASE(T, D);
begin
   procedure APPLY_U_RULE(T, h, i, B)
   begin
      p := MIN(T, {h, i}, B);
      q := {h, i} - {p};
      for each g ε EC(T, q, B) do
         T(g, B) := T(p, B)
      od
   end {APPLY_U_RULE}
   repeat
      T' := T;
      for each pair, h and i, of distinct tableau row numbers do
         X := MATCH(T, h, i);
         for each B ε DEP(X) such that B ⊈ X and |B| = 1 do
            APPLY_U_RULE(T, h, i, B)
         od
      od
   until T' = T
end {UCHASE}
```

4. The Correctness and Complexity of the Algorithm

Let T' denote the state of the tableau after zero or more applications of the U-Rules. In the proof of the validity of the U-Rules, we will need to refer to the sequence of changes made to the tableau symbols, thereby inducing the pattern occurring in T'. Before each U-rule application, for each tableau column, say A, there is a partition of the set of row numbers induced by the symbols which occur in each of the cells in the A-column. As successive changes are made to the A-column, symbols are equated and a new partition of the row numbers is obtained by taking the union of the set of row numbers containing the replaced symbol with the set of row numbers containing the replacing symbol.

Let T_1 = TABLE(R), and let T_i, i = 1, 2, 3, ..., denote the state of the tableau before the ith application of the U-rules. With the ith application of the U-rules, we associate a 6-tuple:

$$S_i = \langle T_i, p_i, q_i, X_i \twoheadrightarrow B_i \mid Z_i, P_i, Q_i \rangle.$$

The above 6-tuple has the following interpretation.

T_i is the state of the tableau just prior to the ith application of the U-rules,
p_i and q_i are a pair of tableau row numbers,
X_i = MATCH(T_i, p_i, q_i), $B_i \in$ DEP(X_i) such that $|B_i| = 1$ and $B_i \notin X_i$,
$Z_i = U - X_i - B_i$,
p_i = MIN(T_i, $\{p_i, q_i\}$, B_i), $q_i = \{p_i, q_i\} - \{p_i\}$,
P_i = EC(T_i, p_i, B_i), Q_i = EC(T_i, q_i, B_i).

When referring to a particular 6-tuple, we shall use subscripted S's; individual items in the 6-tuple will be referred to with the same subscript. The sequence, in order of occurrence, of the first j symbol-equating changes which UCHASE makes to the tableau can be described by a sequence of 6-tuples, namely, $\langle S_1, S_2, \ldots, S_j \rangle$.

For the proof of Lemma 6, below, we define a graph, G = (V, E), for the column, B_k, and the set of row numbers, Q_k, in the tableau state, T_k, just prior to the kth application of the U-rules, i.e. the application which is associated with the 6-tuple S_k. The graph, G, represents the sequence of the merges between the equivalence classes, P_j and Q_j ($j < k$), of row numbers in the set Q_k that occurred as a result of applying the U-rules in the B_k-column. In order to achieve this, we first define the sequence:

$$\text{Merges}(S_k) = \langle S_j \mid 1 \leqslant j \leqslant k \ \underline{\text{and}}\ B_j = B_k \ \underline{\text{and}}\ P_j \cup Q_j \subseteq Q_k \rangle. \qquad (2)$$

Note that (2) is a subsequence of $\langle S_1, S_2, \ldots, S_{k-1} \rangle$.

The vertex set, V, and edge set, E, of G are defined thus: $V = Q_k$. Each vertex in V is labelled by the corresponding row number in Q_k. Where there is no ambiguity, we shall not distinguish between a vertex and its labelling row number.
$E = \{(p_j, q_j) \mid p_j, q_j$ are the row numbers in $S_j \in \text{Merges}(S_k)\}$.

We observe that each 6-tuple in Merge(S_k) corresponds exactly to one edge in E, and we label each edge of E with the corresponding 6-tuple.

Before proceeding to prove Lemma 6, we first prove that G is a tree.

Lemma 4. G is a tree.

Proof. In order to prove that G is a tree, we must prove that G is both connected and acyclic. If $|V| = 1$, the proof is immediate, so assume that $|V| \geqslant 2$. First we prove that G is connected.

Let $q \in Q_k$. Prior to UCHASE, $T_1(q, B_k)$ contains a unique 'b' symbol, thus $|EC(T_1, q, B_k)| = 1$. However, by hypothesis, $|EC(T_k, q, B_k)| \geqslant 2$, so let S_j be the last 6-tuple in the subsequence Merges(S_k) for which $|EC(T_j, q, B_k)| = 1$. Consequently, either $Q_j = \{q\}$, in which case $q_j = q$, or $P_j = \{q\}$, in which case $p_j = q$. In either case, the vertex labelled by q is incident to the edge labelled by S_j. Thus all vertices of G must be incident to at least one edge.

Suppose that G has more than one connected component. Let S_j be the last 6-tuple in the subsequence Merges(S_k). Thus $P_j \cup Q_j = Q_k$. Let $G' = (V', E')$ be the connected component containing the edge labelled by S_j.

Let $G^- = (V^-, E^-)$ be another connected component in G. Let edge $(p_g, q_g) \in E^-$ be such that for any other edge $(p_h, q_h) \in E^-$,

$$P_g \cup Q_g \nsubseteq P_h \cup Q_h. \tag{3}$$

By hypothesis, $j > g$, so from (2), $P_g \cup Q_g \subseteq Q_k$, thus the symbol in $T_g(p_g, B_k)$ was equated with another symbol as a result of some U-rule application. Let S_f be the 6-tuple in Merges(S_k) associated with this U-rule application. Thus either $P_f = P_g \cup Q_g$ or $Q_f = P_g \cup Q_g$, so there is an element $s \in P_g \cup Q_g$ such that either $s = p_f$ or $s = q_f$. In either case, $s \in V^-$ and it is incident to an edge labelled by the aforesaid 6-tuple, S_f, for which $P_g \cup Q_g \subseteq P_f \cup Q_f$, which contradicts (3). Thus G is connected.

Next we prove that G is acyclic. Suppose that we construct G by starting with the vertex set, V, and adding the edges in E one at a time in the order in which the corresponding 6-tuples occur in Merges(S_k). At any stage in the construction, all the row numbers labelling the vertices in a connected component will correspond to tableau rows which contain the same 'b' symbol in the B_k-column. This is because the sets of row numbers labelling the vertices in a pair of connected components joined by the addition of the edge, say (p_j, q_j), labelled by the 6-tuple S_j, are precisely the sets P_j and Q_j.

Let the addition of some edge (p_h, q_h), resulting from some U-rule application, complete the first cycle to occur in G. Then there is a path from p_h to q_h prior to the addition of the edge. Thus vertices p_h and q_h are already in the same connected component and hence the tableau rows corresponding to p_h and q_h have the same 'b' symbol in the B_k-column. Consequently, $B_k \subseteq \text{MATCH}(T_h, p_h, q_h)$ and the U-rule would not be applicable in this case, which is a contradiction. Thus G is acyclic.□

Let T and T' be tableaux over the same attribute set and with the same number, m, of rows. We say that $T \leqslant T'$ if for each pair of rows, h and i,

$1 \leqslant h, i \leqslant m$, MATCH(T, h, i) $\subseteq$ MATCH(T', h, i).

Lemma 5. Let $T_1, T_2, \ldots, T_g$ be the states of the tableau before successive applications of the U-rules effected by procedure APPLY_U_RULE. Then

$$T_1 \leqslant T_2 \leqslant \cdots \leqslant T_{g-1} \leqslant T_g.$$

Proof. Let (T_j, h_j, i_j, B_j) denote the arguments passed to procedure APPLY_U_RULE for the jth U-rule application. We note that $|B_j| = 1$. For any $1 \leqslant j < g$, it follows from procedure APPLY_U_RULE that T_{j+1} is identical to T_j except in each of the rows with row numbers in the set Q_j, where, for each $q \in Q_j$, $T_{j+1}(q, B_j) = T_j(p_j, B_j)$. Thus, for each row, $q \in Q_j$, for any row, h, in T_j, if $B_j \subseteq$ MATCH(T_j, h, q), then $h \in Q_j$. In that case, $T_{j+1}(h, B_j) = T_{j+1}(q, B_j)$, i.e. $B_j \subseteq$ MATCH(T_j, h, q), so MATCH(T_j, h, q) $\subseteq$ MATCH(T_{j+1}, h, q). Hence $T_j \leqslant T_{j+1}$, $1 \leqslant j < g$. □

Lemma 6. If $T_k \subseteq$ CHASE(T, D) then $T_{k+1} \subseteq$ CHASE(T, D).

Proof. T_{k+1} is identical to T_k except in the B_k-column of the rows whose row numbers are in the set Q_k. (See APPLY_U_RULE.) For each $t_i \in Q_k$, $T_{k+1}(t_i, B_k) = T_k(p_k, B_k)$, but $T_k(t_i, B_k) \neq T_k(p_k, B_k)$. Thus, if $T_k \subseteq$ CHASE(T, D), we must prove that, for each $t_i \in Q_k$, the row

$$T_k(t_i, U\text{-}B_k)\ T_k(p_k, B_k) \tag{4}$$

is in CHASE(T, D). We do this by finding a sequence of M-rules whose application to T_k produces a tableau comprising the rows of T_k as well as each of the g rows of the form (4), where $g = |Q_k|$. Such a tableau contains a superset of the rows in T_{k+1}. The proof exploits the fact that G, by Lemma 4, is a tree. The method of proof is by induction on the sequence $< t_1, t_2, \ldots, t_g >$ of the row numbers in Q_k as they are visited in a preorder traversal [2] of the tree, G', which is identical to the tree, G, except that G' is rooted at the node q_k.

In the inductive proof that follows, we use a tableau, Θ. Initially, $\Theta = T_k$, so, at first, Θ has m rows. We let $\Theta_0 = T_k$, thus, by hypothesis, $\Theta_0 \subseteq$ CHASE(T, D). We further let Θ_i, $1 \leqslant i \leqslant g$, denote the state of Θ after the ith row has been added as a result of an M-rule application, so Θ_i has m+i rows.

BASIS: The root node in G' is labelled by q_k, so $t_1 = q_k$. We know that the MVD $X_k \twoheadrightarrow B_k \mid Z_k \in$ Unary(D) matches for rows p_k and q_k in T_k. $X_k Z_k = U - B_k$, so the application of the M-rule with associated 4-tuple $< \Theta_0, p_k, q_k, X_k \twoheadrightarrow B_k \mid Z_k >$ generates the first row of the form (4) (with i = 1), which can be added to Θ_0 to give the tableau Θ_1. Obviously, if $\Theta_0 \subseteq$ CHASE(T, D), then $\Theta_1 \subseteq$ CHASE(T, D).

INDUCTION: Suppose the lemma has been proved for the subsequence $< t_1, t_2, \ldots, t_f >$, $1 \leqslant f < g$. Thus, by inductive hypothesis, $\Theta_f \subseteq$ CHASE(T, D). Let t_a be the parent of t_{f+1} in the tree, G'. Thus, in a preorder traversal of G', t_a is visited before t_{f+1}, i.e. $1 \leqslant a \leqslant f$. Consequently, by hypothesis, row m+a of Θ_f is the string:

$$\Theta_f(t_a,\ U\text{-}B_k)\ \Theta_f(p_k,\ B_k). \tag{5}$$

Let S_j be the 6-tuple labelling the edge (t_a, t_{f+1}) in G'. Thus $\{p_j, q_j\} = \{t_a, t_{f+1}\}$. Row (5) above only differs from row t_a of Θ_f in the B_k-column. Moreover, by Lemma 5, $T_j \leqslant T_k$, so $T_j \leqslant \Theta_f$. Thus MATCH(T_j, t_a, t_{f+1}) $\subseteq$ MATCH(Θ_f, m+a, t_{f+1}). Consequently, the M-rule associated with the 4-tuple $< \Theta_f$, m+a, t_{f+1}, $X_j \twoheadrightarrow B_k \mid Z_j >$ can be applied, generating the row

$$\Theta_f(t_{f+1},\ U\text{-}B_k)\ \Theta_f(p_k,\ B_k),$$

since $U - B_k = X_jZ_j$. This row is added to Θ_f as row number m+f+1, thus transforming Θ_f into Θ_{f+1}. Thus, if $T_k \subseteq$ CHASE(T, D), then $\Theta_g \subseteq$ CHASE(T, D). However, the set of rows in T_{k+1} is a subset of the set of rows in Θ_g; in fact, it is Θ_g with the set of rows $\{t_1, t_2, \ldots, t_g\}$ thereof deleted. Thus, if $T_k \subseteq$ CHASE(T, D), then $T_{k+1} \subseteq$ CHASE(T, D). □

Lemma 7. Let T = TABLE(R) and let T' denote the state of the tableau on termination of UCHASE. Then T' $\subseteq$ CHASE(T, D).

Proof. This is by induction on the changes made to T by the successive applications of the U-rules effected by UCHASE.

BASIS: T_1 = TABLE(R) and since the applications of the M-rules in the Chase algorithm only add rows to the initial tableau, i.e. T_1, it follows that $T_1 \subseteq$ CHASE(T, D).

INDUCTION: Suppose the lemma has been proved for the first k applications of the U-rules. The next application of the U-rule transforms T_k into T_{k+1}. By Lemma 6, $T_{k+1} \subseteq$ CHASE(T, D). □

Theorem 1. Let T = TABLE(R) and let D be a set of arbitrary MVDs. UCHASE will generate a row of all 'a' symbols in T if and only if Unary(D) $\models$ *[R].

Proof. [IF] Suppose Unary(D) $\models$ *[R]. Let T^c = CHASE(T, Unary(D)); by Lemma 2, T^c contains a row of all 'a' symbols. Let T^u denote the state of T on termination of UCHASE and suppose that T^u does not contain a row of all 'a' symbols. By Lemma 7, $T^u \subseteq T^c$ and, by hypothesis, the inclusion is proper. Thus, by Lemma 3, T^u, interpreted as a relation, is not in SAT(Unary(D)). Let $X \twoheadrightarrow B \mid Z \in$ Unary(D) be a UMVD that is violated by T^u, and let h and i be two rows in T^u such that, where W = MATCH(T^u, h, i), $X \subseteq W$, $B \not\subseteq W$ and $Z \not\subseteq W$. Without loss of generality, let $T^u(i, B) < T^u(h, B)$ and assume that the row

$$T^u(h,\ X)\ T^u(i,\ B)\ T^u(h,\ Z) \tag{6}$$

is not in T^u.

Consider the last iteration of the <u>repeat</u> loop in UCHASE when T = T^u. Since $X \subseteq W$, by Lemma 1, $B \in$ DEP(W). By this time, UCHASE would have assigned the symbol $T^u(i, B)$ to $T^u(h, B)$ and row (6) is identical to row h in T^u, which is a contradiction.

[ONLY IF] Suppose UCHASE generates a row of all 'a' symbols. From line 15 of UCHASE, for every 6-tuple, S_i, the MVD $X_i \twoheadrightarrow B_i \mid Z_i \in$ Unary(D) and, by Lemma 7, each row changed by the statement in line 8 of UCHASE is identical to a row in T^c. Thus T^c will also contain a row of all 'a' symbols. □

Theorem 2. Given a set, D, of arbitrary MVDs and a JD, *[R], the implication problem Unary(D) $\models$ *[R] can be decided in $O(m^3n^2s \min\{s, \log n\})$ time, where s is the space required to write down the MVDs in D.

Proof. Each new assignment of symbols may need up to m-1 operations. The initial tableau has no more than nm different symbols, so $O(nm^2)$ assignment operations will be performed by APPLY_U_RULE.

The equivalence classes of row numbers referred to on line 7 of APPLY_U_RULE are trivial to initialise and maintain. For any successful application of the U-rules, the only operation required is to take the set union of two such equivalence classes. For $1 \leqslant h \leqslant m$ and any $B \subseteq U$ such that $|B| = 1$, $|EC(T, q, B)| \leqslant m$.

A dependency basis may have as many as n blocks. Moreover, it takes $O(sn \min\{s, \log n\})$ time [8] to compute the dependency basis of an attribute set. Each time the repeat loop iterates, this operation is performed $O(m^2)$ times. The repeat loop only continues to iterate if at least one pair of symbols has been equated in the previous iteration, so it cannot iterate more than mn times. From the above, it follows that UCHASE executes in $O(m^3n^2s \min\{s, \log n\})$ time. □

5. Converting Problem Instances to Unary Form

In this section, we show how an instance of the JD implication problem can be transformed into an equivalent problem instance in which the MVDs are more unary.

Let $P = \{A_f, A_g\}$ such that $P \subseteq U$. P is an atomic pair of attributes if, for all $X \twoheadrightarrow Y \mid Z \in D$, $P \subseteq X$, $P \subseteq Y$ or $P \subseteq Z$. The ensuing lemma shows why atomic pairs are useful.

Lemma 8. If there exists an atomic pair of attributes, $P = \{A_f, A_g\}$, such that, for each $R_i \in R$, $P \nsubseteq R_i$, then D $\not\models$ *[R].

Proof. Suppose that the condition in the lemma is true, yet D $\models$ *[R]. Let T^c denote the state of the tableau on termination of the Chase algorithm. By Lemma 2, T^c contains a row of all 'a' symbols. Obviously, the said row contains 'a' symbols in the P-columns, yet TABLE(R) does not contain a row with 'a' symbols in both of these columns. Let < T', h, i, $X \twoheadrightarrow Y \mid Z$ > be the 4-tuple associated with the M-rule application in which the Chase algorithm generates the first row containing 'a' symbols in the P-columns. The generated row is:

$$j: T'(h, X)\ T'(h, Y)\ T'(i, Z).$$

By definition, neither row h nor row i contains an 'a' symbol in both of the P-columns, yet row j must somehow 'inherit' 'a' symbols in these columns from rows h and i in T'. Without loss of generality, let T'(h, A_f) contain an 'a' symbol, thus T'(h, A_g) must contain a 'b' symbol. In that case T'(i, A_g) must contain an 'a' symbol, so T'(i, A_f) contains a 'b' symbol. Thus $A_f \in XY$ and $A_g \in Z$, contradicting the definition of an atomic pair. □

The above lemma suggests that it is possible to resolve instances of the JD implication problem without using the Chase algorithm.

We show how the identification of atomic pairs of attributes can be used to generalise the applicability of our results.

Let $D \overset{?}{\models} *[R]\ (U)$ be an instance of the JD implication problem. If UCHASE cannot generate a tableau with a row of all 'a' symbols and Unary(D) $\not\models$ D, then we can attempt to transform this instance into another equivalent problem instance by folding atomic pairs of attributes into a single attribute. This is achieved by the following procedure:

```
procedure FOLD_ATOMIC_PAIR(A_f, A_g);
begin
   {Fold the MVDs}
   for each X ->> Y | Z ε D do
      if {A_f, A_g} ⊆ X then X := X - {A_g} fi
      if {A_f, A_g} ⊆ Y then Y := Y - {A_g} fi
      if {A_f, A_g} ⊆ Z then Z := Z - {A_g} fi
   od
   {Fold the JD's relation schemes}
   for each R_i ε R do
      if {A_f, A_g} ⊆ R_i then
         R_i := R_i - {A_g}
      else
         R_i := R_i - {A_f, A_g}
      fi
   od
end {FOLD_ATOMIC_PAIR}
```

In the computation of CHASE(TABLE(R), D) let the kth application of the M-rules be represented by the 4-tuple

$$\Sigma_k = \langle T_k, h_k, i_k, X_k \twoheadrightarrow Y_k \mid Z_k \rangle .$$

Furthermore, let $D' \overset{?}{\models} *[R']\ (U - \{A_g\})$ be the new instance of the JD implication problem after the attribute A_g has been folded into the attribute A_f by procedure FOLD_ATOMIC_PAIR.

<u>Lemma 9</u>. $D' \models *[R']\ (U - \{A_g\})$ if and only if $D \models *[R]\ (U)$.

Sketch of the Proof. [ONLY IF] Suppose that D $\models$ *[R] (U). For each Σ_j in the computation CHASE(TABLE(R), D), the 4-tuple $< T_j, h_j, i_j, X_j \twoheadrightarrow Y_j \mid Z_j >$ can be used in the computation CHASE(TABLE(R'), D'). (Method: Induction on the sequence of 4-tuples.)

[IF] Assume D' $\models$ *[R'] (U - $\{A_g\}$). For each Σ_k in the computation CHASE(TABLE(R'), D'), the 4-tuple $< T'_k, h_k, i_k, X'_k \twoheadrightarrow Y'_k \mid Z'_k >$ can be used in the computation CHASE(TABLE(R), D). (Method: Induction on the sequence of 4-tuples.) □

Theorem 3. Let D' $\overset{?}{\models}$ *[R'] (U') denote the JD implication problem instance after all atomic pairs of attributes have been removed in a sequence of calls to procedure FOLD_ATOMIC_PAIR. Then D' $\models$ *[R'] (U') if and only if D $\models$ *[R] (U).

Proof. By Lemma 9, after each successive fold, the hypothesis in the lemma holds. Thus the theorem follows by induction on this sequence of changes to the JD implication problem instance. □

6. Concluding Remarks

In the present paper, we have investigated the JD implication problem for the case in which, for each MVD, X $\twoheadrightarrow$ Y, used in UCHASE, $|Y| = 1$ and X is an arbitrary subset of U. The results presented herein are analogous to those in [9], where the computational properties of unary inclusion dependencies were investigated. In contrast to unary inclusion dependencies, however, UMVDs are not restricted to singleton left-hand side attribute sets; such a restriction is a special case of a UMVD.

The results that we have presented are also applicable when computing the representative instance [12]. When two rows, g and h, match for the UMVD X $\twoheadrightarrow$ B | Y, $|B| = 1$, in the tableau, T, it is permissible to use the M-rule for X $\twoheadrightarrow$ B | Y (rather than the corresponding U-rule) so long as either T(g, B) or T(h, B) contains a null symbol. Thus UMVDs can act as either tuple-generating or equality-generating dependencies.

Even where Unary(D) is not sufficient to imply a JD, procedure UCHASE could still be used as a pre-processing phase, prior to the full Chase algorithm. We refer the reader to Example 2 in [4], for which the Chase algorithm generates an exponentially large number of tableau rows. It can be verified that by taking the tableau, T, produced by UCHASE for this example, and then using the Chase algorithm to chase T with respect to the appropriate set of MVDs, the final tableau has exactly two rows.

References

[1] Aho, A. V., Beeri, C. and Ullman, J. D.: The theory of joins in relational databases. ACM Trans. Database Syst. 4, 297-314 (1979)

[2] Aho, A. V., Hopcroft, J. E. and Ullman, J. D.: Data Structures and Algorithms. Addison-Wesley, Reading, Mass., 1983.

[3] Aho, A. V., Sagiv, Y. and Ullman, J. D.: Equivalences among relational expressions. SIAM J. Comput. 8, 218-246 (1979)

[4] Beeri, C. and Vardi, M. Y.: A proof procedure for data dependencies. J. Assoc. Comput. Mach. 31, 718-741 (1984)

[5] Beeri, C. and Vardi, M. Y.: On the complexity of testing implications of data dependencies. Technical Report, Computer Science Dept., The Hebrew University of Jerusalem, 1980.

[6] Fagin, R.: Multivalued dependencies and a new normal form for relational databases. ACM Trans. Database Syst. 2, 262-278 (1977)

[7] Fischer, P. C. and Tsou, D-M.: Whether a set of multivalued dependencies implies a join dependency is NP-hard. SIAM J. Comput. 12, 259-266 (1983)

[8] Galil, Z.: An almost linear-time algorithm for computing a dependency basis in a relational database. J. Assoc. Comput. Mach. 29, 96-102 (1982)

[9] Kanellakis, P. C., Cosmadakis, S. S. and Vardi, M. Y.: Unary inclusion dependencies have polynomial time inference problems. In Proceedings 15th Annual ACM Symposium on Theory of Computing, pp. 264-277, Boston, 1983.

[10] Maier, D.: The Theory of Relational Databases. Computer Science Press, Rockville, Maryland, 1983.

[11] Maier, D., Mendelzon, A. O. and Sagiv, Y.: Testing implications of data dependencies. ACM Trans. Database Syst. 4, 455-469 (1979)

[12] Maier, D., Ullman, J. D. and Vardi, M. Y.: On the foundations of the universal relation model. ACM Trans. Database Syst. 9, 283-308 (1984)

INTERACTION-FREE MULTIVALUED DEPENDENCY SETS

Dirk Van Gucht
Computer Science Department
Indiana University
Bloomington, IN 47405, USA

1. Introduction

Multivalued dependencies [Fag1, Zan] (MVD) and *join dependencies* [ABU, Ris] were introduced to study database design problems. Although join dependencies are more general than MVDs, the latter are easier to work with, both conceptually and technically. A natural question is therefore to study under which conditions and how join dependencies are related to MVDs.

Join dependencies can be divided into two classes: *cyclic* and *acyclic* join dependencies. The latter class contains the MVDs as a proper subclass. One of the fundamental results in dependency theory is the following "semantic" characterization of acyclic join dependencies, obtained by Fagin *et.al.* [FMU]:

A join dependency is acyclic if and only if it is equivalent to a set of MVDs.

In addition to this characterization, Beeri *et.al.* [BFMY] have shown that such a set of MVDs has a *cover* which is a *conflict-free MVD set*, a concept first studied by Lien [Lie] and Sciore [Sci]. Although this result gives considerable insight into the "syntactic" structure of a set of MVDs equivalent to an acyclic join dependency, the definition of a conflict-free MVD set is complex and does not provide insight into what is meant by the "semantic" notion of a set of MVDs free of conflicts.

In this paper we introduce the concept of an *interaction-free MVD set*. In contrast to the definition of a conflict-free MVD set, the definition of an interaction-free MVD set clearly indicates that we are dealing with a set of MVDs which do not interact in an adverse way. Furthermore, we provide a simple syntactic characterization of an interaction-free MVD set and show that a join dependency is acyclic if and only if it is equivalent to an interaction-free MVD set.

In Section 2 we review some of the basic definitions in the relational model. In Section 3 we show the relationship between acyclic join dependencies and conflict-free MVD sets. In Section 4 we introduce the concept of an interaction-free MVD set and give a syntactic characterization. In Section 5 we compare the notions of conflict-free and interaction-free MVD sets. The main result of this section is that a join dependency is acyclic if and only if it is equivalent to an interaction-free MVD set.

2. Basic Concepts

Let Ω denote the *universe of attributes*. Each attribute $A \in \Omega$ has a set of associated values, its *domain*, dom(A). We will assume that each attribute has at least two elements. A *relation scheme* R is a finite subset of Ω. A *tuple* t over the relation scheme R is a mapping from R into

$\cup_{A \in R}(\text{dom}(A))$ such that $t(A) \in \text{dom}(A)$ for each $A \in R$. A *relation* over R is a finite set of tuples over R.

Let t be a tuple over R and let $X \subseteq R$. The *X-value* of t, denoted $t[X]$, is the restriction of the mapping t to X. Let r be a relation over R and $X \subseteq R$, the *projection* of r on X is the relation $\Pi_X(r) = \{t[X] \mid t \in r\}$. Let $r_1, \ldots, r_n$ be relations over the relation schemes $R_1, \ldots, R_n$ respectively. The join of the relations $r_1, \ldots, r_n$, denoted $r_1 \bowtie \ldots \bowtie r_n$, is the set of tuples t over $\cup_{i=1}^n R_i$, such that for each i, $1 \leq i \leq n$, $t[R_i] \in r_i$.

In this paper we will consider two classes of data dependencies, the class of join dependencies and the class of MVDs. Let R be a relation scheme and let $R_1, \ldots, R_n$ be subsets of R such that $R = \cup_{i=1}^n R_i$. If the relation $r = \Pi_{R_1}(r) \bowtie \ldots \bowtie \Pi_{R_n}(r)$, we say that r *satisfies* the *join dependency* (JD) $\bowtie \{R_1, \ldots, R_n\}$. A *multivalued dependency* (MVD) is a special case of a JD. Let X and Y be disjoint subsets of R. A MVD $X \rightarrow\rightarrow Y$ for a relation on R is a JD $\bowtie \{XY, XZ\}$, where $Z = R - XY$.

Let J_1 and J_2 be sets of JDs on R. We say that J_1 *logically implies* J_2, denoted $J_1 \models J_2$, if and only if whenever a relation r over R satisfies the JDs in J_1, r also satisfies the JDs in J_2. We say that J_1 and J_2 are *logically equivalent*, denoted $J_1 \equiv J_2$, if and only if $J_1 \models J_2$ and $J_2 \models J_1$. If $J_1 \equiv J_2$ then J_1 is a *cover* for J_2.

Let r be a relation over R and let $j = \bowtie \{R_1, \ldots, R_n\}$ be a JD on R. We define $\text{CHASE}_j(r)$ as the relation $\Pi_{R_1}(r) \bowtie \ldots \bowtie \Pi_{R_n}(r)$. We can generalize the definition of CHASE to a set of JDs. Let J be a set of JDs on R and let r be a relation over R, then $\text{CHASE}_J(r)$ can be defined recursively as follows:

1. if r satisfies the JDs in J then $\text{CHASE}_J(r) = r$
2. if r violates the JD $j \in J$ then $\text{CHASE}_J(r) = \text{CHASE}_J(\text{CHASE}_j(r))$.

It was shown by Maier *et.al.* in [MMS] that $\text{CHASE}_J(r)$ has the finite Church-Rosser property. Furthermore, it follows from the definition that $\text{CHASE}_J(r)$ satisfies the JDs in J.

3. Acyclic Join Dependencies and Conflict-Free MVD Sets

The class of join dependencies over a relation scheme R contains an important subclass: the acyclic join dependencies. This class can be defined as follows: Let R be a relation scheme and let j be a JD on R, we say that j is an *acyclic* JD if and only if there exists a set of MVDs $\mathcal{M}$ on R such that $\mathcal{M} \equiv \{j\}$. For alternative definitions of acyclic join dependencies and their properties see [ADM1, ADM2, AP, BB, BDM, BFMY, BV, DM, Fag2, FMU, GP1, GP2, GR, MU, PV, Sac1, Sac2, Sci, TY, Yan].

A set of MVDs equivalent to an acyclic JD satisfies some interesting properties. In particular, it can be shown that such a set has a cover which is a conflict-free MVD set. The notion of conflict-free MVD sets was introduced by Lien [Lie], who studied the relationship between the network and relational model. Sciore [Sci] analyzed conflict-free MVD sets in the context of database design and argued that "real-world" sets of MVDs are conflict free. Sciore showed that a conflict-free MVD set is equivalent to a join dependency. Beeri *et.al.* [BFMU] sharpened this result by showing that a set of MVDs has a conflict-free MVD set cover if and only if it is equivalent to a single (acyclic) JD. More results about conflict-free MVD sets can be found in [BK, GT, Kat1, Kat2, Lie, Sci, YO].

We use the formalism of [BFMY] to define conflict-free MVD sets. A MVD $X \rightarrow\rightarrow Y$ over the relation scheme R *splits* two attributes A and B if one of them is in Y and the other is in $R - XY$. A MVD *splits* a set V if it splits two attributes in V. A set $\mathcal{M}$ of MVDs over R *splits* a set V if some MVD in $\mathcal{M}$ splits V. We say that a set of $\mathcal{M}$ over R has the *left intersection property* if and only if whenever the MVDs $X \rightarrow\rightarrow Z$ and $Y \rightarrow\rightarrow Z$ are implied by $\mathcal{M}$, then also $X \cap Y \rightarrow\rightarrow Z$ is implied by $\mathcal{M}$. Let $\mathcal{M}$ be a set of MVDs. The left-hand sides of the MVDs of $\mathcal{M}$ are called the *keys* of $\mathcal{M}$. A set $\mathcal{M}$ of MVDs over the relation scheme R is a *conflict-free MVD set* on R if and only if

1. $\mathcal{M}$ does not splits its keys, and
2. $\mathcal{M}$ has the left intersection property.

Beeri *et.al.* [BFMY] obtained the following important theorem:

Theorem 1. [BFMY] *Let R be a relation scheme and let $\mathcal{M}$ be a set of MVDs on R. $\mathcal{M}$ has a cover which is a conflict-free MVD set if and only if $\mathcal{M}$ is equivalent to an acyclic join dependency.*

4. Interaction-Free MVD Sets

The idea of a *conflict-free MVD set* suggests that the MVDs in that set do not "interact in an adverse way". It is not clear, however, what is meant by "interacting in an adverse way". This lack of clarity arises from the rather complicated, non-intuitive syntactic definition of such sets. In this section we propose an alternative definition of MVD sets "free of conflicts". Therefore, we introduce the concept of interaction-free MVD sets.

Let R be a relation scheme and let $\mathcal{M}$ be a set of MVDs on R. We say that $\mathcal{M}$ is an *interaction-free MVD set* on R if and only if for any relation r over R and any pair of MVDs m_1, $m_2 \in \mathcal{M}$

$$\mathrm{CHASE}_{m_2}(\mathrm{CHASE}_{m_1}(r)) = \mathrm{CHASE}_{m_1}(\mathrm{CHASE}_{m_2}(r))$$

The following example shows that the notion of conflict-free and interaction-free MVD sets are incompatible:

Example 1. Goodman and Tay [GT] give an example of a conflict-free MVD set which is not an interaction-free MVD set. Let $R = ABCD$ and $\mathcal{M} = \{A \rightarrow\rightarrow BC|D,\ AB \rightarrow\rightarrow C|D,\ AC \rightarrow\rightarrow B|D\}$. It can be shown that $\mathcal{M}$ is a conflict-free MVD set, but not an interaction-free MVD set. Indeed, it can be verified that

$$\mathrm{CHASE}_{AB\rightarrow\rightarrow C|D}(\mathrm{CHASE}_{AC\rightarrow\rightarrow B|D}(\mathrm{r})) \neq \mathrm{CHASE}_{AC\rightarrow\rightarrow B|D}(\mathrm{CHASE}_{AB\rightarrow\rightarrow C|D}(\mathrm{r}))$$

where r is the relation shown in Figure 1.

Let $R = ABCDE$ and $\mathcal{M} = \{A \rightarrow\rightarrow BC|DE, ABD \rightarrow\rightarrow C|E\}$. It can be verified that $\mathcal{M}$ is an interaction-free MVD set, but not a conflict-free MVD set since the key ABD is split by $A \rightarrow\rightarrow BC|DE$. □

The following theorem gives a characterization of interaction-free MVD sets:

A	B	C	D
0	0	0	0
0	0	1	0
0	1	1	1

Figure 1

Theorem 2. *Let R be a relation scheme and let $\mathcal{M}$ be a set of MVDs on R. $\mathcal{M}$ is an interaction-free MVD set on R if and only if*

$$\mathrm{CHASE}_{\mathcal{N}}(r) = \mathrm{CHASE}_{n_p}(\mathrm{CHASE}_{n_{p-1}}(\ldots(\mathrm{CHASE}_{n_1}(r))\ldots))$$

for any relation r on R, any $\mathcal{N} \subseteq \mathcal{M}$, and any sequence of MVDs $(n_1, \ldots, n_p)$ such that

1. $p = |\mathcal{N}|$, and
2. $\{n_1, \ldots, n_p\} = \mathcal{N}$.

Proof. If $|\mathcal{M}| \leq 1$, the theorem is vacuously true. Therefore assume $|\mathcal{M}| > 1$. The *if* part is trivial, one merely has to consider two element subsets $\mathcal{N}$ of $\mathcal{M}$. We now show the *only if* part of the theorem. Let $\mathcal{N} \subseteq \mathcal{M}$ and let $(n_1, \ldots, n_p)$ be a sequence of MVDs such that

1. $p = |\mathcal{N}|$, and
2. $\{n_1, \ldots, n_p\} = \mathcal{N}$.

Let $r' = \mathrm{CHASE}_{n_p}(\mathrm{CHASE}_{n_{p-1}}(\ldots(\mathrm{CHASE}_{n_1}(r))\ldots))$. If we can show that r' satisfies the MVDs in $\mathcal{N}$, the result follows immediately from the definition of $\mathrm{CHASE}_{\mathcal{N}}(r)$. Since CHASE_{n_p} was the last CHASE operation, r' satisfies the MVD n_p. Since $\mathcal{N}$ is an interaction-free MVD set, it follows that $r' = \mathrm{CHASE}_{n_{p-1}}(\ldots(\mathrm{CHASE}_{n_1}(\mathrm{CHASE}_{n_p}(r))\ldots)$, which implies that r' also satisfies the MVD n_{p-1}. This argument can be repeated for the other MVDs in the sequence. Thus r' satisfies the MVDs in $\mathcal{N}$. □

Corollary 1. *Let r be a relation over R and let $\mathcal{M}$ be an interaction-free MVD set on R. Then*

$$\mathrm{CHASE}_{\mathcal{M}}(r) = \mathrm{CHASE}_{m_p}(\mathrm{CHASE}_{m_{p-1}}(\ldots(\mathrm{CHASE}_{m_1}(r))\ldots))$$

for any sequence of MVDs $(m_1, \ldots, m_p)$ such that

1. $p = |\mathcal{M}|$, and
2. $\{m_1, \ldots, m_p\} = \mathcal{M}$.

The inverse of Corollary 1 in not true:

Example 2. Consider the MVDs $m_1 = A \twoheadrightarrow BC|D$, $m_2 = AB \twoheadrightarrow C|D$, and $m_3 = AC \twoheadrightarrow B|D$ of Example 1, and consider the relation r shown in Figure 1. It can be verified that for any permutation (p_1, p_2, p_3) of the MVDs m_1, m_2, and m_3

$$\mathrm{CHASE}_{\{m_1,m_2,m_3\}}(\mathrm{r}) = \mathrm{CHASE}_{p_3}(\mathrm{CHASE}_{p_2}(\mathrm{CHASE}_{p_1}(\mathrm{r}))).$$

However, as was shown in Example 1, the set of MVDs $\{m_1, m_2, m_3\}$ is not an interaction-free MVD set. □

Theorem 2 gives a "semantic" characterization of an interaction-free MVD set. A "syntactic" characterization follows in a straightforward way from Theorem 3.

Theorem 3. *Let R be a relation scheme and let m_1 and m_2 be the MVDs $X \to\to Y|Z$ and $U \to\to V|W$ on R. Then*

$$\mathrm{CHASE}_{m_2}(\mathrm{CHASE}_{m_1}(r)) = \mathrm{CHASE}_{m_1}(\mathrm{CHASE}_{m_2}(r))$$

for any relation r on R if and only if

1. *$X = U$, or*
2. *$X \cap V = \emptyset$, $Y \cap U = \emptyset$, and $Y \cap V = \emptyset$ (up to renaming of Y and Z, or V and W †), or*
3. *$m_1 \models m_2$, or*
4. *$m_2 \models m_1$.‡*

Proof. We first show the *if* direction:

1. Assume $X = U$. Let r be a relation over R. Because of the symmetry between m_1 and m_2, we only have to show that $\mathrm{CHASE}_{m_2}(\mathrm{CHASE}_{m_1}(r))$ satisfies m_1. Let $t_1, t_2 \in \mathrm{CHASE}_{m_2}(\mathrm{CHASE}_{m_1}(r))$ be of the form

	X	$Y \cap V$	$Y \cap W$	$Z \cap V$	$Z \cap W$
$t_1=$	x	yv	yw	zv	zw
$t_2=$	x	yv'	yw'	zv'	zw'

We have to show that $\mathrm{CHASE}_{m_2}(\mathrm{CHASE}_{m_1}(r))$ contains the tuple t_3 such that

$t_3=$	x	yv	yw	zv'	zw'

Since $t_1, t_2 \in \mathrm{CHASE}_{m_2}(\mathrm{CHASE}_{m_1}(r))$, we know that $\mathrm{CHASE}_{m_1}(r)$ contains the tuples t_{11}, t_{12}, t_{21}, and t_{22} of the form:

$t_{11}=$	x	yv	δ_1	zv	δ_2
$t_{12}=$	x	δ_3	yw	δ_4	zw
$t_{21}=$	x	yv'	δ_5	zv'	δ_6
$t_{22}=$	x	δ_7	yw'	δ_8	zw'

Since $\mathrm{CHASE}_{m_1}(r)$ satisfies the MVD $X \to\to Y|Z$, $\mathrm{CHASE}_{m_1}(r)$ also contains the tuples:

x	yv	δ_1	zv'	δ_6
x	δ_3	yw	δ_8	zw'

and therefore $\mathrm{CHASE}_{m_2}(\mathrm{CHASE}_{m_1}(r))$ contains the tuple t_3.

2. Let m_1 and m_2 be the MVDs $X \to\to Y|Z$ and $U \to\to V|W$ such that $X \cap V = \emptyset$, $Y \cap U = \emptyset$, and $Y \cap V = \emptyset$. Because of the symmetry between m_1 and m_2, we only have

† Condition 2 can be replaced by either of the following conditions:

- $X \cap V = \emptyset$, $Z \cap U = \emptyset$, and $Z \cap V = \emptyset$, or
- $X \cap W = \emptyset$, $Y \cap U = \emptyset$, and $Y \cap W = \emptyset$, or
- $X \cap W = \emptyset$, $Z \cap U = \emptyset$, and $Z \cap W = \emptyset$.

‡ By Theorem 2 of [FMU], it follows that $m_1 \models m_2$ if and only if $((XY \subseteq UV$ or $XY \subseteq UW)$ and $(XZ \subseteq UV$ or $XZ \subseteq UW))$ and $m_2 \models m_1$ if and only if $((UV \subseteq XY$ or $UV \subseteq XZ)$ and $(UW \subseteq XY$ or $UW \subseteq XZ))$.

to show that for any relation r on R, $\mathrm{CHASE}_{m_2}(\mathrm{CHASE}_{m_1}(r))$ satisfies the MVD m_1. Let t_1, $t_2 \in \mathrm{CHASE}_{m_2}(\mathrm{CHASE}_{m_1}(r))$ be of the form:

	$X \cap U$	$X \cap W$	$Y \cap W$	$Z \cap U$	$Z \cap V$	$Z \cap W$
$t_1=$	xu	xw	yw	zu	zv	zw
$t_2=$	xu	xw	yw'	zu'	zv'	zw'

We have to show that $\mathrm{CHASE}_{m_2}(\mathrm{CHASE}_{m_1}(r))$ contains the tuple t_3 such that:

$t_3=$	xu	xw	yw	zu'	zv'	zw'

Since t_1, $t_2 \in \mathrm{CHASE}_{m_2}(\mathrm{CHASE}_{m_1}(r))$, we know that $\mathrm{CHASE}_{m_1}(r)$ contains the tuples t_{11}, t_{12}, t_{21}, and t_{22} such that:

$t_{11}=$	xu	δ_1	δ_2	zu	zv	δ_3
$t_{12}=$	xu	xw	yw	zu	δ_4	zw
$t_{21}=$	xu	δ_5	δ_6	zu'	zv'	δ_7
$t_{22}=$	xu	xw	yw'	zu'	δ_8	zw'

Since $\mathrm{CHASE}_{m_1}(r)$ satisfies the MVD $X \to\to Y$, $\mathrm{CHASE}_{m_1}(r)$ also contains the tuple

xu	xw	yw	zu'	δ_8	zw'

and therefore $\mathrm{CHASE}_{m_2}(\mathrm{CHASE}_{m_1}(r))$ contains the tuple t_3.

3. Trivial.

4. Trivial.

We show the *only if* direction of the theorem by contraposition, *i.e.*, if the MVDs m_1 and m_2 violate conditions 1, 2, 3, and 4 then we show that there exists a relation r over R such that

$$\mathrm{CHASE}_{m_2}(\mathrm{CHASE}_{m_1}(r)) \neq \mathrm{CHASE}_{m_1}(\mathrm{CHASE}_{m_2}(r)).$$

In fact, it suffices to show that there exists a relation r such that $\mathrm{CHASE}_{m_2}(\mathrm{CHASE}_{m_1}(r))$ violates the MVD m_1. If we assume that $X \to\to Y|Z$ and $U \to\to V|W$ violate the conditions 1, 2, 3, and 4 then

$X \neq U$ and
$(X \cap V \neq \emptyset$ or $Y \cap U \neq \emptyset$ or $Y \cap V \neq \emptyset)$ and
$(X \cap V \neq \emptyset$ or $Z \cap U \neq \emptyset$ or $Z \cap V \neq \emptyset)$ and
$(X \cap W \neq \emptyset$ or $Y \cap U \neq \emptyset$ or $Y \cap W \neq \emptyset)$ and
$(X \cap W \neq \emptyset$ or $Z \cap U \neq \emptyset$ or $Z \cap W \neq \emptyset)$ and
$((XY \not\subseteq UV$ and $XY \not\subseteq UW)$ or $(XZ \not\subseteq UV$ and $XZ \not\subseteq UW))$ and
$((UV \not\subseteq XY$ and $UV \not\subseteq XZ)$ or $(UW \not\subseteq XY$ and $UW \not\subseteq XZ))$.

It can be verified that the truth assignments, shown in Table 1, (and their consequences †) are the only truth assignments to the predicates $X \cap U \neq \emptyset$, $X \cap V \neq \emptyset$, $X \cap W \neq \emptyset$, $Y \cap U \neq \emptyset$,

† We say that a truth assignment $(j_{X\cap U}, j_{X\cap V}, j_{X\cap W}, j_{Y\cap U}, j_{Y\cap V}, j_{Y\cap W}, j_{Z\cap U}, j_{Z\cap V}, j_{Z\cap W})$ is a *consequence* of the truth assignment $(i_{X\cap U}, i_{X\cap V}, i_{X\cap W}, i_{Y\cap U}, i_{Y\cap V}, i_{Y\cap W}, i_{Z\cap U}, i_{Z\cap V}, i_{Z\cap W})$ if $j_{X\cap U} \geq i_{X\cap U}$, $j_{X\cap V} \geq i_{X\cap V}$, $\ldots$, $j_{Z\cap W} \geq i_{Z\cap W}$.

	$X \cap U \neq \emptyset$	$X \cap V \neq \emptyset$	$X \cap W \neq \emptyset$	$Y \cap U \neq \emptyset$	$Y \cap V \neq \emptyset$	$Y \cap W \neq \emptyset$	$Z \cap U \neq \emptyset$	$Z \cap V \neq \emptyset$	$Z \cap W \neq \emptyset$
(1)	0	0	0	0	1	1	1	0	0
(2)	0	0	0	1	0	0	0	1	1
(3)	0	0	1	0	1	0	0	1	0
(4)	0	0	1	0	1	0	1	0	0
(5)	0	0	1	1	0	0	0	1	0
(6)	0	1	0	0	0	1	0	0	1
(7)	0	1	0	0	0	1	1	0	0
(8)	0	1	0	1	0	0	0	0	1
(9)	0	1	1	1	0	0	1	0	0

Table 1

$Y \cap V \neq \emptyset$, $Y \cap W \neq \emptyset$, $Z \cap U \neq \emptyset$, $Z \cap V \neq \emptyset$, and $Z \cap W \neq \emptyset$ which make the above expression true.

By the symmetry of m_1 and m_2, however, there remain only three cases to consider:

a. Truth assignments (1), (2), (3), and (6) cannot be distinguished and correspond to the case where $X \cap V \neq \emptyset$, $Y \cap W \neq \emptyset$, and $Z \cap W \neq \emptyset$.

b. Truth assignments (4), (5), (7), and (8) cannot be distinguished and correspond to the case where $X \cap V \neq \emptyset$, $Y \cap W \neq \emptyset$, and $Z \cap U \neq \emptyset$.

c. Truth assignment (9) corresponds to the case $X \cap V \neq \emptyset$, $X \cap W \neq \emptyset$, $Y \cap U \neq \emptyset$, and $Z \cap U \neq \emptyset$.

For each of these cases, we can construct a relation $\mathbf{r}$ such that $\text{CHASE}_{m_2}(\text{CHASE}_{m_1}(\mathbf{r}))$ violates the MVD $m_1 = X \rightarrow\rightarrow Y|Z$. The relation shown in Figure 2, covers case a. The relation shown in Figure 3, covers case b. The relation shown in Figure 4, covers case c. Using the examples shown in Figures 2, 3, and 4, one can construct, in the obvious way, examples for the truth assignments which are either equivalent to or consequences of those mentioned in a, b, and c. □

$X \cap V$	$Y \cap W$	$Z \cap W$
0	0	0
1	1	1

Figure 2

$X \cap V$	$Y \cap W$	$Z \cap U$
0	0	0
0	0	1
1	1	1

Figure 3

$X \cap V$	$X \cap W$	$Y \cap U$	$Z \cap U$
0	0	0	0
0	1	1	1
1	0	1	1

Figure 4

5. Fitting It All Together

Example 1 shows that the notions of conflict-free and interaction-free MVD sets are incompatible. In this section we will show however that they do have a common ground. To do so, we need the notion of a set of MVDs having the subset property, introduced by Goodman and Tay [GT].

Let R be a relation scheme and let $\mathcal{M}$ be a set of MVDs on R. We say that $\mathcal{M}$ has the *subset property* if and only if for each pair of MVDs $X \rightarrow\rightarrow Y|Z$ and $U \rightarrow\rightarrow V|W$ in $\mathcal{M}$,

$$XY \subseteq UV \text{ and } UW \subseteq XZ$$

up to renaming of Y and Z, or V and W. †

Goodman and Tay obtained the following results:

Lemma 1. [GT] *Let R be a relation scheme and let $\mathcal{M}$ be a set of MVDs on R. If $\mathcal{M}$ has the subset property then $\mathcal{M}$ is a conflict-free MVD set.*

The converse of Lemma 1 is not true. The set $\mathcal{M}$ of MVDs of Example 1 is a conflict-free MVD set, but the MVDs $AB \rightarrow\rightarrow C|D$ and $AC \rightarrow\rightarrow B|D$ violate the subset property. However, the following is true:

Lemma 2. [GT] *Let R be a relation scheme and let $\mathcal{M}$ be a set of MVDs on R. If $\mathcal{M}$ is a conflict-free MVD set then $\mathcal{M}$ has a cover which has the subset property.*

Lemma 1, Lemma 2 and Theorem 1 together imply:

Theorem 4. [GT] *Let R be a relation scheme and let $\mathcal{M}$ be a set of MVDs on R. $\mathcal{M}$ has a cover which has the subset property if and only if $\mathcal{M}$ is equivalent to an acyclic join dependency on R.*

In the remainder of this section, we will show that results, similar to Lemma 1, Lemma 2, and Theorem 4, exists between interacion-free MVD set and sets of MVDs which have the subset property.

Lemma 3. *Let R be a relation scheme and let $\mathcal{M}$ be a set of MVDs on R. If $\mathcal{M}$ has the subset property then $\mathcal{M}$ is an interaction-free MVD set.*

---

† *i.e.*, one of the following is true:

- $XY \subseteq UV$ and $UW \subseteq XZ$
- $XY \subseteq UW$ and $UV \subseteq XZ$
- $XZ \subseteq UV$ and $UW \subseteq XY$
- $XZ \subseteq UW$ and $UV \subseteq XY$.

Proof. Let $X \to\to Y|Z$ and $U \to\to V|W \in \mathcal{M}$. Since $\mathcal{M}$ has the subset property, we may assume, without loss of generality, that $XY \subseteq UW$ and $UV \subseteq XZ$ (cf. the footnote that goes along with the definition of the subset property). Condition $XY \subseteq UW$ † implies that $X \cap V = \emptyset$ and $Y \cap V = \emptyset$. Condition $UV \subseteq XZ$ implies that $Y \cap U = \emptyset$ and $Y \cap V = \emptyset$. Hence $X \to\to Y|Z$ and $U \to\to V|W$ satisfies $X \cap V = \emptyset$, $Y \cap U = \emptyset$, and $Y \cap V = \emptyset$. The result follows from the *if* part of Theorem 3. □

Lemma 4. *Let R be a relation scheme and let $\mathcal{M}$ be a set of MVDs on R. If $\mathcal{M}$ is an interaction-free MVD set then $\mathcal{M}$ has a cover which has the subset property.*

Proof.

Consider the algorithm shown in Figure 5.

input: an interaction-free MVD set $\mathcal{M}$
output: a cover of $\mathcal{M}$ which has the subset property

function **transform**($\mathcal{M}$: **set of MVDs**): **set of MVDs**
begin
case

- $\mathcal{M}$ **contains a pair of MVDs** m_1, m_2 ($m_1 \neq m_2$) **such that** $m_1 \models m_2$:
  return(**transform**($\mathcal{M} - \{m_2\}$))
- $\mathcal{M}$ **contains a pair of MVDs** $m_1 = X \to\to Y|Z$ **and** $m_2 = X \to\to V|W$ ($m_1 \neq m_2$) **such that** m_1 **and** m_2 **violate the subset property**:
  return(**transform**($\mathcal{M} - \{X \to\to Y|Z, X \to V|W\} \cup$
  $\{X \to\to Y \cap V | Y \cap W | Z \cap V | Z \cap W\}$))
- *otherwise*: *return*($\mathcal{M}$)

end (**transform**)

Figure 5

It can easily be seen that algorithm **transform** terminates. We now prove that **transform** returns a cover of $\mathcal{M}$ which has the subset property. The proof will be by induction on the number of times **transform** is called before halting.

Induction Hypothesis: If $\mathcal{M}$ is an interaction-free MVD set and it takes $k \geq 1$ calls before **transform** with input $\mathcal{M}$ halts, then **transform** returns a cover of $\mathcal{M}$ which has the subset property.

Base Step: $k = 1$. In this case, **transform** returns from the *otherwise* clause. Thus, $\mathcal{M}$ is an interaction-free MVD set which contains no pair of MVDs $m_1 = X \to\to Y|Z$ and $m_2 = U \to\to V|W$ such that:

a. $m_1 \models m_2$, or

b. $X = U$ and m_1 and m_2 violate the subset property.

---

† Remember that X, Y, and Z are pairwise disjoint subsets such that $XYZ = R$. A similar remark is true for the sets U, V, and W

It follows form Theorem 3 that for each pair of MVDs $X \rightarrow\rightarrow Y|Z$, $U \rightarrow\rightarrow V|W \in \mathcal{M}$

$$X \cap V = \emptyset, \; Y \cap U = \emptyset, \text{ and } Y \cap V = \emptyset$$

up to renaming of Y and Z, or V and W. Conditions $X \cap V = \emptyset$ and $Y \cap V = \emptyset$ imply that $XY \subseteq UW$. Conditions $Y \cap U = \emptyset$ and $Y \cap V = \emptyset$ imply that $UV \subseteq XZ$. Thus, $\mathcal{M}$ has the subset property. Since $\mathcal{M}$ is a cover of itself, the induction hypothesis is true in this case.

Induction Step: If **transform**, with input $\mathcal{M}$, was called $k+1$ times ($k \geq 1$), then the first call must have been a call that resulted from either the first or the second statement in the *case* statement.

Assume the first call was **transform**$(\mathcal{M} - \{m_2\})$, where $m_2 \in \mathcal{M}$ and such that there exists a $m_1 \in \mathcal{M}$ ($m_1 \neq m_2$) with $m_1 \models m_2$. Clearly, $\mathcal{M} - \{m_2\}$ is a cover of $\mathcal{M}$. Since $\mathcal{M}$ is an interaction-free MVD set, so is $\mathcal{M} - \{m_2\}$. By the induction hypothesis, $\mathcal{M} - \{m_2\}$ has a cover $\mathcal{N}$ which has the subset property. Since $\mathcal{N}$ is a cover for $\mathcal{M} - \{m_2\}$ and since $\mathcal{M} - \{m_2\}$ is a cover of $\mathcal{M}$, the induction hypothesis is true in this case.

Assume the first call was

$$\mathbf{transform}(\mathcal{M} - \{X \rightarrow\rightarrow Y|Z, X \rightarrow\rightarrow V|W\} \cup \{X \rightarrow\rightarrow Y \cap V|Y \cap W|Z \cap V|Z \cap W\}$$

This implies that for any pair of MVDs m_1 and m_2 in $\mathcal{M}$, $m_1 \not\models m_2$ and $m_2 \not\models m_1$. Let $\mathcal{M}' = \mathcal{M} - \{X \rightarrow\rightarrow Y|Z, X \rightarrow\rightarrow V|W\} \cup \{X \rightarrow\rightarrow Y \cap V|Y \cap W|Z \cap V|Z \cap W\}$. It follows from the *right intersection* and *union* properties of MVDs [Ull] that $\mathcal{M}'$ is a cover for $\mathcal{M}$. It can also be verified, by using Theorem 3, that $\mathcal{M}'$ is an interaction-free MVD set (remember $\mathcal{M}$ is an interaction-free MVD set). The induction hypothesis implies that $\mathcal{M}'$ has a cover $\mathcal{N}$ which has the subset property. Since $\mathcal{M}'$ is a cover of $\mathcal{M}$, $\mathcal{N}$ is also a cover for $\mathcal{M}$ and the induction hypothesis is true. □

Lemma 3, Lemma 4, and Theorem 4 together imply:

Theorem 5. *Let R be a relation scheme and let $\mathcal{M}$ be a set of MVDs on R. $\mathcal{M}$ has a cover which is an interaction-free MVD set if and only if $\mathcal{M}$ is equivalent to an acyclic join dependency on R.*

We can now state the main result of this section:

Theorem 6. *Let R be a relation scheme. A join dependency is acyclic if and only if it is equivalent to an interaction-free MVD set.*

Proof. Follows immediately from Theorem 5 and the definition of a cover. □

6. Conclusion

Theorem 6 adds another fact to the arsenal of conditions that characterize acyclic join dependencies. In comparison to the other conditions that relate acyclic join dependencies to MVDs, we feel that the concept of interaction-free MVD sets has the advantage of providing a simple semantic characterization.

We conclude by mentioning an open problem: Is there a simple characterization for a set of MVDs which satisfies the conditions specified in Corollary 1?

References

[ABU] Aho, A.V., Beeri, C., and Ullman, J.D. "The theory of joins in relational databases. *ACM Trans. Database Syst.* *4*, 3 (Sept. 1979), 297-314.

[ADM1] Ausiello, G., D'Atri, A., and Moscarini, M. Minimal coverings of acyclic database schemata. *Advances in Database Theory, 2*, Gallaire, H., Minker, J., Nicolas, J.M., Eds, Plenum Press, New York, 1983, pp. 27-52.

[ADM2] Ausiello, G., D'Atri, A., and Moscarini, M. Chordality properties on graphs and minimal conceptual connections in semantic data models. *Proc. 4th Symp. on Princ. of Database Systems*, ACM, Portland, Oregon, 1985, 164-170.

[AP] Atzeni, P. and Parker, D.S. Properties of acyclic database schemes: an analysis. *XP2 Workshop on Relational Database Theory*, Pennsylvania State Univ., University Park, PA, 1981.

[BB] Biskup, J. and Bruggeman, H.H. Designing acyclic database schemas. *Advances in Database Theory, 2*, Gallaire, H., Minker, J., Nicolas, J.M., Eds, Plenum Press, New York, 1983, pp. 3-26.

[BDM] Batini, C., D'Atri, A., and Moscarini, M. Formal tools for top-down and bottom-up generation of acyclic relational schemata. *Proc. 7th Int. Conference on Graph-theoretic Concepts in Computer Science*, Hanser Verlag, Linz, Austria, 1981, pp. 219-229.

[BFMY] Beeri, C., Fagin, R., Maier, D., and Yannakakis, M. On the desirability of acyclic database schemes. *J. ACM 30*, 3 (July 1983), 479-513.

[BK] Beeri, C. and Kifer, M. Elimination of intersection anomalies from database schemes. *Proc. 2nd Symp. on Princ. of Database Systems*, ACM, Atlanta, 1983, pp. 340-351.

[BV] Beeri, C. and Vardi, M. On acyclic database decompositions. *Information and Control 61*, 1984, 75-84.

[DM] D'Atri, A. and Moscarini, M. On the recognition and design of acyclic databases. *Proc. 3rd Symp. on Princ. of Database Systems*, ACM, Waterloo, Ontario, 1984, pp. 1-8.

[Fag1] Fagin, R. Multivalued dependencies and a new normal form for relational databases. *ACM Trans. Database Syst. 2*, 3 (Sept. 1977), 262-278.

[Fag2] Fagin, R. Degrees of acyclicity for hypergraphs and relational database schemes. *J. ACM 30*, 3 (July 1983), 514-550.

[FMU] Fagin, R., Mendelzon, A.O., and Ullman, J.D. A simplified universal relation assumption and its properties. *ACM Trans. Database Syst. 7*, 3 (Sept. 1982), 343-360.

[GP1] Gyssens, M. and Paredaens, J. A decomposition methodology for cyclic databases. *Advances in Database Theory, 2*, Gallaire, H., Minker, J., Nicolas, J.M., Eds, Plenum Press, New York, 1983. pp. 85-122.

[GP2] Gyssens, M. and Paredaens, J. On the decomposition of join dependencies. *Proc. 3rd Symp. on Princ. of Database Systems*, ACM, Waterloo, Ontario, 1984, pp. 143-153.

[GR] Grahne, G. and Raiha, K. Dependency characterizations for acyclic database schemes. *Proc. 3rd Symp. on Princ. of Database Systems*, ACM Waterloo, Ontario, 1984, pp. 9-18.

[GT] Goodman, N. and Tay, Y.C. Synthesizing fourth normal form relations from multivalued dependencies. Harvard Technical Report TR-17-83, Harvard Univ. (May 1983).

[Kat1] Katsuno, H. When do non-conflict-free multivalued dependency sets appear? *Information Processing Letters 18* (1984), 87-92.

[Kat2] Katsuno, H. An extension of conflict-free multivalued dependency sets. *ACM Trans. on Database Syst. 9*, 2 (June 1984), 309-326.

[Lie] Lien, Y.E. On the equivalence of database models. *J. ACM 29*, 2 (Apr. 1982), 333-362.

[MMS] Maier, D., Mendelzon, A.O., and Sagiv, Y. Testing implications of data dependencies. *ACM Trans. Database Syst. 4*, 4 (Dec. 1979), 455-469.

[MU] Maier, D. and Ullman, J. Connections in acyclic hypergraphs. Stanford Technical Report STAN-CS-81-853, Stanford Univ., 1981.

[PV] Paredaens, J. and Van Gucht, D. An application of the theory of graphs and hypergraphs to the decompositions of relational database schemes. *Proc. of CAAP*, 1983, L'Aquila, 1983.

[Ris] Rissanen, J. Theory of relations for databases—A tutorial survey. In *Proc. 7th Symp. on Mathematical Foundations of Computer Science*, Lecture Notes in Computer Science 64, J. Winkowski, Ed., Springer-Verlag, pp. 537-551.

[Sac1] Sacca, D. On the recognition of coverings of acyclic database hypergraphs. *Proc. 2nd Symp. on Princ. of Database Systems*, ACM, Atlanta, Georgia, 1983, pp. 297-304.

[Sac2] Sacca, D. Closures of database hypergraphs. *J. ACM 32*, 4 (Oct. 1985), 774-803.

[Sci] Sciore, E. Real-world MVDs. In *Proc. Int. Conf. on Management of Data*, ACM, New York, 1981, pp. 121-132.

[TY] Tarjan, R.E., and Yannakakis, M. Simple linear time algorithms to test chordality of graphs, test acyclicity of hypergraphs, and selectively reduce acyclic hypergraphs, *SIAM J. Comput. 13*, (1984), 566-579.

[Yan] Yannakakis, M. Algorithms for acyclic database schemes. In *Proc. 7th Int. Conf. on Very Large Data Bases*, ACM, New York, 1981, pp. 82-94.

[YO] Yuan, L. and Ozsoyoglu, M. Unifying functional and multivalued dependencies for relational database design. To appear in *Proc. 5th Princ. on Database Systems*.

[Ull] Ullman, J.D. *Principles of Database Systems*. Rockville, MD: Computer Science Press.

[Zan] Zaniolo, C. Analysis and design of relational schemata for database systems. Ph.D. Dissertation, Univ. of California at Los Angeles, July 1976.

UPDATING LOGICAL DATABASES CONTAINING NULL VALUES

Marianne Winslett*
Stanford University, Computer Science Dept.
Stanford CA 94305 USA

Abstract. We show that it is natural to extend the concept of database updates to encompass databases with incomplete information in the form of *null values*, or tuple attribute values that are known to exist but whose exact value is not known. Our approach embeds the incomplete database and the updates in the language of mathematical logic, which we believe has strong advantages over relational tables and traditional data manipulation languages in the incomplete information situation. We present semantics for our update operators, and provide an algorithm to perform the operations. The computational complexity of the algorithm is examined, and a lazy evaluation scheme coupled with simple user–supplied cost limits is recommended to avoid undesirable expense during execution. This paper extends results presented in [Winslett 86a].

1. Introduction

Much attention has been paid to the problem of answering queries in databases containing *null values*, or attribute values that are known to lie in a certain domain but whose value is currently unknown (see e.g. [Imielinski 84], [Reiter 84]). Progress on this front has encouraged research into the problem of updating such databases; as one group of researchers aptly points out [Abiteboul 85], the problem of query answering presupposes the ability to enter incomplete information into the database, and, with any luck, to remove uncertainties when more information becomes available.

Reiter [84] sets forth a logical framework for the null value and disjunctive information problems, where databases are represented as logical theories. (Disjunctive information occurs when one knows that one or more of a set of tuples holds true, without knowing which one.) Given a relational database, Reiter shows how to construct a *relational theory* whose model corresponds to the world represented by the database, and extends this framework to allow disjunctive information and null values. The use of a logic framework has three advantages for us: it allows a clean formalization of incomplete information; it allows us to define the meanings of query and update operators without recourse to intuition or common knowledge; and it frees us from implicit or explicit consideration of implementation issues, by not forcing incomplete information into a tabular format. By framing the update question in this paradigm, we will also gain insights into the more general problem of updating general logical theories, and lay groundwork for use in applications beyond ordinary databases, such as AI applications using a knowledge base built on top of base knowledge.

This paper builds on earlier work presented elsewhere [Winslett 86a], which investigated the simplest variant of the update problem, ground updates, and therefore did not address the

---

* AT&T Bell Laboratories Scholar

problem of updating null values. As an example of when null values rather than other types of incomplete information are needed, in the supplier–parts domain, suppose we know that someone is supplying widgets, but have no idea who that mystery supplier might be—whether one of the currently known suppliers, or another supplier as yet unknown. This knowledge cannot be represented by a disjunction, as for practical purposes the set of possible suppliers may be considered infinite. We should be able to phrase this type of information easily in an update request, and the recommended formalization of incomplete information databases should be able to represent the new knowledge. Similarly, if we know that exactly one of the three companies A, B, and C supplies widgets, this information is awkward to express using disjunctions but is easily captured with null values.

In related work, Abiteboul and Grahne [Abiteboul 85] investigate the problem of updates on several varieties of *tables*, or relations containing null values and auxiliary constraints other than integrity constraints. They propose a semantics similar to our own for simple updates, and investigate the relationship between table type and ability to represent the result of an update correctly and completely. They do not consider updates with joins or disjunctions in selection clauses, comparisons between attribute values, or selection clauses referencing tuples other than the tuple being updated. Their conclusion was that only the most powerful and complex version of tables was able to fully support their update operators.

This work is also related to that of Fagin et al [Fagin 83, 84], differing chiefly in the choice of semantics for updates and in the inclusion of a constructive algorithm for update computation. We base the semantics of updates on the contents of the models of the theory being updated; Fagin et al lend more importance to the particular formulas currently in the theory, producing a more syntactically oriented approach. The effect of an update in our paradigm is independent of the choice of formulas (other than schema and integrity constraints) used to represent that set of models. Another difference concerns our identification of two levels of formulas in a theory—axioms and non-axioms—and the provision of very different algorithmic manipulations for the two types of formulas during an update.

In the remainder of this paper, we will set forth an update capability for a formalization of databases with incomplete information. Extended relational theories, presented in Section 2, are an extension to Reiter's theories for disjunctive information and null values in which history predicates may appear in formulas in the theory for the database and in which formulas other than simple disjunctions may appear, thus allowing a much broader class of models for the theories. In Section 3.1 we set forth a data manipulation language for updates to extended relational theories, and give model–theoretic definitions of the meaning of updates in Section 3.2. Section 3.3 presents an update algorithm that implements these semantics. The algorithm is shown to be correct in the sense that the alternative worlds produced by updates under this algorithm are the same as those produced by updating each alternative world individually. Section 4 discusses the computational complexity of the update algorithm, and gives practical methods for controlling and reducing that cost during execution.

This paper is self–contained, and hence overlaps [Winslett 86a] for much of the introductory material. An update algorithm for use under the open–world assumption, along with a discussion of the treatment of dependencies and rules under update in the context of knowledge bases for artificial intelligence, will appear as [Winslett 86b].

2. Extended Relational Theories

We now give a formal presentation of our extension to Reiter's theories, called *extended relational theories*. Extended relational theories are sufficiently powerful to represent any set of relational databases all having the same schema and integrity constraints.

2.1. The Language

The language $\mathcal{L}$ for the theories contains the following strings of symbols:

1. An infinite set of *variables*, for use in axioms.

2. An infinite set of *constants*. These represent the elements in the domains of database attributes, plus extras for internal extended relational theory use.

3. A finite set of *database predicates* of arity 1 or more, representing the attributes and relations of the database.

4. Punctuation symbols '(', ')', and ','.

5. Logical connectives, quantifiers, truth values, and the equality predicate: $\wedge$, $\vee$, $\neg$, $\rightarrow$, $\leftrightarrow$, $\forall$, $\exists$, T, F, and $=$.

6. For each database predicate R (item 3 above), one *history predicate* H_R of arity one greater than R. Also, a unary history predicate H. The history predicates are a convenience feature that will make updates easier to perform.

7. An infinite set of *Skolem constants* ϵ, ϵ_1, ϵ_2, ϵ_3, ... Skolem constants are the logical formulation of null values; they represent existentially quantified variables. For example, if a logical theory consists of the two wffs $R(\epsilon, c_1)$ and $R(c_2, \epsilon) \vee R(\epsilon_2, \epsilon_3)$, then this theory has the same models as the wff $\exists x_1 \exists x_2 \exists x_3 (R(x_1, c_1) \wedge (R(c_2, x_1) \vee R(x_2, x_3)))$. $\diamond$

We now present a few definitions needed in the remainder of this paper.

Atomic formulas are well-formed formulas (wffs) without logical connectives. We consider Skolem constants to be functions; hence Skolem constants may appear in atomic formulas. For the purposes of this paper, *atoms* are atomic formulas without variables as arguments. Similarly, *datoms* are atoms *over database predicates.* For example, $R(\epsilon)$ and $R(c)$ are datoms; $R(x)$, $H_R(c)$, and $\epsilon = c$ are not datoms.

Definition. σ is a *substitution* if σ defines a syntactic replacement of distinct Skolem constants by constants and Skolem constants. In traditional form σ applied to a wff α is written $(\alpha)^{\epsilon_1 \cdots \epsilon_n}_{c_1 \cdots c_n}$ or more concisely as $(\alpha)_\sigma$. The *wff form* of σ is the wff $(\epsilon_1 = c_1) \wedge \cdots \wedge (\epsilon_n = c_n)$. The wff form of the identity substitution (i.e., where no substitutions are specified) is the truth value T. If σ does not substitute any Skolem constants for Skolem constants, then σ is a *constant substitution.*

In the discussions that follow, σ will be assumed to be in wff form whenever that follows logically from the context; for example, assume σ is in wff form when it appears in $\alpha \wedge \sigma$.

On occasion we will speak of a more exotic type of syntactic replacement, that of one datom for another. For example, $(\alpha)^{R(c)}_{H_R(c,d)}$ calls for the replacement of all occurrences of $R(c)$ in α by the history atom $H_R(c,d)$. A datom substitution has no wff form. Datom substitutions will be so designated explicitly in the text.

A datom f appears *explicitly* in a wff α if f is syntactically present in α. For example, $R(\epsilon)$ appears explicitly in the wff $R(\epsilon) \wedge (\epsilon = c)$. If f does not appear explicitly in α, but there is a substitution σ such that f appears explicitly in $(\alpha)_\sigma$, then f appears *implicitly* in α. For example, $R(c)$ and $R(d)$ appear implicitly in $R(\epsilon) \wedge \epsilon = c$. All future references to the appearance of a datom f in a wff mean explicit appearances, unless otherwise noted.

2.2. Extended Relational Theories

Extended relational theories, an extension of Reiter's relational theories [Reiter 84], encode the semantics of databases with incomplete information. A theory $\mathcal{T}$ over $\mathcal{L}$ is an *extended relational theory* if $\mathcal{T}$ has exactly the following wffs:

1. *Unique Name Axioms:* For each pair of distinct constants c_1, c_2 in $\mathcal{L}$, $\mathcal{T}$ contains the unique name axiom $c_1 \neq c_2$.

2. *Completion Axioms:* To implement a version of the closed-world assumption so that we may prove certain atomic formulas to be false, $\mathcal{T}$ must include axioms stating that the only datoms that may be true in a model of $\mathcal{T}$ are those given somewhere in $\mathcal{T}$. This means that

any atom not appearing implicitly or explicitly in $\mathcal{T}$ should be false in all models of $\mathcal{T}$. More precisely, for each n-ary database predicate R of $\mathcal{T}$, either $\mathcal{T}$ contains an axiom of the form $\forall x_1 \cdots \forall x_n \neg R(x_1, \ldots, x_n)$ or else for some nonempty set of constants and Skolem constants $c_{11}, c_{12}, \ldots, c_{mn}$, $\mathcal{T}$ contains exactly one axiom of the form

$$\begin{aligned}
&\forall x_1 \forall x_2 \ldots \forall x_n (R(x_1, x_2, \ldots, x_n) \rightarrow \\
&\quad (((x_1 = c_{11}) \wedge (x_2 = c_{12}) \wedge \ldots \wedge (x_n = c_{1n})) \vee \\
&\quad ((x_1 = c_{21}) \wedge (x_2 = c_{22}) \wedge \ldots \wedge (x_n = c_{2n})) \vee \\
&\qquad \ldots \qquad \vee \\
&\quad ((x_1 = c_{m1}) \wedge (x_2 = c_{m2}) \wedge \ldots \wedge (x_n = c_{mn})))).
\end{aligned}$$

Further, $((x_1 = c_{i1}) \wedge (x_2 = c_{i2}) \wedge \cdots \wedge (x_n = c_{in}))$ is a disjunct of the axiom iff $R(c_{i1}, c_{i2}, \ldots, c_{in})$ appears explicitly in $\mathcal{T}$. In this case we say that $R(c_{i1}, c_{i2}, \ldots, c_{in})$ is *represented* in the axiom.

For example, $\forall x (R(x) \rightarrow ((x = c) \vee (x = \epsilon_1)))$ is a legal completion axiom. Note that the completion axioms of $\mathcal{T}$ may be derived mechanically from the rest of $\mathcal{T}$.

3. *Body:* The body of $\mathcal{T}$ may be any finite set of wffs of $\mathcal{L}$ without variables. For example, with the completion axiom given just above, the body might be the wff $\neg (R(c) \wedge R(\epsilon_1))$. ◇

In an implementation of extended relational theories, we would not actually store the unique name or completion axioms. Rather, the axioms formalize our intuitions about the behavior of a query and update processor operating on the body of the extended relational theory. For example, PROLOG is a query processor that shares our unique name axioms, but has an entirely different closed–world assumption.

Though the models of $\mathcal{T}$ look like possible states of databases consistent with the known information, not everything in a model of $\mathcal{T}$ is an instantiated consequence of known facts, due to the presence of history predicates. For this reason we define an *alternative world* of $\mathcal{T}$ as a model of $\mathcal{T}$ minus the equality and history predicates:

Definition. Let σ be a substitution of constants for all the Skolem constants of a theory $\mathcal{T}$. Then $\mathcal{A}$ is an *alternative world* of $\mathcal{T}$ if $\mathcal{A}$ is a set of truth valuations for all the datoms in $\mathcal{L}$, such that those valuations are satisfied in some model $\mathcal{M}$ of $\mathcal{T}$. If this relationship holds between $\mathcal{A}$ and $\mathcal{M}$, then we say that $\mathcal{M}$ *represents* $\mathcal{A}$. ◇

Intuitively, an alternative world is a snapshot of the tuples of a complete–information relational database. The alternative worlds of an extended relational theory look like a set of ordinary relational databases all having the same schema and axioms.

With the inclusion of history predicates in $\mathcal{L}$ (as a convenience feature that makes updates easier to perform) we depart from Reiter's paradigm. Because these predicates are "invisible" in alternative worlds, there may not be a one–to–one correspondence between the models of a relational theory and its alternative worlds, as two models may give the same truth valuations to all datoms without Skolem constants but differ on some history atoms without Skolem constants, and still represent the same alternative world. Alternative worlds contain just the information that would be of interest to a database user, while models may be cluttered with history atoms of no external interest.

3. A Language for Updates

We now present a data manipulation language based on first–order logic, which is an extension of the language LDML presented in earlier work [Winslett 86a]. Appropriate subsets of traditional data manipulation languages such as SQL and INGRES may be embedded in this language.

3.1. Update Syntax

Let ϕ and ω be formulas over $\mathcal{L}$ without history predicates or variables. Then an *update* takes the form INSERT ω WHERE ϕ.

The reader may wonder what has happened to the traditional relational data manipulation operations of MODIFY and DELETE. Under the semantics presented below, any DELETE or MODIFY request can be phrased as an INSERT request, using negation. To simplify the presentation, DELETE and MODIFY are omitted right from the start.

Examples. Suppose the database schema has two relations, Mgr(Manager, Department) and Emp(Employee, Department). Then the following are updates, with their approximate intended semantics offered in italics:

INSERT Emp(Reid,ϵ) $\wedge$ (ϵ=CSD $\vee$ ϵ=EE) WHERE $\neg$Mgr(Nilsson,CSL). *In those alternative worlds where Nilsson doesn't manage CSL, insert the fact that Reid is in one of CSD and EE.*

INSERT $\neg$Emp(Reid,ϵ) WHERE $\neg$Mgr(Nilsson,ϵ) $\wedge$ Emp(Reid,ϵ). *For some department Nilsson manages, delete the fact that Reid is in that department.*

INSERT F WHERE $\neg$Emp(Reid,CSL). *Eliminate all alternative worlds where Reid isn't in CSL.*

INSERT $\neg$Emp(Reid,CSL) $\wedge$Emp(Reid,ϵ) WHERE Emp(Reid,CSL). *In any alternative worlds where Reid was in CSL, reduce that belief to just believing that he is in some department.*

INSERT $\neg$Emp(Reid,ϵ) WHERE T. *Insert the fact that Reid is not a member of every department.*

3.2. Update Semantics

We define the semantics of an update operating on an extended relational theory $\mathcal{T}$ by its desired effect on the models of $\mathcal{T}$. In particular, the alternative worlds of the updated relational theory must be the same as those obtained by applying the update separately to each original alternative world. In database terms, this may be rephrased as follows: The database with incomplete information represents a (possibly infinite) set of alternative worlds, or complete-information relational databases, each different and each one possibly the real, unknown world. The correct result of an update is that obtained by storing a separate database for each alternative world and running the update in parallel on each separate database. A necessary and sufficient guarantee of correctness for any more efficient and practical method of update processing is that it produce the same results for updates as the parallel computation method. Equivalently, we require that the diagram below be commutative: both paths from upper-left-hand corner to lower-right-hand corner must produce the same result.

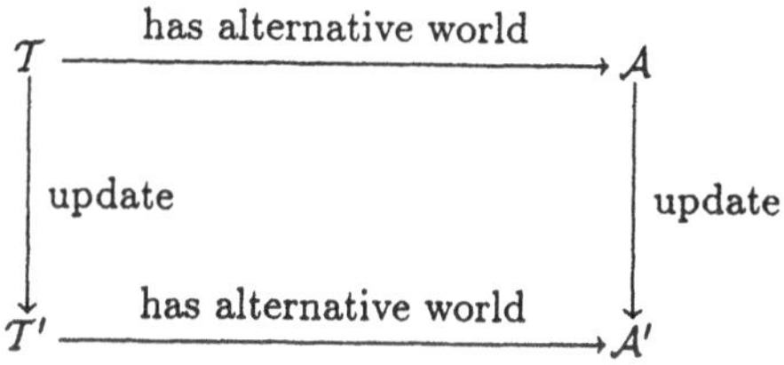

The general criteria guiding our choice of semantics are, first, that the semantics agree with traditional semantics in the case where the update request is to insert or delete a single atom, or to modify one atom to be another. Second, an update cannot directly change the truth valuations of any atoms except those that unify[†] with atoms of ω. For example, the update INSERT Emp(Reid, CSD) WHERE T cannot change the department of any employee but Reid, and cannot change the truth valuation of formulas such as Mgr(Nilsson, CSD).

The other important criterion is that the new information in ω is to represent the *most exact and most recent state of knowledge obtainable* about the atoms that the update inserts; and the update is to *override all previous information* about these atoms. These criteria have a syntactic component: one should not necessarily expect two updates with logically equivalent ωs to produce the same results. For example, the update INSERT T WHERE T is different from INSERT Emp(Reid, CSD)$\vee\neg$Emp(Reid, CSD) WHERE T; one update reports no change in the information available about Reid's department, and the other reports that whether Reid is in CSD is now unknown.

An intuitive motivation is in order for our method of handling Skolem constants. The essential idea is that if the user only had more information, the user would not be requesting an update containing Skolem constants, but rather an ordinary update without Skolem constants. Under this assumption, the correct way to handle an update U with Skolem constants is to consider all the possible Skolem-constant-free updates represented by U and execute each of those in parallel, collecting the alternative worlds so produced in one large set. Then the result of the update the user would have requested had more information been available is guaranteed to be in that set.

For a formal definition of semantics that meets the criteria outlined in this section, let U be an update and let $\mathcal{M}$ be a model of an extended relational theory $\mathcal{T}$. Let σ be a substitution of constants for exactly the Skolem constants of ϕ, ω, and $\mathcal{T}$, such that $\mathcal{M}$ is a model of $(\mathcal{T})_\sigma$, that is, a model of the theory resulting from applying the substitution σ to each formula in $\mathcal{T}$. [††] Then for each pair $\mathcal{M}$ and σ, $\mathcal{S}$ is the set of models produced by applying U to $\mathcal{M}$ as follows: If $(\phi)_\sigma$ is false in $\mathcal{M}$, then $\mathcal{S}$ contains one model, $\mathcal{M}$. Otherwise, $\mathcal{S}$ contains exactly every model $\mathcal{M}^*$ such that

(1) $\mathcal{M}^*$ agrees with $\mathcal{M}$ on the truth valuations of all Skolem-constant-free atoms except possibly those in $(\omega)_\sigma$; and

(2) $(\omega)_\sigma$ is true in $\mathcal{M}^*$, and $\mathcal{M}^*$ still satisfies the unique name axioms.

Example. If the agent observes INSERT Emp(Reid, CSD) $\vee$ Emp(Reid, EE) WHERE T, then three models are created from each model $\mathcal{M}$ of $\mathcal{T}$: one where Reid is in both CSD and EE, one where Reid is just in CSD, and one where Reid is just in EE—regardless of whether Reid was in CSD or EE in $\mathcal{M}$ originally.

Example. If $\forall x \neg R(x)$ is true in $\mathcal{M}$ and we then insert $R(\epsilon_1) \vee R(\epsilon_2)$ into $\mathcal{M}$, then $\mathcal{S}$ will contain every model $\mathcal{M}^*$ such that just one or two Skolem-constant-free atoms of R are true in $\mathcal{M}^*$, with truth valuations for other datoms unchanged.

For simplicity we have defined the semantics of U in terms of its effect on the model $\mathcal{M}$ rather than in terms of its effect on the alternative world of $\mathcal{M}$. However, because the semantics are independent of the truth valuations of history atoms in $\mathcal{M}$, U will have the same effect (i.e., produce the same alternative worlds) on *every* model representing the same alternative world as $\mathcal{M}$.

The remarks at the beginning of this section on correctness of update processing may be summed up in the following definition:

Definition. The execution of an update U against an extended relational theory $\mathcal{T}$, producing a new theory $\mathcal{T}'$, is correct and complete iff $\mathcal{T}'$ is an extended relational theory and

---

[†] In this formulation, two atoms a and b unify if there exists a substitution σ for the Skolem constants of a and b under which a and b are syntactically identical.

[††] Since Skolem constants do not appear directly in models, the purpose of σ is to associate the Skolem constants in U with specific constants in $\mathcal{M}$, so that the agent can directly refer to entities such as "that department that we earlier noted that Reid is in, though we didn't know exactly which department it was."

the alternative worlds of T' are exactly those alternative worlds represented by the union of the models in the S sets.

3.3. The Update Algorithm

The semantics presented in the previous section describe the effect of an update on the *models* of a theory; the semantics give no hints whatsoever on how to translate that effect into changes in the extended relational theory. An algorithm for performing updates cannot proceed by generating models from the theory and updating them directly, because it may require exponential time to generate even one model (since satisfiability testing is involved) and there may be an exponential number of non-isomorphic models. Any update algorithm must find a more efficient way of implementing these semantics.

The *Update Algorithm* proposed in this section for incorporating updates into an extended relational theory T may be summarized as follows: *For each atom f appearing in T that unifies with an atom of ω, replace all occurrences of f in T by a history atom.* † *Then add a new formula to T that defines the correct truth valuation of f when ϕ is false, and another formula to give the correct valuation of f when ϕ is true.*

Before a more formal presentation of the Update Algorithm, let us motivate its workings in a series of examples that will illustrate the problems and principles underlying the algorithm. Let the body of T be ¬ Emp(Reid, CSL), and the new update be `INSERT` Emp(Reid, CSL) `WHERE` T.

One's natural instinct is to add $\phi \rightarrow \omega$ to T, because the update says that ω is to be true in all alternative worlds where ϕ is true now. Unfortunately, ω probably contradicts the rest of T. For example, adding T→ Emp(Reid, CSL) to T makes T inconsistent. Evidently ω may contradict parts of T, and those parts must be removed from T; in this case it would suffice to simply remove the formula ¬ Emp(Reid, CSL).

But suppose that the body of T contains more complicated formulas: Mgr(Nilsson, CSD)↔ ¬ Emp(Reid,CSD) and Mgr(Nilsson, CSL)↔ ¬ Emp(Reid,CSD). One cannot simply excise ¬ Emp(Reid, CSL) or replace it by a truth value without changing the models for the remaining atoms of T; but by the semantics for updates, no datom truth valuation except that of Emp(Reid, CSL) can be affected by the requested update. Contradictory wffs may be ferreted out and removed by a process such as that used in [Weber 86]; however, in the worst case such a process will multiply the space required to store the theory by a factor that is exponential in the number of atoms in the update.

The solution to this problem is to replace all occurrences of Emp(Reid, CSL) in T by another atom. However, the atom used must not be part of any alternative world, as otherwise the replacement might change that atom's truth valuation. This is where the special history predicates of $\mathcal{L}$ come into play; we can replace each atom of ω by a history atom throughout T, and make only minimal changes in the truth valuations in the alternative worlds of T. In the current case, Emp(Reid, CSL) is replaced by H_{Emp}(Reid, CSL, U), where U is a unique ID for the current update. †† For convenience, we will write H_{Emp}(Reid, CSL, U) as H(Emp(Reid, CSL), U), to avoid the subscript. The datom substitution that replaces every datom f of ω by its history atom $H(f, U)$ is called the *history substitution* and is written σ_H.

Let's now look at a slightly more complicated update U: `INSERT` Emp(Reid, CSL) `WHERE` Mgr(Nilsson, CSL), when T contains just ¬ Emp(Reid, CSL). As just explained, the first step is to replace this body by (¬ Emp(Reid, CSL))$_{\sigma_H}$, i.e., ¬ H(Emp(Reid, CSL), U).

---

† These history atoms are not visible externally, i.e., they may not appear in updates; they are for internal extended relational theory use only.

†† If the argument U were not present, then a similar substitution in a later update involving Emp(Reid, CSL) would make big changes in the alternative worlds of T at that time.

Within a model $\mathcal{M}$ of $\mathcal{T}$, this step interchanges the truth valuations of every datom f in ω and its history atom $H(f,U)$; if ϕ was true in $\mathcal{M}$ initially, then $(\phi)_{\sigma_H}$ is now true in $\mathcal{M}$.

It is now possible to act on the original algorithmic intuition and add $(\phi)_{\sigma_H} \rightarrow \omega$ to the body of $\mathcal{T}$, establishing correct truth valuations for the atoms of ω in models where ϕ was true initially. In the employee example, the body of $\mathcal{T}$ now contains the two formulas $\neg H$(Emp(Reid, CSL), U) and Mgr(Nilsson, CSL)→ Emp(Reid, CSL).

Unfortunately, the fact that if Nilsson is *not* the manager of CSL then Reid is *not* in CSL has been lost! The solution is to also add formulas governing truth valuations for atoms in ω when ϕ is false: Add $(f \leftrightarrow H(f,U)) \vee (\phi)_{\sigma_H}$ to $\mathcal{T}$ for each atom f in ω. Then $\mathcal{T}$ contains $\neg H$(Emp(Reid, CSL), U), Mgr(Nilsson, CSL)→ Emp(Reid, CSL), and (Emp(Reid, CSL)↔ H(Emp(Reid,CSL), U)) ∨ Mgr(Nilsson, CSL).

Yet another problem remains, for this theory has models in which Nilsson manages CSL, even though the original theory disallowed that. The solution is for the new completion axioms to represent all atoms in the update, which in this case means adding a disjunct for Mgr(Nilsson, CSL). In addition, ¬ Mgr(Nilsson, CSL) must be added to the body of $\mathcal{T}$. This is best accomplished at the very beginning of the update process, before the history substitution is applied. If we retroactively add this wff, $\mathcal{T}$ now has the desired alternative worlds.

The informal algorithm proposed so far does not work when Skolem constants are present in either the theory or the update. The basic difficulty is that one must update every atom in the theory that unifies with something in ω, since truth valuations for that atom might possibly be changed by the new update. For example, suppose the body of $\mathcal{T}$ contains the formula Mgr(Nilsson, ϵ), and the new update is `INSERT` ¬ Mgr(Nilsson, CSL) `WHERE` T. In other words, Nilsson was known to manage some department, and is now known not to manage CSL, quite possibly because he has just resigned that position.† A moment's thought shows that quite possibly Nilsson now manages no departments (e.g., if he has retired), and so the formula Mgr(Nilsson, ϵ), which unifies with Mgr(Nilsson, CSL), must be changed in some way; ($\epsilon \neq$ CSL)→ Mgr(Nilsson, ϵ) is the obvious replacement. In the general case, it is necessary to replace all atoms in $\mathcal{T}$ that unify with datoms of ω by history atoms as part of the history substitution step.

Let's examine one final example. Suppose the theory initially contains the wff Mgr(Nilsson, CSL) and the new update takes the form `INSERT` Mgr(Nilsson, ϵ) `WHERE` T, implying that Nilsson may now manage another department. As the first step, Mgr(Nilsson, ϵ) is to be added to the completion axioms; but it will not do to follow the suggested procedure of adding ¬ Mgr(Nilsson, ϵ) to the body of $\mathcal{T}$, because this would permanently eliminate the possibility that ϵ is CSL, which is not implied by the update. This problem arises because Mgr(Nilsson, ϵ) already appears implicitly in $\mathcal{T}$. The solution is to add the wff Mgr(Nilsson, ϵ)→ (ϵ = CSL) to the body of $\mathcal{T}$, that is, to add the fact that if Nilsson already manages a department ϵ, then ϵ must be a department already mentioned in $\mathcal{T}$ as a possible candidate for his management.

Continuing with the suggested algorithm, a theory is produced containing the four formulas H(Mgr(Nilsson, ϵ), U)→ (ϵ = CSL), H(Mgr(Nilsson, CSL), U), T→ Mgr(Nilsson, ϵ), and (Mgr(Nilsson, ϵ)↔ H(Mgr(Nilsson, ϵ), U))∨ T. Unfortunately, this theory has models where Mgr(Nilsson, CSL) is false! The problem is that the algorithm does not yet properly take care of the alternative worlds where ϵ is not bound to CSL; in those worlds, Mgr(Nilsson, CSL) must still be true, regardless of what the new information in the update may be. The

† In other words, the update leaves open the possibility that the underlying state of the world has changed. To say that Nilsson does not manage ϵ, while retaining the belief that Nilsson manages some department, the appropriate update is `INSERT F WHERE` ¬ Mgr(Nilsson, CSL); this new update says that the state of the world has not changed, but that we now have more information about its state. Although both updates talk about Nilsson's department, their semantics are quite different.

solution is to add $(\epsilon \neq \text{CSL}) \rightarrow (\text{Mgr(Nilsson, CSL)} \leftrightarrow H(\text{Mgr(Nilsson, CSL)}, U))$ to $\mathcal{T}$, and in fact this new theory has the desired alternative worlds.

The lessons of the preceding examples may be summarized as an algorithm for executing an update U given by `INSERT` ω `WHERE` ϕ against an extended relational theory $\mathcal{T}$. First a bit of terminology: if atoms f and g unify with one another under substitutions σ_1 and σ_2, then σ_1 is *more general* than σ_2 if σ_1 contains fewer substitutions than σ_2.

The Update Algorithm

Step 1. Add to completion axioms. To maintain the closed–world assumption, all datoms in ω and ϕ need to be represented in the completion axioms of $\mathcal{T}$. First change the body of $\mathcal{T}$ to reflect the new completion axioms: for each atom g appearing in ω or ϕ but not in $\mathcal{T}$, let Σ_0 be the set of the most general substitutions σ such that for some datom f appearing in $\mathcal{T}$, f unifies with g under σ. If Σ_0 is the empty set, then add $\neg g$ to the body of $\mathcal{T}$; otherwise, add the wff

$$g \rightarrow \bigvee_{\sigma \in \Sigma_0} \sigma \tag{1}$$

to the body of $\mathcal{T}$. Then for every datom g of $\mathcal{T}$ not represented in the completion axioms, add a disjunct representing g to those axioms. Call the resulting theory $\mathcal{T}'$.

Example. If ω contains the datom $R(a, \epsilon_2, \epsilon_1)$, and the body of $\mathcal{T}$ contains the datoms $R(\epsilon_3, c, \epsilon_4)$ and $R(\epsilon_4, c, c)$, then add $R(a, \epsilon_2, \epsilon_1) \rightarrow ((a = \epsilon_3) \wedge (\epsilon_2 = c) \wedge (\epsilon_1 = \epsilon_4)) \vee ((a = \epsilon_4) \wedge (\epsilon_2 = c) \wedge (\epsilon_1 = c))$ to the body of $\mathcal{T}$, and add the disjunct $(x_1 = a) \wedge (x_2 = \epsilon_2) \wedge (x_3 = \epsilon_1)$ to the completion axiom for R. Intuitively, Formula (1) says that if g is true in some model of $\mathcal{T}$, this must be because g has unified with a prexisting atom of $\mathcal{T}$ in that model.

Step 2. Make history. For each atom f appearing in $\mathcal{T}'$ and unifying with an atom of ω, replace all occurrences of f in the body of $\mathcal{T}$ by the history atom $H(f, U)$. In other words, replace the body $\mathcal{B}$ of $\mathcal{T}$ by $(\mathcal{B})_{\sigma_H}$.

Step 3. Define the scope of the update. Add the wff $(\phi)_{\sigma_H} \rightarrow \omega$ to $\mathcal{T}'$.

Step 4. Restrict the scope of the update. For each datom f appearing in σ_H, let Σ be the set of all most general substitutions σ under which f unifies with an atom of ω. Add the wff

$$(f \leftrightarrow H(f, U)) \vee ((\phi)_{\sigma_H} \wedge \bigvee_{\sigma \in \Sigma} \sigma) \tag{2}$$

to $\mathcal{T}'$. Intuitively, for f an atom that might possibly have its truth valuation changed by update U, formula (2) says that the truth valuation of f can change only in a model where ϕ was true originally, and further that in any model so created, f must be unified with an atom of ω. $\diamond$

Example. Let the body of $\mathcal{T}$ be the wff $\neg$Emp(Reid, CSD)$\wedge$Emp(Reid, CSL)$\wedge$Mgr(Nilsson, ϵ), and the update be `INSERT` Emp(Reid, ϵ)$\wedge(\epsilon \neq$ EE) `WHERE` T. Then the alternative worlds of $\mathcal{T}$ initially consist of all worlds where Reid is in CSL and Nilsson manages some one department. After the update, the alternative worlds should be those where Reid is in CSL and Reid is in a department managed by Nilsson, and that department is not EE.

Step 1. Add the wff Emp(Reid, ϵ)$\rightarrow ((\epsilon =$ CSD$) \vee (\epsilon =$ CSL$))$ to the body of $\mathcal{T}$, and the corresponding disjunct to the completion axiom.

Step 2. Replace Emp(Reid, CSD), Emp(Reid, CSL), and Emp(Reid, ϵ) by H(Emp(Reid, CSD), U), H(Emp(Reid, CSL), U), and H(Emp(Reid, ϵ), U) respectively. The body of $\mathcal{T}'$ now contains the two wffs $\neg H$(Emp(Reid, CSD), U)$\wedge H$(Emp(Reid, CSL), U) $\wedge$ Mgr(Nilsson, ϵ) and H(Emp(Reid, ϵ), U) $\rightarrow ((\epsilon =$ CSD$) \vee (\epsilon =$ CSL$))$.

Step 3. Add the wff $(\phi)_{\sigma_H} \rightarrow \omega$ (i.e., T$\rightarrow$ (Emp(Reid, ϵ)$\wedge(\epsilon \neq$ EE))) to the body of $\mathcal{T}'$.

Step 4. Add to T' the three wffs (Emp(Reid, ϵ)$\leftrightarrow H$(Emp(Reid, ϵ), U)) $\vee$T, (Emp(Reid, CSD)$\leftrightarrow H$(Emp(Reid, CSD), U)) $\vee$ (ϵ = CSD), and (Emp(Reid, CSL)$\leftrightarrow H$(Emp(Reid, CSL), U)) $\vee$ (ϵ = CSL). The update is now complete, and T' has the correct alternative worlds. ◇

The models of T' produced by the Update Algorithm always represent exactly the alternative worlds that U is defined to produce from T:

Theorem 1. Given an extended relational theory T and an update U, the Update Algorithm correctly and completely performs U. In particular,

(1) the Update Algorithm produces a legal extended relational theory T';

(2) The alternative worlds of T' are the same as the alternative worlds produced by directly updating the models of T. ◇

The proof of Theorem 1 is quite lengthy and we omit it here.

4. Controlling Computational Costs

We first examine the computational complexity of the Update Algorithm, then briefly look at ways to control the size of the extended relational theories produced by the Update Algorithm.

4.1. Computational Complexity of the Update Algorithm

Let k be the number of instances of atoms in the update U (its *size*); and let R be the maximum number of distinct datoms of T over the same predicate. When T and U contain no Skolem constants, the Update Algorithm will process U in time $\mathcal{O}(k\log(R))$ (the same asymptotic cost as for ordinary database updates) and increase the size of T by $\mathcal{O}(k)$ worst case. This is not to say that an $\mathcal{O}(k\log(R))$ implementation of updates is the best choice; rather, it is advisable to devote extra time to heuristics for minimizing the length of the formulas to be added to T. Nonetheless, a worst-case time estimate for the algorithm is informative, as it tells us how much time must be devoted to the algorithm proper.

When Skolem constants appear in T or in U, the controlling factor in costs is the number of atoms of T that unify with atoms of U. If n atoms of T each unify with one atom of U, then T will grow by $\mathcal{O}(n+k)$. In the worst case, *every* atom of T may unify with *every* atom of U, in which case after a series of m updates, the number of occurrences of atoms in T may *multiply* by $\mathcal{O}(mk)$. Theorem 2 summarizes these properties.

Theorem 2. Let T be an extended relational theory containing n different datoms (not occurrences of datoms) having Skolem constants as arguments. Let k be a constant that is an upper bound on the size of updates. Then under a series of m updates not contining Skolem constants, the size of T may increase by $\mathcal{O}(nmk)$. Under a series of m updates, the size of T may increase by $\mathcal{O}(nmk+m^2k^2)$. ◇

Proof of Theorem 2. (Sketch) The number of datoms containing Skolem constants determines the size of Σ_0 in Step 1. Any datom of an update U can appear implicitly in at most n datoms of T. If no update contains Skolem constants, then this means that Step 1 can add as many as $\mathcal{O}(nmk)$ occurrences of atomic formulas to T'. If the updates contain Skolem constants, then each update can add k datoms containing Skolem constants to T, so that the first update after U may have a Σ_0 of size $n+k$, the second may have size $n+2k$, and so on. After m updates, the size of this compounding factor is $\mathcal{O}(m^2k^2)$.

Step 4 also involves a set of substitutions, but this set is not asymptotically larger than that of Step 1, in the worst case. ◇

Assuming that any datom may be located in T in $\mathcal{O}(\log R)$ time, it follows that the running time of the Update Algorithm is $\mathcal{O}(kn\log(R))$ worst case. This estimate assumes that the history step (Step 2) is optimized through special data structures [Winslett 86a]: The body of the extended relational theory must be represented as a set of logical relationships between *pointers*. All occurrences of a single datom in the body are linked together in a chain of pointers; only the head of the chain points to the tuple record for the actual datom.

Happily, a large class of common types of updates—those with very simple ω and ϕ—can be performed in $\mathcal{O}(k \log(R))$ time per update; Abiteboul and Grahne [Abiteboul 85] examine a subset of these simple updates. For the general case, however, potential growth of $\mathcal{O}(nmk)$ in the size of $\mathcal{T}$ is much too large, yet is unavoidable if the effect of the update is to be represented directly in the extended relational theory, for every datom of $\mathcal{T}$ that appears implicitly in the update *must* be changed in some way in $\mathcal{T}$. In some sense the information content of a single update is no more than its size, k, and so growth of more than $\mathcal{O}(mk)$ after m updates is too much. We can achieve growth of no more than $\mathcal{O}(mk)$ by simply storing the updates without incorporating them into $\mathcal{T}$. However, since query answering presupposes some means of integrating updates with the rest of the database to allow satisfiability testing, a means of at least temporary incorporation must be offered. We have devised a scheme of delayed evaluation and simplification of expensive updates, by bounding the permissible number of unifications for the atoms of an incoming update. Examples of this lazy evaluation technique are given in the next section.

4.2. Lazy Evaluation of Updates

The algorithms required for delayed execution of updates are very intricate: an inclusion of them here would double the length of this opus. For that reason, we confine our discussion of delayed execution to a high-level overview followed by a series of simple examples illustrating the potential benefits afforded by lazy evaluation.

The first element of a system for cost reduction of too-expensive updates is a cost evaluation function, so that we can decide which updates are too expensive to execute. If an incoming update U is determined to be too expensive, we will not execute U, but instead set U aside in the hopes that either no queries will be asked that require processing U completely, or intervening updates will reduce the cost of U sufficiently before we have to execute it.

The main data structure for this *lazy evaluation scheme* is the *lazy graph*, a directed acyclic graph that keeps track of data dependencies between updates. The lazy graph helps minimize the amount of updating we have to perform before executing an incoming query Q, and keeps track of relevant update sequencing information. Some examples will clarify the potential benefits.

Example. The effect of the two updates `INSERT` Emp(Reid, CSD) `WHERE` T and `INSERT` $\neg$Emp(Reid, CSD) `WHERE` T is dependent upon the order in which they are executed; if we store these two away for lazy execution, we must make sure that any eventual processing of them is done in the order in which they were received. On the other hand, neither of these two conflicts with the update `INSERT` Emp(Reid, CSL) `WHERE` T, which could be performed before, after, or between the other two.

This example suggests a parallel between lazy evaluation sequencing control and concurrency control. The main difference is that in database concurrency control, any execution equivalent to some serial execution is correct, while sequencing control requires that the execution be equivalent to the original update input order.

Example. Suppose the update U': `INSERT` $\epsilon =$ CSD `WHERE` T is received while the update U: `INSERT` Emp(Reid, ϵ) `WHERE` T is still unexecuted. Unlike information about the truth valuations of datoms, information about the bindings of Skolem constants is permanent and once asserted can never be refuted, only refined. (For example, if the user follows U by the update `ASSERT` $\epsilon =$ CSL, then $\mathcal{T}$ will become inconsistent.) This pleasant property of statelessness allows us to use the new information in U' about the value of ϵ to simplify not only $\mathcal{T}$, but also the pending update U: U can now be reduced to `INSERT` Emp(Reid, CSD) `WHERE` T, which may well be affordable enough to execute directly even if INSERT Emp(Reid, ϵ) WHERE T is not.

Example. Another potentially useful feature is the ability to execute only part of an update, leaving the more expensive part for later incorporation. For example, suppose the update U: INSERT Emp(Reid, ϵ)$\wedge$ Mgr(Nilsson, CSD) WHERE T is too expensive only because Emp(Reid, ϵ) appears implicitly in too many datoms of $\mathcal{T}$. If a user later asks a query involving only Mgr(Nilsson, CSD), it is advantageous to split U into the two updates U_1: INSERT Mgr(Nilsson, CSD) WHERE T and U_2: INSERT Emp(Reid, ϵ) WHERE T and only execute U_1 before processing the query.

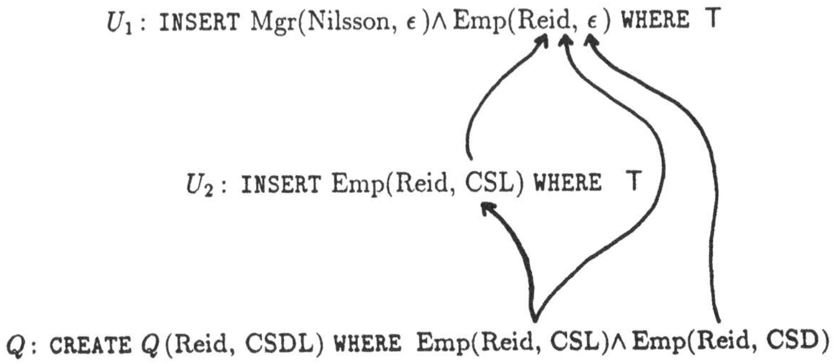
U_1: INSERT Mgr(Nilsson, ϵ)$\wedge$ Emp(Reid, ϵ) WHERE T
U_2: INSERT Emp(Reid, CSL) WHERE T
Q: CREATE Q(Reid, CSDL) WHERE Emp(Reid, CSL)$\wedge$ Emp(Reid, CSD)

Figure 1.

Example. Suppose an update U_1: INSERT Mgr(Nilsson, ϵ) $\wedge$ Emp(Reid, ϵ) WHERE T arrives in the system, followed by the update U_2: INSERT Emp(Reid, CSL) WHERE T. Then there is a write/write conflict between Emp(Reid, ϵ) in U_1 and Emp(Reid, CSL) in U_2; the lazy graph of figure 1 depicts these relationships. Suppose that the query Q: CREATE Q(Reid, CSDL) WHERE Emp(Reid, CSL)$\wedge$ Emp(Reid, CSD) arrives next. (We have not formally defined queries here; think of them as establishing a new relation that gives a view of the current database.) There are read/write conflicts between Emp(Reid, CSL) of Q and Emp(Reid, ϵ) of U_1 and Emp(Reid, CSL) of U_2, and between Emp(Reid, CSD) of Q and Emp(Reid, ϵ) of U_1, as depicted in figure 1.

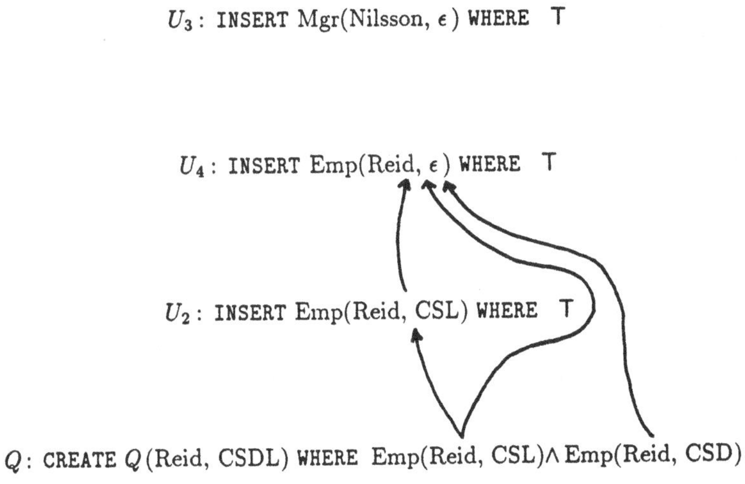
U_3: INSERT Mgr(Nilsson, ϵ) WHERE T
U_4: INSERT Emp(Reid, ϵ) WHERE T
U_2: INSERT Emp(Reid, CSL) WHERE T
Q: CREATE Q(Reid, CSDL) WHERE Emp(Reid, CSL)$\wedge$ Emp(Reid, CSD)

Figure 2.

Assuming that both Emp(Reid, ϵ) and Mgr(Nilsson, ϵ) in U_1 are too expensive to execute because they appear implicitly in too many datoms of T, the best procedure is to first split Mgr(Nilsson, ϵ) out of U_1, as depicted in figure 2, creating updates U_3 and U_4.

Then U_4 needs to be split on the two substitutions $\epsilon = \text{CSL}$ and $\epsilon = \text{CSD}$, creating updates U_6, U_7, and U_8, depicted in figure 3. At this point Q and the updates Q depends upon are more likely to be affordable.

U_3: INSERT Mgr(Nilsson, ϵ) WHERE T

U_6: INSERT Emp(Reid, CSL) WHERE $\epsilon = \text{CSL}$

U_7: INSERT Emp(Reid, CSD) WHERE $\epsilon = \text{CSD}$

U_8: INSERT Emp(Reid, ϵ) WHERE $(\epsilon \neq \text{CSL}) \wedge (\epsilon \neq \text{CSD})$

U_2: INSERT Emp(Reid, CSL) WHERE T

Q: CREATE Q (Reid, CSDL) WHERE Emp(Reid, CSL) $\wedge$ Emp(Reid, CSD)

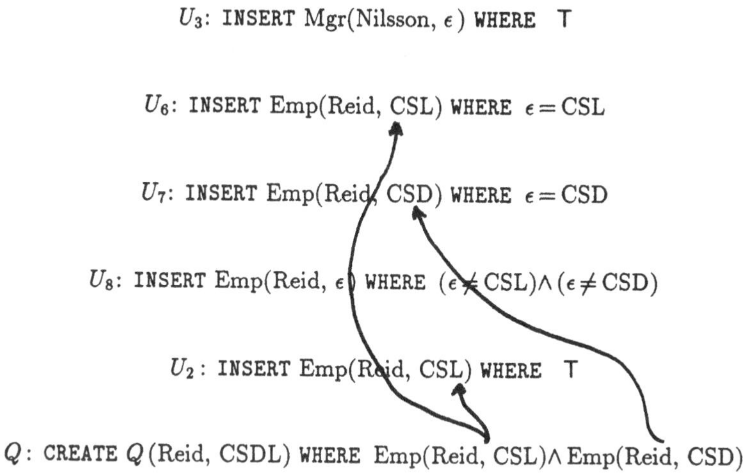

Figure 3.

These examples should suffice to give a flavor of the possible advantages of a lazy evaluation scheme. With the algorithm and data structures we have devised, if a query is rejected due to excessive expense, exact reasons for the high cost are returned to the caller, so that assertions about the possible bindings for Skolem constants may be used to reduce the amount of uncertainty in the database and render the query affordable. Furthermore, any new binding information can be used to reduce the size of the extended relational theory, in effect retroactively reducing the cost of all earlier updates that contained those Skolem constants. In addition, the growth due to update splitting in the lazy graph data structure is limited to a constant factor (k, the maximum size of an update).

5. Summary and Conclusion

In this paper we formalize databases containing incomplete information as logical theories, and view the models of these *extended relational theories* as representing possible states of the world that are consistent with all known information. Formulas in the body of an extended relational theory may be any sentences without universal quantification. Typically incomplete information will appear in these theories as disjunctions or as Skolem constants (a.k.a. null values).

Within this context, we set forth a data manipulation language for updates, and give model-theoretic definitions of the meaning of these updates. We present the Update Algorithm as a means of incorporating updates into extended relational theories, and prove it correct in the sense that the alternative worlds produced under the Update Algorithm are the same as those produced by updating each alternative world individually.

For extended relational theories and updates without Skolem constants, the Update Algorithm has the same asymptotic cost as for an ordinary complete–information database update, but may increase the size of the extended relational theory. For updates involving Skolem constants, the increase in size will be severe if many atomic formulas in the theory unify with those in the update. A simulation program has been constructed for the Update Algorithm.

The Update Algorithm may lead to excessive increases in the size of an extended relational theory $\mathcal{T}$ as expensive updates are incorporated into $\mathcal{T}$. To control the growth of $\mathcal{T}$, we have devised a scheme of lazy evaluation for updates. Lazy evaluation strictly bounds the growth of the extended relational theory caused by each update, via user–specified limits on permissible size increases. Under lazy evaluation, an overly–expensive update U will be stored away rather than executed, in the hopes that new information on costly null values will reduce the expense of executing U before the information contained in U is needed for an incoming query. If an incoming query unavoidably depends on the results of an overly expensive portion of an update, the query must be rejected, as there is no way to reason about the information in the update other than by incorporating it directly in the extended relational theory. When a query is rejected, the originator of the query is notified of the exact reasons for the rejection. The query may be resubmitted once the range of possible values of the troublesome nulls has been narrowed down.

The Update Algorithm may be extended to allow updates containing variables. This reduces to the problem of performing a set of variable–free updates simultaneously. Again, lazy evaluation will be needed to control growth in the extended relational theory, particularly during joins.

We conclude that, first, one may extend the concept of a database update to databases with incomplete information in a natural way; second, that mathematical logic is a fruitful paradigm for the investigation; third, that one may construct an algorithm to perform these updates with a reasonable polynomial running time; and lastly, that a scheme of lazy evaluation is needed to prevent runaway growth in the database under a series of updates.

6. Acknowledgments

I thank Moshe Vardi and Christos Papadimitriou for their insightful comments. Christos Papadimitriou suggested storing rather than executing expensive updates as a strategy for cost reduction, a line of attack that proved most fruitful. Moshe Vardi's liberal use of punctuation ("?") on earlier drafts has led to a much more comprehensible presentation.

7. References

[Abiteboul 85] S. Abiteboul, G. Grahne, "Update Semantics for Incomplete Databases," *Proc. VLDB Conf.*, Stockholm, August 1985.

[Fagin 83] R. Fagin, J. D. Ullman, and M. Y. Vardi, "On the Semantics of Updates in Databases," *Proc. of the 2nd ACM PODS*, April 1983.

[Fagin 84] R. Fagin, G. M. Kuper, J. D. Ullman, and M. Y. Vardi, "Updating Logical Databases," *Proc. of the 3rd ACM PODS*, April 1984; reprinted in *Advances in Computing Research* **3**, JAI Press, 1986.

[Imielinski 84] T. Imielinski and W. Lipski, "Incomplete Information in Relational Databases," *Journal of the ACM*, **31**:4, October 1984.

[Reiter 84] R. Reiter, "Towards a Logical Reconstruction of Relational Database Theory," in M. Brodie, J. Myopoulos, and J. Schmidt (eds.), *On Conceptual Modelling*, Springer–Verlag, 1984.

[Winslett 86a] M. Winslett, "A Model–Theoretic Approach to Updating Logical Databases,"

Stanford Univ. Computer Science Dept. Tech. Report, January 1986. A preliminary version appeared as "A Model–Theoretic Approach to Updating Logical Databases (Extended Abstract)," *Proc. of the 5th ACM PODS*, Cambridge, March 1986.

[Winslett 86b] M. Winslett, "Is Belief Revision Harder Than You Thought?", Stanford Computer Science Dept. Tech. Report, June 1986. A shortened version will appear in *Proc. AAAI Conference*, Philadelphia, August 1986.

A NEW CHARACTERIZATION OF DISTRIBUTED DEADLOCK IN DATABASES

Ouri Wolfson
Technion - Israel Institute of Technology
Computer Science Department, Haifa 32000, Israel

ABSTRACT

The problem of distributed transactions deadlock is analyzed from a new point of view. Consequently we are able to obtain three results. The first is a sufficient condition for deadlock freedom of transactions. The second establishes how many syntactically identical transactions must be analyzed to determine their freedom from deadlock. The third extends the Havender scheme ([3]) for deadlock prevention (locking entities in a fixed order) to the distributed case.

1. INTRODUCTION

Assume that transactions executing in a distributed database control concurrency by locking of entities. The deadlock situation for this popular scenario has been characterized in the context of deadlock detection algorithms [4,6,9]. The characterization demonstrates a circular wait among transaction cohorts (i.e. the processes which execute in behalf of the transaction at different sites). The wait is on resources which may be database entities, or intersite messages. In a centralized database the circular wait is among transactions, on entities alone. In this paper we present a unified approach which eliminates the difference between centralized deadlock and distributed deadlock. Our approach is somewhat similar to the one taken in [10]. That paper deals with centralized processes whose execution is modeled by a path in a tree. We model a transaction by its partially ordered lock-unlock events. The model was originally introduced in [2] to study the serializability issue, and first used for studying the complexity of the deadlock problem in [7]. Our deadlock characterization consists of demonstrating a circular relationship that the order of locks-unlocks imposes on the entities involved in the deadlock.

The new point of view enables us to prove the following three results. First, a sufficient condition for deadlock freedom of an arbitrary set of transactions in a distributed database is obtained. It can be tested in polynomial time but is not necessary. A polynomial time necessary and sufficient condition is unlikely because the problem has been shown NP-complete even for a centralized database (see [8]), while in a distributed database it is NP-complete even for <u>two</u>

transactions ([7]).

The second result we obtain pertains to deadlock of syntactically identical transactions (or copies of a transaction). Copies execute concurrently when a task has to be performed at the same time by multiple database users (e.g., airline seat reservations). In a centralized database, multiple copies of a transaction cannot deadlock (they are modeled by straight line programs). It has been shown in [7] that in *distributed* database they can. For many locking patterns, if multiple copies can deadlock then two copies can do so, regardless of the number of entities referenced (see [7]). Also, consider the other desirable property of transaction sets, namely serializability assurance (see [1,5]). It has been demonstrated that if multiple copies can have a nonserializable schedule then two copies can do so ([11]). This naturally leads to the following question. Is there a fixed number of copies that are sufficient to test for deadlock freedom (in an exhaustive search manner) to determine whether any finite number of copies are deadlock free or not? Unfortunately, we prove that this is not the case. Namely, the number of copies to be tested for deadlock freedom is equal to the number of entities referenced by the transaction.

The third result we obtain extends the Havender scheme for deadlock prevention. The restricted scheme assumes a total order s imposed on the database entities and states that a transaction can issue a lock request for an entity x if it "currently" does not hold a lock on an entity which succeeds x in s. The problem in literally extending the scheme to the distributed case, is with the word "currently". When events are partially ordered it is not clear what it means, and as we show can be interpreted in a way which makes the scheme incorrect. We reformulate the Havender scheme in terms which make the extension to the distributed case natural. Then we prove (based on our first result) that it indeed ensures deadlock freedom.

The rest of the paper is organized as follows. In Section 2 we present the model. In Section 3 we formalize the new deadlock characterization and prove the sufficient condition for deadlock freedom. Section 4 proves the result about transaction copies, and Section 5 discusses the extended Havender scheme.

2. THE MODEL

A *distributed database D* is a finite set of entities partitioned into pairwise disjoint subsets called sites. A *transaction T* over D is a partially ordered set of Lock-Unlock steps referencing the entities of the database [2]. It is clear that for analyzing deadlock only the locking pattern of a transaction is of interest. The lock of an entity x is denoted by Lx and the unlock by Ux. The partial order has to satisfy the following conditions: 1) Lx is in T if and only if Ux is in T, and Lx precedes Ux. 2) All the steps referencing entities which reside at the same site in the database are totally ordered.

The reason for condition 2) is that steps referencing entities residing at the same site are sequentially executed by one computer. Thus, if the database has only one site (is centralized) the transaction is reduced to the popular representation of a centralized transaction as a sequence of steps. Steps executed at different sites may be ordered. If they are, then the order must be enforced by some intersite messages.

Given a set of transactions $\tau = \{T_1 = (V_1, A_1), \ldots, T_n = (V_n, A_n)\}$ we assume that the steps in V_i are superscripted by i (to distinguish between two Lx steps from different transactions). τ can be regarded as the directed acyclic graph (dag) (V, A) where $V = \bigcup_{i=1}^{n} V_i$ and $A = \bigcup_{i=1}^{n} A_i$. It is the partial order in which the steps of all transactions must be executed. S is a *schedule* of τ if it is a linear extension (i.e. a sequence obtained by a topological sort) in which: between every two Lock steps of an entity there is an Unlock step of the entity. Intuitively, a schedule is a possible sequence-of-execution of the transaction steps (a locked entity cannot be locked by another transaction before it is unlocked). Subgraph P' of a dag P is a *prefix* of P if in P there are no arcs from a node which is not in P' to a node in P'. This definition subsumes the regular prefix definition if P is a total order. S is a *partial schedule* of τ if it is a schedule of some prefix of τ, namely a linear extension of some prefix of τ in which the locks are respected. Intuitively, a partial schedule is an incomplete execution of the transactions. A partial schedule S is a *deadlock schedule* if it cannot be extended, i.e. there is no (partial) schedule of which S is a proper prefix. τ is *deadlock-free* if it has no deadlock schedule.

Example 1: Assume that entities x and y reside at different sites. Let $\tau = \{T_1, T_2\}$ where T_1 is the transaction of Fig. 1(a) and T_2 is the transaction of Fig. 1(b). Then the partial schedule L^1x, L^2y is a deadlock schedule. It is an extension of the prefix of τ consisting of the nodes $\{L^1x, L^2y\}$ and an empty set of arcs. []

τ is a set of *copies* of a transaction T if each T_i in τ can be obtained by superscripting the steps of T by i. It means that all T_i's represent the same transaction.

Figure 1

3. A SUFFICIENT CONDITION FOR DEADLOCK FREEDOM

First we will provide the new deadlock characterization (Lemma 1). Assume that S is a deadlock schedule. For each transaction T involved in the deadlock there exist one or more lock steps on which T waits indefinitely. Denote them $Ly_1, \ldots, Ly_k$. They have the following properties: (1) Each y_i is locked in S by another transaction. (2) T executed in S all the predecessor steps of each Ly_i. (3) Any other step which T does not execute in S, succeeds in T some y_i (otherwise S can be extended). Let $Ly_1,...,Ly_k$ be the critical steps defined by S in T.

Assume now that τ is a set of transactions. The *deadlock graph* of τ, denoted $DG(\tau)$, is a directed graph (digraph) having all entities referenced in τ as nodes and an arc $x \rightarrow y$ if and only if there is a transaction in τ where Lx does not precede Ly and Lx precedes Uy.

Lemma 1: Let τ be a set of transactions and S a deadlock schedule of it. Then $Z = \{ x \mid x$ is referenced by a critical step defined by S in some transaction $\}$ induces a cyclic digraph in $DG(\tau)$.

Proof: Denote the transactions of τ by $T_1,...T_q$. Let y be some entity in Z and assume that y is locked by a critical step of some transaction T_j. Then there is another transaction, T_h, such that y is locked by T_h in S and unlocked by T_h after one of its critical steps. (Otherwise Ly is not a critical step of T_j). Assume that the critical step of T_h which precedes Uy is Lx. Since T_h locks y in S but not x it means that Lx does not precede Ly in T_h. Then, by definition, there is an arc $x \rightarrow y$ in $DG(\tau)$. Note also that x is in Z since Lx is a critical step. Therefore, for an arbitrary entity y in Z we found an entity x in Z and an arc from x to y in $DG(\tau)$. If Z induces a directed acyclic graph in $DG(\tau)$, then for a root of this dag there is no incoming arc from an entity of Z.
[]

Theorem 1: A set of transactions is deadlock free if its deadlock graph is acyclic.

Proof: Follows from Lemma 1. []

The condition of Theorem 1 can be tested in polynomial time and is sufficient for deadlock freedom. However the condition is not necessary; namely, it is possible that the deadlock graph of a set of transactions is cyclic, yet the set is deadlock free. To realize it consider the transaction T of Fig 2(a). Let τ be $\{T_1, T_2\}$ where each T_i is a copy of T. By definition $DG(\tau)$ is the directed graph given in Fig. 2(b). It is cyclic, but it is clear that τ is deadlock free. The reason is that the copy T_j which locks z first will prevent the other copy from beginning until T_j completes; so deadlock cannot occur.

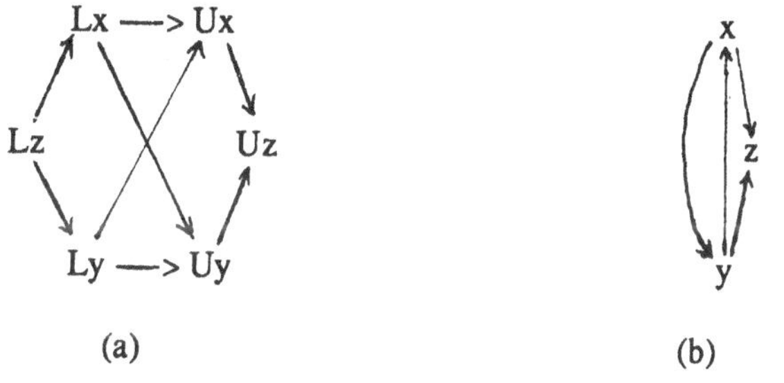

Figure 2

4. DEADLOCK OF TRANSACTION COPIES

Let m be an arbitrary integer. Denote by $F(m)$ the directed graph of Fig.3. We will show in this section that m copies of $F(m)$ are necessary and sufficient to produce a deadlock schedule.

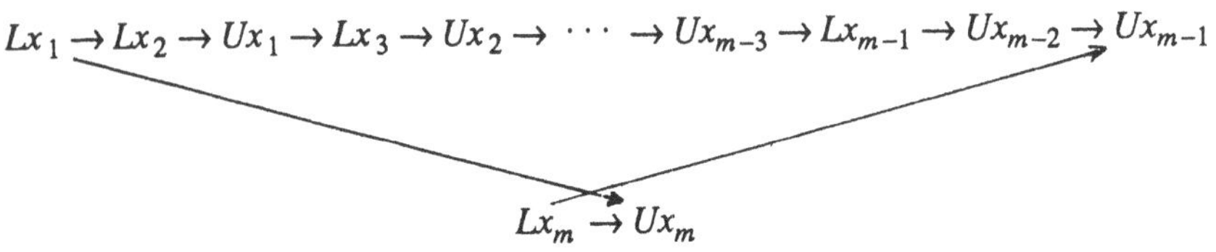

Figure 3

First we have to show in which cases $F(m)$ is indeed a well defined transaction.

Lemma 2: Let D be a database distributed among two or more sites and consisting of $2m-2$ or more entities. Then $F(m)$ is a transaction over D.

Proof: Entities $x_1,...,x_m$ have to be selected from D such that x_m and x_i reside at different sites for any i between 1 and $m-1$ (because Lx_m is incomparable to any other lock step of $F(m)$). x_m is selected from a site b with the minimal (among all sites) number of entities. Each one of the other $m-1$ entities is selected from a site (not necessarily the same one) different than b. If the number of sites is $2m-2$ or more, such selection is possible. Otherwise it is not guaranteed that there exist $m-1$ entities which reside at a site different than b; it may depend on the distribution scheme. []

Lemma 3: Let τ be a set of copies of $F(m)$. τ is deadlock free if and only if the number of copies in τ is less than m.

Proof: (Only if) We will prove that copies $T_1,...,T_m$ of $F(m)$ can deadlock. We do so by exhibiting a deadlock schedule S of the copies. S is defined as follows. Each T_i executes the sequence of steps t_i where: $t_1 = Lx_1$, and $t_i = Lx_1,Lx_2,Ux_1,Lx_3,...,Lx_i,Ux_{i-1}$ for $2 \le i \le m-1$, and $t_m = Lx_m$. S consists of $t_{m-1},t_{m-2},...,t_1,t_m$ executed in this order and without any interleaving. We have to demonstrate two points about S in order to complete the proof. First, that S is "legal" in the sense that in S no transaction locks an entity which is already locked by another transaction. Second, that it indeed results in a deadlock.

S is a legal partial schedule because when each T_i completes the sequence t_i it holds a lock on one entity alone, x_i. Also, t_j does not reference any entity with an index higher than j (these are the only entities which are held locked by copies executing before t_j in S). The fact that S results in a deadlock can be realized by examining Figure 4. It illustrates the steps executed by each T_i in S, (to the left of the vertical line), the entity it holds a lock on (underlined), and its critical steps (to the right of the vertical line). It is clear that S cannot be extended because every critical step references an entity which is held locked in S by another transaction.

$T_{m-1}: Lx_1, Lx_2, Ux_1, \ldots, Ux_{m-3}, \underline{Lx_{m-1}}, Ux_{m-2}$	Lx_m
$T_{m-2}: Lx_1, Lx_2, \ldots, \underline{Lx_{m-2}}, Ux_{m-3}$	Lx_{m-1} Lx_m
.	
.	
.	
$T_2: Lx_1, \underline{Lx_2}, Ux_1$	Lx_3 Lx_m
$T_1: \underline{Lx_1}$	Lx_2 Lx_m
$T_m: \underline{Lx_m}$	Lx_1

Figure 4

(If) We will prove that less then m copies of $F(m)$ cannot deadlock. Assume that S is a deadlock schedule of a set of copies τ. Note that $DG(\tau)$ is exactly the cycle $x_m, x_{m-1}, \ldots, x_1, x_m$. Thus, by Lemma 1, after execution of S the critical steps must lock all entities of the set $\{x_1, \ldots, x_m\}$. If a copy has two or more critical steps then it is easy to see that they are pairwise incomparable in $F(m)$ (i.e., there is no path from one to another). Steps $Lx_1, \ldots, Lx_{m-1}$ are totally ordered in $F(m)$, thus two of them cannot be critical steps of the same copy. Therefore, each one is a critical step of a different copy, which implies that in the deadlock are involved at least $m-1$ copies. Denote the copy which has Lx_i as a critical step by T_i, for $1 \le i \le m-1$. Some copy involved in the deadlock locks x_{m-1} in S. That copy must also lock (and possibly unlock) $x_1, \ldots, x_{m-2}$ in S, therefore its only critical step must be Lx_m. Thus the copy cannot be any of the defined T_i's and there must be an additional copy, T_m. []

For a transaction T let $d(T) = \{ n \mid$ if a set of n copies of T is deadlock-free then an arbitrarily large set of copies of T is deadlock-free $\}$. We are interested in the minimal number in $d(T)$.

Theorem 2: For every positive integer m there exists a transaction T referencing m entities such that $m = \min\{d(T)\}$.

Proof: By Lemma 3 $\min\{d(F(m))\} \ge m$. Left to prove is that $m \in d(F(m))$, namely that if a set of m copies of $F(m)$ is deadlock free then an arbitrarily large set is deadlock free. Assume that a deadlock of more than m copies of $F(m)$ occurs. In the deadlock schedule S there must be copies which do not hold locks on any entities. They can be eliminated from S, with S remaining a deadlock schedule. []

Consider now the important case in which a transaction T is two phase locked, namely all locks precede all unlocks (e.g. the transactions of Figures 2(a) and 5).

Proposition 1: Two copies of a two-phase-locked transaction T are deadlock free if and only if the transaction has a lock step which precedes all other steps.

Proof: (Only if) Assume that T does not have a lock step which precedes all other steps. Then there exist at least two locks Lx, Ly without predecessors in T. A partial schedule S in which copy T_1 locks x as the first step and copy T_2 locks y as the first step, must end in a deadlock; in S, T_1 and T_2 may be able to execute some more lock steps but copy T_1 will not be able to unlock any entity until it executes all locks (including Ly), and the symmetric situation exists for T_2.

(If) Suppose that Lx precedes all other steps. Then a copy T_i which begins execution (seizes x) prevents any other copy from starting until it unlocks x, namely until T_i obtains all locks. Thus T_i will not deadlock. []

Corollary 1: A set consisting of an arbitrary number of copies of a two phase locked transaction is deadlock free if two copies of the transaction are deadlock free.

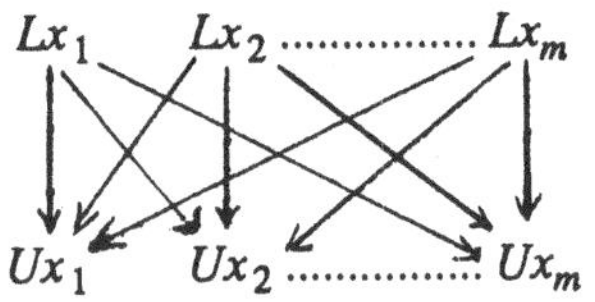

Figure 5

5. EXTENDED HAVENDER SCHEME

For transactions whose execution is modeled by a total order of Lock-Unlock steps Havender proposed the following deadlock-prevention scheme [3]. Impose a total order l on the entities and request that when a transaction issues a Lx step it does not hold a lock on an entity which succeeds x in l. In other words, if a transaction T accesses entities x and y and in T

1) Ly precedes Lx, and

2) Lx precedes Uy

then y precedes x in l. What if the transaction executes simultaneously at several computers and is modeled by a partial order? Then the scheme does not work any more. To realize that consider the transaction T of Fig.5. Any two copies of T obey the scheme, but by Proposition 1 they are not deadlock free.

Now consider the following *extended* Havender scheme of deadlock prevention for arbitrary transactions. Impose a total order l on the entities and require the following. If a transaction T references entities x and y, and in T

1) Lx does not precede Ly and

2) Lx precedes Uy

then y precedes x in l. The difference between the restricted (or traditional) Havender scheme and the extended one is that condition 1) changes. In the extended version it holds if Lx succeeds Ly or *Lx is incomparable to Ly.*

Theorem 3: If each transaction in a set of transactions τ obeys the extended Havender scheme then τ is deadlock-free.

Proof: $DG(\tau)$ is a partial order (having l as an extension). By Lemma 1 τ is deadlock free. []

Observation 1: The extended Havender scheme reduces to the restricted one for transactions modeled by total orders.

Observation 2: It has been pointed out in [7] that a set of transactions τ is deadlock free if the set $\tau' = \{t \mid t$ is an extension of some $T \in \tau\}$, regarded as a set of centralized transactions, is deadlock free. The extended Havender scheme does not ensure deadlock freedom by ensuring that all extensions obey the restricted Havender scheme; it is *weaker*. To realize that assume that T consists of the nodes $\{Lx, Ux, Ly, Uy\}$ and the arcs $\{Lx \to Ux, Ly \to Uy\}$. Then two copies of T obey the extended Havender scheme and are indeed deadlock free. However, the extensions Lx, Ly, Ux, Uy and Ly, Lx, Ux, Uy can deadlock.

Observation 3: In two-phase-locked transactions all locks precede all unlocks. Thus, if such transactions are to obey the extended Havender scheme, two locks cannot be incomparable and therefore all locks must be totally ordered. (Unlocks at different sites can still be incomparable.)

REFERENCES

[1] K.P. Eswaran, J.N. Gray, R.A. Lorie and I.L. Traiger, "The Notion of Consistency and Predicate Locks in a Database System", *CACM,* 19 (11), pp. 624-633, (1976).

[2] P.C. Kanellakis and C.H. Papadimitriou, "Is Distributed Locking Harder?", *JCSS,* (28), pp. 103-120, (1984).

[3] J.W. Havender, "Avoiding Deadlock in Multitasking Systems", *IBM Sys. J.,7(2), pp. 74-84, (1968).*

[4] J.N. Gray, "Notes on Database Operating Systems", in *Operating Systems*, an Advanced Course, Springer Verlag (1979).

[5] J.D. Ullman, *Principles of Database Systems*, Computer Science Press, (1979).

[6] D.A. Menasce and R.R. Munz, "Locking and Deadlock Detection in Distributed Databases", *IEEE TOSE*, 5(3), pp. 195-202, (1979).

[7] O. Wolfson and M. Yannakakis, "Deadlock Freedom (and Safety) of Transactions in a Distributed Database", *Proc. ACM Symp. on Principles of Database Systems*, pp. 105-112, (1985).

[8] M. Yannakakis, "Freedom from Deadlock of Safe Locking Policies", *SIAM J. Comput.*, 11, pp. 391-408, (1982).

[9] R. Obermack, "Distributed Deadlock Detection Algorithm", *ACM TODS*, 7(2), pp. 187-208, (1982).

[10] T. Minoura, "Deadlock Avoidance Revisited", *JACM*, 29(4), pp. 1023-1048, (1982).

[11] O. Wolfson, "Concurrent Execution of Syntactically Identical Transactions", *Technion-IIT TR 387*, November 1985.

Vol. 192: Automata on Infinite Words. Proceedings, 1984. Edited by M. Nivat and D. Perrin. V, 216 pages.1985.

Vol. 193: Logics of Programs. Proceedings, 1985. Edited by R. Parikh. VI, 424 pages. 1985.

Vol. 194: Automata, Languages and Programming. Proceedings, 1985. Edited by W. Brauer. IX, 520 pages. 1985.

Vol. 195: H. J. Stüttgen, A Hierarchical Associative Processing System. XII, 273 pages. 1985.

Vol. 196: Advances in Cryptology. Proceedings of CRYPTO '84. Edited by G. R. Blakley and D. Chaum. IX, 491 pages.1985.

Vol. 197: Seminar on Concurrency. Proceedings, 1984. Edited by S. D. Brookes, A. W. Roscoe and G. Winskel. X, 523 pages. 1985.

Vol. 198: A. Businger, PORTAL Language Description. VIII, 186 pages. 1985.

Vol. 199: Fundamentals of Computation Theory. Proceedings, 1985. Edited by L. Budach. XII, 533 pages. 1985.

Vol. 200: J. L. A. van de Snepscheut, Trace Theory and VLSI Design. VI, 0–140 pages. 1985.

Vol. 201: Functional Programming Languages and Computer Archi-tecture. Proceedings, 1985. Edited by J.-P. Jouannaud. VI, 413 pages. 1985.

Vol. 202: Rewriting Techniques and Applications. Edited by .-P. Jouannaud. VI, 441 pages. 1985.

/ol. 203: EUROCAL '85. Proceedings Vol. 1, 1985. Edited by 3. Buchberger. V, 233 pages. 1985.

/ol. 204: EUROCAL '85. Proceedings Vol. 2, 1985. Edited by 3. F. Caviness. XVI, 650 pages. 1985.

'ol. 205: P. Klint, A Study in String Processing Languages. VIII, 165 ages. 1985.

'ol. 206: Foundations of Software Technology and Theoretical Com-uter Science. Proceedings, 1985. Edited by S. N. Maheshwari. IX, 22 pages. 1985.

'ol. 207: The Analysis of Concurrent Systems. Proceedings, 1983. dited by B. T. Denvir, W. T. Harwood, M. I. Jackson and M. J. Wray. 'II, 398 pages. 1985.

ol. 208: Computation Theory. Proceedings, 1984. Edited by A. kowron. VII, 397 pages. 1985.

'ol. 209: Advances in Cryptology. Proceedings of EUROCRYPT '84. dited by T. Beth, N. Cot and I. Ingemarsson. VII, 491 pages. 1985.

ol. 210: STACS 86. Proceedings, 1986. Edited by B. Monien and G. idal-Naquet. IX, 368 pages. 1986.

ol. 211: U. Schöning, Complexity and Structure. V, 99 pages. 1986.

ol. 212: Interval Mathematics 1985. Proceedings, 1985. Edited by K. ckel. VI, 227 pages. 1986.

ol. 213: ESOP 86. Proceedings, 1986. Edited by B. Robinet and Wilhelm. VI, 374 pages. 1986.

ol. 214: CAAP '86. 11th Colloquium on Trees in Algebra and ogramming. Proceedings, 1986. Edited by P. Franchi-Zannettacci. , 306 pages. 1986.

ol. 215: Mathematical Methods of Specification and Synthesis of oftware Systems '85. Proceedings, 1985. Edited by W. Bibel and P. Jantke. 245 pages. 1986.

ol. 216: Ch. Fernstrom, I. Kruzela, B. Svensson, LUCAS Associative ray Processor: Design, Programming and Application Studies. XII, 23 pages. 1986.

ol. 217: Programs as Data Objects. Proceedings, 1985. Edited by H. anzinger and N. D. Jones. X, 324 pages. 1986.

ol. 218: Advances in Cryptology – CRYPTO '85. Proceedings, 85. Edited by H. C. Williams. X, 548 pages. 1986.

ol. 219: Advances in Cryptology – EUROCRYPT '85. Proceedings, 85. Edited by F. Pichler. IX, 281 pages. 1986.

Vol. 220: RIMS Symposia on Software Science and Engineering II. Proceedings, 1983 and 1984. Edited by E. Goto, K. Araki and T. Yuasa. XI, 323 pages. 1986.

Vol. 221: Logic Programming '85. Proceedings, 1985. Edited by E. Wada. IX, 311 pages. 1986.

Vol. 222: Advances in Petri Nets 1985. Edited by G. Rozenberg. VI, 498 pages. 1986.

Vol. 223: Structure in Complexity Theory. Proceedings, 1986. Edited by A. L. Selman. VI, 401 pages. 1986.

Vol. 224: Current Trends in Concurrency. Overviews and Tutorials. Edited by J. W. de Bakker, W.-P. de Roever and G. Rozenberg. XII, 716 pages. 1986.

Vol. 225: Third International Conference on Logic Programming. Proceedings, 1986. Edited by E. Shapiro. IX, 720 pages. 1986.

Vol. 226: Automata, Languages and Programming. Proceedings, 1986. Edited by L. Kott. IX, 474 pages. 1986.

Vol. 227: VLSI Algorithms and Architectures – AWOC 86. Procee-dings, 1986. Edited by F. Makedon, K. Mehlhorn, T. Papatheodorou and P. Spirakis. VIII, 328 pages. 1986.

Vol. 228: Applied Algebra, Algorithmics and Error-Correcting Codes. AAECC-2. Proceedings, 1984. Edited by A. Poli. VI, 265 pages. 1986.

Vol. 229: Algebraic Algorithms and Error-Correcting Codes. AAECC-3. Proceedings, 1985. Edited by J. Calmet. VII, 416 pages. 1986.

Vol. 230: 8th International Conference on Automated Deduction. Proceedings, 1986. Edited by J. H. Siekmann. X, 708 pages. 1986.

Vol. 231: R. Hausser, NEWCAT: Parsing Natural Language Using Left-Associative Grammar. II, 540 pages. 1986.

Vol. 232: Fundamentals of Artificial Intelligence. Edited by W. Bibel and Ph. Jorrand. VII, 313 pages. 1986.

Vol. 233: Mathematical Foundations of Computer Science 1986. Proceedings, 1986. Edited by J. Gruska, B. Rovan and J. Wiedermann. IX, 650 pages. 1986.

Vol. 234: Concepts in User Interfaces: A Reference Model for Command and Response Languages. By Members of IFIP Working Group 2.7. Edited by D. Beech. X, 116 pages. 1986.

Vol. 235: Accurate Scientific Computations. Proceedings, 1985. Edited by W. L. Miranker and R. A. Toupin. XIII, 205 pages. 1986.

Vol. 236: TEX for Scientific Documentation. Proceedings, 1986. Edited by J. Désarménien. VI, 204 pages. 1986.

Vol. 237: CONPAR 86. Proceedings, 1986. Edited by W. Händler, D. Haupt, R. Jeltsch, W. Juling and O. Lange. X, 418 pages. 1986.

Vol. 238: L. Naish, Negation and Control in Prolog. IX, 119 pages. 1986.

Vol. 239: Mathematical Foundations of Programming Semantics. Proceedings, 1985. Edited by A. Melton. VI, 395 pages. 1986.

Vol. 240: Category Theory and Computer Programming. Proceedings, 1985. Edited by D. Pitt, S. Abramsky, A. Poigné and D. Rydeheard. VII, 519 pages. 1986.

Vol. 241: Foundations of Software Technology and Theoretical Com-puter Science. Proceedings, 1986. Edited by K. V. Nori. XII, 519 pages. 1986.

Vol. 242: Combinators and Functional Programming Languages. Proceedings, 1985. Edited by G. Cousineau, P.-L. Curien and B. Robinet. V, 208 pages. 1986.

Vol. 243: ICDT '86. Proceedings, 1986. Edited by G. Ausiello and P. Atzeni. VI, 444 pages. 1986.